THE
FRENCH REVOLUTION

By

J. M. THOMPSON

TWO strong angels stand by the side of history, whether French history or English, as heraldic supporters: the angel of research on the left hand, that must read millions of dusty parchments, and of pages blotted with lies; the angel of meditation on the right hand, that must cleanse these lying records with fire, even as of old the draperies of asbestos were cleansed, and must quicken them into regenerated life.

DE QUINCEY

BASIL BLACKWELL
OXFORD
1966

BASIL BLACKWELL 1943

FIRST PRINTED 1943
SECOND EDITION 1944
   Reprinted   1966

Printed in Great Britain
By Photolithography
Unwin Brothers Limited
Woking and London

A PRACTICAL PREFACE

IF this book bears any trade-mark, it is that of the Oxford tutorial system. For a good many years it has been the writer's business and pleasure to guide pupils through the revolutionary period. There is no better way of finding out the difficulties of the subject. It is with those that this Preface will deal.

THE BOOKS DIFFICULTY

The first difficulty comes from the books on the revolution. How is the inexperienced reader, faced (even in war-time) with a shelf-full of them, to know which to accept, and which to reject? Accustomed to believe that any statement will pass, if 'the book says so,' he learns with surprise that wrong 'facts' and prejudiced views may go on unchallenged from one historian to another. Accustomed to trust his own eyes and ears, he has to learn that the best witnesses sometimes disagree, and that the most pains-taking research cannot always guarantee 'truths' that histories are accus-tomed to take for granted. He begins to be a historian from the moment that he uses his common sense, and asks himself, 'Is it likely that people would behave as they are said to have done?' or, 'Cannot I discover the reason why they did so?' He becomes a critic from the moment that he ceases to think of books as books, and begins to think of them as persons, some of whom he will learn to trust, and some to distrust.

This book hopes to be trusted. It contains no bibliography, and no foot-notes. Its foot-notes would have been too many for the ordinary reader, and too few for the expert. A bibliography would have been of little use unless it had criticized the books it mentioned; and criticism might have been invidious, or even libellous. So let me give dogmatically, and without more ado, a list of

THE FIFTY BEST BOOKS ON THE REVOLUTION

ACTON. Lectures on the French Revolution (delivered 1895–9, published 1910)
AULARD. Recueil des actes du Comité de Salut public (21 vols., 1889–1911)
—— La Société de Jacobins. Recueil de documents (6 vols., 1889–97)
—— Histoire politique de la Révolution française (1901)
—— Etudes et leçons sur la Révolution française (7 vols., 1893–1913)
—— Les Orateurs de la Constituante, de la Législative, et de la Convention (3 vols., 1882–6)
BOITEAU. Etat de la France en 1789 (1861)

BRAESCH. La commune du dix août, 1792 (1911)
BRUNOT. Histoire de la Langue française (vol. vii, 1926, vol. ix, 1927)
BUCHEZ and ROUX. Histoire parlementaire de la Révolution française
    (40 vols., 1834–8)
CAHEN and GUYOT. L'Œuvre législative de la Révolution (1913)
CARLYLE. The French Revolution (1837)
CARON. Paris pendant la Terreur (2 vols., 1914)
CROKER. Essays on the French Revolution (1857)
DAUBAN. La démagogie en 1793 à Paris (1868)
—— Paris en 1794 et en 1795 (1869)
DESPATCHES FROM PARIS (vol. i, 1784–7, 1909 ; vol. ii, 1788–90, 1910)
DOUARCHE. Les tribunaux civils de Paris pendant la Révolution (3 vols.,
    1905–7)
GOWER, EARL, The despatches of (1885)
JAURÈS. Histoire socialiste de la Révolution française (8 vols., 1901–4)
KROPOTKIN. La grande révolution, 1789–1793 (1909)
KUSCINSKI. Dictionnaire des conventionnels (1916)
LACROIX. Actes de la commune de Paris pendant la Révolution (15 vols.,
    1894–1909)
—— Le département de Paris et de la Seine pendant la Révolution (1904)
LEFEBVRE. Les paysans du nord pendant la Révolution (2 vols., 1924)
LEFEBVRE, SAGNAC, and GUYOT. La Révolution française (1930)
MALOUET. Mémoires (2 vols., 2nd ed. 1874)
MARION. Dictionnaire des institutions de France aux xviie et xviiie
    siècles (1923)
MATHIEZ. La Révolution française (1922)
—— La vie chère (1927)
MAUTOUCHET. Le gouvernement révolutionnaire (1912)
MELLIÉ. Les sections de Paris pendant la Révolution (1898)
MERCIER. Tableau de Paris (1781)
MIRABEAU. Correspondance entre le Comte de Mirabeau et le Comte de
    La Marck (2 vols., 1851)
MORNET. Les origines intellectuelles de la Révolution française (1933)
MORRIS. A diary of the French Revolution (ed. Davenport, 1939)
PAPIERS INÉDITS trouvés chez Robespierre, Saint-Just, Payan, etc.
    (3 vols., 1828)
ROBESPIERRE. Correspondance de Maximilian et Augustin Robespierre
    (ed. Michon, 1926)
ROBIQUET. Le personnel municipal de Paris pendant la Révolution (1890)
ROCQUAIN. L'Esprit révolutionnaire avant la Révolution (1878)
ROLAND. Lettres de Madame Roland (ed. Perroud, 4 vols., 1900–15)
SAGNAC. La législation civile de la Révolution française (1898)
SAGNAC and PARISET. La Révolution (2 vols., 1920)
SCHMIDT. Tableaux de la Révolution française (3 vols., 1867–70)

SELIGMAN. La justice en France pendant la Révolution (1901)
DE STAËL. Considérations sur les principaux événemens de la Révolution française (1818)
DE TOCQUEVILLE. L'Ancien régime et la Révolution (1855)
TOURNEUX. La bibliographie de l'histoire de Paris pendant la Révolution française (5 vols., 1890–1913)
TUETEY. Répertoire général des sources manuscrites de l'histoire de Paris pendant la Révolution française (11 vols., 1890–1914)
YOUNG. Travels during the years 1787, 1788, and 1789 (1792)

THE LANGUAGE DIFFICULTY

The second difficulty—it is a less serious one—comes from the French language, which often uses words closely resembling their English equivalents in senses which are unfamiliar to us. The best way to illustrate this difficulty, and to help meet it, will be to give a list of some of these words, with the necessary explanations.

arrêté, like *arrêt*, means any resolution or decision, not necessarily one involving arrest.

assermenté means one (generally a priest) who has taken an oath of allegiance, *insermenté* one who has not : alternative expressions are *jureur* and *non-jureur, constitutionnel* and *réfractoire*.

bailliage, an ancient administrative and judicial district, sometimes translated as 'bailiwick,' can be rendered during the revolutionary period 'constituency.' So can *sénéchaussée*.

bourgeois need not be given the rude meaning sometimes attached to the adjective 'middle-class'; it means one who enjoys the rights of citizenship, or the whole body of those who do; derivatively, 'the middle classes.'

capitaliste can be used of anyone who possesses capital, whether or not he uses it like a modern capitalist.

citoyen before the revolution meant much the same as *bourgeois*: the revolution gave it a new meaning: it took the place of the old *monsieur*, and stood for the social equality of all, not as townsmen, but as Frenchmen.

coalition is used not only of a coalition of powers, but also of an employers' or workers' 'union.'

comité and *commission* differ much as in English: the first is generally a 'standing committee,' the second a 'special committee' set up to deal with a particular question.

commune means the inhabitants of any place who are bound together by common interests and administration, especially in a town with a municipality: *les communes* may come to be used of 'the common people,' or even their representatives—'the Commons.'

constitution: as in medicine it means the fundamental make-up of the body, or the essential element of bodily health, so in politics it means a fundamental law, whether of state or church; to most eighteenth-century Frenchmen it suggested the Papal *constitution* 'Unigenitus' of 1713: so it would naturally be applied to the 'civil constitution of the clergy,' the church settlement of 1790: but equally well to the fundamental state laws embodied in the state constitutions of 1791 or 1793; and these might include the regulation of matters not strictly 'constitutional' in our sense of the word. An *assemblée constituante* is one which has power to make or to alter such fundamental laws.

curé means 'vicar,' and *vicaire* means 'curate'; the first holds the *cure* or *bénéfice*; the second acts as his substitute (Lat. *vicarius*).

député is the more general and popular term for the *représentant*, the political representative of the people, and might be translated 'M.P.': it does not carry the special theory of representation implied in *mandataire*, our 'delegate.'

enragé is commonest in the phrase *un chien enragé,* 'a mad dog'; and hence applies to anyone excessively angry, or with exaggerated views: for its special application to a political party, see p. 228.

fédération means the association of *citoyens* or *communes* as an expression of national unity; they sent representatives (*fédérés*) to the *fête de fédération* at Paris every fourteenth of July: but when the Girondins stressed the interests of the separate *départements* against those of the capital, the Jacobins called this *fédéralisme*—an attempt to divide the unified country into its component parts.

fermier, a man who makes a contract (Lat. *fermitatem*), can be either one who 'farms' the taxes, or one who 'farms' the land, whether for himself or as agent for the landlord.

feuillant, a nickname for the Cistercian order of monks, was applied to the royalist club which met in their convent near the *manège*; hence it came to mean 'conservative,' if not 'counter-revolutionary.'

jacobin, the nickname of the Dominicans of the rue Saint-Honoré whose premises were occupied by the *Amis de la Constitution,* means a member of the Jacobin club; also, from about August, 1792, onwards, a member of the Jacobin party with which the club increasingly identified itself.

jury is the English word; but the jurymen (*jurés*) are specially elected or appointed officials, not any casual twelve citizens.

lanterne means a street-lamp hung from a bracket, or from a cord across the street; hence a convenient gallows in an emergency.

ministre is 'minister,' and *ministère* is 'ministry.'

parlement (a 'speaking' assembly) means the ancient body of magistrates which had the duty of registering and the right of remonstrating against the laws in Paris and in certain provincial towns: but the

States-general was the only Parliament; and when it recovered its rights in '89 the *parlements* disappeared.

patriote meant 'a man who belongs to my part of the country' (*pays*), a 'compatriot,' long before it implied 'loyalty to the country,' or 'patriotism': this English interpretation of a Latin word was not admitted by the *Académie* till 1762 (cp. p. 121).

peuple, the population of a place or a country thought of *en masse*, acquires the idea of subjection in relation to the government, and of poverty and ignorance in contrast with the rich and educated minority; thus it becomes less like the Latin *populus*, and more like *plebs*; those who liked the people as a whole called it *nation*; those who disliked it called it *canaille* ('rabble,' or 'mob').

république meant the Common-weal (*la chose publique*, Lat. *respublica*), without specifying how it was governed: Napoleon followed the Roman emperors in keeping the word on his coins: but August, 1792, gave France democracy without a king, i.e. a 'republic' in the modern sense of the word.

révolutionnaire means not so much 'belonging to the revolution' as 'revolutionary in character,' i.e. 'emergency,' super-constitutional: thus the *armée révolutionnaire* (p. 395) was not like the rest of the army, and the *tribunal révolutionnaire* was not part of the ordinary criminal jurisdiction of the revolution (cp. p. 488).

salut, as in *comité de salut public*, means the act of saving, not the state of safety that results from it; it is almost 'the committee to save the state': the condition of security is represented by *sûreté*; and *comité de sûreté générale* almost means 'police committee,' anticipating the modern use of *Sûreté* for the French C.I.D. (cp. p. 390).

sansculotte does not, of course, mean one who wore nothing below his shirt, but one who preferred proletarian trousers to aristocratic breeches : and so a working-class republican, especially one living in the Paris slums.

surveillance, as in *comité de surveillance*, has the special meaning of 'police supervision'—our Vigilance or Watch Committee.

terreur is misleadingly translated by 'terror': when *terreur* was put *à l'ordre du jour*, it meant a policy of intimidation: 'the Terror' of 1793–4 was not a time when Parisians or Frenchmen were particularly terrified, but when the government used force instead of persuasion.

tribune is used, not for a leader of the people (*tribun*, Lat. *tribunus*), but for the desk or pulpit (Lat. *tribuna*) from which he makes his speeches (cp. p. 229).

Another part of the language difficulty is the occurrence in French histories, and in some English books that follow them too closely, of weights and measures which do not correspond to ours, and of a coinage and a calendar with which we are unfamiliar.

WEIGHTS AND MEASURES

There were, before 1789, almost endless variations both in the local names of weights and measures, and in the meaning attached to them. The revolution invented the metric system ; but it was not enforced till half a century later; and we, who have never adopted it, can find something familiar in terms which the common sense of the eighteenth century rejected as uncouth and inconvenient.

Land was measured in *ares* of about the size of half a lawn-tennis court: 30 *ares* made a *journal*, or a day's ploughing; 34 *ares* made an *arpent*, which was 85/100ths of an acre, and may be roughly translated by that word.

Length was measured by the *pied*, our 'foot,' and about the same size; the *aune*, or 'cubit' (forearm), of 3–4 feet (there were giants in those days); the *toise*, or 'fathom,' of about 6 feet; and the *lieue*, or 'league,' of about 2½ miles.

Capacity was measured by the *muid* (Lat. *modius*, a measure); the *muid* contained 12 *septiers*, 144 *boisseaux*, and 1728 *litres*: but it is easier to remember that the *septier* was about 4 bushels, and the *boisseau* about ⅓rd of a bushel.

Weight was generally reckoned by the *livre*, roughly equivalent to our 'pound.'

COINAGE

The coinage of the revolution followed, on the whole, that of the monarchy, even retaining Louis' head for a time after the fall of the throne. But the higher denominations disappeared from common use with the introduction of paper *assignats*.

The *livre* or *franc* (not the *livre parisis* of Paris, but the *livre tournois* of Tours, which ousted its more valuable rival in the mid-seventeenth century) was no longer a coin, but a standard of value, used for reckoning incomes, or luxury-values, like our 'guinea.' The standard coins in 1789 were, in gold, the *louis* of 24 *livres* (there was also a double and a half *louis*); in silver, the *écu* of 3 *livres* (there was also a *gros écu* of 6 *livres*), and 30, 24, 15, and 12-*sou* pieces; in copper, the *sou* or *sol*, of which 20 went to the *livre* (there were also 2 and 1½ *sou* pieces), as well as smaller coins worth ½ *sou* (*demi-sol*, or *double liard*), ¼ *sou* (*liard*), and 1/12 *sou* (*denier*).

What was the value of these coins in our money ? Arthur Young reckons the *livre* at 10¼d.; in the years before the war of 1914–18 it was usually worth 10d.; but no great error will be made if it is taken as equivalent to our 'shilling': all that is then needed, to make sense of the huge arrays of francs that disfigure the history books, is to divide them by 20, and they become pounds sterling. That is what I have done in this book. The *louis d'or* of 24 *livres* may roughly be reckoned as a 'sovereign'; the *écu* of 3 *livres* as 'half a crown' in English currency, or a 'dollar' in American; and the *sou* as a 'half-penny,' or a 'cent.' It does not, of course, follow that the purchasing power of the French coins was that of their modern equivalents: it was probably about four times as great.

THE REVOLUTIONARY CALENDAR

The Revolutionary Calendar is confusing for three reasons: it begins 'at the wrong time of the year,' its first year is called 'AN II,' and it does not come into force until the last ten months of the period dealt with in this book.

When the Convention met for its first session on September 21st, 1792, it passed the famous resolution—'The National Convention unanimously decrees that royalty is abolished in France.' The official copy of this resolution, signed next day, was dated 'September 22nd, 1792, the first year of the Republic.' A year later, in October, '93, under decimal and anticlerical patronage, the Revolutionary Calendar was formally adopted. The first year of the Republic had now passed; the second (An II) was reckoned as from September 22nd, '93. The twelve months, at first called '1st,' '2nd,' and so on, consisted of 30 days each, divided into weeks of 10 days, each ending with a Tenth-day (*décadi*). A little later the months were appropriately and prettily named after the weather or the crops that might be expected of them—three autumn months, Vendémiaire, Brumaire, and Frimaire; three winter months, Nivôse, Pluviôse, and Ventôse; three spring months, Germinal, Floréal, and Prairial; and three summer months, Messidor, Thermidor, and Fructidor. There was, it is true, an awkward gap at the 'end ' of the year, between 30 fructidor, An II (September 16th) and 1 vendémiaire, An III (September 22nd) which had to be filled by five supernumerary days called *sansculottides*; but this hardly marred the most sensible calendar ever invented—too sensible for a country which calls the 10th, 11th, and 12th months of the year October, November, and December.

THE MENTAL DIFFICULTY

When all these difficulties have been overcome, there still remains the greatest obstacle to the understanding of the French Revolution. It is the difficulty of realizing that it was French, and that it was a Revolution. Historians too often assume, as Burke assumed, that because the French Revolution of 1789 did not proceed like the English Revolution of 1688, there must have been something wrong about it. They seem to expect Paris in 1789, or France in 1794, to behave with the calm and propriety of London in 1889, or England in 1894. True, our historical imaginations have been jolted by more recent events. Nineteenth-century complacency could hardly survive the shocks that the twentieth century had in store for it. Yet pupils have constantly to be urged: 'Use your mind; think what it would have been like, if you had been there; ask yourself what you would have done, if you had been in Louis' place, or Robespierre's. They were men, not monsters; but men faced with a difficult and dangerous task, as many statesmen are today. Try to understand them, before you either condemn them or excuse them.'

Perhaps the best guide to the revolution of 1789 is the history of the revolutions of 1830 and 1848. Perhaps the Paris Commune of 1871 is the best commentary on the Insurrectional Commune of 1792. Perhaps Dublin is more like Paris than London is. One who is puzzled by the French character can learn what it is like from a hundred sympathetic observers, from Sterne and Young to Edith Wharton and Gertrude Stein. The happenings of the last few years, so full of instruction for historians, have been expounded by a score of intelligent eye-witnesses. It is possible, as it was never possible before, to see the national character and institutions in the crucible, and to assay their worth. The present crisis ends one epoch of national greatness: does it begin another? The study of the French Revolution may suggest an answer.

I have tried to provide illustrations which will help the reader, and to avoid those which can be found in other books. If some of the maps and diagrams seem amateurish, it may be put down to war conditions, and to an incorrigible weakness for doing things for myself.

My gratitude is due to my successor at Magdalen, Mr. A. J. P. Taylor, and to my son, Mr. Anthony Thompson, for their kindness in reading the proofs; and to Mr. Basil Blackwell for making the business of publishing (to the author, at least) a pleasure.

J. M. T.

January, 1943.

CONTENTS

CHAPTER I: STATES-GENERAL (May–June, 1789)

CHAPTER II: NATIONAL ASSEMBLY (May–June, 1789)

CHAPTER III: BASTILLE (July, 1789)

CHAPTER IV: GRANDE PEUR (Summer, 1789)

CHAPTER V: FOUNDATION-DEEDS (August–October, 1789)

CHAPTER VI: PARIS (October, 1789–July, 1790)

CHAPTER VII: FREE FRANCE (1789–1791)

CHAPTER XV: DETHRONEMENT (August, 1792)

CHAPTER XVI: COMMUNE (August–September, 1792)

CHAPTER XVII: CONVENTION (September, 1792–January, 1793)

CHAPTER XVIII: GIRONDINS (September, 1792–June, 1793)

CHAPTER XIX: FEDERALISM (June–October, 1793)

CHAPTER XX: JACOBINISM (June–December, 1793)

APPENDICES

ILLUSTRATIONS

Chapter I

STATES-GENERAL

A man in a revolution resolving to do nothing which is not strictly according to established form resembles a man who has lost himself in the wilderness, and who stands crying 'Where is the king's highway? I will walk nowhere but on the king's highway.' In a wilderness a man should take the track which will carry him home. In a revolution we must have recourse to the highest law, the safety of the state.—(Sir John Maynard, 1689.)

There were good reasons for the enthusiasm with which the French people welcomed Louis XVI's decision, in the fifteenth year of his reign, to summon the States-general. It was the only parliament known to French history. The body which met at Versailles on May 5th, 1789, was the same as that in which representatives of the towns had first sat beside representatives of the clergy and the nobility five hundred years before. It was the same as that which for three hundred years had been consulted at every crisis in the succession, and during every emergency of the national fortunes. When the last Capet king of France died childless in 1328, the States-general saved the throne from Edward III of England, and preserved it for the first of the Valois. After Crécy and after Poitiers the States-general found supplies to carry on a national war. In 1483 it confirmed the succession of Charles VIII.

More than a century and a half had elapsed since this parliament was last summoned to deal with the crisis caused by the death of the most popular of French kings, and was first suppressed by the most tyrannical of French ministers. No one remembered a time when the government had consulted the people, and no one expected that such a time would come again. Were it proposed in our Parliament to revive the Court of Star Chamber, or to place the Anglican Church under a High Commission, what a rummaging there would be in the Record Office, and in the library of the House of Lords! The ignorance of the men of '89 as to the institutions of the seventeenth century was even more profound. No memory, no sure tradition survived of the parliament of 1614. For a hundred and seventy-five years no writs had been issued, no elections had been held. There was no trustworthy map of the old constituencies. No parliament-house existed in Paris or at Versailles. No one could tell how a deputy should be chosen, or what costume he should wear. Every detail of procedure had to be rediscovered and redefined. The statesmen could do nothing until the antiquarians had finished their work.

No one appreciated this more fully than Etienne-Charles Loménie de Brienne, the Archbishop of Toulouse, Louis XVI's Controller-general of Finance. He intended that the necessary research should take a long time;

F.R.—I

and he hoped that its results would discourage those who looked to the Estates for constitutional reform. He accordingly issued a decree (July 5th, '88) inviting the co-operation of as many bodies as possible in the investigation. Archivists and officials all over France were to collect documents and traditions bearing on the history of the national parliament. This mass of material was to be studied by committees representing local authorities and provincial assemblies. Learned men, led by members of the Academy of Inscriptions, were to contribute the results of their deep researches. It was suggested that in seven months' time Barentin, the Lord Privy Seal (*Garde des sceaux*), might be in a position to make a final report upon the outcome of all this learning. The minister's invitation was enthusiastically accepted. A flood of some five hundred pamphlets swept away the barriers of the Censorship. The clerks in Barentin's office were soon busily employed sorting out *dossiers* that came in from all over the country: this was docketed as from Thoumin of Paris, this from Riche of Soissons, this from Rouzet of Toulouse. A sheriff wrote from Houdin that no documents were discoverable in the local records, but that if he could find any old man in the district with the needed information, he would write again.

After two months of these activities, the reactionary Brienne fell from power, and was succeeded by Necker, the nominee of reform. The new Controller-general viewed with alarm an accumulation of evidence which had delighted his predecessor. Every doubt raised as to the constitution and procedure of the Estates made it less likely that they could be promptly summoned, or do their work effectively. One difficulty, in particular, suggested that, as a weapon for extracting supply, they might break in the minister's hands. It appeared that upon every occasion of which records remained the number of deputies summoned to the national parliament had been one for each of the three orders in each constituency. True, the Third Estate had sometimes sent more than its share of representatives. In 1483 they had outnumbered those of the clergy by thirty, and those of the nobility by thirty-two; in 1576 by forty-six and seventy-eight; in 1588 by fifty-eight and twelve; and in 1614 by forty-one and fifty-seven. But this concession to the growing power of the middle class had never been allowed to influence the decisions of the Estates. If matters came to a division, each delegation had cast its three votes, and no more. The representatives of the two privileged orders had always been able to outvote those of the one unprivileged order.

This injustice had continued unchallenged so long as the States acquiesced in the withdrawal of their ancient rights by a succession of rich and powerful monarchs. It could no longer be tolerated by an enlightened age which, in a growing urge of pamphlets, publicly expressed its intention of treating the States-general, as it treated other institutions of its Gothic past, according to the principles of reason and the lights of nature. In its prosperous days the States-general had imposed conditions upon kings. Even in the days of its de-

MAXIMES

MORALES ET POLITIQUES

TIRÉES

DE TÉLÉMAQUE;

IMPRIMÉES

Par LOUIS-AUGUSTE, Dauphin.

A VERSAILLES

De l'Imprimerie de Mᵍʳ LE DAUPHIN,

DIRIGÉE

Par A. M. LOTTIN, Libraire & Imprimeur
ordinaire de Monſeigneur le Dauphin.

M. DCC. LXVI.

LOUIS XVI AS PRINTER

Louis at the age of twelve had a private printing-press at Versailles, on which he set up and printed twenty-five copies of these extracts from Fénelon's 'Télémaque.' He is said to have presented the first copy to his grandfather, Louis XV, who opened it at a passage describing the tyranny of kings, and said, ' M. le Dauphin, you have finished your work; you had better break up the type.'

3

cline it had never ceased to register its complaints, or to voice its demands: it had, indeed, heightened its tone, as the power to enforce its wishes was taken away. Such subservience could no longer be borne. If the States of '89 were to be constituted in the same manner as those of 1614, the rights that might be forced from the hands of a weak king would be snatched by a still powerful aristocracy. The privileges of church and castle would supplant the pre-rogatives of the crown. The interests of the Commons, and of the vast majority of the people, would be ignored. Such a blighting of the national hopes might be averted by two essential and easy reforms. The repre-sentation of the Third Estate must be made at least equal to that of the other two orders combined; and effect must be given to this double representation by voting *par tête* instead of *par ordre*, two votes being cast by the deputies of the Commons in each constituency, instead of one.

Necker supported this claim, both as a philosopher and as a financier. He thought it a reasonable concession to public opinion; and he saw in it a means of using the Third Estate to break down the tax-privileges of the clergy and nobility. But he did not feel himself in a strong enough position to force the measure upon the king and the court without the backing of that kind of opinion which carried weight at Versailles. In his embarrass-ment he had recourse to the expedient so recently tried by his predecessor Calonne. He recalled the Notables of 1787, and submitted to their con-sideration the problems raised by the investigations of Brienne. These exponents of the higher opinion were nominated by the crown. They consisted of seven princes of the blood royal, forty-one nobles, twelve members of the King's Council, twelve ecclesiastics, thirty-four representa-tives of the *parlements*, two of the *chambre des comptes*, two of the *cour des aides*, sixteen deputies of the *pays d'états*, one *lieutenant-général*, and twenty-five *chefs municipaux* of the principal towns. To them the king added his ministers—the four Secretaries of State, and the Controller-general of Finance.

A hundred and forty-two Notables answered the royal summons. They met on November 6th in six panels (*bureaux*) of twenty-four members, each under the presidency of a prince of the blood royal. Each panel had before it such documents as Necker's antiquarian adviser, Pastoret, of the Academy of Inscriptions, considered sufficient, and a questionnaire under twenty-five heads submitted by the minister himself, dealing with the composition, election, convocation, and procedure of the proposed parliament. After a fortnight's discussion it appeared that the higher opinion was hardening in favour of the precedents of 1614. Necker submitted an urgent memo-randum, calling attention to the public demand for the double representation of the Third Estate. His ultimatum was badly received. The Prince de Conti complained that the country was being deluged with scandalous writ-ings, and moved, from the chair of the sixth panel, that ' all new systems be proscribed once for all, and that the constitution and the old forms be maintained in their integrity.' Necker hastily withdrew his memorandum, and left the Notables to answer his questions, which their ingenuity had by now increased from twenty-five to fifty-four. Their reply to the crucial fifth question—What should be the number of deputies of each order ?—was not encouraging. Only one of the six panels—that over which the king's less illiberal brother, the Comte de Provence, presided—showed a majority of one vote in favour of the double representation of the Third Estate.

But Necker was now in a mood to accept any omen. He noticed that minorities on the other five panels, amounting in all to twenty members, had voted in the same sense. He persuaded the King and Queen to accept this view, and the Queen attended Council for the first time to express her approval. The conclusions of the Conference (*Procès-verbal de l'Assemblée des Notables*) were held back from publication till the following year, and the world was informed by Necker's Report (*Résultat du Conseil*) of December 27th that the plan of double representation had the royal consent. The States-general was to consist of groups of four deputies apportioned, according to population, among some two hundred and fifty constituencies. Each deputation was to consist of one cleric, one noble, and two commoners. The report did not insist upon the three orders sitting together; and, on the ground that they should be free to settle their own procedure, the Estates were left to settle the controversy between voting *par ordre* or *par tête* if and as they would. But the essential point was gained. The veto of privilege had been destroyed. A legislature of two Orders had been substituted for one of three Orders. A medieval *Duma* was transformed into a modern Parliament, and the magic of representation turned a people into a nation.

When the first electoral regulations (*règlement*) appeared on January 24th, liberal opinion was further reassured. Not only would the Third Estate have its six hundred deputies, against the three hundred of each of the other orders; but they would also be elected by constituencies in which an attempt had been made to recognize the changes of population during the last hundred and seventy-five years. The industrial cities would at last be adequately represented. Bordeaux, Bourges, Lyons, Nîmes, Rouen, Tours, and Toulouse would each return sixteen members: Paris would be fully, indeed over-generously represented by forty members for the city, and twenty-eight for the suburbs. The franchise, too, was so democratic that one could only suppose that the government hoped to exploit the support of the conservative and royalist country-side against the restive working-class elements in the towns. With a few trivial exceptions, every Frenchman of twenty-five whose name was on the tax-rolls would have a vote.

But how much political power did this in fact imply? Politicians scrutinized with eagerness an electoral procedure which might seem unintelligible to the general public, but which was to determine the fate of the first national Parliament. The elections, they found, were to be carried out under the supervision of the magistrates (*baillis* and *sénéchaux*): the constituencies (*circonscriptions*) were the jurisdictions (*bailliages* and *sénéchaussées*) of the old feudal regime. About two hundred of the four hundred and ninety *circonscriptions* were constituencies by themselves: the rest were grouped as *bailliages secondaires* round *bailliages principaux*, to which they contributed their quota of delegates. In every constituency, whether principal or secondary, the three orders met separately, to nominate their delegates to the general assembly of the whole constituency; and it was here that the deputies were elected, and the address (*cahier*) finally drafted.

The meeting of the clergy could be attended by all clergy holding benefices (*possédant bénéfice*) in the constituency; except that, if they lived more than two leagues from the place of meeting, and could not provide for their work during absence, they must vote by proxy. Chapters and communities were represented by delegates, at the rate of one for every ten canons, one for every twenty members of a chapter, or unbeneficed clergy, and one for each community of monks or nuns. The meeting of the nobility could be attended by all nobles of the constituency who held their land by feudal tenure (*possédant fief*), as well as by such nobles as were acting as proxy for ecclesiastics (who, if appearing in person, did so among the clergy), or for women or minors (who could not appear in person) holding land by the same tenure. Nobles who owned such estates in more than one constituency could vote by proxy in them all.

If the meetings of the Third Estate had been organized in the same way as those of the other orders, they would have been of quite unmanageable size. It was considered that the ideal number for the general assembly of a constituency was about four hundred, made up of one hundred delegates from each of the privileged orders, and two hundred from the Third Estate. In order to keep within these limits it was necessary to subdivide the constituencies of the Commons. In the towns this was done by calling subordinate meetings of trades and professions. The professional and industrial guilds (*corporations*) chose one delegate for every hundred or two hundred of their members; and citizens who belonged to no such association two for every hundred members. In the country-side every village had its primary assembly, which chose two delegates for every two hundred (or less) households (*feux*), and one for every hundred households above that number. This arrangement gave full voting power to the rural population: but, in order to reduce still further the number of delegates at the general assembly, and to spare as many as possible the time and expense involved in journeying to the central place of meeting, it was further provided that only one in four of these delegates should attend the general assembly. Even in *bailliages principaux* which had no satellite constituencies attached to them the same reduction was obtained, if necessary, by excusing from attendance some of the delegates of the Third Estate.

When the general assembly at last met, the three orders sat together, under the magistrate (*bailli*) or his deputy, to call over the names of those present, and to make a declaration of their intention to carry out their duties in good faith. This done, they separated, in order to draw up the address (*cahier*) and to elect the deputies of each order. The address was drafted by a committee, and approved by the assembly of each order. The election was made by open voting in the assemblies of the clergy and nobles ; but the Third Estate, some of whose delegates could not write, or did not wish to publish their views, used the ballot. No candidate could be elected unless he obtained an absolute majority of those present and voting.

Apart from the wide franchise, the most important of these regulations was that which gave a direct vote to all the nobility, and to most of the clergy, but denied it to the Commons. The privilege of direct voting enabled the clergy and nobles to choose representatives whom they knew and trusted: the voters of the middle and lower classes were forced to delegate the choice of their deputies to those whom they nominated as electors. The results of this discrimination must have been disappointing to those who looked for a legislature consisting of three hundred bishops and peers, and six hundred farmers and ploughmen. The *noblesse de la robe* and *de province* so outnumbered the smart aristocracy of Versailles that they were able to elect a majority of noble deputies from men of their own stamp—men who, because excluded from the amenities of their rank, lacked the will to stand against the pretensions of the Commons, and who, because they were without political influence, lacked the power to do so. The numerous rank and file of the parochial clergy, the poorest and most respectable of their order, were enabled to choose representatives who detested both the ease of the monks and the pride of the bishops, whilst they shared the outlook and grievances of the common people.

The complicated regulations governing the elections of the Third Estate produced results particularly galling to the anti-reform party. Few tears, indeed, were shed over the disfranchisement of bankrupts, actors, or domestic servants, the victims of antique social or ecclesiastical taboos. Few members of any class regretted the exclusion from the polls of that eighth part of the population which was too poor to pay even the smallest tax. But there still remained some five out of a possible six million voters—the greatest body of men (it was remarked) exercising the right of election that Europe had ever seen. These five millions voted indirectly. They chose not deputies, but the electors of deputies. Their wishes counted for little in the ultimate selection of the person who was to represent their interests at Versailles. The parson, the village schoolmaster, or the small farmer who secured the suffrages of the primary assembly, and who met other parsons, farmers, or schoolmasters at the county town to draft an address and to elect a deputy, naturally fixed his choice upon someone with more than a village reputation. Influence, education, and knowledge of the world now seemed to him more necessary qualifications than acquaintance with the needs of the poor. In nearly half such cases his choice fell upon a resident in the central town of the *bailliage*.

The result was an over-representation of the trades, the professions, and the interests of property; it was a loss to democracy, but it was a gain to parliamentary leadership. The vast illiterate mass of the lower orders could be spoken for by the most intelligent and responsible members of the middle class. The majority of the deputies, whether clergy, nobles, or Commons, were more nearly of one character, and of one mind, than had ever been anticipated by those who settled the method of their election. It had been expected that the immemorial feuds between town and country, landlord and tenant, farmer and labourer, employer and workman, would enervate and immobilise the Estates. This calculation was upset by the necessities of an enlarged franchise and of an unwieldy electorate. The Commons, with the help of their sympathisers in the other orders, were enabled to build up a democratic block, the nucleus of a National Assembly.

This result was secured no less by the character than by the status of the deputies. There were no party lists, no sponsored candidates, no programmes, no tests, no election addresses. The candidates (it was remarked) were not men, but principles. Each electoral group chose the best men it could, on general grounds of patriotism and public reputation; with some regard, too, to the readiness of the nominee to sacrifice his time and resources to a political mission which would certainly be expensive, and perhaps dangerous. The selection was, in most cases, made with exemplary care. Since each candidate had to secure an absolute majority, only one could be elected at a time, and the choice of a group of deputies might well take a week, or more. This was an additional discouragement to the poorer or busier electors, and an additional guarantee of the choice of middle-class representatives.

Although the first writs (*lettres de convocation*) were issued on Feb. 7th, the last did not reach the constituencies until May 3rd, only two days before the opening of Parliament, and a number of deputies could not be elected in time to be present at this function. The most notable absentees were the twenty deputies for the Third Estate of Paris. The electoral regulations of the capital had been differently drawn from those of the rest of the country. One of the most jealously guarded privileges of Paris was that of sending its deputies direct to the States-general; it would be thought of not as a *bailliage*, but as a *généralité*, a self-contained group of *bailliages*. There was good reason for admitting this claim. The population of the capital was six times that of Bordeaux or Marseilles, and included a mass of the middle and lower classes without parallel elsewhere in the country. Even its clergy and nobility were far too numerous to be gathered into a single electoral meeting. Its vast Third Estate, with its infinite variety of social rank and occupation, could never be grouped under trades and professions. The city must be subdivided into electoral districts, whose voters, like those of the *bailliages secondaires*, contributed delegates to the general assembly of the whole city. Only the clergy were exempted from this arrangement. If beneficed, they voted directly in the general assembly. If unbeneficed, they elected delegates from a single meeting at the rate of one for every twenty of their number. If members of chapters or religious orders, they were represented in the same proportion as in other constituencies. The nobles voted in twenty wards (*quartiers*) of the city, according to their place of residence, and elected one delegate for every twenty of their number.

For the elections of the Third Estate the wards were subdivided into sixty districts, in each of which delegates were elected at the rate of one for every hundred voters. But because the government feared the common people of Paris more than that of other cities, a special franchise was set up. No one was qualified to vote for the Third Estate unless he could prove that he held an official post, or had taken a University degree, or occupied a position of trust (*commission ou emploi*), or was qualified (as *maître*) to teach his trade, or paid taxes at the rate of six shillings a year. The effect of this rule was to disfranchise not merely a sixth part of the population, as elsewhere, but nearly a quarter. As a further discouragement to illiterate or timid voters the ballot was disallowed; votes had to be given in writing, and read aloud by the scrutineers. The electoral assemblies were given very little time in which to do their work, and met in some fear of attack by the government. Less than twelve thousand voters represented a population of half a million at the polls of the Third Estate. But these Parisians already showed their spirit. The primary assemblies rejected the presiding officers appointed by the municipality, and chose four hundred and seven electors, instead of the one hundred and forty-seven to whom they were entitled. The general assembly took its full time over the choice of deputies. Paris had received its writs on April 15th. Electors were chosen in the suburbs on the 18th, and in the city on the 21st: but it was not till May 11th, a week after the deputies should have made their bow to the king at Versailles, that the elections began, and not till the 18th that they ended.

Every electoral assembly, from the original parish or trade meeting to the final assembly of the *bailliage*, whether it consisted of clergy, nobility, or Commons, was entitled to draw up an address to the crown (*cahier de doléances*) embodying its complaints and demands. The opportunity of expressing grievances which had accumulated during two centuries of arbitrary rule, and of airing ideas rendered fashionable by the writers of the day, was not neglected. A committee would be appointed to draft the document; but the expression of its views was often coloured by the sentiments and style of some prominent individual. At Nemours, sixteen Commissioners spent six days compiling the address of the Third Estate;

but their language was that of the Physiocrat Dupont. At Nîmes the *cahier* of the Commons was drafted by the Protestant Rabaut Saint-Etienne. Parts of the address of the nobles of Ponthieu were borrowed from a pamphlet by Thouret. The *cahiers* of the Third Estates of Aix and Chartres show evidence of the influence of their deputies, Servan and Pétion. Where local talent did not suffice to express what was in the minds of the electors, it was natural to copy what neighbouring constituencies were saying; and it was not uncommon to adopt one of the model forms which were in circulation. The Duc d'Orléans, one of the richest men in the country, whose estates were almost as large as his debts, issued a hundred thousand copies of an Instruction to his agents, which he hoped would direct the policy of his tenants all over the country. In some districts the parsons were forward to suggest models to their parishioners. Almost everywhere the influence of the lawyers, from that of the *bailli* or his substitute who presided over the local assembly of the three orders to that of the *notaire* who was called in to advise a handful of villagers, shows itself in the matter and form of the addresses. But a genuine attempt was made to ascertain the views of the electorates. In Paris special boxes were set up at the Châtelet and at the Town Hall into which citizens were invited to put memoranda or suggestions for the use of those who drafted the city address. If a model address, or the draft of some village politician, were adopted by a country assembly, it would be expanded by the addition of local complaints or petitions.

As the votes of the Third Estate were indirect, so were their addresses. Every electoral assembly had the right to draft a *cahier* : but these 'particular' *cahiers*, as they have been called, had to be combined, like the electors who carried them, with the 'particular' *cahiers* of other assemblies, till they were finally merged in the 'general' *cahier* of the constituency. The documents finally presented at Versailles—usually one by the deputies of each order in each constituency—included, along with the *doléances* themselves, the minutes (*procès-verbal*) of the meeting at which they had been drawn up, and the credentials (*mandat*) of the deputies who presented them. The number of these 'general' addresses must have been about six hundred; of the 'particular' addresses some twenty thousand are still in existence— enough to present the historian with a vivid and unique picture of a great country on the eve of revolution. Here is the *cahier* of the Third Estate of the city of Paris—a thoughtful and well-written essay on the burning topics of the day, drawn up by a committee that included six members of the Academy. Here is a plea for an international Court of Arbitration, put into the mouth of a small peasant community by its parson, who has evidently been reading Saint-Pierre's *Projet de paix perpétuelle.* Here are Monsieur Josse's *doléances des Dames de la Halle et des marchés de Paris,* written in characteristic 'Billingsgate'; and here is the illiterate record of the troubles of some remote village. 'This community'—so runs the almost illegible address of a hamlet near Marseilles—'composed of a very few inhabitants, almost all of them unable to read or write, is fortunate in having a *seigneur* of whom it has no complaints to make. He is fond of his tenants, and is kind to them whenever possible. It has a *curé*, too, who is a peace-lover, who sets a good example, and who is good to his parishioners, when-ever opportunity offers. These poor inhabitants have, then, no occasion to exercise their right of complaint against either squire or parson. Their only grievance is their poverty. They are heavily burdened by seigneurial and feudal charges, especially considering the barrenness of the soil. When their rents and taxes have been paid, they have hardly a penny left. They pay, indeed, without understanding what they are paying; though they are entirely convinced that they should pay, and that, if necessary, their landlord would explain to them why they do so. There is only one thing they ask— that the States-general should find a way to ease their lot, and to relieve the poverty of these poor people.'

The *cahiers* were conscientiously studied by the King and the King's ministers. The clergy, in the enforced leisure of the early weeks at Versailles, started an investigation of their own addresses; and the Commons employed Clermont-Tonnerre to summarize the opinions of their con-stituencies on the single subject of a constitution. But they have been re-examined with fresh interest by the archivists who still sometimes disinter them from the dust of municipal libraries. There is nothing in the range of historical evidence quite like them. They reveal with equal clearness the intelligent middle-class visualizing its reform programme, and the deep discontents of the working class, without whose driving force that pro-gramme could never have been carried through. Like an old photograph album, they record with unstudied and unerring accuracy the fashions and features of a society that has long since passed away.

It is a world in which conditions of life and abuses of government that modern taste would consider quite intolerable are borne with a patience and lack of resentment more ominous than red-hot indignation; yet it is a world in which the theorists agree with the practical politicians that nothing is to be gained by revolutionary violence that cannot be got by constitutional reform. It is a world in which there are deep divisions between class and class; yet it is a world in which there is no class war, and little class con-sciousness; a world in which all orders of society, whatever their other differences, are at one in demanding greater freedom from restrictions, greater equality of opportunities, and a larger voice in the government of the country; a world in which men of every shade of opinion profess loyalty to a limited monarchy, and tolerance of a reformed church. In this mood the country looks forward to a golden age in which—as one of the addresses put it—' Frenchmen will have one fatherland, and will be one people—a single family, whose elder members use their superior intelligence and powers only to increase the happiness of the younger, in which the national character will recover its energy, and patriotism will rule every heart, and Frenchmen will show what they can accomplish, once they are at liberty, and can make use of the advantages that nature has given them.' The evidence of the *cahiers* did not stand alone. Ever since Louis' promise to summon the Estates, Paris, and indeed all France, had been deluged with pamphlets (*brochures*), in which many of the sentiments contained in the *cahiers* were more fully and eloquently expressed. In the summer of '89 this flood was in full power. Nearly a hundred pamphlets came out in May. In June they appeared at the rate of more than a dozen a day. Their loosely stitched pages, in every variety of type and paper, still clutter up the shelves of the world's great libraries. Over twelve hundred occupy one section of the *Bibliothèque nationale*: the Chamber of Deputies possesses sixty bundles gathered by Camus: the collection of the indefatigable Croker contains over forty-eight thousand items, and fills five hundred shelves in the British Museum. Some are the undistinguished work of anonymous citizens : some carry the authority of names which hold an honourable place on the roll of the National Assembly. Their ephemeral objects give them a value lacking in more comprehensive treatises. They are instructive in what they say, and in what they fail to say. Their truths are often less enlightening than their falsehoods.

Amongst a mass of less memorable scribblings were a few solid compositions by able men that left a mark upon policy and opinion; and none more so than the *Qu'est-ce que le Tiers État ?* of the abbé Sieyès. Sieyès was already known by a slighter *Essai sur les privilèges*. Now, in six chapters, and some twenty thousand words, he expounded a Catechism for the Commons. What is the Third Estate ? he asked; and answered, It is everything. The Commons are the workers, the privileged classes are drones in the hive.—What has the Third Estate counted for hitherto? Nothing. France is really an aristocracy.—What does the Third Estate demand? To count for something.—What has been done so far? The Ministers have attempted certain reforms, and the privileged orders have proposed certain concessions; but that is not enough.—What ought to be done? The general will of the people, expressed in a national assembly, can and must draw up a constitution defining and limiting the powers of the government. Sieyès put into words that everyone could understand things that everyone was thinking. His catechism became the gospel of the Third Estate in its search for political salvation. He may well have reflected that at the last meeting of the States-general the President of the order of nobles had described the Third Estate as the feudal inferiors (*hommagers et justiciables*) of the two privileged orders, and had rejected their modest claim to be the youngest sons (*cadets*) of the national family of Frenchmen. He realized and proclaimed that the Commons were now in a position to claim the whole inheritance. Sieyès preferred an inactive rôle in the background of a Revolution which he foresaw and forearmed: but there was profound truth in the contemporary caricature which represented him as a giant Gulliver towering above a Lilliputian Tuileries. His democratic idea dwarfed the throne.

A modern visitor to Paris might walk its spacious streets and scan its magnificent vistas without catching sight of the old capital in which the scene was set for the events of 1789. The finest buildings belong to an earlier or to a later date. Many of the winding old alleys, with their steep banks and dingy backwaters, through which imagination can still picture the flowing tide of revolution, have been straightened out into wide thoroughfares, or short-cut by airy unimaginative boulevards. It is as difficult to visualize the *tricoteuses* counting the fall of heads in the Place de la Concorde as it is to reconstruct the Place de Grève, where fashionable women of the previous generation sat at their hired windows to see Damiens tortured to death in front of the Town Hall. There are few public memorials of the greatest episode in French history. The relics of the Revolution have been housed in an aristocratic mansion of the Age of Louis XIV.

Versailles is much less changed. The visitor can follow the street through which the procession of the Estates moved on May 4th: he can enter the tennis court where the deputies took their patriotic oath on June 20th: he can stand under the balcony in which Lafayette kissed the queen's hand on October 6th, and promised to bring the royal family to the capital. Here is the biggest palace in the world, built at a cost of five million pounds, and no one knows how many lives, on a site which once held a sordid village, and a humble shooting-box. Here congregated a court so numerous that its dependants created a town of sixty thousand inhabitants. Here Parisians on holiday frequent the elaborate terraces, fountains, and parterres laid out by the same skilful hand as Greenwich Park and the gardens of the Vatican, where in the summer of '89 eager deputies jostled the elegant ghosts of an age they had come to destroy. Here are the rustic bridges and grottoes, the miniature mill and the model dairy where Marie Antoinette tried to forget that she was the unhappiest queen in the world. Perhaps there was no spot in France where nature and art had been brought into closer harmony, or where greater triumphs had been achieved by intelligent planning: no scene perhaps so well set for the curbing of ancient privileges, and the remodelling of ancient institutions.

Louis XVI, unwilling either to give up his hunting, or to face the discomforts of residence at the Tuileries, had refused Necker's suggestion that the States-general should meet in Paris. It was at Versailles, on May 2nd, that he formally welcomed the deputies of the three orders. The tedious ceremony lasted from eleven o'clock in the morning till eight o'clock at night. The king was bored but benevolent, and had a kind word for old Michel Gérard, who appeared in the dress of a yeoman (*laboureur*). The deputies of the Third Estate were received in the Galerie des Glaces, whose seventeen great mirrors have reflected many historical gatherings—but none more momentous than this. They were offended by ceremonial slights upon their order, and they were shocked rather than impressed by the wasteful magnificence of Versailles. They returned for the week-end to their uncomfortable lodgings in the town with fewer hopes than they had brought with them.

On Monday morning, May 4th—it was a fine spring day, and the streets were already crowded with sight-seers from Paris—the deputies met at Nôtre Dame, to sing the *Veni Creator*, and to escort the Host in solemn procession to the church of Saint-Louis, where the opening of the Estates was to be consecrated by a mass, a sermon, and a *Te Deum*. It was such a gathering as no other country could show: the royal entry heralded by music of drums, fifes, and trumpets; the choir hung with embroidery and cloth of gold; the king enthroned on the right of the choir-screen, with the princes, ministers, and grand officers of the crown below him, on seats upholstered in velvet, and adorned with fleurs-de-lys; on the other side the queen, the princesses, and the ladies of the court, their robes glittering with jewels; the procession of deputies, marching two and two, with candles in their hands—drab, lawyer-like Commons, nobles in black and gold, with plumes in their hats, clergy in cassock and biretta, and bishops in the gorgeous vestments of the Gallican hierarchy. Then the sudden exit from the gloom of the church to the sun-lit street outside; the glittering ranks of Swiss and French Guards, the walls rich with tapestries, the windows gay with coloured frocks and waving handkerchiefs, the bands, the cheers, the clapping of half a million hands.

'Soon,' wrote an impressionable deputy of the *noblesse*, 'I no longer saw the scene before my eyes; my mind was obsessed with thoughts that both saddened and inspired. Here was France, in all her glory. What? (thought I), is it possible that troublesome, ambitious, and designing men should be seeking to destroy this splendid unity of the nation, to dissipate this glory, like smoke before the wind? My heart was overwhelmed with love of my country. Never before had I felt as I did at this moment the tie that binds us to our common soil, and to men who are our brothers. Here and now I make a solemn resolution. This dear France where I was born and brought up, the scene of all my experiences, the source of all my moral ideas—never will I betray the glorious trust it has placed in my hands: no motive shall rule my mind or will but that of the interest and welfare of my fellow-countrymen.' Such feelings were doubtless in many minds; and the crowd cheered as no French crowd had ever cheered before: but they kept their warmest welcome for Orléans, who appeared as a deputy, not as a prince; for Mirabeau, who, though a noble, walked with the Commons; and for the dingy ranks of the Third Estate, rather than for the brilliant array of bishops and peers. Louis had his *Vive le Roi!* For the queen alone there was generally silence, and sometimes abuse.

At Saint-Louis the Archbishop of Paris (de Juigné) and the choir of the Chapel Royal sang mass, and the Bishop of Nancy (de la Fare) preached a sermon two hours long. He was one of the youngest and ablest men on the bench, and in high favour at court. To Mirabeau, who thought that his friend Talleyrand should have been in the pulpit, his discourse seemed an inappropriate patchwork of clerical commonplaces—the baptism of Clovis, Louis XV's illness at Metz, denunciations of luxury, and insulting remarks about philosophy. But its thesis, that religion was the basis of national life, could not be gainsaid; many of its topics recalled the address of the clergy of Nancy, which the bishop had helped to draw up; and one passage referring to the grievances of the peasantry, and the barbarous business of tax-collecting, was greeted with loud applause, a thing unheard of in the presence of the king and the Host.

Louis dozed through the interminable discourse. But when he heard it attacked at court, he sent for the bishop's manuscript, and returned it a week later with a request that it should not be published. He might well have taken more offence: for though it called the queen 'a daughter of Emperors, who shares and emulates the beneficence of her august Spouse,' it also referred slightingly to her 'childish imitation of nature' at the Petit Trianon; and it contained one phrase so subversive that it might have been taken as the motto of the Revolution: *France, ta volonté suffit;* 'It is enough that France will have it so.' The bishop lived to make amends for his radicalism. Thirty-five years later he was chosen to preach at the coronation of Charles X.

Having thus made their bow to the king, and their prayers to Heaven, the deputies met on May 5th for the business that had brought them together. Their meeting-place, the Salle des Menus Plaisirs du Roi, was soon after these events pulled down: only prints remain to show the huge vaulted and pillared hall, which contained without difficulty twelve hundred deputies and (it is claimed) twice as many spectators. The representatives of the Commons had ample time in which to appreciate the discomforts as well as the splendours of the building; for they were summoned for eight o'clock, and were forced to spend over three hours waiting in its dim lobbies, whilst their names were called over, and their places assigned to them, according to rules of precedence drawn up in 1614. At about one o'clock the king arrived, the historic scene was set, and a series of official speeches opened the drama of the revolution.

Louis spoke first. He had carefully rehearsed his oration, and read it well. It was short, and (as even Mirabeau admitted) full of unexceptionable sentiments, and of a fatherly regard for his people. But the fatherliness seemed, to the more sensitive of his children, a trifle overstrained. He spoke of 'a general state of unrest and an exaggerated desire for change, which might completely pervert public opinion, if they were not dealt with at once by a conference of wise and moderate men.' 'A gathering of national representatives (he warned the deputies) will, no doubt, pay attention to wise and prudent advice.' So much stress on wisdom and moderation cast a chill upon the enthusiasm of May 4th; and dutiful applause was modified by doubt as to what precisely the king's intentions might be.

This it was the business of the Lord Privy Seal to expound. But Barentin's speech was not only far too long; it was almost inaudible. He was understood by his impatient audience to confirm the king's acquiescence in the double representation of the Commons, and to announce his willingness to sanction voting *par tête*, if they so desired. The privileged orders, he said, were ready to bear their part of the burden of taxation. The deputies were at liberty to debate a number of subjects—freedom of the press, maintenance of public order, reform of the criminal law, and education—such as were likely to secure 'the internal quiet of the realm, the glory of the throne, and the happiness of the king's subjects.' But there was not a word about the topic nearest the deputies' hearts—constitutional reform; and the speech ended with another warning against 'those dangerous innovations which enemies of the state would like to introduce along with the welcome and necessary changes that His Majesty desires.'

More liberal sentiments were expected from the next speaker, the Controller-general of Finance. But Necker was neither a statesman nor a Frenchman. He made no attempt to accommodate himself to the temper of his audience. He had felt it his duty to prepare a long speech, and to leave nothing unsaid. Fearing that his voice would give out, he had arranged with Dr Broussonnet, whose reading of reports in a loud carrying voice was familiar to members of the Royal Agricultural Society, to finish it for him. The result was disastrous. The bored deputies, after listening to a long financial statement, which admitted a deficit of £280,000, heard with dismay that the remedy for bankruptcy lay, not in Parliamentary control of taxation and expenditure, but in a further instalment of the minister's familiar operations on the money market, conducted 'under the patronage of the people.' The Estates were in fact given to understand that their presence at Versailles was of no account. The minister could do all that need be done without them.

There was another disappointment when Necker came to speak of the method of voting. He still refused to decide this crucial issue. His hope appeared to be that the Commons would leave the nobles and clergy to deal with the deficit by a voluntary surrender of their tax privileges. Then, all being well, they might be rewarded for their good behaviour by being allowed to outvote the privileged orders in the matters of less importance mentioned by the *Garde des sceaux*.

But the passage in Necker's interminable discourse which produced the most painful impression on the Commons was that in which he described the general attitude of the government towards the people. 'The king,' he said, 'enlightened by a long course of obstruction, and by the recent crises, has acquired the experience of a man of twice his age. He is more than ever set on reason, and he is able to judge where it lies. As soon as the first fluctuations of opinion inevitable in so large a body of deputies come to an end, and as soon as the dominant view of the assembly reveals itself, His Majesty will be able to judge the character of your deliberations. If it is such as he hopes, and has a right to expect, if it is such, too, as the sound majority of the nation hopes and asks, then the king will support your wishes and your acts; he will think it an honour to approve them; and from this co-operation of the best of princes with the most loyal of peoples will spring unshakable power, and benefits beyond compare.' The deputies cheered: but this was not at all what they wanted, or what they had been led to expect. They recalled the very different tone of Necker's report of December, and of the January declaration by the king. They could only suppose that the minister had been coerced by the court into modifying his proposals at the last minute. Were they here, they indignantly reflected, merely on sufferance, and to be dictated to? Were they to accept unconsulted, and without comment, reforms which the king threw to them, as a man throws a bone to his dog? Were they gratefully to discuss immaterial issues, without any certainty that they could carry a single effective resolution? Was this to be the futile end of so many debates, so many pamphlets, and such a troublesome and expensive gathering of twelve hundred Frenchmen?

'Let us hope,' wrote Mirabeau the same evening, 'that the Minister of Finance will understand, before it is too late, that the time for shilly-shallying is over; that it is no longer possible to resist the tide of public opinion—one must either swim with it, or be drowned. And let us hope that the representatives of the nation will realize, as never before, the dignity of their functions, their mission, and their character ; that they will put a price upon their acceptance of the king's offer; and that, instead of appearing to the world like schoolboys let off a caning, or wild with joy because they have been given an extra holiday, they will show themselves to be men—the chosen men of a nation which needs no constitution to make it the first in the world.' It was in this spirit that, a few days later, a deputy of the Commons, insulted by a member of the Comte de Provence's body-guard, challenged him to a duel, and ran him through. It was in this spirit that the Third Estate engaged, for the next six weeks, in a silent struggle for the mastery of the orders, and for the coercion of the crown.

Necker, to his bitter regret, had omitted to provide a separate meeting-place for the Commons.   For six weeks they met daily in the great hall which had been intended only for combined meetings of the three orders. There, under the eyes of their masters, the Sovereign People, they silently staked out their claim to be a parliament. For six weeks no letters were opened, no business was transacted, no money was voted, no reforms were discussed, lest the delegates of a people might seem to be acting as members of a class. ' It was not,' they plainly informed the king, 'three separate assemblies of three orders that Your Majesty summoned here, but the National Assembly, to busy itself, along with Your Majesty, in the regeneration of the realm.' Such an assembly could not begin its work until the credentials of its members had been verified in the name of the whole body. Necker had failed to provide any method of carrying out this formality. Until the clergy and nobles consented to sit, for this purpose at least, with the Commons, nothing else could be done. This deliberate inaction was a masterstroke of policy. It put the privileged orders in the wrong. It reduced the government of the country to impotence. Yet it left a still more formidable weapon in the hands of the Commons. That weapon was the power of the purse. Necker might scrape enough money together to avoid bankruptcy for another six months: no more.

While the Third Estate pursued a policy of glorious inaction, the nobles, almost unanimously, and the clergy, by a majority, refused to sit with the Commons. They proclaimed themselves separate orders, and proceeded to verify their credentials by themselves, in committee-rooms which had been prepared close at hand. It would be as tedious to describe as it was doubtless tiresome to experience the comings and goings between the three Houses, the interviews, the conferences, the royal letters, and the loyal answers which punctuated the long contest. It was soon realized that the nobility wished to dictate, but that the clergy were willing to negotiate. The choice made by the almost equally divided clergy would be decisive. Caricaturists pictured their order as a cat in clerical bands, sitting between the emblems of the nobility and the Commons, with the motto, 'I am waiting to see what happens.' Robespierre on May 16th and Mirabeau on May 18th suggested that an attempt should be made to deal with the clergy separately: but the House would not adopt this course. They believed inaction to be a better weapon than intrigue.

Strengthened by the arrival of the Paris deputies on June 3rd, and with Bailly in the chair, the Commons determined at last to verify their own credentials; but they did it deliberately not as representatives of the Third Order, but as representatives of the nation as a whole. Yet if they were not the *tiers état*, who were they? The point had been reached at which they must find another name for themselves. Two considerations guided their deliberations. They wished to win over the minority of waverers in the other two houses; and they wished to outmanœuvre the majority of reactionaries, who still hoped to use the States-general for their own purposes. To do this, they must transform a conference of three orders into a national Parliament, ready to co-operate with a friendly and reforming monarch. For such Louis was reputed to be; and in such a partnership it was reckoned that he would collaborate. Necker, though widely blamed for his lack of leadership, was still powerful at court, still influential with the Estates, and still popular in Paris. He might be able to lead Louis back from his unhistoric *rapprochement* with the privileged orders into the traditional alliance of King and People.

Some such thoughts were in the minds of the deputies when they engaged in the critical debate of June 17th. The Third Estate had already refused to act as an Order. They now refused to act as representatives of their electors, under whatever title, whether *représentans connus et verifiés* or *légitimes* (as suggested by Sieyès), whether *de la majeure partie* (Mounier) or *du peuple* (Mirabeau). They boldly assumed as an official title a term already widely used to describe their character—*Assemblée nationale,* the Assembly of the nation. For, as they proceeded to declare, 'National Assembly is the only title appropriate to the assembly, as things are : first, because its members are the only representatives properly and publicly known and accredited; secondly, because they have been sent here by practically the whole nation; and thirdly, because there can be only one single body of representatives, and no deputy, in whatever order or class he may have been chosen, has any right to exercise his functions apart from the present assembly.'

At the same time as the Commons made this declaration, they brought into play the weapon that they had hitherto kept in reserve. They announced, using a royal formula, *entend et décrète,* that the taxes would continue to be paid, however illegally they might have been imposed, just so long as the National Assembly continued in session: if for any reason it were dissolved, they would cease to be payable, as no longer carrying the free and formal consent of the nation. This was, of course, a direct challenge to the government, the arrogation of a royal prerogative. 'If His Majesty once gives His decided approbation of the proceedings of the Tiers État,' wrote the British ambassador, 'it will be little short of laying His Crown at their feet.'

The challenge came at a moment when private sorrow made Louis even less able than usual to deal with a public emergency. At Meudon, on June 4th, the Dauphin had died, at the age of seven, after a long and distressing illness. As soon as the week's lying-in-state, the ceremonial visits of condolence, and the public funeral were over, the king and queen took the opportunity to drive the few miles that separated the din and distractions of Versailles from the simpler comforts of Marly-le-Roi. But care was their coachman, and questions of state rode behind. Within a few days they were told of the resolutions of the Commons on June 17th. Such defiance, at so cruel a moment, seemed insufferable. Urged on by the queen and by his brothers, Louis determined to apply the only remedy he knew for a disobedient assembly. Orders were sent to close the Parliament-house against the deputies, and to prepare it for a Royal Session (*séance royale*).

The Commons were ready with a counter-move. On June 20th Versailles was placarded with notices of a royal session for the 22nd, and Bailly, the President of the Third Estate, received an official letter saying that its meetings must be suspended while the hall was got ready. The deputies none the less gathered outside the building. It was a wet morning. They found the doors closed, and soldiers, not carpenters, in possession. Determined to resist what was evidently a first step towards their dissolution, they moved on to the royal tennis-court (*jeu de paume*), whose large bare spaces soon echoed with their angry protests. Bailly, perhaps to prevent more provocative action, such as Sieyès' proposal that they should move to Paris, accepted Mounier's suggestion of the oath which was to make them famous, and to become a charter of French liberty.

'The National Assembly,' so their resolution ran, 'considering that since it was summoned to settle the constitution of the realm, to bring about the regeneration of public order, and to uphold the true principles of the monarchy, nothing can prevent it from continuing its deliberations, in whatever place it may be obliged to meet ; and considering that, wherever its members are gathered together, *there* is the National Assembly; resolves that all members of this assembly shall here and now take a solemn oath never to abandon it, and to go on meeting wherever circumstances may dictate, until the constitution of the realm is set up and consolidated on firm foundations; and that when this oath has been taken, all the members, severally and in common, shall confirm by their signatures this unshakeable resolution.' And so they did. Only one deputy, Martin Dauch of Castelnaudary, put after his name the word *opposant*. He could not, he said, conscientiously support measures not sanctioned by the king. It was to the credit of the majority that, being unable to remove his scruples, they agreed, 'as a proof of the liberty of opinion ', to let his signature stand.

Not long afterwards the Constituent Assembly commissioned David, the most famous artist of the day, to immortalize the scene of June 20th. His drawing was hung in the Salon of 1791. True to the taste of the age, it presented a romantic subject in a classical style, and mixed portraiture with symbolism. In the centre Bailly stands on a table, administering the oath, his right hand raised to heaven. From all sides carefully balanced groups of deputies stretch out their arms towards him. But Sieyès sits unmoved, as though pondering on the event; old Gérard, the peasant deputy, is clasping his hands in prayer; Barère, already a journalist, is reporting the scene, pen in hand; and Robespierre, the least demonstrative of men, strikes a dramatic attitude, his head thrown back, and both hands upon his breast, as though (it was the artist's own explanation) he had two hearts beating for liberty. In the foreground a monk (Dom Gerle, who was not there), a priest (Grégoire), and a Protestant pastor (Rabaut Saint-Etienne) are embracing one another. The facts needed no such embroidery of fiction. The oath of June 20th was a gesture that the world could not misinterpret. 'The step that the Commons have taken,' wrote Arthur Young the next day, 'is in fact an assumption of all authority in the Kingdom. They have at one stroke converted themselves into the Long Parliament of Charles I.'

Meanwhile at Marly, on June 19th, the king had called a Council, to draw up the agenda for the royal session. Louis, though inclined to conciliation, was unwilling at such a moment to add to the queen's domestic distress by opposing her political prejudices. Pestered by princes and bishops to make a firm stand against the Revolution, he was too weak to back Necker's policy of concessions. A month ago the minister had warned him against any appeal to force, and had drafted a declaration in which he was to accept an English type of Constitution. It would have been, almost word for word, the Charter granted by his younger brother, Louis XVIII, twenty-five years later. But the opportunity had been let slip. Necker's view now was that, though the assembly could no longer be dismissed, it might yet be divided. He accordingly proposed to ignore the 'National Assembly' resolution and the tax declaration of June 17th; to abolish those privileges (exemptions from taxation, and the monopoly of certain appointments) which the nobility had already shown their readiness to surrender; and to refuse common deliberation and voting *par tête* on the subject of other privileges, whilst allowing it on such constitutional questions as that of future meetings of the Estates. He had shown these proposals to the ministers most likely to give him their support, and he hoped to secure a majority at the Council. But to the party of No Compromise his plan seemed intolerable; and they prolonged the discussion till late at night. As a last resource the queen called the king out of the council-chamber, and induced him to adjourn the meeting.

The Council met again at Versailles on the 21st. The palace was surrounded with troops. The news of a clerical secession to the Commons (June 19th) and of the Tennis Court oath (June 20th) had stiffened the party of reaction. The Comte d'Artois, the king's counter-revolutionary brother, engaged the tennis court, to prevent another meeting of the Commons before the royal session, which was now postponed till the 23rd, in order that the seats provided for the general public might be removed. He and his elder and only less reactionary brother, the Comte de Provence, attended the Council, bringing with them two complaisant State Counsellors, De Gallisière and Videau de la Tour, whose vote, it was hoped, would secure a clear majority against Necker and the three ministers—Montmorin, Luzerne, and Saint-Priest—who were expected to support him. Necker's programme was reconsidered, and decisively turned down. It was agreed that the 'National Assembly' resolution should be quashed; that tax exemptions could be abolished only by resolution of the privileged orders themselves; that their monopolies were to be retained; that all important questions concerning the rights of the orders and the organization of the Estates should be reserved for debate and voting *par ordre*; and that the king might impose extraordinary taxation without the consent of the assembly. There was, indeed, to be an undertaking to consider certain reforms, but only if they were separately recommended by all three orders. The queen's party, as it was openly called, had won the day. Montmorin and Saint-Priest protested in vain. Necker, at the last minute, took the advice of his family, and stayed away from the royal session. But none of the ministers resigned. They were the servants of the king, though their sympathy might be with the Commons.

It soon appeared that the king's stand had come too late, and could only be maintained by arms. A display of force was, indeed, made: when the deputies arrived at the Parliament-house on June 23rd, they found it surrounded by troops. But this threat of violence, and the absence of the popular minister, served only to strengthen the spirit of resistance. Nor did the Commons now stand alone. On the previous day they had been joined by the Archbishops of Vienne and Bordeaux, at the head of a hundred and fifty clerical deputies. After listening to 280 speeches in five days, these representatives of the First Estate had at last decided to throw in their lot with the Third. Thus strengthened, the National Assembly was in no mood either to be intimidated or to be cajoled.

The king's opening speech, after lamenting that the Estates could not proceed peaceably with the task allotted to them, made two declarations. The first dealt with matters of procedure. The Assembly, it said, consists of three separate orders. The deputies are not bound by their mandates: they cannot plead that the electors instructed them to refuse 'supply' until they had secured a constitution. The orders are exhorted to sit together, and to vote *par tête*, in matters not affecting the rights of the privileged classes. Even so, each order may by a two-thirds majority veto the joint proceedings. Finally, the public are to be excluded from all debates. Having thus deprived the Commons of any chance of carrying out their own programme, the king proceeded in a second declaration to offer one of his own. Its heads were: no taxation without consent, except in a national emergency; equality of burdens, by leave of the privileged classes; an annual audit, and control over expenditure; the name *taille* to be abolished—but the hateful tax itself would be retained; reduction of indirect taxation to be considered; and the abolition of requisitioning by the government (*corvée*) recommended. As for private property, all rights and privileges were to be retained, together with all titles—though with some revision of the offices to which they were attached. Hunting rights (*capitaineries*) would be limited. Liberty of the press, and liberty of the person, especially the abolition of arbitrary warrants of arrest (*lettres de cachet*), could be discussed. Serfdom (*main-morte*) was to be done away with. A further provision of provincial assemblies would extend the benefits of local government to all parts of the country. The abolition of internal Customs would encourage commerce.

'Gentlemen,' the king himself concluded, 'you have just heard the formal embodiment of My views. It is an expression of My keen desire to do something for the common good. If by any ill chance (as I should be sorry to think) you fail to support Me in this high endeavour, I shall by Myself do what is best for My people. I shall regard Myself alone as their real representative.

Knowing the wishes of your constituents, and the complete agreement of My intentions with the will of the majority of the nation, I shall put complete trust in that unexampled unanimity, and proceed towards My intended goal with all the firmness and courage it may well inspire.'

Thus, in terms as clear as French could make them, the Assembly was reminded that it was only being allowed to play at reform. Louis could refuse to sanction what the deputies proposed: he could force them to accept what they disliked. He claims to have done everything hitherto by himself: he will, if necessary, dismiss them, and proceed alone. He will do for France what Frederick has done for Prussia, Catherine for Russia, Joseph for Austria. He will be the Benevolent Despot for whom the country has been waiting so long.

If such a declaration had been made six weeks earlier, it would have been acclaimed, and might have been accepted. Now it was too late. Louis, a weak and benevolent ruler, had let himself be persuaded that the Assembly would give way. The queen's party, taking a strong line, and exploiting the popularity of the crown, may really have thought that it would do so: yet they at least were ready for a refusal, which they reckoned would lose the deputies much of their popular support, and enable the king to make a successful appeal to force. But Necker, though he might have agreed that it was a clever move to offer reforms before 'supply' had been granted, showed by his absence, and by his offer to resign, what he thought the outcome would be. It was, in fact, a desperate attempt to regain the initiative for the crown, and to put on the assembly the responsibility for a rupture.

It was a responsibility from which the deputies would have shrunk six weeks ago: now they had good reason for shouldering it. The declaration that the assembly consisted of three Orders destroyed its claim to be national, and undid all its work. Under the procedure proposed by the king all the important reforms reserved for discussion could be vetoed by one or other of the privileged Orders. To accept the royal programme would be to surrender every right for which the Commons had been contending, without any security that its terms would be carried out. Refusal might seem to put them in the wrong. But they had two strong grounds of confidence. The king counted upon the disunity of the Orders: it had already been healed by the adherence of the clergy to the Commons. The king must have 'supply': now that Necker's policy had been disowned by the court, his bluff—the proposal to raise money without the help of the assembly—could be confidently called.

It had not been unheard of, under the previous reign, that when the king retired from a royal session of the Parlement, the magistrates stayed behind, and tore from their records the page on which they had been forced to register a royal decree. When Louis and his train, followed by most of the bishops and nobles, had left the hall, the deputies of the Third Estate sat on thunder-struck, uncertain what to do; they looked one at another, waiting for a suggestion to end their irresolution. Mirabeau gave them the lead that they wanted, and became from that moment the champion of their cause. 'Gentlemen,' he cried, 'I admit that the proposals you have just heard might save the country, were it not for the ever-present danger of despotism, and were it not for this apparatus of war that desecrates the temple of the nation, and would force you to be happy against your will. Who is it that gives these orders, and dictates these laws? It is your own representative (*mandataire*); it is one who ought rather to receive orders from us, the inviolable priesthood of the national policy, from us, to whom alone twenty-five millions of Frenchmen look for a happiness agreed, given, and received by all—a happiness, therefore, certain and sure.'

Mirabeau had hardly finished speaking when the Marquis de Dreux-Brézé, the Master of Ceremonies, reappeared, and said, 'Gentlemen, you have heard the king's orders.' It was a command to adjourn. 'Go and tell those who sent you,' replied Mirabeau, 'that we shall not budge from our places here except at the point of the bayonet.' More diplomatically, but no less firmly, Bailly informed the king's representative that the assembly had resolved beforehand that it would continue its sitting after the royal session, and that he could not adjourn it without a full and free debate. 'Is that the reply,' asked Dreux-Brézé, ' that you wish me to give to the king? '—'It is,' replied the President; 'for I take it (here he turned to the deputies) that no one can give orders to the assembled nation.'

When Louis heard what had passed, he replied peevishly, and with an oath, 'Very well, let them stay.' So they did; and consolidated their victory by issuing a declaration of parliamentary privilege that deserves a place amongst the foundation deeds of the Revolution: 'The National Assembly declares that the person of every deputy is inviolable, and that any individual, corporation, court, or commission that presumes to sue, arrest, or imprison any deputy by reason of any proposal or opinion uttered by him in the States-general, is acting with criminal and treacherous intent towards the nation, and is guilty of a capital crime.'

The resistance of the Commons was well timed. The same evening, after an hour's talk with the king, Necker withdrew his resignation. The next day another large body of clerical deputies went over to the Commons. On the 25th they were followed by nearly fifty nobles, and on the 26th by others of both orders. The reactionaries at Versailles still counselled resistance, and the queen called for arms—*Il faut des troupes!* But the counsel was discredited by failure, and the appeal to force was met by a new fear. Paris was moving. The *Gardes françaises*, upon whom the security of the capital depended, were declaring for the people, there was fear that the mutiny might spread to the Salis-Samade regiment, reputed the smartest in the French army. There was talk at the Palais royal, the parliament-house of the common people, of a march on Versailles; and noble deputies found their doors marked during the night with what they took to be threats of assassination.

When, therefore, on the 27th both clergy and nobility received royal orders to unite with the Third Estate, so that the whole assembly might 'occupy itself with the affairs of the nation,' they yielded, though with a bad grace, to a command which they knew to be inspired by fear of a popular attack on the throne.

A fortnight later, on the recommendation of its Constitutional Committee, the reunited body of the three orders called itself *l'Assemblée nationale constituante*—an assembly representative of the whole nation, whose function it was to enact a constitution. The claim passed unchallenged. It was a complete victory for the party of reform. The occasion was celebrated by one of the inartistic and rudely executed medals of the day, which showed a noble, a priest, and a commoner sitting round a table, with the motto, *Post tenebras lux*: the darkness of tyranny had ended in the dawn of a constitutional day.

An impartial historian must admit that the deputies of the nobles and clergy had good reason for resenting the king's order to join the Commons. The proceedings of the Third Estate, during the weeks between May 5th and June 27th, had been guided by shrewd political sense, and inspired by the highest motives of patriotism. But no acts of the old regime had been more arbitrary than those which the Third Estate deemed necessary in order to overset it. Nothing that Louis XIV or his successors had done showed more clearly than the resolutions of the last six weeks the need for a written constitution. As the nobles protested on June 19th, six hundred deputies had claimed to monopolize the authority of the States-general, without waiting for the co-operation of the other Orders, or for the consent of the king. They had claimed to turn their decrees into the law of the land. They had abolished and reimposed taxes. They had assumed for themselves, in unmistakable language, the privileges of the Orders and the prerogatives of the crown. They had, in truth, carried through a coup d'état, and placed themselves above the law and the constitution. Their acts could only be justified, if at all, by the national emergency: they could only be regularized by national consent.

The deputies of the Commons believed themselves to be so justified, and to be able to count on such consent. They had shown the world that the Third Estate 'counted for something.' They had shown the world that 'the General Will of the People, expressed in a National Assembly, can and must draw up a Constitution.' Moreover, their victory had been won not only for the people, but by the people. 'They have taught the People its powers,' wrote de Ferrières on June 28th; 'they have identified the private interests of six hundred representatives with the public interest of twenty million Frenchmen: it is a movement which will soon spread to Paris, and to the whole of France.'

CHAPTER II

NATIONAL ASSEMBLY

There were many men in the first Constituent Assembly who held sound Whiggish doctrines, and were for settling the Constitution with a proper provision for the liberties of the people.—(SCOTT, *The Antiquary*.)

THE transformation of the Third Estate into the National Assembly was made possible by divisions within the privileged Orders, and by the support of Paris. Its real cause was the clear-sighted policy and the spirited leadership of a group of middle-class deputies. This was the surprising fruit of electoral regulations which were expected to fill the Estates with a crowd of complaisant shopkeepers and ignorant country-folk. Chosen in feudal constituencies at polls presided over by royalist magistrates, and under the eye of the landlord and the priest, the representatives of twenty-four million farmers, peasants, and artisans were found to be the shrewdest heads in the country—lawyers and parsons, professional and business men, the most intelligent members of a minority which composed perhaps a twentieth part of the whole population. The Comte de Lamarck did not much exaggerate when he said that the National Assembly included practically all the ability, the energy, and the wits of the kingdom. 'No political assembly,' agreed Malouet, 'ever contained so many remarkable men.'

The French bourgeoisie of '89 belonged to a class proud of its economic independence, and of its social standing. Its members had earned or inherited a competence derived from honest toil. They cherished a self-respect that set them no further from the *aristos* above them than from the *sansculottes* below. Yet they resembled the English aristocracy, and differed from that of their own country, in being a class, not a caste. Their ranks were not fixed, but fluid. There was always an element in them surging upwards from *roturier* to *bourgeois*, and from *bourgeois* to *noble*. Of the two motives which ruled their lives, it might be doubted which spurred them to greater efforts—the hope of rising or the fear of falling in the social scale. Hitherto they had been kept out of the government of a country which they enlightened and enriched. But nothing had been able to exclude them from the management of its trade, its agriculture, or its administration. Here they had become apprenticed to political power. Here, during half a century of political outlawry, they had been educating themselves for 1789.

The deputies of the Third Estate were neither young men, nor inexperienced in affairs. He who considers the poor expectation of life in the eighteenth century, and the early years at which men qualified for public service, will be surprised to find how many of these legislators were men of mature age. In our present House of Commons ten members out of every hundred are over seventy, sixty-four are over fifty, and only twelve are under forty. Such examples of elderly efficiency could hardly be expected at a time when the average duration of life was believed to be under twenty-nine years. Yet of those members of the National Assembly whose ages are most easily ascertained, seventy-five per cent. were over forty, and only six per cent. under thirty.

If their professions are inquired into, it will appear that out of every hundred of those whom Burke slightingly described as 'country attorneys and obscure curates,' fifty at least were lawyers, twelve administrators, twelve tradesmen and business men, eight landed proprietors, seven agriculturalists, and two clergy, doctors, and officers of the army or navy. The statement that more than half of these men were lawyers needs some qualification. A legal education of some kind was commoner then than a classical education is now; and many of those engaged in business or administration possessed a knowledge of the law. Conversely, so many persons, both clergy and laymen, whether in their own right, or as members of corporations, exercised judicial functions of some kind, that almost everyone might add to his name one of the many qualifications of the legal profession. One good authority has counted among the six hundred deputies thirty members of the *haute magistrature*, thirty *baillis d'épée*, two hundred *magistrats des sièges inférieures*, and over two hundred *avocats*. Here too, as among the representatives of the clergy and nobility, will be remarked the preponderance of the humbler grades of the Order. The future of France was to be determined by the average Frenchman.

These lawyers were by no means the dry and dusty characters of fiction. They were men of action and men of affairs. Many of them had been chosen to represent the interests of the poor, and had a good right to do so. Villagers whose parson was only 'one of themselves' or farmers whose business took them to market went for advice on disputed points of feudal tenure, or in the endless litigation between tithe-owners and tithe-payers, to the solicitor (*procureur* or *notaire*) in the local town. In an age before country doctors were thought of, the lawyer was the friend of the people. In the towns his knowledge of legal forms made him indispensable in business transactions, and in municipal government. There were, too, not a few barristers (*avocats*) at provincial bars who, like Robespierre of Arras, gave their services without charge for the defence of poor clients, or for the championship of the victims of aristocratic or ecclesiastical tyranny.

Not only their knowledge of popular needs, but also their power of expressing them, qualified lawyers to play a leading part in a national Parliament. Many of them owed their professional eminence less to knowledge of the law than to forensic eloquence. Their education generally included a careful training in rhetoric—the classical rhetoric of the schools, the expository rhetoric of the pulpit, the emotional rhetoric of the bar. Much of the oratory of the period is uncongenial to modern taste. But the speakers of '89 knew their audience. Their speeches did the work that they were intended to do.

Some general reflexions will occur to one who looks through the biographies of these men. He will notice how many are of provincial, and especially of country-town origin. Not a few die where they were born, and confine their travels to this one visit to Versailles. They are rooted in the soil of their country-side. They are the products of the old-fashioned parochialism that they have come to destroy. Many of them inherit a local business or practice: they see life, as their fathers saw it, from the office window or the shop counter, and their horizon is bounded by the square of their native town. They have had, almost to a man, a Catholic, classical, and liberal education. Though the Jesuit schools have been closed since the middle of the century, their place has been taken by semi-clerical *collèges*, where education still has a strong religious background. Though French is fast becoming the language of France, the school-boy's model in eloquence is Cicero, in philosophy Seneca, and in morals Plutarch; and he knows more about the history of republican Rome than of monarchical Paris. Though the curriculum is still that of the age of Louis XIV, the teaching is influenced by the Enlightenment, and copies of the *Dictionnaire philosophique* and *Emile* pass surreptitiously from hand to hand. Nor did education end at college. It is remarkable how many future deputies, after a seminary education, threw up the church career for which it qualified them, in order to prepare themselves for literature or the law. The capital was full of clever young men who would rather starve in a Paris attic than grow fat in a provincial canonry.

In a country without professional politicians a legal apprenticeship is the natural approach to public life. The deputies of '89 may not have much political experience ; but they are too familiar with affairs to become mere dreamers or ideologists. They may not be amenable to party discipline; but they are sufficiently men of the world to know when a policy is practicable, and when it is visionary. They may not have read d'Holbach or Helvétius; but they will have dipped into the *Encyclopédie*. They are likely to have more sympathy with Voltaire's championship of Calas than with his attack upon *l'Infâme*. They prefer Beccaria to Mably, and *Qu'est-ce que le Tiers Etat?* to the *Contrat Social*. They are not likely to turn 1789 into *l'An deux mille quatre cent quarante*; but they will apply reason and common sense to each problem of statecraft as it comes before them.

The Third Estate was amazingly fortunate in its early leaders. Sieyès, the hero of June 17th, Bailly, the hero of June 20th, and Mirabeau, the hero of June 23rd, would have stood out in any assembly. Emmanuel-Joseph Sieyès (or, as he preferred to sign himself, Sieys) was a quiet donnish man of forty-one. Forced against his will into a clerical career by poor and pious parents, he consoled himself with political philosophy and music. He was not much interested in the past: French history provided many political warnings, but few political examples. He regarded the present world with cynical detachment. His passion was for an ideal state. His abstract mind was concerned with politics so far as it supplied the raw material for a perfect system of government. As Secretary to the Bishop of Tréguier he had come to hate landlordism, and to pity the Breton poor. As a member of the Provincial Assembly of Orléans he had worked with Lavoisier to reform agriculture, taxation, and commerce. In Paris, refusing to live by the altar, he had become the oracle of a set of younger men interested in the political and economic questions of the day. He admired the political speculations of Spinoza, and emulated his philosophical detachment. An 'ungraceful and uneloquent speaker,' he had an inspired pen, and was master of the *mot juste* which sums up a policy. No one did greater service for the popular cause in the summer of '89, or less for it afterwards. His cynical temper and lack of social gifts drove him back into the silence from which he had emerged. He lived on through the Revolution, waiting for an opportunity for the perfect state. When at last it came, he embodied a life-study of political science—some said that he claimed to know it all—in the liberal constitution which Bonaparte turned by a stroke of the pen into the despotism of Brumaire.

By the side of Sieyès sat another unprofessional revolutionist, Jean-Sylvain Bailly. A year before, at the dangerous age of fifty-two, when any man may make a fool of himself in politics or in matrimony, Bailly had done both. He had married a widow, a woman with no pretensions to culture, and he had thrown up a distinguished scientific career to dabble in municipal politics. Born in the Louvre, where his father had been hereditary Keeper of the king's pictures, he had graduated in art and literature, before devoting his mature talents to astronomy. A monograph on the satellites of Jupiter, and a controversy with Voltaire, earned him the membership of three Academies, and a reputation for orthodoxy which was hardly shaken by the suspicion that he doubted the literal truth of *Genesis*. In politics his first interest was in the planetary laws of official procedure, and he never seemed quite happy unless he had his eye fixed upon rules and precedents. But his house became a centre for young reformers, he was elected a deputy for the Third Estate of Paris, and his age and distinction marked him out both for the Mayoralty and for the first Presidency of the National Assembly.

Seniority might make Bailly a leader, and authorship Sieyès: leadership came by natural right to Honoré-Gabriel Riquetti, Comte de Mirabeau. At court the Mirabeau family might be accounted poor provincials, and out of society. But the grandfather had been to the wars, and had outwitted death on more than one of Louis XV's battlefields. One of the uncles was a distinguished sailor, a Colonial governor, and almost a minister of the crown. The present head of the family, the old Marquis, was at once farmer, administrator, economist, and author. He knew all the philosophers and literary men of the day, and his *L'Ami des Hommes* was accounted one of the most remarkable books of the century.

His eldest son was a thickset bull-headed man, with a shock of hair, and a strong pock-marked face that reminded Chateaubriand of a *Last Judgement* of Michelangelo. The prodigious offspring of a prodigious parentage, which had startled the world with every exaggeration of vice or virtue, the Comte de Mirabeau was the life-long victim of two passions. He could not see a pretty woman without falling in love with her, nor encounter a subject of controversy without writing about it. At twenty-one he had enough ability, said his uncle, to become general, admiral, minister, chancellor, pope, or anything he pleased. By forty a disreputable series of matrimonial scandals had been varied, and sometimes advertised, by a succession of brilliant publications. Pamphlets on arbitrary imprisonment, finance, despotism, music, free-masonry, and other topics of the day, flowed from his pen. As spendthrift in his sympathies as in his purse, Mirabeau defended the Dutch against Joseph II, the press against the censorship, and the Jews against their Catholic persecutors. A venal and vicious man, his reputation was such that he was barred by the not very squeamish society of the Paris drawing-rooms, and distrusted by every party in the parliament-house at Versailles. At first no one would follow him: but he soon forced himself to the head of the deputies by his knowledge of the political world, by his grasp of the issues before the Revolution, and by his genius for expressing the public feeling of the moment. 'Resembling Wilkes (thought Macaulay) in the lower and grosser parts of his character, he had, in his higher qualities, some affinity to Chatham.' He was the first of the revolutionary leaders to form a policy, and to work to a plan. He was the nearest of them all to being a statesman.

Behind these three leaders stood, during the critical days of June, other men of varied and hardly inferior talents. Such was Mounier, the young hero of the Dauphiné revolution, deeply versed in Blackstone and Delolme, and working for the adoption of an English constitution; or Malouet, the Civil Intendant of Toulon, who had made up his mind at the age of twenty-five on every important issue in life and legislation, and was now at forty-nine puzzled to find that France could not be reconstructed according to the maxims of Colbert; or Rabaut Saint-Etienne, following in his father's steps as a devoted pastor and life-long champion of Protestantism.

Beside the representatives of the old world there sat, for a short time, six deputies of the new. In the West Indian island of San Domingo, as early as August, 1788, a secret committee, soon backed by sympathisers in Paris, had begun to work for liberation and self-government. The colonists were invited to send deputies to the States-general. They would have preferred an opportunity of ventilating their grievances without admitting their dependence on the mother country. Nevertheless elections were held, and *cahiers* drawn up, without much regard for the royal regulations; and soon no less than thirty-one deputies disembarked, and arrived at the capital. The six whom the assembly agreed to accept were, however, so alarmed by the subversive votes of August 4th, that within a fortnight the white settlers of the Club Massiac were agitating for the original programme of independence; and this, under the interested influence of the Lameths, and other factory-owning and slave-owning deputies, the assembly at last allowed. Thus the French Revolution repaid in rather dubious coin the debt which it owed to the American rebellion.

In one respect most of the deputies of the Third Estate were at a disadvantage compared with those of the nobility and of the upper clergy. They were not rich men, and could not for long support themselves away from home in the expensive hotels and lodging-houses of Versailles. Sometimes, it is true, their constituents had given them a travelling allowance, and twelve or fifteen shillings a day for their board and lodging: but most of them had to pay their own expenses. It had not been anticipated that the States-general would sit for more than a week or so. When its stay at Versailles, and afterwards in Paris, extended from days to weeks, and from weeks to months, it became apparent that the only way to prevent its break-up was to pay its members. Following a report by its Finance Committee (August 12th), the assembly accepted the principle both of a stipend and of a travelling allowance. The stipend was subsequently fixed at eighteen shillings a day, and the travelling allowance at five shillings a league. So it remained until January, 1795, when the depreciation of the currency had rendered the payments of so little value that they were doubled. It was an arrangement which implied no stigma of class: it raised no party issue. Not to pay the representatives of the nation would be to deprive the national Parliament of some of its best members. The thought that they were paid by the nation, not by a political party, might encourage them to legislate nationally. It would at least relieve them of a suspicion that attaches to all democratic assemblies. 'Without a competence it is not easy for a public man to be honest: it is almost impossible for him to be thought so.'

The payment of members has been adopted, for not dissimilar reasons, by the Mother of Parliaments. Another arrangement which was accepted without question in '89 has never commended itself. At the same time and in the same way as the constituencies elected twelve hundred and twenty-three *députés titulaires* they elected five hundred and eighty-one *députés suppléants*, or supernumerary Members of Parliament. Some of these men came to Versailles with those for whom they were ready, if necessary, to act as substitutes; seats were even provided for them in the parliament-house. Others remained at home till their services might be required. Thus, in a country of political inexperience and bad communications, constant elections could be avoided, and the national representation be maintained in its entirety.

The same electoral regulations which enabled the middle class to represent the Commons also enabled the parish clergy to represent the church. Though bishops presided over the electoral assemblies, and were not uncommonly elected at the head of the poll, their vote carried no more weight than that of the humblest *curé* in their dioceses; and whilst every incumbent who could get away from his parish might cast his one direct vote, a hundred members of the wealthiest community or chapter could not outvote him. The result was that the Gallican church was represented at Versailles by forty-two bishops, fifty-five unbeneficed clergy (*abbés*), seven monks, and two hundred and five incumbents (*curés*).

It was the tragedy of the French church that it had lost the democratic temper of Catholicism, and that its hierarchy was determined no longer by talent or piety, but by birth and wealth. Its bishops in '89 were aristocrats to a man, and ranked with the lay nobility: its parish priests were drawn from the lower classes, and ranked with the peasantry and artisans. All the wealthiest endowments went to the rich; all the worst-paid posts went to the poor. Bishops who consorted with Intendants, and were better known as builders or business men than as preachers or saints, looked down upon the canons and incumbents of humbler birth whom their aristocratic scorn drove into counter-alliance with the people. Bishops who were zealous to live in their dioceses, to visit their parishes, to confirm, and to ordain, were often pluralists, exactors of tithes, and intolerant in proportion to their piety. This was the more noticeable at a time when, even in such devout provinces as Brittany, the monasteries were deserted, and there was a shortage of candidates for ordination, whilst the produce of the tithe was barely enough to secure an incumbent his *portion congrue* of thirty-five pounds a year. It need hardly be added that a church which was unable to support itself had ceased to proselytise. The glorious title of *convertisseur*—it is Gibbon's phrase —so much coveted by churchmen of the age of Louis XIV, was now obsolete.

An episcopate which ranged from the radical bishop of Chartres to the reactionary Evêque-comte de Léon could not be content with a single type of representative. No parliament could have contained two men more dissimilar than Champion de Cicé, Archbishop of Bordeaux, and Talleyrand-Périgord, Bishop of Autun. De Cicé had been in episcopal orders for nearly twenty years. He bore the reputation of a worldly, ambitious man, but one jealous for the rights of his clergy, and a devoted worker for social reform. Talleyrand, thrust into Orders against his will, had at the age of thirty-five just acquired a bishopric as a reward for his wit, his social gifts, and his unblushing careerism. A sly, cunning, and malicious man (it is the malicious judgement of another cripple, the American, Gouverneur Morris), he was soon to exchange a rôle in which he was entirely miscast for one in which his talents and ambitions could be indulged without reproach. Both men had this in common: they stood apart from the reactionary clergy; they saw that concessions must be made to the spirit of the age. They belonged to the minority of the episcopate which had favoured the granting of civil rights to Protestants, which led the reunion of the clergy with the Commons, and which initiated the renunciation of clerical privileges on August 4th. They made no protest against the suppression of the monastic orders: they were willing to accept the Civil Constitution of the Clergy. They comforted themselves with the reflexion that none of these things seriously interfered with the autocratic administration of their dioceses.

The representatives of the lower or parish clergy, who outnumbered their ecclesiastical superiors by two to one, might seem to be lacking in the varied experience, as they were certainly lacking in the worldly advantages of the Commons. But in truth this was hardly more so than it would be with any modern gathering of town and country clergy. Their uniformity of dress concealed deep differences of outlook and experience. Their seminarist education, the hourly obligation of office and mass, the class-badge of cassock and tonsure, and the rule of celibacy separated them from the world, and sometimes produced an austere and even fanatical intolerance. But among them might be found men of learning and men of affairs. They were at least as likely to have read the philosophers and the economists as most of their lay brethren; and more likely to know at first hand the grievances of the poor. Voltaire's *bon curé* had mastered enough medicine to prescribe for the minor ailments of his parishioners, enough agriculture to give them good advice on farming, and enough jurisprudence to prevent their ruining themselves by unnecessary litigation.

The leaders of the lower clergy included men of very different types. When Thomas Lindet became a constitutional bishop in 1791, his episcopal ring bore on one side the emblems of his faith, and on the other side the symbols of agriculture and economics. His reputation for secular views was such that, when he died, the clergy of the Bourbon restoration refused his body Christian burial. His antithesis was Jean-Siffrein Maury, a cobbler's son, who became a popular preacher, and the author of a famous essay on Eloquence. The Revolution knew him as the ablest and most exasperating defender of reaction, and the Empire as Napoleon's Cardinal-archbishop of Paris. To the Assembly he seemed a coarse violent man, with something of Luther in his make-up, and an equal master of vituperation and repartee. Henri Grégoire resembled Maury in nothing except sincerity. The recognized leader of the liberal clergy, he was perhaps the only one of them to be fired by an almost personal hatred of the crown. He preached with equal conviction charity towards the Jews, and respect for the rights of the people. A constitutional bishop, like Lindet, in '91, and one of the most popular figures in France, he remained a good Catholic without ceasing to be a good Jacobin, and still wore his bishop's dress in the President's chair of the Convention.

Such were the leaders. Among the rank and file of the clerical deputies were men of varied tastes and attainments. Here would be a counterpart of Mr. Abraham Adams, an excellent scholar, and 'a man of good sense, good parts, and good nature, but as ignorant of the ways of this world as an infant just entered into it'; and here of Mr. Trulliber, who was 'a parson on

Sundays, but all the other six days might more properly be called a farmer.'
Here might be an abbé Bérenger, a high authority on the cultivation of
silk-worms; and here the sensible and worldly abbé Barbotin of Prouvy,
half of whose mind was occupied by dislike of the bishops, and half by
anxiety for the pigs, the vegetable garden, and the pet canaries that he had
left behind him.

The reputation of the French clergy in the eighteenth century has been
allowed to suffer from the sins of a small minority. Chateaubriand admitted
that they were ignorant and narrow-minded, but said that their 'simplicity,
sanctity, poverty, and charity made them the worthiest part of the nation.'
His evidence is corroborated by that of a great English orator and a great
French historian. 'I found the clergy in general,' says Burke, 'persons of
moderate minds and decorous manners.' 'I am not sure,' writes de Tocqueville, 'whether, in spite of the crying faults of some of its members, there
was ever a more remarkable clergy than that of France at the moment when
it was overtaken by the French Revolution—more enlightened, more
national, less limited in the exercise of private virtue, or better provided with
public morality and religious faith.'

The Commons had certainly less opposition to fear from the clergy
than from the nobility. These too were a caste; but the root of their class-
loyalty was in this world, not in the next; and it was nourished by property,
tradition, and family pride, not by poverty, religious discipline, and service
for others. The old aristocratic families (*noblesse de l'épée*) had long ago lost
any direct part or power in the government of the country. Duties of local
magistracy or administration which were still performed by their counter-
parts in England had been transferred to lawyers and officials of middle-
class origin. They were shut up within a privileged pale of court pensions,
army commands, and ecclesiastical sinecures. They consoled themselves for
the loss of their functions by the reflexion that they had also lost their responsibilities. They lived, often extravagantly, on what their land-agents and
game-keepers could extract from ill-managed and impoverished estates; and
they made the most of privileges which placed them almost beyond the
reach of their creditors, and of the police. During his occasional visits to
the country the Duc de Brissac might dine and hunt with the *bourgeoisie*;
but if such humble acquaintances presumed to call back at his town house,
they would expect to feed in the servants' hall. Men of pedigree pointed
proudly to the portraits of remote ancestors that hung in their picture-
galleries; and would explain with complacency the superiority of a *grand
seigneur* to a mere *présenté*, who had occasionally appeared at court, whilst
agreeing that such a man was infinitely above the *non-présentés*, or *nouveaux
anoblis*, who ranked almost as low as commoners.

To such men it was bitter to think that they were far outnumbered by the
petite noblesse, country gentlemen with long pedigrees and short rent-rolls,

who lived proudly and penuriously in tumble-down *châteaux*, and found it less troublesome to alienate than to collect the feudal dues upon which they kept their sons in the army, or their daughters in nunneries. These *hoberaux* or *gentillâtres de province* were sometimes scholarly men, who quoted Horace, and subscribed to the *Encyclopédie*; but more often persons of rustic mind and manners, living on good terms with tenant-farmers not much worse off or much worse educated than themselves. They were probably more popular than those prosperous merchants who bought a country estate in order to put a *de* before their name, and aped the airs without having acquired the manners of a *grand seigneur*. They were certainly more popular than the *capitalistes* who, in the name of agricultural reform, enclosed commons, sold up unsuccessful farmers, and suppressed the villagers' right to fuel or fodder.

It has become traditional to think of the nobility of '89 as standing for nothing better than outworn loyalties and indefensible privileges—for the feudal rights, social monopolies, and fiscal exemptions in revenge for which the Revolution persecuted their Order. There were doubtless a few whose disorderly and indulgent way of life might seem to readers of Gibbon to presage the decline and fall of another Roman Empire. There were a few who, like the old Comte de Quélen, would reach down a rusty sword from its hook over the mantelpiece to fight for a formula, and would rather die than allow the King of France to be called the King of the French. But the old regime was falling to pieces around them, and many of them knew that reform was inevitable. Indeed, the medal struck to commemorate the presence of their order at Versailles bore the inscription, *Legi Regique Fideles*: even the *noblesse* put loyalty to the law before loyalty to the king.

But this was not all. If there were a revolution in England to-morrow, the old aristocracy would stand for something more than its entries in Debrett, and the amenities of its country-house life. It would stand, a little self-consciously, for *noblesse oblige*. It would stand for a cultivation of mind, a moral decency, and a loyalty to principles more easily grown from an old stock than grafted on a new. It was so with the best of the French nobility in '89. Their superior manners were the mark of a superior mind. Their taste, their fortunes, and their homes were the main security of the culture, the art, and the social amenities of the most elegant of all ages. It is possible, whilst understanding the cry, *A bas les aristocrates !*, to sympathize with the desire to preserve a society so decorative, so witty, and so humane, and to deplore the waste of so much that the old aristocracy might have contributed to the new France.

Within a year (June 19th, '90) the abolition of hereditary nobility gave legislative sanction to the liquidation of the aristocracy. The privileges of rank had gone long ago: why should its forms be retained? Of what use now were liveries, titles, or armorial bearings? Aristocracy would still survive from father to son as a family tradition, a way of life, a code of manners. Nothing could prevent the noble from thinking, behaving, and dying as a gentleman. It would need more than a decree to destroy the stamp of centuries, or the subtle effect of leisure, and lovely houses, and wide estates. What the men of '89 could not foresee was the substitution of a new privilege and a new snobbery for the old; the cult of official position and of commercial success; the promotion to places of high authority of men whose view of life was bounded by the solicitor's office, the counting-house, or the barrack-square; who had been forced by narrow circumstances to cultivate the art of getting on in life; and to whom obscurity, the lot of so many of the world's greatest men, would always be anathema.

A considerable number of the old nobility, either from conviction or from policy, and sometimes under English or American influences, accommodated themselves to the new regime. The Comte de Châteauneuf-Randon, a member of one of the oldest families in France, passed from the royal into the revolutionary army, sat on the Left in the Constituent Assembly, and in the Convention, and voted for the death of the king. The Marquis de Châteaurenard, who had, under another name, acted as secretary to Voltaire, lived to hold administrative posts during the Jacobin regime, and to serve under the Empire. The Marquis de Sillery, after a distinguished naval and military career, became a member of the Jacobin club and the Convention, but was involved in the treachery of Dumouriez, and executed during the Terror. One of the most prominent members of the Assembly was the Comte de Clermont-Tonnerre, a clever young aristocrat, who had exchanged the boredom of army and embassy life for the excitements of politics, and was chosen as first deputy for the Paris noblesse in '89. He led the secession of the nobles to the Commons, and supported the abolition of feudalism; but was soon suspected of royalism, and perished in the disorders of August, '92.

Others were more fortunate. The Duc de Bouillon was commandant of the Town Guard at Evreux in '89, and lived on there undisturbed until his death in '92. The Marquis de Ferrières was a soldier by profession, but by taste a scholar and a country gentleman. With easy convictions and conciliatory manners, he sat on in an assembly which many of his friends had deserted, resided in Paris during the events of '91–93, and from '93 onwards at his country seat, where he was a member of the local municipality, and bore the reputation of a good husband, a good landlord, and a good citizen.

None of these men was so well known outside his order, or had so captured the public imagination, as the young Marquis de Lafayette. Married at an age when his English contemporaries were leaving Eton for King's, and with wealth enough to enter the best company in Europe, Lafayette had deliberately turned his back on society to pursue adventure overseas. His refusal to grow up and his air of self-conscious rectitude have made it easy for historians to belittle a Peter Pan of revolution, an imitation Washington. But there is discernible in his American correspondence a genuine enthusiasm for liberty, and a gallant and even quixotic spirit, which the people of Paris were prompt to appreciate. 'Consecrated at the age of nineteen'—so he wrote of himself—'to the destruction of despotism and the liberty of mankind,' he had hoped, as he returned from America, that the revolution in the New World 'might serve as a lesson to the oppressors and an example to the oppressed' in the Old. He had visited England; he had toured the continent; he had talked with William Pitt and Frederick the Great; and he had only refused an Imperial invitation to the Crimea because he thought it his duty to join the Notables of '87. He found nothing in the old world that was not better in the new. Now, at the age of thirty-two, he confidently and even complacently expected a gradual and peaceful change from feudalism to social equality, from absolutism to limited monarchy, and from the rule of privilege to representative government.

To most of the deputies the situation did not seem to offer such a simple solution. They embodied, and they were conscious that they embodied, the rank, religion, and wealth of the greatest state in Christendom. Yet they were painfully aware that all their reforming efforts would be in vain, unless they could conciliate, exploit, or destroy one institution which, by immemorial tradition, stood outside and above them all—the French crown. The monarchy which Louis XVI inherited was still what it had been made by Henri IV, Louis XIII, and Louis XIV, by Sully, Richelieu, and Colbert. It called itself unique, inalienable, and absolute. The liberty, the property, and the lives of French citizens were held on sufferance from the king, and the king was responsible to none but God, by whose church he was anointed, and whose vicar he was upon earth. France owed everything to its kings, and had grown accustomed to expect everything from them.

But one thing had been neither expected nor given. The monarchy had never become democratic. There had always been a gap between the will of the king and the wishes of the people—a gap which during the eighteenth century had widened into a deep gulf of misunderstanding. As the people had acquired power to stand without the king, the king had lost power to support the people. There is at Windsor a charming building by Sir Christopher Wren, whose ceiling is apparently supported by two rows of substantial columns. They were added to the building—so tradition asserts—because the townspeople feared that the ceiling was not safe without them. Wren placed them there, as he was desired to do: but he left a gap between them and the roof they were intended to support. They do no work: the ceiling supports itself. It was so with the French monarchy and the French nation in 1789.

Louis XVI had now been on the throne for fifteen years. He had been given every opportunity to raise the crown from the discredit into which it had fallen owing to the disastrous end of Louis XIV's reign and the long inertia of Louis XV. In 1774 he had all France at his feet. He might have

guided, if he could not have suppressed, the liberalism which was beginning
to demand a more popular and enlightened form of government. The
throne, like the altar, might have outlived the beliefs it was designed to
express, and the institutions that had misinterpreted them. The King of
France might have headed a national revival, like the King of Poland. Had
he not declared for *une manière fixe d'être gouverné?* But Louis had shown
himself unable to keep in office the most enlightened ministers that France
had ever possessed. He had turned his back on the people, the traditional
friends of the crown, and had allied himself with the privileged classes,
its traditional enemies. When he came to the throne, Parisians had expressed their hopes of him by chalking on the statue of Henri IV, the most
popular of French kings, *resurrexit*—'he is risen again.' Now, in 1789,
Louis is not unpopular, but he has earned no gratitude, and he commands no
respect. The anger of the nation is not directed against the monarch, but
against the monarchy—against the system of which Louis is the heir and the
victim. His heart is with the people; but he is as much the prisoner of
Versailles as the Pope is the prisoner of the Vatican.

This absolute ruler of twenty-five million Frenchmen, this almost
miraculous personage, is pathetically unsuited for the part he has to play.
His countenance, remarks an English traveller, is agreeable and benign, and
bears more marks of sincerity in it than most of his countrymen. But he
holds his head stiffly, and peers short-sightedly at people only a few yards
away, with an appearance of pride foreign both to his real feelings and to his
undignified bearing. For at thirty-five, in spite of constant hunting, Louis is
getting fat. He walks like a man accustomed to horseback; and the figure
reflected in the gilded mirrors of the Salle des Glaces is that of a country
squire stumping round his stables. His mind is less stupid than slow. He is
fond of reading history; he is interested in maps; his hands are skilled in the
use of tools. He has from time to time encouraged his friends and surprised
his critics by deserting boar-hunting, and devoting himself to books. In '81
he perused Necker's dull and difficult *Compte Rendu* three times. He has a
good memory, and can follow complicated affairs in Council, and keep his
head at a ministers' meeting: but after a day with the hounds his snores have
been known to disturb the decorum of a *lit de justice.*

Louis is, above all, a benevolent and religious father of his people. His
charities have made him popular at Versailles, and in Paris the royal name
heads every philanthropic subscription-list. But in spite of fifteen years'
experience of kingship he is happiest when out hunting—an occasion of
state exactly organized, to which everything must give way. He still hates
court functions with the hatred of a shy, awkward, and tongue-tied young
man; and he dully regards the staring crowds that invade his bedroom and his
dinner-table, unable to frame the kind word or the appropriate gesture which
would express a friendliness he really feels. His passive courage, his stub-
bornness, and his lack of initiative are German rather than French. So is a

MARIE-ANTOINETTE IN 1791

From an unfinished pastel by Kucharski. The holes in the canvas are said to have been made by the bayonets of revolutionaries.

strain of greediness and brutality which, though less noticeable as he grows older, may still show itself in drunkenness, over-eating, and cruelty to animals.

Louis was not so simple as he seemed. It was soon discovered by those who had many dealings with him that his dullness concealed a deep duplicity, and his weakness an immovable obstinacy. He had the chief failing of Charles I without his charm, and the chief failing of James II without his capacity. Yet, with it all, he remained, both to the minister he dismissed and to the mayor who assisted at his execution, a good, simple, friendly man, better fitted, perhaps, for a mitre than for a crown. His dream was of retirement to some pleasant house in the country, where he could live undisturbed, with his family and his books around him. He should never have sat upon a throne; yet he might have done better as King of England than George III would have done as King of the French.

It was a tragic chance that bound Louis, whilst still only half a man, to a girl who at fifteen was already wholly feminine. Marie-Antoinette, graceful, impetuous, and pleasure-loving, had the strength of will that her husband lacked, but not the wisdom. The king came all the more easily under her influence because he had never been attracted by women, and could not be induced to follow the Bourbon custom of furnishing his drawing-room with a French mistress, whilst leaving the cares of his nursery to a foreign wife. After too many years of misunderstanding, a family and affection came together. Unhappily Louis' new devotion to Marie-Antoinette coincided with a time when the political situation made her influence over him doubly dangerous. She could never have been a political nonentity, like the last queen—the homely daughter of a dethroned prince. Her beauty made an instant appeal, especially to foreign eyes. 'It was impossible,' wrote Horace Walpole in 1775, ' to see anything but the Queen. Hebes and Floras, and Helens and Graces, are street-walkers to her. She is a statue of beauty when standing or sitting; grace itself when she moves.' She could not forget that she was a Habsburg, a princess of the proudest house in Europe. But her birth had been heralded to the world by the disastrous earthquake of Lisbon, when thirty thousand people lost their lives. Nor was she allowed to forget that she was a pledge of the unpopular Franco-Austrian alliance of 1756. Her youth was dogged by the malice of an anti-Austrian cabal, which magnified her least indiscretion into a crime.

Nor was her conduct such that it was difficult to find occasion for scandal. Made a wife and a queen at an age when she should have been at school, and removed from the staid economical atmosphere of Schönbrunn to the luxurious suppers and card-parties of Versailles, she slipped all too gaily into a life of frivolity and wastefulness. Her martinet mother, the Empress Maria-Theresa, made matters no better by treating her as a naughty child: her letters, based upon monthly reports from the Austrian ambassador, are full of admonitions to say her prayers, to read pious literature, and to clean her teeth. The Queen of France must pay more attention to her manners, spend less on dress, and correct her spelling. Her brother Joseph, the only one of her family who sees that she has grown up, and surrenders to her charm, cannot forbear to lecture her on the duties of her station, and to urge the use of her influence over the king to maintain the Franco-Austrian alliance, and to forward Habsburg interests in Bavaria and the Netherlands.

It must be added, in order to explain her position, that ever since the notorious 'necklace affair' Marie-Antoinette's enemies had not been content to attack her extravagance. Her supposed immorality, too, was the subject of a hundred scurrilous pamphlets on sale in the arcades of the Palais-Royal. Few people in Paris society, when they heard her name coupled with that of the Duc de Coigny or the Duc de Biron, believed that the charges were untrue. Popular dislike easily added another indictment against her.

In the early years of her marriage Paris could not fail to recognize in the new princess a charm which was as French as Louis' stolidity was German, and would have forgiven all other failings, if she had been the mother of a Dauphin: when the first child came, and was a girl, she was beyond forgiveness. She could be touched by the demonstrations of goodwill that rarely came her way: she was bitterly hurt by the common coldness. 'What harm have I done them?' (*Mais que leur ai-je donc fait?*), she cries, after one of these experiences. Yet she shows little understanding of the common people, and little sympathy with their troubles. The claims of the Commons rouse her to nothing but blind resentment. In a word, no one was more to blame for the fall of the French throne: indeed, the judicious Jefferson always maintained that but for her there would have been no Revolution: but nothing is more distasteful than to indict her.

Surrounding the young monarchs, living on them, shielding them, and compromising them, was ranged the vast hierarchy of the court. The king, the queen, the Dauphin, the Comte de Provence, and the Comte d'Artois all had their own Households (*maisons*) of civil, ecclesiastical, and military officials, monopolizing in all some fifteen thousand appointments, and blocking the throne with a shifting population of sixty thousand dependants. The King's Household alone comprised twenty-two departments, and occupied forty-five pages in the *Almanac de Versailles*. The salaries of the court, the upkeep of the royal residences, and the varied expenses of food, heating and lighting, hunting, travelling, and the rest, constituted nearly a quarter of the civil expenditure of the country. The Grand Falconer received fifteen thousand pounds a year, the Master of the Royal Wolf-hounds ten thousand pounds, and the Head Equerry twenty thousand pounds. At Versailles everything belonged to the king. He was the resident *seigneur*, whose favoured tenants enjoyed exemption from the property-tax (*taille*), and from the duty of billeting troops, and could count on royal subscriptions to their churches and charities. Until 1787 Versailles had no mayor and no municipality: its police and public services were in the hands of impoverished crown departments; and the economic interests of the growing middle class were sacrificed to the privileges of the court. When the Revolution came, the *cahiers* of the local tailors', cobblers', barbers', and innkeepers' Unions were no less outspoken than those of unroyal towns; even the eighty members of the palace band (*musique du roi*) petitioned for the right to present their complaints.

As behind the dignity of a royal town there lay disorder and discontent, so behind the magnificent façade of the court lay boredom, back-biting, and deep dissension. 'Versailles,' says Gouverneur Morris, 'is the most *triste séjour* on earth.' It was a life from which Louis XIV had sought escape in the Grand Trianon, Louis XV in the *petites appartements*, and Marie-Antoinette in the gardens of the Petit Trianon; a life which turned young Dubois-Crancé, after fifteen years' service in the royal guard, into a hot revolutionary. But whilst the social stresses of Versailles have been fully exploited by the memoirists and diarists of the time, historians have paid too little attention to the silent and constant pressure of court influence upon a king and ministers insulated from the public opinion of the capital. The queen's circle had increasingly and insidiously taken the place of a king's will, a king's mistress, and a king's ministers. Its influence was specially dangerous in an age which knew of no appeal to educated opinion through parliament, or the press. It was thus that Louis' ablest advisers had fallen—Turgot and Malesherbes, because they did not know how to appeal to the nation, and Necker, because he offended the court by attempting to do so.

It is not easy to pierce through the barrage of false sentiment with which royalist writers have attempted to hide the realities of Versailles. The Comte de Paroy, ordinarily a rational being, devotes eight pages of his memoirs to an account of some magic-lantern slides that he made for the young Dauphin. Madame Campan, in after-life a sensible school-mistress, meets attacks upon the queen's morals by stating that she never entered a bath without wearing a long flannel robe buttoned up to the chin. Candidly examined, the court dissolves into a series of social cliques, supping and gossiping in their separate apartments, competing for royal favour and patronage, spreading rival rumours and scandals, and each imagining that its own taste sets the fashion of the town.

Of Louis XV's seven daughters, only Mme Adelaide and Mme Victoire still resided at court in '89. They had shown their spirit when they nursed their father through his last dreadful illness. Their portraits, painted at an age when they could be flattered, still adorn the walls of Versailles. Faded and rather formidable old ladies, they were now the centre of a circle that intrigued against the Austrians and the anti-clericals, and slandered, if they could not exploit, the inexperience of the young queen. Monsieur, the Comte de Provence, thrived on a too easily earned reputation for liberalism and learning, and had become the head of a selfish but cautious counter-revolutionary clique, which aimed at supplanting the king in the favour of foreign courts. As Louis XVIII he lived to be sorry for his disloyalty. Louis' younger brother, the Comte d'Artois, had once been the favourite of the people, who saw in his talents and disposition some resemblance to Louis XIV. But he had suffered more than most from the bad education given to princes, and was now a stupid and provocative reactionary. A patron of the Die-hards, as his brother was of the Intelligentsia, he was a more determined foe of the Revolution, and a more vindictive enemy of the king and queen.

Other groups surrounded the king's younger sister, the pious reactionary Madame Elisabeth, the Pope's unofficial ambassador; Madame de Lamballe, a faithful friend of the queen, who came back to share her fate in the winter of '91; the smart extravagant Polignacs and de Noailles, who helped her to waste her money; and—politically the most important of all—the Orléans family, the traditional pretenders to the throne, and the recognized centre of opposition at court. At its head was an immensely rich but as immensely indebted and ineffectual prince, whose evil reputation rendered almost innocuous attempts to popularize his claims, and intrigues supported by his wealth, and inspired by his hatreds rather than by his ambitions.

France might have forgiven, and fate overlooked, a king's weakness, the frivolity of a queen, and the quarrels of a court, if there had been a body of ministers strong enough to support the crown, and to defy intrigue. There was not. The ministerial system created by Louis XIV needed a masterful and hard-working monarch at its head. Without such a centre of gravity the erratic relations between the five *conseils* and the four *secrétaires d'état* might at any moment dissolve into chaos. The development from Privy Council to Cabinet which was possible in England under the Hanoverians was not possible in France under the Bourbons. The appointment of enlightened and competent ministers in 1774 came, like other gestures of Louis XVI's unhappy reign, too late: it was, in any case, soon nullified by court intrigue, and the antipathy of the queen.

In one respect the position of a French minister was particularly hazardous. 'One of the causes of the ruin of this country,' wrote the Spanish ambassador in 1789, 'is the constant intrigues against the ministers, and the pensions available for any one who, for however short a time, has succeeded in becoming a minister. The result is that the country shows more confidence in the minister of to-morrow than in the minister of to-day; the personnel of the ministry is perpetually changing; and it never has a serious and definite policy.' During thirty-one years of public life Nuñez had seen only eleven ministers hold office in Spain. During the twenty-six months he had spent in France seventeen had come and gone, not counting those still in office: all were alive, and all drawing pensions. During the same thirty-one years France had employed fifty ministers, only three of whom had died in office.

Of the seven men who were nominally in power during the summer of '89, Montmorin (Foreign Affairs), Saint-Priest (Minister without portfolio), and Luzerne (Navy and Colonies) were reckoned to be reformers: Barentin (Keeper of the Seals), Villedeuil (Royal Household), and Puységur (War Office) were reckoned to be reactionaries. The minister to whom the king's constant need of funds gave pre-eminence, and the only one on whom he could count for a policy, was Jacques Necker, the Genevan banker, his Controller-general of Finance.

Brought into the government in 1776 to avert a national bankruptcy, Necker could not forget how he had climbed the dark staircase to Maurepas' cramped apartments under the roof of the palace at Versailles, with a mind full of ambition, and a portfolio full of projects of reform. He could not forget how he had been dismissed in '81 for suggesting a policy which he was recalled to introduce, seven years later, as the one hope of saving France from revolution. A Protestant, and the son of a Prussian lawyer, Necker has been hardly more misrepresented by the slanders of his enemies at court than by the flattery of his wife and daughter—the philanthropic Suzanne Curchod and the literary Germaine de Stael: nor do his own voluminous apologies remove the impression that he was a prig and a bore. A man of high principles, he was rich enough to indulge them by taking no salary, refusing the commissions and perquisites usual to his office, and lending a large part of his private fortune to the Treasury at a nominal rate of interest. There was nothing in him that made a natural appeal to Frenchmen. He owed his popularity, as Robespierre did after him, to qualities peculiarly uncommon in time of revolution—incorruptibility and moral courage. But he was a financier, not a statesman; he planned expedients; he had no long-term policy. 'He could never make up his mind to any move,' wrote his daughter, 'without long consideration and reflexion, in which he consulted both his conscience and his judgment, but never his personal interests.' He was too often uncertain what to do, and sorry afterwards that he had done it. Gibbon, who had nearly married his Suzanne, and knew him well, thought him 'an honest man—too honest, perhaps, for a minister.' 'A good bank-manager, no more,' is the judgement of de Ferrières. Napoleon, who called at Coppet on his way to victory at Marengo, reported that he was 'a regular don (*régent de collège*), with a heavy and pompous manner.'

Of the other ministers, Montmorin was an honest, unimpressive little man, overwhelmed by scruples and hesitations—more fitted to be a minister's clerk than a minister; but a loyal friend of the royal family, and always trying to find a way out of their troubles. Saint-Priest, too, was genuinely attached to the king, and thought of little but his safety. With him stood Luzerne, a veteran of the Seven Years' War, and a man of sense, but more occupied with botany than business. The feeble Barentin, Puységur—another soldier—and Villedeuil did nothing but compromise the royal cause, and disappeared from office before the summer was over.

The final argument of a Bourbon king had always been an appeal to force. Both the hesitation and the heroism of the Commons, during the summer of '89, turned on the use that Louis might make of the army. If the troops could have been trusted, the Revolution might have been brought to an end in six weeks. But they could not be trusted. The French army in '89 consisted of three elements: seventy-nine infantry regiments of the line, recruited by drink, bribery, and the press-gang; twenty-three regiments of foreign mercenaries; and a territorial militia, conscripted by lot from among the peasant population. The cavalry, artillery, and engineers attached to the regular forces were the best of their kind in Europe. Together with the Mounted Police (*maréchaussée*) and coast-guards, these standing forces numbered some two hundred and seventy thousand men. They had been reorganized and freshly trained in methods suggested by the Seven Years' War, and they were a formidable army. But this army was partly stationed on the frontiers, and partly frittered away in provincial garrisons. It had less experience of waging war than of suppressing bread-riots, and convoying food-waggons. In a sudden crisis the king could never count on being able to mobilize more than ten thousand men.

Nor could the officers be relied upon in an emergency. The aristocratic majority were already throwing up their commissions, and joining the exiles at Trier or Coblentz. The minority which sympathized with the revolutionary rank and file disliked the new-fangled German discipline they were expected to enforce, and would have refused to fire on the people. The royalist general de Bouillé wrote to Louis that, of the hundred and twenty battalions of infantry and the eighty squadrons of cavalry under his command, there were only five battalions of foreign troops on which he could rely. Necker warned the king a fortnight after the meeting of the States-general to put no confidence in the army. Even the Household troops (*garde du corps*) could not be trusted. In practice, then, the king could count only on his mercenaries—a sorry argument to use against a national Parliament, or a Paris mob.

CHAPTER III

BASTILLE

Then shame to manhood, and opprobrious more
To France than all her losses and defeats
Old or of later date, by sea or land,
Her house of bondage, worse than that of old
Which God avenged on Pharaoh—the Bastile.
Ye horrid towers, the abode of broken hearts,
Ye dungeons and ye cages of despair, . . .
There's not an English heart that would not leap
To hear that ye were fallen at last, to know
That even our enemies, so oft employed
In forging chains for us, themselves were free.

(COWPER, *The Task*, 1785.)

THE sentries who guarded the Parliament-house on June 23rd were a threat to the liberty of the assembly. The regiments which now surrounded Paris were a threat to the liberty of the people. He who controlled Paris controlled France, and could control the Revolution. It was from Paris that the Third Estate had drawn support and encouragement during its struggle with the privileged orders. Paris had celebrated the victories of the Commons on June 17th, 23rd, and 27th. No stroke against the assembly could be attempted unless Paris were overawed, and none would be decisive until Paris was disarmed. The forces of reaction had been defeated at Versailles, the seat of the King; they might yet be victorious in Paris, the seat of the Sovereign.

The Parisians knew very well that such was the king's design, and they were ready to meet it. At no moment during its long history had the capital of France been so truly the capital of the nation. In earlier crises of the national history it had too often been behind public opinion, or ahead of it. In the fourteenth century, in the days of Étienne Marcel and the Ordinance of 1357, it had been so far ahead as almost to anticipate the ideas of 1789. In the English wars of the fifteenth century it had been so far behind that France had been saved, not by Paris, but by Domrémy and Orléans. In the Wars of Religion Paris had been so strong for the old church against the new crown that it had to be captured by its king before it could become a national capital. So seriously had it become alienated from the throne during the troubles of the Fronde that never, since the flight of young Louis XIV, had it provided a home for the royal family.

Lately, during the long unviolent process of eighteenth-century change, the city had lost its reputation for standing out of the national life. Whilst the centre of fashion had shifted from Paris to Versailles, the centre of power had shifted from Versailles to Paris. The home of privilege was overshadowed by the home of wealth. During a century and more all the energy and talent of the provinces had flowed into the capital along the deep-cut channels of Colbert's centripetal road-system. Since the end of the Seven Years' War there had been such an influx of foreign visitors, foreign industries, and foreign gold as had never been known before. During half a century of growing prosperity and rising prices Paris had become the authentic capital of a new France—a capital in which a wealthy and progressive middle class ousted the landlords from their superfluous estates, the ecclesiastics from their half-empty churches and convents, and the municipality from its control of the public services.

This new Paris might be too far from the Mediterranean to understand the interests of the southern ports and manufacturing centres: it might be too absorbed in the business of feeding its vast population to consider the needs of the agricultural provinces: it might be too near the north-east frontier to view with detachment rumours of war or of foreign intrigue: it might even—as some thought—be too near Versailles successfully to defy the crown. Yet it remained the only possible capital of the country, the only possible centre of a national revolution. No city in France could approach it in size, wealth, or magnificence. There was little exaggeration in the claim of a guide-book popular in '89, which declared that 'Paris, this great city, this centre of art, this rendezvous of Europe, grows bigger and finer every day. It lays itself out to be the most beautiful city in the world. Its churches, its shows, its walks, its libraries, its museums, its men of learning and culture, attract a crowd of travellers, whose presence adds activity to the busy scene.'

Good Parisians never grew tired of guessing the population of the capital. Its most accurate citizens calculated that it contained 23,565 houses, 71,114 families, and 576,630 inhabitants. Gibbon, reckoning its area as 1160 *toises*, decided that it yielded only to London in the modern world, and to Babylon, Thebes, and Rome (which he credited with a population of 1,200,000) in the ancient world. It is generally agreed that its citizens must have numbered between five and six hundred thousand souls—a population still some three hundred thousand short of that of London, but five times as large as that of any other city in France.

Yet this monstrous wen of humanity, as Cobbett would have called it, viewed from the grey towers of Notre Dame, or from the green eminence of Montmartre, still bore the aspect of a fortified town of the Middle Ages. Its walls, indeed, had recently been pulled down: but the narrow twisting streets, the overhanging tenement-houses, six or seven storeys high, with their steep roofs and dormer windows, the dark courts and stairways, the rough *pavé*, the muddy kennel, and the noisome *égout*, showed little advance upon the discomforts of the seventeenth century. 'It is the most ill-contrived, ill-built, dirty stinking Town that can possibly be imagined,' writes a candid visitor: 'as for the inhabitants, they are ten times more nasty than the inhabitants of Edinburgh.' Francis Burdett had the intolerance of nineteen. The builders of the eighteenth century thought it more important to put up a fine new

De par le Roy

Cher et bien-amé, Nous vous mandons et ordonnons de recevoir dans votre Maison le S. Jean de S.te Sajullon et de l'y garder jusqu'à nouvel ordre de notre part, au moyen de la pension qui vous sera payée par notre trésor royal jusqu'à nouvel ordre Si n'y faites faute: Car tel est notre plaisir. Donné à Versailles le 5 avril 1777.

A LETTRE DE CACHET
See p. 139.

structure than to improve an old slum; and most travellers were prepared to overlook the dirt and discomfort of a town that could boast the portico of the Théâtre français, the dome of Sainte-Geneviève, and the pyramided Pont de Louis Seize.

In any event the picturesque squalor of Paris ended at the boulevards which marked the site of the old walls. Between them and the still unfinished *enceinte* and *barrières*, set up for the stricter enforcement of the *octroi*, lay the *faubourgs*—part slum areas, part suburban villas, part monastic buildings and enclosures, part fields and market-gardens. Directly the traveller passed the *barrières*, white dusty roads led him afield into an unsullied country-side. So sudden was this transition that it caused more scandal than surprise when, one April day in 1787, the hounds and horsemen of the Duc d'Orléans' hunt chased a deer past the Bastille, and up the rue Saint-Honoré, scattering and injuring citizens in the narrow streets, and killed it in the Place Louis Quinze, almost under the windows of the Tuileries.

An Englishman might have found many features in Paris to remind him of London. A river divided the place into two complementary but dissimilar parts; but the Seine was a more intimate and less stately stream than the Thames—one to bathe and fish in, not an ocean-going highway. On its north bank lay the City of Paris, with a cathedral, a law-court, and a town-hall. A Strand-like rue Saint-Honoré followed the north bank to a West End, with its royal palaces and its public parks. Eastwards a Tower-like Bastille guarded the approach from the slums and wharfs of the faubourg Saint-Antoine. On the south bank the academic and artistic quarters, unlike Bloomsbury and Chelsea, neighboured one another; whilst south-eastwards lay another poor quarter corresponding to Bermondsey and Greenwich. For Paris, like London, was pre-eminently a home of the common people.

In a society that was turning from the criticism of minor verse to the study of social and economic issues Paris presented unrivalled material for observation and experiment. Its preoccupation with finance, with business, with trade; its air of consuming everything and producing nothing; the toll it seemed to take of the wealth and skill and intelligence of the country; were more often an occasion of censure than of praise. 'Paris,' exclaimed Mirabeau, 'has been swallowing up for a long time past taxes raised all over the kingdom. It is the headquarters of a fiscal system that the provinces abhor. It has created the national debt. Paris by its shameless stock-jobbing has ruined the public credit, and compromised the national prestige. Paris is interested only in finance; the provinces are interested only in agriculture and commerce. Paris wants to make money; the provinces want to make laws.'

But a city that consisted entirely of consumers, financiers, and idlers would be an economic absurdity. In fact, every rich Parisian kept a troop of servants, and provided work for dozens of employees in the building, decorating, and clothing trades. Every journalist, politician, and lawyer needed board, lodging, and entertainment. Every visitor and sight-seer must have his cafés, theatres, and places of public amusement. The town must be kept, however inadequately, cleaned and lighted; news-vendors, pedlars, and water-sellers must go about their business; *fiacres* must ply for hire in the streets, and *diligences* carry their patrons into the country. The thousand needs of daily life must be supplied. Thus there grew up, in this city of consumers, the tanneries of Saint-Marcel, employing some thirty thousand tenement-dwellers, or the working-class suburb of Saint-Antoine, whose teeming population, close-packed at a hundred to the acre, supplied labour to the royal glass factory, and to the lesser employers in cabinet-making, paper-printing, and other luxury trades of the East End. When Dr Johnson paid his grudging visit to Paris, he was shown the 'Hortensia' brewery in which, with the help of steam and imported machinery, Antoine-Joseph Santerre brewed the British ales and porters so popular in the Anglicized clubs and cafés of the day.

Thus it came about that in a city whose rates (*contribution mobilière*) in 1791 yielded £386,000, or ten shillings per head of the population, and where nearly five hundred pounds could be asked for a piece of land in the city not a hundred feet square, at least one citizen in ten lived on charity. Indeed, official returns made in March, 1790, showed that a hundred and twenty thousand Parisians—one in five of the population—were at that time indigent, and in receipt of public relief. The Quinze-vingts contained over eight hundred blind people, the Enfants-trouvés nearly six thousand foundlings, and the city's hospitals and almshouses a shifting population of some twenty thousand inmates—the moraine-heaps of a vast mass of humanity worn down by the weight of bad housing, bad food, and bad sanitation.

The slums of Paris had their counterpart in every large city, and their inhabitants were not often seen north of the bridges, or west of the Bastille. The truly Parisian atmosphere of the streets depended on the *petite bourgeoisie*, upon the clerks, traders, shopkeepers, and small professional men, upon the artists, students, journalists, and minor exponents of the law, who filled the cheap lodgings and attics of the Marais, or of the rue Saint-André des Arcs. It has been held that the custom of living in flats or apartments militates against individualism, and lends itself more easily than the separate house system to mass-hysteria and mob-rule. Those who accept this view point to revolutionary Paris as one of their most convincing examples. Apart from a minority of rich *hôtel*-owners, few Parisians possessed a house or garden of their own. Most of them lived as a matter of course rather than of choice in *appartements*. This enormous aggregation of lodgers and flat-dwellers, whom lack of elbow-room obliged to spend their leisure and to take their meals in public, filled the Tuileries gardens, the boulevards, and the Palais-Royal with the most restless, intelligent, and talkative crowd in Europe.

The philosopher Hume, not many years before, had complained that 'the immense greatness of London renders the people fractious, mutinous, seditious, and even perhaps rebellious': but he considered that Paris, under an absolute government, was less liable to popular disorder. In spite of conditions of life that to modern ideas seem intolerable, in spite of a general disregard for the rights of the man in the street, in spite of an inquisitorial police-system, and the not uncommon spectacle of criminals done to death in public, Paris was regarded as a home of liberty for the ordinary citizen. Every provincial town envied the reputation that Paris bore for good manners: there was said to be no place in France where the people were better dressed, better washed, and more amiable. Rétif de la Bretonne, who spent his nights exploring the more sordid streets and cafés of the capital, calls it 'the freest, pleasantest, and happiest city in the world.' Even Mercier, whose satirical pen spares the reader no detail of nastiness, is compelled to admit that, whilst a country life may be very well for a disciple of Rousseau, no place but Paris can supply the company and conversation needed by an intelligent man.

An eloquent passage in Chateaubriand's *Essai sur les révolutions* (1797) compares modern Paris with ancient Athens. There flourished all the wit and talent of the provinces. There French intelligence blossomed in the endless talk of the *salon*, the café, and the club: there it came to flower in plays, pamphlets, and epigrams: there its exuberant growth clothed with new verdure the dead branches of the old order. 'Never,' wrote Madame de Stael, 'was Parisian society as a whole so brilliant and so serious-minded as between 1788 and 1791. Those who lived through those years are bound to admit that never was so much life and wit centred in one place.' Gibbon, looking for an effective climax to the volume which was to bring him fame, found it in a contrast between the Paris of the fourth century and the Paris of the eighteenth. 'If Julian,' he wrote in 1776, 'could now revisit the capital of France, he might converse with men of science and genius, capable of understanding and of instructing a disciple of the Greeks; he might excuse the lively and graceful follies of a nation whose martial spirit has never been enervated by the indulgence of luxury; and he must applaud the perfection of that inestimable art which softens and refines and embellishes the intercourse of social life.' It would be possible to quote a dozen passages from Gibbon's contemporaries expressing, though with less felicity, the same experience. Only those who had known Paris before the Revolution could understand what Talleyrand meant by his regretful phrase, *la douceur de vivre*. They had inhaled the last fragrance of a life which was already passing away.

But Paris was not only the focus of French culture: it was also the focus of French society and politics. 'This agglomeration, which is scarcely five miles across, controls the whole existence of the nation. Out of every seven Frenchmen, one lives there, and the other six depend upon what people think there, and what they do there. Doctrines, power, reputations, fashions, money, the fruits of the soil, the products of industry, flow into it, and are redistributed by the currents of thought, of opinion, and of transport, of which the capital is the focus. Its welfare or its downfall are very nearly commensurate with the health or ruin of the state itself.' The words are those of the leader of Fighting France; they explain the fall of his country a century and a half later: but they apply, with hardly a reservation, to the France of 1789; and they explain why Paris became the centre of the revolution.

For two months before the critical third week of June the government had been exercised about the state of affairs in the capital. During the elections of April the king received daily reports from the Lieutenant of Police as to what went on in the streets and at the polls; and unusual precautions were taken to prevent disorder. At first all was peaceful; but on the 27th an incident occurred serious in itself, and ominous for the future.

There was in the faubourg Saint-Antoine a wall-paper factory whose proprietor had from humble beginnings built up a business enjoying royal patronage, and employing three hundred and fifty hands. Réveillon may have been as good a master as he asserted himself to be: but at an election meeting a few days before he had been unwise enough to say that his workmen lived less well on the forty *sous* (1s. 8d.) a day he was now forced to pay them than on the fifteen *sous* (7½d.) that they had previously found sufficient. This remark was twisted by trade rivals into the statement that no workman was worth more than sevenpence-halfpenny a day, and an agitation was organized against Réveillon as though he were an enemy of the people. A certain abbé Roy was also accused of having incited the crowd, and fled rather than face a trial. On the afternoon of April 27th a mob of five or six hundred workers appeared in the streets, hanged Réveillon in effigy, armed themselves with clubs and torches, and began to pillage the shops in the Gobelins district, and in the Place de Grève. Troops were soon on the scene; but they could not prevent the mob from sacking the house of another un-popular employer, the powder-manufacturer Henriot, or from burning his furniture in the street. The next day more soldiers were out; but more rioters were out too. They served Réveillon's house as they had served Henriot's, they engaged in hand-to-hand fighting with the troops, and they answered the summons to surrender with cheers for the king, the Controller-general, and the Commons, and with cries of 'To Hell with the nobles and clergy!' By night-fall the riot was over: but some twenty bodies, which rumour multiplied into four hundred, lay dead upon the ground, and the wounded numbered at least twice as many as the killed.

In the summary vengeance or after the judicial inquiry that followed, several of the rioters were hanged, and many were sent to the galleys. There could be little doubt upon which side public sympathy lay. It was sufficiently expressed by the clergy of Saint-Paul, who wrote to Necker hoping that 'the king's great design of general amelioration would not be stopped by the intrigues of a handful of malcontents trying to raise revolt among the vilest of the people.' Réveillon, who had taken refuge in the Bastille, was compensated for his losses by the king himself; and the assembly, at a cost of a hundred pounds, presented him with a replica of a royal medal which had been looted from his house. Even the people forgave him, when he interceded on behalf of one of the rioters, a mother of seven children, and saved her from the gallows: three years later he is found supplying decorations for a patriotic fête in the capital.

This 'little Riot' (so Morris makes light of it) was significant.   The historian Taine describes those who were responsible for it as bandits and starving men: in fact most of them were the ordinary poor of Paris, roused to sudden violence by rumour, indignation, and the unaccustomed excitements of a general election. The affair scandalized fashionable Parisians, who found their way to a race-meeting at Vincennes barred by noisy crowds, which hurled abuse at them, and relieved them of their watches and purses. To the government it was a warning that they could on longer count on the traditional good temper of the capital.

By the electoral regulations of April, '89, Paris had been divided into sixty districts, in each of which enfranchised members of the Third Estate voted together, irrespective of class, profession, or trade. This arrangement had results unforeseen at the time, but of immense importance for the subsequent course of the Revolution. It gave to the Commons of the capital a local solidarity, and a germ of self-government, which grew into the organized independence of the districts, and of their later equivalent, the sections. It provided the common people with a voice and a weapon which both the assembly and the municipality were forced to respect.

At the moment, the fate of Paris was in the hands, not of the sixty districts, but of the four hundred electors whom they had appointed to choose their deputies for Versailles. The immediate work of the electors was, indeed, finished when, between May 11th and 18th, they had appointed twenty actual and twenty supernumerary deputies. Nevertheless they continued to meet, first at the Museum, and then at the Town Hall, almost daily. The royal nominees who were the legitimate rulers of the city found themselves pushed out of the municipal nest; and from this centre of administration their supplanters kept in touch with their representatives at Versailles, supported the stand of the National Assembly against the king, and provided revolutionary Paris with an organ of common opinion and common action.

Who were these electors, that they should take charge of the destinies of the capital? Their average age was forty-two. By profession fifty per cent of them were lawyers, and twenty-five per cent tradesmen: the remaining twenty-five per cent were equally divided between administration, art, learning, medicine, and other callings less easy to classify. Both in age and occupation they belonged to the same class as the deputies of the Commons; but they came from its more specialized city representatives. Their politics, too, were of the same stamp. Although they belonged to districts of Paris as different as Westminster is from Whitechapel, they spoke the same language, and held the same ideas—not those of a political party, but those of a capital which feels that it has a nation behind it. As Parisians, no doubt, they stood for the interests of property and profession; for those who had a stake in the country; for the bankers, business men, and tradesmen; for the *rentiers*, the holders of national stock, who pocketed every year, in the form of interest on their investments, half the revenue of the nation; and for the financiers whose fear of bankruptcy or civil war caused the shares of the *caisse d'escompte* to fall in May and June, and to rise in July:—in a word, they stood for all those who, in the hope of social stability and safe money, were ready to finance and support a popular revolution.

But let there be no mistake about it. These electors are more than Parisians: they are Frenchmen. They include, besides traders and business men, ecclesiastics, royal officials, artists, doctors, scientists, members of learned Academies, and men of letters. Camus, Condorcet, Marmontel, Guillotin, Bertholet are names that would do honour to any assembly. At their head, as President, stands no native Parisian, but a distinguished lawyer and historian of the West Indies, Moreau de Saint-Méry, as determined a champion of the popular cause in Paris as he was an opponent of it in the Antilles, and a living reminder that France is—as its people are proud of saying—an *empire*.

'The whole business is now over,' wrote Arthur Young on June 27th, ' and the revolution complete.' He left Paris on the 28th, without the least anticipation of what was to follow. Such indeed was the general state of mind. True, the popular demonstrations after the victory of the Commons were marked by some acts of violence. On June 30th a mob attacked the Abbaye, and, before the troops ordered up by the Duc de Châtelet could intervene, released fifteen men of the French Guard imprisoned there for desertion, theft, and other offences against army discipline. Two days later Louis graciously pardoned the liberators. The shortage of food in the capital (it was established that on July 14th only enough flour remained for three days' baking) increased the anxiety of a government long accustomed to regard the price of bread as a thermometer of the public temper. The *messageries*, too, brought alarming reports of rioting at Lyon and Metz.

Near Chalons, on July 9th, Young met a regiment marching to Paris. 'Maréchal Broglie (their officer told him) was appointed to command an army of fifty thousand men near Paris: it was necessary: the *tiers état* were running mad, and wanted some wholesome correction.' This was on the day after Mirabeau had moved that the king be asked to withdraw the troops already encamped between Paris and Versailles. The Assembly feared disorder in the capital no less than the king. But up to the very eve of the crisis it seems to have occurred to nobody that the twenty regiments by now encamped around Paris would be unable to control the situation, or that there was anything to fear from the respectable electors and docile districts of the capital. 'The stocks,' notes the British ambassador on July 2nd, 'continue to rise.'

On Saturday July 11th the king launched his attack. Necker, who since June 23rd had been cold-shouldered at court, was suddenly dismissed from office, and replaced by the dictatorial Baron de Breteuil, who had received his summons and instructions two days before. There could be no doubt that Breteuil's mission was to collaborate with de Broglie and Besenval in re-establishing by armed force the initiative, if not the absolute power of the crown. The stroke was cleverly timed. Necker left for the frontier at 5.30 on Saturday evening. On Sunday the assembly would not be sitting; the Bourse and the banks would be closed; and all good Parisians would be taking a week-end holiday. It was not, in fact, until the morning of the 12th that the news reached the beleaguered capital. It spread dismay in the *salons* of the financiers, who hurriedly decided to close the Bourse again next day, and sent a representative to Versailles to keep in touch with the situation. There were gloomy anticipations that the government might repudiate its debts, and the notes of the *caisse d'escompte* depreciated rapidly in a few hours.

The news spread dismay, too, amongst the crowds dancing at the *Fer à cheval*, or displaying their Sunday finery in the alleys of the Palais-Royal. Here might be seen a lively irresponsible young man from Guise, Camille Desmoulins by name, a graduate of Louis-le-Grand, who had for the last eight years tried in vain to make a living as a barrister attached to the Paris *parlement*. About half-past three on this Sunday afternoon Desmoulins stood with a group of friends deploring the cowardice of the city in face of the king's attack, when three young men came along, holding hands, and crying *Aux armes!* He joined them, and was persuaded to mount a table, and harangue the crowd. There were, he says, six thousand of them. His head was bursting with ideas, but he could not express them in an orderly way. He could only denounce the dismissal of Necker as an insult to the nation, and as the omen of another St Bartholomew's Eve, a massacre of patriots. He ended by repeating the call to arms. 'Let us take as our badge,' he cried, 'green cockades, the colour of hope!' He drew a pistol, and defied the police to arrest him. He would die a glorious death, sooner than see France enslaved.

The cry *Aux armes!* was taken up, and thousands of excited Parisians rushed from the garden into the streets. They forced the theatres to close their doors as a sign of public mourning. They paraded wax busts of Necker and Orléans from Curtius' gallery in the Palais-Royal. They forced the passers-by to cheer the Third Estate. They came to blows with German mercenaries under the Prince de Lambesc in the Place Vendôme, in the Place Louis Quinze, and by the *pont-tournant* over the Seine. Here a number of them were wounded. The cry of massacre was raised, and maddened the crowd. The foreign troops soon found themselves forced back, not only by citizens armed from the plunder of gunsmiths' shops, but also by the French Guard, who broke from their barracks with their arms and ammunition, and declared for the people. To lose command of the Guard was to lose command of Paris. At one o'clock next morning Besenval ordered a retreat to the Champ de Mars, and left the capital to its own resources.

Whilst the troops were in action, the police had disappeared. Their place was taken by armed citizens and French Guards, who limited the immediate disorder to the burning of the hated *barrières*, and the pillaging of a grain-store at the convent of Saint-Lazare. Private property suffered; but it was impossible to proceed against the rioters—as was pointed out by the law officer responsible for their prosecution—without arraigning the whole Revolution. Early next morning, July 13th, the electors took command of the situation. A standing committee, under one of the old municipal officers, the *prévôt des marchands*, Jacques de Flesselles, was to carry on the administration of the capital. Every district was to contribute two hundred citizens of good repute, and fit to bear arms, to form the nucleus of a Town Guard (*milice bourgeoise*). Their uniform was to be the red and blue of the city colours. The quotas were soon raised to eight hundred, and the total strength to forty-eight thousand. It need not have caused surprise that the supply of arms gave out; but the rumour was that Flesselles had withheld them. One way or another, order was maintained, the streets were lighted and patrolled, and offenders against the new authority met with summary punishment. Gouverneur Morris noted in his journal for the 13th that it was the first day since the troubles began on which he had dared to walk the streets, though he took the precaution to ornament his hat with a green bow in honour of the Third Estate. Yet security was only skin-deep. Whilst the American was writing up his diary, one of the electors, the abbé Lefebvre, sat in an office at the Town Hall, doling out rations of gunpowder to a threatening crowd, whose drunken carelessness might at any moment have blown the building sky-high.

Several times during the morning of Tuesday the 14th there were rumours that the royal troops were returning to the attack. The electors ordered barricades to be thrown up, and every step to be taken to block the entrances of the town. But soon it was found that the only soldiers to appear at the barriers were deserters from the king's troops; and the energies of the crowd turned to the search for arms and ammunition.

It had already been discovered that there were none at the Carthusian monastery to which Flesselles had directed attention, and none at the Arsenal, whose stores had been transferred two days before to the Town Hall and the Bastille. A deputation sent the previous evening to the Invalides, the Chelsea Hospital of Paris, reported that it contained enough muskets to arm thirty thousand citizens. A crowd gathered outside the building. The Governor, the old Marquis de Sombreuil, tried to refuse admission, and was only prevented by lack of time, and the insubordination of his men, from carrying out the order given by the War Office a few days earlier to render the weapons unusable. Before he could do anything the crowd forced its way in, and seized all the arms it could find.

Next, powder. Part of the Arsenal supply had already been distributed at the Town Hall; most of it was known to be in the Bastille. The governor of this formidable old fortress, the Marquis de Launey, was making ineffectual preparations for defence. His ordinary garrison of a hundred Swiss Guards and pensioners (*Invalides*) had been reinforced a week before by thirty men of the Salis-Samade regiment; but he was seriously short of food. The sight of unaccustomed gun-muzzles thrust out between the antiquated battlements that overlooked their crowded streets set the inhabitants of Saint-Antoine in a ferment. Complaints were made; and at ten o'clock on the morning of the 14th deputies arrived from the municipality—the first of many such during the day—begging the governor not to fire on the people. De Launey received the delegates courteously, asked them to share his *déjeuner*, and ordered the guns to be withdrawn. Meanwhile a crowd of sightseers had gathered in the unfortified outer court (*cour avancée*) of the fortress, and there was talk of an attack.

To prevent this, the municipality, about midday, sent a second deputation, under the elector Thuriot, to summon the governor, in the name of his country and nation, to surrender. De Launey took Thuriot up on to the battlements, to show him that the guns had been withdrawn. He guaranteed that, so long as the fortress was not attacked, its garrison would not fire. But he refused to surrender to a mob of civilians. Thuriot took this answer back to the Town Hall, and an order was given to proclaim it to the people: but as the herald raised the trumpet to his lips a sound of gunfire came from the direction of the Bastille.

No impartial account tells how hostilities began, or justifies the charge that de Launey fired treacherously on the crowd. But that he did so unnecessarily seems to be beyond doubt: and this provocation was the chief cause of what followed. About one o'clock a third deputation arrived from the Town Hall, with the proposal that a detachment of the *milice bourgeoise* should be admitted, to occupy the Bastille along with the royal troops. But these delegates were unable to reach the fortress; and when another party approached, in a vain hope of stopping hostilities, its drum and white flag were fired upon by the defenders.

The fighting now grew fierce and fatal. Between two and three in the afternoon the French Guard and the City Militia brought up guns, and an almost professional attack was made on the main defences of the fortress. Citizen volunteers led the way. It is related that Elie and Réole dragged away, at risk of their lives, some blazing hay-carts with which the garrison attempted to provide a smoke-screen; and that Hulin, with great daring, shot down the chains of the outer drawbridge. The attackers now occupied the inner approaches (*cour du gouverneur*), and the attack on the main drawbridge and gate could begin. In this close fighting the civilian assailants again showed a bravery which was acknowledged by their professional opponents, and lost heavily: eighty-three of them were killed outright, and eighty-eight wounded, fifteen fatally.

After two hours' cannonade, a white handkerchief fluttered from one of the towers, and a scrap of paper was pushed through a crack in the main gate. The assailants threw a plank over the moat. The first who tried to cross it fell, and was killed. The second, a man whom history later knew as Stanislas Maillard, succeeded. The paper was found to contain a threat to blow up the fortress, if an honourable capitulation were not granted. The crowd were now determined to capture the place at all costs. Their guns opened again on the bridge and gateway. The governor was prevented from carrying out his threat by his own men, who insisted on surrender. At last the footbridge was lowered, and then the main drawbridge, and the crowd rushed in. The Bastille had fallen.

The people used its right of conquest to destroy the fortress, but not to plunder it. Doors, furniture, and wood-work of all kinds were demolished. Papers were tossed out of the windows. The dungeons were opened, and the prisoners found in them—only seven remained since Malesherbes' merciful visitation of 1775—were released. Two of them, said to be the Comte d'Auche and Major White (Whyte de Malleville), an Englishman, were taken to the house of Santerre, the popular brewer of Saint-Antoine, and spent the night there. One had to be removed to an asylum: the other appeared at a window on the 17th, and waved his hat when the king passed by. De Launey, saved from immediate vengeance by Maillard, Elie, and Hulin, was pursued through the streets, and murdered by an angry crowd, before his protectors could convey him to the Town Hall. His fate was shared by three of his officers, and three of his men. Flesselles was shot down as he left the Town Hall to answer the charges of treachery brought against him.

Amid the almost incessant ringing of bells and firing of muskets, the shouting of excited crowds and the marching to and fro of the City Militia to which Paris had by this time grown accustomed, the siege of the Bastille passed almost unnoticed outside the remote district in which it took place. Dr Rigby of Norwich, who was staying in Paris at the time, was first made aware of what had happened when he met an immense crowd marching, or rather running—such is the impression produced by the rapid step of a French mob, or of a French regiment—along the rue Saint-Honoré towards the Palais-Royal. As it came nearer, he saw 'a flag, some large keys, and a paper elevated on a pole above the crowd, in which was inscribed '*La Bastille est prise et les portes sont ouvertes!*' This sight was greeted with 'shouts and shrieks, leaping and embracing, laughter and tears,' and every sign of frantic joy. But in a few moments another crowd followed. It was welcomed with equal signs of joy, but produced a very different impression upon the English visitor; for instead of trophies of victory it carried trophies of revenge —the bleeding heads of de Launey and Flesselles raised aloft on pikes.

The capture of the Bastille seemed miraculous to an age accustomed to scoff at miracles. That a massive medieval castle like Conway or Corfe, strengthened with guns and a garrison, should have surrendered after a few hours' fighting to a civilian crowd stiffened by a few soldiers, might well puzzle a professional mind. There was little food in the fortress; but the garrison was not starved out. Both besiegers and besieged realized that, if the affair dragged on, de Broglie's troops would be bound to intervene. The civilians had a few guns : but what could they have done against so rock-like a building? The governor soon lost what little discretion he possessed: but he need never have surrendered. The day was, in fact, won, not by guns or gunpowder, but by the moral force of the people. It was the enthusiasm of the people which inspired Hulin and his fellows with legendary courage. It was disdain of the people which inspired de Launey's threat to blow up the fortress. It was sympathy with the people which forced the garrison to surrender. The apparent miracle was the result of unwonted but not unnatural causes.

Couriers who set out for England on July 14th heard the firing of cannon for four hours after they left the capital, and believed that the Bastille was beating off its assailants. The sound of its fall was heard all over the world. The fortress, as old and dark as the feudal system it symbolized, had hung like doom over the poor inhabitants of the East End. To all Europe Linguet's memoirs had made it a sombre legend, a bogey to frighten school-children. With its destruction a new world seemed to come into being. Patriots dated their letters from July 14th as 'the first day of the first year of liberty.'

A key of the Bastille was presented by Lafayette to George Washington, the foster-parent of the French Revolution: he showed it, with some pride, to Chateaubriand, two years later. The bells from its clock-tower were to be seen, not long ago, in a workshop at Saint-Denis: the picture from its chapel altar hung in a Paris church. Of the mass of papers found in its cupboards—three centuries' accumulation of feudal and criminal records—some were thrown on to bonfires, some carted away by tradesmen to wrap their goods, some saved by collectors, and some gathered into carts by the Commune, to be sorted out by commissioners at the Town Hall. During the disturbances of August, '92, this deposit—the largest of all —was transferred to the Arsenal, where it furnished material for Manuel's *Bastille dévoilée*, and for his edition of Mirabeau's *Letters to Sophie*. Villenave's collection was the source of Jacob's speculations about the Man in the Iron Mask: Dubrowski's collection is in a library at Leningrad.

Whilst the contents of the Bastille were scattered to the winds, every stone of the building itself was torn down. The work of demolition was entrusted to one of its six hundred and thirty-three *Vainqueurs*, the builder Palloy, an ingenious and ubiquitous patriot, who exploited his opportunity to he full, and turned a contract into a career. A thousand workmen, helped by volunteers of both sexes, flung down the battlements that had so lately threatened them with destruction. Eighty-three envoys calling themselves Apostles of Liberty carried models of the Bastille carved out of its stones into every department of France. Its bolts and bars were fashioned into figures of Freedom, busts of popular heroes, snuff-boxes, ink-pots, and paper-weights. Its various relics were exhibited in what remained for many years one of the most frequented shows in Paris—Palloy's Liberty Museum. Stones from the Bastille were built into the new bridge over the Seine, and into the stairways of private houses, so that they might be trodden under foot by patriots. Every deputy was given a medal made of chains from the demolished dungeons. The little Dauphin played with a box of dominoes carved out of the marble mantelpiece from de Launey's apartment.

Not content with starting an industry which filled the antique-shops of Europe with bric-à-brac from the Bastille, Palloy proposed to erect on the site, which had been conceded to him in lieu of payment, a Column of Liberty. The first stone was laid on the third anniversary of the famous 14th: but the column, like the liberation it commemorated, was never completed. Fifty years later, when the project was revived, in his search for popularity, by Louis-Philippe, nothing was to be seen on the site but a plaster model of a fountain in the form of a life-sized elephant spouting water from its trunk, with which Napoleon had intended to divert Parisians from memories of the liberty he had taken away. The column which now stands over the buried dungeons of the Bastille commemorates the victims of another July revolution—the men who fell in the street-fighting of 1830.

The night of July 14th was the most anxious of the whole week. It seemed certain that the royal troops would now attack the city, which was full of rumours of their approach. The Town Guard ceaselessly patrolled the streets. The citizens were warned to stay awake, and to keep their lights burning. The night was noisy with gun-fire and bell-ringing. Householders sat up till dawn on their roofs or at their windows with piles of missiles at hand, to hurl on the invaders' heads.

In reality the danger was over. At Versailles the news of the arming of Paris, and of the capture of the Bastille, had worked another miracle. On July 13th the assembly had answered the king's challenge by declaring their unanimous confidence in Necker, and in the ministers who shared his fall; they protested against the march of troops on the capital; and they declared that no power, not even the king's, could pronounce 'the infamous word bankruptcy.' But Louis had stood firm; and every hour the deputies expected to hear the tramp of royal troops sent to close the parliament-house, and to order them back into the provinces. On the afternoon of the 14th, when the first news of the fighting reached Versailles, the king was twice asked to withdraw his troops from the capital, and twice refused. Even after it was known that the Bastille had fallen, the Comte d'Artois and the Duchesse de

Polignac continued their efforts to win over the wavering mercenaries. When Louis went to bed that night after hearing of all that had happened, he could think of nothing to write in his diary but the single word which had become so monotonous recently—*Rien*. The crisis had once more deprived him of his customary day's sport, and he had not killed a single stag or boar.

But at *levée* the next morning the Duc de Liancourt was able to convince Louis that what he had to face was 'not a revolt, but a revolution,' and that his only safety lay in immediate co-operation with the National Assembly. Thus it happened that, just as a deputation was starting from the assembly to protest against the action of the king's brother and the queen's favourite, Liancourt arrived with the news that the king himself was coming across from the palace to the parliament-house. Making an informal entry, he announced that he had given orders for the withdrawal of the troops. The deputies cheered, in spite of Mirabeau's warning that silence was the only lesson a king could understand (*le silence du people est la leçon des rois*): but Louis' request that they would help to restore order in Paris was not so well received; and Bailly had the hardihood to remind him that the cause of the trouble was his own dismissal of ministers who had the confidence of the people. The king returned to the palace through a cheering crowd; and when the queen appeared on a balcony with the Dauphin in her arms, the mob in the Marble Court was moved to tears.

But when popularity can only be won by concessions to violence, or by appeals to sentiment, the end is near. Marie-Antoinette was already burning her papers, and packing her jewel-boxes. The only question before the privy council next day was whether or not the court should flee to Metz, and raise the country against the capital. Louis was nearly persuaded to this course, and lamented, two years later, a lost opportunity. 'But what could I do,' he complained to Fersen, after the failure of the flight to Varennes, 'when Monsieur himself begged me not to go, and when Marshal de Broglie, who commanded the troops, said "We can get to Metz all right ; but what are we to do when we have got there?"'

So the king once more capitulated to the people. His signature to an order dictated by the assembly brought Necker back from the Rhine-side comforts of the *Three Kings* at Bâle. As he returned, he passed the first refugees posting towards the frontier—d'Artois, who had fled at daybreak on the 15th, the Condés, the Contis, Lambesc, Barentin, Breteuil, the Polignacs, the abbé Vermond (the queen's tutor), and many others who had good reason to fear the vengeance of the people. Louis remained, to welcome back the minister whom they had persuaded him to dismiss less than a week before.

The king had made amends for his treachery: but might not Paris also demand a public penance? Already on the 16th a deputation of eighty-eight members of the assembly had been joyfully received by the citizens, who still half expected to be attacked. A *Te Deum* had been sung at Notre Dame, and

speeches had been made at the Town Hall by the least democratic of the
deputies, blessing the work of the people. On every side voices had been heard
calling for the dismissal of the new ministers, and for the recall of the old.
Now that it was known in Paris that the troops were in retreat, and that
Necker was on his way back from exile, Louis made a resolve which may
have been dictated by fear, but which was certainly carried out with courage.
He determined to visit the capital in person, and to bless a revolution that he
could no longer control.

On Friday, July 17th, whilst de Broglie led away his useless army, the king,
after hearing mass, and empowering Provence, if he did not return alive, to
rule in his stead, set out with a handful of officers and members of his body-
guard in the modest carriages in which he ordinarily drove to the hunt, and
with no convoy but the slovenly Town Guard of Versailles. This mournful
procession seemed to the British ambassador that of a captive rather than a
king: indeed it put him in mind of 'a tame bear led along by its keepers.' It
was met at the gate of the city by Bailly, at the head of the electors and the
municipality. Standing as President of the assembly, not kneeling as mayor of
Paris, he presented Louis with the keys of his capital, in words that recalled
the entry of Henri IV two centuries ago. 'Then (he said) the king reconquered his people: now the people has reconquered its king.'

The procession set off again to the democratic Town Hall, which Louis
had chosen, rather than the Tuileries or Notre Dame, the sanctuaries of
the old regime, as the scene of his penance. 'If one is to do the thing at all,' he
had said to Bailly, 'one may as well do it properly.' The unrehearsed progress
afforded a spectacle that no art or organization could have surpassed. The
streets were lined with forty thousand men of the city militia, armed and
uniformed in such fashion as time and means could afford. Thousands more of
the citizens stood by their side, carrying rude pikes, scythes, or clubs. Behind their ranks were crowded nearly half a million Parisians of every rank
and calling—ladies of fashion at the windows, priests with their congregations at the church doors, and sight-seers perched in the trees and on the
roof-tops. The continuous shouts of *Vive la nation! Vive le roi! Vive
Bailly . . . Lafayette . . . les électeurs!* almost drowned the music of the
military bands, and the salute of the guns.

The king entered the Town Hall under an inscription that read 'Louis
XVI, the Father of the French, the King of a Free People.' He fixed in his
hat a blue and red cockade, the city colours; he listened to speeches by Moreau de Saint-Méry, Ethis de Corny, and Lally-Tollendal; and he read a reply
agreeing to the establishment of the Town Guard, and approving the appointment of Bailly and Lafayette as the mayor of Paris and the commander
of its armed forces. But when he went on to tell the electors that they could
best please him by arresting and punishing the 'malefactors' of July 14th,
they could not think that this advice (with which many of them secretly
agreed) would be palatable to the crowd that thronged the Place de Grève,

and was already pressing into the Town Hall.   Urged to say something more conciliatory, Louis could only stammer, 'You can count upon my affection.' The words were sincerely meant: and when he stood at a window facing the square, wearing the city colours, he was cheered to the skies.

It was ten o'clock at night when the king returned, weary but safe, to Versailles. He had made his *amende honorable* for blasphemy against the people. He had not won back their respect, but he had retained what (unluckily, for a king) he rated more highly—their affection. If he remembered Bailly's ironical comparison between his position and that of his great ancestor, he may have comforted himself with the reflexion that Paris was worth a penance. Perhaps Marie-Antoinette, who had hardly expected to see him back alive, was sorry now that she had let him go alone. It was an opportunity of regaining personal popularity which the unhappy queen could ill afford to lose.

'Thus, my Lord,' wrote the Duke of Dorset, in his despatch of July 16th, 'the greatest revolution that we know anything of has been effected with the loss of very few lives: from this moment we may consider France as a free country, the King as a very limited Monarch, and the Nobility as reduced to a level with the rest of the Nation.' 'The whole conspiracy against freedom,' Morris noted in less diplomatic language, 'is blown up to the moon.' But Paris, with good grounds for suspicion, was not so convinced that Louis' repentance was sincere, or that the revolution was over; and from Lyon Madame Roland wrote to her friend Bosc, warning him that there could be no security until the king and queen were put out of the way, either by execution or by assassination.

The events of the week left bitter and gruesome memories behind:—of the identification of bodies in the dungeons of the Châtelet; of the severed heads of de Launey and Flesselles that the grave-digger of Saint-Roch wrapped in a dish-cloth, and put away under his church-tower; of the armourers' shops robbed of their stock; or of private property destroyed in the burning of the barriers and the sack of the Bastille. It was not until a week had passed that the electors felt it safe to order the relaying of paved streets torn up to provide missiles and barricades. Ten months later the public was startled by the discovery of a number of skeletons at the bottom of a cellar staircase in the still half-demolished Bastille.

To such grim reminders of the past was added a present shortage of food. In the Saint-Antoine district there had been literal starvation for twenty-four hours on July 15th; and it was the more felt since work in the city had stopped during the crisis, and the usual number of empty mouths was increased by military deserters and undesirable characters (*gens sans aveu*, or *sans asile*) whom the events of the last two months had drawn into the capital. Though the price of bread fell a week later, the general discontent blazed up into a further outrage on July 23rd.

Joseph-François Foullon was an unpopular landlord, and a contractor for the commissariat of de Broglie's army. The king had appointed him in Necker's place as Minister of Finance. He was an obvious object of popular vengeance. He tried to save himself by putting his family into mourning, and giving it out that he was dead. He was discovered, seized by an angry crowd, summarily tried, and hanged by a builder's labourer and a greengrocer on a lamp-bracket outside the Town Hall. His son-in-law Berthier de Sauvigny, the Intendant of Paris, was likewise dragged from hiding at Compiègne, and soon afterwards shared his fate. Chateaubriand says that he happened to be at his window when the heads were carried by on pikes. 'Brigands!', he cried, 'is this how you understand liberty?' Had he a gun, he would have shot them down like the wolves of his native Brittany. The communist Babeuf, another eye-witness, though he applauded the punishment, condemned the crime. But what else, he reflected, could one expect from a populace accustomed to the public spectacle of torture and execution in the Place de Grève? 'These outrages,' wrote Thomas Paine, 'were not the effect of the principles of the Revolution, but of the degraded mind that existed before the revolution, and which the revolution is calculated to reform.'

However this might be, the Foullon-Berthier murders had an important effect on the municipal life of Paris: for they proved the necessity and they led to the formation of a properly organized city government and city police. It had already been proposed that the improvised authority of the electors should be replaced by that of formally appointed delegates of the sixty districts. This was now done; and on July 30th these hundred and twenty citizens succeeded to the difficult task which their predecessors had not unsuccessfully begun. The electors spent another nine months drawing up an account of their stewardship. Their last act was to present their successors with a bust of Bailly, the mayor of Paris. It was placed beneath that of Louis, and opposite that of Lafayette, as though to signify that the capital still clung to its faith in the happy co-operation of King, Commune, and National Guard.

The provisional municipality thus set up lasted for fifteen months, till it was replaced by the commune constitutionally elected under the municipal law of May, 1790. But it was twice reorganized. In August, in view of the number of calls on their time, the hundred and twenty were given the help of sixty more delegates, one from each district; and in September this body of a hundred and eighty was replaced by one of three hundred. The municipal personnel changed less than this double enlargement might suggest; for nearly a third of the three hundred were chosen from among the hundred and eighty. The proportion of lawyers (about a third of the total), of business men and tradesmen (about a fifth), and of members of the liberal professions (about a sixth) shows how consistently the control of Paris remained in the hands of the middle class.

Nor did municipal business vary much from month to month. There was always the food shortage, the lack of currency, the influx of 'brigands' from the suburban country-side. There was always the difficulty of policing a net-work of narrow ill-lit streets. There was always the indiscipline of the districts, which respected the orders of their own representatives on the commune as little as the commune itself respected the orders of the assembly. The three hundred had plenty to do. Their Committees of Administration (i.e. Finance), of Public Works, and of Police were always fully occupied; and the degree of public anxiety could be judged by the number of applications dealt with by the Passports Committee.

For there was still fear of disorder. The three hundred had scarcely been installed when they had to deal with the François affair. A baker named François refused to sell to his ordinary customers six dozen loaves which had been ordered for the use of the National Assembly. The bakery was under military guard: but the crowd brushed aside the sentries, dragged the baker from his shop, lynched him, and cut off his head (October 21st). This outrage could not be passed over. The murderer was apprehended, and hanged in the Place de Grève. A decree *contre les attroupements*, or *loi martiale*, was hurried through the Assembly, and was signed by the king (pleased at last to find something of which he could approve) the same evening. It was to have fatal results nine months later. At the same time the Commune set up a committee of investigation, whose ominous title (*comité des recherches*) was too easily associated with terrorism. From this date the relations between the Commune and the districts became so strained that Bailly reported in favour of a new municipal constitution, and even gave his support, in February, 1790, to a rival body of district deputies (*comité centrale*) which tried to take the place of the official Commune. Fortunately the municipal elections of August provided a fresh outlet for the quarrelsomeness of Parisians.

If the City Militia had been more than ten days old, it might have prevented the Foullon-Berthier murders. But it was still in the making. Collenot d'Angremont, one of the obscurer organizers of the revolution, who for nearly two years sat at his desk in the Town Hall, directing the Military Committee (*bureau militaire*) of the commune, had hardly begun to transform the casual volunteers of July 13th into the well-armed and well-drilled National Guard which policed Paris during '90-'94. Lafayette's extemporized appointment as commandant (some would have said, as King) of Paris had not yet been confirmed by the districts. He took the failure to prevent the lynchings of July 23rd as a kind of *lèse-majesté*, and threatened to resign. When he gave way to the electors' desire that he should remain, he was more than ever resolved to keep the control of the Guard in the hands of the responsible middle class.

Within a few days provisional rules had been drawn up, requiring every resident *bourgeois* to do his turn in the force. In case of unexcused absence, the district might provide a substitute at the delinquent's expense. 'Passive' citizens were soon excluded by law (May, '90). In any case the cost of uniform and equipment, which amounted to nearly five pounds, automatically excluded poor recruits. Early in August the Guard was put on a permanent footing, and its regulations were approved by most of the districts; for even those which resented class-discrimination, and feared an armed oligarchy, were in no position to enforce their objections.

The National Guard, as it was henceforth called, consisted of seven divisions—six of infantry, and one of cavalry. Every infantry division consisted of ten battalions—one drawn from each district of the city. Every battalion comprised five companies of fusiliers, one company of grenadiers, and one company of chasseurs. The cavalry battalion consisted of eight companies. As the complement of a company was a hundred men, the total force numbered, on paper, 68,000. The original members were all volunteers, but those who later transferred from the French Guard, and other regular forces, were paid for their services; and this treatment was extended to the chasseurs, to one of each five companies of fusiliers (called *compagnie du centre*), and to the whole of the cavalry. Before long the cost of uniforms and equipment was taken over by the municipality, and a bonus of twenty-four shillings was offered to each recruit. By such means it was hoped to provide a professional nucleus for what must be in the main an amateur army, with sixty centres of loyalty. With the same idea in view the commandant and officers of higher rank were appointed by the commune, whilst the junior officers were chosen, generally from among the non-commissioned officers of the French Guard, by the district to which each battalion was attached, and whose motto and emblem it carried on its colours.

But the most significant article of the decree of August 10th was that which bound the officers of the Guard to employ their troops only under the orders of the civil or municipal authorities. When this rule was extended to the whole army (February 28th, '90), the king was completely disarmed. Thus the revolution had solved at its outset the problem which had puzzled both Montesquieu and Blackstone. It had created a standing army which could not be used by the king against the people.

On Sunday September 27th all sixty battalions appeared for the first time on parade. They marched from the Town Hall to the cathedral of Notre Dame, where their flags were blessed by the Archbishop, and their officers took the national oath, and the abbé Fauchet, the popular preacher of the day, delivered a 'sublime and touching' address. It was remarked by critics of the proceedings that most of the banners, worked by the women of Paris, were in royal white; that few showed the red and blue of the city; and that, whilst the word *Liberté* appeared commonly enough in their inscriptions, there was no mention of *Egalité* or *Fraternité*. The National Guard wore its democratic uniform with an aristocratic air.

In spite of some pretensions to professionalism, the National Guard remained an amateur force on an experimental footing. Two years after its formation it was still without a standardized uniform. It armed itself by degrees. Six thousand muskets were provided by the king, seven thousand by the fortress of Maubeuge, and three thousand by the factory of Saint-Etienne. Two guns were procured from the country house of the Comte de Ségur. Guardsmen who did not live at home had to content themselves with such barracks or billets as the districts rather unwillingly supplied. But without its extemporized Home Guard the revolution could not have gone on. It was at once an army and a police force. It not only mounted a guard for the king, the assembly, and the commune; not only did its chasseurs man the barriers, and police the Town Hall; it also provided detachments for every public function, from a *Te Deum* at Notre Dame to a rout at Ruggieri's, or an execution in the Place de la Révolution. It guarded the bank on the night before a distribution of lottery prizes: it convoyed cash or corn coming in from the provinces: it would even lend its band to supply music for a patriotic fête. Most of its duties took it no further afield than the prisons, the bridges, or the quays of the capital: but upon occasion Bailly would persuade Lafayette to send a detachment as far as Nemours or Neuilly-sur-Marne to put down a food-riot, or to take part in a presentation of colours. The old police forces—*maréchaussée, guet-à-pied,* and *garde des ports*—were gradually absorbed into the new body, until it became, in effect, the capital under arms.

In the provinces a decree of June 10th, 1790, ordered a similar amalgamation of the *milices bourgeoises.* Whilst all enfranchised citizens and their sons over eighteen had to register for service, every existing body of Town Guards was incorporated in the local battalion of the National Guard. Its old flag was hung up in the parish church, its old uniforms went back into the wardrobe, and it appeared on parade in the same uniform, the same cockade, and the same equipment as the Town Guard of Paris. Thus there came into being all over the country a new volunteer army—not eighty departments, but a single nation under arms; and it wore a badge that combined the white of the crown with the red and blue of the capital—the tricolor which, as Mirabeau was bold to prophesy a year later, would fight its way round the world.

Nevertheless it could not be ignored that the new force had been created principally for the defence of the middle class; for the defence of its privileges, which were challenged, of its property, which was envied, and of its security, which was threatened by the discontents of the poor. It was not to be expected that the workers of Saint-Marcel or Saint-Antoine, who had already been disfranchised, would allow themselves for long to be disarmed. The Bastille, the symbol of an old tyranny, had fallen, and by their own hands. Might not the National Guard become the symbol of a new tyranny even more difficult to overthrow?

CHAPTER IV

GRANDE PEUR

Mon fils, nous sommes aujourd'hui roturiers, et je m'en félicite sincèrement. Le roturier est l'homme par excellence: c'est lui qui paie les impôts, qui travaille, ensemence, récolte, commerce, bâtit, fabrique. Le droit d'être inutile est un pauvre droit! Ne le regrettons pas.
—(RÉTIF DE LA BRETONNE: *La vie de mon père.*)

THERE were three French revolutions in 1789—a revolution in the capital, a revolution in the towns, and a revolution in the villages. In Paris the revolution was political before it became municipal. In the towns it was municipal before it became political. In the villages it was neither political nor municipal, but economic.

The towns were the oldest part of France. Some of them had been Roman, Imperial, or even English long before they could call themselves French. They had old memories of past glory. When they joined in the movement of 1789, it was not to assert the natural rights of man, or the political rights of Frenchmen, but to recover liberties that had once been enjoyed by citizens of Bordeaux or Marseille, of Lyon, or Rennes, or Reims. They wanted to elect their own mayors and magistrates, to spend their own money, and to manage their own affairs. They watched with deep interest whilst the Parisians elected a municipality and recruited a City Guard, and they hardly waited for the crucial events of July 14–17th to try similar experiments themselves.

Bordeaux was a rich and busy seaport of some eighty-five thousand souls. Arthur Young could not too much admire its fine modern buildings, its vast theatre, and its tidal corn-mill. He saw it at a fortunate moment. The low tariff regime introduced by the Eden treaty of 1786 had ruined the cloth-traders of Amiens and Abbeville; but it had brought prosperity to the wine-merchants of the Gironde. Never had the town been so flourishing. Its magnificent river-front was crowded with the ships of every western nation, and with all the queer rigs of the Levant. Greeks, Syrians, and Egyptians thronged its quays, and did business with the Flemish, German, Irish, and Dutch firms who had offices in the Place des Quinconces. Every year its vessels carried to England alone twelve thousand tons of wine, and brought back cargoes of leather-work, ironmongery, and Staffordshire pottery. Fortunes were being made in its dozen sugar-refineries, and in its sixty shipyards, where every fortnight a new ship was on the stocks. Ambitious young men learnt with envy of one merchant who, a penniless clerk in 1740, now owned a fleet of forty ships, and a fortune of eight hundred thousand pounds.

It might be expected that so much middle-class prosperity would be viewed with bitterness by the men who built and manned the Bordeaux fleet. But in fact wages were reasonably high, and employment was plentiful; so that the town suffered little from labour troubles or class war. It was not thought strange when, in '89, the local electors of the Commons were invited by representatives of the parishes, led by a prominent merchant, to co-operate with the municipality in a reformed administration. It was doubtless because they were accustomed to this easy association of bourgeois and popular interests that the deputies of the Gironde found it difficult to understand the more class-conscious atmosphere of Paris.

Arthur Young, who thought Bordeaux a finer town than Liverpool, was disgusted with the dirty crowded streets of Marseille, and called its port 'a horse-pond compared with the Gironde.' Yet Marseille was at this time the largest city in France, after Paris and Lyon, with a population that ran into six figures, and a commerce amounting to a fifth part of that of the whole country. Its geographical position, its freedom from the customary harbour-dues, the progressive policy of its Chamber of Commerce, and the high tariff which protected its shipping against foreign competition gave it a monopoly of the Levantine trade, and made it the first port of the Mediterranean. Its thousand ships, its sixty thousand workmen, and its annual turn-over of fifteen million sterling were evidence of its immense prosperity.

Here, as at Bordeaux, there had been no serious labour problem, or enmity between class and class. The old provincial families and the new Swiss, Italian, and Corsican immigrants who made their fortunes at Marseille seemed able to do so without antagonizing their workmen. In political matters the *patrons* and *ouvriers* made common cause with the *capitalistes*. Whether the Marseillais were working or fighting, they would do so as one man. It was thus that they united in '89 to defend their property and privileges against the government, the clergy, the nobles, and the municipality. A body of two thousand four hundred armed citizens enabled them first to defy, and then to dispense with a military garrison. Electing deputies, drafting *cahiers*, and keeping local interests before the National Assembly, their Chamber of Commerce—the oldest in the country—was for three years almost a provincial Parliament. Not till 1792 was this characteristic body replaced by the departmental and municipal authorities which its championship of local interests had hitherto kept at bay.

Nevertheless there were signs that Marseille could not much longer be exempt from the economic troubles that were hurrying the country into revolution. An address recently sent to the Lieutenant-general of Provence over the signatures of ninety thousand Marseillais called the city a whited sepulchre, whose apparent prosperity covered a serious shortage of food, and declared that a system of official graft had reduced the poorer inhabitants to the depths of misery.

The great inland city of Lyon, the French Manchester, was troubled with social and economic problems unknown to the more adaptable seaports.

AORLEANS | *Bon nous voila daccov* | CHEZ·LE TOURMI·

A NATIONAL TRIO

The priest, the commoner, and the noble are at last playing in tune:
'Bon, nous voilà d'accord.'

The most populous, and, as many thought, the most magnificent place in the provinces, with a long-established silk industry employing sixty thousand hands, Lyon was also a great business and banking centre, whose richer citizens admitted to incomes of six figures, and whose capital was swollen by foreign gold. But the employers of Lyon seldom enjoyed the social calm or the stable economy of their rivals at Bordeaux or Marseille. For here it was customary for the rich merchant to buy a title of nobility, or a municipal sinecure, so that the bourgeoisie lost their natural leaders, and the commercial policy of the town was framed by those who had little sympathy with the interests of the workers. No city in the land had so many strikes. None was so prone to rise against its rulers.

The traditional government of the town had been re-enacted under new forms by the royal regulations of 1764. It consisted of a Consulate (a Provost and four Sheriffs), a Town Council (*corps de ville*) of twelve members, and certain Notables, representing the church, the nobility, the magistracy, and the commercial aristocracy. The old regime had at least embellished the town with quays and fountains, and with a theatre, a hospital, and an Exchange second to none in France. It had named, cleaned, and lighted the streets. It had provided a service of cabs, and a fire-brigade. The new regime had nothing to its name but a discreditable record of financial decay, municipal feuds, and labour troubles. It had the misfortune to coincide with a decline in the silk industry, due to new fashions in dress materials, and to the growth of rival establishments under government protection in Spain. Within ten years the municipal debt had risen to £170,000, and the annual deficit to nearly £50,000. The Consulate was at loggerheads with the magistracy (*sénéchaussée*); and the magistrates, in the name of the general public, carried on a campaign against the Consuls not unlike that which the Paris *parlement* carried on, in the name of the people, against the government of Louis XV. An age-long quarrel between the master-merchants (*maîtres-marchands*) and the master-workers (*maîtres-ouvriers*) blazed up into a series of strikes, of which those of 1744 and 1785 resounded throughout France.

The strikers of '85 published a working-class budget, which anticipated the researches of Booth and Rowntree. They showed that the average earnings of a family of five members amounted to seventy-six pounds a year, and its expenses of living to a hundred and two pounds. They inferred, in language new to the eighteenth century, that if the Lyon silk industry could not be carried on without reducing its workers to a state of destitution, it had become a national scandal (*un vice dans l'état*), and had better be destroyed. The only reply that occurred to the city authorities was to call out the police and to shoot down the strikers. When the revolution of '89 broke out, more than a third of the workers were on the streets; whilst the interest on the municipal debt swallowed up the whole revenue derived from the unpopular and rapidly diminishing dues on imports (*octroi*).

Yet even under these circumstances the Lyonnais closed their ranks in view of the crisis of '89. Three months after the elections (July 17th) the local representatives of the clergy and nobles declared their solidarity with Third Estate, and promised their support to the National Assembly. A standing committee was set up, consisting of delegates of all three Estates, to co-operate with the municipality in keeping order, and in carrying on the public services. It was only with the approach of war and with the increase of unemployment that this *rapprochement* broke down.

The conditions of life in the great ports and manufacturing centres were, in their different ways, as exceptional as those of Paris. How did the revolution begin in the smaller and more typical provincial towns? Reims, with a population of thirty thousand, was still a walled town in '89, though some of its streets had been widened, and fountains played in its squares, and the citizens prided themselves upon the hundred and eighty-three new oil-lamps which, on nights when there was no moon, lighted its dark and twisting alleys. A famous and venerable provincial capital, it boasted an archbishop, a university, the biggest textile industry, and the most extensive wine-cellars in north-eastern France. Nor could it be forgotten that at every royal accession the cathedral of Reims became the Westminster Abbey of the nation, the scene of the most sacred and magnificent function known to French history.

The town itself was hardly worthy of its destiny. It suffered from a chaos of jurisdictions—financial, judicial, and administrative—whose rival exactions pressed heavily on the mass of the citizens. Its municipal government had become the monopoly of a few mercantile families, who combined with the clergy to exclude from power not merely the aristocracy but also the professional class and the artisans. Outside the fifty-four privileged Unions (*corporations*) with their three thousand skilled workmen was a mass of thirty thousand largely unskilled and unemployed labourers. Of these it had been recently reported that as many as one in three was without food, and in need of immediate relief.

Such misery would not initiate but might carry on a revolution. Already in the spring of '89 there had been serious riots in the town itself, and in some of the surrounding districts. When election-time came the working class clamoured in vain for a more generous franchise. The deputies were chosen, and the addresses drawn up, by the commercial magnates of the town, and by members of the Unions, who were more interested in their trade privileges than in questions of social reform. Their *doléances* might include some recommendations that appealed to the workers, such as provision for the recovery of overdue wages, or for the settlement of disputes between masters and men; but the deputies they sent to Versailles were the leaders of the anti-democratic party—the archbishop, the commandant of the garrison, the seigneurial judge, and the lieutenant of police. It was not until the elections of 1792 that the working-class grievances of

Reims were represented by almost the only working man in the National Convention.

There could hardly be a greater contrast than that between the reactionary cathedral city of Reims and the emancipated half-foreign frontier city of Strasbourg. Here the upper classes lived an easy elegant life, whilst the lower classes shared in a prosperity which did not depend upon a single source, but upon the varied requirements of travellers, and the changing needs of international trade. Such a place provided an ideal scene for one of Brienne's experiments in local government. Its Provincial Assembly provided a generous non-party programme of reform, and a political training which made Strasbourg men and Strasbourg opinions important throughout the revolution. In the elections of '89 there was little disposition to question the conduct of the city authorities. The greater part of the local address was taken up with rights and claims common to all classes. But when they saw the old municipal regimes tumbling all over France, the unprivileged Strasbourgers demanded reforms which were unacceptable to the municipal monopolists. The news of the fall of the Bastille led to scenes of rioting and incendiarism which, thanks to the fortuitous presence both of an English and of a Russian traveller, have been recorded in unusual detail.

One more example. Rennes, towards the end of the eighteenth century, was the fifteenth place in France, with a population of some thirty-two thousand souls. It was an important market and administrative centre. It boasted a *parlement* and a school of law. It was one of those 'parliament towns' which Adam Smith had described a few years before as living idly and poorly on the pickings of expensive courts and assemblies. It comprised a fashionable quarter, rebuilt early in the century, and inhabited by well-to-do lawyers, manufacturers, and professional men; an 'old town,' where the small tradesmen and artisans were crowded from basement to attic in medieval squalor and picturesqueness; and *faubourgs* in the same style, outside the town wall, abandoned to the lowest part of the population. More than half the town and most of the big buildings belonged to the church. Every twentieth person encountered in the street was either a cleric or a lawyer. The needs of the rich were provided for by a bank, five doctors, and a group of prosperous clothiers, builders, and wine-merchants. The mass of the citizens made their humble purchases from the seventy-five bakers, the forty butchers, the sixty-three tailors, the seventy hairdressers, and the hundred and fifty bootmakers who competed for their unremunerative custom, and were little better off than themselves. Their children, if they could afford the luxury of education, were sent to small and ineffectual elementary schools kept by dames or private schoolmasters. The social distinctions of such a town rested almost entirely on comparative degrees of poverty. Only in the building trades was the new relationship of employer and employee beginning to show itself.

To an age which regards living in a town as more natural than living in the country, but which is losing the local loyalty that once dignified town life, it may seem strange that civic patriotism played so large a part in the origins of the French revolution. The men of '89 were commonly born and buried under the shadow of their parish church. They were shut up nightly within the city walls. They seldom travelled beyond sight of the city gates. It was natural for them to think first what the revolution might do for local interests. It was therefore unwise to quarrel prematurely with the bishop, the mayor, or the capitalist, however unpopular they might be; for these privileged citizens alone would be listened to at Versailles. The mass of the citizens would stand firm behind deputies who were not of their class, and could not be expected to sympathize with their troubles, but who could at least be trusted to further the common interests of the town. In maintaining this inter-class discipline, this at any rate superficial solidarity, the towns did an immense service to the national cause. If the party of reaction had been able to isolate the upper from the lower middle class, and the skilled from the unskilled workers, as they had isolated the privileged from the unprivileged order, they might have denied liberty to them all.

Historians of socialism may think that the working class in '89 showed too little consciousness of its rights and of its power. They may lament that its cause was allowed to go by default in the hands of its natural enemies. But this was in fact the only way in which a vantage-ground could be won for a wider emancipation. Only by submitting to middle-class leadership now could the workers learn ultimately to lead themselves. Again, historians who, like the Girondins, dislike reducing a national revolution to the scale of a Parisian *émeute* may reflect that neither at Bordeaux, nor at Marseille, nor at Lyon could the revolution overstep the frontiers of class and calling, but only in Paris. Only in Paris could it combine all that the country had to give of intellect and experience, and become a truly national, indeed international crusade.

The interests of the towns, with all their differences, were pursued in much the same way. Nearly everywhere the opportunity was taken to replace a privileged and non-elective municipality by one representative of the commercial and professional classes; to turn out *intendants*, military governors, *parlements*, and other embodiments of the old regime; and to form town guards on the model of the Paris militia, manned by the better citizens, and armed by the looting of some government arsenal, to protect the lives and property of the *bourgeoisie*. Soon the towns will come to see that their interests are much the same as their neighbours', and will form the patriotic leagues (*fédérations*) which provided the basis of the great fête of federation in Paris the following year. From the provincial reading-rooms (*salons de lecture*), where prominent citizens meet to hear and discuss the news, hard-headed merchants and tradesmen, self-educated in politics, will bring to the capital their notions of a 'business government,' and will play their part in the republic of '92. But whatever the National Assembly might later accomplish, here in the provincial towns was a civic revolution, a popular revolution, almost a national revolution, already in being.

Neither the Paris revolution nor the revolution in the towns would have won its way without the revolution in the villages. Out of a total population of twenty-six million Frenchmen only five and a half millions lived in towns. Eighty out of every hundred persons were country-born and country-bred. With us the proportion is exactly reversed: eighty out of every hundred live in urban or suburban areas. Even village life has become so assimilated to town life that it is difficult to picture the experiences of those whose only world by day was the field, the farmyard, and the country lane, and by night the candle-lit fireside or the moon-lit meadow, where no sound was heard but that of some wild animal in wood or hedgerow.

The country population of France was increasing, though slowly, and with regional exceptions, at the rate of a hundred thousand a year: it was half as large again in 1789 as it had been at the beginning of the century. Only unhealthy conditions of life and a huge infant mortality kept it within bounds, at a time when two brothers had been known to father thirty-nine children. In one district of the Loire valley whose records have been studied it is found that one child in four died before it was ten, and one in fifteen between the ages of ten and twenty. In another district only half the population reached the age of twenty-one.

As the population increased, the old food-shortage was aggravated by a new land-hunger. It was the ambition and pride of the peasant to own his little plot of ground. A high proportion of all the cultivated land in the country, perhaps on an average thirty per cent, had passed from its lay or clerical landlords to so-called peasant proprietors. They had bought the land: they were freeholders. But this did not mean that they had no charges to bear. It must sometimes have seemed to the *roturier* (*ruptuarius*, one who breaks up the ground), *cultivateur*, or *fermier* (one who holds his land on a contract, *fermitatem*) that his lot was barely preferable to that of the *métayer* (*mediatarius*, one who shares the produce), whose spade and plough were on loan from his landlord, or to that of the *laboureur*, or *travailleur*, the hired workman, who lodged with the farmer, and could not call an inch of ground his own; or even to that of the serf, who had no more property rights than a pig or a sheep. For what the landlord lost in personal hold over the tenant he more than made up in charges attached to the land—charges mysteriously fixed by his lawyer, and mercilessly exacted by his agent.

The more scandalous and picturesque feudal dues were already, in '89, part of the stock-in-trade of medieval romance writers: but the farmer's small profits were still seriously reduced by payments in respect of the inheritance, sale, or exchange of property; by payments for the compulsory use of the seigneurial wine-press, mill, or bakery; or by payments in lieu of labour upon fields that the landlord no longer cultivated. The peasant proprietor was still unable to protect his fields against the huntsmen from the *château*, or the herds of deer that roamed the country-side. He was still liable, up to the age of forty, unless he were married, to conscription in the hated militia.

Such trials might perhaps be borne, if the *seigneur* (*seniorem*, elder) resided upon his estate, and looked after his tenants. Talleyrand's grandmother played Lady Bountiful in her village, summoning to the *château* after Sunday mass all who needed medical treatment or relief; but the cantankerous *seigneur* of Salency disputed at law the harmless right of his parishioners to choose and crown a May Queen. In very many places neither good nor evil could be expected from 'the rich man in his castle.' Chateaubriand's family lived at Combourg like a garrison in a beleaguered fortress. Landlordism had indeed, in many districts, ceased to coincide with land-ownership. The *seigneur* in whose name the feudal charges were exacted need no more reside in the *château*, he need no more own a square yard of the estate, than the lay impropriator of the tithe need show his face inside the parish church. The payer of rent, like the payer of tithe, felt that he was the victim of a system without a soul.

Even if unburdened by feudal charges and tithes, the countryman's holding was very often too small to afford a living. Out of every hundred peasant proprietors, from fifty to seventy-five were forced to make up their income by working as paid labourers on other men's land, or by allowing their families to take in piece-work such as weaving or lace-making from the nearest industrial town. Infinitely worse was the position of those who had no land of their own. In some districts one family in five was in this case; in some as many as three or four in five. Over the whole country every fifth to tenth man made his living by begging. In a land which had no Poor Law, and regarded mendicancy as an honourable profession, this floating population of the unemployed, swollen by pedlars, mountebanks, horse-thieves, and highwaymen, not only presumed on the charity of people hardly better off than themselves: it preyed upon the farmers' crops, poached the landlords' preserves, and terrorized the unprotected homesteads of the country-side.

A farmer's life under the old regime might occasionally be as pleasant and patriarchal as it appears in Rétif's *Vie de mon père*. Generally it was little better than a round of wasteful servitude. Arthur Young was loud in his praise of peasant proprietors in Flanders or Béarn. The magic of property, he thought, turned sand into gold. On the other hand, small properties meant small farming, whose narrow scope and out-of-date methods could never make the best of the land as a whole. In vain the Agricultural Societies of Paris or Tours, of Laon or Limoges, read papers and published programmes. In vain the National Assembly appealed to Nature and Reason. In vain was the bee-like activity of *M. le Secrétaire* Abeille. The peasant persisted unmoved in the ways of his father and his grandfather. Neither

Physiocrat nor Ideologue could disturb the immemorial rhythm of country life.

In England the sixteen hundred Enclosure Bills passed during the eighteenth century had introduced an agricultural revolution which in the long run benefited those who most bitterly opposed them. In France enclosure was merely another form of feudal exploitation. It was associated with the filching of common lands, the withholding of villagers' rights, and the erection of huge hunting reserves. It discredited the case for big farming, and encouraged the small cultivator to go on digging his little plot of ground in his own way.

One result of agricultural poverty, land shortage, and bad farming was the dreaded *disette*, the famine which in every year of a bad harvest afflicted some part of the country, large or small. Not that it was attributed to natural causes. It was God's will, and perhaps the king would provide a remedy. Yet it must have been easier to feel confidence in God's kindness than the king's. His representative, the *curé*, was at least a fellow-sufferer, and would do what he could to move the Intendant to pity. There was nothing to hope from the tax-collector, whose demands for *taille, vingtièmes, décimes,* and *capitation* could only be met by pretending complete destitution. There was nothing to be expected from the army of *gabelous* who extorted the hateful salt-tax (*gabelle*) as oppressively as the chimney-man had extorted hearth-money in this country a hundred years earlier. There was nothing to be expected from the king's officers who commandeered the peasant's ox and cart for the transport of military stores, or carried off his able-bodied sons into the army. What with tax, tithe, and feudal rents, the peasant's lot was almost too hard to bear. An inquiry made in the Carcassonne area in 1791 showed that out of a population of 214,000 no less than 67,000 (exclusive of children) were unfit to work, or unable to earn a living: nearly one man in three was a pauper.

A contemporary cartoon shows the villager with his fork and flail feeding his chickens, and compares his lot unfavourably with that of his pig, his cow, and his bees. It is headed 'Born for trouble,' and has the lines :

> All day upon the land
> In heat and cold I stand,
> Though poor, to have enough in hand
>   To pay the Rector:
> I work the whole year round,
> Producing from the ground
> What may content, when he comes round,
>   The tax-collector.

In the background the peasant's ambition in life is signified by a stone cottage, at the door of which he is receiving a quittance for his *taille* from the local *collecteur*.

It is easy, without drawing on the more antiquated feudal abuses, and without denying the existence of humane landlords, to paint an almost intolerable picture of the peasant's sufferings towards the end of the eighteenth century. It is difficult to believe that his lot had been harder a hundred or even fifty years ago. Yet so it was. The country-side shared with the cities the gradual increase in wealth and the rising standard of living which characterized the eighteenth century.

Recent investigations have shown more clearly how, if not why, this change came about. It has been established that the revolution of '89 broke out at the moment when prices had reached their maximum, after an unprecedented rise of fifty-six years. The economic conditions of the eighteenth century were, of course, very different from our own. In a country in which small-scale production was the rule both in industry and agriculture, and in which market was cut off from market by local tariffs and bad communications, there could be no general level of prices. An accurate graph of the prices of corn, wine, or meat during the years 1733–1789 would show a steady rise throughout the period; but it would also show such zig-zags due to seasonal, cyclical, and other variations that it would resemble a seismographic chart. One conclusion is beyond controversy. Prices rose most of all in the cheapest and commonest commodities; not in the rich man's luxuries, but in the poor man's necessities—his food, his fuel, and his clothing. It has been estimated that in the twenty years preceding the revolution the cottager's household budget went up by fifty-five to sixty-two per cent. It is certain that the cost of his two chief comforts during the terrible winter of '88—wood fuel and candle-grease—reached a figure that it had never reached before.

With this rise in prices went, no doubt, a rise in nominal wages; but it always lagged behind. Arthur Young, writing in 1792, believed that in Normandy the rate of wages had doubled in twelve years, but that in Anjou it remained what it had been half a century ago. Labourers' wages as a whole had risen twenty per cent within a generation. Yet the average earnings of a French working-man were still no more than 9½d. a day, as against 1s. 5d. in England. Young, who was quick to notice this circumstance, found a Malthusian explanation for it. The excessive growth of the working-class population, he thought, prevented their obtaining a due share of the national prosperity. A simpler explanation is that they had neither the spirit nor the education to organize, and to enforce their demands.

The question of wages stood by itself in the towns: in the villages it was merged in the general problem of existence. The whole country-side lived in a state of dull resentment against feudalism and privilege, which might at any time break out into a local *jacquerie* or *bacchanale*. At any time a band of hungry villagers might break up a market, plunder a barn, or pillage a baker's shop. Such disorders might be particularly hard to repress during the summer of 1788, when the only courts which could inflict a death sentence were, by the king's order, no longer in session, and when it was notorious that the king's troops could not be relied upon to take action against the people.

But no fear was entertained of widespread or organized insurrection. It was admitted that in an agricultural country, where twenty out of twenty-six millions of the people lived on the land, the land question was the most urgent of all. It was admitted that a contented peasantry meant a quiet country, and that a discontented peasantry might turn a local revolt into a national revolution. Yet noble and *bourgeois*, magistrate and landlord, without being actively cruel, preyed habitually and unfeelingly upon the rural population. Few of them realized what the peasant was thinking, if, indeed, they considered him capable of thought. Few of them hated or feared him: they merely ignored him, as they might his horse or his cow. There grew up a more dangerous condition than class-hatred—the isolation of class from class. Revolution was not expected. Yet, if a revolution were to come to such a society, it would be a revolution that freed the land, and gave it to the people; a revolution that would last, because it was deep-rooted in the people's family life, and property, and freedom; a revolution that would strengthen the country equally against extreme reaction and extreme reform.

The history of peasant revolts in France was, as might be expected, a long one. Gibbon had related, only a few years before, how ploughmen and shepherds had risen against the Gallic nobles of the third century, and had asserted the natural rights of man, until the Imperial legions 'obtained an easy victory over a licentious and divided multitude.' Ever since the thirteenth century the word *jacquerie* had associated civil disorder with Jacques Bonhomme, the typical rustic. Men were still alive in '89 who remembered the troubles of '47, '50, and '52. Those of '64–68, '70, '75, '82 and '85 (so frequent had they become during the last half century) were vivid in the mind of the government, which went in constant fear of fresh outbreaks.

When Necker returned from exile in '88 his first care was to find a remedy for the severe hailstorm and bad harvest of which he had seen evidence on every stage of his journey. How, he asked himself, could the best use be made of the supplies still available? The question of distribution involved an old and difficult dilemma. If grain were moved from districts of surplus to districts of shortage, suspicion arose that it was being sold to some foreign country, or hoarded by profiteers; and there followed attacks upon the corn-convoys. If the movement of grain was prohibited, the villages which were temporarily short of flour and the towns which nearly always needed it were in danger of starvation, and food-riots had to be feared. In the spring of 1789, whilst the deputies were travelling towards Versailles, the first outbreaks warned them of what might be in store. For a time Jacques Bonhomme tightened his belt, and prayed that the new assembly would provide him with bread. It was the disappointment of this hope which led to the more serious insurrections of the summer.

It would be a mistake to suppose that the trouble always began in the villages. True, agricultural life and work were, in most parts of the country, more communal and co-operative than they would be nowadays. The harvest, the threshing, and the Sunday mass brought together a crowd which any common excitement might turn into a mob. But the towns too were implicated in the rural revolution. The market-place was the meeting-ground of town and country opinion, where the butcher buying pigs and the cottager selling milk and eggs exchanged views with the farmer and the farmer's wife; where the crimes of the mayor were matched with the sins of the *seigneur*; and where the differences between country producers and town consumers might be temporarily forgotten in a common grievance against Paris and the wheat corner (*pacte de famine*). In hundreds of places up and down the country there could be heard every market-day the same political rumblings that sounded in the Halles and at the Palais-Royal.

When the electoral edict of January, '89, invited the primary assemblies to draw up *cahiers* and to appoint electors, the peasant felt that now at last the king would discover and redress his wrongs. When the Commons resisted the crown, and Paris armed, and the Bastille fell, the food-riots of the spring easily turned into the political risings of the summer. All over France, but particularly in the east and south, estate-owners, both lay and clerical, were attacked, cellars and larders were looted, legal documents—the source of almost superstitious fears—were destroyed, and sometimes *châteaux* were burnt down, with all the traditional accompaniments of a *jacquerie*.

The reaction of the authorities to this situation was such as might have been expected. Whatever happened in the villages, the massed property of the towns must be protected, the superior lives of the bourgeoisie must be preserved. If the king's troops can no longer be trusted, the municipalities must organize their own defence. A town guard of respectable citizens must be set up to keep order within the walls, and to repel any attack by armed bands from without.

Already in May a new and alarming feature marked the peasant risings. At Montpellier on the 12th, and at Beaucaire fair, where rumour was always cheap, a fortnight later, it was confidently asserted, with every sign of alarm, that 'the brigands were coming.' Who the brigands might be, or where they came from, was not stated: but it sufficed for Catholics to recall how, during the Camisards troubles of 1703, a band of Protestants had roamed the countryside, burning the churches, plundering the villages, and terrorizing the people. What had happened once could happen again. Alarm began to run through the land. It spread, as news can spread among an illiterate and superstitious community, whether in the fields of Catholic Europe or in the forests of pagan Africa: it spread, not in print or writing, but by word of mouth, and with a speed that outran the royal courier. Wherever it came, the cottagers drove in their cattle from the fields, and barred their doors; the townsmen shut their gates, armed their citizens, and manned their walls. Everywhere men waited for an attack—an attack which never came.

Such was the great panic (*grande peur*) which overran France during the second half of July, 1789. It did not start from a single centre, or at the same time; but from five different places (of which Paris was not one), at different moments, and in different ways. It spread along the ordinary travel-routes, from house to house, and market to market, by relayed rather than direct broadcasting. Everywhere it developed in much the same stages, from the first rumour that the brigands were coming to the final discovery that they did not exist. The brigands were, in fact, a myth, like the Rapparees of Feversham's army who were supposed to be marching on London during the Irish Night of 1688. But there was a genuine peasant rising, a spontaneous outbreak, born of poverty, hunger, and the elections; a rising that began without waiting upon events in Paris, though it was later enlarged by them; a rising that had aims hardly understood by the peasants' own representatives in the National Assembly. For it was a movement of the conservative masses, whom the government of the old regime had enfranchized more generously than the townspeople, because they counted on the influence of the squire and the priest to keep them on the side of privilege and order.

But there was more at stake than this. The *jacquerie* of '89 was a rising of the illiterate and unpropertied majority, whose views had been ignored, and whose spokesmen had been outvoted in the middle-class scramble for representation. The burning of the *châteaux* was their plain way of saying what they wanted. 'The aristocrats make a great noise about it,' wrote Madame Roland, rather unfeelingly, 'but really it is not such a bad thing. . . . I see no cause for public lamentations, however unpleasant it may be for the individual.' She might have put it more strongly. The peasant insurrection not only ensured the rout of aristocratic feudalism: it also attacked the throne from behind, and made it impossible for the king to hold out any longer against the frontal attack of Paris, and of the big towns. It needed just this to make the revolution irresistible.

CHAPTER V

FOUNDATION DEEDS

The Homunculus, Sir, in however low and ludicrous a light he may appear, in this age of levity, to the eye of folly or prejudice;—to the eye of reason in scientific research, he stands confessed—a Being guarded and circumscribed with rights.—(STERNE: *Tristram Shandy*.)

THE National Assembly crowned its victory over the king by drawing up the foundation-deeds of the revolution. In less than three weeks it enacted three great measures—the Declaration of Rights, the Abolition of feudalism, and the suspensive Veto. The Declaration, the creed of the revolution, was the work of Versailles: the Abolition, the creation of a new social order, was the work of the provinces: the Veto, the key-point of the new constitution, was the work of Paris. The joint effect of these measures was so revolutionary that the king could see no answer to them but a third appeal to arms. His failure, and his forced acceptance of them, put them irrevocably on the statute-book of democracy, and ended the first stage of the revolution.

The Declaration of Rights came before the assembly on a report of the Constitutional Committee on July 27th. It was discussed, intermittently, for a month: the last clause was passed on August 27th. The Abolition of feudalism was proposed and carried through in the course of a single night's debate on August 4th. The Declaration involved philosophical questions, which could not be decided in a hurry, and difficult problems of definition and drafting. The Abolition was a practical expedient to meet a dangerous crisis, and could be put through in outline in a few minutes.

The deputies had barely begun their discussion of the Rights of Man when they were interrupted by an alarming reminder that there were Frenchmen whose rights had been taken away from them, and who were minded to recover them by force. The peasantry were up in arms. They were reported to be attacking the *châteaux*, seizing the land, and shooting the game. A committee was appointed to investigate these reports. When the deputies learnt how serious the situation was, their first reaction, as a cynic might have observed, was remarkably like the king's reaction towards the rising in Paris. They issued a strongly worded declaration against disorder, and (remembering their claim of June 17th) against the non-payment of taxes. Next day they called on the troops to suppress the rioters. A week later they authorized the municipalities to requisition any armed forces that might be available (*milices nationales, maréchaussées, troupes*) to disperse 'seditious gatherings' of all kinds.

Nor were these mere threats. The inhabitants of Cluny, led by one of the monks, trapped a body of 'brigands' in the town, and shot them down without mercy. At Mâcon an illegal tribunal hanged twenty peasants for refusing to pay tithe and feudal dues. The National Guard of Lyon killed eighty rioters, and took sixty more prisoners. In Dauphiné the law-officers travelled round the country with troops and police, holding inquiries, and summarily executing those whom they found guilty of disturbing the public peace. In this policy of repression the provincial authorities had the sympathy not only of the privileged classes, but also of the *bourgeoisie*, whose representatives were at this very moment declaring property to be one of the 'natural and imprescriptible, inviolable and sacred' rights of man, and were asserting that 'no one can be deprived of it except by public necessity, under legal forms, and with provision for fair compensation.'

Nevertheless it soon became apparent that repression would not solve the problem. Practically, there were not enough troops: morally, the peasants had too strong a case. On August 3rd the austere Malouet, after speaking of the economic crisis likely to follow the revolution, put in a plea for the out-of-work classes, and suggested that their needs might be met by relief committees and labour bureaux. On August 1st the Baron de Montchenu renounced all feudal rights in certain parts of his estates. The situation was a matter for urgent discussion in the newly formed Breton Club; and it was here that a drastic remedy was first formulated.

When the assembly met on the night of August 4th, Target, an eminent lawyer, but no statesman, introduced proposals for the enforcement of the law, and the continued payment of all taxes and dues. The Vicomte de Noailles at once opposed this motion in a speech boldly advocating equality of taxation, and the abolition of all feudal charges. He was supported by the Duc d'Aiguillon, who said that the Vicomte had anticipated his own proposals. Next a Breton deputy, Le Guen de Kerangall, in the language and dress of a peasant, denounced feudalism in terms which were no less moving because his facts were out of date. La Poule of the Franche Comté followed in the same strain. The deputies were moved to deep indignation. In a spirit of impulsive and sometimes generous sacrifice, landowners, clergy, magistrates, and representatives of local authorities offered to surrender their rights and privileges. So infectious became their enthusiasm that an agitated aristocrat passed a note to the President saying that the deputies were out of their minds, and begging him to suspend the sitting.

The original intention of the speakers may have been to save something from the wreck that private property was suffering all over the country: the effect was to turn French society upside-down. Consider some of the changes proposed by the resolutions of August 4th. Serfdom was abolished. All feudal rights could be extinguished by purchase. The privileges of the seigneurial court, the seigneurial hunt, the seigneurial pigeon-cote and rabbit-warren were suppressed. All tax-exemptions and tax-privileges were done away with, and taxation was to be made fair and equal for all as from January 1st, '89.

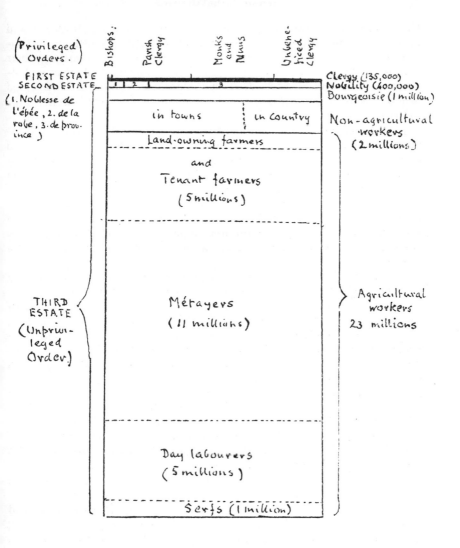

THE FRENCH NATION
in 1789
(the figures are only approximate)

Civil and military posts were thrown open to all citizens. Justice would in future be administered gratis, and the sale of legal appointments discontinued. Provinces and towns abandoned their separatist claims and their pecuniary and administrative privileges. Tithes, annates, and other ecclesiastical charges were suppressed, and pluralism was prohibited. Undeserved pensions were to be withdrawn. Trades unions (*jurandes*) were to be reformed.

No wonder the deputies ordered that a medal should be struck to commemorate so great an occasion, that a solemn *Te Deum* should be sung, and that the king himself should be associated with the acts of the assembly under the title of 'Restorer of French Liberty.' For although cool reflexion suggested doubts as to the wisdom of some of these measures, and many of them were whittled down in the process of statute-drafting, yet nothing could efface the first impression produced by so great and in many cases so generous a surrender of private interests to the public good. It was a gesture, perhaps, rather than an attitude; but a lightning-flash is the gesture of a thunderstorm.

In view of what was going on in the provinces, it was permissible to view the landlords' calculated proposals with a cynical eye. It cost them nothing to sacrifice serfdom, a wasteful type of labour which survived on few of their estates. It cost them little to sacrifice feudal rights, which constituted, on the whole, only a quarter of their income, if they could secure compensation for them. The abolition of tithe would benefit the large landowner even more than the small farmer; whilst the church counted on a moratorium, and looked forward to some arrangement under which its remaining revenues would be better administered, and its salaries paid on a more generous scale by the state. But no reasons of self-interest could be alleged for the sacrifice of tax-exemptions or hunting-rights by the gentry, of privileges by the towns, or of pensions by the army. Ferrières was not wrong when he traced beneath the worldly motives of August 4th 'that love of his country which is born in every French heart, and which makes it the imperative duty of the *noblesse* to dedicate its property and its life to the king and the nation.'

To the peasantry—there can be no doubt about it—one night had brought a freedom which it would take a life-time to appreciate. At first, like the prisoners lately released from the Bastille, they stumbled into liberty, dazzled by the unaccustomed daylight, and half frightened to be at large in a world of which they had no experience. Some of the emancipated serfs are said to have regretted the *main-morte* system, under which their lands could not be bought up by rich towns-people, or their children reduced to the status of mere day-labourers. Some took liberty for licence, and plundered the landlord's orchard and kitchen garden as readily as they would have looted a shop-window. But to the vast majority the disappearance of old obligations and the discovery of new rights—were it only freedom to slaughter the fat hares and partridges that browsed by the roadside—brought a new self-respect, and a new incentive for living.

One considerable grievance remained. The redemption of feudal dues would cost a sum—it has been reckoned at about three hundred and thirty millions sterling—quite beyond the resources of the country-side; and meanwhile payment was to go on. But though instances can be quoted in which feudal charges—and tithes too—were still being exacted in 1790, '91, or even '92, it appears that in most places little attempt was made either to pay them or to collect them. It was not long before the nationalization of the church lands and their sale in small plots for depreciated paper money provided a happy appeasement of land-hunger. The peasant proprietor was soon a landlord, and as good a man as his neighbour—tenacious of his newly won rights, suspicious of government interference, and, with all his obstinate old-fashioned ways, the backbone of the country. There was truth in the caricature which showed the peasant before August 4th bowed down by the weight of the priest and the noble, who rode upon his back; and after August 4th himself riding on the back of the noble, clapping his hands, and saying 'I knew my turn would come some day!'

The abolition of feudalism not only swept away an old society: it created a new one. The positive side of its measures—equal taxation, equal opportunity, equal justice, and the drastic reform of civil and ecclesiastical bodies—gave birth to the equal citizenship which became the strength of modern France. The old feudal ideas might reappear in the officialism that mars French administration; for they have their root in a will to dominate and to be dominated which even democracy cannot destroy. But they could never again be used to defy the government, or to exploit the people.

Again, the social revolution of '89 counteracted a dangerous tendency of the political revolution of '89. The latter, in its reaction against the centralization of the old monarchy, became individualistic. The former, in its reaction against feudal particularism, became *étatiste*. The levelling, consolidating effects of the abolition of feudalism might have been exploited by Louis XVI, as Mirabeau suggested, in the interests of a stronger monarchy. They made possible, under stress of war, the Jacobin dictatorship of 1793–4. They played into the hands of Napoleon. But August 4th had an ultimate effect of even greater importance. It redistributed land, as the eighteenth century had already redistributed wealth and wits. It gave to a vast number of small proprietors a stake in the country which has kept France fundamentally faithful to the principles of 1789.

A revolution, like a church, must have beliefs: but need it embody them in a creed? It cannot live without ideals: but is it wise to publish them to the world? The deputies of '89 had little doubt as to the answer to this question. They definitely desired a declaration. But few of them were philosophers or moralists: their reasons for desiring it and the ideas which they expressed in it sprang from authentic roots in the character and history of their country. They believed, as they said in the preamble of their manifesto, that all misgovernment and all public ills were due to a failure to recognize the rights of man. They did not need Locke or Hobbes, Mably or Rousseau, to teach them this truth. They did not much care whether rights had existed before the state, or the state before rights. They only knew that for centuries Frenchmen had been forced to do this and prevented from doing that by their landlords and their kings. The Declaration was neither the manifesto of a new nation, like that of 1776, nor a revolutionary class programme, like that prefixed to the Russian constitution of 1918. It was a Bill of Rights, reasserting liberties which had been overruled, establishing rights which had been obscured by wrongs. The design may have been inspired by the *Contrat Social*: the material was supplied by the *cahiers* of '89. In those very human documents the French people had passionately demanded social equality, freedom of opinion, security of property, a career open to talent, a fair assessment of taxes, and a hundred other reversals of the old order of society and government.

Some of these changes had already been enacted in the spirit, if not in the letter. Article VII of the Declaration, prohibiting arbitrary imprisonment, was a commentary on the destruction of the Bastille. The useless social distinctions denounced in Article I had disappeared on the night of August 4th. The 'natural and imprescriptible rights of man'—liberty, property, safety, and resistance to oppression (Article II)—were precisely those which Paris had won for its people a month before. Why not, then, proclaim them? The National Assembly had asserted two months ago its right to give or to withhold the taxes: why not, then, claim (Article III) that the principle and essence of sovereignty resides in the nation? It need not be denied that these practical and purely French ingredients of the Declaration were mixed with foreign influences of a more speculative kind. The influence of Blackstone (Article IX) and Beccaria (Article VIII) cannot be overlooked. But the ideas of these writers had been so absorbed into French thought that their alien origin was forgotten.

Thirteen years before, the American states united at Philadelphia had declared that 'when it becomes necessary for one people to dissolve the bands which have connected them with another, a decent respect to the opinions of mankind requires that they should declare the causes which impel them to the separation': and they had proceeded to draw up that Declaration of Independence which was already famous in '89 as the only printed charter of democracy. The circumstances, indeed, were not now the same as in 1776. France was not a new state justifying its existence before an old world: it was an old state advertising a change of political faith; a war-worn battleship nailing new colours to its mast. America, as was pointed out by more than one speaker in the debate on the Declaration, had little in common with France. It was a country of small farmers and equal citizens. It inherited no feudal institutions. Its taxes were light. It had no extremes of poverty or wealth. Its people were ready-made for democracy. Yet France had contributed to the liberty of America, and might learn from America how to win its own. It seemed to the Constitutional Committee that the assembly could not do better than preface its own constitution by a Philadelphian manifesto of its political faith. One of the many drafts which it considered— that submitted by Lafayette—had been drawn up in consultation with Jefferson, the American ambassador, and may still be read in a copy annotated by his hand.

On the other side was the older but less congenial example of England. England, said Durand de Maillane, in the debate of August 1st, had substituted free institutions for constitutional freedom. She had been content to secure political rights by safeguards and remedies. She had omitted to state the natural rights anterior to any such measures, upon which they really depend. On the contrary, argued Malouet, it was precisely from English writers—from Locke, from Cumberland, from Hume—that France had derived the notion of natural rights. But the English had avoided the error of supposing that freedom ever had existed, or ever could exist, apart from free institutions. It was not the naked savage, Man Friday, but the clothed and civilized Crusoe, with his gun in his hand, and his dog by his side, who was in a position to assert and defend his rights as a man. 'Our business,' Malouet concluded, 'is not so much to announce human freedom, as to make men free. The prohibition of *lettres de cachet* will do more towards this end than all the preambles in the world.'

The deputies agreed with this view. Their whole conduct shows that most of them were practical men, not dreamers. But they believed that a declaration of abstract rights would be a help, not a hindrance, to the enactment of laws and the setting up of institutions designed to secure the liberties of Frenchmen. 'The better men know their rights,' said the Comte de Castellane, 'the more they will be attached to the laws that protect them.' Not only so. A declaration of political rights would set a standard of political achievement. It was the intention of the Constitutional Committee that 'these ineradicable principles should always be inscribed before our eyes, and in our thoughts, and that at every juncture the nation should be able to compare them with each article of the constitution, and to make sure that we have faithfully carried them out.' This was indeed grasping the nettle: for what code could ever express the legislative ideal? But it was good to have such an aim on record. Lafayette, himself the most rigid embodiment of 1789 constitutionalism, was always proud of his part in the Declaration, and assured Washington a year later that of the immense number of decrees passed by the National Assembly few were inconsistent with it.

Here a fresh doubt arose. If the French citizen, in compensation for so many centuries of wrongs, was to be presented with a charter of rights, might he not also, for the good of his soul, and for the greater peace of his government, be presented also with a decalogue of duties? Does not the right of liberty of opinion or worship carry with it the duty of tolerating other people's opinions and forms of religion? Does not the right of property involve the rich in the duty of paying taxes? Does not the right of collaborating in a representative government involve the poor in the duty of accepting disfranchisement? Such abnegations might seem inevitable, when the language of natural rights is translated into the terms of political institutions. In no other way, perhaps, can rights of any kind obtain civil status. But if rights coupled with duties look suspiciously like wrongs, would it not be better to say nothing about this side of the matter? So, in fact, the deputies decided, by a considerable majority, on August 4th.

Some would have gone further, and would have had no declaration at all. It was better, Malouet thought, not to allow the people a Pisgah-view of a Promised Land which they might never inherit. Alternatively, the rights might be reconsidered along with the institutions in which it was hoped to embody them, and both be published together. But the deputies stood by their creed. They determined to publish it first, and to let it stand for what it was—an ornamental and perhaps grandiose entrance to the constitution. Never mind if the constitution, like a modern *Exposition*, is a long time building: something at least stands there to challenge attention.

These preliminaries having been settled, the House proceeded on August 17th to consider a number of rival proposals for a declaration, including those of Mirabeau, Lafayette, and Sieyès. The draft finally chosen as the basis of discussion was modelled on the American declaration, and proposed by the Archbishop of Bordeaux's committee. After ten days' discussion the seventeen Articles of the Declaration were accepted in their final form.

It is a Declaration of the rights *de l'homme et du citoyen*:—not of men as such; not of men who fail or refuse to share a common life; but of men who are also citizens, who accept the duties (*devoirs*) as well as the rights (*droits*) of membership of a community (*corps social*). It is made 'in the presence and under the auspices of the Supreme Being';—a mild concession to religion in the language of pagan Rome and philosophical Deism.

Its underlying ideas are four in number. First, there are certain human rights older than any existing society—liberty to act as one likes, equality with other men in all the affairs of life, and freedom to possess property, to live safely, and to resist oppression. Secondly, it is the duty of every 'political association,' from the family or the tribe to the city or the state, to defend these rights. It does not, of course, defend them in their pre-social form, as natural rights, but in their social form, as political rights: for as soon as the individual becomes a member of a political association, his liberty to act as he likes must be reconciled with the liberty of other members to act as they like; his freedom to hold property must not interfere with their freedom to do so too, his claim to protection must not override theirs. Thirdly, the state is nothing else than the community of citizens, expressing their common will (*volonté générale*) in the laws that embody their rights, their common action in whatever government they choose to set up, their common use of force in an army, and their common need of money in taxation. Fourthly, as there is a danger that the community in action may abuse its power against individual members, this power must be limited in scope and means, and its agents must be held to a strict account.

Like all attempts to catch human nature on the run, the Declaration has notable omissions, and is capable of unintended uses. Saying nothing of a right of association or of a right of employment, it leaves capital and labour unevenly matched. Speaking only of private property, it affords no comfort to the communist. It limits freedom of speech and worship in the name of public order under circumstances determined by the law: but no such law was ever drafted. It promises that public officials shall be held to account:but it does not provide the means of doing so. The general colour of the Declaration is that of a middle-class individualism. By equality it means the lowering of the old privileged aristocracy to the level of the new privileged bourgeoisie, not the raising of the unprivileged working class to that level. But it is a double-edged weapon, which may later be turned against those who forged it. It is, indeed, a virtue rather than a fault if a declaration of principles or ideals is incomplete, and capable of more than one interpretation. Otherwise the Declaration of 1789 would hardly have become a model for the constitution-makers of Switzerland, Belgium, Piedmont, Denmark, Austria-Hungary, or Spain. In its own country it has been slowly and very imperfectly embodied in a century and a half's legislation. But the government which forty years ago ordered that a copy of the Declaration should be put up in every school-room bore witness to the place it still holds in the heart of French democracy.

The Declaration of Rights was passed on August 27th. On the 28th the assembly went on to discuss the royal veto. This was the popular description of what ultimately appeared in Tit. III, Cap. III, Sect. III of the Constitution of 1791, under the heading *De la Sanction royale*. There were practical reasons why this part of the constitution should be regarded as urgent, and taken before others which were logically antecedent to it. On August 5th, as soon as he heard of the proceedings of the 4th, Louis wrote to the Archbishop of Arles, saying that he would never give his sanction to decrees despoiling the clergy and nobility. The deputies had foreseen this contingency, and had drafted the decisions of August 4th not as decrees (*décrets*) requiring the king's formal acceptance (*sanction*), but as resolutions (*arrêtés*) that only needed publication (*promulgation*) by his orders. They thus gave effect to a feeling which they shrank from putting into a formula—that during the framing of the new constitution the king's legislative power was in abeyance: the crown was brought even lower than the old *parlements*. But

Louis' threat could not be allowed to pass unchallenged. It was already assumed that the executive power in the coming constitution must consist of the king and the king's ministers. It had never been anticipated that they would be given unlimited power to veto the proceedings of the legislature. Not only would the principle of the separation of powers be violated: the sovereignty of the people, the corner-stone of the constitution, would be in danger.

Mounier, so lately the hero of the Tennis Court oath, had already begun to fall out of line with the majority of the assembly. As *rapporteur* of the Constitutional Committee he was fighting a losing battle for a limited monarchy, an Upper House, and a royal veto on the English model. He knew that the *cahiers*, which most of the deputies read as instructions from their constituents, recognized some kind of royal sanction as necessary for the validity of a law. He proposed that Article II of the first part of the constitution, entitled *Principes du gouvernement monarchique*, should read, 'No legislative act has the force of law unless it has been passed by the deputies of the nation, and sanctioned by the king.' In view of Louis' attitude towards the resolutions of August 4th it was impossible for the House to accept such a formula. If any foreign precedent were followed, let it be taken from democratic America. A series of stormy debates, lasting, with some diversions, till September 11th, ended in the granting by 673 votes to 325 of a suspensive veto like that enjoyed by the President of the United States.

This was the first issue on which the Commons lost their unanimity, and broke up into a Left and a Right. Mirabeau, the most effective speaker for the Right, plagiarizing de Casaux's recent *brochure* on the English constitution, argued that the ultimate power to give force of law to the decisions of the assembly could be more safely entrusted to a single king with an army at his back than to six hundred deputies supported by the people. The king's use of the veto could be restricted by withholding supply, especially from the army. Take away his veto altogether, and he may be driven to worse courses. For the Left Sieyès replied that an assembly was in a better position than a king to know the mind of the nation; that the business of the executive was to carry out the will of the legislature, not to obstruct it; and that a royal veto on the proceedings of a national assembly 'is nothing less than a *lettre de cachet* issued against the will of the people.' The question might have been debated for ever; but on September 11th, after transactions of none too clear a character between Necker, Lafayette, and a group of moderate deputies, it became known that the king would consent to promulgate the resolutions of August 4th if he were granted a veto valid for two sessions. Under this gentleman's agreement the suspensive veto (*véto suspensif* or *itératif*) became part of the constitution the same day.

It had in fact been carried less by the arguments of the speakers than by the urgency of the political situation. It was feared that the differences of opinion among the deputies of the Commons might be exploited by the royalist party for its own ends. It was feared that the authority of the assembly might be endangered by another intervention on the part of the capital. Day by day, as the debate dragged on at Versailles, indignant meetings were held in the alleys of the Palais-Royal. Day by day petitions arrived at the Parliament-house, and at the Town Hall. Threats were heard that the people would nominate new deputies. A notorious agitator, the Marquis de Saint-Huruge, set out one evening with fifteen hundred men to march to Versailles, and to offer violence to the Assembly, if it did not at once renounce its 'liberticide' plan of a veto. 'The veto,' declared a popular manifesto, 'belongs to no individual, but to twenty-five million people.' This was undeniable; and the leaders of the agitation—they included along with the usual lawyers and business men a writer, a scientist, and a *curé*—were citizens of such respectability that they could hardly be suspected of seditious intentions. But the deputies would not be dictated to by their constituents. They had survived the threats of the king: they were determined to resist those of Paris. The deputations were coldly treated, or refused an audience. The café de Foi in the Palais-Royal was raided and closed. Only the king's refusal to budge prevented the removal of the assembly to some place beyond reach of the Parisians. In so strained a situation the deputies were willing enough to trust the king, to closure the debate, and to compromise on a suspensive veto.

In opposing the veto popular instinct was not far wrong. In England, with its long history of constitutional growth, with a monarchy limited for the last hundred years, with a king able to dissolve Parliament, and with an Upper House ready to carry the odium of obstruction, a royal veto might be practicable—though it was not in fact agreed whether George III had this power. In France, just emerging from centuries of absolutism, and staking all its liberties upon a single assembly, it was unworkable. Even in peacetime a measure which enabled the king to hold up legislation until a third session would have been intolerable. In a time of revolution, and (as it was so soon to be) in a time of war, it could only lead to disaster. The veto might be applied not only to long-term constitutional laws, but also to the routine decrees by which the assembly was remodelling the old regime, and dealing with the emergencies of the hour. Under such circumstances a suspensive veto amounted to an absolute veto of a most objectionable kind. To hold up urgent legislation for six years was to hold it up for ever. To put such a power into the hands of a mere king of cards (*roy des cartes*), as Madame de Nemont called him, was to tempt Louis into a series of peevish and provocative gestures, which could have but one issue. The king's use of the right given him on September 11th brought about within three years the erection of a republic on the ruins of his throne. Mounier did not live to see the enactment in 1814 of the Anglicized constitution he tried to introduce in 1789.

A week had passed since the granting of the suspensive veto; yet the king's promise to publish the resolutions of August 4th was still unfulfilled. Pressed by the assembly to carry out his part of the gentleman's agreement, Louis replied that, though he approved the general sense (*esprit général*) of the resolutions, there were some of them to which he could only consent conditionally: and he proposed to take time to consider his decision. Meanwhile he submitted a number of criticisms, which the assembly could hardly do less than examine in committee. At this the deputies not unnaturally lost patience. The president was sent next day to ask for immediate *promulgation*. Louis tried to put him off with a promise of *publication*. Three days later he ordered the resolutions to be printed. They never issued from the royal press.

Why all this prevarication and delay? The reason was simple. The king had once more been persuaded to appeal to force, and he wished to gain time whilst troops were summoned to Versailles. Three days after his promise to publish the resolutions of August 4th, he ordered up the Flanders regiment from Douai. It arrived on the 23rd. It became necessary to justify what, after the events of July, could only be regarded as an insult to the National Guard, and a reflexion on the loyalty of the capital. Saint-Priest claims credit for persuading the municipality of Versailles to authorize the protection of the king against attacks from Paris, or his safe removal to Rambouillet. Pressure was put upon the Town Guard of Versailles to welcome the Flemish troops, and to assist them in the defence of the court. The queen presented every company with a new flag. Lafayette himself was approached with an offer of the Lieutenant-generalship of the Kingdom, if he would pledge the support of the Paris Guard.

On October 1st, the Flemish officers were given a complimentary dinner by their comrades of the king's body-guard. The toast was the royal family, not the nation. The king and the queen, her young son in her arms, walked among the guests, who received them with shouts of *Vive le roi! Vive la reine! Vive le Dauphin!* The regimental band played Grétry's air, *O Richard, O mon roi, l'univers t'abandonne!* It was alleged that in the drunken excitement of the banquet the national cockade had been trampled under foot, and the black badge of Austria donned in its place; that many officers of the National Guard, by reason of this incident, had refused a similar invitation to dinner two days later; and that on October 4th ladies of the court had tried to distribute white cockades, the Bourbon colours, to increasingly resentful patriots.

Paris was in no mood to take such provocation calmly. The capital was disturbed during these weeks not only by the political struggle at Versailles, but also by domestic troubles—municipal elections, emigration, unemployment, and a growing shortage of food. Within less than two months the government of the city had changed hands three times. Each change was the occasion of manifestos, demonstrations, and intrigues. Each successive body of representatives was criticized and obstructed by those who had put it in power. Parisians bitterly resented the institution of the *comité des recherches*, and the threat of Martial Law. The control of municipal affairs was disputed by the semi-independent districts, amongst which some counted as most troublesome the Palais-Royal, the favourite meeting-place of the forty thousand foreigners who lodged in Paris, and enjoyed an easy French citizenship, but who were excluded from the deliberations of the district assemblies.

In spite of a good harvest, there was a serious shortage of flour. The hot weather which ripened the crops also reduced the level of the Seine, and put the Paris water-mills out of action. Already in June Necker had been driven to purchasing corn in Burgundy and Morocco. At the beginning of September Paris had only enough flour for ten days' baking. A month later it became necessary to place large orders at Hamburg. Italy, Sicily, Flanders, and England were ransacked for supplies. Bread, even of the worst quality, was almost unobtainable, and the queues at the bakery doors grew longer every day.

The emigration—it was said that two hundred thousand passports were issued between July 14th and September 10th—threw great numbers of domestic servants and workers in luxury trades on the streets. The Spanish ambassador estimated the financial loss from this source alone at ten millions a year, enough to pay the wages of three hundred thousand workmen. As wages diminished credulity increased. The poor people who grumbled at the street-corners were ready enough to believe that the twenty thousand unemployed for whom work was being provided at Montmartre were no better than brigands, and might at any moment loot the city and massacre its inhabitants. The truth needed no such exaggeration. Things were so bad that in the early days of October—providentially, it must have seemed, to Madame Roland, who was at that moment outlining just such a plan to her friend Bosc—there broke out a popular insurrection which completed the work of July 14th, and made Paris, once and for all, the head and stay of the revolution.

In the official report (*exposé*) of the Representatives of the Commune, published a year later, these three hundred good citizens show themselves hard at work, from September 18th onwards, trying to keep order in the capital by the same means as their predecessors of July. On September 23rd comes news of the arrival of troops at Versailles. They send commissioners to verify the report. They are informed that the Flanders regiment has come at the request of the municipality, and to help the Town Guard. When the districts of Paris refuse to credit this official excuse, and demand means to defend the city against another royal attack, they order the transport of powder from the magazines at Essonnes, and the purchase of bullets and cannon-balls; they make grants in aid of bakers who cannot otherwise purchase enough flour to satisfy their customers; and they petition the king to safeguard the grain-convoys on their way to the capital.

But Paris will not be appeased. On Sunday October 4th Morris notes in his diary 'serious suffering from want of bread,' and records that a woman speaking in the Palais-Royal has denounced 'plaster-of-Paris bread, sacrilegious opera-dinners, green uniforms, and black cockades.' Early on the morning of the 5th the Town Hall is surrounded by a hungry mob of women calling for the mayor and councillors, and declaring their intention to march on Versailles. Soon they break into the building, seize all the money and arms they can find, and nearly lynch the abbé Lefebvre for refusing to re-enact his rôle of July 13th.

When the Guards at last restore order, the women find a leader for the next part of their adventure in Stanislas Maillard, a tall thin young man of twenty-six, who works with his elder brother, a mounted officer (*huissier à cheval*) of the Châtelet, and who has already distinguished himself as one of the heroes of the Bastille. He will lead the march to Versailles. The procession gathers recruits as it goes—working women of all kinds, some of the middle class, and here and there a lady of fashion, forced to leave her carriage and to join in the march. 'Wearing ribbons of all colours, and armed with long sticks, pitchforks, pikes, even a few muskets and pistols,' and marching 'very clamourously, but in order and determined step,' they tramp off under a wet sky along the fifteen miles of muddy road that lead to Versailles. 'A ludicrous sight,' thinks the Duke of Dorset: but Paris is in a ferment, and who knows what the result may be?

Whilst the women are on the march, the tocsin (*touche-sin*, touch-bell) is still ringing, the district assemblies are still talking, and the municipal council is still debating the demand of the National Guard to be allowed to follow them. Why do the Guard want to go? Not to defend the king; but to support the demand of their women-folk for more food, to revenge on the Flemish regiment its insult to the tricolor, and to bring the royal family, the ark of the constitution, back to Paris. A fortnight before, an individual who had made this last suggestion had been indicted for treason (*propos séditieux*): now it is the programme of the people. At four o'clock Lafayette, hating so unsoldierly a command, but threatened (it was said) with the fate of Foullon, at last gives way, secures an order from the Town Hall, and sets out at the head of fifteen thousand Guards, and as many more irregular volunteers. He cannot now hope to arrive at Versailles much before midnight; but he sends a messenger ahead to tell the king that he is coming, and to urge him not to let the royal body-guard fire on the mob.

That morning at Versailles the National Assembly had been faced with another, and perhaps not the last, instance of royal obstruction. It had received a letter in which the king refused to promulgate isolated fragments of the constitution, but 'acceded to' those articles of it (the resolutions of August 4th) which had already been voted, on condition that no attempt was made to diminish his executive power (the decree of September 11th). He added that he would decide about the Declaration of Rights after the constitution as a whole had been passed. This fresh act of deceit and defiance caused such an uproar that Mounier, who was in the chair, was on the point of suspending the sitting, when (at three o'clock in the afternoon) the Paris women arrived, and asked to be heard. A deputation was admitted. Maillard, speaking for them, explained that they had come to ask for food, and to punish the insult to the patriotic cockade: they hoped to do so, it seemed, by securing the dismissal of the Flanders regiment.

The deputies were not unwilling to make use of these new, if unconventional, allies. Mounier, as President, led a party of them to the palace, with instructions to demand the king's signature not only to a decree providing food for Paris, but also to the Declaration of Rights, and to the nineteen articles of the constitution already passed, including that on the suspensive veto. By this time the king had come back from his hunting at Meudon, and the queen from the last visit that she would ever pay to her beloved Petit Trianon. Louis received the women amiably, embraced the least ill-favoured of them, and sent them away with promises of food. Supplies hitherto held up, presumably by royal order, at Senlis and Lagny were hurried to the capital.

But for five hours Mounier and his fellow-deputies waited in the palace, whilst the king tried to make up his mind. Should he give way to the demands of the assembly, or should he slip away—the royal carriages were at the door —to Rambouillet, where everything was prepared for him? Had the moment come to appeal to the country against Paris and the assembly? At last, with tears of vexation in his eyes, he handed Mounier a paper drawn up by his advisers in which for the third time in three months he capitulated to the people. 'I accept without qualification'—such was the formula dictated to him—'the articles of the Constitution and the Declaration of Rights presented to me by the National Assembly.'

The king's signature to this document might seem to end the crisis. The deputies of France and the people of Paris had what they wanted. But when Lafayette and his men arrived, not long before midnight, Louis was informed of the further desire of the Paris commune that he would make his home in the capital. True, neither court nor people could return to Paris that night; and the most that *le général Morphée* could do at the moment was to persuade the deputies to go home to their lodgings, and the women to use what hospitality the town offered, or to bivouac in the palace court. But the royal family must at least give up their last-minute plan for flight to Rouen, and rely upon Lafayette's word for their safety. Louis, having assured the assembly that he 'would never desert them, and had never thought of doing so,' retired for the night; and at three o'clock in the morning the tired deputies did the same.

The king indeed had nothing to fear. But among those who had followed Lafayette's men were some who had sinister aims against the queen, and amongst the women was one—Reine-Louise Audu—who afterwards suffered a year's imprisonment on the charge of having threatened 'to bring back the queen's head on the point of her sword.' At daybreak on the 6th some of these creatures found an unguarded way into the palace, exchanged shots with the sentries, and rushed up the main staircase towards the royal apartments. Warned by the shouts, the smashing of doors, and the shrieks of her women, Marie-Antoinette fled half-dressed to the king's room, just in time to save her life. There the royal family gathered, listening to the cries of their assailants, and wondering from which side the attack might come. At last the National Guards came to their rescue, and drove out the rioters. Quiet was restored in the palace.

Meanwhile the courtyard filled with a noisy and excited crowd, which did not know quite what had happened, and clamoured to see the king. When he appeared on a balcony with the queen and the Dauphin, they cried *Vive le roi!* When the queen appeared alone with her children there were cries of *Pas d'enfants!* and someone levelled a musket at her. It needed courage— but she never lacked that—to come out again, this time with Lafayette, who bowed, and kissed her hand. The crowd was touched, and cheered them both. When Louis reappeared there were repeated cries of *A Paris!* 'Yes, my friends,' he replied, 'I will come to Paris with my wife and children. I entrust my most precious possessions to my good and faithful subjects.' An informal meeting of the Council agreed that nothing else could be done. The assembly declared that it was inseparable from the king, and chose a hundred of its number to accompany him to the capital.

Paris had waited anxiously during the night of October 5th for news from Versailles. Some report of the king's capitulation may have reached the city early the next morning: but nothing certain can have been known of the attack on the palace until the return, about midday, of a first party of assailants, carrying what was by now recognized as the trophy of a popular victory —the heads of two of the royal body-guard, raised on pikes. Two hours later a second body followed—some soldiers, and a mixed crowd of civilians, riding in cabs, carts, and gun-carriages, and carrying helmets, sword-pommels, and bandoliers taken from the defeated troops. It was not till seven or eight in the evening, after six weary hours on the road, that the main procession arrived in the darkening streets of the capital.

Three months ago Louis had come by the same way, almost alone. Now the carriage in which he rode with his wife, his children, his elder brother, his sister, and the royal governess, was preceded and followed by a bizarre convoy of thirty thousand citizens— women bearing pikes or branches of poplar, some of them on horseback, some sitting astride gun-barrels; National Guardsmen with loaves stuck on the points of their bayonets; soldiers who a few hours ago had been firing at one another—French Guards, men of the Flemish regiment, and members of the king's body-guard—now fraternizing, and exchanging cockades; and carriages containing the representatives of the assembly. The victors of Versailles were too tired to be dangerous; but sometimes they fired shots into the air; and their marching-song was, 'Here come the baker, the baker's wife, and the baker's errand-boy!'

It was a lovely day, after yesterday's rain: a breeze that hardly stirred the leaves by the road-side: sunshine that lit up every beauty of the landscape. Madame de Staël, driving into Paris by the Bois de Boulogne, could moralize on Nature's failure to fit her moods to human affairs. Few, perhaps of the spectators of October 6th recalled how differently Louis and Marie-Antoinette had first entered Paris together fifteen years ago:—dressed in jewels and white satin, riding in a great gilt coach, surrounded by Gentlemen of the Household, and Officers of the Royal Hunt, and escorted by picturesque Suisses, and Gardes du Corps in their uniforms of red and blue and gold.

At the barrier Bailly, for the second time in three months, welcomed the king to his capital. At the Town Hall he repeated Louis' reply that 'it was with pleasure—and with confidence, added the queen—that he found himself among the citizens of his good city of Paris'; and Moreau de Saint-Méry spoke of the occasion as a family reunion. When, by the light of two flickering torches, they could all be seen standing at a window overlooking the Place de Grève, there was such cheering as had not been heard since July 17th. Once more Paris had reconquered its king.

At Versailles—a royalist letter sadly recalls—a sudden silence reigned, and the only sound heard in the palace was that of the doors, blinds, and window-shutters being closed for the first time since the reign of Louis XIV.

It is not easy for a visitor to modern Paris to reconstruct in imagination the Tuileries as it was in 1789. Then the palace closed the whole eastern end of the Tuileries gardens. Now only its two extremities remain—the Pavillon de Marsan on the north, and the Pavillon de Flore on the south. Both have been twice rebuilt—first by Napoleon III, and again after the fire of 1871; and they form the western ends of the new Louvre. The long narrow building which once stretched between them, the old palace of Catherine de Medici, had originally, like the Louvre itself at an earlier date, been outside the city wall. Its front therefore faced west, towards open country so delectable that it was named after the Homeric paradise, the Elysian Fields. At its back, where the city walls had been pulled down, was a courtyard surrounded by stables and outbuildings; then the open space of the Place du Carrousel (so called from an equestrian fête held there by Louis XIV in 1662); and behind this again a medley of old lanes and houses encumbering what is now the garden front of the Old Louvre. Difficult of approach from the east, the palace was almost invisible from the west. The 'magnificent perspective,' the 'towering pavilions,' the 'warm grey colour' of the stone, and the 'long range of windows glistening in the evening light' so much admired by early Victorian visitors were then obscured by high walls. The garden was overgrown with trees. On the south side, where things are least changed, the steep scarp of the Seine prevented close approach. To the west were terrace-walls, and a moat, across which a bridge led to the Place Louis Quinze, now known to every traveller as Place de la Concorde. Northwards what is now Napoleon's rue de Rivoli was in 1789 a lane enclosed between the high walls of the Tuileries garden on one side and of properties whose buildings faced the rue Saint-Honoré on the other. This space was used as an exercise-ground for the horses employed in Louis XV's riding-school (*manège*), which stood at its western end, opposite the present rue Castiglione.

Disused by the court since the minority of Louis XIV, the Tuileries, together with parts of the Louvre and of the surrounding buildings, had gradually been filled with a crowd of lodgers—royal pensioners, poor aristo-crats, retired army officers, and actors connected with the three theatres to which its huge apartments also gave hospitality. Many of these persons were turned out on October 6th, or gave up part of their accommodation, to make room for the royal family and its retainers. Their rooms were rearranged, their furniture and fittings adapted or removed; with results as uncomfort-able for the new inmates as inconvenient for the old. Even so, it was found at the time of the king's flight two years later that the palace contained more than two thousand persons, many of them unconnected with the court. It was not until a month after October 6th that the distracted M. Angivillier, *directeur général des bâtiments du roi*, could find room in the palace for the twelve boxes which contained the queen's books from Versailles.

'*Consummatum est*: it is finished,' wrote Desmoulins, not long after October 6th: 'the king is in the Louvre, the National Assembly is at the Tuileries, the channels of circulation are being cleared, the market is crammed with sacks of grain, the Treasury is filling up, the corn-mills are turning, the traitors are in full flight, the priests are under foot, the aristocrats are at their last gasp, the patriots have triumphed!' The revolution might well seem over.

But one condition had never been certain, and met with difficulties in its fulfilment. The assembly had declared itself inseparable from the king. But when Louis had been asked by Lafayette on the 6th to say that he would now live in Paris, he had cautiously replied, 'I don't refuse to; but I haven't made up my mind.' He may have felt something of the foreboding Mirabeau expressed, when he wrote next day to his friend Lamarck that unless the king left Paris both country and court were doomed. But what could he do, or where could he go? On the 8th the deputies were warned by the Duc de Liancourt to be ready to move their sessions to Paris. The next day an official letter informed them that the king had made up his mind to remain in the capital, and instructed them to find a place of meeting there.

At this point fresh difficulties arose. Some of the deputies already imagined themselves in danger at Versailles. Thibaudeau bolted his bedroom door at nights, and made his son sleep in an ante-room, with pistol and sword by his side. In view of the recent demeanour of the Parisians—their demonstrations at the Palais-Royal, their threats against the assembly, their attempt on the queen's life—less timid deputies might well fear to trust themselves within the capital. It was, no doubt, more than three months since they had solemnly declared their inviolability. But at that time they had only their enemy the king to fear: now they had to reckon with their friends the people. Their snuff-boxes had not been safe in the Salon d'Hercule: would their lives be more secure in the dark alleys behind the Tuileries? The declaration of June 23rd might protect them from their creditors, and from the police: would it be more than a scrap of paper to the roughs of the Paris slums? The names of ninety deputies who voted against the 'National Assembly' resolution of June 17th had been placarded in the Palais-Royal. What vengeance might not be in store for a deputy who had voted for a second chamber, or for an absolute veto?

On October 8th Mounier sent in his resignation, and set off—the first of the federalists—to his native Dauphiné, to rouse provincial revolt in defence of the liberty of king and assembly. He was followed by many others. The President found himself overwhelmed with applications for passports—two hundred were asked for within two days. The deputies were urged to show more courage. Difficulties were put in the way of obtaining leave of absence. Cowardly representatives were denounced by their constituents. The Paris commune went bail for the good behaviour of the citizens. These steps were on the whole successful. Lally-Tollendal, indeed, retired in indignation from an assembly that he denounced as a den of cannibals (*caverne d'anthropophages*): but others, like de Ferrières, were content to send home for their wives and their pistols. Malouet, even, stayed on to be the last royalist commoner, still insisting that France must change for him, not he for France.

Thus the assembly which held its first meeting in Paris on October 19th, though smaller by some three hundred members, was substantially the same as that which had held its last meeting at Versailles on the 15th. It was as national, it was as patriotic. The authors of the foundation-deeds of the revolution became the architects of the new France. As for the Parisians, they were so proud to have the assembly with them, and so pleased at the arrival of a thousand new customers, that they treated the deputies with unwonted and unanticipated respect. The deliberations of the assembly, Lafayette told Mounier, were less interrupted from the public gallery than they had been at Versailles.

Nevertheless the transference of the king and the assembly to Paris radically altered the conditions under which the government was carried on. Of the changes it brought about the most obvious was, perhaps, the least real. The prisoner of the Tuileries had in fact been, ever since July, a prisoner at Versailles. The impression produced upon the royal family by the half-dismantled apartments of their new home was gloomy and oppressive. Its back windows were overlooked by shabby tenements. Its front windows showed a terrace crowded with the general public. The garden afforded so little privacy that for ten days Louis could not venture out. Yet the king's political position was no worse than before: it was, indeed, in one respect better. He was more able to know what his country and his capital were thinking; he could be quicker to lead, or it might be to follow, the general will. The deputies, too, could see from the south windows of their new parliament-house the garden front of the palace, and hear through its north windows the street-cries of the rue Saint-Honoré. They were better placed to gauge the public temper, and to mediate between the capital and the court, than they had been in the quiet suburbs and green garden-vistas of Versailles.

Paris had changed too. Its citizens were not likely to forget that October 6th was a victory for the policy of direct action. They would not be backward in reminding either king or assembly that the organs of government were accountable to the sovereign people. A capital which had under its protection both the executive and the legislature was in a position to dictate a policy to the whole country. Military control was passing from the army to the National Guard. Political control was passing from the intellectuals to the demagogues. The general will was contracting to the scale of the personal and party relationships of city life. These invisible changes were to alter the whole course of the revolution.

They would not necessarily denationalize it. Efforts were made during the tedious inquiry conducted by the Châtelet into the incidents of October 5th and 6th to prove that the attack on Versailles had been incited by Mirabeau, or by the Duc d'Orléans. The charges, based upon the hearing of nearly four hundred witnesses, were carefully considered by the *Comité des rapports* of the assembly, which exonerated both deputies. Mirabeau took the occasion (October 2nd, '90) to produce an *alibi*, and to prove his innocence. Meanwhile Orléans had been advised by Lafayette to leave the country, and was employing himself on an imaginary mission in London. His credit as the head of a party, or as a candidate for a Regency, was destroyed. His only future lay within the ranks of Jacobinism. But neither Orléans nor Mirabeau had been needed to inspire the march on Versailles. It was the spontaneous act of the Paris people.

In the same spirit as the Châtelet historians have been found to attribute the later blunders and crimes of the revolution, if not to Orléanism or Communism, if not to the Jews or to the Freemasons, then at least to 'the Paris mob,' which they suppose to have dictated its will, at every turn, to a terrorized and servile government. What exactly the influence of the capital was upon the revolution is a question still to be examined. But it can already be said that there was more hope in Paris than in any other part of France that a truly French revolution would go forward, and not back; that the hopes expressed in the *cahiers*, and the faith embodied in the Declaration

of Rights, would come to fruition in a constitution: and that the deliberations of the assembly would be guided by the best intellects in the country,
inspired by the most national because the most comprehensive outlook. Paris
was the brain and the heart of France. By what organs could it be better
ruled?

Chapter VI

PARIS

I walked up gravely to the window in my dusty black coat, and looking through the
glass saw all the world in yellow, blue, and green, running at the ring of pleasure. The old
with broken lances, and in helmets which had lost their vizards,—the young in armour
bright which shone like gold, beplumed with gay feathers of the east—all—all tilting at it
like fascinated knights in tournaments of yore for fame and love.—(Sterne: *A Sentimental Journey: Paris.*)

For nearly two years after the exciting summer of '89 the march of the
revolution slowed down. Nothing occurred to alter the essential relations
of crown, country, and capital until the king's flight in June, '91. But this
was not an unimportant period. It was a period of national reconstruction,
which saw far-reaching reforms carried out both in church and state. It was
also a period of disillusionment, counter-revolution, and a growing conviction that the new France could not come into being under its present
constitution.

Even before its move to Paris the assembly had lost some of its early
naïvety, its other-worldly enthusiasm. Its homogeneity had been compromised, since July, by the adherence of clergy and nobles who did not
agree with its aims. Its unanimity had been broken during August by the
debates on feudalism and natural rights. Its prestige had been lowered
during September by the quarrel about the veto and by the tactless intervention of Paris. The defection of so many members of the Right on the
eve of the transference of its sessions to Paris restored some of its solidarity,
but removed many of its best minds. The revolution lost in intelligence what
it gained in power.

In speaking of differences of opinion within the assembly the word
'party' can hardly be avoided. It is a very misleading expression. To an
Englishman, accustomed to the two-party or three-party subdivision of a
Parliament that may sit for five years, the word suggests party funds, party
whips, and a party programme. To an Englishman parliamentary government depends upon the party in power being able to count upon a majority
of members who will 'vote straight,' unless too great a strain is put upon
their loyalty. This assumption would have seemed strange to the deputies of

'89. Though they reported from time to time to those who had elected them; though they did what they could for local interests; yet they looked upon themselves as representatives of the nation. They belonged to no party in our sense of the word. Political Quakers, they sat in their places waiting for the inspired word to be spoken: they allowed no one to dictate their opinions: they decided every issue as their reason and conscience directed.

At first this austere attitude prevented the formation, not only of parties, but even of clubs. At Versailles the Breton Club, the first of its kind, found it advisable to open its membership to deputies of other provinces, if it were not to be accused of secret and seditious practices. Its successor, the Jacobin Club, soon admitted the general public to its meetings. The political societies which grew up in the more clubbable atmosphere of Paris were parliamentary parties in embryo. It amused the public to talk of the *côté de la reine,* or of the *côté du Palais-Royal.* But, generally speaking, the movements of political fragments within the kaleidoscopic assembly only formed a pattern when reflected in the fixed mirrors of a crucial issue, or when jolted by a great oration. The truest account of parliamentary opinion in 1789 would be to say that most of the deputies wanted the revolution to go forward, some of them wanted it to go back, and some of them wanted it to stop where it was.

The formation of parties was due in no negligible degree to the arrangements of an impromptu parliament-house. The *salle des menus plaisirs* at Versailles, in which the Commons first sat alone, and subsequently with the clergy and nobles, from May 6th to October 15th, '89, was so large that it encouraged a loud and flamboyant style of oratory, well suited to the birth of a revolution, but regretted by the government which acted as its unwilling *accoucheur.* The President's table, placed in the centre, divided the House in half, and already the terms Right and Left were in popular use.

When the assembly followed the king to Paris, it had to be content for three weeks (October 19th—November 9th) with a big room in the Archbishop's palace (*archevêché*) near Notre Dame. Soon the need for more accommodation, and the fall of a public gallery, made it necessary to look for easier quarters. These were found in the *manège* on the north side of the Tuileries gardens. A riding-school built for the young Louis XV became the home of the Constituent Assembly during the rest of its career, and the scene of its most famous debates.

The building was more convenient in its surroundings than in itself. It stood close to the rival centres of political passion—the Tuileries and the Palais-Royal. It was easily reached from those parts of the city in which most of the deputies lodged, on either bank of the Seine. There were neighbouring buildings—the Feuillant, Capucin, and Jacobin monasteries, and the smart *hôtels* of the Place Vendôme—where clubs could meet, committees confer, and secretaries file their correspondence. The nearer of these premises were soon connected with the *manège* by covered passages, so that the members could come and go without regard to the weather. The Tui-

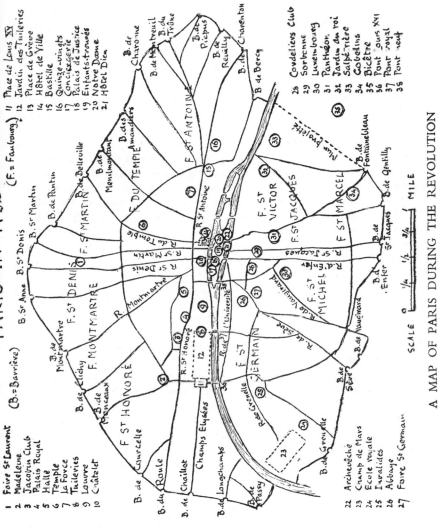

A MAP OF PARIS DURING THE REVOLUTION

Showing the principal streets, buildings, barrières, and faubourgs.

(F. = Faubourg) (B. = Barrière)

1 Foire St Laurent
2 Madeleine
3 Jacobin Club
4 Palais Royal
5 Halle
6 Temple
7 La Force
8 Tuileries
9 Louvre
10 Châtelet
11 Place de Louis XV
12 Jardin des Tuileries
13 Place de Grève
14 Hôtel de Ville
15 Bastille
16 Quinze-vingts
17 Conciergerie
18 Palais de Justice
19 Enfants-trouvés
20 Notre Dame
21 Hôtel Dieu
22 Archevêché
23 Champ de Mars
24 Ecole royale
25 Invalides
26 Abbaye
27 Foire St Germain
28 Cordeliers Club
29 Sorbonne
30 Luxembourg
31 Panthéon
32 Jardin du roi
33 Salpétrière
34 Gobelins
35 Bicêtre
36 Pont Louis XVI
37 Pont royal
38 Pont neuf

leries gardens afforded a pleasant refuge from the bustle of business, where deputies could talk over their opponents' speeches, and think out their replies.

The new parliament-house itself was small, and badly lit; it was of an inconvenient shape; and it was difficult to speak in. A long, low, narrow building, it was seated like our House of Commons, so that the members faced one another across a gangway. But one side was broken by the President's seat and the secretaries' table, and the other by the speaker's desk. Thus the members found themselves divided, whether they wished it or not, into a Right and a Left. It was not long before certain blocks of seats were appropriated by certain groups of deputies. Those on the right belonged, roughly, to the royalists, those on the left to the democrats. The extreme members of each party tended to sit in the highest seats at the back of their block, the moderates in the centre, and those who belonged to no party in the front rows, whence they could easily cross the floor of the House.

The room had no source of heat except a stove—in later days a porcelain model of the Bastille—placed in the centre of the floor. The atmosphere was so bad (*malsain et méphytique*) that the health of the deputies suffered from it, and the ingenious Dr. Guillotin suggested the sprinkling of vinegar and scent twice a day. The public galleries, which seated some three hundred spectators, were very cramped compared to those of Versailles, and could easily be monopolized by the *claqueurs* of a political party. Mirabeau, in April ,'90, seems to have been the first to employ this device. By January, '91, some two hundred agents (*mouchards*) drawn from the artisan and shop-keeping class earned fifteen shillings a week by 'policing' the public galleries in the interests of his royalist policy.

Such were some of the drawbacks of the new parliament-house. From time to time proposals were made to transfer the assembly to the Madeleine, or to the Louvre, or to a building specially designed for its sittings. But nothing was done. The deputies remained in their uncomfortable quarters until the fall of the throne, in August, '92, made it possible to move to the Tuileries the following May.

The deputies adopted no rules of procedure until the end of July, '89. For the first six weeks the Third Estate had refused to act as a representative body, and deliberately kept the informal procedure of a debating society. During the six weeks following June 17th the National Assembly was fighting for its existence, and could not tie its hands by rules that might hinder an urgent decision, or handicap an impromptu debate. But customs were inevitably formed; and it was these which the *comité de règlement*, one of the first four committees set up by the assembly, embodied in the regulations of July 28th. The *règlement* was not particularly effective; but as Frenchmen and revolutionaries the deputies not unnaturally preferred their own arrangements to such ready-made rules as they could read in Romilly's account of the procedure of the House of Commons.

Arthur Young's well-known descriptions of noisy and disorderly debates belong to the unregulated period; things were better afterwards. But not always: for two English visitors, Lord Mornington and Miss Berry, describe sessions a year later in which a number of speakers were on their feet at the same time, and the President in vain attempted to keep order. There was even an occasion (April 8th, '90) when (as the British Ambassador put it) 'the Assembly was converted into an absolute bear-garden,' and the public in the galleries pelted the deputies with apples and oranges. The truth is, any French assembly is apt to regard the rules of debate as a belliger-ent nation regards the Hague Conventions: they are excellent in peace-time, but inapplicable in time of war. Many sittings in the Constituent Assembly were as edifying and orderly as the House of Lords. But certain speakers, certain subjects, certain words might at any moment rouse a storm which swept away the frail regulations, and turned a debate into a riot.

In some important points the assembly of '89 defied both the experience of St Stephen's and the common sense of mankind. The chair was occupied, not by a permanent Speaker, but by a fortnightly President. He might have been chosen to represent the dominant party in the House. He might have been chosen in recognition of some service recently rendered, or of his special interest in some subject before the House. He was not expected to be impartial: whether he could or could not keep order was hardly considered. There were the ushers (*huissiers*): there was the President's bell (*sonnette*). If both failed, he could put on his hat, and suspend the sitting. The six secretaries were a little less transitory than the President—only three of them changed fortnightly: but they had no authority to direct the debates.

Again, it was a good democratic custom that allowed any member to propose a motion or an amendment. But the precautions against hasty legis-lation and ill-considered diversions of a debate were too easily over-ruled. The House was often entangled in such a web of resolutions and alternative resolutions, amendments, and counter-amendments, that it did not know what it had to decide. Yet again, deputations were received, not by His Majesty's ministers, but by Parliament. Their leaders were allowed to de-liver addresses from the bar of the House. Their members sometimes marched through it, and received a presidential embrace (*accolade*), coupled with a complimentary speech. This democratic custom made possible some moving incidents, such as the reception on October 23rd of Jean Jacob, the oldest patriot in the country, whose baptismal certificate showed that he had been born a hundred and twenty years ago. But more often it was not only a waste of time, but also an opportunity for party demonstrations for or against the petitioners.

Another custom, but one that led to boredom rather than to disorder, was that of delivering set speeches. The Constituents had great themes to expound, and all time at their disposal. They rejected with scorn the pro-posal made by one of the silent members that their eloquence should be limited to five minutes by the hour-glass. They seldom spoke without a manuscript. Many of the so-called debates consisted of a series of essays, each of which was carefully thought out, and elegantly expressed, but dealt with the subject under discussion *de novo*, without reference to what had been said by previous essayists. Extempore speaking was a rare and envied accomplishment. Those who could achieve it—Mirabeau, Barnave, Maury, Rabaut Saint-Etienne—passed for prodigies. Few debates hit the happy mean between instructive dullness and unedifying abuse. At their best moments the deputies seemed to be addressing a friendly universe, and the result was not unlike what it would be if the proceedings of the House of Commons were to be broadcast. At their worst moments they seemed to think, and had no hesitation in saying, that anyone who differed from them was a traitor and an assassin. There was plenty of good rhetoric: but few debates could show what was not uncommon in the contemporary House of Commons—the finer eloquence that comes from the unrehearsed clash of able minds.

For its ideas, revolutionary rhetoric drew on the rich stocks of Montesquieu and Rousseau, Mably and Raynal. Its clichés, its metaphors, and the tricks of expression which make it monotonous and unreal to a modern reader, came from the stilted tradition of the Comédie française, from Jesuit *Conciones* learnt by heart at College, and from the study of Thomas' popular *Essai sur les éloges*. The manner and gestures of the speakers were modelled on those of the bar, the pulpit, and the Academy. Their expansive egoism flowed with their French blood, and borrowed something from the early habit of the confessional. Within this general tradition of oratory there was, of course, room for wide differences of method and taste. No reader is likely to confuse Mirabeau's speeches with Danton's, or to be unable to distinguish Vergniaud's style from that of Robespierre.

Customs of procedure and debate had not unimportant effects upon the work of the assembly. More serious was a characteristic inherent in the very nature of a body which claimed to be a direct emanation of the sovereign people. Though the deputies faced one another across the floor of the House, there was no Government, and no Opposition. A Bill would be introduced by a committee composed of members of all parties. There was no guarantee that it would be carried. No one outside the committee was pledged to support it. Those who disliked it could criticize it unreservedly, without the restraining fear that the Government might resign, and leave it to them, as the Opposition, to introduce alternative legislation. Yet it must be admitted that this drawback was not very seriously felt. Few legislatures have produced a weightier series of reports, or an acuter body of criticism, than the Constituent Assembly of '89-'91. Here is a genuine attempt by the best minds of an exceptionally enlightened age to think out a democratic system. It contains a rich store of political wisdom.

One result of the transference of the assembly to Paris was the multiplication of newspaper reports of its proceedings. At Versailles the *Moniteur* had enjoyed the monopoly of a press-box (*loge grillée*) from which it could report the debates undisturbed. The representatives of other papers had to do as best they could in the public galleries: they might have to wait, as they complained, all night to make sure of a seat. The smaller galleries of the *manège* were confined to ticket-holders. The *Journal national* was accordingly given a *chassis grillé* in a corner of the hall; and Dr Guillotin, the *commissaire*, found places for other reporters, with increasing difficulty, by the steps on the right and left of the raised platform that bore the President's seat. The speakers had now some hope that their names would be correctly spelt, and their remarks properly reported. They spoke less to their fellow-deputies, and more to the invisible audience of citizens.

In any case the best work of the assembly, as of many such bodies, was not done in public, and in the presence of reporters, but behind the scenes, in committee. For many deputies the two morning and evening sessions were only a part of the day's work. The most important of the thirty-one standing committees of the House—the constitutional, diplomatic, military, feudal, ecclesiastical, and financial committees—met, singly or jointly, almost every day. Their business was constantly increasing: their powers were progressively encroaching upon those of the executive. Their *rapporteurs* resembled departmental ministers; their *rapports* initiated legislation; their *instructions* guided local administration. The *comité des recherches* issued warrants of arrest. The *comité des finances* controlled the printing of *assignats*. The *comité ecclésiastique* imposed the clerical oath. The *comité diplomatique* read ambassadors' despatches. The *comité d'aliénation* settled every detail of the sale of the *biens nationaux*. The much-advertised principle of the Separation of Powers might prohibit such executive activities on the part of a constitutional legislature. It was powerless to check a Constituent or constitution-making Assembly. During an instructive debate on October 20th, '90, it was maintained that the Military Committee had usurped the functions of the Minister of War. As Cazalès observed, 'the only means of restoring the executive power of the crown was to suppress all the administrative committees of the assembly.'

Deputies who had never before lived in Paris were probably less conscious of stresses within the structure of the assembly than of pressure impinging upon it from outside. Within the four walls of the parliament-house they could enjoy, save for occasional interruptions from the public galleries, a lively illusion of freedom. They could hardly go outside its precincts without being reminded that their little world revolved in a Parisian universe.

The legislative and executive powers, so recently at issue with one another, were now no further apart than the Tuileries and the *manège*. Both were under the suspicious survey of the Palais-Royal across the way, the headquarters of the sovereign people. That the deputies were conscious of hostile supervision is shown by their eagerness to exclude each other from office under the crown. But this could not save them. They must all bear the odium of being part of the government, the suspicion of being an enemy rather than a friend of the people. From October, '89, until June, '91, every stage in the decline of the throne is a stage in the discrediting of the assembly.

The ministers too are of no account: even Necker will soon be forced to resign. But they still have a hand on the administrative machine. The civil service is packed with reactionary officials. The reforms of the assembly can be sabotaged almost at will by the local administration. Only, perhaps, at the Foreign Office, under Montmorin, the least unpopular of the ministers, the old traditions and the old personnel are helpful to the new regime. As the standing committees of the House get to work, they grow increasingly impatient of departmental obstruction and delay.

In Paris, again, the deputies are feeling the pressure of those financial interests which had hitherto identified themselves with the ups and downs of Necker's ministerial career. 'The capitalists,' Ferrières told his wife, 'are the real influence behind the Estates.' This was an exaggeration. But big industrialists of the day—Diétrich the Strasbourg iron-master, Ternaux the cloth manufacturer, or de Fontenay, who owned the cotton-mills at Rouen —dined with Lafayette, and worked for the construction of a 'business government,' under which property might be secure, and profits easy. If their wishes were ignored, they were as ready to turn against an irresponsible democracy as against an autocratic king. Again, whilst the capitalists are intriguing to secure new profits, the refugees are intriguing to safeguard old gains; foreign bankers are speculating in the funds; and foreign emissaries are rumoured to be financing the agents of public disorder. Yet little of this appears on the surface. To Morris, himself a business man, business seems to be at a standstill. 'Pleasure,' he writes, 'is the great affair: everybody has his country seat, and comes to town to do business once in three or four days.' The centre of revolutionary society is not the bank-counter or the lawyer's office, but the coffee-house and the club.

Ever since the peace of '83, Paris had been invaded by English clubs, English clothes, and English manners. The young Parisian welcomed the informality of a society in which he need not change his morning coat or boots, and to which his women-folk were not admitted. The club provided the professional and middle classes with that easy-going intercourse which the shopkeepers had already found in the *cafés*, and the workers in the *tavernes* and *guinguettes*. 'A Frenchman,' remarked a satirist of the time, 'is a man who cannot hold his tongue. Whatever the subject, he must be talking. He is never heard to say, " I don't know anything about that."' On every side clubs sprang up to satisfy this craving. Already, before the revolution, Paris had a *Club politique* and a *Club de Boston*; and the temporary police ban of '87 only resulted in a fresh crop of clubs two years later—a *Club de Viroflay*, a *Club de Valois*, a *Club de Montrouge*, and many others. The old salons had talked about literature, religion, and natural science: the new clubs talked about politics, and again politics. Their chief forcing-ground was the Palais-Royal, where every flower in the political catalogue flourished, and scattered its seeds over the country.

Two societies were of superior and independent origin. The *Club breton*, founded at Versailles by Breton deputies of the States-general, had enlarged itself, since the National Assembly came to Paris, into the *Société des Amis de la Constitution*. It had hired the premises and inherited the nickname of the Dominican monks of the rue Saint-Honoré, and was generally known as the Jacobin club. Here deputies of all shades of opinion, and such politically minded Parisians as could afford time enough, and an annual subscription of twenty-four shillings, met nightly to debate the questions of the day.

The Jacobins was not a party club. It reflected the dominant opinion of the general public. Whilst Paris was monarchical, the Jacobins swore by the constitution. When Paris overthrew the throne, the Jacobins became republicans. The meetings were at first held in the Dominican refectory; then in the library; and finally in the chapel. The changes did not signify an increasing spirituality of outlook; only a growing need for space. From October, '91, onwards the Jacobins debated in public, and their galleries were as crowded as those of the assembly. By means of an official journal, and a system of affiliation with similar bodies in the provinces, their ideas were spread all over the country.

The *Société des amis des droits de l'homme et du citoyen* was known as the Cordeliers club because it met in the Franciscan monastery in the street of that name, on the south bank of the river. It was of later foundation than the Jacobin club, and of lower social status. Here the shopkeepers, students, and artisans of the Quartier Latin could, in less formal surroundings, and for a subscription of a penny a month, learn the Declaration of Rights, hear the case against the government of the day, and turn the eye of vigilance which was the badge of their society upon the misdeeds of city officials. For if the Jacobin club was the Government club, the Cordeliers was the club of the Opposition.

It was largely to counteract such opinions that other clubs of a more aristocratic and conservative type were founded—the *Impartiaux* of Malouet and his circle, Lafayette's *Club de '89*, whose exclusive entry fee was five pounds, or the *Club monarchique* in which Lally-Tollendal tried to rally the remnants of the Moderate party. The unqualified royalism of the *Amis du roi* was, in its turn, offset by the *Cercle social*, or *Amis de la Vérité*, whose vaguely socialistic and republican doctrines were expounded in the *Bouche de fer*, and in the abbé Fauchet's popular lectures in the circus of the Palais-Royal. Soon, in July, '91, the Feuillants would be disputing the heritage of the Jacobins, compromised by republicanism; and to the list of lesser clubs would be added a *Cercle municipal*, issuing *Ephémérides* for the discussion of civic administration, a *Club des indigents*, whose heroes were

Rousseau and Robespierre, and a *Portique français*, which proposed to study art and literature alongside politics beneath the dome of the Panthéon.

A few clubs, such as the Cordeliers, the *Société de l'harmonie sociale*, and the two *Sociétés fraternelles des patriotes des deux sexes*, admitted women; and there was one, the *Société des citoyennes républicaines révolutionnaires*, whose officers and members were all female. The Club Massiac, or *Société des colons français*, represented the interests of the West Indian planters; and the objects of some other societies were sufficiently indicated by such names as *Société du serment du jeu de paume; des victimes du pouvoir arbitraire; du club littéraire des loyalistes* (later known as *Club helvétique des patriotes suisses*); or *des fédérés des gardes nationales du royaume*.

As for the cafés of Paris—who could keep account of them all? President Routh of Magdalen, at the age of ninety-three, was fond of recalling the coffee-houses which catered for the University of his younger days. Tom's, he would say, was the most gay and expensive: Horseman's was patronized by Merton, All Souls, Corpus, and Oriel: Harper's catered for Queen's and Magdalen, Bagg's for New College, Hertford, and Wadham; Malbon's was the centre for Trinity and other neighbouring Colleges. In the same way every café in the centre of Paris had its special *clientèle*.

The Palais-Royal—once the town house of the Duc d'Orléans, now laid out in alleys and piazzas like Covent Garden, and become a place of public entertainment—was described by Macaulay forty years later as 'the spot in all the earth in which the good and evil of civilization are most strikingly exhibited.' M. Billecocq, the Director of the national lottery, who doubtless disliked unofficial competition, reported in April, '91, that it contained more gambling-houses, cafés, taverns, and prostitutes than all the rest of Paris put together. The police proceedings of the time are full of references to this neighbourhood. Seditious and indecent *brochures* are being sold in the arcade outside the café du Berceau-Lyrique. Certain persons foregather at the café du Conti with intention to insult the money-changers (*agents de change*); others force the orchestra of the café du Caveau to play 'various tunes, including *Nina*.' At the café de la Rotonde a customer is apprehended whilst passing forged notes. The café de Valois is the scene of a violent quarrel between the Marquis de Saint-Huruge and a fellow-officer about the affair at Lille. Secret gaming-tables are known or suspected to exist at the café Mécanique, the café du Roi, and the café des Variétés. The police have orders to clear out the customers and to close down all these premises an hour before midnight. The café de Foy, the best-known resort of politicians, has a reputation to keep up. Its proprietor, the *limonadier* Pierre Jousseran, reports a lodger for keeping a *jeu de biribi*, and prosecutes a client for the theft of a silver spoon. But even here *propos incendiaires* are not uncommonly heard, and a dispute may end with the drawing of pistols ; whilst the old staircase and the stone arcade outside are a favourite haunt of pick-pockets, who help themselves to the watches and snuff-boxes of those who enter or leave the café. Such was the rather disreputable background of the political life of the capital —the subsoil into which the roots of the transplanted assembly were pushing down for nourishment. Nor was that the end. Wherever the clubs cast their seed upon the working-class quarters of the capital, they gave rise to a rich parasitical growth of Popular and Fraternal Societies, whose members listened to readings from Rousseau, drew up manifestos about the right of petition or universal suffrage, and would seldom refuse an opportunity to loot a baker's shop, or to lynch an enemy of the people.

The deputies viewed some of these bodies with natural apprehension. They could have no objection to the progress of revolutionary ideas in more academic circles. At the Collège de France M. Gournand's lectures on the *Contrat social* attracted a crowd of young students, who enjoyed his denunciations of the ecclesiastics, and his sarcasms at the expense of the Sorbonne. The Lycée, founded in '85 as a centre for free lectures, concerts, and exhibitions, reopened under revolutionary auspices in January,'91. In its well-filled library three hundred subscribers studied the *Monthly Review* from England, and perused the periodicals of the day. In its comfortable sitting-rooms, which were open from 9 a.m. till midnight, they could discuss the latest rumours from the Palais-Royal close by, or pass round copies of the evening *Postillon*, with its Stop Press reports of the day's debate in the assembly. So the revolution spread to the younger generation.

The National Assembly might rule France. Paris was ruled by the Commune, and the Commune was ruled by the Districts. They were the real springs of revolutionary life during the nine months following July, '89. They had come into being in April, '89, as electoral subdivisions of the capital. When the elections were over, the electors did not disappear. Neither did the districts. In the critical days of July, when the electors took over the government of Paris, the electoral assemblies of the districts also assumed new powers. Not content to appoint municipal officers, they became units of local self-government. Each group of lawyers, merchants, clergy, and literary men formed itself into a district legislature (*assemblée générale*) and a district executive, whose various committees dealt with Police, Highways, Poor Relief, Finance, and such other matters as come within the scope of a modern City Council. For twelve months these sixty little republics enjoyed a rich and independent life. They did not hesitate to impose their views upon the municipal body which they had elected, or to make them known to the representatives of the sovereign people.

A body of regulations (*règlement général*) drawn up in April, '90, clearly explained their attitude. They acknowledged that the municipality was a corporate association of all the citizens for the preservation of liberty, property, and security, and for resistance to oppression. But they held that each district within the civic commonwealth (*commune*) should be free to exercise autonomous legislative and executive powers. It was as though the discipline and teaching of a Public School were to be managed by its House-masters;

or as though the multifarious business of the University of Oxford were to be taken out of the hands of Council and Congregation, and directed by twenty-two College Meetings. This civic federalism was an exaggeration of democracy characteristic of the ideas of '89, but no more likely than departmental federalism to survive the double pressure of war and counter-revolution.

The most original and characteristic source of revolutionary ideas was the Paris press. The Paris press was at once the child and the father of the revolution. A few years before, only five periodicals had been on sale, by permission of the *directeur-général de la librairie*, in the bookshops of the capital. These were a court gazette, a literary weekly, a church paper, a political and literary review, and the *Journal de Paris*. A rising young lawyer like de Sèze might also read the *Mercure*, the *Année littéraire*, and the *Journal encyclopédique*. The first was dull, and the second obscurantist; but the third might be enlivened with an article by Voltaire.

With the approach of the revolution official encouragement was given to the authors of *brochures*. It could not long be withheld from the editors of gazettes. The government had started on a wrong line by prohibiting (May 5th-6th) Mirabeau's *Etats-généraux*. It retrieved its mistake a fortnight later by authorizing certain papers—the *Gazette*, the *Mercure*, the *Journal* —to publish reports of the proceedings of the assembly. It even tolerated the unauthorized accounts that appeared in the *Point du jour*, the *Journal des Etats-généraux*, the *Courrier français*, and some other papers.

During the summer of '89 Parisians were bewildered by the appearance of a fresh paper every week. The municipality raged in vain against street-sellers (*colporteurs*), caricaturists, and anonymous publishers. The director-general found it impossible to stem the invasion of unauthorized printing-presses. On the same day (November 12th) that he refused leave to Mlle de Kéralio—though her father had been a *censeur royal*—to start a National Press, he was obliged to point out to the *chambre syndicale de Paris* how difficult it had become to stop unlicensed printing. With that apologia he disappeared from the scene. To a regime of ineffectual censorship succeeded a state of journalistic anarchy. In the end the assembly was asked to do no more than limit the number of printers by some test of technical skill.

The earliest of the new papers were edited by self-taught journalists exploiting public interest in the States-general, or by amateur politicians who wished to put their views before a wider public. Soon the deputies themselves discovered that they could more easily get a hearing in the press than in the rostrum, and could supplement their official allowance with the profits of a newspaper. Few of these publications involved much organization or outlay. Pancoucke's semi-official *Moniteur*, Brissot's *Patriote français*, Prudhomme's illustrated Sunday paper, the *Révolutions de Paris*, Barère's *Point du Jour*, which appeared daily during the first twenty-eight months of the revolution, or Mallet du Pan's *Mercure*, with its local correspondence and its circulation of twelve thousand copies a week, were undertakings of some magnitude.

They corresponded to the *Times*, the *Morning Chronicle*, the *Morning Post*, and the other leading English newspapers, which at this time sold for three-pence-halfpenny or fourpence a copy.

The rest were very unpretentious publications. Their eight or twelve pages of octavo or even duodecimo size were vilely printed on poor paper. They came out only once or twice a week. They contained no more matter than one man could write, and another man print, in the time he spared from his shop, or from his seat in the assembly. They needed no capital to start them, and no advertisements to keep up their circulation. Yet they sold at a price higher than our immense penny papers: their readers were prepared to pay a subscription of from thirty-six to forty-eight shillings a year.

A few months before, Arthur Young, accustomed to the substantial and well-informed journals of the English county capitals, had complained that he could not find a single paper in the French provinces. Now the *Affiches de Dijon* and the *Affiches de Rennes*, hitherto content to announce local sales, government orders, and shipping items, interspersed with a few trade advertisements, began to print political news from the capital. Soon a public reading-room could be found in every large town. The *salon de lecture* at Lyon took in twenty-five periodicals. Jacobin clubs subscribed to approved periodicals, both Parisian and provincial, and changed their subscriptions as frequently as an Oxford Common Room. Foreign admirers of the *philosophes* and the *Encyclopédistes* were interested in the political ideas of the revolution. Even the Pope subscribed to the *Moniteur*, the *Ami du roi*, and the *Journal des débats*, and had himself supplied with all the more important pamphlets as soon as they appeared.

The revolutionary press profited by a freedom such as had never been known before, and might never be known again. Though sanctioned by the Declaration of Rights, and embodied in the Constitutions of '91, '93, and '95, this freedom was not a thoroughfare secured by law, but a right of way granted on sufferance. At any moment the political party in power might deny it to their opponents, and there would be no redress. In fact, Sieyès' Censorship Bill (January 20th, '90) was not even discussed. Liberty of the press gave currency to irresponsible rumours, and gross personal abuse. But it enabled every idea to be aired, and every grievance to be exposed. Without it the revolution might not have survived.

To the political influence of the press was added that of the stage. Under the old regime actors had been outlawed by the church. Under the new regime they were patronized by the state. As a community they had, perhaps, more to hope from the revolution than any other: and they were not slow to seize their opportunity. On July 14th Beaulieu of the *Variétés* took part in the attack on the Bastille, and Mlle Contat looked on from a safe distance. Very soon actors played prominent rôles on the political stage. True, the respectable *bourgeoisie* were indignant that a *comédien* should hold a commission in the National Guard. It was not until the end of December that the civil disabilities of the profession were removed, and not till a month later that the censorship of plays was done away with. Talma could not find a priest to marry him until April, '91.

The stage showed its gratitude for these liberties, however long delayed, by giving performances in aid of patriotic charities, and by lending itself to political propaganda. For this it was admirably adapted. An audience too poor to subscribe to the clubs, too ill-dressed to be admitted to the galleries of the assembly, and too illiterate to understand the newspapers, could take up a political allusion from the pit of the Théâtre Montansier, or from the gallery of the Théâtre Italien. The spectator of a play was in a more receptive and uncritical mood than the auditor of a speech, or the reader of a gazette. Sentiments which sounded commonplace on the lips of a Danton or a Robespierre acquired a new meaning when put into the mouth of Cato or Brutus. Patriotism made a fresh appeal when reinforced by the magic of theatrical scenery and costumes, stage-lights and music.

Second-rate talent could, under such conditions, produce results out of its reach in other forms of literature. Chénier's *Charles IX*, first produced in November, '89, baptized the stage in the name of the nation, the law, and the constitution. It was followed by a flood of topical plays, whose titles—*Prise de la Bastille*, *Chêne patriotique*, *Fête de la Liberté*, *Triomphe du Tiers-Etat*, and so forth—sufficiently proved that the stage was now as free and patriotic as the press. Soon there were few houses that did not find it profitable to put on shows, or to interpolate speeches, that afforded cues for the cheers and counter-cheers of citizens quick to notice any allusion to current affairs. The armed guards whom it was customary to place amongst the audience could not always prevent disorder, or even bloodshed. The abolition of privilege had made it possible for anyone to set up in theatrical management. So popular did political playgoing become that within two years the number of theatres in the capital had doubled, whilst the Palais-Royal, the fairs, and the boulevards abounded with political skits and revues of the lowest and most provocative character.

It was the same in the provinces. Most of the larger towns maintained a municipal theatre, and produced the plays that had been popular in Paris. At Metz, when the officers of the garrison objected to the revolutionary tone of the Comédie, and withdrew their subscription, the municipality made themselves solely responsible for the management and policing of the theatre. Every crisis in the revolution had its commentary on the civic stage. Performances of *Le serment civique* and *Châteaux en Espagne* became occasions for demonstrations in honour of de Bouillé, the military governor, who was personally popular, or officially worth courting. The suppression of the Nancy mutiny, the abolition of royalty, and the publication of the Constitution of '93 each had its echo on the municipal stage. The plays, however, were still what the public wanted. When the Jacobin dictatorship was set up in the autumn of '93, they were chosen by authority, and the Metz theatre was drilled, like the theatres of Paris, in the goose-step of Robespierrist orthodoxy.

None of these plays better illustrates the part borne by the stage in the revolution than Chénier's *Charles IX, ou l'Ecole des rois*. In his Dedication the dramatist declared that his aim was to transform the stage from 'a school of flattery and libertinism' into a 'school of virtue and liberty.' In his preface he criticized the taste and morals of Corneille and Racine, and professed himself a follower of Voltaire. There is hardly a scene in the play which does not condemn tyranny, fanaticism, and treachery as crimes of the court, and exalt the cause of justice and the rights of the people. Revising his text, which was written before the revolution, in view of the events of October, '89, Chénier urges Louis to break with the court, and to ally himself with the People:

> Trust your own heart, rule of your own accord,
> And if your subjects' love is your desire,
> Be King of France, not Despot of Versailles.

In Act III the Chancellor de l'Hôpital, who is evidently meant for Necker, prophesies in rather pedestrian verse the time

> when to the grandeur of the throne
> There shall succeed the grandeur of the state,
> And when the People, glorious again,
> Shall banish every prejudice and lie,
> And repossess themselves of Natural Right.
> Then shall these living tombs, these dread Bastilles,
> Crumble to dust beneath their generous hands
> Which give the Prince his duty, and the clown,
> And fix for e'er the limits of their power.
> Then shall our sons and heirs, a prouder race,
> Many a leader, ne'er a master own,
> Happy beneath a justice-loving King
> Who gives them back their Liberty and Laws!

The end of the play shows Charles struck with remorse as a vision of his victims passes before him. The moral hardly needs pointing:

> I have betrayed my country and its laws:
> May my sad fate make other Princes pause!

It is not surprising that *Charles IX* played for over three weeks to crowded audiences. It was the most effective revolutionary propaganda of the year.

This Paris of the first year of revolution is not a quiet or restful place of residence. Every café has its groups of earnest and excited talkers. Every street-corner is covered with posters (*affiches*) announcing the latest regulations of the commune, or advertising the views of the newest publicist. Every print-shop window displays *libelles* and caricatures. Colporteurs cry their papers and pamphlets under the arcades of the Palais-Royal, or by the doors of the *manège*. Mingling discreetly among the crowd, noting their looks, and recording their remarks, are Sieur Goisset and his gang, the spies of the *comité des recherches*. The most casual visitor cannot fail to be aware of the tense atmosphere, of the heavy pressure of city life. The ringing of a church bell, the beating of a drum, or the tramp of a patrol down a darkened street suggests every kind of hidden danger. 'All Paris,' writes an English visitor at this time, 'is still in a ferment. The last sound which dies away upon the sleeping ear is the rattle of the patriot drums, and the first murmur which disturbs our rest is the martial music of the national militia. It is like living in a citadel besieged.'

Political excitement may act as a sedative to criminal tendencies. Yet the proceedings instituted during the winter of '89 by the Châtelet under the comprehensive charge of *lèse-nation* show nothing that need have been very alarming to the deputies. One Deschamps was sentenced to three days in the pillory and nine years in the galleys for obstructing the transport of grain from La Brie to Paris. A certain Delcros was banished for nine years for attempting to enlist soldiers for the Spanish army. Martin and Duval were discharged with a caution, after two months' imprisonment, for denouncing martial law. Curé, who received a life sentence in the galleys for libelling the queen, was not the only person guilty of such disloyalty. A weekly gossip paper, the *Sottises de la semaine*, and Fréron's weightier *Orateur du peuple*, had attacked the king and the assembly. Monsieur, the king's brother, and Lafayette had not escaped serious libels. Political controversy ended not infrequently in a duel in the Bois de Boulogne.

The most ominous fact was, perhaps, that the course of justice was so often obstructed by the democratic journalists and districts of the capital. When the Englishman Rutlidge was charged with inciting the Paris bakers to demand a higher subsidy from the commune, Desmoulins defended him. When he attacked Necker, he was incited by the Cordeliers club. Noël's 'incendiary statements' on the same subject were inspired by a pamphlet of Marat's; and when Marat himself was indicted by the Châtelet, he was hidden from arrest by his friends in the Quartier Latin, and his case was so effectively championed that the unpopular court was discredited and destroyed.

The civic authorities were at some pains to reassure the deputies, who were still disposed to regard a demand for higher wages by the *garde soldée*, or an *attroupement* of glass-workers in the faubourg Saint-Antoine, as the beginnings of another insurrection. The Police Department pointed out that under the old regime the police had been paid by the number of arrests they made, and had enjoyed the help of an efficient spy system: under the new regime they had no spies, and though there were fewer arrests, there were more convictions. During three months of '89-90 a hundred and twenty-two robberies had been reported, and a hundred and seventy-six arrests made: the corresponding figures for the same months in '88-9 had been five hundred and sixty reports and two hundred and sixty-one arrests. Moreover many of the hundred and twenty-two robbers had merely broken into eating-houses: very few had aggravated robbery with violence. The public might conclude that, even if the revolution had increased the amount of petty crime, it had diminished the more serious dangers to life and property.

Another cause of alarm was dispelled by a report issued in May, '90, by the *comité de mendicité*. Nervous deputies still supposed 'brigands' to be flooding into the city, with the intention of plundering the goods of respectable citizens. It was found upon inquiry that the number of beggars and vagabonds in Paris, which rumour put at twenty thousand, was actually between fifteen and eighteen hundred—not an excessive number in a city of more than half a million inhabitants. The 'brigands,' in fact, were almost as legendary as Falstaff's 'men in buckram.'

Paris had made itself, by the winter of '89, the mainspring of the revolutionary movement. Its leaders were full of ideas. Its rank and file were upon their best behaviour. But how could Paris impress its ideas and its demeanour upon the country? This was the problem that the assembly had to face during the months that followed. It was the more difficult, because there was as yet no authorized programme, no accepted design for the new France. The revolutionaries had pulled down the old fabric before inquiring whether some parts of it might not be embodied in the new. The new building had to be constructed on ground encumbered by the debris of the old. The sovereignty had been transferred from the king to the people: but Louis XVI was still on the throne. The assembly was enacting, clause by clause, a new constitution: but each regulation had to make its way not merely against official obstruction, but against the age-long habits of a people unaccustomed to self-government.

Gradually, during the two years following October, '89, royal prerogative, municipal privilege, feudal right, and political monopoly gave way to the equal citizenship of the new order. But until the constitution was codified and enacted as a whole, it could not be said for certain—This is constitutional: that is not. Church tithes and seigneurial charges might be exacted until substitutes were found for them, or until provision was made for their redemption. A new franchise was in force for municipal elections; but it would not come into force for a general election until the dissolution of the National Assembly. The old currency of *louis d'or* and silver *écus* was hoarded or exported, whilst the new *assignats* flooded the country with depreciating paper money. During this period of transition, everything would depend upon co-operation between Paris and the provinces. There were many old reasons—political, social, and economic reasons—for doubting this happy alliance. There were at least two new reasons for anticipating it.

The French language, once the literary prize of an educated class, was now the property of the people. Latin would survive as the language of the church and of the law. Provincial patois would survive as the language of the peasant. French would be the language of the nation in revolution, the medium in which the ideas of the new France would be interpreted.

As the French language had won its way without compulsion, and without a system of education, so there were springing up spontaneously all over the country political associations, through which the impulse given by Paris could be imparted to every corner of the provinces. The eleventh article of the Declaration of '89 had affirmed that 'the free communication of thoughts and opinions is one of the most precious rights of men.' The sixty-second article of the Municipal Law of December 14th had recognized the right of 'active' citizens to meet for the purpose of drawing up petitions. The revolutionary spirit did not indeed wait for such sanctions. For years past, Academies, National Societies, reading circles, and Masonic Lodges had given a political turn to their proceedings. One of the first effects of the revolution was to impart fresh life to these centres, and to create many more like them. In the smaller provincial towns a group of citizens would take out a joint subscription to the Paris *Patriote*, and meet to discuss the news. At Dijon a club was founded under the leadership of Guyton-Morveau. At Bayeux five or six friends meeting at M. Toustain's house formed the nucleus of a society which, to avoid any suspicion of secrecy, invited members of the general public to attend without payment.

In the big towns the patriots organized themselves on a larger scale. The Friends of the Constitution at Bordeaux rivalled the Friends of the Constitution in Paris. They met in the local Jacobin monastery. They proudly compared their speakers, Vergniaud, Guadet, and Ducos, with Mirabeau, Pétion, and Barnave. Although their hall of meeting contained nearly twelve hundred persons, it was far too small for all those who wished to attend the debates, and women would wait three hours for admission to the public gallery. Neither birth nor position, neither wealth nor professional eminence were admitted as qualifications for membership; only patriotism and a good reputation. Even Jews were not excluded.

In many towns the electors of '89, having drafted their addresses, and appointed their representatives, organized a Town Guard, set up Patriotic Committees, or Communal Councils (*conseils de commune*), and sat in the seats of the old municipality. Such was the commonest origin of a provincial Jacobin club. In the enthusiasm of the moment these activities might pass without opposition. The municipal elections of '90-91 produced a fresh crop of revolutionary clubs; they also produced tares among the wheat—societies for the defence of monopoly or privilege, whose programme and proceedings might be frankly counter-revolutionary. At Montauban political controversy was inflamed by religious discord. At Dax a quarrel between the municipality and the club was referred to the arbitration of the National Assembly, which decided in favour of the club.

Whatever the origin of a local society of patriots, and whatever its name, its keenest members were drawn from the professional and lower middle classes—from the active minority who in every small community 'run' the local organizations. To these might be added some elements of upper-class patronage and lower-class aspiration—people who could afford the time and the subscription, and who could hold their own in a political debate. There might be others who, embarrassed by newly won liberties, and puzzled as to the duties of citizenship, found comfort in friendly association. Sometimes an elaboration of rules, or of mysterious initials, suggests a masonic background. Perhaps the affiliation of the Jacobin societies was suggested by that of Mesmer's *Harmonie universelle*, which the philosophic Dupont and his friends took so seriously. Always there is the desire to adopt the terms and forms of parliamentary debate.

By the end of 1790 some two hundred of these clubs existed in provincial towns up and down the country. They were evidence of a reforming zeal, a thirst for political education, and new zest for dangerous living without which the revolution might well have become a dull and donnish affair. As time went on the number of these clubs increased, till in the Year II (1793–4) there were certainly three thousand of them, and perhaps twice as many. They passed under what was once a description, and had now become a name—*sociétés populaires*.

The voluntary association of patriots for conference in the clubs, and for action in the National Guard, inspired the provincial Federations, and culminated in the Parisian Fête of Federation on July 14th, 1790. The idea of celebrating the anniversary of the fall of the Bastille by an armed demonstration of representatives from the new departments was first suggested by the Paris districts, and was enthusiastically taken up in the provinces. Pleasure, profit, and patriotism all pointed the same way. No citizen of Nancy or Rennes would miss a chance of a free trip to the capital. Every tradesman and lodging-house keeper in Paris would welcome the chance of making extra money. The liberty and unity of the nation, so recently achieved, would be strengthened and advertised.

This was in May. During the next month many additions were made to the original programme. The king was asked to allow troops of the line to march with the volunteers. It was proposed that, whilst the soldiers took an oath of fidelity to the Nation, the Law, and the Crown, the women of Paris should swear to bring up their children in the same faith. On the suggestion of the self-appointed ambassador of Europe, the Baron de Cloots, it was agreed that a thousand foreign guests should watch the ceremony from a special tent. It was debated whether the four chained figures of conquered peoples round the pedestal of Louis XIV's statue in the Place des Victoires should be removed, as 'monuments of despotism and slavery,' or should merely be deprived of their fetters, M. Gouchon with an eye on the profits of his silk business, suggested the ascent of a monster balloon painted with the emblems of patriotism. The 'artist-painters' of Paris offered to decorate the site free of charge. The Chapter of Notre Dame allowed their choristers to lead the singing of the *Te Deum*. M. Naudier, a print-seller, provided an illuminated missal from which the sceptical Bishop of Autun, who was not so familiar with the service as he might have been, would celebrate a solemn mass at the Altar of the Country.

When it appeared that the workmen in charge of the preparations would never have the great amphitheatre ready in time—it was nine hundred yards long, with a raised platform in the centre big enough to contain two thousand people—Parisians of every class marched out to help, to the sound of fife and drum, carrying picks and spades, or wheeling barrows, with a zeal that to a patriotic fancy seemed magnificent, but to the philosophic eye a little absurd. Lafayette himself visited the busy scene, and put in two hours' work with the spade. Two days before the ceremony five hundred copies of the order of procession were posted on the walls of the capital. From every corner of France the *fédérés*, as they were called, marched into Paris and were billeted on patriotic citizens.

There might be some doubt as to the temper of these provincial patriots. Constitutionalists feared that the king might consent to undergo a form of re-coronation, and change a hereditary into an elective monarchy. Royalists hoped that he would exploit the anti-Parisian feeling of the *fédérés*, and use their help to get rid of the assembly. Both hopes and fears were disarmed by the simple loyalty of the countryside. Fifteen hundred Breton *fédérés* insisted on being admitted to the Tuileries. Their commander laid his sword at the king's feet, and they swore that they would shed their last drop of blood to defend the royal family. Outside in the garden they found the little Dauphin picking flowers. The 'pretty boy' insisted on distributing them to the *fédérés*; and when none were left, 'gathered lilac leaves, and for fear they should not last, tore them in two, and gave half a leaf apiece to the rest.'

At half-past eleven on July 14th, not in the capital alone, but in every town in the country, the church bells were rung, the oath of loyalty was taken, and the *Te Deum* was sung, with an enthusiasm which took no heed of the heavy rain that Nature contributed to the festival. In Paris the whole population appeared to be on the Champ de Mars. It seemed to the American William Short a 'really sublime and magnificent' spectacle. Only Louis let the weather hinder him from taking the oath at the open altar, in sight of the people. Could not Lafayette, it was urged, ask him to do it again? *Mes enfans*, he replied, *le serment n'est pas une ariette; on ne peut pas le jouer deux*

THE FÊTE OF FEDERATION, 1790

From a contemporary water-colour. Note the fashions.

fois—'an oath can't be encored, like a song.' But there was dancing by the National Guard, arm in arm with girls, or with cassocked priests; and the following Sunday saw a review on the Champ de Mars, a fête in the Champs Elysées, and another on the site of the Bastille. These spectacles, being less vast than that of the 14th, were perhaps more enjoyable, and everything passed off in good order and good temper. But part of the temporary bridge over the Seine collapsed, two men were killed by a ramrod carelessly discharged during a salute of artillery: and two federals were drowned when crossing the river in a boat to view the illuminations.

Talleyrand, after saying mass, singing the *Te Deum*, and blessing the banners of the eighty-three departments, spent the evening dining and dicing; he always remembered the day as that upon which he had twice broken the bank at a fashionable gaming-table. He is said to have written the next day to his mistress, making fun of 'that ridiculous fête.' There was disillusionment, too, in the minds of some contractors whose bills were still unpaid three years later. Nevertheless no event of the time, unless it were the fall of the Bastille, left happier memories behind it. More medals were struck for this than for any other event of the revolution. The windows of the print-shops were full of pictures of the scene on the Champ de Mars. Innumerable plates, jugs, and other mementoes were sold in the fairs and at the Palais-Royal to commemorate the great day on which Frenchmen, for the first time in their long history, knew themselves to be equal citizens of a free and united country. So potent was the urge towards unity that at a small town in the Montauban district, rent by an age-long feud between Catholics and Protestants, the *curé* and the *pasteur* administered the oath from the same altar, led the combined singing of the *Te Deum*, and joined in setting light to an interdenominational display of fireworks.

Within a few weeks of the Federation a new paper, the *Feuille villageoise*, circulating among 'land-owners, farmers, clergy, and country-lovers,' and not uncommonly read aloud by the priests to their parishioners, instructed the country-side in the history and geography of the new departments and their capitals, in the articles of the constitution, in the reformed system of justice, in the new currency, and in the duties of local officials. The clergy were given advice on points of religion and morals; the farmers were taught how to improve their crops; and every number contained parliamentary reports. Cérutti's publication had an immense success. France was 'finding herself.' Instead of a collection of *pays* she had become a single *patrie*. *Patrie* was indeed a Latin word; a word first heard at school, not in the home; a word associated not with French but with Roman history. *Royaume* had been till this moment the word that best described the territory and subjects of the King of France. As late as 1776 the Academy had defined *patrie* in terms of *pays*: a Frenchman's country was merely that part of it in which he happened to have been born. It was the revolution which first gave *patrie* and *patriote* a national meaning. There had been medieval federations to defend oneself against the local despotism of the *seigneur*. There had never before been a federation to proclaim a national emancipation from the feudal system. July 14th, 1790, celebrated the coming-of-age of the heir of the French monarchy—the French people.

CHAPTER VII

FREE FRANCE

The purpose of the National Assembly of France is to abolish every contrivance and pretence by which one or a few may be privileged, first to benefit, then to injure millions; to destroy the principle of all modern governments, that a part is greater than the whole, and instead of applying a machine, denominated either Monarchic, Aristocratic, or Democratic, to govern the community for the advantage of individuals, orders, or professions, to organize the community itself; to form it into an actual body; to diffuse a lively and poignant sensibility over its surface; to connect the extremities with the seat of reflection and thought; and to introduce that general sympathy which ever prevents a well-constructed body from injuring any of its parts.—(*Lessons to a Young Prince by an Old Statesman*, 1790.)

THE first principle of the constitutional revolution of 1789 was the sovereignty of the people. *Le principe de toute souveraineté*, it had been stated in the Declaration of Rights, *réside essentiellement dans la nation*. In place of the will of one stood the will of all (*la volonté générale*). The old formula of arbitrary rule, *Le roi le veult*, was to be replaced by the guarantee of an agreed code of law. But how could a nation of twenty-five millions think and act and speak as one man? Only through a national assembly, freely appointed and fully empowered to represent it.

This had been achieved. At present the people were content with the body of twelve hundred representatives of the Orders summoned under the January regulations, and refashioned nearer to the heart of France by the events of June and July. For the future legislatures contemplated in their new constitution the deputies believed that the six hundred representatives originally allotted to the Commons, with a margin of a hundred and fifty more, would be enough to satisfy the needs of the new electorates. Some such number, it is generally agreed, is the greatest that can conveniently sit together and debate together in one place. The last Chamber of Deputies and the last freely elected Reichstag contained a little over six hundred members. It is the present number of the House of Commons.

The size of the Legislative Body settled itself. The franchise upon which it was to be elected could not be so easily determined. Upon this franchise depended not only a general election at some future date, but also the impending local elections, at which departmental and municipal officers, mayors, magistrates, and parsons were to be appointed all over the country. The Declaration of Rights had expressly stated that every citizen was eligible for 'all public dignities, posts, and employments.' It had carefully refrained from promising a universal franchise. 'The law,' it had said, 'is the expression of the general will.' 'All citizens,' it had said, 'have the right to take part (*concourir*) in its formation, either personally, or through their representatives.' But unless a political vote was one of the ' natural rights' guaranteed by the state to the individual—and it was not mentioned among them—no Frenchman could appeal to the Declaration against a limitation of the franchise.

Some such limitation had long been anticipated by the philosophers in the name of reason, by the economists in the name of property, and by men of common sense who believed that the best precedents for a French constitution were to be found, not in the tiny city-states of ancient Greece, but in republican Rome, monarchical England, or democratic America. The franchise of '89, designed to catch the conservative vote of the countryside, yet excluded non-taxpayers. In the municipal and provincial elections of '87-9 taxpayers of less than ten shillings a year had been disqualified. There was every reason to expect that these precedents would be followed in the constitution of '91. Yet the events of the summer of '89 had altered the situation. The active intervention of Paris on July 14th and October 5th, and the open claim of its citizens to have saved the revolution, could not but plead for a manhood suffrage. On the other hand the alarm which the deputies felt at the political activities of the Palais-Royal and of the districts strongly prejudiced them against the enfranchisement of the Paris proletariate. The issue was fought out in a series of debates during the last three months of the year, and the new law was enacted in time to govern the local elections of '90-91.

The basis of the new franchise was a distinction between 'active' and 'passive' citizenship first propounded by Sieyès six months before. Passive citizens were those who enjoyed natural and civic rights: active citizens were those who also enjoyed political rights. Active citizens could vote : passive citizens could not. One would look in vain for this distinction in the Declaration of Rights. But it could be found strongly embedded in the minds of those who drew up the Declaration. It was unbelievable that a middle-class assembly would not make the right of voting depend in some form upon the possession of property and the payment of taxes. This principle was in fact embodied in Thouret's report of September 29th, and became the main issue in the debate which began on October 20th.

The case for the opposition was best put by the abbé Grégoire, one of the five deputies who voted against the disfranchisement of passive citizens. All that is needed, he declared, to make a man fit either to elect or to be elected is that he should be 'a good citizen, with a sound head and a French heart.' But few of the deputies set so much store by mental and moral qualifications.

To be elected, even to be an elector (they thought), a man must have 'a stake in the country': he must have a proprietary interest in the 'raw material of politics.'

It was pointed out that the property qualification might create a new aristocracy of wealth no less objectionable than the old aristocracy of birth. The somewhat cynical reply was that it would stimulate the poor man to make himself rich, and so to qualify for active citizenship. And thus, almost unanimously, it was enacted. The vote was confined to active citizens, and active citizenship was defined in terms of tax-paying capacity.

It might be thought that the requirement specified in the Act was so small that almost everyone would get the vote. A tax-payment equivalent to three days' wages of a labourer (*journalier*) turned a passive into an active citizen. But even this meagre requirement disqualified nearly two million out of six million adult Frenchmen. Moreover the remaining four millions still exercised only an indirect vote, as they had done in '89. The direct elector, the representative of a hundred indirect electors, needed a tax qualification equivalent to ten days' wages. In the whole country there were only fifty thousand individuals rich enough to satisfy this requirement—one in five hundred of the population.

The first franchise enactment of democratic France might be thought decidedly ungenerous. Yet in Scotland the representatives of two million people were appointed by less than four thousand electors; the hundred members who represented fifty-one English and Welsh boroughs were chosen by less than fifteen hundred electors; and the county franchise (which was considered democratic) was confined to owners of a forty-shilling free-hold. In all, not more than four Englishmen in a hundred had a vote. In 1817 the French electorate was still only three per cent of the population; in 1831, five per cent; and in 1848, seven per cent. The Reform Bill of 1832 enfranchised thirty-two per cent of the British people.

Nevertheless some concessions had to be made. The franchise was extended without question to members of the National Guard serving at their own expense, to all soldiers of sixteen years' service, and to the clergy, who did not pay taxes, and who might have found it difficult to do so. In any case the problem of fixing the standard value of a day's wages, either centrally or locally, proved insurmountable. The regulations were sometimes evaded at a general election : in '91 the town of Nantes so reduced the qualification for active citizenship that it nearly doubled its electorate. In the local elections they were pretty generally ignored.

The limitation of the electorate had met with little opposition. The proposal to limit eligibility roused wide protests. That measure might be contrary to the spirit of the Declaration of Rights: this measure violated its express wording. The highest tax-qualification demanded before one could elect was the lowest demanded before one could stand for election. A candidate for municipal office had to produce a receipt for taxes equivalent to ten days' wages, a candidate for election to the Legislative Assembly had to produce a receipt for taxes equivalent to no less than fifty days' wages. This sum was represented by the so-called *marc d'argent*, and amounted to about fifty-four shillings in our money.

Is it surprising that so small a sum should rouse so great a storm? It was stated by serious speakers that the *marc d'argent* would exclude from the assembly nineteen-twentieths of the population, including all the parochial clergy. It was indignantly alleged that under this regulation neither Corneille nor Rousseau nor Mably could have represented their country. But opposition availed nothing. Indeed, the representatives of Physiocrat theory and the land-owning interests were still unsatisfied. They demanded that intending deputies should be possessed of an income from property in land amounting to sixty pounds a year. The requirement was accordingly added, though without specifying so high a figure; and in this form, on October 29th, the *marc d'argent* became law. It did not remain long on the statute-book. Whilst passive resistance made the three-day and ten-day requirements a dead letter, a series of attacks in the House and in the press led to the ultimate abandonment of the fifty-day requirement in the final revision of the constitution two years later.

It must be added, to complete the electoral scene, and to give the deputies their due, that they enfranchised several classes of citizens hitherto regarded as political outlaws. The vote given to the Protestants in '89 was confirmed. It was given, in spite of the protests of the abbé Maury, to actors. It was given, in spite of the opposition of the Bishop of Nancy, to public executioners. It was given in two instalments (January 28th, '90, and September 27th, '91) to Jews. The Jews had been excluded on religious, not on racial grounds from the enfranchisement of 'non-Catholics' in January, '89: now their social exclusiveness seemed a greater affront to the principle of national unity than their religious separatism seemed to that of unity of worship. The vote which was thus extended to Jews and Protestants, actors and executioners, was still withheld from those relics of the feudal system, domestic servants. A cook or a valet was thought to have no more stake in the country than a convict or an undischarged debtor.

The obvious criticism of the franchise law of '89 was that it set up a plutocracy. 'In place of Commons, Nobles, and Clergy,' complained Cambon, 'we have now the Rich, the Richer, and the Richest.' In place of the three orders of the old regime, remarked Babeuf, there are now four—'the Pence, the Shillings, the Crowns, and the Sovereigns' (*L'ordre des patards, celui de l'écu, celui de la pistole, et celui du marc*); and the Pence (he considered) were even worse off than the Tiers Etat. This was a little unfair. If a three-days' wages qualification disfranchised nearly two million Frenchmen, the poverty of the country was more to blame than the prejudices of the assembly. It would be difficult to put the wage-limit lower without enfranchising a mass of illiterate peasants whom no government of the eighteenth century would

have considered fit for political responsibility. It was not in the disfranchisement of indirect electors, but in the high qualifications demanded of direct
electors and candidates for office that the attempt to monopolize power by
the bourgeoisie was most evident. Even here the ten-day test set a comparatively modest standard of plutocracy, and excluded few whom the primary
electors would have chosen as their representatives.

It is instructive to compare the social status of the deputies of '89 or of the
local officials of '91 elected under the Act of '89 with the deputies of '92,
elected after it was done away with. All of them, so far as can be ascertained,
came from the same class: many of them were in fact the same men. The
worst effect of the *régime censitaire* was not seen in its electoral unfairness,
but in the suspicion it aroused, and in the retaliation it suggested. Too
often since 1789 electoral legislation in France has been designed to keep
in power the political party of the moment.

The aim of the new franchise was to nationalize the central government.
The aim of the new departments was to nationalize the administration.
France in 1789 was a composite but not a unified country. It had been
pieced together during eighteen centuries by nearly a hundred *réunions* of
detached estates, beginning with the Counties of Paris and Orléans in
987 A.D. and ending with the island of Corsica only thirty years before
the revolution. These territories had been absorbed into its common life,
and enclosed within its common frontiers. But a patchwork map still
showed the evidences of this process in four inconsistent systems of sub-
division.

Ecclesiastically France consisted of a hundred and fifty-six bishoprics
(*diocèses*), which still preserved the shapes of the old Roman *civitates*. For
military purposes it consisted of thirty-three *gouvernements*, based on the
history of its wars of conquest. For administration and the collection of taxes
it had consisted since the sixteenth century of from twenty to thirty-five
intendances or *généralités*. Its judicial system, based on feudal land-tenure, cut
up the country into nearly five hundred *bailliages* and *sénéchaussées*, whose
boundaries were so uncertain that more than eighteen hundred parishes did
not know to what district they belonged, and no map could be relied upon
to show them correctly. The word *province* was popularly and even officially
used to cover up the ambiguities of a chaotic system. In the plural it meant
everything outside Paris, as to an Englishman 'the provinces' means everything
outside London. Used in the singular of Brittany, Gascony, or any of the old
'Counties' of France, it conveyed a meaning, but could not be defined upon
a map.

In the background of all these divisions, like the water-mark in the paper
on which they were inscribed, existed another series of divisions:—France
of the *langue d'oc* and the *droit romain*, and France of the *droit coutumier* and
the *langue d'oil*: France that formed a customs union (*cinq grosses fermes*), and

France that did not: France that recognized the Papal *concordat*, and France of the *pays d'obédience*: France of the *pays d'élections*, and France of the *pays d'états*.

Old land-divisions have a deep historical interest, and preserve differences in the customs and speech of a people which it would be a mistake to destroy. England would be a less interesting country if the old counties had been abolished by the Reform Bill. It will become a less interesting country if they are replaced by Regional Planning Areas. But there were good reasons why the Frenchmen of '89 should wish to destroy their *bailliages* and their *généralités*. They wished to destroy the old sub-divisions because they were chaotic and confusing to a degree that ours never were, especially to the tidy mind of the eighteenth century. They wished to destroy them because they were bound up with a centralised administration incompatible with revolutionary freedom—a royal bureaucracy (the *intendances*), a feudal jurisdiction (the *bailliages*), an ecclesiastical enclave (the *diocèses*), and a military system (the *gouvernements*) used to keep down the people. They wished to destroy them because in no other way could the old regionalism be subordinated to the new nationalism: in no other way could the *patrie* be put before the *pays*: in no other way could Bretons, Gascons, and Dauphinois be shown that they were all Frenchmen.

Turgot, remembering his fantastically shaped *intendance* of Limoges, had believed that this result could be achieved by a system of sub-divisions just so large that a man might travel from the furthest point of each to its central town and back in twenty-four hours. Sieyès' mathematical mind visualized a symmetrical division of the map of France, like the squares of a chess-board, into fifty provinces, two thousand *arrondissements*, and forty thousand parishes. The committee set up to investigate the problem did, in fact, work from a map in which the country was, for purposes of convenience, squared up into nine regions and eighty-one counties. On the other hand, the Provincial Assemblies of '87 had been based on an ungeometrical sub-division of the old *généralités*.

Thouret, whose *rapport* introduced the question to the assembly, tried to combine reason and nature into a single system. He proposed that France should be divided into eighty approximately equal *départements* (with a supplementary department for Paris), and sub-divided into seven hundred and twenty districts or *communes*, and six thousand four hundred and eighty *cantons*. Each canton would form an electoral assembly of about six hundred and eighty active citizens. Each department would be administered by a departmental assembly, meeting annually as a *conseil*, and carrying on during the rest of the year as a standing committee (*directoire*) with executive powers, chosen by and from the council. For electoral purposes the cantons would act independently. For administrative purposes they would be grouped into communes, and administered by communal assemblies, under the control of the departments.

It was not difficult to pick holes in this plan. Deputies looked in vain for their constituencies on Thouret's neatly squared map. Some critics thought there were too many sub-divisions: some thought there were too few. Mirabeau enjoyed pointing out that local needs had been overlooked, and variations in the density of population ignored. Little thought seemed to have been given to the problem of changing over from the old system to the new. But Thouret successfully defended his plan, and on December 22nd it was accepted as a basis for discussion, with the proviso that the number of departments and districts should at present be left open. A committee of four was set up to work out the details in consultation with the deputies of the *bailliages*.

This was the most delicate part of the business. It says much for the intelligence and good sense of the men of '89 that, in spite of the stubborn and sometimes bitter rivalry of local interests, the map of France was successfully redrawn. It was comparatively easy to secure agreement upon the boundaries of the new departments. It was pleasing and even flattering to find one's local fishing-stream—Allier or Ain, Loiret or Lot—immortalized as the name of a department on the national map. It was more difficult to conciliate the rival claims of departmental capitals and cathedral towns, and to deal with endless applications for the administrative assembly or the law-court which was expected to bring custom and prestige to some local centre. Tarn was constituted a department in spite of the protests of Toulouse: it had to defend itself against the encroachments of Haute-Garonne, Lot, and Hérault. Castres became the capital: Albi obtained the bishopric and the *école centrale*; Lavour could not even obtain one electoral assembly in three. But by the middle of February these difficulties had been overcome, and Dupont was able to report that France had been successfully divided into the departments which still figure in a modern atlas. The statistical *tableau général* given in the convenient *Dictionnaire géographique et méthodique* issued a few years later shows, with the addition of Paris, Corsica, and the territories newly acquired in 1793–4, eighty-eight departments, containing 556 districts, 4,770 cantons, and 41,007 municipalities.

It only remained to get the new areas and authorities into working trim. This task was entrusted to men of high local standing appointed by the crown. Three *commissaires du roi* were despatched into each department. It was their business to draw up the rolls of active citizens, to convoke the electoral assemblies, and to settle any problems that might arise in the interpretation or working of the new system.

Paris presented problems all of its own. In point of population the city might have become a department outright. But the position of the capital had been enhanced by the destruction of the old provinces, and the sub-division of their administrations. In Paris alone more than half a million Frenchmen, more than a fiftieth part of the whole population of the country, kept their historical identity and their traditional forms of government. If to so great a city there were to be added a surrounding area at all equivalent to that of the other departments, it would become too preponderant. Yet if it were deprived of its traditional control over the corn-lands of the middle Seine the government would be embarrassed by a constant threat to its food-supply. The assembly tried to solve this dilemma by extending the city boundaries three leagues beyond the *barrières*. So came into existence the *département de Paris*, an authority constantly at loggerheads with the Paris commune, and adding another to the embarrassing number of legislative and executive bodies in the capital—the king, the assembly, the municipality, and the districts.

The opportunity was taken to give definitive form to the Paris municipality, and to strengthen its hands against the districts. The deputies were encouraged to do this by more than one expression of approval. A report of the Constitutional Committee presented by Démeunier on April 27th attacked the 'federal' tendencies of local government, and declared that steps ought to be taken to prevent the disorderly districts of the capital from disturbing the repose of its citizens and the business of its tradesmen. An article in the *Moniteur* asserted: 'The capital belongs to the state: it is the seat of government, the centre of power, the strong-house of public wealth, the residence of the sovereign. The whole country is therefore equally concerned that nothing in the capital should subvert order, hinder business, or alarm the throne.'

The assembly was not slow to exploit this feeling. By the Municipal Law of May 21st, 1790, the sixty districts whose independent ways had been the root of the trouble were rearranged into forty-eight sections, each containing about twelve thousand five hundred persons. The active citizens of these sections might not meet except for electoral purposes or, peaceably and unarmed, to present a petition. Their armed force, the National Guard, was under the control of the municipality, which could, if necessary, neutralize it by calling out other forces as well. The sections were allowed their full share of administration; but every difficulty was put in the way of their independent action, or their interference in the political affairs either of the capital or of the country. By such measures it was hoped to prevent the recurrence of another July 14th, or another October 5th.

Meanwhile time had been wasted—too much time, in the view of those who considered Paris the storm-centre of the revolution. The municipal elections did not end until September, '90: the departmental elections did not begin until January, '91: the organization of the capital was nearly a year behind that of the country as a whole. What might not happen during such as interregnum?

Such delays were not, indeed, confined to Paris. The transition from the old to the new France was neither so sudden nor so complete as it looked on Thouret's map. The departments set up by the decree of February 26th were at first used for administration only, not for taxation or for justice. The old municipal and parochial authorities did not at once disappear; still less the extemporized bodies which had so often replaced them during the summer of '89. Many months passed before the municipalities authorized by the decree of December 14th had elected their *maires*, their *bureaux*, and their *procureur-syndics;* before the departmental administrators set up by the decree of December 22nd took over the management of taxes, poor law, education, and police; or before it was possible to settle the numerous problems of procedure and precedence which arose amongst rival authorities during the transition period. Everywhere the new system overlapped the old. But in due course these irregularities were smoothed down; the new order was at work; and it could be judged as a whole.

It is not easy for an Englishman to understand the urgency of the problem that had been faced, or the importance of the solution that had been found for it. Our counties and dioceses ceased long ago to stand for feudal and ecclesiastical privilege. They have continued essentially unchanged from the sixteenth century down to the present day. They have not hindered the political and social revolution of the last hundred years; and they have not been endangered by it. The Borough Councils and Rural District Councils which correspond to the new *municipalités* of '89 have not displaced the County Councils based on the old divisions of the country: they exist side by side with them. We have not needed to destroy an old provincialism in order to create a new patriotism. They coexist. They are the obverse and the reverse of the national character.

In France this was not so. The provinces stood not merely for differences of dialect and culture, but also for ideas of political independence which had endangered the state, and might still endanger it. Regionalism was too nearly allied to separatism. The *intendances* represented an imposed and artificial attempt to unify the provinces, not as co-operative members of a nation, but as contributory estates of the crown. The *intendant* was the king's schoolmaster, who made loyalty unpopular by enforcing it, and duty distasteful by putting it into the curriculum. The *bailliages* were the seats of a hateful seigneurial jurisdiction. The municipalities were strongholds of middle-class monopoly. Even the dioceses were associated with a rich and aristocratic episcopate. Gradual reform was not impossible: in fact it had begun. But the opportunity and the temper of '89 hurried reform into revolution. The old order was swept away, and the new order was put in its place, without sufficient thought for continuity.

The new system was an honest attempt to substitute what seemed to its authors a natural division of the country for an artificial one. They hoped by grouping the population in relatively small units round prehistoric and unpolitical features—a river, a coast-line, or a mountain-range—to break down traditional feuds and local rivalries, to bring the country-side into

riendlier relations with the towns, and to encourage the free collaboration
f every member in the life and work of the body politic. Many a sleepy
rovincial town was now restored to its rightful position as the *chef-lieu* of a
epartment or of a district. Many a *hôtel de ville*, hitherto overshadowed by the
athedral, gained new importance and self-respect. Through its locally
lected authorities the new order created a sense of civic responsibility.
Through its departmental and municipal bodies it brought into being a new
lass of administrative officials. There were soon (it was reckoned) a million
nd a quarter civil servants whose interests would perpetuate the new regime,
nd prevent the return of the old.

It has been objected that where the old system of administration had been
oo centralized, the new system was too decentralized; that the departmental
irectories inherited the unpopularity of the *intendant* without his powers;
nd that there was now no effective link between the national assembly and
he municipalities. It was not long before the Jacobins found it advisable to
end travelling agents of the government into the provinces, to provide a
aison between the single legislature and the multiple executive. It was not
ong before Napoleon restored, in his *préfets*, the *intendants* whom the revo-
ition had destroyed.

Centralization might have given greater efficiency to the new depart-
ients. But the liveliness, the spontaneous patriotism, and the happy informa-
ty of the revolutionary spirit would have been lost. Nearly all that was
est in the revolution came from the circumference to the centre. It was
he work of free Frenchmen. It was made possible by the policy of trusting
he people. The revolution might have taken shape in a federal France, the
ucleus, as Mirabeau sometimes hoped, of a federal Europe. But this dream
as destroyed by the faults of the Gironde. The Napoleonic system, and
wo wars for life or death, led to an over-centralization not unlike that from
hich France was delivered in '89. She may need to be delivered again.

Liberty and Equality are dreams: Justice is something which even the
ave, even the prisoner at the bar, expects. To Frenchmen in '89 justice
emed the most important part of good government. There is nothing about
hich the *cahiers* are so unanimous as the need for judicial reform. When
ey speak, as they constantly do, of a single law for the whole country
der which abuses of authority will be impossible, they are thinking chiefly
a civil and criminal code to put an end to the cruelties and injustice of the
d courts. No educated Frenchman was ignorant of the judicial scandals con-
ected with the names of Calas, Sirven, and La Barre, to which Voltaire had
voted fourteen of his most devastating pamphlets. Beccaria's *Dei Delitti*
d gone through seven editions in a French version with a preface by
oltaire. Prizes had been offered for essays on judicial reform by respectable
cademies, and had been competed for by Robespierre and Marat.

Only four years ago a fresh and notorious miscarriage of justice had shown how necessary it was that Voltaire's work should be embodied in statutor reform. In August, '85, the *bailliage* of Chaumont had convicted a peasar named Lardoise, with two companions, of housebreaking and assault, and ha condemned him to penal servitude (in the galleys) for life. On appeal, th Paris *parlement*, by the vote of nine judges against six, varied the sentence t that of breaking on the wheel—the cruellest form of execution known to th criminal law. One of the six, believing in the men's innocence, started campaign for the revision of the sentence, and secured the interest of hi brother-in law Dupaty, a famous lawyer of Bordeaux. Dupaty outraged th traditions of the bar, and risked his reputation, by issuing a *mémoire justificat* to the general public. Whatever the rights of the case, none could den that the men had now lain two years in prison under a cruel death-sentenc Even the queen was moved to send them alms. But the only reply of th *parlement* was to order the burning of Dupaty's memorandum. At last, i December, '87, the conviction was quashed by the *conseil du roi*. It is a pit to have to add that Lardoise, for whom Dupaty found a home in the countr reappeared before the courts on a charge of theft in one of the first trial held under the new regime, and profited by the milder treatment which hi case had done so much to bring about.

The old system of justice was incredibly cumbrous and complicated. A over the country summary jurisdiction was nominally exercised by seventy o eighty thousand seigneurial courts, which could inflict penalties rangin from small fines to execution by hanging. There were on the average tw seigneurial courts in every township in the country. Quite small place might well have as many courts as they had churches, and each with its ow judges, counsel, and staff. The *bailliage* of Versailles comprised twenty-fou *justices locales* in villages of from twenty to two hundred households. Some o these possessed a gaol and a court—it might be in the mansion of the *seigneur* Some were unable to obtain justice without a long journey to Versailles The court was generally presided over by a *bailli* or *procureur-fiscal* paid t do so by the *seigneur*. Its main concern was to secure the landlord's rents, an to protect his game. Its methods were too often tyrannical, and its decision arbitrary and unjust.

In Paris summary justice was exercised by the *commissaires du Châtele* (police magistrates), of whom two or three sat in each of the sixty district of the city. It was also exercised by the *Lieutenant de Police*, the repre sentative of the crown in its dealings with the municipality. Behind thes courts stood the Châtelet, presided over, in the name of the *Prévôt d Paris*, by a Civil Lieutenant, a Criminal Lieutenant, and the Lieutenan of Police, and employing a crowd of minor magistrates and lawyers. Thi Central Criminal Court exercised a wide jurisdiction, both civil and crimina not only in the capital, but also over cases referred to it from other par of the country.

Behind the Châtelet stood a group of even more formidable courts—thos

f the *parlement de Paris*. They were housed, as they are now, in the Palais
e Justice, the judicial heart of France. Their prison was the Conciergerie,
nce a royal dining-hall, now a favourite thrill for sightseers. Their almost
oyal personnel of fifty-two peers and a hundred and sixty hereditary magis-
rates was swollen into a judicial army by the enrolment of six hundred bar-
isters (*avocats*), two hundred and fifty attorneys or solicitors (*procureurs*),
nd the notaries-public (*notaires*) and other minor lawyers who made up
he uncounted crowd of the legal underworld (*basoche*). Its jurisdiction
overed about a third of France, and a population of ten millions—more
han three times as large as the *ressorts* of the rival *parlements* of Rennes or
Louen, of Bordeaux or Toulouse. Finally, behind both Châtelet and Parle-
nent stood the ultimate court of appeal, the *Conseil du Roi*, presided over by
he Chancellor and the Lord Privy Seal.

Such was the centre of justice. Its circumference embraced a complicated
ystem of departmental courts, with subordinate and embarrassing jurisdictions.
'he *cour des comptes* dealt with Treasury cases. The *cour des aides* was
tached to what we should call Somerset House; the *cour des monnaies* to
he Mint. Five courts in Paris and twenty in the provinces heard cases about
Waters and Forests. Six specialized in the Game Laws. There was a *grand
nseil* to protect royal privileges. There was a *tribune de commerce*, whose
nsuls dealt so successfully with business disputes that it had sixty-seven
aughter-courts in different parts of the country, and was exempted from the
eneral liquidation of the judiciary in '89. There was an Admiralty court, a
ourt to settle disputes affecting builders and contractors, courts to deal with
ffences committed in the royal palaces or gardens, courts to deal with 'affairs
f honour,' with the Swiss Guard, with the university, and of course with the
hurch.

This preposterous system survived partly by the force of habit, and partly
y the traffic in legal appointments, which enabled a small class to live in
thenian elegance, and to cultivate their minds, whilst the work of the
ountry was done by a mass of underfed clerks and officials. Fabulous sums
ad been paid, during the last century, for the prizes of the legal profession.
ven now the higher appointments were worth from five thousand to seven
ousand five hundred pounds a year, and the lower appointments from a
ousand to four thousand. Necker had calculated that in '84 it would cost the
ate twenty-five millions sterling to buy out the vested interests of the bar.

The English bar was organized as a series of Colleges or clubs—the Inns
' Court. The French bar, as befitted a power in the state independent of
e legislature and of the executive—the only power which could limit the
solutism of the crown—was a separate caste, with a hereditary and
ivileged position akin to that of our House of Lords. A position conceded
the name of public liberty was exploited in the interests of private gain.

Lawyers have been venal in this country, and litigation has been expen-
ve. But never have the services of our lawyers or the mysteries of our law

been so shamelessly traded as they were in France under the old regime
Adam Smith, in a passage defending the system, declares that, were it no
for court fees, the salary of a judge in the *parlement* of Toulouse, which
ranked next to that of Paris, would have been only seven pounds a year. The
natural result followed. Legal appointments were valued not for the legiti
mate fees they carried with them, but for the opportunities they offered of
illegitimate pickings and perquisites. In almost every case brought before the
courts it was necessary to bribe the judges, and the verdict went to the client
who bribed most. An agent of the East India Company trying to extract
trading concessions from a native potentate was in no worse position than
land-owner seeking to establish his title to a property before the Paris
parlement.

The scandal was increased, during the eighteenth century, by the habit of
employing attorneys, or (as they were beginning to be called in England
solicitors (*procureurs*), to look after the interests of the business man and the
landlord. It was increased by the custom of arguing and settling cases out of
court in a series of intricate and expensive opinions and judgements. The
solicitor and the consulting lawyer grew rich at the expense of their clients
It was in their interest to drag out a case to the interminable lengths of
Jarndyce *v.* Jarndyce. In 1789 there was a universal demand that such
scandals should end.

Reformers were generally agreed as to what should be done. The number
of courts must be reduced. There must be an end of private and privilege
jurisdictions. Magistracies must no longer be obtainable by heredity or by
purchase. The expenses of litigation must be reduced. Bribery must be
abolished. The assumption of the prisoner's guilt, and the hostile procedure
based upon it, must no longer disgrace the criminal courts. Torture
already abolished in name (the *question préparatoire* in '80 and the *questi*
préalable in '88), but still practised by some courts, must be finally done
away with.

The ground had been cleared during the summer of '89 by the resignation
of the Lord Privy Seal and of the Lieutenant of Police (July 15th); by
the abolition of seigneurial courts and of the custom of purchase (August 4th
and by the declarations of August 21st against unjust arrest and arbitrary
imprisonment. More recently the summer vacation of the *parlements* had
been indefinitely extended. Their attempt to pose as champions of the people
had not deceived an assembly of lawyers. They would never again encumbe
the legal stage.

The first proposals for reform came from the same moderate group as had
backed a Second Chamber and an Absolute Veto. Nicolas Bergasse was a
rich man's son from Lyon whom the scandals of the Kornmann case had
turned into a partisan of judicial reform. His political views made him a
ally of Malouet, Mounier, and Lally-Tollendal. Whilst Mounier draft
his proposals for a new constitution, Bergasse presented the assembly with t

outline of a new judicial system (August 17th). His plan was to keep the judiciary quite independent of the legislature; wholly to abolish purchase; to do away with all expenses of litigation; to conduct all judicial proceedings in public; to institute judges of assize, juries, and poor men's lawyers; to confine capital punishment to cases of murder and high treason; to abolish the penalty of confiscation; and to introduce an element of popular election into the appointment of judges.

These proposals were the basis of the report of the Constitutional Committee presented by Thouret on December 22nd: they came up again in a revised form the following summer, and became law on August 24th, 1790. The long legal debates which produced this measure were conducted by an assembly of lawyers at a high level, and provide material for thought on many aspects of judicial theory and practice. No legal system is beyond the need of reform. It is still worth while to know what eighteenth-century legislators thought about Justices of the Peace, Assizes, Trial by Jury, Courts of Appeal, the appointment and qualifications of Judges, the use of special Courts, or the functions of Counsel.

When agreement had been reached, it was decided that the main judicial reforms should be included in the unalterable Constitution of 1791. Titre III, Chapitre V, *Du pouvoir judiciaire*, lays down in twenty-seven articles the charter of revolutionary justice. The Judiciary is to remain independent of the Legislature and the Executive. Justice will be administered free of charge by judges elected by the people. They will sit in local and assize courts, as well as in courts of appeal. Criminal trials will be conducted in public, and before a jury. Every person arrested will be questioned within twenty-four hours, and released, if no case can be shown against him. Henceforth civil justice was to be administered by a *juge de paix* in each *canton* of the country, and in each section of the capital, and by a court of five *juges* in each district of the country, and in each of the six *arrondissements* of Paris. These courts were to act both as courts of first instance, and as courts of appeal against each other's decisions. A law of October 12th, '90, gave them criminal as well as civil jurisdiction, until separate criminal courts consisting of a President and three judges were set up in each department by the law of September 16th, 1791. Each *arrondissement* at Paris had already been provided, under a decree of March 13th, '91, with a criminal court corresponding to its civil court, but with seven judges instead of five.

The new system worked well. True, a long time was spent in electing five judges for each of the five hundred and fifty districts: it took a month to elect thirty in Paris. But they were carefully chosen. Some were qualified lawyers. Others, though without legal qualifications, were such men of good judgement and reputation as might sit on the magistrates' bench in any country, and prove themselves fit to deal with the simpler issues of the law. The influence of the new magistracy upon public opinion in the provinces was so great that it became an essential part of Mirabeau's great plan (August

24th, '90) to secure the appointment of royalist nominees. For the same reason, two years later (September 25th, '92) Danton urged the necessity of appointing new judges of a more republican character.

In deference to a petition from the sections of Paris, the new judges discarded the wig and gown of the old regime. But here, as in some less trivial respects, there was a tendency to fall back into the old ways. Before long it was common talk that bribes were once more being accepted, that the courts imposed unduly severe sentences, and that there was overcrowding in the prisons. It would have been impossible to prevent such things, Mirabeau ironically observed, without abolishing the whole tribe of lawyers. But there is no reason to doubt that most of the new courts took their duties seriously, and carried them out conscientiously. They set a standard of revolutionary justice against which the later and better known methods of the Revolutionary Tribunal were a deliberate reaction, and a notorious offence.

The new criminal courts of Paris installed in April, '91, were at first embarrassed by the mass of cases they took over from the Châtelet. Fifteen hundred trials had to begin again; and only one official (*greffier*) remained with a knowledge of the old routine. The Conciergerie was full of prisoners whom the Minister of Justice wished to be tried as soon as possible. But the new judges were soon at work: from May onwards there was a steady flow of judgements; and by the end of August the first of the six tribunals had nearly come to the end of its list.

On May 1st the new Appeal Court (*cour de cassation*), with judges elected by the departments, was welcomed by the king, and began its work. Some improvement had already begun, under pressure of public opinion, within the old appeal system. It was more than maintained by the new court. It is instructive to compare the reports of actual cases which have survived among the archives of the revolution. Here, first, are a few of the seventy-five judgements rendered on appeal by the Paris *parlement* between July 14th and September 8th, '89.

Simon Ricoux, a sawyer, convicted at Riom of burglary, and sentenced to be whipped, branded on the shoulder with a 'G' (*galères*), and sent for nine years to the galleys: altered on appeal to a life sentence.

Antoine Renaudot, aged eighteen, a carpenter, convicted by the Châtelet of stealing a piece of cloth, and condemned to a whipping, branding with a 'V' (for *voleur*), and five years' banishment: the sentence varied to five years in the galleys.

Mathieu Bonhomet, aged forty-eight, a labourer, convicted at Le Mans for drunkenness and violence, and condemned to the pillory: the *parlement* adds three years' banishment.

Ducare, aged fifty, a day-labourer, convicted for murder, and sentenced to breaking on the wheel: varied to hanging.

J. B. Tremblay and Michel Deschamps, convicted of robbery with attempted murder, and sentenced by the Châtelet to branding and the galleys for life: altered to torture (to extract evidence) and breaking on the wheel.

Jacques Redereau, aged twelve or thirteen, a pig-herd, convicted at Saint-Suzanne of theft, and condemned to the pillory, branding, and three years' banishment : committed to the Bicêtre (the Paris Borstal) till the age of twenty.

Alexis Collin, aged forty-five, a priest, convicted of raping and abducting his *seigneur's* daughter; admonished, and fined ten shillings, by the court at Langres: the *parlement* decides to rehear the case.

Here is another list of cases which were heard by the vacation court of the Paris *parlement* between September 9th, '89, and May 21st, '90.

Claude Maillet, aged forty-five, a cutler, of Riom, convicted of homicide: acquitted, but fined six shillings, of which three went to provide bread for poor prisoners, and three to pay for a mass for the repose of the soul of his victim.

André, aged twenty-nine, a forester, and his sister, aged 20, convicted of homicide; he was sentenced to be hanged, and she to be present at the hanging: sentence commuted to one year's imprisonment.

Marche, aged twenty-eight, a day-labourer, convicted of homicide at Montluçon, and condemned to be hanged: after inquiry, set free.

Veik, aged forty-four, and Guérin, aged twenty-eight, day-labourers, convicted of robbery and attempted murder, and condemned to breaking on the wheel: sentence confirmed.

Aveline, his wife, his son, and a widow named Deaurin, convicted at Chartres of attempted murder, and the man sentenced to breaking on the wheel: sentence changed to a year's imprisonment.

Mardant, of Magny-en-Vixin, convicted of homicide, and condemned to one year's imprisonment: sentence varied, after seeing the evidence, to breaking on the wheel.

A comparison of these two lists suggests that the disappearance of the old *parlement* was followed at once by a more lenient regime. Evidence was reconsidered; sentences were revised; and the crueller punishments were generally avoided. But it is significant that the courts did not hesitate to inflict the brutal punishment of breaking on the wheel so late as January, 1790, when the revolution had already run eight months of its course towards a humaner society. It would undoubtedly be found, if reports of criminal trials by the new courts were available, that this progress continued, and that an offender stood a far better chance of fair treatment under the revolutionary regime than he could ever have hoped for under the monarchical system of justice.

In one important branch of judicial reform—that which concerned the army and navy—there was general agreement as to what should be done, but extreme delay in doing it. The brutal and arbitrary methods of discipline used by the old courts-martial had become intolerable long before '89. The *cahier* of the Paris *noblesse* said no more than was in every mind when it called on the States-general to find means to 'reconcile the duties of military service with those of citizenship, and the needs of discipline with the rights of liberty.'

The simplest method of doing this was propounded in Alexandre de Lameth's report of February 9th, '90, and embodied in the law of September 22nd. This measure drew a sharp distinction between the soldier's offences against common law and his breaches of military rules. The first were to be dealt with by the courts of the land: the second were to be dealt with by military courts-martial. The cruel repression of the Nancy mutineers in September, '90, when de Bouillé's *conseil de guerre* executed thirty ring-leaders, and his troops were said to have cut down over three thousand of their followers, forced this reform on to the statute-book. It was followed a year later by a new penal code, which, though still rigorous, abolished the worst punishments of the old. This had been done in the navy a year ago (October 27th, '90). A system of reformed courts-martial already introduced on board ship was now supplemented by similar bodies set up in the naval ports.

Unfortunately the exigencies of war led to the erection of additional courts of summary jurisdiction. In the crisis of May, '93, all attempts at reform were swept away by a new system of *tribunaux criminels militaires*. Two of these were set up in each army. They were modelled on the Revolutionary Tribunal of Paris. Their civil judges and military juries administered a penal code specially directed against the crimes of a soldiery on active service. This system, though somewhat modified in January, '94, remained in force throughout the Terror.

When a Frenchman demanded justice, he was thinking mainly of the lawyers: when a Parisian demanded justice, he was thinking mainly of the police. The resignation of the last Lieutenant-general of Police in July, '89, brought to an end one of the most treasured and hated features of the old regime. Mirabeau wondered that his countrymen could speak with pride of the 'thirty *inspecteurs des quartiers,* the fifty *commissaires,* the hundreds of *exempts* (police officers), the thousands of spies, the crowd of *sbires* (police agents), and the legion of clerks (*commis* and *sous-commis*),' who instead of confining themselves to cleaning, lighting, and policing the streets of the capital, formed an unholy Inquisition, enslaving the lives of its citizens. Their spy system and their censorship of the post (*cabinet noir*) enabled the police to know every-thing that was going on. Suspicious characters were followed, and their most private affairs reported on. Domestic scandals that might nowadays be hinted at in the gossip columns of the less reputable newspapers then circulated in unbowdlerized *nouvelles à la main*. No secret was safe from the fashionable *salon,* or from the royal breakfast-table.

The threat to privacy was backed by a more serious threat to liberty. An indiscretion begun at a letter-box might end in the Bastille. The system under which any citizen might be arrested upon an arbitrary warrant, and kept in prison without trial or power of appeal, was not a major cause of the revolution, but it was one of the most notorious scandals of the regime which the revolution sought to destroy. The *lettre close* or *lettre de cachet* was a warrant signed by the king, and counter-signed by one of the Secretaries of State. It was written on a single sheet of paper, and folded so that it could not be read without breaking the seal (*cachet*).

Here is one (*see p. 47*), issued by Louis XVI in 1777. It is headed *De par le Roy*. It orders the *cher et bien-amé* governor of one of the state prisons to receive into his establishment (*maison*) a certain Jean-Baptiste Sagrillon, and to keep him there until further orders. All expenses will be paid by the crown (*trésor royal*). The document ends with the formula of absolutism, *Car tel est nôtre plaisir*. It is signed *Louis*, and countersigned *Amelot* (Bishop of Vannes, 1775). In the top left-hand corner are two notes by a later hand, presumably the governor's. The first says that the prisoner was received into custody on April 6th, 1777: the second says that he died on April 7th, 1780.

Some of these warrants were issued by the government against political offenders, some were issued by the police against ordinary criminals, and some were issued at the request of powerful personages against their private enemies, or their errant relations. But whether the motive was good or bad, whether or not the system met a need that could not otherwise be provided for, nothing could justify the right of imprisonment, without cause shown, without trial, and without means of redress or release, which the *lettre de cachet* put into the hands of any minister of the crown. If the system was, as Mirabeau maintained in one of his most elaborate writings, so essential to the Bourbon government that it would never be voluntarily surrendered, it was yet, as he went on to insist, contrary both to natural and state law, destructive of liberty, and utterly tyrannical.

Under Louis XV the secret police had been mainly concerned with moral delinquencies. The victims of the hundred and fifty thousand *lettres de cachet* that he is said to have signed were largely undutiful sons such as Mirabeau himself, or authors of libellous verse, like Voltaire. In the more sultry atmosphere of the eighties the fourteen thousand warrants issued by Louis XVI may well have caused more discontent, by striking at the political opinions of the moment; whilst the victims of government alarm roused more public sympathy than those of private spite. Nevertheless the chief sufferers were not the lower or even the middle classes, but the intelligentsia and the aristocracy. The abolition of *lettres de cachet* was not an act of popular vengeance, but of democratic self-respect.

The Lieutenant of Police was at first replaced by a committee of the sixty districts of Paris. When the court moved to the capital, the inquisitorial tradition of the police was inherited by a municipal *comité des recherches*. After a month's experience this committee issued a report (November 30th) which may well have made good democrats rub their eyes, and wonder whether they were not back in the worst days of the old regime. For these champions of the new order complained that they had not enough spies—an odious resource (they admitted), but one rendered necessary by the indiscipline of the districts. They exhorted members of the public, as a matter of patriotism, to denounce one another to the police. Under the old order, no doubt, denunciation had been disliked, because it meant reporting the innocent failings of one's friends to a hostile authority. Now everything is changed. It becomes a public duty to denounce activities directed against the country to a popular authority which will give them humane and impartial consideration.

This disingenuous plea was rejected by the good sense of the deputies. Under the new municipal arrangements of 1790 police authority was divided between the department and the commune. The forty-eight police commissioners of the municipality were put under the control of the department. The department was put under the control of the Executive Power—the king, and the king's ministers. Since, however, the forty-eight commissioners were elected by the sections, and were assisted by sixteen more *commissaires* in each section, it was in effect the active citizens who controlled the department, the commune, and the king. So far as the municipality was concerned the hated system of *espionnage* disappeared. For three happy years Parisians could do what they liked, write what they liked, and say what they liked without serious apprehension. France was free.

CHAPTER VIII

CHURCH SETTLEMENT

I do not know what the Lord's anointed, his vicegerent upon earth, divinely appointed by him, and accountable to none but him for his actions, will either think or do, upon these symptoms of reason and good sense, which seem to be breaking out all over France; but this I foresee, that before the end of this century, the trade of both King and Priest will not be half so good a one as it has been. God's Vicegerent, and Christ's Vicar, will only be obeyed and believed as far as what the one orders, and the other says, is conformable to reason and to truth.—(LORD CHESTERFIELD, 1752.)

As the dioceses were the oldest divisions of the French soil, so the Catholic church was the oldest institution in French society. It was older than the three Orders, older than the feudal system, older than the crown. In any contest of national loyalties, it might well carry the day. Custom and emotion are stronger springs of action than reason and the hope of change.

The Catholic church pervaded the life of eighteenth-century France to an extent which is difficult to understand in a Protestant country where only one person in four is an active member of any religious body. Its hundred and

CATHEDRALE

DE METZ,

A   LOUER.

LES Citoyens font avertis que le 4 floréal, de l'an trois de la République . françoife, une & indivifible, ou le 2ɟ avril 1795 (vieux ftyle), les neuf heures du marin, pardevant les citoyens Adminiftrateurs du Directoire du Diftrict de Metz, il fera procédé à l'adjudication, au plus offrant & dernier enchériffeur, de la laiffe a bail, pour trois, fix ou neuf années,

Du local de la ci-devant Cathédrale de Metz

A CATHEDRAL TO LET
This was the end of the revolutionary church settlement, in 1795.

fifty dioceses provided four bishops to one intendant. Its thirty-five thousand benefices were three times as many as England provides for a population twice as large. Every fiftieth adult in the country, perhaps every tenth person met in the street, was a priest, a monk, or a nun. The value of the land and buildings belonging to the church was variously estimated as between a fifth and a half of all such property in the country. Its annual income might be anything from fifty to a hundred millions sterling. If the Scottish church at that time, with an income of £68,000, supported nearly a thousand clergy, an income of four millions should have sufficed to support the sixty thousand priests of the French church.

But such figures have little meaning. What mattered most for the Frenchman of '89 was a spiritual monopoly so familiar that it had ceased to strike the mind. Every public function was associated with a sermon, a *Te Deum*, or a mass. At every event of family life, from birth to marriage, and from sickness to burial, the priest must be called in. When a man was young he looked to the church for education; when he was middle-aged, for employment; and when he was old, for charity. All matters of conduct were the concern of the church. If his priest disapproved of him, a man might starve in this world, and burn in the world to come. The church exercised a spiritual dictatorship beside which the temporal tyranny of the crown was of little account.

The control of these tremendous powers was nominally vested in the Pope and the king. The king chose the bishops, and through the bishops the clergy. The Pope consecrated the bishops, and through them ordained the clergy. As holders of land and revenues both bishops and clergy were answerable to the king: as trustees of creeds and sacraments they were amenable to the Pope. But during the second half of the eighteenth century the real control of the church had fallen into the hands of an aristocratic episcopate. Ecclesiastical patronage was by now so unevenly distributed that there was little chance for a *curé* of humble birth and reduced circumstances to rise to places of high responsibility and rich emoluments. The decline of theology, and the new importance attached to social problems, led to the filling of bishoprics with men of birth, good administrators and good chairmen, rather than men of piety or learning. The great preaching tradition of the seventeenth century had died with Massillon in 1742. The expulsion of the Jesuit order loosened the papal grasp upon the church. The king handed over the selection of bishops to the official in charge of the *feuille des bénéfices*, and hardly knew by sight those who were appointed.

If the king knew little about his bishops, the bishops, in their turn, knew little about the troubles of their clergy. The country parson of the eighteenth century was not only poor: his poverty was made burdensome to him by the custom of patronage, and by the law of tithes. If he held a *cure à bénéfice*, he had the choice of exploiting his glebe-lands and collecting his tithe either personally or through an agent. By doing so personally he got exemption from *taille*; but it was difficult to secure the necessary labour, and he might be involved in legal disputes with his parishioners on the innumerable problems involved in the assessment and collection of the tenth part of the produce of their land. If he employed an agent, his receipts were liable to taxation; and the tax-collectors showed little charity towards the clergy. If he was not a *curé bénéficier*, he had to live as best he could on the *portion congrue* allowed him by the tithe-owner. This had been fixed by law in 1686 at fifteen pounds a year, and refixed in 1768 at twenty-five, and in 1786 at thirty-five pounds, to meet the decrease in the purchasing value of money during the last hundred years. Both *bénéficier* and *congruiste* were provided with a parsonage by the parish. They had certain perquisites, such as *offrandes* (collections), *casuel* (fees), and payments for masses. Out of their small means they had to contribute their share, on a sliding scale of from a half per cent to six per cent of their income, towards the *don gratuit* by which an enormously wealthy church compounded for the non-payment of property-tax.

It was not surprising that the country clergy looked with much envy and some hatred upon the comfortably lodged and richly endowed ecclesiastics of the cathedral establishments. One of them put his thoughts into verse.

> A country parson, by God's grace,
> I take the tithes of this poor place.
> But of my troubles let me speak.
> Here, six days out of every week,
> I stump about the country-side
> —I have no horse to drive or ride;
> On Sundays, when I preach in church,
> The clerk may leave me in the lurch;
> I ring the bell myself; I hear
> Confessions daily all the year;
> On Saints'-days and Rogation-days
> I urge my flock to mend their ways;
> And all my working hours I spend
> In every kind of odd and end,
> While morning turns to afternoon,
> Till January ends in June.
> One recompense remains; 'tis that
> We country parsons can't grow fat:
> A corporation, sure, is apter
> (You'll own it) for a Dean and Chapter.

But in spite of many symptoms of decay, in spite of philosophic attacks upon ecclesiastical fanaticism and intolerance, in spite of the incredulity which had become fashionable among educated people, the church had not lost its hold upon the mass even of middle-class Frenchmen. The same writers who condemned the church for superstition believed in the soundness of its moral influence. The same writers who held that society must be regenerated by reason and good legislation also held that there was a rôle for the church to play in the new order, as the spiritual partner of the state. To the average deputy of '89 it remained not merely a rich corporation, whose wealth should be used for the benefit of the nation, but also a great spiritual force, which should be exploited as a source of social morality and good citizenship. It was in this spirit that the National Assembly consecrated its opening ceremonies with a mass, a religious procession, and a sermon; that it recorded its political victories by solemn singing of the *Te Deum*; and that it celebrated the national reunion of July 14th, '90, by an open-air mass on the Champ de Mars.

Yet the same body repeatedly rejected proposals, of which Dom Gerle's motion of April 12th, '90, was the most determined, to declare Catholicism the established religion of the country; and a memorial in favour of the proposal was signed by less than half even of the clerical members. Some of the deputies were nominal Catholics, who made their confession and communion once a year. Some were nominal Deists, like Thibaudeau, who 'said his morning and evening prayers, hat in hand, either in his study or in his garden, according to the weather.' Whatever their private beliefs, they regarded themselves, before all else, as Frenchmen with a mission to reform what they reverenced, and to accept no part of the old regime, however venerable, upon its own valuation. There must be an end to fanaticism, intolerance, and superstition. Protestants and other non-Catholics must be given freedom of worship. A purged episcopate, a reformed clergy, a simplified and more Apostolic church would have a part to play in the national revolution.

Many of the clergy themselves shared this view. They were alarmed by the failure of recruits for ordination, and by the rarity of vocations for the religious life. They were distressed at the hostility they encountered in some parts of the country from the working classes who should have been their friends. Their study of the philosophers and their knowledge of the lives of the poor brought them into sympathy with the secular movement for social and economic reform. The rank and file of the lawyers supported judicial reform, because the prizes of the profession went to the *parlementaires*. The rank and file of the clergy had much to gain by the reform of a system which left them starving, whilst their leaders divided the spoils. The expulsion of the Jesuits in '64, the dissolution, during the next sixteen years, of several decadent religious orders, and the movement, towards the end of the century, for the use of French in church services, all had clerical support. The Oratorian colleges in Paris and the provinces were a training-ground for the future leaders of the revolution. It was in these establishments that

Joseph Fouché and others of his stamp acquired that union of republican politics with a monkish austerity and the ruthlessness of the Inquisition which marked the character of the most successful terrorists.

But the clerical reformers were not all of one type. Some, like Nicolas Armez, the organizer of the Côtes-du-Nord department, had entered the Catholic ministry as their ancestors had entered a monastery, in order to indulge a taste for philosophy or science, and were little concerned with ecclesiastical affairs. Others, like Talleyrand, forced into orders against their natural bent, cynically combined a worldly life with occasional priestly functions. Sieyès, who had never preached a sermon or heard a confession, and whose attitude in the assembly was anything but ecclesiastical, remained a priest at heart. The letter he wrote (March 10th, '91) declining the arch-bishopric of Paris shows how conscientiously he would have pontificated, had he been able to overcome his fear (*sorte d'effroi*) of a public profession of religion.

It is instructive to compare the careers of the brothers Lindet. Robert, the layman, busies himself with organizing his brother Thomas' diocese of Evreux: 'I congratulate you,' writes the grateful bishop, 'on the way you carry out your pastoral functions.' One could read Thomas' letters on the clerical oath, or on the religious Orders, without suspecting that he was anything but a layman and an anti-clerical.

But it would be an error to suppose that the French ministry in '89 was full of spiritual misfits. There were many who felt that a Catholic priest could be a good democrat. The abbé Fauchet's tract *De la religion nationale* forecasts an almost socialistic state, in which, nevertheless, only Catholics will have full civic rights. The abbé Grégoire accepted the liberty and equality of the revolution as corollaries of the Christian faith. There were others whom Jansenism inspired, not with theological heresies (for theology was out of fashion), but with high moral and social principles, fit to reinforce the secular Puritanism of a Robespierre or a Saint-Just.

That church reform must come, was clear to anyone who studied the *cahiers* and *brochures* of '89. In these writings it was assumed that the church, like the throne, would be a mainstay of the new order. But it would be a church reformed and regenerated. There must be no more payments to the papacy. Bishops must in future reside in their dioceses. The constant holy-days interfere with business, and must be reduced in number. Clerical fees for marriage and burial must be abolished. The mendicant orders, perhaps all religious orders, must be dissolved. Tithes, if not abolished, must be dras-tically reformed. When dioceses and parishes are rearranged, when forms of worship are standardized, when church revenues are redistributed, and church property (perhaps) nationalized, then Catholicism can be transformed from a privileged corporation within the state into the state itself in its spiritual capacity. But there is in these same writings hardly any demand for religious toleration. To the eighteenth century, non-Catholics were hardly less alien than they had been in the seventeenth century. It was still doubtful whether a Protestant was quite a Frenchman.

The ground had been cleared for ecclesiastical reform, as it had been cleared for judicial reform, by the abolition of feudalism, and by the Declaration of Rights. On August 4th tithes (Article V) and fees (Art. VIII) had been abolished, clerical offices had been democratized (Art. XI), Annates and other payments to Rome had been discontinued (Art. XII–XIII), and pluralism had been made illegal (Art. XIV). On August 21st it had been laid down that no one might be persecuted for his opinions 'even in matters of religion,' or prevented from expressing them in public. It was also provided that religious vows should no longer be recognized at law: they were in fact prohibited, and all religious orders dissolved, by a further law of February 13th, '90.

But it was generally felt that behind all such details of church reform lay the bigger issue of the ownership and use of church endowments. When the assembly, on June 17th, had claimed control over taxation, it had done so to embarrass the crown. The 'power of the purse' had played a large part in its victory. But the purse which it had withheld from the king was now empty. The taxes were not being paid. The market for loans had been exhausted. Trade and industry were almost at a standstill. How could the deputies not look towards that immense store of wealth, the property of the church, which had always been regarded as available for common use in times of national emergency? Were they likely to forget the plundering of the Jesuits, or the spoliation of the suppressed Orders? Were they likely to overlook the suggestion made in nearly forty *cahiers* that the monastic estates should be sold to pay off the National Debt? Church lands had been used by the old kings to satisfy the nobles and to check the Third Estate. Might they not be used by the new sovereign to check the nobles, and to satisfy the people?

When, two days after its abolition, the clergy tried to maintain the collection of tithe, Buzot of Evreux protested that the property of the church did not belong to the clergy, but to the nation, and quoted clerical pronouncements to that effect. The proposal that the ecclesiastical revenues should be taken over by the country was first made in the House by the lawyer Dupont of Nemours on September 24th. The debate on Talleyrand's motion that a third part of these revenues should be alienated to state purposes began on October 10th. Three weeks later (November 2nd) it was decreed in terms intended to soften the blow of confiscation that 'all church property is at the disposal (*disposition*) of the nation.'

It was argued in support of the decree that the state has the right to suppress all subordinate corporations, and to confiscate their property; that if it takes over social services such as education and charity from the church, it can take over the resources that support them; and that, whilst the state can make wiser use of such revenues, an Apostolic church is better off without them. The opponents of the decree replied that church endowments had been given to particular bodies or institutions, not to the church as a whole; that a corporation has the same right to hold property as an individual; and that the money taken away from education and charity would be spent on socialistic schemes of which its donors would never have approved.

Such arguments have been heard in every debate on disestablishment. They came mainly from the dignitaries of the church. But attempts were also made to mobilize public opinion. Parishioners were asked to sign printed forms protesting against the spoliation of charitable endowments, 'the patrimony of the poor.' The views of many, perhaps of most parish priests were better expressed by Grégoire. The clergy, he said, did not own their endowments, but held them on trust. They could hardly be said even to live on them—so meagre was their yield. It was a matter of principle that the state should apply them to their proper uses, and administer them in what it considered the best way.

It was, indeed, well understood that if the state took over the church property, it would make itself responsible for the payment of the clergy. Agricultural reformers voted for the decree because they hoped that the confiscated land would be marketed in small lots for the benefit of peasant proprietors. Clerical reformers voted for the decree because they hoped that the state would pay the clergy on a more generous scale than they had enjoyed under the old regime.

The assembly, having made the nation the owner and administrator of all the ecclesiastical property and revenues in the country, was faced with some difficult problems. It dealt with them, on the whole, in a practical and impartial spirit. The deputies had no great sympathy with the clerical point of view. But they had no wish to hamper the work of the church; and no desire to antagonize a class which could so strongly influence the people for or against the revolution. It had first to be settled—for this had been left open by the formula of November 2nd—whether to deal with the confiscated wealth as capital or as revenue; whether to realize its total value by selling it, or to be content with the use of the income derived from it. It would not be easy to put such a vast property on the market; and there might be some danger of being forced to sell at a loss. Nevertheless the first plan was the only one that promised immediate returns on a scale proportionate to the financial embarrassments of the government.

It was therefore determined to put the property as a whole up to auction, and to provide for the clerical salaries, and other church expenses, by special taxation. It was objected that under this arrangement a sum of about six and a half millions sterling needed for the support of the Catholic church would have to be provided every year by taxpayers who were not all Catholics. It was answered that the churches were open to all who cared to use them, and that the clergy were a 'holy militia,' analogous to the National Guard. So, with some protests, this plan was accepted.

Next it had to be settled how the clergy were to be appointed and paid.

The assembly had refused to constitute itself an Ecclesiastical Commission for the administration of church revenues. It did not feel itself bound to provide out of taxation the same income as the church had received from its endowments. It saw no necessity to apply the new revenue in the same way as the old. It had a duty to the taxpayers to make the best use of their money. It intended to use its position as paymaster of the clergy to introduce reforms which were generally desired, and to bring the church into reasonable relations with the state. Accordingly a report of the Ecclesiastical Committee proposed a number of changes, not of course in the faith, but in the organization of the French church. These changes took shape, after a long debate, in the Church Establishment Bill of July 12th, 1790. Its title (*constitution civile du clergé*) showed that the word *constitution* still retained some of its old physical sense, and had not yet acquired the political meaning of its English equivalent. The *constitution civile* of July, '90, was not included in the *constitution française* of September, '91.

The first part of the document (*Titre I, Des offices ecclésiastiques*) provided for a rearrangement of the old dioceses and parishes. The old dioceses had varied in size from twenty to fifteen hundred square leagues. The new dioceses coincided with the homogeneous departments. The old town parishes were unnecessarily small and numerous. They were now united, so that there should not be more than one parish in places of less than six thousand inhabitants. At Saint-Denis, for instance, five parishes were amalgamated into one—that of the Abbaye. The number of parishes in the capital was reduced from forty-four to thirty-three. The unwanted churches were closed, and their altar plate was distributed amongst others that had need of it.

The second part of the Bill (*Nomination aux bénéfices*) ruled that all bishops and clergy should in future be appointed by local election. Bishops would be elected in the same way as departmental officials, and clergy in the same way as district officials. It also prescribed that, before admission to his office, every beneficed clergyman, whether bishop or *curé*, must take a solemn oath 'to watch over the faithful of the diocese or parish entrusted to him, to be loyal to the nation, the law, and the king, and to uphold by every means in his power the constitution decreed by the National Assembly and accepted by the king.'

The third part of the Act (*Du traitement des ministres et de la religion*) fixed the stipends of bishops and clergy. A bishop received from six hundred to a thousand pounds a year, according to the size of his cathedral town, of which he also acted as *curé*. The Bishop of Paris received two thousand and fifty pounds. *Curés* were paid from sixty to two hundred and forty pounds; *vicaires* received thirty-five pounds—the old *portion congrue* of the *curé*.

The fourth part of the Bill (*De la loi de la résidence*) ruled that bishops and clergy must not be absent from their dioceses or parishes for more than a fortnight at a time without special leave, and prohibited their holding certain secular offices which might interfere with their clerical work. The most important measure of all, perhaps, was that which gave the departmental authorities power to punish an incumbent who persistently disregarded these regulations by deprivation of his stipend, or of his cure. This destroyed the last vestiges of the 'parson's freehold,' and put the clergy under the disciplinary control of the state.

In the debate upon the Bill comparatively little stress was laid upon the proposed changes. Some of them seemed no more than corollaries of the Gallican propositions of Francis I or Louis XIV. Others that broke with the Gallican tradition seemed likely to make the French church more popular and more efficient. It was indeed argued that elected clergy would be under the thumb of their electors, who might include any kind of non-Catholic: in Alsace the majority would be Protestants. The heretic Arius was an elected bishop—a bad precedent. But opposition concentrated on the underlying assumption of the Bill that it was in the power of the assembly to make any such changes. The office and jurisdiction of the bishops, said the Archbishop of Aix, descend through the Apostles from Jesus Christ himself. The state cannot touch them; only a national synod. Dioceses cannot be rearranged without an appeal to the Pope. Voidel's report of November 26th, '90, represented this as a principal cause of opposition to the Bill. On the other side the Voltairian Treilhard and the Jansenist Camus argued that the rearrangement of dioceses and the election of bishops and clergy has nothing to do with faith or morals, the special domain of the Pope. The church has no temporal or territorial rights against the state. The assembly can deal with all matters of a non-spiritual character. It is doing no more than St Paul did, when he bade Titus appoint elders in the cities. If Arius was an elected bishop, so were St Gregory and St Ambrose.

This was the view of the majority. But to many Catholics, lay as well as clerical, the Civil Constitution seemed an unwarrantable break with church tradition, an intolerable interference of the laity in matters which should have been left to the decision of the bishops and clergy. In the Lozère department more than a third of the electors showed their disapproval by refusing to take part in the election of a bishop. There were parish priests all over the country like Cormaux of Brittany, who rang his bells for the fall of the Bastille, and lent his church for the municipal elections of 1790, but who resigned his living as a protest against the Civil Constitution, and became a fanatical leader of the 'refractory' clergy. Others, like Besnard of Doué, set themselves a course of reading in theology and ecclesiastical history before they could make up their minds to take the oath prescribed in Article XXI.

It was on this point that the bitterest controversy arose. Unfortunately, by the time the question of the oath came up for discussion at the end of November, '90, clerical opposition to the basis of the Bill was so pronounced that the deputies were beginning to lose patience. Paris, too, was on the move. There was a danger that anti-clerical agitation in the capital might compromise the settlement of the church question as it had already compromised the settlement of the royal veto. Voidel, who proposed the oath, did so frankly on the ground of clerical opposition to the bill. When Mirabeau ventured on a theological argument about Bossuet's Articles, he was easily worsted by the abbé Maury; but when he roundly declared that there were too many clergy in the country, and that too few of them were patriots, he evoked enthusiastic applause. The deputies looked to the oath to weed out the undesirables. Some of them cynically reflected that the greater the number of the clergy who refused this test, the cheaper the new establishment would be. Some regarded it as a first step towards the separation of church and state which was to come about five years later.

But most of the deputies had no wish to antagonize the clergy. They honestly could not see why a priest should object to an oath which was taken by the soldier and the magistrate who, like him, received a salary out of the taxpayer's pocket. They could not see why a priest should object to a form of words which put spiritual duties first, or why he should refuse a pledge of loyalty to the revolution which secured his liberties, and to the settlement under which he drew an improved stipend. But many of the clergy felt themselves to be faced by a cruel dilemma. If they accepted the oath, the state might force them into a schism. If they refused it, their own action might precipitate one. Attempts were therefore made to ease matters as much as possible for that sensitive organ, the clerical conscience. The abbé Dillon maintained that one might take the oath as a public official, not as a Christian. Grégoire declared that the assembly was not asking for an *ex animo* undertaking (*assentiment intérieur*), but merely for an external compliance with the demands of the law. There was at least one diocese, that of Viviers, whose bishop took the oath with reservations, and allowed his clergy to do the same, until Roland, in August, '92, insisted upon the literal meaning of the test, and undid all the bishop's work for unity.

The majority of the deputies had little sympathy with a subtlety of mind or conscience which enabled an undertaking to be accepted in one spirit and carried out in another. In their view the issue was the same as in the matter of the veto. The first principle of the revolution was at stake—the sovereignty of the people. If the people was sovereign, it could claim rights over the church that had been exercised by all French kings since the sixteenth century. Any refusal to recognize these rights could be treated as an act of *lèse-majesté* against the revolution. The assembly therefore insisted that the law must be enforced. By a decree of November 27th, '90, all clergy exercising public functions must take the oath after High Mass on Sunday morning in the presence of their congregation and of a representative of the General Council of the Commune. If any incumbent refuses to do so, he is deemed to have resigned his living, and can be replaced by an elected priest

Je soutiendrai la Constitution   Je détruirai la Constitution

Le Roi Janus, ou l'homme à deux visages

LOUIS FACING BOTH WAYS

To the deputy he says, 'I will support the Constitution'; to the priest he says, 'I will destroy it.' But as he says it, the crown is falling from his head.

who has taken the oath. If he fails to carry out his undertaking, or tries to go on with his work without taking the oath, he can be deprived both of his stipend and of his rights as an active citizen. If he organizes resistance to the decree, he can be prosecuted and punished as a disturber of the peace (*perturbateur du repos public*).

After doing his utmost for a month to hold up a measure which went so much against his conscience, Louis, on December 26th, sanctioned the decree. The king feared that he was sanctioning a schism. The assembly hoped that he was preventing one. January 2nd, '91, was put down as the day upon which the clerical deputies should give a lead to their brethren by taking the oath before the National Assembly. The President reads out the names, one by one. 'The Bishop of Agen.' The bishop rises. 'I ask leave to speak.' 'You can't make a speech,' shout the deputies of the Left: 'Are you taking the oath, or not?' He tries again: 'It is with a heart torn by grief . . .' ('Hear, hear,' from the Right); but he is again shouted down. 'The mayor ought to stop this rioting,' exclaims the Marquis de Blacons. 'He isn't here: he has left the House' is the reply; and there is wild agitation on the Right. 'I myself shall see that order is enforced,' says the President. Another deputy jumps to his feet: 'Listen to these rebels,' he cries: 'they have destroyed the monarchy, and now they are destroying the church, I protest. . .' But his voice is drowned by a general demand from the deputies to 'get on with the roll-call.'

The bishop of Agen is now allowed to finish his speech; the upshot of it is that he will not take the oath. The Marquis de Fournès congratulates him on his bold lead. The abbé Leclerc of Alençon is the next on the list. 'The Catholic church,' he begins, 'is my mother.' Roederer of Metz objects: 'The invitation to take the oath allows nothing but a plain acceptance or refusal.' 'The answer,' rules the President, 'must either be, I take the oath, or I refuse to take it.' The Marquis de Foucault-Lardimalie exclaims, 'This is sheer tyranny! Even the Roman Emperors who put the Christian martyrs to death allowed them to testify to their faith.' The President reads out the form of oath. The abbé Landrin takes it, amid applause. Couturier, the *curé* of Châtillon-sur-Seine, says he is ready to take it with reservations. There are cries of 'You must take it as it stands.' There is a pause. 'Is no one else going to take the oath?' asks the President. At last the old Bishop of Poitiers rises. 'I am seventy,' he says, 'and I have been a bishop for thirty-five years. Though bowed down with age and study, I will not dishonour my grey hairs. I refuse the oath.' There is applause from the Right. And so the scene goes on.

In Paris, on the appointed Sunday, January 16th, the streets were full of expectant crowds going to mass, and of troops patrolling to keep order. Some clergy stayed in their presbyteries. Some entered their pulpits at the end of the service, took the oath, and became 'constitutional' *curés* by acclamation. Some bravely stated their reasons for refusing to swear what their consciences would not allow. They were greeted by cries of '*A bas l'aristocratie!*' or '*A la lanterne !*'

The *curé* of Saint-Sulpice, had, as the law required, given notice beforehand that he intended to refuse the oath. The church was packed. At the end of an emotional address on Hell he began to attack the National Assembly. There were cries of 'Order!' and his remarks were soon drowned by the organist, who, with all his stops out, played the revolutionary song *Ça ira*. When the *curé* retired from the pulpit, a municipal officer took his place, and said, 'Citizens! The law does not oblige this man to swear allegiance to the nation. By his refusal he has only incurred his dismissal from the public employment which was entrusted to him. He will soon be no longer your pastor, and you will be called upon to name another more worthy of your confidence.'

Such was the hesitation of the clergy in taking the oath and of the assembly in enforcing it, that it was not until February 5th that a full list could be drawn up of those who had complied with the law. No time was then lost in ordering the election of new incumbents in place of those who had sacrificed their cures. On the 24th Talleyrand, who had resigned his own bishopric of Autun a month before in order to become a member of the Paris department, consecrated the first two bishops under the Constitution. On March 3rd, at Notre Dame, the induction of the newly elected *curés* was combined with the consecration of nine more newly elected bishops. Three weeks later (March 24th) the deputies officially attended the installation of the first bishop of Paris appointed under the Act—the clerical deputy for Belfort, Joseph Gobel. Sieyès, whom public opinion designated for the post, had refused to stand. Grégoire, who best deserved it, obtained only a few votes.

A footnote to the first draft of the Civil Constitution had suggested that the king should be asked 'to take any steps he might think necessary to ensure the full and complete execution of the decree.' It was for him to negotiate with the Pope. When the decree was passed at the end of July the clerical party asked that this suggestion should be carried out. The assembly, distrusting the king, and jealous of its independence, took no action. The deputies hardly supposed that at a time when Catholic prestige stood so low the Pope would reject an arrangement which re-established the old church in close alliance with the new state. They remembered that in 1774 Clement XIV had sanctioned the reorganization of the Catholic church in Poland by Catherine the Great. They remembered that five years ago Pius VI, under Jesuit pressure, had recognized her creation of the archbishopric of Mohilef, and had given it jurisdiction over all the Latin churches in Russia. If the successor of St Peter, the fountain of orthodoxy, had allowed the schismatic Empress to nominate bishops to Catholic sees, he would surely not risk a schism with the oldest branch of the Roman church rather than accept reforms intended to restore it to the purity of primitive Christianity.

Pius VI, a handsome, cultivated, and ceremonious old man, was also vain, weak, and stubborn. He was the last man in the world to understand the revolution. Yet he might have compromised with it, and returned to the draining of the Pontine Marshes, and to his delightful digging at Pompeii, had it not been for circumstances which overruled his natural inertia. One of these circumstances was his official sympathy, as Pope and prince, with the spiritual and political troubles of the king of France. Another was the influence of the French ambassador at the Vatican. Old Cardinal de Bernis could never forget that he had once been the confidant of Mme de Pompadour. He hated this new-fangled ill-mannered revolution. Montmorin, the Foreign Minister, had talked of replacing him by the agnostic and adaptable Bishop of Autun: but Louis refused to be represented by such a man. A third circumstance, perhaps the decisive one, was the Pope's anxiety over his rights in Avignon and the Comtat Venaissin, where economic interests and dislike of papal misrule, exploited by the press and the University, by German *illuminés* and French secret societies, were driving the inhabitants into rebellion, and encouraging their reunion with France.

Yet Pius was slow to move. The abolition of Annates on August 4th meant a loss of eighteen thousand pounds a year to the papacy; and it implied that French bishops would in future be instituted without reference to Rome. This occurred at the very moment of the Avignon revolt. Neither Pope nor bishops protested. The decree for the confiscation of church property (November 2nd), for similar reasons, passed unchallenged. Up to February, '90, the papacy had still made no pronouncement against the revolution. All but a few bishops were still willing to take the civic oath of loyalty to the constitution. There was good reason to hope that an accommodation might still be arranged. But at the end of March it became known that Pius, encouraged by his recent suppression of Joseph II's religious reforms in Belgium, had decided to make a stand. He would not give up his right under the Concordat to nominate candidates for certain French bishoprics. He might be driven to denounce the whole revolution. His first move, though definitely hostile, was not made in public. A Secret Allocution (March 29th) condemned the whole work of the National Assembly, from the Declaration of Rights to the Civil Constitution of the Clergy. His second move struck at the source of Orders in the constitutional church: he excommunicated the Bishop of Autun.

Considering the manner in which these steps were taken, the assembly might be excused for thinking that the Pope was merely saving his face, and that he might yet be brought to accept a reasonable compromise. This feeling was encouraged by a letter which arrived from the Vatican on July 23rd, urging the king to take serious counsel with the archbishops of Vienne and Bordeaux before accepting the Civil Constitution. The advice in fact came too late, for Louis had sanctioned the Bill on the 22nd. Yet it was neither without hope, nor without some encouragement from the Papal

Nuncio, that the bishops asked the king to write to the Pope. Meanwhile the deputies, remembering Louis XIV's tactics in 1664, held up their decision of the Avignon question, in the hope that they might yet be able to use it to coerce the papacy.

On August 1st a special courier left Paris, carrying official instructions from the assembly to the cardinal, and a private letter from the king to the Pope. These documents make three things quite clear. First, Louis has given way to the urgent demand of the assembly and of the people for the immediate enactment of the Civil Constitution, so far as concerns the rearrangement of the dioceses and the filling up of the vacant sees. Secondly, he might have summoned a national synod to discuss the other provisions of the Bill, but he prefers to consult the Pope. Thirdly, Pius is urged, for the sake of religious peace in France, and from fear of a schism, to give provisional sanction to the new dioceses and the new bishops, and to negotiate with representatives of the French government on the other points at issue. On the French side, then, the door to a settlement was still kept open.

There followed three months' delay, from mid-August to mid-November, during which any possibility of agreement gradually disappeared. Bernis, in close touch with the clerical opposition, misrepresented his instructions, and concealed the urgency of the situation. Pius, indignant that Louis should have sanctioned the Civil Constitution before consulting him, and alarmed at the prospect of losing his possessions at Avignon, grasped at any excuse for doing nothing. He noted the hardening of clerical opinion against the settlement. He watched the *rapprochement* of the Catholic powers, due to their growing fear of revolutionary propaganda. He could not ignore the pressure exercised by refugee princes, and by prelates hostile to the assembly. He went on hoping that he might be able to make the best both of the spiritual and of the temporal world.

The result was that he lost both. The manifesto (*Exposition des principes*) published by Cardinal de la Rochefoucauld and twenty-nine episcopal deputies on October 30th drove the assembly into the decree of November 29th, enforcing the clerical oath. Thus religious war was declared, and the schism that Pius so much dreaded, but did so little to avoid, had begun. Meanwhile, as a result of the debate of October 27th, troops were sent to Avignon, and the first step was taken towards its annexation.

On February 24th, '91, without public notice, and in the remote church of the Oratory, Talleyrand, 'ex-bishop of Autun,' with his brethren of Lydda and Babylon, consecrated constitutional bishops to the sees of Quimper and Soissons. There had been threats of assassination, and the altar was surrounded by armed guards. Three weeks later (March 10th) Pius publicly condemned the Civil Constitution: but the Apostolic succession of the schismatic church was already secure. It was not till the end of May that he withdrew his Nuncio from Paris, and refused to receive de Ségur, whom Louis would have sent, too late, in place of the treacherous Bernis.

Looking back on a long and tiresome controversy, the deputies may well have been conscious of mistakes. They might have consulted the Pope about the arrangement of the new dioceses and the selection of the new bishops. They might have invited the clergy to settle the less urgent details of the Civil Constitution in a national synod. They might have modified the terms of the clerical oath. They might have refused to listen to the complaints of the Pope's rebellious subjects at Avignon. Some of these concessions might have strengthened the patriot party among the bishops and clergy; some of them might have divided the opposition. But probably no concession would have appeased the radical hostility of the reactionary party in Paris and in Rome. Nothing would suit them but that the assembly should give up its claim to reorganize the church. The only attitude the assembly could have adopted without criticism was one that necessity and conviction alike forbade—that refusal to intervene in ecclesiastical affairs which the United States of America were at this moment embodying as an amendment in their new constitution : 'Congress shall make no law respecting an establishment of religion.' The assembly, therefore, cannot fairly be blamed for the unlucky results of the Civil Constitution. Both parties were at fault. The counter-revolutionary acts of the refractory clergy, the penal legislation designed to deal with them, and the anti-clerical excesses in Paris and some parts of the provinces, may be attributed to the peculiar bitterness always aroused by a religious quarrel.

One serious result of the controversy had probably not been foreseen by either party to it. The expulsion of the Jesuit order in the middle of the eighteenth century had still left most of such national education as existed in '89 in the hands of the church. The provincial universities, the Oratorian seminaries, the ecclesiastically endowed colleges in the towns, even the village schools managed by *curés*, schoolmasters, nuns, or *dames régentes*, which kept up an unequal fight against the massed illiteracy of the country-side—all were under church control. The abolition of tithe, *octroi*, and other old sources of educational revenue had so impoverished many of these establishments, that already they were half empty, if not entirely closed down. At Toulouse the *collège* had lost two-thirds of its revenue. The universities of Dijon, Caen, and Aix could no longer afford to pay their lecturers. Even Louis-le-Grand at Paris was poorer, owing to the suppression of tithes, by three thousand pounds a year.

But now the personnel of education was to suffer, as well as its endowments. Not many schools might be affected by the abolition of the religious Orders (February 15th, '90). The requirement of the oath from every teacher in a place of public education (March 22nd, '91) split the teaching profession, as it had split the ministry, from top to bottom. In the University of Paris only forty-one out of a hundred and sixty-one *professeurs* would take the test. At Nancy eight out of twelve refused it. In the Bernay district only six out of fourteen nunnery schools had enough teachers left to carry on. No doubt the old educational system needed reform, and one of the obstacles to reform was a clerical and counter-revolutionary body of teachers. Yet the action of the assembly did nothing but hurry on the death of a sick institution. The Legislative Assembly re-examined the case, and made a small grant towards its treatment. It was not until the second year of the Convention that the diluted extract of a series of ambitious Reports was administered to a patient by that time almost dead, and that the first step was taken towards a state-controlled system of national education.

Fortunately education is not a monopoly of the educationists. The essential condition of popular instruction in '89 was the use of the French language. This was being spread more widely every day by revolutionary news, revolutionary laws, and revolutionary institutions. The desire expressed in the *cahiers* that French should oust clerical Latin and provincial *patois* was being realized without legislation in the *culte de la patrie*, at the electoral assemblies, and at the Fêtes of Federàtion. The new departments cut across the old linguistic frontiers. Latin was discredited by the counter-revolutionary attitude of the clergy. *Patois* was discredited by Girondist federalism. The *Marseillaise* carried French triumphantly all over France. It soon became as unnecessary as it was inconvenient to translate the decrees of the assembly into the dialects of eighty-three departments. Representatives on mission in the provinces might still find the *patois* useful for polemical purposes against non-jurors and rebels. Constitutional priests might find it necessary to preach and catechize in the language of the country-side. In Alsace the revolution always remained bi-lingual. But a cultural and political movement for the use of French progressed rapidly, even in the church; though it was noticed that some congregations were still reciting the *Salvum fac regem* in Latin three months after the fall of the throne.

The criticism most commonly urged against the work of the National Assembly is that it destroyed the old regime, instead of incorporating it into the new. Here, in the church settlement, is an instance of the opposite procedure; and the critics are equally loud in their condemnation. Only a few clear-sighted fanatics, it is true, have been found to urge, with Mazzini, that the revolution should have thrown over the Catholic church, and created a new religion of Brotherhood to take its place. But many historians seem to think it strange that the deputies of '89 were unable to solve outright a problem which has baffled so many governments before and since—how to adapt a Catholic church to a democratic state.

Perhaps the problem is insoluble. At any rate the men of '89 made their attempt in all honesty, believing that their countrymen wished it so. They made it with such patience and good sense as they could command. They failed because, whilst they steered a straight course for port, deeper currents which they could neither calculate nor control were carrying their ship out to sea.

Chapter IX

LAND AND LABOUR

Where a great proportion of the people (said he), are suffered to languish in helpless misery, that country must be ill policed, and wretchedly governed: a decent provision for the poor is the true test of civilization. Gentlemen of education, he observed, were pretty much the same in all countries; the condition of the lower orders, the poor especially, was the true mark of national discrimination.—(SAMUEL JOHNSON, 1770.)

'Mons. Melon, in his political Essay on Commerce, asserts that, if you divide France into twenty parts, sixteen are labourers or peasants; two only artisans; one belonging to the law, church, and military, and one merchants, financiers, and bourgeois. This calculation is certainly very erroneous. In France, England, and indeed most parts of Europe, half of the inhabitants live in cities.' So wrote David Hume. But Hume was wrong, and Melon was right. In eighteenth-century France four out of every five people lived in the country. To thousands of French families the land was their only home, their only wealth, their only security. Yet their holding in it was too small, their means too poor, and their profits too heavily taxed by king and tithe-owner, to afford them a living. A happy settlement of the land question was the first condition of national prosperity.

It was the aim of the revolution to free the land from its burdens, and to redistribute it more fairly amongst those who needed it. The land settlement of '89 was closely connected with the church settlement. Both were designed to reassert national rights over a great national possession, and to use it for the benefit of the nation. Neither was a class policy, or a Utopia; both were practical attempts to solve a difficult problem in the interests of the country as a whole.

The problem had been set by the peasant revolts in the spring and summer of '89. The outlines of its solution had been laid down by the resolutions of the night of August 4th. To what extent the land should henceforth be free and accessible depended upon the effect given by subsequent legislation to the 'abolition of feudalism'. The first article of the decree of August 11th showed just how little abolition might mean. The feudal regime was said to be 'entirely destroyed'; but this was explained to mean three things. First, the most degrading personal and rental obligations of feudalism, those defined as *ceux qui tiennent à la main-morte réelle ou personnelle*, were indeed abolished without compensation. Secondly, all others could be extinguished by redemption (*rachat*). Thirdly, until this was done, these obligations would still remain in force. The remaining articles showed that all game-law restrictions—*colombiers, capitaineries*, and the like—were abolished without compensation, purchase, or moratorium; so were all personal and corporate privileges. The seigneurial courts, tithes paid to laymen, legal charges, and clerical fees were to disappear as soon as they were otherwise provided for; but all rents, and tithes due to the clergy, would remain payable until redeemed.

Further action was postponed by the king's refusal to print the decrees till September 19th, or to promulgate them till October 5th. The *comité féodal* appointed on August 12th to carry out the measures of the 11th could not begin its work till October 9th. The committee was fairly representative of all three Orders, but it had a bias towards vested interests in land. There was little hope that it would simplify or expedite the provisions of August 11th. The decree of March 15th, '90, in which its decisions were embodied, contained such a mass of legal terms and technicalities that it was almost unintelligible to the general public. Its reclassification of feudal dues as between person and property seemed merely to confuse the issue.

The first part of the document reaffirmed in unnecessary detail the social equality resulting from the abolition of feudal privilege. The second part gave an elaborate list of all the *droits seigneuriaux* abolished without compensation, and noted certain exceptions. The third part dealt with the crucial question of redemption. Here for the first time it was provided that proprietors whose cartularies had been destroyed, or who had been forced to surrender their rights during the peasant risings of the previous year, could nevertheless reassert their claims. It was not for the old owner to prove his title, but for the new owner to disprove it. Unless or until he could do this, he must either redeem the feudal charges at twenty or twenty-five years' purchase, or go on paying them.

Measures so favourable to lawyers and land-owners led to renewed outbreaks during the winter of '89–90. Had the peasants been left to deal with the situation alone, there would have been no remedy but force. Actually, as soon as the new municipalities came into being at the elections of January, '90, they started an attack on seigneurial privilege. Here they disputed the seigneur's right to nominate the beadle, to take precedence in the parish church, or to put poachers in the village stocks. Here they protected the peasant against attempts to make him pay tithe, or feudal dues. Here they acted as middle-men in buying out the landlord's rights, or in buying up his estates.

Such was, in fact, the beginning of a process familiar enough in the succeeding century—the transference of private rights and private duties to the state. Seigneurial justice was transformed into a system of national courts. Seigneurial *corvées* were replaced by a road-tax. Monopolies passed from private individuals to districts or communes. Charity became a social service, and was paid for out of the public purse. Feudalism, in fact, was not abolished; it was municipalized. Its few picturesque relics stood, like the old turnpikes beside our own high-roads, as idle reminders of an extra penny or two on the rates. But though this timely intervention eased the situation,

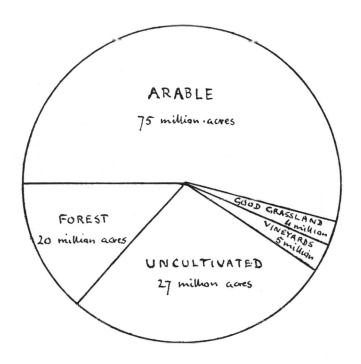

ARABLE
75 million·acres

FOREST
20 million acres

UNCULTIVATED
27 million acres

GOOD GRASSLAND
4 million

VINEYARDS
5 million

FRENCH AGRICULTURE IN
1789
(from Arthur Young)

there was still a bitter feeling in the provinces against the *rachat* regulations; and it was feared that more *châteaux* might go up in flames.

The problem of tithe was old and troublesome. The *dîme*, once a voluntary gift, had for a thousand years or more been a tax on the produce of the soil paid to the church in kind or in cash as a return for its services and its charities. Nominally due from rich and poor alike, it could be evaded by anyone wealthy or powerful enough to defy the tithe-owner. Theoretically a tenth of the gross produce of the land, tithe in fact varied from place to place, and averaged a thirteenth. Its total yield was about five millions a year.

These local diminutions in the tax, and the fact that it was not levied on some newer crops, such as potatoes, whose introduction tithe-owners therefore opposed, made the tithe less onerous in France than it was in England; but, like other French taxes, it fell most heavily on those who could least afford to bear it. Meanwhile a system which starved the clergy, and provided next to nothing for the needs of the parish, gave rise to an infinity of lawsuits. Its abuses were denounced with equal anger by Physiocrats and agricultural reformers. The *cahiers* of the nobles agreed with those of the clergy and the Commons in demanding its abolition, or at least its reform. Tithes should at any rate be paid by townspeople as well as villagers; the proceeds should be funded; and the clergy should receive a living wage. But this could hardly be done so long as salaries varied with the yield of the soil, and were fixed in terms of chickens and cabbages instead of cash.

The decree of August 11th distinguished tithes paid direct to the clergy from those paid to alien tithe-owners. The first were redeemable: the second were abolished without compensation. But both were still to be paid until other arrangements had been made to meet the liability for clerical salaries, the upkeep of church buildings, charities, education, and other expenses that had hitherto been borne by the church. This transitional period was extended during the long debates on the Civil Constitution, and did not end with the passing of the Bill. The last of a series of fresh decrees (June 18th and August 3rd, '90, March 11th, '91) ordered tithes still to be paid two months after the date fixed for their abolition (January 1st). It was not till after the fall of the throne in August, '92, that the land was finally freed from this unpopular burden.

Long before that date tithes had in fact ceased to be paid, except perhaps in a few out-of-the-way places. The evidence on the point is not complete; but it suggests that the passive resistance of the tithe-payer, and the unwillingness or inability of the tithe-collector to coerce him, generally combined to make the law a dead letter. Already during the bad winter of '88 it had been impossible to stop the wholesale killing of game and cutting of timber by which the peasant kept his pot full and his fire burning. It was not likely that, after the liberating decrees of August 4th, he would be content to go on paying either tax or tithe. Soon the sale of the church lands promised a better investment for his meagre capital; and he would have to be taxed in a new way.

It was not only the small tenant who benefited by the freeing of the land from feudal and ecclesiastical charges. On the contrary, the chief beneficiary was the owner of large estates, who not only had much less to pay himself, but could also raise the rents of tenants who benefited as he did. Nevertheless the new land settlement brought real boons to the small proprietor. He gained almost as much by the simplification of his tenure as he gained by the reduction of his charges. He could now count upon being the real possessor of all that his little plot produced, of all his labouring time, and of all his cattle. It only remained, for his full satisfaction, that the land thus made free should also be made accessible, and that he should be able to widen the frontiers of his new freedom. For this, fresh funds were now becoming available. No more state loans were being floated. It was not a favourable moment to invest in business. Savings that had previously been swallowed up in tithes, dues, and taxes, could now be invested in the purchase of land. Money hitherto hidden from the *collecteur* reappeared. Poor men who had simulated destitution now began to inquire how they could add a *toise* or two to their little holdings.

This further step was made possible by the decision to take over the property of the church, and to put it up for auction. When to the church lands were added (December 19th) the lands of the crown, the king's personal domain (March 9th, '90), and the estates of the emigrants (July 17th, '92), an immense amount of land and buildings, now the property of the nation (*biens nationaux*), was available for sale to the public. But how to dispose of it so as to benefit both the state that sold and the citizen who bought was a problem not easily solved.

A beginning was made with the decision (December 19th) to put up to auction twenty million pounds' worth of church and crown lands, and at the same time to issue twenty million pounds' worth of interest-bearing certificates (*assignats*) of the face value of fifty pounds, which could be used for the purchase of the land. It soon became clear that this step would involve others. It was imperative for the government to raise a large sum in a short time. To do this it must appeal to the small purchaser. The small purchaser would have no scruples about offending the crown: but he might hesitate to incur the ban of the church. It would therefore be advisable to employ the local authorities as middle-men in the land-purchasing market.

The departmental and district councils, to which this rôle was assigned, would not be elected until late in July. During the interim their part was played by the municipalities, which were not unwilling to forward the purchaser's interests in return for the commission of six per cent on sales allowed them by the government. Paris led the way (March 17th) by boldly buying up half the total amount of property on the market; and the provinces were not slow to follow the example of the capital. The conditions of sale were fixed and refixed in a bewildering series of decrees issued during the next eighteen months. In September, '91, the retiring deputies passed on the problem, only half solved, to their successors of the Legislative Assembly.

The fear of incurring the enmity of the church was not entirely fanciful. In some parts of France, where clerical influence was unusually strong, the traffic in church lands became a religious issue. At Strasbourg it was announced in the name of the Prince-bishop that anyone purchasing church property would incur a major excommunication. In the Nord department the clergy worked on popular feeling by suggesting that the new owners of the land would evict their tenants, or at least raise their rents, and discontinue the local charities. When these arguments failed, they organized passive resistance to the sales, or reduced the value of their land by letting it go out of cultivation.

Nevertheless the auctions were a great success. Two-thirds of the *biens nationaux* were sold between November, '90, and December, '93. The big lots, especially in the towns, went to the *bourgeoisie*. The small lots, especially the clerical glebe-lands, went to the peasantry, who often formed syndicates to buy up more than they could individually afford. In the Nord department as a whole 8,490 peasant proprietors purchased forty-three thousand *hectares* of land and a hundred and twenty buildings, whilst 2,143 *bourgeois* purchased twenty-two thousand *hectares* and twelve hundred buildings.

The land was mostly sold at less than its market value, and was considered an attractive investment. The queen herself advised her Swedish friend, the Comte de Fersen, to use some of his money in this way. This was partly due to the desire to make things easy for the small purchaser. It was partly due to the depreciation of the *assignats*. To the purchaser by fixed instalments each deferred payment cost less than the last. Phelip, a business man of Bordeaux, bought in February, '91, a property that had belonged to the Ursuline Sisters at Bassens. The price was five thousand and fifty pounds, payable in eight instalments spread over four years. What he had actually paid for the property when he came into possession of it at the end of the period was £2,635. This was under the regulations of November, '90, which only allowed four years' grace. Earlier purchasers had been allowed as much as twelve years, and profited in proportion. After November, '93, with the *assignats* still losing in value, the land was sold in specially small lots, to encourage small buyers. It can be imagined how easy it became under such conditions for comparatively poor men to enter the class of landed proprietors.

This was, of course, no new thing. Long before the revolution it had been a common practice for townspeople who had made money in trade to invest it in land. With all its drawbacks, land was, under an arbitrary government, a safer investment than Consols (*rentes*). In those days the price of land had been kept up by a number of causes—the failure to make the best use of such areas as were under cultivation, or to bring new areas under the plough; a growth of population out of all proportion to the amount of land available; and the competition of new purchasers whenever an old estate was broken up. In those days the profits of farming had been reduced by the complicated burdens on the land. Now all this was changed. The land was on the market. The price was low, and the yield was high. It is not surprising that all classes of society tried to improve the occasion.

Attempts have been made (so far without finality) to ascertain which class profited most from the sale of the *biens nationaux*. In two departments—one in the south-west (Gironde) and one in the centre (Cher)—the most important buyers, especially of the larger properties, were *bourgeois*; next to them came the working class, who bought a great number of small lots. Perhaps those who benefited most were well-to-do peasants, farmers, or tradesmen who had already put part of their savings into land, and who were now able to purchase a little more. In the neighbourhood of Toulouse artisans and employees (*ouvriers*) were considerable buyers. In the Saint-Gaudien district small farmers (*cultivateurs*) took the lead. Officials often invested their savings in real estate. Speculators bought in order to sell at a profit.

In the Nord department the peasant probably gained most. The land was purchased collectively, and its purchase opened the way to a movement for the restoration of the collective rights of the villagers. They would not be content until the common lands which had been enclosed were again under cultivation, until their cattle were once more grazing by the roadside, and until they were free to cut what timber they needed in the neighbouring forest. This movement was not without its drawbacks. Communal cultivation might enliven the social virtues of the countryside: it did not make for good farming. There was more to be hoped from the individual efforts of new farmers, fresh from the town. On the other hand, the old peasant proprietor who now secured enough land to make himself independent was likely to carry on the worst traditions of small farming. His methods had shocked the Agricultural Societies of the eighteenth century: they remained the despair of Ministers of Agriculture during the nineteenth century.

The effects of the sale of the *biens nationaux* were seen all over the country. In the provinces, if there were now fewer big estates, there were more small farms. The *château* might be in ruins, but the park was under the plough. The process that can be seen going on all over England under the pressure of surtax, death duties, and higher wages was then suddenly imposed upon France by a scheme of compulsory purchase. This may have been bad for the narrower amenities of life: it was good for its wider happiness and efficiency.

In the towns, too, both land and buildings were changing hands. Their old owners had been cathedral chapters, ecclesiastical seminaries, and monastic orders. Their new owners were business men, builders, and speculators in real estate. Their old owners had been good neighbours, perhaps, and kind landlords; but their chapels and cloisters cumbered the town, and their privileges stood in the way of social and economic progress. The new owners might well be harsher landlords, who 'let the poor go on the rates'; but they developed the land, they put up new buildings, and they increased the prosperity of the town.

What were the political effects of this land settlement? They were analogous to those of the constitutional settlement. The redistribution of power transferred sovereignty from the king to the people. The redistribution of land transferred property from the aristocracy of church and state to the middle and lower classes. What had been the monopoly of one Frenchman in a hundred was now shared between twenty-five. The magic of property —of property freed from old encumbrances, and guaranteed by new laws—was now within the reach of any thrifty and hard-working citizen. Between the rich landowner and the poor labourer there was now a new class of small farmers, a French yeomanry, which balanced the old class of *rentiers*, and gave the state a fresh and deep foundation of security in the soil of the country. This was a permanent guarantee of political stability. In the Bourges district the purchasers of land in 1791 belonged in almost equal numbers to the Terrorists of 1794 and to their victims. It was likely that, when the revolution was over, their common interests as proprietors would bring these political extremists together in support of the First Empire, and of the Third Republic.

The troubles of the peasantry forced themselves upon the attention of the assembly, and led to a land settlement that left a deep mark on the country. The no less real grievances of the town labourer found little expression in the *cahiers* of '89, and less sympathy among the deputies. No labour settlement emerged from the revolution.

Only one French family in five lived in a town; of working-class families, probably not more than one in ten. Even after the readjustment of urban representation under the electoral regulations of January, the town workers' vote carried little weight at the elections of '89. It carried still less in the elections of '91, when the disfranchisement of 'passive' citizens took effect. It was only in the cities that they could hope to make themselves heard. Yet in Paris, by far the largest working-class constituency in the country, half the adult male citizens, including much more than half the workers, were deprived of the vote. The interests of the town workers remained almost unrepresented in the National Assembly. Their case was never fairly brought before Parliament.

True, the country workers too were almost unrepresented. But the *jacquerie* during the summer of '89 had shown that their complaints could not be ignored; and the land settlement was a bid on behalf of the propertied classes for their political support. Paris, as the deputies found in July and in

October, could be dangerous too. But its political interventions had been organized by middle-class leaders, and its economic demands could, it was believed, be met by the muskets of the middle-class National Guard.

Such had been the experience of labour troubles in the capital during the last fifty years, and more. In 1724 the Paris stocking-makers had struck against a reduction in piece-rates. In 1737 the weavers had struck against the conditions of *maîtrise*, the employment of women, and the inventions of Vaucanson. In 1776 the bookbinders and gilders had struck for a fourteen-hours day. In 1786 the carpenters had struck against a new rule prohibiting the free use of wood, and the *gagne-deniers* (porters, or carriers) had struck against the competition of a more up-to-date organization called the *fourgons*, to which the government had conceded a monopoly of the carrying trade in Paris. None of these strikes had led to more than minor disorders, which were easily dealt with by the police. True, some eight hundred *gagne-deniers* had marched to Versailles, in order to appeal to the king. But the king was out hunting, and they marched back again. Their ringleaders were put in the pillory, and banished from the city. The rank and file gave no more trouble. It was not unreasonable to argue that what had happened in '86 would happen in '89. The police would keep order. There would be no need to bribe the worker with higher wages or shorter hours, or to pacify the pauper with free food.

Such calculations might hold good so long as the workers remained leaderless, unorganized, and unconscious of their power. But what if they became aware of themselves as a class? What if they freed themselves from middle-class patronage, and found leaders in their own ranks? What if they used the power of the strike against the assembly, as the assembly had used the power of the purse against the king?

Though the small workshop was as much the rule in industry as the small farm was the rule in agriculture, there were already in some towns the beginnings of capitalism and the factory system. Hitherto, for various reasons, there had been few reactions to the new conditions of employment. The socialistic and sometimes communistic opinions of the *philosophes* had never been translated into popular terms ; and they were still in advance of the age. The church had always discouraged political activities among working-men's sons who took Orders. The philanthropists of the 'eighties had persuaded the poor, without much difficulty, to accept charity instead of asking for justice. The demand for bread could not be quieted; but it never became a class issue.

There could be no Labour Front against the *bourgeoisie* so long as the Third Estate was united in the struggle against the privileged classes. In the early stages of the revolution the town workers let themselves be represented and led by tradesmen, merchants, and lawyers; sometimes instinctively, as at Bordeaux, sometimes grudgingly, as at Lyon. There had been no *jacquerie* in the cities, no seizure of private property, no refusal to pay rents. How long would this moratorium last? How soon would the revolt of the country labourer against feudalism find its echo in a revolt of the town labourer against capitalism? Might not the municipality, in the interests of public order, find it necessary to meet the demands of the poorer citizens? Might not the assembly be forced to make a labour settlement?

As far as can be ascertained, in the absence of full statistical evidence, there were in Paris at this time nearly sixty-three thousand employees (*ouvriers*), who worked under nearly four thousand employers (*patrons*) in small businesses employing on an average sixteen men each. On the usual reckoning of four or five to a family, this would give a working class numbering nearly three hundred thousand souls, or about half the population of the capital. It would still exclude other kinds of workers. The problems involved in this ominous situation varied from year to year, according to the food-supply, the price-level, the rate of wages, and even the state of the weather.

The year 1789 was a bad one for the Paris workers. A climax of high prices coincided with the aftermath of a bad harvest, a hard winter, and an influx of unskilled labour. There was, no doubt, a boom in the building trade and its allied industries, and the demand for skilled labour was good. But wages were low, and conditions of work were bad, both for the organized and for the unorganized workers. Industrial workers who in England would have earned 1s. 8d. a day could only earn thirteen pence ; and women sevenpence-halfpenny as against ninepence. Those who belonged to workers' unions (*compagnonnages*) could do little against their masters (*patrons*); and few of them could afford the fee—it might amount to as much as two years' wages—to become *maîtres* themselves. Those who belonged to trades' unions (*corporations*) could not use them to better their economic position without falling foul of the police. Those who belonged to unorganized industries had no protection against the arbitrary action of an employer backed by the law of supply and demand.

The Réveillon riot in April had been the first sign of protest against this state of affairs. It was followed during the summer by a series of labour troubles—a strike by the tailors, both masters and men; a strike by the hairdressers' and bootmakers' apprentices; a strike by domestic servants; the bread-riots of October; the François affair; and the march of the market-women to Versailles. Necker's slumbers, he afterwards asserted, were so disturbed by these worries that he woke up every morning with palpitations of the heart, from fear of what might happen if Paris went for twenty-four hours without bread.

Yet nothing was done to raise the level of wages, and little was done to lower the price of bread. The only remedy attempted for unemployment was to set up Labour Camps (*ateliers de charité*). In the largest of these, at Montmartre, twenty-two thousand men were paid tenpence a day for as much work as they cared to do: it was an economic experiment easier to initiate than to abandon, and universally condemned.

The labour troubles of the following year, 1790, were those of a transitional period. Economically, the workers were beginning to organize and to agitate. Politically, the assembly and the commune were beginning to discover that there was a problem to solve. There were recurrent food-riots, beginning in January at Versailles. In March there were meetings of the workers, and some talk of violence due to poverty and lack of food. In March, too, Bailly, the mayor of Paris, was moved to report on the economic needs of the capital, and to claim financial help from the assembly. In May came fresh reports of 'brigands'. In June the printers formed a Union (*corps typographique*), and drew up a constitution (*règlement général*). At harvest time, in many parts of the country, there were troubles between farmers and harvesters known by the picturesque name of *bacchanales*. In December the *perruquiers* struck again. By this time the price of bread had at last fallen to nearly half what it had been a year ago, and the assembly tried to close the Labour Camps, which had already lowered their rate of wages below that current in the open market. But the municipality dared not agree to this. Winter conditions increased the number of men who would work for any wage to twenty-six thousand. Nor were they the only applicants for relief. Employment had to be provided for out-of-work women, in Weaving Shops (*ateliers de filature*). It was not until June, '91, that the *ateliers* were finally closed down.

In February, '91, a step was taken which the Paris workers would have welcomed before. The tax on food and other goods brought for sale into the city (*octroi*, or *droits d'entrée*) was abolished. This was not done for charitable reasons. The work on the new wall (*enceinte*) was still unfinished, and the *barrières* occupied by the employees of the tax-collecting syndicate (*ferme générale*) had proved quite insufficient to prevent smuggling. 'Every night,' wrote the British Ambassador, 'some *barrière* is forced, and prodigious quantities of smuggled goods, particularly wine and brandy, are brought into the town.' A month later the work of construction was stopped, and the land and buildings were sold. But whatever its motive, the abolition of the *octroi* was as great a boon to the poor of the capital as the abolition of tithes had been to the poor in the provinces. It was defended, too, on grounds which would hardly have been urged a year before—the debt of the revolution to the people of Paris.

This was not the only respect in which 1791 improved the position of the working class. The third year of the revolution was a year of better trade. The emigration of so many rich families had certainly caused some loss of custom and employment. But there was immigration as well as emigration. The revolution brought to Paris not only twelve hundred deputies, with many of their families and friends, but also a flood of sightseers and fortune-hunters. All these had to be housed and fed. Thanks to the talkativeness of authors and politicians, the paper-making and printing trades had expanded beyond all precedent. The sixty thousand men of the National Guard had to be uniformed and armed, and there was great indignation among local manufacturers when it was found that their tunic-buttons were being ordered from England. At the Jacobin club in November Roederer was able to speak of a boom in manufactures, and of money returning to the country.

The labour troubles of '91 were therefore due not so much to worse as to better conditions of labour. They represented a first attempt by the workers to use strike federations (*coalitions*) to obtain a share in the profits of improved trade. In an interesting manifesto on this subject (April 29th), the municipality declared that it would be unjust to reduce the workers' wages on the ground that the abolition of the *octroi* had lowered the cost of food; that it was equally unreasonable to expect wages to be raised; that it was going against nature to suggest that all workers in the same trade, whatever their capacity, should be paid alike; and that a federation with any such object in view was an offence against the law. This statement was followed (May 4th) by another in more severe terms, denouncing the workers' attempts at picketing, declaring that wages must be fixed in a friendly way (*de gré à gré*) between employers and employees, and instructing the police to arrest anyone interfering with blacklegs.

Whilst the commune talked, the assembly acted. Within a week of the manifesto of May 4th the first blow was struck at the *coalitions*. At the request of the Paris department a decree was passed prohibiting collective petitions. A collective petition was the obvious means by which a popular association of any kind could bring its views before Parliament, or before the public. The decree was drafted in very wide terms. It applied to 'electoral, administrative, judicial, and municipal bodies, communes, sections of communes, and citizens' societies.' It was based upon the principle that collective action is the action of a number of individuals, each of whom is individually responsible. Its operative article laid it down that a petition must bear the signature of every person subscribing to it.

This was equally embarrassing to all associations. It was aimed at political as well as economic associations; not only at *coalitions*, but also at clubs. It appeared to threaten the workers no more than those who were seeking to stifle the workers' claims. The bias of the decree appeared in two articles which followed, and which would have been more appropriate as the preamble of a bill yet to come. Communal assemblies, it was laid down, cannot meet except to discuss matters of municipal administration; and the municipality (subject to an appeal to the department, or to the assembly) is the sole judge of what constitutes an unlawful meeting. The first of these additional articles struck at the Paris sections: the second struck at workers' demonstrations.

The man who presented this measure to the House was no common reactionary. Isaac-René-Guy Le Chapelier was a deputy for the Commons of Rennes, where he had practised as a lawyer, and had assisted in the foundation of the Breton club. He had presided over the assembly on the famous night of August 4th. He had voted for the popular election of judges. He had supported the adoption of red, white, and blue as the colours of free France. He had proposed the abolition of titles of nobility. If he now led the attack upon the right of public meeting and collective petition it could hardly be through any lack of sympathy for the popular cause. A matter of principle was at stake.

That this was Le Chapelier's view is evident from the reasons given for a second law, a companion to that of May 10th, which followed a month later, and which is even more closely associated with his name. The *loi Le Chapelier*, passed by the assembly on June 14th, prohibited, in a comprehensive series of articles, all professional or class corporations, all associations of employers, workers, or shopkeepers, all collective petitioning, all strikes, all picketing, and all workers' meetings.

The first reason given for this drastic measure, in Le Chapelier's opening speech, is that, whilst citizens as such have the right to hold meetings, it does not belong to citizens as members of particular professions. Article XI of the Declaration of Rights, which guaranteed 'the free communication of thoughts and opinions', had said nothing about the right of meeting or of petition. It might be argued that those who drew it up were thinking simply of the freedom of the individual. To extend this liberty to a public meeting or to an association would be to interpose the claims of a class or of a corporate body between the interest of each and the interest of all, to encourage an *esprit de corporation* inimical to the *chose publique*.

The second reason that Le Chapelier gives is that, if unemployment and poverty exist, it is for the nation, not for any sectional body, to provide work or relief. 'It is but equity,' Adam Smith had written, 'that they who feed, clothe, and lodge the whole body of the people, shall have such a share of the produce of their own labour as to be themselves tolerably well fed, clothed, and lodged.' The third reason is that wages and hours of work should be fixed by free discussion between employer and employee (*aux conventions libres, d'individu à individu*). Once this has been done, it is the duty of the worker to abide by the terms so agreed upon.

Much of this is idealistic: none of it can fairly be called undemocratic. If it is hostile to the workers' unions, so it is to any association of citizens, in the name of their common loyalty and common rights. It forbids corporate action, in the name of liberty. It denies it to all alike, in the name of equality. It prohibits any appeal to force, in the name of fraternity. Only the last clause of the Bill discriminates against the workers; and that is because they are the only class likely to hold meetings leading to a breach of the peace.

In the *code rural* of July 20th, which applied the provisions of the *loi Le Chapelier* to the countryside, this absence of discrimination is particularly plain. 'The proprietors or farmers of any canton (says Article XIX) are forbidden to unite (*se coaliser*) for the purpose of lowering or fixing at an insufficient level the day's wages of workmen or domestic servants.' 'Harvesters, domestic servants, and country labourers (says Article XX) are forbidden to form unions (*se liguer entre eux*) in order to raise or fix the level of wages or salaries.' Nothing could be more impartial. Nothing could be more damaging to the unpopular *jurandes, compagnonnages,* and *maîtrises* of the old regime. Nothing could be more favourable to the freedom of labour which the workers so much desired.

Such considerations might be urged in favour of the view that Le Chapelier's law was an attempt to carry into the sphere of labour politics the general principles of a democratic revolution. It might be as necessary for the revolution to prohibit, in the name of political liberty, the mediation of the demagogue as it was for the Reformation to abolish, in the name of religious liberty, the mediation of the priest. It might be thought as important in the eighteenth century to ban trades unionism for the sake of national unity as it has been thought important in the twentieth century to discourage nationalism for the sake of international concord.

Those who cannot credit the National Assembly with such wide views may justly point to the practical results of the *loi Le Chapelier.* The prohibition of petitions and public meetings affected the workers more adversely than any other class. An occasional and uneasy combination of employees could make little headway against the permanent tacit agreement of the employers. Another assumption underlying the Bill was that the present rate of wages was always the best that the workers had any right to expect; that their condition of life was fixed by circumstances outside the purview of Parliament; and that the constitution of society should be as unalterable as the constitution of the state.

Nevertheless, like the Combination Act of 1799, the Bill could not unreasonably be defended and attacked as a measure designed to deal with a particular crisis, rather than a piece of long-term legislation. This, indeed, may have been the reason why it met with so little opposition from those who might have been expected to oppose it, either on the Left of the assembly, or in the popular press—either from Marat or from Robespierre. The democratic leaders at this time went in constant fear of popular excesses which might justify acts of repression by the government. They may have seen in the provisions of the Bill a salutary constraint, if not a measure of emancipation.

If they had been able to look further ahead, they might have thought differently. The circumstances which brought the law into being changed; but its provisions remained. They remained under the Legislative Assembly, they remained under the Convention, they remained under the Directory, they remained under the Consulate. Le Chapelier's law tied a burden on the back of the working class which it did not shake off for nearly a hundred years. It was not formally abrogated until March 21st, 1884.

The whole incident was significant, not so much of the strength of middle-class prejudice, as of the weakness of working-class consciousness. It was not a forcible disarming of the proletariat by the bourgeoisie, but a failure of the workers to combine, and a short-sighted connivance in their own subordination. The incident was significant in another respect. It showed that the revolution was beginning to turn back from the individualism of the new regime towards the *étatisme* of the old. The destruction of the privileged orders was already leading to the suppression of political minorities. It might soon be found that the tyranny of one king was less onerous than the tyranny of twelve hundred representatives of the people.

There was no Labour Settlement in 1789. The new state refused to allow any interference with the laws of nature, whether morally exemplified in the Rights of Man, or economically exemplified in the workings of Supply and Demand. The government dealt with the working classes as a policeman and a relieving officer: nothing more.

CHAPTER X

CONSTITUTION

Those only who have been in France during the Revolution can tell how powerful an engine the *assignats* have been: had some celebrated emigrants taken my advice in the year 1791, in making war upon the credit of France instead of combating her troops, we should not have had now to arm in England: so many brave men would not have bled in the field, nor so virtuous a monarch on the scaffold.—(WILLIAM PLAYFAIR, 1793.)

'THE capitalists,' wrote de Ferrières to his wife on August 20th, '89, 'lead us, without our knowing it, in the way they want to go. They are the power behind the Estates.' The Marquis, who did not like the prospect of paper money, was exaggerating. But there was solid fact behind his fancies. The revolution arose out of a financial crisis, and could not continue without a financial reconstruction. The land question, the church question, and the labour question were all closely connected with the question of money. It would be useless to set up the ideal state, if it could not pay its way. The national constitution and the national credit must stand and fall together.

Ever since Necker, in his *Comte rendu au Roi* (1781), had taken the country into his confidence, the French public had shown a surprising interest in the uncongenial subject of finance. Three years later his *Administration des finances*, by no means light reading, sold eighty thousand copies, and lay beside *La nouvelle Héloise* and *Le Vicaire de Wakefield* in ladies' drawing-rooms. There was no lack of amateur economists, from the Marquis de Mirabeau to the Marquis du Crest, prepared to teach the Controller-general how to balance a budget.

It was an age of industrial and commercial prosperity, in which iron-masters and cloth manufacturers exchanged views with politicians and

economists at Lafayette's dinner-table. It was an age of financial speculation, in which Paris bankers with foreign names—Koch, Abbema, Schweit-
zer, Proly, Pereira—showed society ladies how to invest their profits
from the *fermes* or from the *rentes*. It was an age of realistic statesmanship,
in which financiers expected to play a political rôle; for commerce required
credit, and credit required security, and security depended upon a 'business
government.'

Necker, like his predecessor Calonne, and the rest of the seventeen Con-
trollers-general who had held office during the last twenty-five years, found
it almost impossible to understand the financial system of the old regime—its
caisses, its *trésors*, and its *exercices*, its arrears and its anticipations, its unaudited expenditure, and its extravagant methods of raising revenue. Economic experts still differ in their interpretation of the evidence: but it appears
from the statements drawn up by Lamoignon in March, '88, and by Necker
for the year beginning on May 1st, '89, that at the moment when the
assembly made itself responsible for the national budget about sixty per cent
of the gross revenue never reached the Treasury; that the interest on the
National Debt accounted for more than half the annual expenditure; and
that at the end of every financial year there was a deficit amounting to not
less than one-fifth of the total outgoings.

The States-general of '89 was itself the latest and forlornest attempt of
the government to devise an effective tax-collecting and tax-spending
authority. The only important powers left to the Estates which still survived
in the provinces called *pays d'états* were financial. 'The states of Languedoc
are met,' reports Laurence Sterne in 1764; "tis a fine raree-show, with the
usual accompanying of fiddles, bears, and puppet-shows.' But the deputies
found time to consent to the tax imposed upon them by the crown, to vote a
grant from its proceeds (*don gratuit*) to the Treasury, and to assign what was
left to local expenditure. This system had two advantages over that obtaining
in the provinces called *pays d'élections*. There was less unwillingness to pay
taxes, if a proportion of them was spent locally; and administration gained
from being to this degree decentralized.

Attempts had therefore been made by a succession of finance ministers
—Turgot, Necker, Calonne, Brienne—to extend the system to other parts
of the country. The new Provincial Assemblies of Berry in '78 and Haute-
Guyenne in '79 were intended to interest themselves chiefly in taxation. In
Berry, for instance, compulsory road-making (*corvée*) was reorganized, and
made a charge on the taxpayer. But the experiment was ill-timed. It came
too early for the Intendants, who were not yet prepared to see their authority
set aside. It came too late for public opinion, which preferred to stand by the
old Estates, where they still existed, or to call for their restoration, where,
as in Dauphiné, they had ceased to meet.

As '89 drew near, the government and the people were more and more at
cross purposes. The government thought in terms of devolution and reform:

Gold louis of 1789.

Gold 24 livres of 1793.

Silver écu (3 livres) of 1789.

Silver écu (6 livres) of 1793.

ROYAL AND REPUBLICAN COINAGE

the people thought in terms of replacement and revolution. With the break-down of the provincial assemblies nothing remained for the king but to summon the States-general. He would mobilize at Versailles, where they would be most under the royal influence, all the forces of provincial taxation —the old Estates, whether still alive, or dying, or already dead; the new Provincial Assemblies; the unprivileged Order, which paid too much, and the privileged Orders, which paid too little. If the appeal to loyalty failed, the appeal to force might prevail. Somehow the national credit would be re-established.

The deputies' instructions squared with the desires of the crown. Their *cahiers* were as insistent as Necker himself on the necessity for financial reform, and for a balanced budget. But they saw what the king would not admit—that constitutional and financial reform must go together. By refusing supply until they obtained recognition as a national Parliament, they laid the only possible foundation for a sound finance. 'I think they will soon establish their credit,' wrote Gouverneur Morris, ten days after the tax-resolution of June 17th, 'which, among other things, will bring the exchange between France and foreign nations to be more favour-able. If the money of this country is brought into free circulation, I think it will lower interest everywhere. The sum is immense, and its effects must be commensurate with its activity and mass. At present it lies dead.' The Paris banks, Morris had already noted, were in the habit of paying ten or even twelve and a half per cent for loans.

Certain principles, or certain prejudices which a natural reaction against the old regime raised to the dignity of principles, directed this operation. It was agreed that the old taxes must go—the direct taxes because unjust, and the indirect taxes because uneconomical. Both were complicated and oppres-sive. Both broke all the canons of taxation laid down by that clever Scotch economist whom Turgot and his friends were so fond of quoting. Their total yield per head of the population was (Adam Smith believed) less than half what was raised, without any public opposition, in England. But des-truction was not enough. There must be new taxes to take the place of the old. On what system should they be raised? Three operations were involved —assessment, imposition, and collection.

Hitherto the direct taxes had never been fairly or efficiently assessed. The taxable value of property in land could not be determined, because no ade-quate survey of it (*cadastre*) had ever been made. The taxable value of income could not be determined, because (except for the *vingtième*) no tax-payer was ever required to make a return. All that the Treasury could do was to estimate the taxable capacity of each *généralité*, according to reports on the state of the crops and other varying circumstances. All that the local assessor of taxes could do was to take last year's contributions as a basis, and to modify them according to the total sum to be raised, and the presumed means of the taxpayer.

As to the imposition of the taxes; it had always proved impossible to equa-lize the burden of taxation as between landed (*foncier*) and funded (*mobilier*) property. Land was always heavily taxed: income derived from other sources was elaborately but more lightly taxed under a number of schedules, such as *capitation* and *vingtième*. These taxes had originally been designed to reach the richer classes: but so many offices carried exemption, and so many powerful interests compounded at lower rates, that the burden of the new tax fell on the old *tailleables*.

Collection, the third problem, depended in the last resort upon local *collecteurs*, men who thought themselves even worse off than the majority of those from whom they had to force or wheedle the quota imposed upon their district. It would have been a miracle if such a system had worked equitably. It did not. A detailed study of the Puy-de-Dôme department has shown some instructive results. Although its population was between a twenty-sixth and a thirty-sixth of that of the whole of France, the tax for which it was assessed amounted to a twenty-first or twenty-second part. The richer areas of the district were taxed less heavily than the poorer areas. Town-dwellers, such as tradesmen and officials, were as a whole taxed more lightly than country people.

Nor was indirect taxation in any better way. The salt-tax (*gabelle*) had long been a public scandal. The country was divided into six areas. In each area households were compelled to buy a fixed amount of salt per head at a price which varied widely (from a farthing to sixpence-halfpenny a pound) from one district to another. The contract for collecting the revenue of the tax was let for about three millions a year to a syndicate of Paris financiers. Payment was enforced and smuggling punished by an army of officials (*gabelous*), backed by the courts, the convict-gang, and the gallows. The tobacco tax was levied in the same way, and was only less oppressive because no one was forced to buy. The reform of this iniquitous system was unanimously demanded. But when the *fermes* disappeared the taxes ceased to be paid. The revenue from salt sank from nearly two hundred thousand pounds in July, '89, to not much more than forty thousand pounds in December. Necker was insistent that something should be done.

Some important repairs were in fact carried out upon the monuments of financial corruption. Local privileges and tax-exemptions were removed. The new income and property taxes (*contributions mobilières et foncières*) were assessed and collected by the municipality, whose knowledge of local conditions did something to correct the unfairness of the old system. The long-desired land-survey was at last begun. But it would be a long time be-fore the main object of these reforms could be achieved. The new taxes must at present be assessed upon the same arbitrary basis as the old—a valuation of the land which did not exist, and returns of income which were never made. It might easily happen, as it happened in Auvergne, that a new *département* was taxed more heavily than an old *généralité*. There was, however, a way of escape for the new taxpayer that had not been open to the old. Under a regime of liberty he could refuse to pay, without much fear of being punished.

France in 1789 was full of silver and gold. But it was seldom deposited in banks. It was seldom lent on interest, or invested in business. It lay as unused *écus* or *louis d'or* in the boxes of thrifty merchants. It was displayed as cups and salvers on gentlemen's side-boards. Cathedral sacristies treasured price-less monstrances and reliquaries. French wealth was like the fabulous gold in a sunken treasure-ship; and the Controller-general might think himself fortunate if he recovered a few ingots at a time. If the state could not collect money, it might either save it, or create it. The deputies believed in economy, but only on condition that it was carried out at the expense of the court and the ministries, with their bad tradition of unaudited extravagance, not at the expense of the *rentier* class to which they and their friends belonged. Interest on the National Debt, they insisted, must be secured, until the bond-holders could be paid off without loss to themselves. Under such conditions the amount that could be saved was unlikely to be large.

Why not, then, create new money? The prospect could not fail to be attractive. Yet the deputies recalled with alarm what they had read at school in their Velly or Anquetil about the disasters of the Mississippi Company. They remembered the lively pages in which Voltaire described the rise and fall of that notable Scotch 'gambler and calculator whom we call Jean Lass.' They were sadly familiar with the recent history of the Discount Bank (*caisse d'escompte*), whose depreciated note-issue of some six million pounds' value based on a metal reserve of less than twenty-five per cent was only kept in circulation by a Treasury guarantee. They had acquired, under the regimes of a series of finance ministers, a deep suspicion of banking opera-tions.

The man in the street—and in monetary matters most of the deputies belonged to this class—dreamed of a new finance as simple and sound as the new constitution. It should be something analogous, on a larger scale, to the accounts of his household and of his business. The householder's ideal is to keep an account of every penny he spends, and to show a balance on the right side at the end of the year. This golden rule of finance had never been observed under the old regime. The men of '89 at any rate attempted to incorporate it in the new order. Their system was carried on by Napoleon. It stood France in good stead from 1803 to 1914. It compares favourably, according to an important school of French historians, with the methods in vogue in their country during more recent years.

To the *premier ministre des finances*, as he is now called, the National Assembly is little more than a new kind of money-making machine. Necker seems not to care what financial ideas may be in the heads of the deputies. He imagines that they are dazzled by the legerdemain which has reduced Brienne's deficit of eight millions to two and a half, and will soon make it vanish altogether. But they can see arrears and anticipations up his sleeve. They notice that he is counting upon the voluntary contributions of the privileged orders. They are offended by the suggestion made in his speech of May 5th that he has his own ways of raising money, and will not need their help after all. Almost criminally optimistic, he goes on squeezing the dry skin of the Discount Bank for loans. He budgets as though the national credit would remain unshaken by the earthquaking events of '89.

The assembly sees things less expertly, but more realistically. It exploits its influence over the taxpayers to coerce the King (June 17th). It rejects Louis' tempting financial programme (June 23rd), because it is coupled with political conditions it cannot accept. It reassures the *rentiers* (July 13th) against a repudiation of the National Debt. It is, in fact, putting forward a rival financial policy. It is rewarded by the support of the capital against the king and the Controller; and it wins the day.

After July, '89, it might have been expected that all parties to the financial quarrel—king, minister, assembly, and taxpayer—would combine to deal with a crisis which involves them all. But the yield of the taxes diminishes with every defeat of the government. The deficit in the Treasury increases at the rate of forty-five thousand pounds every month. Louis raises fresh difficulties. The assembly is increasingly suspicious of Necker's methods. Had not Condorcet, at the time of his first dismissal from office, slightingly compared him with France's only other foreign finance minister? It was not such ancient history that the deputies missed the allusion: Maurepas, Louis XVI's first minister, had served both with Necker and with John Law. Accordingly the expedients which Necker proposes during the autumn of '89 in order to fill the fast-emptying Exchequer are hotly disputed, and come to a bad end. The million and a half loan proposed in August is killed by criticism, and by the reduction of the rate of interest from five to four and a half per cent. A second loan of four millions is not much more than half subscribed. In September there follow a bank loan, an attempt to reimpose a modified salt-tax, a forced loan (*contribution patriotique*) of twenty-five per cent on income spread over three years, and a scheme of voluntary subscriptions (*dons patriotiques*).

The loan might have succeeded, had there been enough money left in the banks. The new *gabelle* was nullified by a general refusal to purchase salt at any price. The forced loan which Necker's old enemy Mirabeau ironically urged upon the House (September 26th), as a last defence against the horrors of bankruptcy, yielded no more than a hundred thousand pounds a month. The *dons patriotiques* were a picturesque gesture, which led to a few substantial gifts, along with many pathetic and rather absurd instances of private generosity. Thus the actors of the Comédie française subscribed £1150, the Paris printers and publishers £1000, the mounted officers (*huissiers*) of the Châtelet £270, and the pupils of the Academy of Music £750. The Irish College sent its Chapel plate, the women artists their jewellery, the instructors at the Royal Fencing School their rapiers, and the scholars of Louis-le-Grand forty-five pounds, along with their silver shoe-buckles. 'An old woman who has only a shilling in the world' subscribed sixpence. The total yield from such gifts in six months was less than three hundred thousand pounds. It could do little to fill up the huge gulf of public indebtedness.

Finally, it was proposed that the *ci-devant privilégiés*—those who before the revolution had enjoyed exemption from taxation—should make a special contribution equivalent to the amount they had previously evaded. But this tax, decreed against the advice of the Finance Committee, it proved impossible either to assess or to collect.

Such was the situation when the assembly faced the alternative which was by now in everybody's mind—the nationalization of the almost fabulous wealth of the church. There were two ways in which it might be used to finance the revolution. Dupont de Nemours wished the state to take over the administration of the property and endowments of the church, and to use what could be saved from church expenses (he put them at two and a half millions a year) to guarantee a fresh loan on favourable terms. Talleyrand proposed that the whole of the church property should be put on the market. He estimated that it would yield enough to buy out the judicial office-holders, to pay off a large part of the National Debt, and to finance the church. Mirabeau threw Talleyrand's suggestion into practical form by proposing to treat ecclesiastical property as the property of the nation, on condition that provision was made for the upkeep of the church, and that no *curé* was paid less than sixty pounds a year. Helped by this bid for clerical support, Mirabeau's motion was agreed to on November 2nd.

The need for money was urgent, and the sale of so much property might well take a long time. It was therefore determined that part of the yield of the 'national property' should be anticipated by issuing certificates exchange-able for the land and buildings put up for sale. It was not intended that these certificates should themselves be used as money, like the already discredited notes of the Discount Bank. Both Dupont and Talleyrand disclaimed any such design. Some of the speakers in the debate, like the Comte de Seneffe reminded the House of the unhappy experiments in paper currency made in French Canada, in the Ile de France, in Russia, and in the United States and prophesied a national bankruptcy. Others argued that if the certificate were treated as currency they would stimulate trade, and augment the public wealth. To most of the deputies economic arguments seemed of minor importance compared with political considerations. A widely spread owner ship of money, like a widely spread ownership of land, would unite all classes in defence of the revolution. The certificates would be the cement of the constitution.

But the experts still shrank from the risk. For this reason it was decided to issue the new certificates like notes through a bank, and not like coins from the Mint, or from any state department. The Committee set up to work out the details of the plan reported against making use of the unpopular and discredited Discount Bank. But they hoped that its note-issue might be saved, if it were guaranteed by a new bank, and by a fresh issue of certificates backed in a new way. They proposed to create an Emergency Bank (*caisse de l'extraordinaire*), into which should be paid the proceeds of Necker's recent experiments in taxation, and of the sale of the confiscated church property. On this security the bank would issue twenty million pounds' worth of *assignats* in denominations of fifty pounds.

The name *assignat* came from Russia, where it had already been used by Catherine the Great in 1768. It meant, not a currency note, but an assignment, or bill of exchange. It was in fact a Treasury bond, bearing interest at five per cent, and realizable in the possession or in the proceeds of the sale of 'national property.' The piece of paper on which it was printed was headed, in large letters, *Domaines Nationaux*. On the left and right were medallions bearing the head of the king and the fleur-de-lys, with the inscriptions, *Louis XVI, Roi des Français*, and *La Loi et le Roi*. Below was the designation, *Assignat de Cinq Cents liv.*, and the guarantee, *Il sera payé au Porteur la somme de cinq cents livres à la Caisse de l'Extraordinaire, conformément aux décrets des 16 et 17 Avril et 29 Septembre 1790*. So the great experiment began.

It was not long before circumstances, some of which were exceptional, and some of which might have been foreseen by any economist, forced the assembly to go further. The new certificates did not restore the credit of the old notes. Holders of *assignats* hesitated to exchange them for land still encumbered by the debts and mortgages of the clergy. When this difficulty was got over by transferring to the state all the liabilities of the church (March 17th, April 17th), the *assignats* assimilated themselves more than ever to a paper currency. The expectation that they would soon be made legal tender led to the hoarding of gold and the export of silver.

Meanwhile the government was incurring fresh liabilities, and feeling the shortage of ready money. Pensions had to be paid to monks extruded from their cloisters, and stipends to clergy deprived of their tithes and fees. The fleet had to be refitted during the Nootka Sound scare of a naval war with England. The new administration created a host of minor officials, to all of whom salaries had to be paid. There was a growing shortage of currency in the country and in the capital. During September one Paris section after other asked for paper money, particularly in small denominations.

On the other side of the account, revenue fell sadly below the estimates. Though it had been decreed (January 30th) that the old taxes should be levied, and though the oath of Federation (July 14th) included a promise to pay them, the finance minister spent an unhappy summer trying to squeeze revenue out of a people blandly determined to exercise the rights of property-holders without the duties of taxpayers. On March 6th Necker reported that there was already a deficit on the first two months of the year amounting to three millions sterling.

It seemed to most of the deputies, who were not financial experts, and distrusted those who claimed to be such, that it was the height of pedantry not to meet the demand, and to fill the void in the Treasury by the easy expedient of manufacturing paper money. They had only, as Necker ironically pointed out, to provide themselves with a paper mill and a printing press to make the nation solvent. Accordingly on April 17th the original twenty millions' worth of *assignats* were declared legal tender, their denominations were varied to fifty, fifteen, and ten pounds, and, in order to encourage their realization in land, the interest they bore as certificates was reduced from five to three per cent. The new currency was at once used to pay the creditors of the government—bond-holders, contractors, officials, and the rest; and many of these persons were among the earliest purchasers of national property.

Within six months this first step towards the benefits and dangers of a paper currency was followed by another. On September 29th it was decided after a long debate, and by a small majority, to issue another forty millions' worth of *assignats*, in denominations of five pounds and two pounds ten, bearing no interest. This was paper money without disguise. It was intended for the redemption of the National Debt. But it appeared by the middle of the following May that less than fifteen millions had been used for this purpose. The rest had gone to meet the current expenses of government, which now amounted to over seven millions a month. So urgent by this time was the need for cash that on May 6th the assembly authorized the issue of another five millions, and on June 16th of thirty millions more. Half the currency in the country was now in paper. The Legislative Assembly followed the lead of the Constituent Assembly, and issued another five millions on September 28th, five more on November 11th, and fifteen more on December 16th. By the end of 1791 the amount of *assignats* in circulation exceeded the value of the national property on the market. They were issued in sheets, like our postage-stamps, and cut off as required with a pair of scissors. Inflation and depreciation were in full swing.

The chief reason for this was of course the reckless issue of more and more *assignats*, without any attempt to call in the old currency, or to prevent its sale and purchase as a marketable commodity. Good money was inevitably driven out by bad. But this was not all. By decrees of October 30th and November 7th holders of certain classes of state bonds (*créances sur l'état*) could use their certificates as though they had been *assignats* for the purchase of national property. At Lyon, Tours, Orléans, and other large towns the municipalities were allowed and even encouraged to issue paper token-money (*billets de confiance*). Their example was followed by big business firms and banks. The tokens issued by Monneron of Paris were valid at Bordeaux,

Lyon, Marseille, Nantes, Rouen, and Strasbourg, and had a large circulation. Sixty-three varieties of banknotes circulated in Paris alone. By the end of 1791 these unofficial issues were said to total two millions pounds' worth in Paris, and five millions in the provinces.

As a result of this multiplication of unfamiliar notes the forging of paper money became easy and remunerative. The criminal courts of the capital were kept busy during the summer and autumn hearing charges against the inmates of La Force and the Conciergerie, who spent their compulsory leisure in printing false *assignats*, or against coiners whose more comfortable quarters were in London or Limoges. As the quantity of paper money increased, and its quality became more suspect, its exchange value went down.

One of the expected checks upon inflation proved a failure. It had been anticipated that large quantities of *assignats* used for the purchase of national property would return to the Treasury, and be destroyed. But since the purchases could be made by instalments, this amount was much less than it should have been. All that the Treasury received between January 1st and May 15th on account of the sale of property valued at twenty-nine millions was five and a quarter millions. The burning of these notes did little to reduce the immense mass of paper now in circulation.

Again, the exchange of *assignats* of the higher denominations into small metal coins, which was necessary for so many business transactions, was practised by the government, and not discouraged among the general public. But the large notes lost from four to six per cent of their face value in exchange; and the supply of small metal coinage soon gave out. Even copper disappeared; and the government was driven to using bell-metal (*métal de cloche*) as a substitute for it. As early as December, '89, it had been proposed that religious communities should be allowed only one bell, and suburban churches (which usually had four) only two, so that the rest might be turned into coinage. *Dixains* and other small coins in this metal were soon being minted at the Barnabite convent in Paris. The smaller notes were commonly refused, especially in the frontier provinces; or if taken, they were promptly exchanged at whatever rate the money-changer, whose business was made increasingly difficult by the hoarding and exporting of silver currency, would allow.

Contemporaries who were honestly puzzled by the depreciation of the *assignats*, and later writers who wished to exculpate the assembly, put it down to political causes. They blamed the hostility of the church, the fear of counter-revolution, or the machinations of foreign powers. They pointed, as proof of this view, to the way in which the value of the *assignat* rose and fell, during the years '90–94, in sympathy with political changes, and the fortunes of the war (see p. 337). Such causes account for the minor variations in the rate of exchange. But these variations are insignificant compared with the steady downward trend throughout the period as a whole. For the cause of this there is no need to look beyond the elements of economics. A paper currency which increases out of all proportion to the stock of commodities for which it is exchangeable inevitably loses its value, according to what good Rousseauists should have been quick to recognize as a natural law.

But the deputies were not thinking of Rousseau when they persisted with their paper currency. They deliberately defied economics in the name of politics. They broke the laws of nature, if they were such, for reasons of state. They wanted to encourage the sale of the national property, and to create a large class of landed proprietors. They needed ready money to stimulate trade, to meet the charges of church and state, and to pay off the interest on the National Debt. They were already financing a revolution: they were soon to be faced with the necessity of financing a war. Whatever the dangers of the *assignats*, they could see no practicable alternative to them. Nor are our economists so infallible that they have much right to blame the tentative finance of French deputies a hundred and fifty years ago. Right or wrong, it saved the revolution.

There are some countries in which the people know what the government allows them to be told; there are some in which they know what it pays the press to tell them; and there are some in which they know what they happen to hear. France in 1789 fell under the last head. A few events flooded the country with rumour, excitement, and fresh experiences: the news of most minor happenings percolated into provincial backwaters, where illiterate mayors puzzled their heads over a series of complicated and sometimes contradictory decrees.

The Declaration of Rights and the Abolition of Feudalism led to changes so widespread and fundamental that no one can long have remained ignorant of them. The new administrative divisions and the new franchise must have been forced upon the attention of every voter in 1790. The meaning of the church settlement was brought home to every parish on the exciting Sunday when its *curé* either accepted or refused the oath. The benefits of the land settlement came to mind every time the peasant added a few square yards to his plot of ground; and its drawbacks every time he found a false *assignat* among the money he brought back from market. But it may be doubted whether the petty offender or the common litigant found as much difference as he should have done between the new justice and the old; whether the ban on petitions and associations caused much serious concern outside the big towns; or whether anyone except politicians and journalists was moved by the debates on the minor issues of the new constitution.

The political basis of the new regime had been enacted during the autumn of '89: the new electoral and administrative system had been in force since February, '90; yet, when the *Constitution Française* could at last be read as a whole, there must have been many who turned over its pages

DÉCRET

DE L'ASSEMBLÉE NATIONALE.

Du *trois Septembre* 1791.

La Constitution française —

Déclaration des droits de l'homme et du Citoyen.

Les Représentans du Peuple Français, constitués en Assemblée Nationale, considérans que l'ignorance, l'oubli ou le mépris des droits de l'homme sont les seules causes des malheurs publics et de la corruption des Gouvernemens, ont résolu d'exposer, dans une Déclaration solemnelle, les droits naturels, inaliénables et sacrés de l'homme, afin que cette déclaration, constamment présente à tous les Membres du Corps social, leur rappelle sans cesse leurs droits et leurs devoirs ; afin que les actes du pouvoir Législatif et ceux du pouvoir —

THE CONSTITUTION OF 1791

The first page, containing the preamble to the Declaration of Rights, with Louis'
signature in the margin.

with fresh interest, and with some anxiety, to see what was or was not included in it of the feverish legislation of the last two years.

After the Declaration of Rights, which now stood in its proper place as the preamble to the constitution, came a reiteration—but not in the legal language of the decrees of August 11th or March 15th—of the benefits won by the abolition of feudalism. Amongst these were cleverly included the destruction of the *corporations*, and the abolition of religious vows. The reader, were he of an ironical or prophetic turn of mind, might notice that, when all other inequalities disappeared, one remained. The *supériorité des fonctionnaires publics dans l'exercice de leurs fonctions* sanctioned the formidable privileges of officialdom, and forecast the *droit administratif* of the Third Republic.

The first part (*Titre I*) of the constitution reaffirmed, in general rather than in legal terms, the Declaration of Rights. It explained that these rights now included freedom to emigrate, which had been more than once debated in the assembly, freedom of individual petition, and the right of compensation for property confiscated by the state. It added a promise of other benefits not yet put into statutory form—a Poor Law (*secours publics*), an Education Bill (*instruction publique*), national festivals, and a code of Civil Law.

Titre II summarized the new territorial divisions—departments, districts, cantons, and communes—and laid down the conditions of civic status. What is remarkable here, and in pleasant contrast to the exclusiveness of modern nationalism, is the generosity shown to aliens. A foreigner's son born in France, or any descendant of a French religious refugee, willing to settle in the country, and to take the oath of civil allegiance, can become a French citizen. A foreigner who buys land, manages a factory or farm, or marries a French wife, can obtain citizenship by five years' residence, and by taking the oath. Under exceptional circumstances the assembly can allow French citizenship to any foreigner wishing to reside in the country, and willing to take the oath. In another part of the Constitution (*Titre VI*) the ignominious *droit d'aubaine*, under which the goods of an alien dying in France were confiscated by the crown, is abolished. Foreigners can inherit from Frenchmen, and acquire or dispose of property. Their persons, possessions, and rights of worship are protected by the state.

The greater part of the constitution is of course taken up by the system of government gradually worked out during the past two years, and revised on the eve of the king's acceptance of it. This is the subject-matter of *Titre III*. It is none too well arranged. The *réunion* of the assembly (Cap. I, Sect. V) is separated from its *pouvoirs et fonctions* (Cap. III, Sect. I) by a long passage (Cap. II) *de la royauté et du roi*; and the latter is cut off from its natural sequel, *de l'exercice du pouvoir exécutif* (Cap. IV). But the main outlines are clear enough.

It is first laid down in a preamble which contains the essence of the whole constitution that the national sovereignty is exercised by representation through an assmebly (the legislature) and a king (the executive), and by delegation through a judicature. The age-long monarchy is no more than the second of three emanations of the sovereign people. The constitution goes on to define the three powers, roughly in this order.

The unicameral National Assembly sits for two years, and cannot be dissolved by the king. It consists of seven hundred and forty-five deputies from the eighty-three departments, and an unspecified number from the colonies. It is to meet on the first Monday in May—the anniversary of the first session of the States-general in '89—but it cannot function until an absolute majority of the deputies are present, or, if there is still no quorum, until the end of the month. Deputies are privileged in act and speech whilst exercising their functions, and without the leave of the House no criminal charge can be pursued against them.

The powers of the assembly are those of most legislatures under a limited monarchy: but it is to be noticed—for the point was not settled without hot debate (May 22nd, '90)—that the king cannot declare peace or war without the ratification of the assembly. It is also laid down—for the deputies did not forget the summer of '89—that the king shall never station or move troops within thirty thousand *toises* (about forty miles) of the place of meeting of the assembly.

A procedure is then prescribed for the making of decrees, including the royal sanction (the suspensive veto): and provision is made for the immediate enactment, without royal consent, of decrees affecting the constitution and privileges of the assembly, or dealing with taxation. Regulations are also made to secure friendly relations between the king and the assembly. There is no relaxation of the rule excluding deputies from the ministry, and ministers from membership of the assembly. But it is arranged that places shall be reserved for them in the House; they have the right to address the assembly on matters belonging to their departments, and can be allowed to do so on other subjects.

The 'King of the French' is no longer the 'King of France,' for he has exchanged his royal domains for a Civil List salary. He reigns in virtue of heredity, but in the name of the law. His person is 'inviolable and sacred'; but his household troops have been replaced by not more than eighteen hundred men chosen from the army or from the National Guard. The arrangements made for a regency, and for the royal family, are chiefly interesting for the anxiety they show lest the Flight to Varennes should not be the last attempt to escape from the country.

The section dealing with the ministers (Cap. II, Sect. IV) had roused strong feeling among the deputies. It might have been expected that an assembly which had constitutionalized the king would also constitutionalize the king's ministers. It did indeed recognize the orthodox doctrine of ministerial responsibility. No order of the crown, says Article 4, is valid unless countersigned by the appropriate minister; and no minister can escape responsibility for his acts (Article 6) by pleading that he acted under the king's orders. But the deputies definitely refused to try the consequential experiment that was still being worked out in England. They refused to let the king choose ministers from among the deputies. They refused to set up a council of ministers as a *liaison* between the executive and the legislature. So obsessed was the assembly with the traditional distrust of ministers, so fearful was it lest a deputy who accepted office under the crown should be corrupted by wealth and power, that it forbade any member of the present or of any subsequent National Assembly—or, for that matter, any judge or juryman in the Court of Appeal—to accept any kind of appointment or payment from the king (*pouvoir exécutif*) or his agents until two years after ceasing to hold his present position.

The Decree of November 7th, '89, was aimed at the ambitions of an individual statesman. Its first aim was to prevent Mirabeau from becoming a Walpole or a Pitt. But its inclusion in the constitution shows that it was also a matter of principle. Whether, if this ban had not been imposed, the king would have chosen deputies as ministers, is more than doubtful. It is certain that, the disposition of Louis and of the assembly being what they were, deputy-ministers would have lost the confidence of the House without gaining that of the king. The assembly can hardly be blamed for shrinking from so dubious an experiment.

The constitution ends with sections on the judiciary, the fighting forces (*la force publique*), taxation, and foreign relations. *Titre IV* defines the armed forces of the nation as the regular army and navy, the troops confined to home service, and the National Guard. Little is said of the first two, except that they cannot ordinarily be called out for police purposes save by civil officials acting under regulations of the assembly. The National Guard appears in the constitution in order that its democratic character may be put beyond question. It elects its own officers, and discards rank as well as uniform off parade. Yet it remains, like the rest of the armed forces, nothing if not disciplined (*essentiellement obéissante*). No armed citizen, it is added, may take part in a public debate. By the time this provision became law, civilian deputies were beginning to carry daggers and pistols under their coats. But they still dreaded nothing more than armed interference with their freedom, unless it was the overthrow of democratic government by a military dictatorship.

In the final revision of the constitution the church settlement of 1790 had been excluded. This was not because it was less important than the new departments, or the new judicial system, but because the deputies were not entirely satisfied with it, and realized that some of the provisions of July 12th might require revision within less than ten years.

Nevertheless there was, hidden away in a short and easily overlooked Article of the constitution, a revolutionary denial of one of the prerogatives of the church. 'The law,' says *Titre II, Art. VII*, 'regards marriage as nothing but a civil contract.' What was this but a denial of an age-long right, and a first step towards the complete secularization of society? In the chaos of legal codes under which Frenchmen had hitherto lived, a gleam of coherence had seemed to come from the canon law of the church. Through canon law the church exploited its partnership with the crown, and kept a close hold on the legal status and civil rights of every Frenchman. But it could not be long before this monopoly was broken down, and a remedy found for the legal inequality of persons under the old regime.

Soon women gain every right the revolution has to give, except the vote. Monks and nuns, hitherto the slaves of the cloister, with no civil or legal existence, become members of society. They can renounce their vows: they can marry: they can inherit. Non-Catholics, whether Protestants or Jews, are admitted to all public employments. Protestants may reclaim any property confiscated from them since 1685—the year of the Revocation of the Edict of Nantes. The emancipation of the Jews is not so sure: but the confirmation of certain long-standing rights of their race in the Midi cannot long be withheld from other parts of the country; and a codicil is added to the constitution (September 27th, '91) extending its provisions to any Jew who takes the oath of allegiance.

Slavery no longer exists in France. But there are slaves on French soil in the West Indies. For five years the supposed interests of the planters prevent their liberation. Only when the commissioners of the Convention free the black men of St Domingo in order that they may fight in the republican ranks against the English (February, '94), is it recognized that black men as well as white men 'are born and remain free and with equal rights.'

The constitution had broken the church's monopoly of marriage: but public opinion was not yet ready for secularization. It was not till September 20th, '92, that one of the last acts of the Legislative Assembly made civil marriage and civil registration the law of the land. At the same time many obstacles to marriage and divorce set up, in the supposed interests of order and morality, by royal and canon law, were destroyed. The priest had said— The man may marry at fifteen, the woman at fourteen, but not (without an expensive dispensation) within the prohibited degrees of relationship.—Yes, added the magistrate; but (thinking of aristocratic *mésalliances*) they must have their parents' consent, unless the man is thirty and the woman twenty-five. Hitherto marriage had been a bargain between the parents. Now it was to be a free contract between free citizens.

Divorce too would be made easier. The law of September 20th, '92, allowed it on seven grounds—insanity, criminal conviction, cruelty, immorality, desertion, five years' absence, or emigration. Mutual consent provided an eighth way of escape; but here the family could intervene, and insist upon delay, unless or until both parties clearly wished for the dissolution. These reasonable grounds for divorce were unreasonably extended by the Convention, until a few months' separation, or a supposed incompatibility of temper, enabled couples to be unmarried and remarried with almost American ease.

Meanwhile the principles of liberty and equality removed some causes of domestic friction. The wife had hitherto been under the rule of her father or her husband. Now she became the joint administrator of the family fortune. A family council could secure a settlement from the estate in favour of a widow or widower left without other resources. Orphans and minors were put under the care of the family as a whole until they reached their majority at twenty-one. Adoption was encouraged, and the legal status of bastards was improved.

Finally a limit was put to the arbitrary disposal of property by will. All but a fraction of the estate went automatically in equal shares to the family. Even the testator's disposal of the one-sixth to one-tenth part that remained was restricted. The democratic intention was to prevent the accumulation of too much wealth in too few hands. So far did the Convention carry its zeal for equality of inheritance that in '94 it made these provisions retrospective, and applied them to all testamentary acts since the day of the fall of the Bastille, with special provisions favouring the claims of poor dependants.

The British constitution is, like Methuselah, without beginning or end of days. It admits no origin, and it foresees no finality. Yet it can be altered by an ordinary Act of Parliament, and it provides no safeguard against revolutionary change. The French constitution of 1791 had not been in existence two years earlier. It was the work of an assembly from which there was no appeal except to the people; and the only way in which the people could answer an appeal was by a fresh revolution. There was good reason, therefore, why the deputies should take precautions against any sudden or inconsiderate change of the institutions they had so carefully set up.

Nevertheless the machinery for revision provided in *Titre VII* cannot but strike the reader as fantastically cumbrous and slow-moving. Neither the present assembly nor its successor can even propose an amendment to the constitution. Afterwards three successive assemblies must pass unanimous resolutions in favour of the revision of this or that Article. But they can do no more. The sixth legislature—that is to say, since each sits two years, the Legislative Assembly of 1801—may then proceed to amend these Articles. But it can only do so under further safeguards. It has to be augmented by two hundred and forty-nine special deputies chosen by the departments on a population basis. Amongst these no deputy of the last legislature that demanded revision may be included. The members of this revisional assembly swear collectively to live and die for liberty (*vivre libres ou mourir*), and undertake individually to deal only with the amendment of the stated Articles, and to maintain unaltered the rest of the constitution. Revision must be the first item on their agenda. As soon as this business is done, the two hundred and forty-nine must retire.

It would have been difficult to devise surer means of making constitutional change impossible. Yet an assembly of Solomons would hardly have expected its decrees to need no revision for ten years; and after ten years to need it so badly that four successive companies of seven hundred and forty-five Frenchmen would be unanimously of that opinion. The inevitable result of this arrangement was that when the critics of the constitution became numerous enough it was forcibly amended by a fresh revolution.

Chapter XI

VARENNES

Madam, all is in your hands. The moment you begin to negotiate with the traitors, you lose your greatest strength, which is wholly in patience, firmness, silence, and refusal. You cannot take an active measure which does not lead to destruction.—(EDMUND BURKE: Sketch of a letter to the Queen of France, 1791.)

BETWEEN October, '89, and June, '91, the revolution seemed to be marking time. Madame Roland found that the text of the Declaration of Rights was still unknown in her village more than a year after its epoch-making publication. The British ambassador reported in February, '90, that two-thirds of the mayors elected by the new municipalities came from the *noblesse*. A revolutionary movement that has ceased to go forward is in effect going back. A close observer might have remarked counter-revolution advancing under cover of reform.

The new constitution was being steadily enacted—here a little and there a little—up to the end of 1790; and the 'patriots' carried every division in the House. But they were already beginning to show signs of the party spirit of '92, the intolerance of '93, and the disillusionment of '94. By the time that their work was finished, few of the deputies felt satisfied with it. The land settlement had become involved in the technicalities of compensation. The Civil Constitution of the clergy had led to a schism. The finance which paid for the revolution produced high prices, inflation, and speculation. The workers were not allowed to combine for the improvement of their condition. Signs began to appear of the first real class-war within the revolutionary state—that between the gainers and the losers under the new regime.

Madame Roland's letters during the spring of '91 are full of lamentations about the corruption of public life, and the incompetence of the government.

PLANS FOR FLIGHT

On hearing of the death of her brother, the Emperor Leopold (March 1st, 1791), Marie-Antoinette sent Goguelat (who afterwards played a part in the flight to Varennes) to the new Emperor, her nephew Francis. She and Louis were so closely watched that they could write no more than these hasty lines to accredit their messenger.

The Jacobin club, she says, is in the hands of a reactionary clique (*bureau*). Even the best of the so-called patriots are men of little ability, more concerned for their private reputations than for the public good. As the revolution lost impetus, and its first genuine but fortuitous enthusiasm gave place to an *ennui* equally characteristic of the nation, the initiative passed to a party in the country which at any rate knew what it wanted, and believed that it might exploit the differences of the rest to secure it. This was the party of reaction or counter-revolution. Its figurehead was the king.

In May, 1790, Louis had expressed himself as gratified to receive from the mayor a medal struck to commemorate his residence in Paris, with the inscription, *J'y ferai désormais ma demeure habituelle.* In fact, he had never reconciled himself to residence at the Tuileries. He missed his hunting, and was too indolent to find other forms of exercise. The royal family had perforce settled down to a regime that they disliked. As much as possible of the routine of Versailles had been re-established. Visitors to the palace found the royal apartments crowded with dukes, bishops, deputies, planters from San Domingo, and Knights of Malta. The king and queen were respectfully greeted by the bourgeois citizens who thronged the royal gardens. Some of the ministers tried to ingratiate themselves with the leaders of the assembly: the Minister of War, La Tour du Pin, entertained them, without their wives, two dozen at a time.

Yet Louis had never really accepted his defeat in the summer of '89. He was still hoping and planning, with the persistence of a weak and stubborn man, to escape from a position which a stronger or a more pliable character would at least have made tolerable. The events of the two years following October, '89, may therefore be studied from the windows of the Tuileries. Their meaning is most easily interpreted as the development, climax, and catastrophe of a counter-revolutionary movement. Its central figure is the king: its main theme is the flight to Varennes.

It was the view of the king's circle at Versailles that he ought to have escaped into the provinces on October 5th. The King of Sweden had confidently instructed his ambassador to follow the court to Fontainebleau. Within ten days of the transference of the royal family to Paris, Mirabeau addressed a *mémoire* to the Comte de Provence urging that Louis was neither free nor safe in the capital, and discussing alternative plans for his escape. He insisted that the king must not go to any such frontier town as Metz: he must do nothing to suggest collusion with the emigrants, or with a foreign power. Rouen had more advantages than Coblentz, and fewer dangers. It was nearer at hand. It was rich, royalist, and ecclesiastical. It controlled the Paris corn supply. It provided an easy means of escape from the country, through Havre, if the king's plans miscarried. At Rouen, once more free, and with his loyal nobility around him, Louis might appeal to the nation, and invite the assembly to join him. He would not undo their work, but he might allow them to consummate it under his leadership.

This memorandum Mirabeau himself described as a *ballon d'essai*. He was probably not surprised when the Comte de Provence told him that not even the queen could persuade Louis to adopt a course which led straight towards civil war. Only a civil war would restore the king's authority, was his uncompromising reply. Did the king shrink from the expense? It could be paid for by promising rewards to faithful supporters of the crown.

Mirabeau's intervention had been dictated both by policy and by ambition. Nearly a year before (December 28th, '88) he had offered Montmorin a plan to save the throne. Every event since the outbreak of the revolution had strengthened his desire to become the king's adviser, and to have his debts paid out of the royal purse. He dreamed of a ministry of all the talents, recruited from the assembly, and including himself as a minister without portfolio. But for the moment his hopes were scotched. Louis rejected his advice, and he could not work with Louis' confidants. Montmorin, the mildest of men, could not forgive the publication of the *Histoire secrète de la cour de Berlin*, and snubbed his advances. Necker's attitude, at a meeting arranged for him by Malouet, made him despair of co-operation. With Lafayette he contrived, during October, a few weeks of stiff and fruitless intercourse.

Upon the top of these disappointments came the decree of November 7th, excluding deputies from office under the crown. This rebuff was the more bitter because Mirabeau had reason to believe that, though moved by Lanjuinais, it had been inspired by one of the king's ministers, the new Lord Privy Seal, Champion de Cicé, Archbishop of Bordeaux. He was, in fact, distrusted by the court and disliked by the Commons. The king could not forget his leadership of the assembly during June and July, or his rumoured connexion with the affair of October 5th. The deputies who had hissed him on May 5th, cheered him on June 23rd: but they could not forgive his domineering ways, and his too evident desire for power. Only a radical change in the situation could put him in a position which no one so much coveted, and no one was so fit to use.

In any case the plan of removal from Paris would have to be reconsidered. The trials for the new crime of *lèse-nation*, conducted, in default of a special court, by the unpopular Châtelet, had revealed plans for a royal flight far less discreet than Mirabeau's, and no less compromising. Augeard, the queen's private secretary (*secrétaire des commandements*), had spent part of his *fermier's* fortune on preparations for a flight to Metz. He was denounced to the *comité des recherches*, tried, and acquitted. The Comte de Maillebois was accused of planning a royal retirement to Lyon. This scheme was to be financed by the Kings of Spain, Naples, and Sardinia; it was to be supported by twenty-five thousand Savoyard troops, the nucleus of an army that would raise the Midi, and march on Paris. Maillebois escaped before trial; his agent, the Chevalier de Bonne-Savardin, was acquitted: perhaps so fantastic a design was hardly taken seriously.

The Marquis de Favras was not so fortunate. Arrested in November, '89, he was charged three months later with plotting to assassinate Bailly, Necker, and Lafayette, to carry the king and queen out of the country, and to bring them back in the train of a foreign army, which would dismiss the assembly, and restore the royal power. If this was the real plot, it was a foolish one: Fersen, the queen's Swedish friend, would have nothing to do with it. Its discovery compromised the court. Rumour accused the king's brother, the Comte de Provence, of being implicated in it. It was in fact known to others besides Lamarck, the king's confidant, who had seen the document, that Favras held a compromising letter from the Comte: Talon, the President of the Châtelet, persuaded him not to use it. Provence took a course which no Bourbon, however liberal, would have dreamed of before 1789. In a speech said to have been dictated by Talleyrand he declared his innocence, and pledged his whole-hearted support of the revolution, before a special meeting of the Paris commune (December 26th).

A month later (February 4th) Louis himself thought it wise to make a speech to the assembly. No mention was made of Favras, Augeard, or Maillebois. His rôle was that of a patriotic and paternal ruler, distressed by recent evidences of counter-revolution. He urged the deputies to persevere in a course of reform which he had himself initiated. He exhorted them to respect the crown, the privileged orders (though now deprived of their privileges) and the national tradition. This too transparent *démarche* was well enough received by the revolutionary press. 'The King,' wrote Brissot, 'is now the head of the revolution.' The mayor took the opportunity to urge Louis to appear more in public, to visit factories, hospitals, and exhibitions, and to show an interest in the concerns of the people. The deputies solemnly renewed their oath of fidelity to Nation, Law, and King. But Mirabeau called it a farce, and his reactionary brother broke his sword, declaring that Louis had broken his sceptre. A royalist attempt to exploit the incident by giving the king special powers to repress disorder was stopped with a decisiveness that showed how little effect the King's apologia had really produced.

Such was the position when Lamarck returned to Paris, after a short absence, in March, 1790. Mirabeau at once resumed his soundings in the shifting channels of royal favour. At the end of April he made up his mind that it was useless to have any more dealings with Lafayette, who seemed to think that the power of the crown could be maintained by a policy of picturesque inaction. A rude and patronizing letter (April 28th) asking for the post of ambassador to the Porte having met with the snub it deserved, he turned from Lafayette to Mercy d'Argenteau, the Austrian ambassador, and offered his services to the French court, in return for a salary and a promise to pay his debts. The salary was to be at the rate of three hundred pounds a month: the debts, which included a tailor's bill at the time of his wedding, twenty years ago, amounted to ten thousand pounds. His terms were accepted. On June 1st he penned two letters. One was a last appeal to Lafayette, in which he adjured him to be another Richelieu, and asked for employment in the rôle of the Capucin agent, Father Joseph. The other was the first of his Notes to the court. In it he described Lafayette as the slave of Paris opinion, and suggested that he should be supplanted by de Bouillé, acting under his own (Mirabeau's) advice.

Such was the interested and ambiguous origin of the series of fifty Notes, which Mirabeau dispatched to the Tuileries every four or five days until the middle of November, '90, and then occasionally until February, '91. It may be doubted whether the transaction benefited anyone so much as the impecunious statesman, who now felt at liberty to enlarge his collection of books, seals, watches, snuff-boxes, and Sèvres porcelain, and to open his lodgings, on an ever-increasing scale of prodigality, for the entertainment of libertines and liberals. If, by the same contract, he gained the privilege of addressing his facile ideas to royal ears, it was without any certainty that they would be attended to. Louis liked perusing projects of all kinds; but he was quite incapable of concentrating his mind on any one of them, or of turning it into action. Nor need it be supposed that Mirabeau was putting any strain upon his political conscience. He accepted payment for saying what he believed.

It was asked then, and may still be a matter for surprise, why Mirabeau could not co-operate with Lafayette—the man of ideas with the man of action, the controller of the National Assembly with the commander of the National Guard. Both believed that the revolution must go on. Both stood for the maintenance of a popular legislature and a royal executive. Both advised the king to throw in his lot with the people, and follow the opinion of the capital. There are passages in Lafayette's correspondence at this time which are at once a reflection and a criticism of Mirabeau's notes to the court. 'Devoted as I am (he writes to Mounier on October 23rd) both from duty and inclination to the popular cause, I shall oppose with equal zeal aristocracy, tyranny, and party spirit. I know the faults of the National Assembly; but it seems to me very dangerous, indeed culpable (*this was Mirabeau's plan*) to discredit it. I hate personal predominance; but I am much more impressed than you are with the necessity of restoring the executive power of the crown. I hold that the only way to avoid civil war (*which Mirabeau would have risked*) is to exploit the present situation, and to work with and through the partnership of the king and the assembly in Paris (*not at Rouen*).'

Sometimes Lafayette was less critical. In a memorandum addressed to the king, and discovered two years later in the 'iron chest' at the Tuileries, he said, 'The establishment of a free constitution, in which every interest is sacrificed to that of the people, is the only hope of safety either for the nation or for the king'; and the advice that he proceeded to give for the cultivation of easy and efficient collaboration between the legislative and executive powers could hardly have failed to win Mirabeau's consent.

F.R.—13

Why then could not the two men co-operate? They had no points of
contact with one another: Mirabeau was a profligate; Lafayette was a prig.
Neither of them would take orders from the other: Mirabeau could not help
domineering; Lafayette could not bear to be outshone. He knew that he
would be at a fatal disadvantage, if he once exchanged his sword and his
white charger for a pen and a desk-chair. There were points in the programme of the mercurial politician that the stolid soldier could not accept.
His honesty rejected the plan to discredit the assembly; his knowledge
of Paris showed him the fatal results of a flight to Rouen; his experience
as a soldier taught him to dread a civil war. In any case the link that
might have bound the two men together was lacking. Both were distrusted and disliked by the king and queen. Their separate services were
unacceptable: they would have been no more acceptable if they had served
together.

The summer of 1790 passed peacefully, if not happily. The king took
Bailly's advice, and appeared more in public. He reviewed his troops on the
Champ de Mars. On June 3rd (the *Fête Dieu*) he walked in a procession
through the streets with the deputies and the National Guard. On May 22nd,
when the assembly deprived the king of his prerogative of declaring war,
the little Dauphin was remarked at a window of the Tuileries, clapping his
hands. Louis' demand for a Civil List allowance of a million and a quarter
sterling was granted almost without question. 'We are all in good health,
thank God,' writes the queen to her brother Leopold, 'and it is a miracle,
considering all our worries, and the frightful scenes we are told of every day,
and often see with our own eyes. We must try to win the confidence of this
unhappy people. Nothing but patience and good intentions will restore our
popularity.'

In June the royal family moved as usual to Saint-Cloud, and stayed
there till October. It was their last holiday in the country. Louis no longer
hunted: he had put down most of his horses and hounds; and the park was
full of poachers, killing off his unprotected game. Not all the beauties of the
place—the lawns, the fountains, or the famous view of Paris—could make
its inhabitants forget the painful past, or ignore the ominous future. Above
all they dreaded another winter in the Tuileries.

All these months a stream of notes from Mirabeau proposed alternative or
supplementary schemes for saving the situation. Now it was an appeal to the
nation, and the possibility of civil war. Now it was an appeal to the army,
with de Bouillé as adviser in place of Lafayette. In one note he would suggest the formation of a royalist party in the assembly; in another the removal
of the court to Fontainebleau; in another the influencing of public opinion
in the king's favour by journalistic propaganda. Always the same object is in
view—to restore the king's executive power; for 'to manage is to rule, and
to rule is to reign' (*administrer, c'est gouverner: gouverner, c'est regner*).
Bright-eyed ideas popped in and out of Mirabeau's brain, like rabbits in a

hedgerow. The court liked to see them play, but made no attempt to catch them.

It was in the gardens at Saint-Cloud, on July 3rd, that Mirabeau had his one interview with the queen, and went away (if the partial Madame Campan is to be trusted) with the remark, 'Madame, the monarchy is saved.' Marie-Antoinette was agitated by the meeting, but satisfied with it. In her heart of hearts she thought little of Mirabeau or of his plans. She hoped to save the monarchy by foreign help; and she preferred the company of the handsome Swedish officer, Count Axel von Fersen, who had been admitted privately to the Tuileries once or twice a week during the previous autumn, and might now be seen riding in the park at Saint-Cloud.

The Franco-Swedish alliance of the seventeenth century, and companionship in arms during the wars of the eighteenth century, had led to the formation of a *Royal-Suédois* regiment, and to the residence of a series of young Swedish noblemen at Versailles. Always candidates for court favour, it was believed that they were at this time candidates also for the hand of the wealthy daughter of the Controller of Finance. Like Stedinck and de Stael (who was in fact successful in marrying Mlle Necker) Fersen had been kindly received by the queen. Marie-Antoinette preferred foreigners to Frenchmen, and was attracted to Fersen by features of an almost feminine beauty, and a Byronic blend of passion and melancholy which lesser women had already found irresistible.

Fersen began by admiring the queen of France, and ended by loving Marie-Antoinette, as well as he was able to love anyone but himself. His letters to his sister describe on his side a comradeship hardly to be distinguished from courtship, and on her side a pleasure in his company that might easily become a passion. 'I see her occasionally,' he writes, 'quite informally in her own apartments, and it comforts us a little for the trouble she is in. Poor soul! her conduct, her courage, and her sympathy are angelic. Never was such affection!' He asks his sister to send three dozen Scanian gloves of the finest quality, and of a special size: the price is no object. Can they really be, as he tells her, for the Queen of Spain? Later he sends his sister a lock of the queen's hair. 'She is so kind and perfect (he adds): I think I love her all the more now that she loves you too.'

With the coming of winter, and the return to Paris, things took a more alarming turn. It was with the greatest reluctance that Louis sanctioned the Civil Constitution of the clergy, which the Pope told him was the work of Protestants disguised as philosophers. He was too irresolute to prevent a measure that he detested. He was too stubborn to pretend that he approved of it. He would receive constitutional bishops as though they were nothing more than state officials. He would turn his back on his parish *curé*, who had taken the oath. He would scheme to make his Easter confession, and receive his Easter communion, at the hands of a non-juror priest. Such conduct only made Louis more unpopular, and strengthened public feeling against the refractory clergy. His ministers were forced to resign, under pressure of a campaign started by the Paris sections, and were replaced by nominees of Lafayette (Duportail, the new War Minister) and of the Lameths (Duport-Dutertre, Keeper of the Seals). It was evident that little value attached to the king's constitutional rights in face of a popular agitation. Public opinion, as Madame Roland reminded her friend Bosc, had made the revolution, and public opinion would save it. If only the people had arms!

There was little now to lighten the gloom behind the curtains of the Tuileries. 'Our health is still good,' writes Marie-Antoinette again; 'but it would be better, if we could see a gleam of happiness in our surroundings. For ourselves there is no more hope of it, whatever happens. It is a king's duty, I know, to suffer for others; and, heaven knows, we are doing it to the full. Perhaps some day people will realize this.' The isolation of the royal family was increased in September by the departure of Mercy d'Argenteau, and its apprehensions by the arrival in Paris two months later of the woman Lamotte, the victim of the unfortunate 'necklace case.' She had evidently been brought to plague the king and queen.

There is now a new urgency in Mirabeau's proposals. His defence of the crowd which sacked the Duc de Castries' house, after his duel with Charles de Lameth (November 13th), has made him a popular hero, and given his ambition a fresh range. He is terribly overworked. He receives a hundred letters a day, and innumerable pamphlets. He is employing several secretaries to prepare his speeches for the assembly. Yet he finds time to send the court seven notes in September, and eleven in October. All are variations on the theme of a new ministry, excluding Necker and Lafayette, and directed by himself. Ministry-making has by this time almost become a parlour game in the Parisian *salons*. Lists are passing from hand to hand. Names are eagerly canvassed.

Necker, indeed, has excluded himself. The king no longer consults him. His opposition to paper money, and his refusal to publish the royal pension list (*livre rouge*) have lost him the confidence of the assembly. Early in October, '90, the hero of the summer of '89 is driven out of the country by threats of popular violence. 'He is abused by all parties,' writes his friend Gibbon, 'and none of the French at Geneva will set their foot in his house.' Lafayette—'Simple Cæsar' (*Gilles-César*), Choiseul called him; and Mirabeau has elaborated the witticism—is discouraged, and might easily be discredited. He reports 'a long and useless talk' with the queen. He has no influence now at court. His prestige among the general public depends upon opportunities of military intervention. There is always the risk that they may carry him too far, and make him unpopular with the crowd. It would not be beyond the wit of Mirabeau to bring about such a situation, in order to remove his rival. According to Gouverneur Morris, who talked to Lafayette on November 25th (the American was just back from London with a

Newfoundland dog for the Duchess of Orléans, and a new copper leg), he suspects just such an intrigue, and might even counter it by contriving a situation to his own advantage.   In any case, Mirabeau cannot take his place so long as the decree of November 7th stands.

The constituent assembly, thinks Mirabeau, is becoming so unpopular that perhaps it might be dismissed. Alternatively, now that the constitution is practically ready, it will soon be dissolved, and the elections can be so managed as to secure the return of a royalist majority in the new legislature. This is the policy outlined by Montmorin in a conversation with Mirabeau reported in the note of December 6th. Mirabeau clasps Montmorin's hand, 'not as a minister, but as a man of honour,' and promises to help him with all the means in his power. He sets to work at once on the forty-seventh note, and presents it on December 23rd.

It is his longest and most elaborate analysis of the situation, and a compilation of all the plans he has thought of to deal with it. Paris, he says, is so incendiary that there is no remedy but to isolate it from the rest of the country. A new military force must be organized in the provinces to counteract the 'Jacobin' National Guard. The assembly cannot be controlled: it must therefore be discredited, dismissed, and replaced by another of more royalist tendencies. The constitution must be revised in the king's interests. In order to carry out this plan, centres of propaganda (ateliers), must be organized, to prepare the ground among the police, the press, the assembly, and the provinces.

The scheme was stillborn. Mirabeau's anti-clerical speeches during the debates on the Civil Constitution of the clergy so offended his friends at court that it had to be supposed that they concealed a design to discredit the assembly, and hurry on its dissolution. His attacks on the ministers offended even his friend Lamarck, who found him more and more difficult to deal with. Mercy d'Argenteau thought the great plan too complicated to carry out. Talon, one of its chief agents, tried to explain it to the court. He found the king listless, the queen bored, and Montmorin too feeble to play any effective part. Mirabeau himself was discouraged. He had sometimes wondered why he went on giving advice to which no attention was paid. He saw that unless he changed his tactics he would soon be discarded by the king. He feared that he might have to sell his books in order to pay his debts. He accepted posts in the Paris department and in the National Guard, which added little to his income, and much to his disfavour at court. On February 3rd, after one more fruitless meeting with Lafayette, he penned his final note.

Two months later, to a day, Mirabeau died, worn out by excesses both of body and mind. The deputies voted him a grave in Soufflot's still unfinished masterpiece, under the dome of Sainte-Geneviève, or, as it was now re-named, the national Panthéon. He was the first Frenchman thought worthy to lie under the proud inscription, *Aux grands hommes, la Patrie reconnais-*

sante. His funeral was followed by a vast crowd of common citizens, who rightly honoured his leadership in the summer of '89, his immortal gesture of June 23rd, and his untiring championship of the revolution. It was not they, but lesser demagogues—a Marat, a Fréron, and a Desmoulins—who would look askance at his moral character, or resent his domineering manner, or grudge him the royal favour that paid his debts. So popular was Mirabeau in the provinces that the artists of the Lyon mint issued trial-pieces with his head in place of that of the king, and with the inscription *Le Démosthènes françois*. No other Frenchman was so honoured. If some critics, since his day, have doubted the greatness of the statesman, few have denied the genius of the man. But the deputies' instinct was right, when they barred his way to the ministry. His idea of the revolution was not theirs. If he had lived, he would have been one of the first victims of the Terror.

Mirabeau, then, as the pious Madame Elisabeth bitterly remarked, 'had gone to another world, to see if the revolution was approved of there.' It was not without significance for the court—it deprived them at the same time of a second source of advice—that Montmorin was forced to pay off the staff of the *cabinet noir*, or postal censorship, upon which Louis, like his predecessors, had relied for secret information from all over Europe. The censors were old men: their average age was sixty-six, and several of them had spent over forty years in the office. But the assembly saw its way to saving a salary-list of eight thousand pounds a year, and the Diplomatic Committee thought that it could do without them. Montmorin was careful to preserve the papers and paraphernalia of the department. They might be wanted again. It was perhaps a loss to the country as well as to the king that Intelligence should now depend upon the casual services of hired spies.

During the last two months of his life Mirabeau had been engaged with Lamarck and de Bouillé in working out plans for a withdrawal of the king, under armed escort, to Compiègne or Fontainebleau. But this was not the only scheme on foot. As soon as Mirabeau was dead, the king and queen turned back with relief to another, and, as they believed, a better plan than any he had put forward. They would escape from Paris to the north-eastern frontier, and appeal to the Catholic princes of Europe to restore them to freedom and power. Whether this plan would necessitate the use of arms, either French or foreign; whether the National Assembly need be dissolved, or merely coerced; or what kind of settlement should be imposed on the country—these were questions which might be discussed in letters to the King of Spain, or to the Austrian ambassador. They seemed of little importance beside the urgent and personal craving for liberty.

A king is always a prisoner, though his cell be walled with flattery, and barred with gold. In the old days Louis had been able to escape for a while to Gamain's workshop, or to the royal kennels. It was with difficulty that he now reconciled himself to the crowded and uncomfortable domesticity of the Tuileries. Though Paris gossip reported that at this anxious time (March, '91) he was eating a prodigious dinner, sleeping heavily, and perusing the royalist *Postillon de Calais*, he was in reality longing to get away.

The king, Montmorin himself told Morris, was absolutely good for nothing, and it was no use trying to do business with him unless the queen were by his side. The queen, in every fibre of her being, was a rebel and a prison-breaker. From the moment of her arrival in France she had struggled against the etiquette of the court. She had made her own friends, and her own fashions. She had put aside duties of state to indulge her day-dreams—child as she still was—in the doll's-house rusticity of the Petit Trianon. The prisoner of a loveless marriage, and of a sickly family, the partner of a throne she hated, and of a husband she could not respect, she was now doubly entrapped in a city that loathed her, and in a revolution that she did not try to understand. Little wonder that memories of Schönbrunn and Vienna mixed with a desire for the quiet cool leisure of Versailles. Little wonder that she turned from the common disdainful Parisians who thronged the *salons* of the Tuileries to almost any foreign face—the romantic Fersen, the kindly Mrs Swinburne, or Thomas Blaikie, the devoted Scotch gardener. Little wonder that she rejected Mirabeau's dubious Rouen expedient, with its alien background of Dover cliffs and Kent hop-fields, in favour of Montmédy, the Rhine valley, and an Austrian army.

All through the winter and spring of '90–91 plans were being made. The Marquis de Bouillé, in command of the troops at Metz, Mercy-d'Argenteau and de Breteuil at Brussels, and the Comte de Fersen in Paris were the principal actors. The scheme was concealed from the ministers, even the faithful Montmorin, but was known to de Bouillé's agent, the Duc de Choiseul, to the Bishop of Pamiers and the Comte de Lamarck, who acted as King's messengers, and to Quentin Craufurd, a rich Scot who was spending a fortune made at Manila and Madras in amassing an art collection in Paris. Craufurd's mistress, Mrs Sullivan, allowed part of his house and of her favours to his friend Fersen. Craufurd lent his purse and his stables to the queen's cause, and was rewarded with her friendship.

Amongst others whom she took into her confidence or entrusted with her service was the Spanish ambassador, the Count de Fernan Nuñez. Louis had no secrets from his Catholic cousin, the King of Spain. As early as October 12th, '89, he had deposited with him two important documents. One was a 'solemn protest' against all acts contrary to the royal authority forced upon him since July 15th. The other was a statement of his intention to carry out the promises made in his declaration of June 23rd: that was to stand as his ultimatum to the French people. Besides, Spanish money, if not Spanish arms, had always been essential to any foreign intervention in France; and Spanish influence was constantly needed to restrain the indiscretions of the Comte d'Artois and his friends across the frontier.

So now (January 5th, '91) the queen sends for Nuñez, and tells him of her plans. The schemes of the Bourbon princes, she says, supported by this or that isolated power, can do nothing but exasperate the assembly, and endanger the royal family. Spain, Switzerland, Sardinia, and the Empire must act together. A threat of arms will be enough: it need not come to fighting. But, to make the threat effective, Louis must first escape to the Rhine frontier, where he will be within reach of his rescuers, and they will be within striking distance of Paris. Nuñez shook his head over this plan. He feared that, once arms were invoked, it would be almost impossible to avoid a frontier incident, and a civil war. He recognized that the queen was 'a desperate woman, at the end of her tether'; yet he doubted whether she would find anyone at court capable of carrying out her designs.

Perhaps nothing more would have been done, but for certain happenings during the following months. On February 4th the king's orthodox aunts, Madame Adelaide and Madame Victoire, their Catholic feelings outraged by the Civil Constitution, asked for passports to Rome. Their departure on the 20th caused fresh rumours of a flight from the Tuileries. So great was the alarm that they were stopped on their way by the municipal authorities of Arnay-le-Duc, as Necker had been stopped, the year before, at Arcis-sur-Aube, whilst the assembly hotly debated the issue. Maury claimed their liberty to leave the country. It was a right guaranteed to every citizen by *Titre I* of the Constitution. At last, unwillingly, the deputies allowed them to proceed.

This success encouraged the queen to think that escape, if carefully planned, would not be impossible; and she was soon busy sending out of the country some fifty thousand pounds in cash, together with jewellery and notes of exchange. On February 19th Lamarck returned from a mission to de Bouillé at Metz and reported that the omens were propitious for the attempt. There was much political discontent, he said, amongst the country-people on that side of Paris, and the queen herself was not unpopular. De Bouillé was Prussian rather than Austrian in his sympathies, and no common counter-revolutionary; but he could be relied on to help in the escape.

It was still not too late to draw back, and to conciliate the revolution, instead of defying it. As late as February 21st the queen and the royal children received an ovation at the theatre. On the very eve of the flight (May 25th) Morris wrote to Montmorin that, if the royal family could endure for another month or two, all would be well. But ten days after Lamarck's return (Feburary 28th) occurred the disquieting incident nicknamed the *journée des poignards* (Dagger Day). The Paris municipality had just voted a large sum for the restoration of the *donjon* of Vincennes, so that it might take some of the prisoners from the overcrowded Châtelet. This establishment was regarded by its inmates (of whom Mirabeau had been one) as a *pension* rather than a prison—a Hampton Court, not a Tower of London; but in the popular mind it ranked with its fellow-monument of feudalism, the

Bastille, and deserved the same fate. There was a story that it was connected
with the Tuileries by an underground passage, and that it might be used to
facilitate a royal flight. The march of a mob to Vincennes was magnified by
rumour into another July 14th, or October 5th. The Tuileries was soon
filled with enthusiastic nobles, some of whom brought arms to defend the
king.

Lafayette hurried back from the arrest of sixty-four rioters to arrest eight
royalists, and to rebuke the Duc de Villequier, who was responsible for
admission to the Tuileries. An English traveller saw him there, 'mounted
on his white charger, galloping to and fro, as if the fate of the world depended
on him.' Paris was beginning to make fun of him. His throne was as insecure
as his master's. The people took the *journée des poignards* as an abortive
attempt at a royal flight. The pamphleteers took it as a plot to murder the
patriots. The court took it as a hint that escape could not be much longer
delayed. Their purpose was confirmed by the debate on the Regency clauses
of the constitution (March 22nd–25th), when it seemed that the hereditary
monarchy itself was in danger.

The Saint-Cloud affair, three weeks later (April 18th) was decisive.
On the 15th four convent churches in Paris had been closed by the police,
as the result of a public protest against their use by refractory clergy. Louis
refused to take the hint. He would stand by the toleration the law allowed,
whatever Paris might say. On Palm Sunday, two days later, he persisted in
hearing mass said by a non-juror priest in the chapel of the Tuileries. The
presence of Bailly and Lafayette did little to mitigate this indiscretion. When
a patriot sentry was dismissed for protesting, his case was taken up by the
Cordeliers club, and in the popular press.

The following day Louis had planned to take the royal family to Saint-
Cloud. His recent illness might excuse an early beginning of the usual summer holiday. At Saint-Cloud he could make his Easter confession to a refractory priest, and receive his Easter communion without risk of public interference. He had taken the advice of the Bishop of Clermont. But he had not
reckoned with the tenacious common sense of the capital, which saw nothing
in his conscientious manœuvres but counter-revolution, and took his journey as another attempt at flight. He had not asked for an armed escort, which
would have given the journey official sanction. A riotous crowd surrounded
the carriage in which the royal family tried to leave the inner court of the
palace, and for over two hours would not let it proceed. For over two hours
Louis persisted in his attempt. Bailly and Lafayette harangued the crowd in
vain. The *Gardes soldés* of the Oratoire section refused to intervene, and
paid no more attention to their mayor than to their general. At last the
royal party returned defeated to their rooms in the palace. A harsh letter
from the Paris department, now under the influence of Talleyrand, warned
the king that on this issue the whole country was against him.

After April 18th there could be no question that the king and queen were as truly prisoners as any wretch who lay in the dungeons of the Châtelet. As cunningly they perfected the plans for their escape. The first thing was to pretend acquiescence in their lot. On the 19th Louis appeared before the assembly, and protested his loyalty to the Civil Constitution. On the 23rd a note from Montmorin instructed his diplomatic representatives in every court of Europe to deny the report that he was not a free agent, and that he had been forced to accept the constitution of '91 against his will.

If there are any limits to what a good man will do for the sake of his conscience, Louis must have had some qualms when he signed this document. 'The enemies of the Constitution '—thus it ran—'constantly repeat that the king is not happy; as though a king could enjoy any happiness but that of his people! They say his authority is set at naught; as if authority based on force were not less powerful and sure than that based on law! They say the king is not free; a cruel calumny, to imagine that his will can ever have been coerced, and an absurd one, if it is supposed that there is any lack of liberty in the king's free consent, so often expressed, to remain amongst the citizens of Paris, in deference to their patriotism, their submission, and their affection!'

Exactly how little this declaration meant may be judged from a letter the queen had written to Mercy d'Argenteau only three days before. 'This last incident,' she says, referring to the Saint-Cloud affair, 'makes us more than ever determined to go on with our plan. We must behave as though we were giving way in everything, until we are ready to act. Our imprisonment shows that we are not free in anything we do. But before we act we must know for certain whether you can find some excuse to move fifteen thousand men to Arlon and Virton, and the same number to Mons. M. de Bouillé is very anxious for this to be done, as it would give him a reason for mobilizing troops and munitions at Montmédy.'

A month later (May 22nd), in reply to difficulties raised by the Emperor, she outlines the now completed plan. 'We are to go to Montmédy. M. de Bouillé has made himself responsible for the provision of troops and munitions at that place. But'—and how ominously the plan has developed!— 'he is very anxious that you should give orders for a body of eight or ten thousand men to be at Luxembourg, under our orders, but of course not till we are in safety, to march on Paris (*entrer ici*: what else can it mean but an invasion of France?), both as an example and as a restraint to our own troops. I have written about this several times to M. de Mercy; but, though he can order troops to the frontier, he cannot sanction their march on Paris (*les laisser entrer ici*) without your leave. The time is getting very short, and I hope you will give your orders at once.'

Leopold's answer, dated only ten days before the flight, makes it quite clear what the plan implies. Till the royal family are in safety, he will make no compromising move, and will prevent the princes from doing so. But 'if the plan succeeds (he writes), and if you ask him, Mercy has orders to help you, and to supply all you want. Money, troops, everything is at your disposal.' The place of refuge is now not Montmédy, but the neighbouring *château* of Thonelle, still half a day's journey from the frontier. It is surrounded by an armed camp, and Austrian troops are a few miles away. Once he is there, Louis' first step will be to dismiss the assembly, and to restore the property of the church. This will at one blow destroy the political and financial credit of the revolution. There may then (it is admitted) be a pause, to await the result of these measures. If they are not successful, the next step will be to march on Paris at the head of an Austrian army.

All this would take time, and involve a long absence. The preparations for the flight were therefore elaborate and costly. The Emperor had been asked to advance three-quarters of a million sterling; but he had refused to do so. In addition to the money she had already sent to Austria, the queen supplied Fersen with seventy-five thousand pounds. This he supplemented with thirty thousand of his own, fifteen thousand borrowed from Craufurd, and twelve thousand from his friends Madame Stegelmann and her daughter, the Baronne de Korff. In later years he tried in vain to recover these debts from Leopold's parsimonious successor. The accounts of the king's Civil List shows that this source, too, contributed to the expenses of the flight. A hundred thousand pounds were drawn out between January and May, in addition to another sixty thousand borrowed from a friendly banker, Duruey. Even so, the date of departure was postponed till the payment (due on June 12th) of the next quarterly instalment of the King's stipend of a million and a quarter a year: and Louis drew out a final thirty-six thousand pounds on the 18th. The flight was postponed again, more than once, for other reasons. Now the queen could not trust one of the servants who took turns of duty at the palace. Now it was necessary to allow time for the movement of Austrian troops towards the frontier. But these delays did not compromise the plans, which had been carefully laid, and which, in this respect, little deserved their disastrous end.

At six o'clock on the evening of Monday, June 20th, Fersen left the palace for the last time. The final arrangements had been made for escape that night. The queen was in tears. The king said—'M. de Fersen, whatever happens, I shall not forget all that you have done for me.' An hour later Fersen went to Craufurd's house, to see that the travelling-coach was ready to carry the royal family to the frontier. At eight o'clock he wrote a last note to the queen, asking her to change the rendezvous for the two *femmes-de-chambre* who were to accompany her. He left the note himself at the palace, and found all quiet there. At 8.45 he gave final instructions to the three *gardes-du-corps* who were also going with the party.

At a quarter past ten, an hour before the appointed time, Fersen, dressed as a cab-driver, brought an inconspicuous hired carriage round to the Cour des Princes at the back of the south wing of the Tuileries. There had been persistent rumours of escape, and a warning was received only two days before from one of the queen's maids. A special guard had therefore been set. Bailly the mayor of Paris and Gouvion the commandant of the palace guard were spending the night in the building. Officers were on duty at every turn. But one door had been left unguarded. It was in the south-east corner of the palace, and it led through the private quarters of the Duc de Villequier by an unlighted passage (*corridor noir*) into the royal apartments. It had been discovered and investigated by the police at the time of the *journée des poignards*; but apparently no further action had been taken. Fersen had frequently used it during the last few weeks. Now it was cautiously opened, and the royal children slipped out to the waiting carriage—Madame Royale ('Amélie'), and the Dauphin, dressed as a girl ('Aglae'), with their governess, Madame de Tourzel, who passed as the Baronne de Korff. At this moment Lafayette drove past, on his way to the king's *coucher*, but noticed nothing.

Three-quarters of an hour later, after driving round the quays, Fersen returned—this time to the Petit Carrousel, at the north end of the Tuileries—and picked up Madame Elisabeth. She was dressed as a nursery-maid, and called 'Rosalie.' A little later, when he had got rid of Lafayette, and was thought to be safe in bed, the king himself slipped out of the palace, dressed as a valet ('Durand') in a grey coat and wig. Last, after an anxious time of waiting, came the queen; she passed as the children's governess, 'Madame Rocher.' It was now midnight. It took another hour, and more—for it would have been dangerous to appear in a hurry, and Fersen drove by a round-about route, in order to make a final call at his stables in the rue Saint-Honoré—to traverse the dark clattering streets to the *barrière* Saint-Martin. Here the travelling-coach was waiting.

Carlyle's misleading narrative makes such play with this 'huge leathern vehicle—huge Argosy, or Acapulco-ship,' that it is as well to know what it really was:—a big, but not unusually big, four-horsed *berline*, built to the Baronne de Korff's orders at a cost of three hundred pounds. Far from 'lumbering along with its mountains of band boxes,' it was fitted with the bare necessities for a long journey, and moved, not at 'a snail's pace,' but at seven miles an hour. A three-horsed *cabriolet*, carrying the two *femmes-de-chambre*, Madame Brigny and Madame Fourville, had gone ahead as far as Claye, the second posting-stage on the road to Chalons. The Comte de Moustier ('Melchior') was on the box of the *berline*, with Fersen by his side. M. de Valory ('François') rode ahead, to make sure that the relays were ready. The Comte de Malden ('Jean') jumped up behind. Fersen's own coachman, Balthasar Sapel, rode as postilion on one of the leaders. The whole party was covered by a duplicate passport for Frankfort issued to the Baronne de Korff, Fersen's Russian friend, by the Foreign Office, at the request of the Russian ambassador, who accepted her statement that the original document had been accidentally destroyed. They were a conspicuous company, over-conspicuous perhaps, for speed or secrecy, on a road frequented by emigrants. But rich foreigners might be excused for travelling eccentrically.

At half-past one, already an hour late, they set out on their first hundred miles' journey to Chalons. At Bondy, a few miles outside Paris, Fersen left them, very unwillingly, while it was still dark, to make his own escape on horseback to Mons (where he would meet Craufurd) and to Arlon, where he hoped to rejoin the king, on the German side of the frontier. At Claye the coach caught up the *cabriolet*, which followed it for the rest of the journey.

All that long summer day—the longest of the year—they jolted and rattled on, along the hot, dusty high-road, stopping only a minute or two at the posting-stages to change horses. They took what meals they could in their crowded quarters: sometimes the children got out to walk up a hill. At Meaux the sun rose, and their hopes rose with it: but the day remained overcast until the evening. At Etoges, beyond Montmirail, between nine and ten, another hour was lost through an accident to the horses, and a broken trace. But they pushed on through the heat of the day, and about four o'clock bumped over the *pavé* into Chalons. To stop and change horses in so large a town, where the king might well be known by sight, was a risk that the fugitives could not avoid, and chiefly feared. They were, in fact, recognized; but the mayor shrank from the responsibility of stopping them. It was not till six hours later, after consulting the district and departmental authorities, that he reported their flight to the assembly at Paris. The travellers knew nothing of this, and went on, almost light-heartedly.

They were now within reach of armed protection. Contrary to the wishes of Fersen, who feared that any use of troops might lead to trouble, de Bouillé had stationed bodies of cavalry at various points on the route east of Chalons, with instructions to safeguard a convoy of treasure on its way to the frontier. The movements of these detachments had been carefully co-ordinated. The first was to meet the coach at Pont-de-Somme-Vesle, a small post-house eleven miles beyond Chalons. It was under the command of the Duc de Choiseul, a royalist officer of wealth and pedigree, chosen against the advice of Fersen, who thought him too young and indiscreet. He had travelled from Paris ahead of the king, to take over his command. Miscalculating the speed of the coach, and making no allowance for contingencies, he assumed that the king would arrive at half-past two. He waited till four o'clock, and then made three fatal mistakes. He did not wait for Valory, the out-rider, who was to bring news of any change of plan. He withdrew his cavalry up the road eastwards, in front of the travellers. Worst of all, he sent ahead Léonard, the royal *perruquier*, who had come with him from Paris, to tell the troops further along the road that the convoy would not arrive to-night. Thus, when the tired travellers reached Pont-de-Somme-Vesle, there were no troops to meet them.

They were now entering a district where the country-people, always hostile to *aristos*, had grown unusually suspicious of late because so many emigrants were making for the frontier. Between six and seven-thirty they pushed on another fifteen miles to the little town of Sainte-Ménehould. Here de Bouillé had stationed a detachment of dragoons under D'Andoins. But this officer, misled by Léonard's message, had ordered his men to unsaddle, only half an hour before the coach arrived. The place was in a state of ferment. A second body of cavalry, under Goguelat, had entered the town the same day, without warning the municipality, and without sounding the customary fanfare. The authorities were alarmed, and took the opportunity to order out the Town Guard—three hundred men newly armed and uniformed—for their first parade. Whilst the coach-horses were being changed, there was some confusion and delay. The king and queen incautiously showed themselves, and were recognized. Jean-Baptiste Drouet, the posting-master (*maître de poste*) an ex-dragoon of Condé's regiment, happened to return at this moment from working in the fields, and identified the king from his head on the *assignats* with which he was paid for the relay. The alarm spread. When the coach moved on, D'Andoins' men were prevented from following it. One of them, named Lagache, cut his way through the crowd: but he lost the road, and did not arrive at the next stage, Clermont, till eleven o'clock at night. The municipal authorities of Sainte-Ménehould were of a different stamp from those of Chalons. They at once despatched Drouet, and one of their own men named Guillaume, to ride after the fugitives.

At Clermont was stationed another detachment of cavalry, under an officer named Damas. They too were allowed to unsaddle half an hour before the coach arrived. They too were prevented from following, when it drove on. One of them, too, Rémy by name, forced his way out of the place, with a few companions: but he missed the turning to Varennes, and rode on along the main route to Verdun.

Meanwhile Drouet and Guillaume, before they reached Clermont, met the postilions returning with the old relay of horses. These men had heard the order given to the postilions who took over from them, *à Varennes*. Varennes is a small town lying ten miles north of the main road to Verdun, at a point where the side-road to Montmédy dips steeply into the valley of the Aire. Hearing this news, Drouet and Guillaume jumped their horses off the road, galloped across country by a short cut that no carriage could have taken, and dropped into the sleeping town, only a little ahead of the royal coach, as the church clock struck a quarter past eleven. With the help of the landlord of the Bras d'Or, and four of his guests, who were just going home for the night, they blocked the bridge at the foot of the hill with a cart full of furniture that happened to be standing there; they armed themselves as best they could; and they prepared to stop the coach at a point where the street was spanned by an archway between the church and the bell-tower of Saint-Gengoult.

They would hardly have had time to do this, had not further mischances befallen the fugitives. Varennes was off the main route, and had no post-house. It had therefore been arranged that fresh horses, paid for by Choiseul, should be ready at the top of the hill at the near end of the town. The travellers spent more than half an hour looking for them. They were not there. Goguelat had moved them to the *hôtel* Grand Monarque, beyond the bridge, at the further end of the town. Here they were waiting, in charge of Charles de Bouillé (a son of the Marquis) and another officer named Raigecourt. Close by was a detachment of hussars under a junior officer named Rohrig.

A messenger was sent to the top of the hill; but he rode past the royal party, and told them nothing. The king's *gardes-du-corps* walked down the hill to look for the horses, but did not cross the bridge. The two officers, waiting at their window at the Grand Monarque, heard a disturbance, but did not trouble to investigate it. The postilions who had brought the coach from Clermont had instructions not to take the horses beyond the entrance to Varennes, because the post-mistress wanted them for carrying hay the next morning. At last they were persuaded to drive on down the hill. When they came to the archway, they were halted by the small group of armed men. The mayor was away, in Paris; but Sauce, the *procureur* of the commune, exercised his authority to stop the travellers, and to demand their passports. The fugitives were forced to alight within a few hundred yards of De Bouillé's horses and Rohrig's hussars, who could have carried them into safety.

Exhausted by nearly twenty-four hours' continuous travel, and worried by the failure of their plans, the royal family let themselves be taken to a room over Sauce's grocery. There Louis admitted to Destez, a local judge, who had been roused from sleep to identify him, that he was indeed the king. Even now a rescue might have been attempted. Choiseul, Damas, and Goguelat were in the town, with more than fifty of their men. Rohrig had ridden off: but his detachment, under Boudet, should not have found it difficult to force a way through the local Guard. Unluckily Louis had passed into his habitual mood of apathy, and dread of violence. He would give no orders till de Bouillé came; and none of the officers dared carry him off by force.

But de Bouillé was not coming. After waiting most of the night by the roadside beyond Varennes, ready at any moment to ride into the town, he returned to Stenay, and heard nothing of what had happened until four o'clock in the morning. Nevertheless the last chance of rescue came from this side. By one of Goguelat's blunders Rohrig's superior in command, an officer named D'Eslon, had been recalled from Varennes. At five o'clock he came up again with a fresh body of hussars, ignored Louis' refusal to give orders, and tried to concert with Boudet an attack on the Town Guard. But his message went astray; and Boudet's men were already drinking and fraternizing with the patriots. At eight o'clock Charles de Bouillé rode up with more men, half an hour after the king had started back for Paris. When the Marquis himself arrived, with the main body of cavalry, the coach was already two hours on its journey to the capital.

Louis' indecision wrote *Finis* to a chapter of accidents for none of which, perhaps, he was to blame. If any one of a score of mistakes had not been made, he might have escaped, and history would have taken a different turn. If two hours had not been lost during the first part of the journey; if Choiseul had waited a little longer at Pont-de-Somme-Vesle, or if he had not sent Léonard on to say that the coach was not coming; if Goguelat had sounded his trumpets when he entered Saint-Ménehould; or if the king and queen had not shown themselves there; if Drouet had not come back from work at that moment; if D'Andoins had followed the coach, or if Lagache had not lost his way; if Damas had waited another half hour before unsaddling, or if Rémy had not missed the turning to Varennes; if the order to the postilions at Clermont had not been overheard; if Goguelat had left the relay at the place arranged; or if the post-mistress had not wanted her horses for carrying hay; if young de Bouillé's messenger had stopped the coach, or if the *gardes du corps* had crossed the bridge; if D'Eslon's message had reached Boudet; if de Bouillé had waited longer by the roadside; or if any of the cavalry officers had shown a little more determination; then the flight to Varennes might have been the escape from France.

Now it was too late. The tocsin was rung, the citizens roused, the entrances of the town barred. During the night the place filled with peasantry from the country round—five thousand, perhaps ten thousand of them—anxious to see and to secure the king. At two in the morning the municipal authorities sent off young Mangin, a local doctor—his father, a native of Varennes, was deputy for Sedan—to ride to Paris, to report the king's arrest, and to ask what was to be done. At six o'clock there arrived two emissaries from the National Assembly; they had ridden after the fugitives, and carried orders for their return to the capital. At half-past seven no further delay was possible, and the long journey began all over again.

Meanwhile the Comte de Provence and his wife, after dining as usual at the Tuileries on the evening of June 20th, had set out by another road, travelling as the Stegelmann family, with a passport provided in the same way as the king's, and had safely reached the Belgian frontier. So fate set the stage for the succession of Louis XVIII.

Chapter XII

REPUBLICANISM

I am now a wanderer again in this kingdom, and it may be supposed, able to form, if not to give to my English friends, some idea of a great kingdom *bouleversé*, as it certainly is, but whether for the better or worse, the wisest man living is as yet unable to determine. I can compare it at present to nothing more like than Montgolfier's balloon; it is a great and astonishing elevated spectacle, at which strangers and natives look up, without being able to determine to what height it will ascend, or where or when it will settle.—(PHILIP THICKNESSE, Paris, July 19th, 1791.)

EARLY on the morning of June 21st, 1791, a rumour began to go round the capital that the king had fled. Parisians had heard this so often during the last few weeks that they thought little of it. But at ten o'clock the firing of three alarm guns told them that it was true. Soon the streets were full of excited crowds. Some hurried to the Tuileries, to stare at the closed doors, and the sentries still at their posts. Some thronged round the *manège*, to see what the deputies would do. Some busied themselves tearing down from the shop-fronts and street-corners every name and emblem of royalty.

At the Town Hall Bailly announced that he had been informed of the flight since seven o'clock, and had already reported it to the President of the assembly, and to the departmental directory. The commune at once issued a proclamation. The king, it said, had been carried off (*enlevé*), but it was not yet known in what direction. The citizens were asked to remain calm, and to keep their lights burning, when night fell, as a safeguard against disorder. During that day—the first of five days' continuous session—a number of emergency measures were taken. Regulations were made as to passports and police. Seals were placed on the royal apartments at the Tuileries and the Luxembourg. Investigation was made into the cellars (*catacombes*) under the royal palace. Servants of the royal household and other suspected persons were protected by arrest from the more dangerous attentions of the sections.

The National Assembly, not knowing as yet which way the fugitives had gone, sent couriers into every department to close the frontiers, and to prohibit the export of specie or arms. It issued a proclamation calling for public confidence. It authorized the raising of an emergency force of a hundred thousand paid volunteers. It directed the ministers for the present to carry out its commands, under the direction of the Diplomatic Committee. It ordered the Minister of Justice to stamp its decrees with the seal of state, which Louis had lacked the resolution either to take with him, or to throw into the Seine. The deputies rightly earned praise for their dignity and calm in face of the sudden crisis. Yet the constitutional change made by the king's flight was almost insignificant. They had but to amputate an organ of government which had long ceased to do its work.

Before long, officers of the National Guard, despatched by every road
from Paris, had discovered the direction of the king's flight. During the
morning two of Lafayette's men were hurried off—Romeuf by the assembly,
and Baillon by the municipality—to pursue the fugitives, and to secure their
arrest. M. de Valory had ridden the hundred and fifty miles to Varennes in
twenty-three hours. Romeuf and Baillon travelled so much faster that they
arrived at Varennes less than seven hours behind the king. Baillon, it seems,
rode back again to Chalons, and thence despatched a local deputy, and the
ubiquitous Palloy, with news of the arrest. This message reached Paris soon
after eleven o'clock on the evening of the 22nd, anticipating that sent off
four hours earlier by the municipal officers of Varennes. The next day a
second letter from Baillon announced that the royal family were on their way
back, and would spend the night of the 23rd at Chalons—the first stage of
their lamentable return.

Thus for more than thirty-six hours Paris lay under a cloud of uncertainty, and a threat of war. Hastily printed *brochures* suggested that Louis
had gone by Compiègne and the Ardennes into the Emperor's territory, to
join the army of the ex-Prince of Condé. It was known that the King of
Sweden had ordered all his subjects to leave France. It was said that Catherine the Great had refused an audience to the French chargé d'affaires. It
was rumoured that Frenchmen were being expelled from Spain, and that
Spanish troops were moving to the frontier. In this emergency the Cordeliers club declared itself ready to exterminate all tyrants. Marat, not content
with denouncing the perfidy of the king, incited his readers to a general
attack on the heads of the government and army. Danton was afterwards
accused of having declared to a crowd, 'All your leaders are traitors, and are
deceiving you.' Even the Paris department, anxious to keep on the popular
side, busied itself with the collection and distribution of gunpowder. It was
fully believed that Austrian troops and revengeful emigrants might at any
moment cross the frontier, and march on the capital.

With the news of the king's capture and return this fear gradually gave
way to a deep resentment against the cause of it. The theory that the king
had somehow been kidnapped (*enlevé*) was accepted both by the assembly and
by the commune. At the Jacobin club only Robespierre challenged it. The
deputies decreed that every step should be taken to provide for the safety of
the royal family during their return journey, and commissioned three of
their number to accompany them on the road. Yet nothing could prevent
the nation from showing its feelings. No one was likely to forget that this was
the third time in two years that Louis had been brought back as a prisoner to
his capital.

The flight had occupied under twenty-four hours: three and a half days
were spent on the return. Escorted by Sauce, the king and queen reached
Clermont at ten o'clock on the morning of June 23rd. Here the crowd that

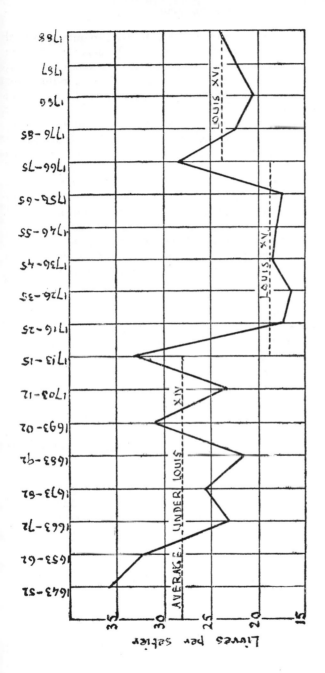

THE PRICE OF WHEAT IN PARIS

during the 150 years before the revolution

(from Arthur Young)

accompanied them from Varennes was swollen with fresh volunteers, who, with the mayor of Clermont, convoyed them to Sainte-Ménehould. At the town of their betrayal they listened to a municipal address, and lunched in the *hôtel de ville.* That Wednesday night was spent at Chalons, in the *préfecture* where Marie-Antoinette had slept as Dauphine on her way to Paris twenty-one years before.

Thursday, June 24th, was the feast of Corpus Christi, which the king and queen had hoped to celebrate at Montmédy with an act of thanksgiving for their escape. Now they were hurried from their ungrateful devotions by a fresh multitude from Reims. Such was the desire of this part of the country to see them, and to make sure of their safety, that they were taken by the alternative northern road from Chalons through Epernay, Dormans, and Château-Thierry, rejoining their old route at La Ferté. Thursday night was spent at Dormans, and Friday night at Meaux. Except between these two places, the coach was forced to go at a foot's pace by the detachments of National Guards, some six thousand in all, and by the crowds of country people who formed its unwieldy escort. Amongst the volunteers from the district of Chauny marched the future regicide and terrorist, young Saint-Just.

No violence was attempted against the royal prisoners: but near Sainte-Ménehould M. Dampierre, a local landlord unpopular with his tenants, who helped one of the ladies into the carriage, and attempted to ride by its side, was shot off his horse, and killed, and his head carried along by the crowd. Near Epernay, it was said, the queen offered one of the escort a piece of meat from her provision-basket. A voice at once cried, 'Don't touch it! you may be poisoned!'

On the third day, between Epernay and Dormans, the procession was met by Latour-Maubourg, Pétion, and Barnave, who announced themselves as the representatives of the assembly, and by Dumas, who took command of the military escort. Latour-Maubourg considerately refused a seat in the already crowded carriage: but room had to be found in it for the other two deputies. Barnave's high character and good manners impressed both Madame Elisabeth and the queen: both were offended by the coarse familiarities (*rudesse républicaine*) of Pétion, who had the conceit to suppose, and the unbelievably bad taste to suggest in his memoirs, that the king's pious sister had half fallen in love with him.

At last, on Saturday, June 25th, the terrible journey ended. From six in the morning till seven in the evening the coach had driven with blinds drawn against the heat and dust. When it reached Paris, it was taken for greater safety round the boulevards to the Champs Elysées, and thence to the west gate of the Tuileries gardens. The National Guards who formed the escort carried their muskets under their arms, as they would have done at a funeral. The route was crowded with sightseers:—several foreigners have left records of the scene. An order had been issued forbidding either insults or applause, and the royal family entered their palace-prison amid a silence even more ominous of the feelings of their subjects.

A few days later Morris noted in his journal, heartlessly enough, 'Vicq d'Azyr says that the Queen's Hair is turned grey by her late Adventures.' Louis, with his usual imperturbability, had kept a diary of the journey.

The king had counted on escape. He left behind him, under cover to La Porte, the minister of the Civil List, an autograph address to the French people; another copy had been entrusted to Fersen, for the Emperor's eye. In this ill-advised document Louis gave the lie to everything he had said in the declaration of April 23rd. He criticized the constitution to which he had so recently professed his loyalty. He complained of the imprisonment that his ambassadors had been instructed to deny. He reiterated the grievances of February 22nd, February 28th, and April 18th. He gave no reason for his flight except to say that in view of all these facts 'it is natural that the king should have sought to put himself in a place of safety (*se mettre en sûreté*).'

The strange inconsequence of this account, and the desire to discover who or what was behind the plot, led the assembly to appoint commissioners to take depositions from the king and queen. To these men Louis asserted that he had no intention of leaving France, and had made no such plan with relations, refugees, or foreign powers. He was going to Montmédy, because it was a safe place in which to leave his family, and a convenient centre from which to oppose any attempt to invade France. If he had meant to leave the country, he would not have published his declaration until he was across the frontier. But what of his brother (it was objected), who had undeniably, and with his connivance, fled to Brussels? He had only done so, Louis replied, in order that they might not both follow the same route; and his intention had been to rejoin the king inside French territory. On the same showing, were the commissioners expected to believe that Fersen had crossed the frontier at Arlon only in order to recross it to Montmédy? Louis ended by saying that his journey had convinced him that public opinion was in favour of the constitution; he had thereupon returned of his own free will.

What could the unhappy queen add to this farrago of improbabilities? Nothing; except that it was affection which constrained her to follow the king; and that, if he had tried to leave the country, she would have done everything to stop him. She added, with characteristic generosity, that the governess, couriers, and *femmes-de-chambre* who had accompanied the royal family were not to blame.

Three days after these declarations the assembly received a letter from de Bouillé, in which he tried to take upon himself the responsibility for the king's flight, and gave yet another account of what would have followed Louis' safe arrival at Montmédy. The king, he said, would have summoned a fresh assembly of 'wise men, who would at last have made an end of the crimes due to popular tyranny, and would have re-established the rule of reason, lit by the torch of freedom.' Meanwhile he would have interceded with the powers to postpone their legitimate vengeance on the French people. Bouillé ended with the threat that, if any harm were done to the king and queen, he would himself lead a foreign army into the country, and leave not one stone of Paris upon another.

This missive, as Lord Sheffield remarked, 'might have been well enough for a Captain of Grenadiers, but did not smell of the grand politician.' It blew the king's apologia sky-high. No need now of Fersen's diary, of the queen's letters to Leopold, or of the indiscretions of the Comte de Provence, to prove that Louis would have crossed the frontier, and returned at the head of an Austrian army. At this moment (July 5th–6th) the Emperor at Padua and the Pope at Rome were writing to congratulate the king on his escape, and were calculating the next step against the revolution. It was more than ever apparent how real was the threat of war.

To counter this threat, two steps must be taken. The king must be kept a prisoner; and he must be kept a prisoner on a throne. His dethronement on the ground of insanity—the only cause hitherto provided in the constitution—would afford almost as good an excuse for foreign intervention as his escape. The setting up of a Regency for the Dauphin would be a more difficult operation than the reinstatement of a perjured king. Indeed, reinstatement would lose much of its sting if it were made conditional on the acceptance and enactment of the new constitution. Louis would reappear, after a decent interval, not as the traitor king, but as the *pouvoir exécutif*; not as a person whom the people no longer honoured or trusted, but as a principle without which the revolution might dissolve into anarchy and civil war.

Other reasons induced the deputies to exculpate and restore the king. There was the prospect of endless accusations, if once the fiction of royal inviolability were destroyed. There was the risk of a struggle between rival claimants to the throne. There was, above all, the fear of republicanism. 'If the king escapes,' Morris had noted on the 25th, 'it means war; if not, a republic.'

Republicanism was not an 'ideology' in '89, like Fascism or Communism a century and a half later. *République* meant a state governed in the interests of the majority of its inhabitants, or a state in which the people has sovereign power. This might happen in a monarchy, or in an oligarchy, or in a democracy. Republican institutions did not necessarily involve a republican constitution. In 1789 nearly all respectable authorities, nearly all recognized writers, nearly all sensible politicians wished to retain the monarchy. But they thought of it as a stock on which republican institutions could be grafted. Only if the stock proved repugnant to this process, would they consent to root it up. The number of deputies who were not monarchists could have been counted on one hand. French republicanism was not a ready-made doctrine or programme imported from outside. It was home-made, and grew out of the political nature and needs of the country.

But every creed begins in a believer. It would not be true to say that there were no theoretical republicans in France before the flight to Varennes. Occasional pamphlets, beginning, perhaps, with Carra's *Orateur des Etats-généraux* ('89), had discussed the abolition of the throne. Certain clubs, papers, and societies were remarked for their anti-monarchical opinions. Republican sentiments might be found in Marat's *l'Ami du peuple*, and in Desmoulins' *Révolutions de France et de Brabant*. The young Belgian, Pierre Robert, who oddly combined the teaching of law with the management of a grocery business, helped his talented wife, Mlle Kéralio, and the future minister, Lebrun, to edit the *Mercure national* ('90-91), which echoed the most advanced views of the Cordeliers club. His pamphlet, *Républicanisme adapté à la France* (January, '91), popularised Lavicomterie's *Des peuples et des rois*, published four months earlier. The *Bouche de Fer*, edited by Nicolas Bonneville and the abbé Fauchet, was the organ of the *Cercle social*, a society which began in Freemasonry, and ended in something like Christian Socialism. Among its activities were the abbé's lectures in the *grand cirque* of the Palais-Royal. Here as many as four or five thousand Parisians would listen to republican propaganda tinged with an almost quakerish pietism. James Rutlidge, the Franco-Irish journalist, had been imprisoned for championing the master-bakers of Paris against Necker's food policy in '88. He came out of prison an extreme Cordelier, and a fervent admirer of Robespierre. In *Le Creuset*, of which he was now the editor, a federal republic was advocated three weeks before the flight to Varennes.

To this paper campaign was added the propagandist work of the Popular and Fraternal Societies. These organizations sprang up in great numbers during the winter of '90-91, generally under the patronage of Marat, and as off-shoots of the Cordeliers club. Their aim was to popularize, amongst those who could not educate themselves, Rousseau and republicanism. So the new ideas spread.

They would hardly have done so, but for economic distress, the treachery of the king, and fear of war. 'As things are,' wrote Cabanis, the latest adviser of the court, on April 21st, 'and during the king's lifetime, no party either in the assembly or out of it would dare to propose another form of government. The republicans have different hopes; but so long as the king himself is safe, the situation can be saved.' This safeguard Louis had now deliberately thrown away. The quite unprecedented protest of public opinion against the flight to Varennes opened the mouth of republicanism. Nor was it an accident that popular excitement found fresh expression in the dancing rhythm of the *Ça ira*, which was first heard in Paris at this time.

On June 21st, as soon as they heard of the king's flight, Robert, Momoro, and some other hot-heads of the Cordeliers published a manifesto of their beliefs. The people, they claimed, had long regarded the monarchy as a tyrannical institution. Kingship, they asserted, was not consistent either with liberty or with equality. Louis, by his flight, had in effect abdicated the throne. They appealed to the assembly 'either to declare outright that France is no longer a monarchy,' or at least to consult the constituencies before restoring Louis to the throne. On the 22nd a petition demanding the king's *déchéance* (forfeiture of the crown) was presented to the assembly by Fournier, called *l'Américain*, one of its six signatories.

Ten days later Tom Paine, whom Morris reported in Paris 'inflated to the Eyes, and big with a litter of Revolutions,' posted on the door of the *manège* an address to his French 'brethren and fellow-citizens.' In this manifesto he summarised the opinions published in London three months before in the first part of the *Rights of Man*. 'The absence of a king (he argued) is more desirable than his presence, and he is not only a political superfluity, but a grievous burden, pressing hard on the whole nation.' 'Let France, then,' he concluded, 'arrived at the age of reason, no longer be deluded by the sound of words, and let her deliberately examine if a king, however insignificant and contemptible in himself, may not at the same time be extremely dangerous.'

This manifesto was backed by the prestige of a champion of the American rebels, a refuter of Burke, and a republican victim of the British government. But it gained little support in the assembly. In the debate to which it gave rise the great majority of the deputies were found to be by policy, if not by conviction, on the side of monarchical government. Sieyès, once more their spokesman, engaged in a press controversy with Paine. It was not habit or sentiment, he declared, which kept him a monarchist, but the conviction that 'there is more liberty for the individual citizen under a monarchy than under a republic.'

Such sentiments now seemed fantastic to the mass of patriotic opinion. Nearly all the papers agreed in denouncing Louis' conduct. Nearly all agreed in demanding his replacement by some other form of Executive—the *Bouche de Fer*, of course, the *Mercure*, the *Creuset*, and the *Babillard*, but also Brissot's *Patriote*, under the influence of Madame Roland, Prudhomme's *Révolutions de Paris*, Desmoulins' *Révolutions de France et de Brabant*, and Fréron's *Orateur du peuple*. Not all of these ventured to use the word *république*. Yet there already existed what might easily become a dangerous breach between the constitutional outlook of the government and of the capital.

The sight of the Duc d'Orléans' *cabriolet* driving up and down the Carrousel on June 21st reminded Paris (as it was intended to do) of a third alternative to a restoration or a republic. But though he was cheered at the Jacobins on the 23rd, and dissociated himself from the royal family by changing his name to Egalité, Parisians showed no desire to adopt this discredited and disillusioned prince either as king or regent.

The deputies shared to the full the revulsion of popular feeling against the king. But they realized, as the general public could not, the danger of deposing him. To dethrone Louis would be to invite foreign attack, and to throw the constitution into the melting-pot. The people could see only that the king had betrayed his trust. They believed that those who wanted to reinstate him were actuated by royalism, or by love of office. Nor was this all. As the assembly lost prestige, so did the constitution. When the moment came for the enactment of the new regime, which the assembly had been elaborating, and the country expecting for two and a half years, too many Frenchmen had ceased to believe or even to be interested in it.

The explosion of these dangerous tendencies came within three weeks of the return from Varennes. On June 26th the king had been provisionally suspended from his royal functions, but no more. He might at some future date be reinstated. For the present the assembly would forget its lip-service to the Separation of Powers, and assume the executive as well as the legislative functions of government. France thus became in effect a republic, and remained so until the king's acceptance of the constitution on September 14th. Its three months' experience of kingless government was an invaluable apprenticeship for the *maîtrise* which fell to it by default a year later. But there hung over this interim regime the memory of Varennes, and the fear of counter-revolution.

On July 13th the deputies began to debate a proposal put forward by the Besançon lawyer, Muguet de Nanthou, on behalf of a strong group of committees, to regularize the provisional suspension of June 26th. The implication of this proposal was that, whatever Louis might have done, the king was, in the terms of the constitution, 'inviolable,' and should be restored to the throne. It was soon seen that this was the view of the vast majority of the deputies. Brissot might ridicule the idea that, whilst Louis sinned, the king could do no wrong. Vadier might clamour for his deposition. Robespierre might declare that 'inviolability' was a myth. The last word lay with Grégoire, the old friend of the people, or with Barnave, the new friend of the queen.

Grégoire maintained that Louis had forfeited his inviolability by his own denunciation of the constitution; but he did not think he could be punished by any lesser body than a national Convention. Barnave pointed out that to depose the king would be to destroy the new constitution, the work of so many laborious months, and the masterpiece of eight hundred national legislators. Barnave spoke for all, when he warned the country against the danger of living any longer without a constitution. He voiced the less creditable thoughts of some of the deputies when he went on to say that now was the time to end the social revolution, before it degenerated into a general attack upon property. On July 15th the assembly confirmed the provisional suspension of the king: it added, as though affirming his inviolability, that his accomplices should be brought to trial. At the same time, on the proposal of Salle, it passed a series of decrees, afterwards embodied in the constitution, defining the conditions, including flight from the country, that constituted abdication.

Meanwhile, fed by tributary discontents, the flood of republicanism was rising fast in the clubs, the sections, and the slums of the capital. On July 3rd-4th there had been trouble with the workmen preparing the Champ de Mars for the ceremony of the 14th. Petitions were received demanding work for those still unemployed. On the 7th the discontented labourers were reported to be fraternizing with the National Guard. On the 15th it was rumoured that the king was planning yet another flight. Bailly was for ever urging Gouvion and Lafayette to call out the Guard, and to repress disorders that hardly existed outside his nervous imagination.

On July 11th Voltaire's remains were transferred in an elaborate procession from their unhallowed grave at Scellières to Mirabeau's side in the Panthéon. It was a wet day, and the second Lord Palmerston, who was then staying in Paris, was not impressed. 'A figure of Voltaire (he wrote) very like him, in a gown, was carried first, sitting in an elbow chair, and afterwards came the coffin on a very fine triumphal car drawn by twelve beautiful grey horses four abreast. The coffin was covered, and over it a waxen figure was laid on a bed.' The procession was very long, 'but a great part of it consisted of very shabby, ill-dressed people whose appearance was made worse by the mud and dirt they had collected.' The ceremony was transformed, however, as Parisian funerals so often have been, from a theatrical pageant into a political demonstration. 'Republican principles,' Palmerston notes, 'are now avowed in every street; and the Palais-Royal is filled with groups who are listening eagerly to a number of little orators who are zealous and indefatigable in propagating sedition.'

On the 14th the fête of Federation was celebrated for the second time with a procession to the Champ de Mars, and choral mass at the altar of the country. But Louis was not there, and his brother, the Comte d'Artois, had not unnaturally refused an invitation from the *Dames de la Halle* to return from Turin to be present at what was no longer a demonstration of loyalty to his family. The Cordeliers Club and the Popular Societies chose the occasion to issue a petition with a hundred signatures calling for a plebiscite on the fate of the king. This petition the assembly refused to receive. Next morning the signatory societies called a public meeting at the altar of the country on the Champ de Mars, and drew up another petition, asking the assembly not to settle the fate of the king without first consulting the wishes of the nation. This document too was carried to the parliament-house. But the petitioners were informed that they came too late. The assembly had just passed Muguet de Nanthou's decree, providing for the reinstatement of the king.

The protesters had now to go warily. The assembly was the nation in council. The constitution provided no appeal against its decisions. An unconstitutional move at this juncture might rouse all the latent fears of

epublicanism. It might alienate those who wished to be rid of the monarchy,
ut not in this way. In their embarrassment the Cordeliers consented to co-
perate with the more cautious Jacobins. The Jacobin view had been well
xpressed by Robespierre two days before in words that might have come from
ny page of the *Rights of Man*. 'The word republic,' he had said, 'does not
1ean any particular form of government. It is applicable to every form of
overnment under which men can enjoy freedom and a fatherland. One may
e as free under a king as under a senate. What is the French constitution at
1e actual moment? It is a republic with a monarch. It is neither a monarchy
or a republic: it is both.'

With this convenient formula in their minds, and with the proviso that
1eir members would be acting only as individuals, the two clubs agreed next
10rning, the 16th, to publish for signature on the Champ de Mars another
etition, which Brissot had drafted in legal form: 'WE the undersigned,
eing Frenchmen, and members of the Sovereign People. . . WHEREAS
1ere followed a recital of Louis' crimes) it would be contrary both to the
1ajesty and to the interests of the nation to entrust the reins of government
ny more to a perjured traitor and fugitive, DEMAND that the National
Assembly shall accept in the name of the nation Louis XVI's abdication on
une 21st of the crown delegated to him, and shall provide for his replace-
1ent by such means as the constitution may allow.' The last phrase (*par tous
s moyens constitutionnels*) had been drafted so as to cover any solution of the
roblem, such as a Regency, or an Orléans succession, except a republican one.

This petition was read aloud from the four corners of the huge altar in the
entre of the Champ de Mars. It met with little favour from the republican-
1inded crowd. Some refused to sign the last clause. Others put their hand to
val petitions calling clearly for a republic. During the night the Jacobins,
:arful of compromising themselves, withdrew their support. The Cordeliers
vere left to go on alone.

Early on Sunday morning, July 17th, a young man visited the Champ de
Aars to copy the patriotic inscriptions which still remained on the altar of
1e country since the apotheosis of Voltaire. He discovered two men con-
ealed beneath the wooden platform, and informed the Guard of the Gros-
Laillu district close by. The men were arrested, interrogated, and marched
ff to the Town Hall. On the way they were set upon by an angry crowd,
nd lynched. There was no immediate sequel to the incident. Six men were
vanted by the police; but no arrests were made. Nevertheless the day had
:arted badly.

All that morning, whilst pious Parisians were going to mass, expectant
roups of patriots gathered round the altar of the country, waiting for the
etition which they still hoped would by some miraculous means remove
1eir fears of treachery and war. It was not until after midday that the defec-
on of the Jacobins became known. There and then Robert and his friends
rafted a new petition. This document recited the previous attempts to

approach the assembly, and warned the deputies of the anarchy which might result from disagreement between the representatives and those they represented. It then went on to ask the deputies, in the name of all French men, to revoke Muguet de Nanthou's decree, 'to consider that Louis' crime has been proved, and that he has abdicated the throne; to accept his abdication, and to convene a new constituent body, which may proceed in genuinely national manner to try the criminal; above all, to replace him and to organize a new executive power.' The new formula (*l'organisation d'un nouveau pouvoir exécutif*) still avoided mention of a republic: but it did not, like that of the day before, exclude it.

Encouraged by their leaders, the people pressed forward to sign the petition. In a short time eighteen or twenty *cahiers* were roughly tacked together containing over six thousand signatures. Some of these were neatly written the names of educated middle-class citizens. Most were the stiff scrawls of illiterate workmen and their women-folk. Sometimes it was a child's hand guided by its parent. Often there was no more than a cross within a circle the mark of those who could not write their names. A few names were there not unknown to fame:—Maillard, the hero of July 14th and October 5th Chaumette, 'medical student,' the future champion of the commune; Brune Napoleon's marshal; Hébert, the notorious editor of *Père Duchesne*; and the handsome popular brewer, Santerre, one of the best horsemen in Paris, and not long afterwards commandant of the National Guard. But most of the names were the stuff of which so many famous crowds have been made—the raw material of unwritten history. The *cahiers* were laid up in the Town Hall, and perished in the flames of 1871; but there must have been many who boasted in later life, 'I was one of the petitioners of July 17th.'

For these illiterates were making history. Their refusal to recognize a *fait accompli* had angered the assembly, and alarmed all good constitutionalists The municipality had feared for the past fortnight that some such trouble would occur. Only the night before it had determined to take action against those whom Bailly misleadingly described as 'intriguers, foreigners, and aristocrats.' A proclamation was issued, forbidding *attroupements*. A strong detachment of the National Guard was posted on the site of the Bastille where the demonstrators were expected to assemble. About eleven o'clock reports were received of the lynching episode, and rumours of an attempt to assassinate Lafayette. Martial Law was at once enforced. The red flag— the symbol of authority, not yet converted into the symbol of revolt—flew for the first time, in accordance with the decree of October 21st, '89, from the principal window of the Town Hall.

After that, events moved slowly but inexorably towards the fatal outcome that all might have foreseen and some desired. About half-past seven in the evening, when the heat of the day was over, and the peaceful and unarmed crowd of holiday-makers was preparing to go home, the municipal officer marched onto the Champ de Mars, with cavalry, artillery, infantry, and

he hated symbol of martial law. There were cries of 'Down with the red
flag!' and stones began to fly: perhaps there were a few pistol-shots. The
soldiers fired over the heads of the crowd: then, as it would not or could not
disperse, they emptied their muskets into the defenceless civilians. A dozen
fell dead: thirty or forty were wounded. Such was the 'massacre of the
Champ de Mars.'

The significance of July 17th, 1791, lay in its exposure of the state
of the public mind. The shocking thing was not so much the death of a
few unknown citizens, as the way in which their killing was regarded—
the complacency with which it was reported by Bailly, and approved by the
assembly; the vindictive terms in which the Minister of Justice demanded
that the courts should prosecute the authors of the petition; or the letter in
which the queen said to him, 'I have seen with pleasure the determination and courage with which you and your friends have upheld the
monarchy.'

Nor was anything lacking in the ferocity with which the deputies and the
municipal officers followed up their easy victory. The Minister of Justice
wrote next day to the Public Prosecutor of the Abbaye tribunal urging him
to use all diligence in 'saving the state and constitution from the attacks aimed
at it by a mob of rebels, whose only objects were murder, pillage, disorder,
and anarchy, which they called liberty.' It was three weeks before the red
flag, the symbol of martial law, was replaced, at the window of the Town
Hall, by the white flag, the symbol of peace. In almost every section of Paris
citizens were arrested for insulting remarks against Lafayette and the
National Guard. Democratic papers were suppressed, and their editors went
into hiding. Brune, Momoro, Santerre, Legendre, Robert, and Desmoulins
were proscribed. Denunciations, arrests, imprisonments, and other arbitrary
acts were practised in the name of public safety. Every day the royalist *Chant
de coq* crowed over the defeat of *les factieux*. Old charges too were revived.
Writing on the 21st, Madame Roland, whose letters are almost a diary of the
period, said that she had just seen three carriages go past her window, carrying to prison Marat and others suspected of complicity with the events of
October 5th–6th.

The leaders of the Jacobins were not proscribed, though Robespierre,
whose caution had saved them, thought it prudent to shift his lodgings from
the distant Marais to the rue Saint-Honoré, close by. But for some months
the club was under a cloud. A large secession of its members formed a rival
society at the Feuillants. The Robespierrist Madame Jullien thought that
nothing short of 'a new and final miracle' would make the country safe for
Jacobinism. It was not till the following winter that Jacobin policy once
more dominated the assembly.

The massacre of the Champ de Mars was never forgotten or forgiven.
'Neither the red flag,' wrote Prudhomme, with excusable rhetoric, 'nor the
miserable excuses of the mayor, nor the president's congratulations, nor the

wordy minutes of the municipality, will wash your official scarves clean of the
indelible stain of your brothers' blood. It has dropped on your hearts. Its slow
poison will corrupt you till you die.' Lafayette might remember these words
when he languished in an Austrian prison. Bailly might remember them
shivering in the rain, whilst the crowd set up his guillotine on the spot where
his men had shot them down, and burnt before his dying eyes the flag that
he had hoisted on the Town Hall. The people knew what the massacre meant.
June 21st had destroyed their faith in the king. July 17th destroyed their
faith in the assembly. The only policy of the constitutionalists seemed to be
to stop the revolution, to repress democratic liberty, and to stabilize a pluto
cratic regime.

This interpretation seemed to be justified by the proceedings of the
assembly during the two months that still remained to it. The first care of
the deputies was to select out of the mass of decrees passed during the past
two years those which were most important, and to codify them into a
constitution, which could be accepted by the king, and submitted for the
recognition of the Powers. Their second care was to fasten this constitution
upon the country in an unalterable form for the longest possible term of
years.

The touch-stone of the constitution was the franchise. As this stood, before
July 17th, the tax-paying qualification for a parliamentary elector was
fairly low (the equivalent to ten days' wages) and that for a deputy (the
marc d'argent, the equivalent of fifty days' wages) correspondingly high. The
committee now set up to codify the constitution seized the opportunity to
revise this arrangement. As a sop to the democrats the *marc d'argent*, which
they had bitterly denounced, would be dropped, and any 'active' citizen would
be eligible as a deputy. On the other hand the qualification of an elector
appointed by a primary assembly would now be the possession of landed
property or house property bearing a tax which varied, according to the
locality, from twice to eight times that of the *marc d'argent*.

This meant that, whilst any 'active' citizen could vote in the election of a
mayor, a parson, or a Justice of the Peace, the election of deputies, of depart
mental and district directors, or of bishops and judges, would rest with a
very small minority of the nation, all belonging to the propertied class. So
few large property-owners were there, that the number of these electors in
the department of Loir-et-Cher, with a population of two hundred and
seventy-five thousand, was only two hundred, and in the Aveyron depart
ment, with a population of four hundred thousand, only two hundred and
ten. Fortunately for French democracy this reactionary measure was not to
come into operation for two years. When the time came, the whole constitu
tion had disappeared.

The deputies would have been greatly surprised if anyone had prophesied
this; for they took the utmost precautions to prevent any change in the

constitution which was to keep their class in power. If the elaborate provisions of Titre VII, *De la révision des décrets constitutionnels*, were strictly observed, not one of the thirteen thousand words of the constitution could be changed for ten years, and even then it would be an extremely difficult operation. The deputies would have been even more surprised if they had been able to look forward those ten years, and to see France living under its fourth constitution, with as many still to come. Yet what else could be expected? A series of rigid regimes constructed in the interests of a class or of a person could only be liquidated by a series of national revolutions.

One objection might be raised to this reading of the situation. Had not the deputies rejected the easiest method of keeping themselves in power, and of perpetuating a propertied regime, when they excluded themselves from re-election? Perhaps if Robespierre's proposal had been made after the flight to Varennes, instead of before it, the vote would have gone differently. A good many deputies no doubt supported it, as Malouet did, because they were tired of parliamentary wrangling.

But in any case the 'self-denying ordinance' of May 16th may legitimately be read in connexion with another measure that closely followed it. A decree of May 28th laid it down that all the departmental administrations so recently and painfully appointed for two years should go out of office with the assembly itself, and that new elections to replace them should be held as soon as the parliamentary elections were over. Thus the outgoing deputies provided themselves with a large number of influential and well-paid posts all over the country—posts from which they could criticize and obstruct the policy of their successors. They could live on the reputation of a great piece of legislation, without the discredit which would probably come to those who tried to carry it out. They could propagate in the country the creed of propertied constitutionalism which they were finding it increasingly difficult to impose on the capital.

To Parisian republicans the revised constitution was now anathema. It might as well have been proclaimed from the altar of the country over the dead bodies of the victims of July 17th. There were two other parties in the field to whom, on very different grounds, it was equally objectionable. To the emigrant princes and their friends, who recognized none but an absolute monarchy, it was utterly unacceptable; if Louis sanctioned it, their allegiance to him would become more than doubtful. To Malouet and his *Impartiaux*, who still hankered after an Upper House and an absolute veto, it seemed little better than republicanism. There were among these men not a few whose dislike was tinged with the feeling that they themselves would have been acceptable candidates for promotion to an elective Second Chamber.

But all these parties were minorities. The majority of responsible politicians neither liked the new constitution nor disliked it; but they clung to it as the only *via media* between the dangers, partly seen, and partly suspected, of royalist counter-revolution on one side, and republican anarchy on the other; or they held, like Morris, that to execute the constitution was 'the only rational Mode of pointing out its defects.'

It only remained to secure the king's consent to the constitution, and to replace him on the throne. As early as July 31st Louis had invited his brother, the Comte d'Artois, to return to France, and to lend his support to the acceptance of the constitution. His letter urged that the new France would resist, and probably defeat, foreign intervention; that an attack upon the constitution would be an attack upon the crown; and that d'Artois' return would restore confidence in the government, and enable Louis, in time, to correct the vices in the constitution. But this line of argument, as Lamarck explained to Mercy, was no more than part of the royal policy of dissimulation. Louis himself still doubted whether he should accord or refuse his signature. If he accepted the constitution, he would finally alienate the *émigrés*, who had the ear of the Emperor, and the intransigent royalists, who were already shaking their heads over him in the alleys of the Luxembourg gardens. If he rejected the constitution, he must either abdicate in his son's favour, or endanger his dynasty, and perhaps his life. He had on his desk a letter from Edmund Burke (August 6th) urging him to take a strong line. But how could he ?

When this painful choice had been made, there still remained a controversy about the form of acceptance, to which Lamarck and other well-meaning advisers attached undue importance, and which Louis redrafted as often as he changed his mind. The queen was impatient, and practical. What did any set of words matter, compared with the daily acts of the court? Pellenc's draft, put forward by Montmorin, was needlessly verbose. 'I remain convinced,' she wrote, 'that the king's speech must be short, dignified, and benevolent. Above all, he must not give the impression of apologising, or show embarrassment when he mentions his journey (*to Varennes*), or his personal feelings. The purity of his intentions will always save him from that.' Nevertheless he was signing under compulsion; and everyone knew it. A cartoon of the time pictured him seated, pen in hand, inside a large cage surmounted by a crown. 'What are you doing?', asks the Emperor from outside.—*Je sanctionne*, replies the king.

On September 13th Louis handed to a deputation of the House a letter signifying his acceptance of the constitution. The next day he appeared in the assembly to make a speech from the throne, and to take an oath of loyalty to the constitution. Royalists were scandalized to see the President of the assembly seat himself by the side of the king, and the deputies remain sitting in the royal presence. They were outraged to hear Louis accept the constitution without amendment or reserve. To many of the audience this complaisance seemed to argue some sinister design. Others were half puzzled and half conciliated by the king's benevolent bearing, and by his refusal to take offence. They wondered how an apparently humble and guileless man could be so tortuous and implacable an enemy of the revolution.

On Sunday, September 18th, the king's acceptance of the constitution was proclaimed from the Town Hall, and Parisians gave themselves up to public rejoicings. The *Te Deum* was sung at Notre Dame, and there was a balloon ascent in the Champs Elysées. On the 30th the National Assembly met for the last time, and Louis reaffirmed his loyalty to the constitution, amid cries of *Vive le roi! Vive la nation!* and *Vive la liberté!* But it could not be ignored that, of all the thousand deputies, only two were chaired and crowned by the waiting citizens—Pétion of Chartres and Robespierre of Arras, the most stubborn champions of popular rights, and the most persistent opponents of middle-class privilege.

Writing to Robespierre after her return home from Paris (September 21st) Madame Roland drew pessimistic conclusions from the reactionary conduct of the deputies. It proved, she said, that 'the least aberration from the orbit of perfect equality and complete liberty necessarily tends to degrade human nature.'

It was not unnatural that politicians who had lived in close touch with Paris opinion should sympathize with the point of view of the man in the street, and condemn much of the work of the assembly. They could not easily forget the red flag of July 17th, or the undemocratic revision of the franchise, or the restoration of a traitor king. They could not easily forgive the betrayal of the people's interests by representatives whom the people had saved from disaster at every crisis of the revolution. What was the working man's reward for July 14th and October 6th? What boon had the active citizen received from the lawyers and journalists whom his overwhelming vote had placed in power? A franchise which became less effective as it became more important: a ban upon the only available means of improving the conditions of the worker: a land-purchase scheme whose chief aim seemed to be to save the interests of the landlord: and a bureaucracy which provided thousands of well-paid posts for the sons of middle-class parents.

Men so disillusioned might easily overlook the real and general advantages won since '89—the destruction of an obsolete and arbitrary regime; the enthronement of the nation in place of the king; a new social equality and self-respect; a new responsibility in local government; a new hope of justice; and a new interest in living.

For what was obviously defective in the constitution of 1791 two circumstances were more to blame than the selfishness of the middle class. One was the speed with which the political revolution had been carried through. The other was the completeness of its break with the past.

Mirabeau, writing to a friend in August, '88, had anticipated a gradual revolution. 'The first States-general,' he said, 'will be disorderly, and will perhaps go too far. The second will establish its right of way (*assureront leur*

marche). The third will achieve the constitution.' Mirabeau's three sessions had been compressed into one. Work that might well have been spread over ten years had been completed in two. Before one reform was launched, another was on the slipway.

But this was not all. It is as true of revolutions as it is of wars that those who have won the victory in the field are not the most fit to sit round the table at the peace conference. The bitter memories of the old regime which the deputies brought with them to Versailles, and the just resentment with which they regarded the conduct of the king during the summer of '89, made it difficult for them to view the situation realistically. Mallet du Pan was saying both too much and too little when he declared that France needed thirty years of preliminary training before it would be fit to support political liberty:—too much, if thinking of the leaders; too little, if thinking of the rank and file. But almost every divergence between the revolutions of 1688 and 1789, so often too complacently contrasted by English historians, may be attributed to the different political antecedents and education of two great peoples.

It has become fashionable to condemn 'a bourgeois revolution.' There is a sense, and one creditable to the intelligence and energy of the middle class, in which every revolution is a bourgeois revolution. The French nation at the end of the eighteenth century was not exceptional in having to rely on its professional and propertied minority for liberalism and leadership. It was unusually fortunate in that this minority was too weak to establish its rule without the help of the majority, and too patriotic to exploit its private interests until it had carried through a programme of national reform.

No narrowing of the franchise, no obstacles to the revision of the constitution, could deprive the mass of the people, the sixteen millions who were the families of 'active' citizens, of the power to call their representatives to account, or to settle the national affairs in a national way. They had overthrown the old privilege of class: they could overthrow the new privilege of cash—if only by another revolution. Meanwhile a bourgeois constitution was infinitely better than none. It protected their lives, their labour, and their land. It prevented the return of the royalist refugees, and of the ecclesiastical monopolists. It saved the country from a foreign invasion designed by its own royal and aristocratic families. It provided for the first time the possibility of an ordered and peaceful existence.

True, these benefits were not given in full measure to the 'passive' citizens, the disfranchised third part of the people. But what other state in Europe would have enfranchised them? Or in what country, having no vote, would they have received so much consideration? If they were excluded from political responsibility, it was not by the propertied and professional minority only, but by their own comrades of the *petite bourgeoisie*—the tradesmen and artisans who were the bulk of the 'active' citizens. If they were benefited, it was not by their own violence, but by the legislative action of deputies drawn from the whole hierarchy of the middle classes, who for a while forgot their class interests and enmities in a genuine zeal for national regeneration. The alliance of the middle and lower classes against tyranny and privilege may have been a *mariage de convenance* rather than a love-match. It did not long outlast their common victory. But its offspring was the liberal-thinking and liberal-living France of 1875–1939.

CHAPTER XIII

LEGISLATIVE ASSEMBLY

There never did, there never will, and there never can, exist a Parliament, or any description of men, or any generation of men, in any country, possessed of the right or the power of binding and controlling posterity to the end of time, or of commanding for ever how the world shall be governed, or who shall govern it. . . Every age and generation must be as free to act for itself in all cases as the ages and generations which preceded it.—(THOMAS PAINE: *The Rights of Man*, 1791.)

THE Legislative Assembly (*corps législatif*) set up under the constitution of 1791 should have been chosen by some forty thousand electors, the nominees of four and a quarter million active citizens. Actually, not more than one active citizen in three in the best constituencies, or one in ten in the worst, took the trouble to go to the polls. Such figures as are available suggest that the forty thousand did little better than the four million. In Paris, the most politically minded city in the country, only seven thousand out of eighty-one thousand primary electors, and only two hundred out of nearly a thousand secondary electors recorded their votes. They were tired of constant and prolonged elections; they shrank from committing themselves; or they were not interested in the new assembly.

The backwardness of the voters did nothing to accelerate the clumsy machinery of the elections. They spread themselves over so long a period that the primary assemblies met (June 12th–15th) before the flight to Varennes, and the nomination of deputies did not take place until August 29th —September 5th, six weeks after the massacre of the Champ de Mars. In the middle of June republicanism was hardly heard of: at the beginning of September the campaign for the repression of republican opinions was in full swing. It was doubtful whether such electors as Danton or Desmoulins would be able to exercise their franchise, whilst warrants were still out for their arrest.

'The new Assembly,' Morris reported to Washington on September 30th, 'is deeply imbued with republican or rather democratical Principles. The Southern Part of the Kingdom is in the same Disposition. The Northern is ecclesiastical in its Temper. The Eastern is attached to Germany and would gladly be reunited to the Empire. Normandy is aristocratical, and so is Part of Britanny. The interior Part of the Kingdom is monarchical.' About two hundred and sixty places went to constitutional royalists and Feuillants of the Right; a hundred and thirty-six to opposition Jacobins of the Left; and about three hundred and fifty to moderate or independent members of the Centre. This gave a large working majority to the supporters of the monarchical constitution. But whereas the Right was divided into a court party and an anti-court party, and the Centre had no definite policy, the Left had enthusiasm, a clear aim, and the support of the capital.

It is natural to use the word 'party' in speaking of the Legislative Assembly; for within a few weeks of its opening session party names were being shouted across the floor of the House, and popularized in the press. The broad division of deputies into *indépendans*, *modérés*, and *patriotes*, was not enough. They must be named after their leaders, with every degree of familiarity or contempt, *Brissotins*, *Dantonistes*, and the like. *Jacobin* soon came to be used as a mark of political opinion as well as a badge of club-membership. *Girondin* soon lost its geographical sense, and was used to label a type of opinion found all over France. The small fraction of the extreme Left became, from its point of vantage in the highest seats, the *Montagne*, or from its likeness to the untrained horses of the old riding-school, the *Enragés*.

This growth of party feeling alarmed men accustomed to the comparative unanimity and good manners of the Constituent Assembly. It was not long before Pétion wrote to the *Patriote* (February 10th) urging the bourgeois deputies to keep up their traditional alliance with the people, and not to endanger public peace and the new constitution by internal strife. 'So long as the *Tiers Etat* is united,' he declared, 'the country is safe.' But the country, as Madame Roland remarked, had grown two centuries older in two years. The new deputies were drawn from a second generation of revolutionaries. They had lost the youthful complexion of '89; but they had not acquired a compensating thickness of skin. They asked for nothing better than unity and a quiet session: circumstances soon conspired to make both impossible.

Who are these new deputies? 'They are young men,' asserts a distinguished constitutional historian, 'and it is disconcerting to find that the majority is composed of men not yet thirty.' This opinion is commonly held, but it is quite erroneous. Out of the two hundred and fifteen members of the Legislative Assembly who afterwards sat in the Convention, and who were certainly no older than the rest, a hundred and ninety-two are found to be over thirty, and only fifteen under that age. The average is, in fact, just what it was in the Constituent Assembly—nearly forty.

As to social and professional status, the aristocratic Lamarck might sneer at deputies whose only *équipages* were galoshes and umbrellas, and whose total income did not amount to fifteen thousand pounds a year; but most of

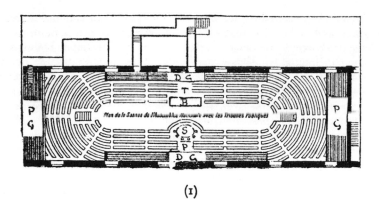

(1)

PLAN DE LA CONVENTION

AUX TUILERIES

(2)

GROUND-PLAN OF THE ASSEMBLY

(1) The Manège. (2) The Salle des Machines. In both plans T is the speaker's tribune, B the bar of the House, S the secretaries' table, P the president's chair, DG the deputies' gallery, and PG the public gallery.

them, like their predecessors, were lawyers of some kind; and nearly all had held office under the new regime as mayors, magistrates, or members of district and departmental bodies. Orthodoxy was still represented by twenty-six clergy, including ten bishops; and dissent by two Protestant pastors. There were a number of officers, especially from the most intelligent branches of the service—the artillery and the engineers. There were some learned men and teachers, twenty-eight doctors, and a fair proportion of landed proprietors, business men, and manufacturers. It is often said that these men were inexperienced. Certainly they lacked their predecessors' knowledge of parliamentary life. But they started with a political education and a ready-made experience of revolution which the Constituents had painfully acquired during two and a half years.

The exclusion of the old deputies (but not of the *suppléants*, of whom Cambon was a notable instance) deprived the House of many well-known figures. But it contained men of real ability, such as Arbogast, the mathematician, and Koch, the professor of History and Diplomatic, from the University of Strasbourg; Buffon's pupil and successor, the naturalist Lacépède; Dr. Broussonnet, a Fellow of the Royal Society, whom Napoleon made Consul at Mogador; Guyton-Morveau, author of a Dictionary of Chemistry, who turned his skill to the production of military balloons; Cérutti, the ex-Jesuit editor of the *Feuille villageoise*: the architect-archæologist Quatremère de Quincy; Dusaulx, the translator of Juvenal, who had served in the Seven Years' war; and François de Neufchâteau, the dramatist-author of *Paméla*.

Amongst the soldiers sat Carnot, the future 'architect of victory,' with several clever writings to his credit, and a reputation for silent and mathematical efficiency. Another tongue-tied mathematician, but of a mental, not of a mechanical turn, was the philosophic Condorcet—a systematizer of the sciences, an architect of national education, the ablest and the least appreciated apologist of Jacobinism. On the Right, amongst the constitutional royalists, were Mathieu Dumas, who had brought Louis back from Varennes, and lived to write distinguished memoirs of the Napoleonic wars; the Protestant ex-Marquis de Jaucourt, Talleyrand's understudy at the Foreign Office, and Louis XVIII's Minister of Marine; Beugnot, the administrator of Westphalia; the memoirist Pastoret; and d'Averhoult, a distinguished Dutch refugee. The ablest legal champion of the constitution which he had helped to frame was Bigot de Préameneu; ten years later he became one of the authors of the *Code Napoléon*.

But in the public eye, and to the press, none of these were so prominent as a little group of intellectuals from Bordeaux, who gave the name of their department to the Girondin party, and who expounded to a public already tired of talk the republican platitudes of a provincial debating society. Their Burke was a clever protégé of Turgot and Dupaty, the inspired but indolent Vergniaud. Their political chief was the grave Gensonné. Their most formidable debater was Guadet, whose legal talents confounded his opponents, but carried no message to the people. Their most determined and clear-sighted leader was the hostess of the party, Madame Roland. A native of Paris, she knew its people better than they did; she held a low view of the Constituent Assembly; and she had come back to the capital convinced that she could show the Girondins how to conduct a revolution.

The romantic appeal of Girondism, which inspired Lamartine's ill-judged apologia, and which has misled some later historians, may be read, as Madame Roland herself read it, in the expansive soul of the virtuous and handsome Buzot. His self-portrait might stand as frontispiece for any history of his party.

'My head and heart,' he writes, 'were filled with Greek and Roman history, and with the great figures which, in those old republics, were the honour of the human race. From my earliest youth I professed their maxims, and lived on the study of their virtues. As a boy I almost ran wild. My passions were tight-packed in a fervent and sensitive heart. But their violence and excess were turned inwards. My soul was never seared by the foul breath of libertinism. I always had a horror of debauchery. Until I was quite grown up, my lips were never soiled by an improper remark. I made acquaintance early enough with misfortune; but only to become more attached to virtue, in whose consolations alone I found relief. With what pleasure I can still remember that happy period of my life, now gone beyond recall—the day when I wandered silent across the mountains and woods of my native place, reading with delight something of Plutarch or Rousseau, or reminding myself of the most precious features of their moral and philosophical teaching! Or the times when, seated on the flowery turf, under the shadow of branching trees, I gave myself up in sweet melancholy to recalling the pleasures and pains that had influenced my early days!'

Such was the genesis of Girondism. But it would be a mistake to suppose that the Girondins held a monopoly of the silliness and sentimentality of youth. The Jacobins of that generation had suffered from the same juvenile introspection. The difference between Buzot and Robespierre was perhaps that Buzot's character never grew old enough to become immune to maladies that Robespierre outlived. A Girondin was a Jacobin who 'had not lived': a Jacobin was a Girondin 'man of the world.'

It remained to find an apostle for these self-centred saints of republicanism. He appeared, a little unexpectedly, in Jacques-Pierre Brissot. Brissot's father, who kept a cook-shop at Chartres, brought him up for the bar. In virtue of a tiny property he added the equivalent of 'Esq.,' to his name, and set out to make a career as Brissot de Warville. During the ten years preceding the Revolution he had written pamphlets or edited papers in England, Switzerland, and America: he had studied law with Nolleau, and science with Marat: he had helped the Belgians to make a revolution, and the Duc d'Orléans to spend a fortune: he had founded a society to liberate the slaves of the West Indies: he had been imprisoned for debt in London, and for seditious writings in the Bastille. An incurable romantic and busy-body, he was just the man to lead France into war, and the Girondins to the scaffold.

Brissot's future rivals and victors of the extreme Left were inadequately represented, at present, by the lawyer Merlin of Thionville, the ex-Capucin Chabot, and Basire of Dijon. All three passed for Dantonists, and the last two perished three years later in the 'purge' of Danton's more disreputable following.

The deputies of 1791 were, then, on a general view, neither better nor worse than those of 1789, but merely different. It needed Gibbon's preju-diced eye to see their predecessors, in comparison with them, as 'a senate of heroes and demi-gods.' They were as truly the representatives of a nation; but of a nation in its third year of revolution; of a nation within six months of war.

After a few disorderly meetings, the new assembly adopted the procedure of the old. It sat every day from nine in the morning till two or three in the afternoon, and again from six to half-past nine at night. It sat on Sundays as on week-days, and did not even take a holiday at the New Year, or on the anniversary of the fall of the Bastille. Such assiduity put too great a strain upon the nerves of the deputies. They saw too much of one another in public, and too little in private. They thought too little, and spoke too much. They wrote newspaper articles about their opponents, when they should have written letters to them. Parliamentary life was corrupted and embittered by a too exclusive and partisan addiction to politics. The *manège* was a worse parliament-house because it was so poor a club. The deputies, too, lost touch with their constituencies. France almost ceased to exist for them outside the Tuileries. Only the representatives of Paris were at home in the capital, and could instruct and be instructed by their electors.

The procedure of the assembly provided further occasions of friction. It might be reasonable for a democratic body to receive petitions from the citizens: but not at the rate of sixty to a hundred a day; not at the beginning of business, where they wasted valuable time; and not with leave to make speeches at the bar of the House, whilst the friends of the petitioners crowded the public galleries, and applauded their demands. Generally petitioners were allowed 'the honours of the session': sometimes the President made them a complimentary speech, or conferred an honorary embrace (*accolade*) upon their leader : sometimes they were permitted to march through the hall, or to seat themselves among the deputies. Occasionally, though the constitution forbade it, they carried arms. Frequently, though the rules of the House prevented the debating of a petition, the question of its treatment gave rise to heated altercation among the deputies.

Again, it was the custom to propose that successful speeches should be printed at the public expense. This practice gave extra publicity to the views of the majority, and sometimes to personal and partisan debates. So did the fortnightly choice of Presidents, who were now party nominees, and used their position to forward party interests.

One more point. The committees of the Constituent Assembly had been semi-executive bodies of experts. The committees of the Legislative Assembly were confined to legislative functions, and came under the suspicion of complaisant partisanship. They were the accomplices, Brissot declared, rather than the critics of the ministers. They were now more frequently renewed: one of the most important, the Diplomatic Committee, consisted of twelve members, half of whom retired every three months. Meanwhile they spread from their narrow quarters at the Capucins to the Feuillants and other neighbouring buildings, with the fecundity of war-time White-hall: one of them changed its address four times in three years. Their proceedings were, indeed, less important than before; but they were not always more peaceful. Robert Lindet, a diffident financier, found it as difficult to get a hearing on the *comité de liquidation* as in the parliament-house itself.

Early in '92, J. F. Reichardt, a court organist whom Frederick the Great had dismissed, after ten years' service, as a ' Jacobin,' came to Paris, and visited the assembly. His tidy Prussian soul was shocked by the casual dress and manners of the deputies. They looked, he thought, like greengrocers' or tailors' apprentices; and they did not improve that appearance by the habit of wearing flowing silk overcoats, like dressing-gowns, with dirty boots, or slippers trodden down at the heel. He describes the hall of meeting, the deputies' green leather seats rising in tiers to the walls, the projecting galleries for the ticket-holding public, and the ten or twelve rows of free seats. In some of these were ten women to one man, and faces of a criminal type worthy of a Hogarth's pencil. The President sat on a high platform, with two ushers by his side, who repeated his frequent cries of 'Silence!' Opposite the President was the bar, and above the bar the pulpit (*tribune*) used by the speakers.

'In the free space on the floor of the House,' Reichardt goes on, 'four ushers in black with smartly curled hair, their hats off, and carrying gold swords, walk up and down, crying incessantly, "Silence! Take your places!" The deputies, carelessly dressed, and a good many of them booted and spurred, block this broad passage. They come and go, slapping their boots with their canes, coughing, spitting, speaking at the tops of their voices, and calling to one another across the hall. The President is constantly ringing his huge bell, and shouting, "Take your seats, Gentlemen!" till he has no voice left. The ushers clap their hands in vain, and cry "*Chut*," till they are tired out. The deputies pay no more attention than schoolboys who have got out of hand, and know that the old master will not strike them. An orator may be making a speech, or a *rapporteur* reading his report: hundreds of deputies go on talking just the same. Somebody may interrupt him, or make loud remarks: often the uproar becomes intolerable.'

Under such conditions, Reichardt thinks, it was almost impossible for a deputy to deliver a properly argued speech. The extremists would put up one of their friends to make an impassioned appeal, and call for a vote directly he sat down. If an unpopular speaker hesitated, or used a wrong word, he would be jeered at. When the minority stood up to vote, they would be greeted with hisses and cat-calls from the free seats, and even from the deputies on the other side.

Nevertheless, Reichardt admits, even the worst sittings had their good moments. When a deputy who commanded respect spoke really well or to the point, he was listened to. Nor can an Englishman who naturally and excusably condemns the disorderliness of the French assembly forget that there have been times, as during the Irish debates of 1840–1841 (not to mention more recent occasions), when the House of Commons itself behaved with no greater dignity or self-restraint.

There was no slackening of the pressure of the clubs, papers, and public upon the deliberations of the new deputies. Fresh embarrassment, indeed, arose from the presence in Paris, and even in the parliament-house, of their predecessors, the ex-deputies of the Constituent Assembly. Some of these men had prudently abjured a publicity which was becoming dangerous. Sieyès, denounced at the Jacobin club (June 19th) for a proposal to divide the assembly into two sections, had retired into the country, and took no further part in revolutionary politics. But others were exploiting a bubble reputation. Brissot himself proposed at the Jacobins (October 5th) a motion to exclude from the *manège* 'the crowd of functionaries (*la foule d'hommes à épaulettes*) which is flooding it, and to get rid of the privileged seats,' which were being improperly reserved for ex-deputies. A speech by Ballet two days later further exposed this scandal. He was supported by a petition signed by two hundred electors, including Desmoulins and Dubois-Crancé; and the offending seats were removed.

It was more difficult to check the growing influence of the Jacobin club, and of the Jacobin press. The prestige of the club increased as that of the assembly declined. As the assembly became less constructive, the club became more critical. Under the sour influence of Robespierre, its attitude towards the Brissotin majority became more and more that of an unofficial Opposition. Nor was Robespierre content with the spoken word. He became the proprietor and editor of a journal, the *Défenseur de la constitution*.

It was as easy to found and edit a paper in 1791 as it is difficult and expensive nowadays. It cost six hundred thousand pounds to start the *Tribune*, and two millions to float the *Daily Herald*. The running costs of the *Daily Express* are five millions a year. Robespierre could carry on the *Défenseur* with what he had saved during the past two years from his deputy's salary of ive pounds a week. A comparison must therefore be looked for not in our great co-operative newspapers, but in the literary periodicals of the eighteenth century. These were not uncommonly the work of one pen. Dr Johnson, deeply immersed in his dictionary, found time to produce the *Rambler*, which he wrote entirely himself, every Tuesday and Saturday for two years.

Not all these papers reported the proceedings in the assembly, but the new legislature was inundated with demands for seats in the reporters' galleries which had been contrived by the old legislature. The *Logographe* wanted fifteen places; the editors of the *procès verbaux* wanted four; five were asked for by the *Journal du Soir*. The *Journal du père Gérard*, the *Gazette Universelle*, and the *Moniteur anglo-français* applied for seats: even the Paris correspondent of the *Morning Chronicle*.

The revolutionary papers did not as a rule contain much matter; but some of them had circulations that would be considered large even to-day. The usual issue was from two thousand to five thousand copies: but at the time when *Père Duchesne* was subsidized by the Jacobin government its circulation is said to have reached a million. The financial risk would be borne by the printer. The reading-matter was not more than an editor and a sub-editor could produce between them twice a week. Nor need politics be sacrificed to journalism. A modern editor must be at his desk early in the evening, and stay there most of the night. In 1791 he could remain in the House till it rose, and write his leading article, which was in effect the whole paper, before he went to bed. Above all, he was his own master. He had no shareholders who might quarrel with his views, no advertisers who might withdraw their custom. He need have no care for the tastes of an illiterate public, and no fear of actions for libel. Only the smallness of the reading public and the difficulties of circulation limited the power of the press.

It was significant of the changed political situation that during a temporary retirement from parliamentary life, in the reduced circle of a discredited club, and as a writer instead of a legislator, the leader of forlorn hopes in the National Assembly should become the champion of the Paris people.

Maximilien Robespierre had appeared among the deputies of 1789 as the singular and aggressive spokesman of an extravagant liberalism. He was poor, discontented, and suspicious of ridicule; but he was consumed by a little man's ambition to play a big part. He forced himself to the front by the assiduous cultivation of second-class talents. His solemn air, his carefully composed speeches, his mastery of revolutionary technique, the bourgeois respectability of his conduct, and the touch of aristocracy (always irresistible to the bourgeoisie) that he gave to his dress and manners, made him the idol of middle-class Jacobinism. Tradesmen and artisans relied on his persistent championship of their rights. Their women-folk found his speeches as comforting as sermons. His limited outlook and mediocre mind mirrored the thrifty virtues which had built up their small businesses. His vague and

rhetorical platitudes hung like illuminated texts in their tidy parlours. They
did not foresee that self-flattery and the need of power would turn his
liberalism into a dogma, his cult of virtue into an Inquisition, and his shrinking
from violence into the regime of the Terror. A cold, enigmatic, unattractive
man, he repeated within the limits of his small study and of his narrow soul
the full-blooded experiments of the revolution, and extracted nothing from
them but gall and wormwood.

Robespierre made it his mission in the autumn of '91, to save the country
from dangers which he saw gathering round it, and especially from the
threat of war. The first six months of the Legislative Assembly may well
seem the most depressing period of the whole revolution. It was a time of
reaction not unlike that which contemporary writers describe as succeeding
the great Reform Bill. But the legislators of 1791 were in a less fortunate
position than those of 1832. They were handcuffed to a defective constitution, which the king's treachery made it impossible to work, and
the selfishness of their predecessors impossible to revise. They were discredited by their association with the anti-republican reaction succeeding
July 17th. They were decried by the very men whose faults they were
expiating. They were faced by the most dangerous moment of any revolution—the back-wash of the first great wave of progress.

In Paris the issue lay between royalism and republicanism: in the provinces it lay between revolution and counter-revolution. The capital showed
its feeling about the affair of July 17th by rejecting Lafayette and electing as
its new mayor the popular and democratic Pétion (November 18th). It was
feeling the benefits of better trade, and of lower prices, though it was
still necessary for the assembly to vote the municipality fifteen thousand
pounds a month out of the national treasury. The provinces remained a
prey to deep and complicated disorders.

The citizens of Brie-Comte-Robert complained of brutal treatment by
the soldiery: Pétion suspected them of designs on the Paris food supply. The
administrators of the Basses-Pyrénées department were disturbed by movements of Spanish troops near the frontier. The municipality of Bayeux and
the Bishop of Charente-Inférieure accused the abbé Fauchet of preaching
anarchy and insurrection. There were disorders at Arles, and debates about
the agitated affairs of Avignon. Many troubles were due to the insoluble
food-question. At Douai a food-riot led to two deaths. The authorities of
Dunkirk begged the help of the assembly in dealing with attempts to prevent
the export of grain. Simoneau, the mayor of Etampes, when trying to
appease a food-riot, was shot dead in his own market-place.

Speculation in *assignats*, and the hoarding and exporting of currency, were
other sources of trouble. It was reported that the year 1791 showed a shortage of twelve and a half million pounds in tax-receipts, compared with the
yield under the old regime, and a deficit of twenty-one and a half millions

on the year's working. On February 18th, '92, Cahier de Gerville, the Minister of the Interior, reviewed the economic situation of the country. He laid particular stress upon the shortage of currency, and upon the difficulty of regulating the food supply. Food, he said, would never be satisfactorily distributed until the public were brought to understand four facts. They must realize that the duty of the administration is to provide bread, but not to fix the price of it; that grain is not the private property of the district that grows it, but belongs to the whole nation; that no human endeavour can alter the laws of supply and demand; and that if a shortage of supplies produces high prices, high prices in their turn produce abundance of supplies. If these bleak and questionable doctrines did not strike grain out of the rock, the minister was prepared to encourage the purchase of corn from Poland, or from Italy. But he warned the departments against putting up the price of grain by competitive buying. So the food-shortage and food-riots went on.

'I am a priest and a citizen,' wrote Thomas Lindet in May, 1790; 'the interests of my country, as I see them, are identical with the interests of my religion.' Not all the clergy saw things so simply. The controversy about the Civil Constitution and the clerical oath split the church into two parts, and gave rise to bitter feelings all over the country.

It is not easy to be sure of the proportion of jurors to non-jurors, of 'constitutional' to 'refractory' clergy. Conditions varied from diocese to diocese. Only two bishops in the National Assembly, and only five outside it, took the oath. In the clerical strongholds of the Nord, the Pas de Calais, the Bas-Rhin, Brittany, and the Vendée, between eighty and ninety clergy out of every hundred refused allegiance. In Normandy, the Moselle district, and the Midi they were equally divided on the issue. But the figures can be differently reckoned, and have been distorted by theological zeal. Some clergy who at first took the oath afterwards repudiated their action. Some took the oath with reservations, or substituted for it formulae of their own which were subsequently disallowed. Some stood by their oath, but refused to recognize the constitutional bishop who was placed over them. In the department of the Ain no less than six hundred and sixty-two out of seven hundred and seventy-two clergy originally took the oath; but many afterwards retracted it, or refused obedience to their new bishop. Viewing the country as a whole, and making allowance for these difficulties, it seems likely that of every hundred *curés*, *vicaires*, and *professeurs* who had to make their choice (other clergy were exempt from the test), about fifty accepted the oath, and fifty refused it.

The clerical oath not only split the church: it split the nation. All over France a breach was made in the old loyalties of the village home and the parish church. The priest was the political as well as the spiritual adviser of his people. If he took the oath, he might feel more deeply committed to the revolution; he would hardly feel more enthusiastic about it. If he refused th oath, he might think it his duty to decry and to obstruct the new regime. I was not an accident that the chief 'refractory' regions were also the region in which counter-revolution was most prevalent and disastrous.

Writing in October, '91, Salamon, the papal chargé d'affaires, took a gloom view of the prospects of the refractory clergy. He need not have done so There may have been villages like that in Périgord where the people force the priest to wear a tricolor cockade during mass, and to leave the tabernacle door open, so that *le bon Dieu fût libre*. But in most country parts the con gregation was likely to be less liberal than the *curé*. It was likely to be eve more opposed to any interference with centuries of church custom. Th position of the constitutional bishop or of the *curé intrus* (as a new constitutiona incumbent was called) was often made intolerable by persecution. At Bloi Grégoire obtained possession of his cathedral and of his palace: but his prede cessor organized an opposition regime in all the convent chapels of th diocese. Lafayette's rustic retirement at Chavaniac was disturbed by th quarrels of constitutional and refractory clergy. The fanatical Père de l Clarivière preached against *assermentés* priests as 'excommunicate, heretics and schismatics,' and forbade the faithful to hear their masses, to go to then for confession, or to receive any sacrament at their hands.

In Paris both sides were to blame for intolerance and persecution. Th 'conformist' nuns of the Cordelières convent in the Arsenal section com plained that propagandist literature was forced upon them by their 'non conformist' sisters-in-God. At the convent of Dames de la Croix in th Palais-Royal section a group of holy women who had refused the oat forced their company upon those who had taken it. The beatification o Sister Marie of the Incarnation, the foundress of the French Carmelites whose chief claim to sanctity lay in blind obedience to papal authority was turned into a demonstration against the Civil Constitution. The con stitutionals retaliated (May 4th) by burning the Pope in effigy.

The church of Saint-Louis-du-Louvre, authorized for Protestant worshi by the municipality, bore the inscription, *Edifice consacré au culte religieu. par une société particulière*. A body of non-juror Catholics hired the Theatin chapel, put up a similar notice, and sang mass there on Ascension Day (Jun 2nd). A crowd broke into the building, stopped the service, and smashed th altar. Even toleration became intolerant. On June 13th–16th processions o children who had just made their first communion at the hands of the con stitutional bishop, Gobel, came to the *manège*. Some of the infants were pu up in the assembly, and prompted to utter surprisingly mature sentiment on religious toleration. The demonstration was denounced by the abb Maury as not *enfantine* so much as *puérile*: but the House ordered th printing of the childish addresses, and of the President's complimentar reply.

Religious differences were so wide that it was impossible to conciliate them

One Sunday at the end of October Bailly and twelve members of the municipality attended a *Te Deum* sung by Huguenots and Lutherans in the church of Saint-Louis-du-Louvre. The papal chargé d'affaires expressed himself as highly scandalized. To an ultramontane toleration seemed outright anti-clericalism.

By the autumn of '91 the position of the non-juror clergy was further compromised by the king's flight, and by the growth of republican feeling. Controversy ran so high that the assembly called for a report, and held a debate. The reporters, Gallois of Aix and Gensonné of the Gironde, declared that the dispute about the oath was the chief cause of public unrest. They instanced the Vendée, whose distant and devout peasantry were being instructed by refractory priests to ban their constitutional rivals. It is a mortal sin, they were instructed, to partake of an *assermenté* sacrament. Children born of a constitutional marriage are bastards. They had better bury their dead like dogs than let a constitutional priest give them a schismatic funeral. Anyone who takes part in the induction of a *curé intrus*, from the mayor to the beadle or the bell-ringer, shares his apostasy. Meanwhile refractory priests were being instructed by the ex-bishop of Luçon to find a barn or other building in which to go on saying mass, with whatever vessels and vestments they could procure. They were to keep separate parish registers: they were to protest against the induction and the acts of their constitutional successor; and they were to maintain a foothold in the neighbourhood, so as to encourage the faithful in their resistance to the new regime.

There was at least one town in Brittany whose priest was stoned by one party of his parishioners when he took the oath, and by another party when he recanted it. There was at least one village whose parishioners divided their allegiance between one *assermenté* and two rival *insermenté* clergy. The constitution was never fully enforced. There were some parishes in which the non-juror cult continued without interruption till 1801. These parochial troubles (Gallois reported) were dividing husbands and wives, fathers and sons, and breaking up family life. Municipalities were embarrassed by the difficulty of finding new clergy to take the place of those deprived for refusing the oath: they were discredited if they did so. The magistrates who enforced the law earned the hatred of the countryside: the National Guard which carried out their orders could not find recruits.

The reduction of church establishments put a number of people out of work, from the 'cello-player of the Sainte-Chapelle to Mademoiselle Filleul, organist of the abbey of Longchamps. Sieyès found his retirement compromised by an appeal from the church choirs of the capital (grandiloquently styled *choristes des nouvelles paroisses de la métropole de l'empire*) to help them recover their wages, which, owing to the troubles, were three months in arrears. Even the ecclesiastical printers and publishers complained that the suppression of sixty-two bishoprics and the issue of a standardized liturgy would ruin their business.

In the debate on the Gallois report the abbé Fauchet put the case in its simplest terms. The question was, he said, how to combine liberty of religious opinion with the suppression of fanaticism, the antithesis of true religion. But the only remedy he could suggest was that the refractory clergy should be deprived of their stipends as well as of their cures. Some would then take the oath; the rest could look for employment outside the church. The assembly agreed with Torné, the Jacobin Bishop of Bourges, that this would be a cruel and unjust discrimination. It was the business of the government to keep order, and to enforce toleration on both parties.

But there was a limit to the patience of the deputies. A week after the debate there came fresh complaints from the department of Mayenne et Loire. Night-time processions were being organized by seditious priests. The demonstrators were no longer armed with rosaries, but with guns, and scythes, pitch-forks and pikes. They were attacking the National Guard. Constitutional priests had been mobbed, and even murdered. Churches closed by government order had been broken open for use by non-juror clergy. The people were refusing to pay their taxes. There were all the symptoms of a civil war.

This time the assembly instructed its *comité de législation* to make proposals for action. A week later the Girondin Isnard, a bitter anti-clerical, called for the exile of all counter-revolutionary priests. On November 20th was passed the first 'Decree relating to the troubles caused on the pretext of religion.' Its eighteen articles provided that the oath should be enforced, and that lists should be made of those who refused it; that non-jurors should be deprived of their stipends, treated as suspects, and, if necessary, removed and imprisoned; and that their churches could be assigned to other cults. Louis, moved by the protests of the Paris department, and of the archbishops of Paris and Aix, vetoed the decree. From this moment war was declared between the revolutionary government and the refractory church. There was already talk of the solution found three years later, when the government disclaimed further responsibility for any religious denomination, and church and state went their separate ways.

The French word *émigré* has the same derivation as the English word 'emigrant,' but a different meaning. Both languages have another word— *réfugié*, 'refugee'—for one who is driven abroad by political or religious persecution. An 'emigrant' is one who leaves his native land to better his condition elsewhere. An *émigré* leaves his native land because he dislikes its government. An *émigré* works for the overthrow of the new regime. An *émigré* is ready to join in a foreign invasion of his country in order to regain his position and power.

The *émigré par excellence* was the French aristocrat of the revolutionary period. He had been demoralized by lack of political responsibility. He was cut off by his caste from every-day contacts with other classes. He was often unfit to adapt himself to the ideas and institutions of a regime which asked him to share liberty and equality with his banker and his baker. That he should flee the country hardly seemed unpatriotic to an age which remembered the Huguenots and the Pilgrim Fathers. It hardly seemed unpatriotic to an age which still spoke of France as *nation* or *empire* more naturally than it spoke of it as *patrie*, and which used *patriote* as the name of a political party. Chateaubriand, to whom the matter had a personal interest, claimed that no one should denounce political refugees until he has experienced political persecution. Yet the *émigrés* of the revolutionary period were rightly reproached for their association with the enemies of their country. They were justly blamed for deserting not only their country, but also their king. No theory of class excused them for treating their fellow-countrymen as revolted vassals. No theory of patriotism excused them for preparing armed vengeance upon the state they should have defended against foreign attack.

It is reasonable to distinguish the first emigration of July and October, 1789, from the second emigration of 1791, and the third emigration of 1792. The first emigration was led by the Comte d'Artois, the Polignacs, and others whose way of life had done much to bring on the revolution, and whose policy had inspired the king's ill-judged resistance to it. They fled the country because they feared the vengeance of the people; but their temper was that of rebels rather than of refugees.

The *émigrés* of 1791 were men who went in no danger of their lives, but who could not face an existence shorn of the privileges, the wealth, and the amenities to which they had grown accustomed. They were men who put class before country, rights before duties, and property before patriotism. Their self-exile deprived the throne of a support which might have restored political balance to the constitution. The *émigrés* of 1792, on the other hand, were for the most part men who had done all they could for their creed, and could not have stayed longer without inviting martyrdom.

The first emigration went partly to Brussels, and partly to Turin; but its headquarters was in the Rhineland. This district had become increasingly French since its penurious rulers accepted the patronage of Louis XIV, and was well known to fashionable tourists. Here were German towns— Saarbrücken, Zweibrücken, Landau—which had given their citizens and names to famous regiments in the French army. Here were German rulers —an Elector of Trier, a Prince-elector of Köln—who were close relations of the king and queen of France. No other district was so accessible or so attractive. The gaming-tables of Aix and the post-house at Coblentz were soon crowded with refugee nobles from across the French frontier. They lived a dull and quarrelsome life. Their morals were often as bad as their debts. But they did not as yet arm or intrigue against their country.

The second emigration bore a different character. Already during 1790 d'Artois and Condé had tried to organize counter-revolution from Turin.

When a plan for revolt at Lyon failed, they turned (November, '90) to the idea of calling in foreign help. By June, '91, d'Artois had made Coblentz the centre of a propaganda which seriously embarrassed the king's attempt to escape from Paris. In July he was joined by his brother, the Comte de Provence, and by a fresh batch of refugees, whose flight was due to the king's recapture, and to the fear of war. During the autumn there was a steady flow of titled emigrants both from Paris and from the provinces.

The smart, expensive, and disorderly life led by these persons at Coblentz reproduced the scandals as well as the quarrels of Versailles. Their political attitude is well enough expressed by a letter from d'Artois to the King of Sweden, dated July 22nd. 'We shall refuse,' he writes, 'to obey our king's orders until the day when he is restored to the throne, under the true constitution, giving him full power, so that he can rule according to the ancient laws of the kingdom. Till then we shall regard all his acts as sealed under compulsion; and our affection and devotion to him, as well as our sense of duty, will make us reject every proposal, determined as we are to shed our last drop of blood for the genuine restoration of the throne of our ancestors, and of the French monarchy.'

Loyal refugees like Augeard doubted the 'affection and devotion' of the princes, and hated the royalists of Coblentz almost as bitterly as the Jacobins of Paris. Others preferred action to intrigue. At Worms Condé had been mobilizing since May the military men who were prepared to fight. They probably numbered two thousand by the end of the year. They lived the simple strenuous life of the parade-ground. They were quixotic and fanatical, and they held a poor opinion of their half-hearted friends at Coblentz. They looked forward to the moment when they would recross the frontier, sword in hand. Vengeance would be cheaply won at the price of the pillaging of their estates, the burning of their homes, and the prescription of the relatives and friends they had left behind them.

Paris rumour multiplied the *émigrés* like Falstaff's men in buckram. Their published intentions were less alarming than their imagined intrigues. Their armed adherents (it was said) lurked in the cellars of the Tuileries. Their secret agents carried cypher messages to and from the frontier, or smuggled boxes of specie out of the country. Their allies, the refractory priests, crept back to Paris disguised as National Guardsmen, to hatch plots for the assassination of patriot leaders. Was it surprising that, whilst on the German side of the frontier the refugees became increasingly unwelcome guests, there should have come from the French side of the frontier ever louder demands for their expulsion?

As early as February, '91, questions were raised in the assembly about the emigration laws. In August a decree against the *émigrés* was only annulled by the general amnesty that followed Louis' acceptance of the constitution. In October the king, in order to prevent further penal legislation, exhorted generals, port commandants, rich proprietors, and other notable refugees, to return to their duties. On October 20th there was a full-dress debate of a rather academic character on the whole subject. To Vergniaud emigration seemed a breach of the *pacte sociale*, the basis of the state. Pastoret quoted Montesquieu and Rousseau in support of some restriction on liberty of movement. Condorcet thought a free country could not prohibit it.

But the deputies cared as little for Condorcet's philosophy as for Isnard's fiery rhetoric. They were determined to do something, and only wondered what steps would be the most effective. Should they enforce stricter passport regulations? Should they prohibit the export of munitions? Should they confiscate *émigré* property? Should they require the refugees to return, or their foreign protectors to expel them?

The first result of the debate was a decree requiring Monsieur, the king's elder brother, to return to France. If he failed to do so within two months, he would lose his right to the Regency, and his succession to the throne. This invitation produced no effect. It was followed by the first penal legislation against emigration in general. A decree of November 9th declared all *émigrés* to be suspected of conspiracy. If they were still mobilized (*en état de rassemblement*) on January 1st, their guilt would be regarded as proved, and they would be liable to the death penalty. The property of the *émigré* princes was sequestrated, and all payments to them were stopped. Refugee officers and officials lost their posts and their emoluments. Any officer emigrating after the date of the decree would be treated as a deserter.

A month later, Louis vetoed this decree. He preferred, he said, to make a solemn appeal to his brothers to return. He expressed his surprise that they had paid no attention to his invitation of October 16th. He asserted that the revolution was over, and that he intended to uphold the constitution. He claimed that their proper place was by his side. 'I invite you to take that place,' he ended: 'if need be, I order you to do so.' The replies showed how useless it was to ask a Bourbon to change his mind. Both princes pretended not to recognize the style in which their royal brother had addressed them, in accordance with the terms of the new constitution: *prince français, frère du roi*. Both insisted that Louis was not a free agent. Both categorically refused to return. It was, in effect, a declaration of war between the emigration and the revolution, between the Bourbon family and a traitor to the dynastic tradition.

The capital mistake of the *émigrés* was to emigrate. They could have done much more harm to the revolution from inside the country than from outside it. History should have taught them that France was peculiarly susceptible to civil war, but that it would unite against any threat of foreign invasion. The most dangerous enemy the Legislative Assembly had to face was neither the enemy troops, nor the enemy court beyond the frontier, but the civilian forces of counter-revolution all over the country, with their centre of intrigue at the Tuileries. 'All intelligent Frenchmen,' said Robespierre on January 2nd, '92, 'know that Coblentz is really in France.'

The counter-revolution was not a new thing: it was as old as the revolution itself. It rested upon the discontents of a nobility deprived of titles, exemptions, and privileges; of a church robbed of its wealth, and resentful of secular control; and of a magistrature ousted from profits and emoluments. There was, indeed, a sense in which the counter-revolution was even older than the revolution. The efficiently organized rising in Brittany in '89 was based on a provincial separatism which had not forgotten the Cellamare plot of 1718. La Rouerie was as ready to call in George III against Louis XVI as Cardinal Polignac had been to call in Philip V against Louis XV. La Rouerie's plot had appealed not merely to the traditional factiousness (*frondisme*) of the country gentlemen, and to the inherent fanaticism of the country clergy, but also to the less reputable motives of the smugglers, vagabonds, and other adventurers who became the Chouans of a later and more formidable insurrection. It antedated the attack on feudal privilege, as the peasant risings antedated the attack on the Bastille.

It needed a negative as well as positive terminal to produce the spark of counter-revolution. This was provided by the bad state of the country in the second year of revolution. Everywhere the old regime was still partly intact, the new regime still partly unenforced. In '91, and even in '92, the national mints were still coining the old Bourbon *louis* and *écus* of '89 alongside the new coinage, with its winged figure writing *constitution* on a tablet resting on the altar of the country. This slowness to change was due to a number of causes: the inertia of a society so long unaccustomed to change; the obstructiveness, sometimes inveterate, sometimes deliberate, of government officials; and the lack of material and mental lines of communication.

Another factor which might have been expected to make for progress really hampered it. The anxiety of the assembly to conduct an orderly advance prevented the free play of those popular forces which had fought for the revolution in its early struggle against the king, and which might have been enlisted to carry on its later struggle against the counter-revolution. The anxiety of the leaders of the middle class to preserve a structure of society in which they were at home, and in which their interests were secure, precluded social and economic experiments which might have won them the active support of the lower classes. Here lay the seriousness of the events of July 1791. In its dread of republicanism the assembly had committed itself to the repression of its best ally, the people of Paris. By its constitutional policy it had alienated the working class in the towns. By its church policy it had alienated the working class in the villages. The bonfire it had started to entertain the public was in danger of setting the whole town ablaze.

Only two things prevented a conflagration. One was the conduct of the counter-revolutionaries themselves. The other was the outbreak of war. In the middle of July *fédérés* from all over France, the representatives of the two million members of the National Guard, were celebrating on the Champ de Mars the anniversary of the fall of the Bastille. In the middle of August a counter-revolutionary army, which some estimated at forty-eight thousand men, led by royalist nobles, and wearing the Bourbon cockade, assembled at Jalès, near Nîmes, and swore 'to reinstate the king in his glory, the clergy in their possessions, and the nobility in their privileges.' At various points of the Midi, during the following months—at Perpignan, at Arles, at Montpellier, at Mende in the Vivarais—there were risings, in which counter-revolutionaries fought patriots on this fundamental issue, town against town, and village against village; and sometimes they prevailed.

In these districts, at least, France knew that it had to fight for its revolution, and learnt that it was worth fighting for. Thus it may be said that the counter-revolution saved the revolution from the decay into which it was in danger of falling during the winter of '91. It was saved even more effectually by the war which broke out in the spring of '92.

CHAPTER XIV

WAR

C'est une chose cruelle à penser, mais qui devient tous les jours plus frappante, que nous devons rétrograder par la paix et que nous ne saurions être régénérés que par le sang. Caractère léger, mœurs corrompues ou frivoles, voilà des données incompatibles avec la liberté, qui ne peuvent être changées que par l'adversité.—(MADAME ROLAND, 1791.)

THE last thing any Frenchman expected in May, 1789, was that within three years his country would be at war. The community of ideas which united the governing classes of Europe at the end of the eighteenth century was, indeed, no better guarantee of peace than the community of commercial interests or the athletic rivalry which was expected to prevent war at the beginning of the twentieth century. But France was the dispersion-centre of the Enlightenment. It was to be expected that with the advent of a benevolent king, and the appointment of philosophic ministers, the country which had taught reform to Europe would at last reform itself.

Even the prospect of a French revolution held no special menace for a world that had applauded dynastic revolution in Sweden, and democratic revolution in America. Had not France itself, with the connivance of a Bourbon ruler, helped to free rebels from a regime not unlike its own? Before 1789 the benevolent despots of Europe had welcomed in Louis XVI a new recruit to their ranks. After 1789 they were hopefully aware of advantages to be won from a country weakened and divided by revolution. This observant attitude might have altered sooner than it did, if the revolution had shown itself provocative or hostile to foreign interests. But from the first it professed pacifism, and opened its arms to aliens. Nothing could have been less alarming. Nothing could have been better calculated—though in fact it sprang from sheer lightness of heart—to win the confidence of the cynical old eighteenth century.

Meanwhile, there was hardly a state in Europe whose government did not rest upon the support of the landlords, and the subjection of the peasantry. There was hardly an aristocracy which might not be alarmed to hear of the *jacquerie*, or of the *grande peur*. There was hardly a middle class which might not be inspired by the political victory of the French *bourgeois* assembly, or by the national enthusiasm which staged the fête of Federation.

In Europe as a whole the situation was not unlike that which history records in the sixteenth century. The countries then open or closed to the Protestant Reformation were the countries now open or closed to the French Revolution. Southern and eastern Europe, except for a minority of travelled merchants in north Italian towns, and of Frenchified counts in Austrian or Polish castles, had as little in common with Rousseauism as with Lutheranism. In the west and north, where the rift between landlordism and commercialism gave a root-like hold to some shoots of popular liberty, religious toleration pointed the way to political liberalism.

Nowhere was this more evident than in England. Though France was a hereditary and a recent enemy, war had stimulated rather than retarded the flow of travellers and ideas across the Channel. Though we were ruled by landlords, and gloried in the bloodless revolution of 1688, yet we could not forget that our most famous Parliament had cut off the head of our most respectable king. Though religious revivalism was diverting the minds of the new working class from earthly grievances to hopes of heaven, yet they might at any moment find a political Gordon to lead them to something more serious than the burning of the Sardinian chapel or the plundering of the Sessions-house at the Old Bailey.

The news of the fall of the Bastille was welcomed in England by Price for the moralists, by Priestley for the theologians, and by Southey and Wordsworth for the young idealists. Scottish philosophy, by the pen of Mackintosh, answered Burke's indictment of so un-English a revolution. 'Friends of the People' memorialized the National Assembly, and prided themselves on affiliation to the Jacobin club. These sympathizers were doubtless a small minority. If their influence spread, it was owing to the growth of working-class feeling, and to the preoccupation of the government with the financial troubles following the American war.

In any case England would never fight a war against mere ideas, however alien. There must be some threat to the City of London, or to the King's peace. But if such a threat could be proved, the government would have less scruple in finding a *casus belli* against an opponent who held subversive views on property or religion.

THE NORTH-EAST FRONTIER

To illustrate the journey
to Varennes
and the campaigns of
1792 – 4

Scale in miles
0 10 20 30 40 50   100

EAST
FRIESLAND

BENTHEIM

BISHOPRIC
OF MUNSTER

Münster

Amsterdam

The Hague
Rotterdam

LEK
WAAL
Nimwegen

DUTCH
FRONTIER

Dordrecht
Breda
Bergen-op-
300m
Walcheren
Flushing

MAAS
Cleves
CLEVES
Wesel

UNITED
NETHERLANDS

Gelders

RHINE

Essen
MARK

BELGIAN
FRONTIER

Ostend
Dunkirk
Calais
Boulogne

Bruges
Ghent

Antwerp

Venloo
GUELDERS
Roermonde

Düsseldorf

BERG

AUSTRIAN
NETHERLANDS

SCHELDT

Louvain

Maestricht

JÜLICH
Aachen

Köln

Bonn

Hondschoote
Ypres
St Omer
Lille

LYS

Tourcoing
Tournai

Brussels

Neerwinden

Liège
LIÈGE

ARCHBISHOPRIC OF KÖLN

Coblenz

Abbeville
Arras
Bapaume
Cambrai

Douai
Valenciennes
Condé
Mons
SAMBRE
Jemappes
Maubenge
Watlighies

Charleroi
Namur

Dinant

ARCHBISHOPRIC OF TRIER

Peronne
St Quentin
Guise

SOMME
Amiens

Rocroy

LUXEMBOURG

Trier

Mezières
Rethel
Sedan

OISE
Laon
Soissons
AISNE

Compiegne

Reims

MEUSE

Montmédy
Longwy

Luxembourg

Sarre louis

Thionville

SARRE

GERMAN
FRONTIER

Chateau
Thierry
Epernay
Dormans
LaFerté
Châlons
Montmirail

Valmy
St Menehould

Varennes
Clermont
Verdun

Metz

MOSELLE

Meaux

Paris
MARNE

SEINE
AIRE

Toul

Nancy
Lunéville
MEURTHE

THE NORTH-EAST FRONTIER

Prussia and Austria, Russia and Scandinavia, had, since the middle of the century, been inoculated with the virus of the Enlightenment. Revolutionary propaganda, though heralded or pioneered by such names as Kant and Fichte, Humboldt and Forster, penetrated with difficulty into the jungle of feudal institutions east of the Rhine valley, and did little more than interest the intelligentsia of Vienna and Copenhagen. Regular subscribers to the Encyclopaedia became admirers of Mirabeau, and adorned their mantel-pieces with stones from the Bastille. When the news of July 14th arrived, liberals embraced one another in the streets of St Petersburg; and at Tzarskoe-Selo a brother of Marat, who was teaching French to Catherine the Great's ladies-in-waiting, began to speculate on the possibility of a career in Paris.

But the Enlightenment had always fallen like manna from heaven. It had never grown out of European soil. No continental country had a middle class fit to lead a political crusade, or a working class ready to follow it. Nowhere did the revolution find a mirror to reflect it, except in the Austrian Netherlands; and there it was, ironically enough, a looking-glass revolution, in which Right was Left, and Left was Right. The *révolution de Brabant* that Desmoulins' journal coupled with the *révolution de France* was a reactionary revolt of Catholic and provincial privilege against the liberating ideas of Joseph II.

Nothing was more unpopular in France than the thirty-year old alliance with Austria. It had begun in military disaster, and had ended in diplomatic defeat. It had made possible, in the last few years, an understanding between England, Holland, and Prussia, embodied in the Triple Alliance of '88. Yet no move was made to support the Belgian revolt of '89. The Nootka Sound crisis of May, '90, nearly brought on war between England and Spain for the control of Vancouver island and its Chinese trade. For some weeks it was expected that France would back its dynastic ally, Spain; and Gouverneur Morris wrote from London urging the opportunity to attack British commerce. Naval and military preparations were made on both sides of the Channel. War fever was fomented by those who wished to destroy the Eden treaty, and by those who wished to destroy the revolution. A dangerous situation was resolved by the pacific intentions of Mirabeau and Pitt, and the secret mission of Sir Hugh Elliott. The occasion was taken to make a public profession of non-intervention. 'The National Assembly,' it was announced, 'declares that the French nation will refuse to undertake any war of conquest, and will never employ its forces against the liberty of any people.' This declaration was not, as it might be nowadays, a move in the war game. It was an honest expression of a pacific policy. The deputies heard unmoved Mirabeau's warning that, unless other nations could be induced to adopt their point of view, France might find herself unarmed in the midst of an armed Europe, and international peace would remain a pleasant dream.

But French enthusiasm can always be deflated by a *reductio ad absurdum*. There was in Paris at this time a French-speaking Dutchman from Cleves who had recently, in a fit of anti-clericalism, changed his name from Jean-Baptiste to Anacharsis Cloots (after the Scythian friend of the Greek legislator Solon) and had shown his emancipation from religious intolerance by presenting the assembly with a work in praise of Mohammedanism. On June 19th this man led through the House a deputation of thirty-six so-called foreigners in national costumes borrowed from the wardrobe of the Opera, and made a harangue in honour of 'France, the new mother of all peoples.' The deputies, to whom this eccentric 'member for the universe,' with his long hair and frantic gestures, appeared to be out of his mind, reacted against Cloots' romanticism, and began to think more realistically.

Nationalism in the old dynastic sense was worse than meaningless. But might it not be re-expressed in terms of popular sovereignty? The Family Compact with Spain might persist as a friendly agreement between two neighbouring nations. No historical claims by the papacy could prevail against the wish of the Avignonese for reunion with the French people. No legal documents drawn up in 1648, no diplomatic guarantees given in 1756, could entitle the Alsatian landlords to prevent the free absorption of their tenants into the revolutionary land-system. What if the *supremum dominium* had been ceded to the French king without the *superioritas regia*? What if property rights in land admittedly French were derived from and guaranteed by the Emperor? Let the rich absentee owners—princes, perhaps, in the Empire, but in France no better than other nobles: Margrave of Baden, Landgrave of Hesse-Darmstadt, Prince-Bishop of Strasbourg, or whatever their outlandish names might be—protest as they liked, and work up indignation among the clergy, magistrates, and industrialists of Alsace. It was enough if the mass of the small farmers and country-people regained their liberty and their land.

German diplomatists thought such views absurd. But the new Emperor Leopold (February, 1790) distrusted the zeal with which the King of Prussia urged him to take up the cause of the Alsatian landlords. He suspected that Frederick William II was hoping to partition another Poland—a province which bargained in French, prayed in German, and opposed whatever might be the government of the day. He would have welcomed a peaceful settlement; and this might have been secured, if the landowners had accepted the monetary compensation proposed by Louis XVI's agent de Ternant in May, and repeated by the assembly, under Mirabeau's influence, in December.

But by this time opinion had hardened on both sides. France, since the fête of Federation of July 14th, was in a more missionary mood. The Diet of Ratisbon was pressing the Emperor to take up arms. Leopold temporized; and the question was allowed to drag on, until it became entangled with the problem of the *émigrés*, and compromised by the flight to Varennes.

The Declaration of Pillnitz (August 27th, '91) contained a threat of armed intervention at some more convenient time by the Emperor and the King of Prussia, and provided a *casus belli*, if the assembly chose to make it so. It was the opening move of a twenty-five years' war.

The position of Avignon was almost as complicated as that of Schleswig-Holstein seventy years later. The town of Avignon itself, and the Comtat Venaissin, whose capital was Carpentras, had been papal territory ever since the 'captivity' of the fourteenth century. Orange, seventeen miles north-west of Avignon, and inside the Comtat—an enclave within an enclave— once belonged to the German princes of Nassau, but had been French since 1715. Carpentras was as papal and aristocratic in sympathy as Avignon was democratic and French. Whilst Avignon was asking for reunion with France, Carpentras petitioned the Pope to grant it a constitution. Orange wanted French protection against both its neighbours. Negotiations in this tangled affair began after the Avignon revolt of June, 1790, and ended in the annexation of both territories in September, 1791.

The assembly proceeded cautiously. It did not wish to act without the unanimous vote of the Avignonese or the consent of the Pope. But the negotiations were complicated and delayed by the controversy about the Civil Constitution. Menou's report (April 30th, '91) advised annexation. A plebiscite showed that a hundred and two thousand out of a hundred and fifty thousand citizens were in favour of this step. Matters were held up, during the next few months, by the king's flight, and by the revision of the constitution. At Avignon itself a military rising under 'Executioner' (*coupe-tête*) Jourdan set up an insurrectional commune, which avenged the death of its patriot mayor by a particularly brutal mass-murder of aristocrats.

Thus, when the annexation came, it was welcomed as an act of pacification rather than denounced as an act of conquest. But though it was carried through with the consent of the annexed populations, and accepted as a *fait accompli* by the powers, it could hardly be squared with the non-interventionist declaration of May, 1790. It offended the Emperor as well as the Pope. It suggested the establishment under French protection of a federal union open to all peoples desirous of liberation from their established rulers. The whole incident created suspicion of French aims, and increased the danger of war.

Marie-Antoinette's first thought, after the return from Varennes, was for Fersen. 'Don't be alarmed on our account,' she wrote to him three days later; 'we are still alive.' 'I am still alive,' she wrote again the next day; 'but I have been worrying about you, and what you must have suffered from not hearing about us.' Her second thought was how to resume the line of conduct which had already led to disaster. Before June, '91, the Tuileries had been a prison. After June, '91, it became a fort. It was now an outpost of the Austrian line; and its garrison was the royal family. Neither the *émigrés*, nor the refractory clergy, nor the food troubles, nor the political embarrassments of the Brissotins, contributed so much to the causes of war as the suspicion, which history has long since justified, that the king and queen were still plotting against the revolution. Throughout the autumn of '91 and the winter of '91–2 a double intrigue went on. There were, as before the flight, two plans. One was designed to throw dust in the eyes of the politicians. The other was designed to secure intervention by the powers.

In October, '91, Lamarck left Paris to join Mercy d'Argenteau at Brussels. Cabanis had now ceased to offer the court advice which was not accepted. During the months of the king's suspension from office he was deprived of the advice of his ministers, who met without him at the residence of the Minister of Justice. It was under these circumstances that Mirabeau's place as counsellor and dupe of the court was taken by the handsome and arrogant young politician who had attracted and been attracted by the queen during the journey from Varennes.

Antoine-Joseph-Marie-Pierre Barnave was the son of a Protestant solicitor and a penniless aristocrat. He inherited blue blood without a thick skin, and bitterly resented the exclusion of his father's family, both as bourgeois and non-Catholic, from the society to which his mother belonged. Practising as a barrister at Grenoble, he disliked the *fin-de-siècle* society in which Choderlos de Laclos had found material for his *Liaisons dangereuses*; but he appreciated the anti-monarchical temper of the provincial *parlement*. The author of some able and provocative pamphlets—his *Introduction à la révolution française*, published fifty years after his death, has been held to anticipate Saint Simon and Comte—Barnave became Mounier's lieutenant in the pre-revolutionary movement of the Dauphiné, and was from the first one of a dozen marked men in the National Assembly. He was a born orator. Arthur Young picked him out immediately as one who 'spoke without notes with great warmth and animation.' It was an over-ready tongue which betrayed him into the brutal and famous retort to Lally-Tollendal's sentimentalizing of the Foullon-Berthier murders—*Ce sang était-il donc si pur?* It was an over-ready temper which led him to attack Mirabeau and Brissot, and to fight a duel with Cazalès. It was a generosity, perhaps over-ready too, which prompted his defence of Lafayette on June 22nd, and made him now the champion of a desolate and despairing princess.

But his mind went with his heart to the help of the queen. He was convinced that a revolution which had not gone far enough at Grenoble had gone too far in Paris. He believed that the throne was in danger. He was ambitious to carry on Mirabeau's policy as the confidant of the Tuileries. He cannot have had much private talk with the queen during the publicity of the return from Varennes; but she had guessed enough of his sentiments to suggest a correspondence. She thought that he might advise her as to the best steps to secure the king's full restoration to power. Between the first week of July, '91, and the first week of January, '92, nearly a hundred letters passed between them. The intermediaries were the Comte de Jarjayes, himself a Grenoble man, and his wife, who acted with Madame Campan as *femme-de-chambre* to the queen. Behind Barnave were his two partners in what has been called a Triumvirate—Adrien Duport, deputy for the Paris *noblesse*, and Alexandre de Lameth, deputy for the Commons of Péronne. D'André of Aix and Mathieu Dumas completed the inner circle of those taken into the confidence of the three. Perhaps ten more, including Lafayette, knew what was going on.

Barnave's advice to the king was that he should accept and hold to the constitution, as the only means of re-establishing his power. His advice to the queen was that she should give up her opposition to the revolution, and her plans for escape. 'A clever government,' he writes on August 28th, 'enjoying public confidence, and the advantage that permanent ministers have over a legislature whose members cannot retain office more than four years, would practically become the legislating power ... whilst the executive is entirely in the king's hands.'

There were three good reasons why this policy could not possibly be successful. First, it paid no regard to the change in the situation since Varennes. 'The People of this City,' wrote Morris on October 10th, 'are become wonderfully fond of the king,' and described how the groundlings (*parterre*) at the Italian Comedy had 'cried out continually *Vive le roi! Vive votre Majesté!*' But there was little in this. The king's apparent popularity in '91 was as unmeaning as his apparent power in '89. If it had been useless for Mirabeau, a year ago, to tell Louis to be wise, and Marie-Antoinette to be prudent, it was doubly useless for Barnave to do so now, when no wisdom or prudence in the world could efface the impression of one disastrous mistake.

Secondly, whilst the king never answered even Montmorin's letters, the queen herself, whatever the motives with which she began the correspondence with Barnave, soon ceased to take it seriously. 'The *Grande Dame* is mistaken,' writes the papal *chargé d'affaires* on August 28th, 'if she thinks one can influence the opinion of twenty-four million excited Frenchmen as one might that of a tiny province. She has learnt nothing from the failure of her various advisers to control the assembly. . . . Nothing but force can now change the situation.' By the end of the year, if not before, the *Grande Dame* herself had ceased to expect anything of the correspondence. This appears plainly enough in her letters to Fersen. After speaking, on December 7th, of her various advisers, she goes on to say, 'I want you to understand my position, and the part I am forced to play every day. Sometimes I scarcely know what I am doing, and am hard put to it to realize that it is I who am speaking. But what else can I do? We should be even worse off than we are, if I hadn't adopted this line from the first. It will at least enable us to gain time, and that's the essential thing. How I should love some day to be in a position to prove to these beggars (*gueux*) that I was never taken in by them!'

There was a third reason why Barnave's post-Mirabeau plan could not but fail. The king and queen had once again placed all their hopes elsewhere. A new secret diplomacy (*secret du roi*) in the best Bourbon tradition was expected to work a miracle of deliverance. It was pursued with the advice of Montmorin, Malouet, and de Moleville, the nucleus of the so-called *comité autrichien*, through a clandestine correspondence with Vienna. Its cyphered messages offered strange contrasts both to the official despatches dictated to Montmorin by the Diplomatic Committee, and to the letters that Jarjayes conveyed to the bemused Barnave.

Whilst d'Artois is being officially informed, on the king's orders (July 31st), that foreign intervention is so unlikely, and France so strong, that he should return to the country, Louis is writing personally to Leopold, saying that the government is in a state of chaos, and that 'he had no doubt the Emperor will do all that his generous heart dictates to come to the help of the king and the French kingdom.'

On November 23rd Barnave advises Louis (as the Paris department did a fortnight later) to veto the decrees against the priests and *émigrés*, and propounds a plan of monarchical propaganda *à la Mirabeau*. On the 27th he dictates a note to Mercy, intended for the Comte de Provence, urging the return of the refugees, as the sole safeguard against civil war. But only the day before (November 26th) Fersen had sent the queen a long memorandum advising an armed congress of the powers, not, indeed, to invade France, but to invest it (*seulement pour entourer et jamais pour entrer dans le royaume*, as Salamon puts it); and he had drafted the appeals that Louis should send to the Emperor, the Empress of Russia, and the Kings of Prussia and Sweden. A letter from Louis to the King of Spain, written on the same day as this memorandum, shows that he saw nothing inconsistent in accepting the constitution and proposing a congress of powers to overthrow it. Throughout these negotiations Barnave's advice was ignored, and Fersen's prevailed.

Early in the new year Barnave retired to his native Dauphiné, still professing belief in the queen's honesty, and in the soundness of his advice. Yet it is difficult not to think that he had at last discovered her dupery, and his danger. To the public eye he had been a man of the people in '89, and a man of the court in '91. Caricaturists depicted him as 'Mr. Facing-both-ways,' with the lines—

> Now hot, now cold, now black, now white,
> Now left-wards turning, and now right,
> I said 'Good morning': now I say 'Good night.'

When he was on trial for his life nearly two years later, Barnave denied his connexion with the queen, and swore that he had never set foot in the Tuileries. It would have been better for him if it had been true.

By the time that Barnave left Paris the international barometer had fallen from 'change' to 'stormy.' Both his plan for a revived monarchy and Fersen's plan for a congress of the powers had been swept away by the rising wind of war. Already (December 4th) the king, tired of friendly appeals, and under pressure of the assembly, had sent an ultimatum to the Elector of Trier demanding the expulsion of the *émigrés*. He consoled himself with the fantastic idea that he might with profit engage the country in a war of limited liability (*guerre politique et d'observation*). Such a war might unite the people behind their traditional leader in times of national emergency—the king. Louis might head a national movement against the universally unpopular *émigrés* and their foreign protectors. This might be done without involving the danger of total war on the Empire, and without focusing public attention on what was now openly called the Austrian Committee at the Tuileries.

Louis found no support for this policy of despair among his Feuillant ministers. They had hitherto backed Barnave's advice, and worked for peace. Having nothing else to stand by, they feared above all the overthrow of the monarchical constitution. But early in December Louis replaced his inactive Minister of War, Duportail, by the bustling Comte de Narbonne. Rumour made Narbonne an illegitimate son of Louis XV. An able soldier, with more than a soldier's knowledge of foreign languages and foreign affairs, he had ingratiated himself at court by convoying the king's aunts during their flight to Rome. He was supported by the reputation of Lafayette, and by the influence of his mistress, Necker's daughter, now the wife of the Swedish ambassador, the Baron de Stael.

With these encouragements, Narbonne welcomed a chance of military service and political power. As soon as he became minister he carried out a hasty inspection of the frontier fortresses. A plan of campaign was settled with the newly-appointed marshals Luckner and Rochambeau. The assembly was assured (January 11th) that an army of over a hundred thousand men was ready to defend the frontier.

Nor did the activities of Narbonne's mistress pass unnoticed. Paris gossip declared that a 'female Triumvirate'—the queen at the Foreign Office, Madame de Lamballe at the Home Office, and Madame de Stael at the Ministry of War—now managed the affairs of the nation. Caricaturists represented the king as a weather-cock on the roof of the Tuileries, now blown eastwards towards Austria by the queen's *côterie*, and now westwards by prudence and fear towards—a royal scaffold in Whitehall.

Two years ago the presence of Lafayette at the head of a French army would have been sufficient proof that it was being used solely for national defence. Now this was not so certain. The air was full of sinister rumours. It was said that Lafayette was in league with Mercy d'Argenteau, the Lameth brothers, Clermont-Tonnerre, the two Duports, de Moleville, and others of the Feuillant party, to march his army on Paris, to dissolve the Jacobin club, and to revise the constitution in the interests of the king and the privileged orders. The papers of Dumouriez include a letter of April 27th in which he warns Biron, then serving under Rochambeau, that attempts will be made to corrupt his loyalty, and in which he accuses Lafayette of aspiring to a dictatorship. He was at worst ante-dating by a few months a conspiracy which contributed to the *débâcle* of August, '92.

Whilst the politicians were calculating how to use the war to increase their power, the financiers were calculating how to use the war to increase their wealth. The bankers decided that war would on the whole be more profitable to them than peace. 'The evil resulting from war,' wrote one firm to another, 'will be less than from a continuation of the present situation: but it must always mean some loss. When a business man has done his duty by his country, it is time for him to consider his own interests.'

Narbonne, with his soldierly ambition, and Brissot, with his missionary zeal, either ignored or were ignorant of the selfish and seditious undertones of war. Since the middle of December, Brissot, with the confidence of a man who knew nothing of military affairs, and with the irresponsibility of a legislator who could never be a minister, had been advocating the war he opposed a year ago. His reason for doing so was perhaps worse than that of the bankers or of the generals. He did not call Frenchmen to a Garibaldian adventure. He did not call them to coldly calculated conquests. He preached war as a means of national regeneration. 'I have been meditating,' he declared, 'for the last six months—indeed, ever since the revolution began— what course I ought to follow. . . The force of reason and of facts has persuaded me that a people which, after a thousand years of slavery, has achieved liberty, needs war. It needs war to consolidate its freedom. It needs war to purge away the vices of despotism. It needs war to banish from its bosom the men who might corrupt its liberty.'

The majority of the deputies, with their eyes fixed on their constituents, applauded this justification of war-fever. The majority of the newspaper editors, with their eyes fixed on their subscribers, glorified this philosophy of a war-purge. Brissot's doctrine was backed by the fascinating Madame Roland, and the eloquent Vergniaud. It would be a disaster, he declared on January 14th, if war were averted. It was denounced only by a small group at the Jacobin club, whose spokesman was Robespierre.

Robespierre's shrewd leadership during the troubles of the summer, his imperviousness to any bribe except flattery, and his flair for high-sounding democratic sentiments, had won him the enthusiastic support of a class hitherto overlooked, but soon (as he saw) to control the revolution—the lower middle class (*petite bourgeoisie*). These decent self-respecting folk resented, even more than the so-called working class, the monopolizing of wealth and power by people a little above them in the social scale. They disliked a constitution that gave them nothing but an ineffective franchise. They were ready to impute the worst motives to soldiers and politicians who sent their sons to be killed in an unnecessary and un-national war.

To this audience Robespierre declared, amidst applause, that Brissot's war was 'not a war of liberation, leading to freedom, but a war waged by a despot against foreign princes, *émigrés*, and priests.' The king, he said, hoped to use the war to restore the old regime; Brissot hoped to use it to set up a bourgeois republic; Lafayette hoped to use it to enslave the country under a military dictatorship. In any case, he maintained, neither the army nor the government was prepared for war; it could only lead to disaster.

Robespierre found an unconscious ally in the enemy. Leopold's intention, after Varennes, had been to lead a crusade for the rescue of his brother-in-law. He soon found that of his five likeliest followers only one, the King of Sweden, would support him unconditionally. When he learnt that Louis was to accept the constitution, and to be reinstated on the throne, he felt no further call of honour to act immediately. He was content to join the King of Prussia in issuing (August 27th) the Declaration of Pillnitz. This ambiguous document left him a diplomatic loop-hole for inaction; but it might be taken as a threat of war in the spring of '92. Early in January the Elector of Trier undertook to expel the *émigrés* from his territory, and thus deprived the French government of its most promising *casus belli*. The Emperor did his best not to furnish them with another. The unwarlike attitude of the smaller states of Germany gave him an adequate reason for refusing the demands of the *émigrés* for armed intervention.

It was a fixed idea with Brissot and his followers that their revolutionary principles were of universal application. They imagined that when French troops crossed the Rhine they would be received with acclamation by the oppressed subjects of the princes of western Germany. This belief was shared by some good observers in that country. The Prussian traveller Reichardt wrote in January, '92: 'If the French cross the Rhine, if they preserve strict discipline, if they are careful not to molest the peasantry, and if they pay cash down for what they need, all the chances are in their favour.' 'The peasants of the Palatinate and Maintz,' he asserted, 'say openly that, directly the French arrive, they will join them.'

Such too was the confident creed of the 'orator of mankind.' On December 13th Anacharsis Cloots followed up his demonstration of the previous year by proclaiming that within a month three great armies would be on the march against Brussels, Liège, and Coblentz. The tricolour and the *Ça Ira* would be the delight of twenty liberated peoples. The peasants of Germany and Bohemia, the Catalans, the Allobroges, the Dutch, the Lombards, and the Scandinavians would rise against their tyrants, and break off the chains of a detested slavery.

Almost at the same time Brissot, a political Peter the Hermit, proclaimed that the time had come for another crusade, 'a crusade whose aim is nobler and holier, a crusade on behalf of universal liberty.' When, three months later, Brissot's friends came into control of the ministerial funds, an elaborate propaganda was organized. Papers and pamphlets were distributed by every post. Republican agents were to be met crossing the Rhine, and climbing the passes of the Alps and the Pyrenees. Plans were set on foot for a republican mission to South America.

Nor did the appeal go unanswered. At the moment when war was declared Cloots reappeared at the bar of the House to offer six hundred pounds towards the expense of equipping a Foreign Legion. Within a week a regiment had been formed by the men of Liège, who had been waiting four months for the opportunity. A Belgian corps fought under Luckner at Courtrai. A Dutch legion was on foot by July. Another force, embracing men from Savoy, Switzerland, Piedmont, and the Valais under the name of their supposed common ancestors, was called the legion of the Allobroges. Cloots himself, and Saiffert, a Saxon doctor attached to the royal household, organized a German regiment. John Oswald, the republican poet and pamphleteer, perished with two sons by his side, fighting in the Vendée, in September, '93, at the head of a battalion armed only with pikes, and including a number of English volunteers.

A questionable element in some of these enterprises was the use of bribery to encourage desertion from the enemies' ranks. At first a bonus of forty-five shillings was offered for a man, and ten pounds for a horse. Later the inducement for desertion was increased to a pension of five pounds a year, with reversion to one's wife, and without any obligation to bear arms on the French side. Good terms of service were also offered to the Royal Swiss regiment, when their contract ended with the revolution of August 10th.

These provocative and unprofessional means of raising an army were matched by the methods of Brissotin diplomacy. If 1792 failed to provide a *casus belli*, it was possible that 1756 might do so. The Franco-Austrian alliance of that year had long been dishonoured, but never disowned. On January 14th Gensonné, in the name of the Diplomatic Committee, proposed that the Emperor should be asked to declare his adhesion to an engagement made by his mother at the beginning of the Seven Years' war, thirty-six years ago. If France were attacked, would he come to her help? It was added that, if a satisfactory answer to this demand were not received by February 11th, it would be regarded as an unfriendly act. Vergniaud and Guadet supported this motion, and it was carried enthusiastically. On January 25th, without waiting for an answer to his first ultimatum, Brissot despatched a second, in even more provocative terms. The Emperor was now asked to state 'whether he intended to live on conditions of peace and good understanding with the French people, renouncing any treaty or agreement directed against the sovereignty, independence, or safety of the nation.' Anything less than a 'full and entirely satisfactory reply on all points' would be regarded as a declaration of war. But here a remarkable parallel to the diplomacy of 1870 breaks down. The time limit set for Brissot's ultimatum was March 1st. On March 1st the Emperor Leopold lay dead.

The war-mongers would not be stayed now—no, not by a sign from heaven. Some of them, indeed, took the Emperor's death as a stroke of Providence on their side. If the Empress of Russia had died, or the King of Poland, there would have been little chance of war with Austria. But now fate had removed the only obstacle to it. 'Leopold is dead,' wrote Barbaroux, 'there is no king of the Romans. The King of Sweden totters on his throne. The Queen of Portugal has gone mad. The King of Spain has been stoned by his people.' Monarchy would soon be as extinct as the volcanoes of Ollioules. Kaunitz need no longer labour to put the French government in the wrong. Brissot would do his work for him. On March 9th the king had dismissed Narbonne—his fall was attributed both to the ambition of the minister and to the indiscretions of his mistress—and had substituted an aristocratic nonentity, the Marquis de Grave. Brissot promptly led an attack against Delessart, a ministerial hack, who had held with equal incompetence almost every office in turn, and was now mismanaging the Foreign Office. On March 10th, when the news of Leopold's death reached Paris, the whole Feuillant ministry had fallen. Louis, seriously alarmed by this attack, took the advice of Radix de Sainte-Foy, the Comte d'Artois' *surintendant des finances,* who had already sounded the leaders of the assembly, and appointed a ministry of Brissotin nominees.

The intention of this unconventional move was explained, not without a touch of irony, in the king's message to the House. 'I had previously chosen,' he said, 'men commended by their high principles and sound opinions. . . . I have now thought it my duty to replace them by men whose title to office is that their views are those of the popular party. You have so often told me that this party is the only one that can re-establish order, and carry out the laws, that I have thought it right to give it my confidence. Thus there will remain no excuse for ill-wishers to doubt my sincere desire to collaborate in the prosperity and happiness of my country.' It was a clever move. It was indeed the first statesmanlike thing Louis had done since the beginning of the revolution. It made possible that co-operation between the legislature and the executive which the new government had hitherto lacked. It pointed the way to a Cabinet system. But it came too late. The machinery for good government was provided: the goodwill that might have worked it was missing.

The only young man among the new ministers was de Grave—a professional soldier, who had held an appointment in the Duc de Chartres' household, and was suspected of an aristocratic inefficiency. The rest were decidedly elderly—their average age was fifty-five—and their republicanism burnt with a dim light. Lacoste (Minister of Marine), Clavière, Necker's

rival and fellow-countryman, the expert on *assignats* (Finance), and Duranthon (Justice) would never set the Seine on fire.

Only two of the five were likely to take a strong line. Charles-François
Dumouriez was a lively and ingenious military adventurer of fifty-three, who
might have filled any office in the ministry—'a bold determined man,'
thought Morris, whose policy it had long been 'to destroy the clubs, but to
effect a change in the government.' Gensonné had put him forward, on
account of his travels and his foreign studies, as Minister for Foreign Affairs.
The sober, censorious Roland had been dragged by the political ambitions
of his young wife from the third volume of his *Dictionnaire des manufactures*
to become Minister of the Interior. Both appointments were blunders from
the Girondin party point of view. In the long run they embarrassed the
party more than they embarrassed the court.

The claims of younger or more democratic statesmen had been canvassed
—Diétrich of Strasbourg, Louvet, the *protégé* of the Rolands, Collot
d'Herbois, Danton, and even Robespierre. But the Jacobin party, as Brissot's
critics were beginning to be called, had to rest content with minor posts in
the ministries.

Louis soon regretted his change of front. He was with difficulty dissuaded
from forming a secret and rival ministry of Montmorin, Malouet, Champion
de Cicé, and the abbé Montesquiou. The easiness and affability of his manner
barely concealed the deep repugnance with which he viewed his new ministers and their policy. Whilst they drafted and discussed their decrees, the
king read the newspaper, or attended to his correspondence. When his
decision was asked, he would raise difficulties, or adjourn the business to
another day. Debates on matters of policy he was apt to turn off with an
anecdote, or to distract into a side-issue. At the end of two or three hours'
sitting, says Madame Roland, the conversation was rather that of a café
than that of a council-chamber. If he had been better advised, he might have
used his new ministers to establish more friendly relations with the assembly,
and to recover some degree of control over the government. It was such an
opportunity as Mirabeau had dreamed of. But Louis could make nothing
of it.

The blame was not all on the king's side. The ministers made little attempt to ease a difficult situation. Roland's refusal to wear court dress, or
buckles in his shoes, and the 'republican frankness' of the memoranda
dictated by his wife, were part of a considered policy. Brissot's nominees
would stand no nonsense from a *pouvoir exécutif* whom they intended to use
for their own ends, and then to throw aside.

The public temper, too, was rapidly rising, and so many interests favoured
war that the public funds rose with it. The *bonnet rouge*, the symbol of
militant patriotism, began to appear in the Jacobin club. Aristocrats who
assumed this unbecoming head-dress consoled themselves with the thought
that it would at any rate keep their heads warm, if it were a cold winter:

republican heads, they reflected, were hot enough already. Royalists who went into mourning for the Emperor were in some danger of being mobbed. Passive citizens could now be enrolled in the National Guard, though armed with nothing better than extemporized pikes. The appearance of a fresh crop of Popular Societies suggested that the people were preparing to intervene more actively in the political arena.

The English publicist Sampson Perry, who was in France during the autumn of '92, reckoned the forces of revolutionary propaganda before August 10th in terms of 'public attendances,' thus:

National Assembly (members and spectators)	2,000
Jacobins (club and gallery)	2,400
Cordeliers, Hal au Bled, and meetings of that sort	7,000
Municipality of Paris, and spectators	800
Forty-eight sections	24,000
Total	36,200

Perry might have added the audiences at more than thirty theatres.

Dumouriez, who never forgot that he had once served in the Prussian army, and who shared the anti-Austrian sentiments of his diplomatic friend Favier, rejoiced in these danger-signals. He welcomed the accession of the inexperienced and incautious Emperor Francis II (March 1st) as an opportunity to push on the war policy. Whilst the court sent desperate messages to Vienna and Berlin, and whilst the queen passed on to Mercy (March 26th), for the information of the enemy, the plans of campaign just settled by the Royal Council, the Minister for Foreign Affairs presented a report reviewing the whole course of the negotiations, and asked the assembly (April 20th) for an immediate declaration of war.

Dumouriez based his demand for war upon the Emperor's supposed breach of the treaty of 1756: far from coming to the help of his ally, he had organized a league of powers against her. Kaunitz's reply to this charge was, diplomatically speaking, unanswerable. The Emperor's promise to support the Elector of Trier had been made inoperative by his dismissal of the *émigrés*, as the French government desired. The Declaration of Pillnitz had been 'suspended, so far as its effects went,' when Louis accepted the constitution. Kaunitz was also on strong ground when he censured the 'incompetent decree' (he might have used stronger terms) in which the assembly had presented Leopold with a second ultimatum before he had time to answer the first. His insistence on the Emperor's refusal to take offence put the Brissotins entirely in the wrong.

But not even Kaunitz's ingenuity could explain away the offensive terms in which he had spoken of the French republican party. Language which might have been applauded by the assembly in October, '91, was received with *murmures* by the deputies in March, '92. Expressions which might have been passed off with a smile by the chancelleries of the last generation, to whom the octogenarian statesman was accustomed to address himself, roused hot anger when recited in a representative parliament. It was not the Emperor's attitude towards the obligations of an out-of-date treaty, but the suspicion that he despised a National Assembly, and disdained a national army, which finally drove the deputies into war.

When the House debated Dumouriez's proposal on the evening of April 20th it was soon evident that there would be a large majority for an immediate declaration of war. All the applause went to the speakers for the motion. It was therefore to the credit of the assembly that it gave the opposition a fair hearing. Hua of Mantes, Becquet, deputy for Haute-Marne, and the future *montagnard* Basire were allowed to plead for further consideration. Becquet's speech in particular fully deserved the attention it received. It was a solemn warning against the danger of war for a newly constituted state.

'War,' said Becquet, 'is a state of emergency, incompatible with the orderly movements of the body politic. It follows that a country which has just reformed its institutions ought to avoid war with the greatest care.' He went on to ask what would happen at home, when all the troops were fighting on the frontiers. He warned the House that the contest could not easily be localized. Any attack on Brabant would challenge the intervention of England, who 'regards the maintenance of the *status quo* in that country as a national interest, and fears that if the commerce of the Netherlands over-reaches its present limits it may rival her own.' If England comes into the war, he added, France may find herself faced by a European coalition. Austria does not want to fight. The questions of Alsace and Avignon can be settled without recourse to arms. A free nation should be above going to war on any but the most serious issues. 'We shall earn the reputation of being an aggressive and a restless people, who disturb the peace of Europe, and disregard treaties and international law.'

These prophetic words carried more weight than votes. War was decreed by a vast majority of the deputies, and confirmed by the cries of the Sovereign People. To secure an overwhelming vote, and to give protective colouring to an obvious act of aggression, the decree included a statement, with reference to the pacific declaration of May, 1790, that France was taking up arms 'only to defend her liberty and independence,' and that this was 'not a war between nations, but the war of a free people defending its just rights against the unjust attack of a king.' It was added that 'the French would never confuse their brethren with their real enemies, and would take every care to mitigate the scourge of war, to observe the rights of property, and to see that the evils inseparable from hostilities fall only on those who are in league against the liberty of their country.'

These fair words salved a few consciences. In the final division only seven deputies, of whom Becquet was one, voted against a contest which was destined to last nearly twenty-five years, and to undo half the work of the revolution.

When Louis entered the House to make his formal declaration of war, he looked round vaguely, and read his speech with an unexpressive voice, as though it were a matter of indifference. Yet with the declaration of war the king and queen lost their last hope of liberty, and began to fear for their lives. They were now shut off from the world by sentries who stood in the very windows of the Tuileries. Sightseers were shown the door, now securely walled up, by which they had escaped ten months before. It was the door, too, by which their few remaining friends outside the palace had visited them with difficulty, and for the last time.

The Spanish ambassador had taken his leave in the middle of September. Louis, he reported, had lost his appetite from lack of exercise, and looked thin and pale. In November Mrs Swinburne, an Englishwoman whose son had served as a royal page at Versailles, was forced to leave Paris. She was allowed to say good-bye to the queen. 'She received me graciously, indeed kindly,' she wrote afterwards. 'She wished me every happiness. "You are going," she said, "to a happy family, and to a quiet country, where cruelty and calumny cannot pursue you. How I envy you!"' When Mrs Swinburne spoke of happier times to come, she shook her head. When, with a generous impulse, she offered to find the queen a passage to England, disguised as her maid, 'She thanked me, and smiled faintly, but said that nothing would induce her to leave her family. . . . "Besides," she said, looking round, "I could not, if I would: there are too many spies."'

The queen's best friends were still foreigners. On February 13th, at risk of his life, the Comte de Fersen paid a last visit to the Tuileries. He had travelled to Paris in disguise, and had lain concealed in an attic at Craufurd's house. Admitted after dark by the secret way which he had used the year before, he stayed in the palace that night, and all the next day. Marie-Antoinette talked of the past, telling him details about the flight to Varennes, and the return. The king, whom Fersen saw in the morning, discussed the possibilities of retrieving a forlorn situation. 'He refuses to leave,' writes Fersen in his diary; 'and indeed he cannot; he is too well guarded. But really it is a matter of conscience; he has so often promised to stop, and he is a man of his word (*un honnête homme*). But he has agreed that, when the armies arrive, he will go with some smugglers, keeping always to the woods, and will put himself into the hands of their patrols. His wish is that the Congress should at first confine itself to presenting demands; if they are granted, it must insist on his being allowed to leave Paris for whatever place is fixed for the ratification; if not, he agrees to the powers taking action, and will risk any personal danger; but he does not believe there would be any, as the rebels need his person to bargain with (*pour obtenir une capitulation*). He sees there is no remedy but force; yet, in his weak way, he thinks it impossible to recover all his old authority.'

Fersen tried to stiffen his resolution. 'I know,' he replied, 'that I am charged with weakness and irresolution; but no one has ever been in a position like mine. There *was* one opportunity that I missed, I know—July 14th: then I ought to have got away. There has never been another since. Now everyone has deserted me (*'J'ai été abandonné de tout le monde*).' So poor Louis planned and counter-planned to the last—consistent only in his inconsistency. Fersen left the Tuileries at half-past nine that evening. He never saw his friends again.

Just a month later, on April 14th, Craufurd, who had often used the same private entrance to the palace, went to say good-bye to the queen. 'She received me,' he wrote afterwards, 'in her room on the ground floor. I left her about nine o'clock. She let me out by a small room containing books, opening on to a poorly lit corridor. She opened the door herself, and lingered talking to me; but hearing steps in the corridor, begged me to go, and closed the door. As was natural, seeing how things were with her, I was suddenly overwhelmed with the idea that I should never see her again. The melancholy thought struck me for a moment motionless. Roused from my stupor by the approaching footsteps, I left the palace, and returned home. In the darkness of the night, and the confusion of my mind, my imagination was constantly haunted by her figure, and by the last look she gave me as she turned away; and so it is to this day.'

Chapter XV

DETHRONEMENT

I asked a genteel looking man who had just arrived at this place in the Diligence, whether he thought there was any danger in being at Paris? 'Pas le moindre,' answered he. They talk, said I, of dethroning the King. '*Tant pis pour lui*,' said the man, '*mais cela ne vous regarde pas*.' To hear a Frenchman talk with so much indifference of dethroning a King, however petty the Monarch might be, was what I did not expect; but to hear him speak with the same indifference of dethroning his own King, that, I confess, astonished me.—(JOHN MOORE: Clermont, August 6th, 1792.)

VISITORS to Paris in April, 1792, when the country was on the eve of war, were surprised to find one body of patriots organizing a demonstration in honour of a convict-gang, and another denouncing it as counter-revolutionary. Such was the affair known as the Fête de Châteauvieux.

On April 15th, incited by Marat, 'the People's Friend,' financed by the Electoral Assembly, organized by Tallien, Palloy, and Santerre, and

patronized by the popularity-hunting mayor Pétion, the democratic sections
of the capital staged a public procession for the Nancy mutineers, sentenced
eighteen months before to the galleys at Brest, and tardily released under the
amnesty of September 14th. They were welcomed on the site of the Bastille
by deputations of the *Vainqueurs*, of 'Apostles of Liberty,' of 'Pupils of the
Fatherland,' and of foreigners, including a Pole, an Armenian, and a negro.
As a sign of their liberation the *ci-devant* convicts wore the *bonnet rouge*,
the traditional red cap of the poor man who was a free citizen. The fête,
if it did nothing else, popularized a patriotic emblem as old as the revolution,
which had already made a tentative appearance on the banners of the
sections, and on designs for the constitutional coinage of '91.

But less patriotic motives were at work. To the democratic eye nothing
could be more reassuring than to see Pétion and Robespierre marching hand
in hand, surrounded by a troop of girls and musicians, behind Voltaire's
funeral car, refurbished for this more cheerful occasion, to the Champ de la
Fédération—the *ci-devant* Champ de Mars. To the democratic temper
nothing could be more pleasant than to spend three hours dancing *farandoles*
round the altar of the country. But sympathy with the Swiss mutineers
could hardly be called spontaneous. Their act had been disowned by the
mass of French opinion, and by their own countrymen. It was being
exploited by politicians who wished to discredit not only the royalists and
reactionaries who had been responsible for the brutal repression of the
mutiny, but also the Brissotin war party, and the old-fashioned military
discipline associated with de Bouillé, the villain of Nancy and Varennes, and
with that discarded hero of the revolution, Lafayette. The loyalty of the
army was attacked from two sides. The assembly proceeded to issue warrants
(*actes d'accusation*) against Marat's *Ami du peuple* and Royon's *Ami du roi*
simultaneously.

But it would have been a mistake to suppose that the demonstrators of
April 15th were likely to oppose the declaration of April 20th. War was
welcomed with enthusiasm. It brought, indeed, a fresh outburst of crime in
the capital; but it also brought a fresh flow of *dons patriotiques* to the Treasury. It was a cause which all embraced, and few understood. If the assembly
remained disunited, the fault lay with its leaders, who seemed less concerned with the public danger than with the contest for party power. It was
at this time that the Brissotins arrogantly called themselves *patriotes*, the
Feuillants *modérés*, and the Robespierrists *enragés*, defining the *patriotes* as
'friends of the people and of the constitution,' the *modérés* as 'false friends of
the constitution, and enemies of the people,' and the *enragés* as 'false friends
of the people, and enemies of the constitution.' Amidst such omens of
dissension France embarked on a war which was to bring it military defeat,
the fall of its government, and the moral reprobation of Europe; until five
months later, Valmy and the Convention gave the first hope of a republican
victory, and of the recovery of national self-respect.

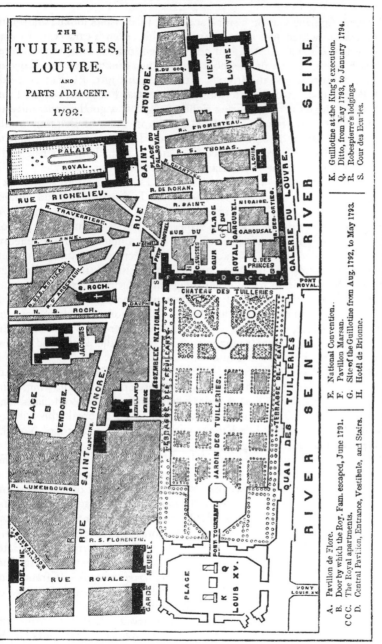

PLAN OF THE CENTRE OF PARIS, 1792

From Croker's *Essays on the French Revolution.*

A. Pavillon de Flore.
B. Door by which the Roy. Fam. escaped, June 1791.
CCC. The Royal apartments.
D. Central Pavilion, Entrance, Vestibule, and Stairs.
E. National Convention..
F. Pavillon Marsan.
G. Site of the Guillotine from Aug. 1792, to May 1793.
H. Hotel de Brionne.
K. Guillotine at the King's execution.
Q. Ditto, from May 1793, to January 1794.
R. Robespierre's lodgings.
S. Cour des Écuries.

The early fighting was on a small scale, but its disasters looked enormous to a generation which had almost forgotten the Seven Years' war. Prussia was not yet mobilized. Austria had not intended to fight until the summer. The death of the Emperor Leopold and the assassination of the King of Sweden had disorganized the friends of the French court. Russian proceedings in Poland distracted the attention of the central European powers from the affairs of the west. Dumouriez rightly judged it a good opportunity to strike a sudden blow. It was calculated that an invasion of Belgium would cause an anti-Austrian rising. It was hoped that Talleyrand would be able to persuade the British Foreign Office to overlook a challenge to England's traditional interests in the Netherlands. So the move was made.

It met at once with a disastrous check. Dumouriez despatched two columns to begin the invasion. One, under the Irishman Theobald Dillon, advanced from Lille on Tournai: the other, under the Duc de Biron, whose military experience had been won in America, advanced from Quiévrain on Mons. Both fell into confusion at their first contact with the enemy. Dillon's men added to the disgrace of flight the crime of murdering their general. Fortunately for France, neither the Austrian nor the Prussian troops were in a position to take advantage of a disorganized army and an open frontier. But the extent of the defeat was shown by the number of officers who deserted their posts, and by the resignation of Rochambeau, the commander-in-chief, and of de Grave, the Minister of War. When the news reached Paris, popular anger turned against the king, and almost attempted an attack upon the Tuileries.

Who was to blame? The court, whose *comité autrichien* was rumoured to be in favour of a defeat which would turn the nation towards the king? The generals, who were denounced as traitors and royalists? The politicians, who had made the war? Or Dumouriez, who had failed to break the Austro-Prussian alliance, and had left France without friends in Europe? No: the fault lay rather with the army.

The army had been disorganized by too many ill-considered reforms during the last thirty years. It had been disarmed by gross mismanagement at the War Office. It had been weakened by the emigration of its most competent officers, by the friction between the old soldiers who still remained and the new recruits who served by their side, and by the discontent and indiscipline of the revolutionary rank and file. Dumouriez's report on the military situation, made two months after the disaster, and two months too late, showed how shallow had been the grounds for the complacency of Narbonne. It spoke of a serious shortage of men and *matériel*. It spoke of fraudulent contractors, and of officers and their staffs sold to the enemy. It spoke of a complete disproportion between the aims and the means of the campaign.

Lafayette, writing to Washington on January 23rd, had described the rank and file of his army as patriotic, but undisciplined. Of the officers, he said, a third had already thrown up their commissions, and another third might be expected to do so soon. But he hoped, by enforcing discipline, to make something of this unpromising material. Brissot himself received more than one letter from Vieusseux, the Adjutant-general of the Rhine army, complaining that his troops were 'distrustful, mutinous, and ill-disciplined.' They refused to obey orders which there was no proper means of enforcing. Their 'French courage' too easily gave place to 'an unexampled despondency.' It was said (but this may have been a royalist myth) that when Biron ordered a bayonet charge, two grenadiers turned to their comrades, and said, 'Let us vote on the general's proposal.' The vote went against Biron, and he had to countermand his order.

The blame for the disaster was thrown first upon the king and his ministers, and secondly upon the Brissotin party. Neither was in a position to support it. The ministers had never been happy together; and perhaps Louis was not sorry to see them quarrelling. They were handicapped by a Civil Service inherited from the old regime, which was not only incompetent and corrupt, but which had also been encouraged by their Feuillant predecessors to obstruct the work of the assembly. They lacked the technique to deal with the petty intrigues (*intrigailleries*, Madame Roland calls them) of Louis and his advisers. Soon they were divided among themselves by the attempt of the Rolands to dictate a policy to the ministry. Contemporary gossip attributed this attempt to the wife of the Minister of the Interior; and history confirms the judgement.

Manon Phlipon was born in Paris, but owed to an uncle, who brought her up in the country, a store of natural vitality that gave force to her affectations, and charm to her features. She was no more than a step-child of nature. The quickness and shallowness of her mind were a Parisian birthright. A serious and impressionable girl, she imagined herself in turn a Jansenist, a Cartesian, a Stoic, a Deist, and a Republican. At heart a courtesan, and always happy in front of her mirror, she became by fastidious self-culture, and a preference for the society of elderly men, a political blue-stocking, and the wife of a prosy Inspector of Commerce twenty years older than herself —a man whose thin clerical features and bald forehead rendered him (it is her own account) 'respectable rather than seductive.'

Her essays and travel-diaries, which include a Swiss tour and a trip to England, blend the fashionable *sensibilité* of the day with some shrewd remarks on political and economic questions. Her letters, many of which her admirers printed as leading articles in their papers, show that even before the revolution she was anti-royalist, anti-aristocrat, and anti-clerical. A meal in the servants' hall of a *fermier-général* had set her against the moneyed classes. A week's stay in a privileged garret in the palace of Versailles, in the same unsavoury corridor as the Archbishop of Paris, had made her hate the monarchy. Her nunnery school had given her religious feelings without religious faith. When the revolution came, she embraced the popular cause, but distrusted the popular leaders, the democratic assemblies, and the influence of the capital. She paid her first visit to Paris after her marriage in February, '91, and returned to her country home near Lyon seven months later completely out of love with constitutionalism.

At the end of the year her husband revisited the capital to claim a pension due for his thirty-eight years' service, and was offered a place in the Brissotin ministry of March, '92. Madame Roland seized the opportunity to use his position and her talents, of which she was more than sufficiently aware, in the cause of republicanism. It was she who most successfully exploited a new technique of ministerial dinners, in rivalry with Vergniaud's richer but less cultivated hostess, Madame Dodun, or with the parties that Pétion gave in his charming garden opening on to the boulevards. Her guests were not only the leaders of her husband's political set, but also such journalists as Dulaure of the *Thermomètre* and Louvet of the *Sentinelle*. Together they discussed, over her frugal and elegant board, every question of Girondin policy.

Already in March the leaders of the Jacobin Left stood aloof from Madame Roland's circle. Collot d'Herbois had fancied himself for the office held by Roland. Robespierre had consistently opposed Brissot's war policy. Later, when war broke out, it was too late to make up these quarrels. It was unlikely that those who had been immune to the blandishments of the pretty hostess of the Hôtel Britannique would succumb to the more solid inducements offered by the minister's wife who adapted herself so modestly to the pillared magnificence of the official residence in the rue Neuve-des-petits-champs.

When de Grave resigned on May 8th, unable to repair the defeats at the front, he was replaced by Joseph Servan de Gerbey of Romans, a friend and almost a neighbour of the Rolands. This appointment increased the friction in the ministry, and antagonized Lafayette. He had not been consulted, and he probably resented taking orders from an undistinguished veteran from the West Indies, who had acquired notoriety by substituting the *Marseillaise* for the *Te Deum* as the official form of thanksgiving for victories in the field. Lafayette was now fully committed to a course of intrigue with Feuillant politicians and royalist officers of the northern command. It began with disobedience to orders, and ended in a plan to march on Paris, close the Jacobin club, and restore the power of the king.

How had Lafayette's loyalty and integrity come to this pass? The clue to his conduct throughout the crises of July 14th, October 5th, June 21st, and July 17th is to be found in the illuminating letters that he addressed to his hero and friend George Washington. It appears from these confidences that he never regarded himself as a mere participant in the revolutionary struggle, but as its democratically if not divinely appointed referee. He stood apart. His duty was to keep order, to enforce fair play, and to see that justice was done to both sides. King, assembly, and people were all one to his self-conscious and superior rectitude. He had used the National Guard, and he would use the army, if need be, to prevent the dangerous predominance of any one party, in the name of the liberty and equality of all. He could not co-operate either with Brissot or with Mirabeau. The one left too little power in the king's hands: the other would have given him too much. Lafayette was too simple or too stubborn to waver from a formula which circumstances forced suppler men to revise: 'Royalism through the revolution, and the revolution through royalism.'

After the flight to Varennes, the massacre of the Champ de Mars, and his defeat by Pétion in the contest for the mayoralty of Paris, he returned to Auvergne. 'His Sun,' wrote Morris, 'seems to be totally set.' A soldier at heart, he had welcomed his recall from retirement in December, '91, to command the army of Metz. He made a point of thanking the assembly for giving him this chance of public service, and he kept on good terms with a series of War Ministers of whom he could hardly approve—Narbonne, de Grave, and even Servan. But it was clear from an otherwise admirable address to his troops on May 1st that he was already thinking of the opportunity his new command gave him to recover the refereeship he had lost after the flight to Varennes, and the massacre of the Champ de Mars. During his absence from the field the rules of the revolutionary contest had been broken. One side was having an unfair advantage over the other. The Brissotin government and the Jacobin opposition were combining to compass the fall of the throne. It was his duty to intervene in the name of the national settlement of 1789–91. If Louis were to abandon the constitution, Lafayette would be the first to co-operate in the overthrow of the monarchy: but meanwhile nobody else must be allowed to do so. He would use his army to safeguard the constitution, to rescue the king from the toils in which the Brissotins had involved him, and to restore the balance of political power.

But events moved too fast for him. On May 28th the assembly considered the state of affairs serious enough to call for a four days' continuous session. Within a week it had presented the king with two measures, the result if not the intention of which was to put the Tuileries entirely at the mercy of the *manège*.

Under the constitution the king was allowed to maintain out of the Civil List, in addition to his formal Guard of Honour, a force of twelve hundred infantry and six hundred cavalry, chosen from the regular army, or from the National Guard, but kept on a separate establishment. It was rumoured that Louis had recently reinforced these men by summoning four hundred and fifty Swiss to the Tuileries. It was notorious that the twelve hundred were too royalist in sentiment for their comrades. On May 29th the assembly decided that, in view of its 'unpatriotic spirit', this force should be dismissed, and its duties provisionally performed by detachments of the National Guard. Its commandant, Cossé-Brissac, was indicted for unconstitutional action before the *haute cour nationale* at Orléans.

A few days later (June 4th) Servan proposed that the National Guards from the provinces who were expected in Paris for the annual fête of July 14th should be given several months' training under canvas near the capital, before they went on to the front. This measure was welcomed by the assembly as an augmentation of the army by twenty thousand men, and by the republicans as a precaution against any armed move by the court. It was a corollary of the suppression of the Royal Guard, and a first step towards the attack on the Austrian outpost in the Tuileries.

But this was not all. The decree which disarmed the King also disarmed the commune. For a long time past the Paris sections had been trying to reorganize the National Guard, and to regain the control over their own affairs which they had lost under the municipal law of May, 1790. The chief author of this movement in the democratic sections and at the commune had been the Jacobin journalist Pierre-Gaspard, or, as he preferred to call himself, Anaxagoras Chaumette. On May 4th this man had induced the municipality to call a conference of the sections to consider what steps should be taken. It was with the intention of over-bidding Chaumette that Roland's protégé, Louvet, presented a petition from the Lombards section in the same sense on May 30th. It was in order to forestall any attempt to exploit the National Guard against them that the Brissotin deputies a few days later accepted Servan's decree for a Paris camp of *fédérés*.

The move was, for the moment, successful. Chaumette even welcomed Louvet's proposal, and was one of a sectional deputation that gave its allegiance to the assembly on June 19th. But Servan's decree caused suspicion and jealousy in the ranks of the National Guard. Some of them signed the so-called Petition of the Eight Thousand against it. The king, who had already imposed his veto on a decree against the refractory priests, was encouraged to intervene again.

This second revolt against his Brissotin masters was not allowed to pass. A letter, or rather a lecture, dictated from the Ministry of the Interior by the minister's wife told the king that unless he withdrew his veto he would endanger the constitution, and be responsible for a fresh insurrection. 'The revolution,' wrote Madame Roland, 'is complete in men's minds: unless wise provision is made against evils which can still be avoided, it will be accomplished at the price of bloodshed, and will be cemented with blood.' This unmannerly missive precipitated, as it was probably meant to do, a ministerial crisis. Within a week the month's experiment of something like Cabinet government—an experiment which might have saved the constitution—came to a fruitless end.

It would require a White Book to do justice to the correspondence in which this ministerial drama was played out, during the days following June 12th. There had been a time when a minister's stipend and pension had been coveted and contested by every clique at Versailles. Now it was the main endeavour of the king's friends to avoid a distasteful and perhaps dangerous employment. After a week of resignations, suggestions, invitations, and refusals, the king informed the President of the assembly that he had appointed the Marquis de Chambonas (*maréchal de camp*) as Minister of Foreign Affairs, Lajard (Lafayette's deputy in the command of the National Guard) as Minister of War, the Marquis de Terrier de Monciel as Minister of the Interior, and Beaulieu as Minister of Finance: Duranthon was to continue for the present in the Ministry of Justice. When these changes were completed, Dumouriez left Versailles, to serve at the front as a Lieutenant-general in the army of Marshal Luckner.

Thus the executive government of the country was once more in the hands of a group of Feuillant nonentities, nominees of the court party. When, three weeks later, all these ministers resigned, and were replaced by others even less distinguished, the change was hardly noticed. The attempt to establish constitutional and personal relations between the king, the assembly, and the people had completely broken down. Nothing now intervened between a discredited government and an indignant nation. Both sides prepared for an appeal to force. 'We stand,' wrote Morris to Jefferson on June 17th, 'on a vast volcano. We feel it tremble, we hear it roar; but how and when and where it will burst, or who may be destroyed by its eruptions, it is beyond the ken of mortal sight to discover.'

Three great buildings had stood out from the crowded, tortuous streets of Old Paris—the Tuileries, the Hôtel de Ville, and the Bastille. Since July 14th the empty site of the Bastille, once a symbol of feudalism, had become a centre of popular revolution. The Town Hall remained, like the constitution, as a link between the West End and the East End—between the seat of the *bourgeois* government and the home of the Sovereign People. A few hundred yards to the south of the Town Hall, on the Ile de Notre Dame, or de la Cité, were the Mairie (the Mayor's official residence), and the Evêché (the Bishop's Palace), the meeting-place of the Paris Electors. The assembly, the ministries, the Paris department, and the Jacobin club met almost under the shadow of the Tuileries. The Palais-Royal was an outpost occupied by patrols of the popular party. The Pont Neuf, at the west end of the Ile Notre Dame, provided a strategical bridge-head, by which the democratic sections of the south bank could reinforce those of the north bank at the central point of municipal government. Thus the Hôtel de Ville looked east and south rather than west or north; and the newly elected municipal authorities of March, '92, were fully aware that they held office by leave of the semi-independent sections that hemmed them in.

No one was more conscious of this than the new mayor, Jérôme Pétion, who had succeeded the discredited Bailly on November 17th, '91. A genial vulgar popularity-hunter, Pétion was a barrister from Chartres, 'a well-looking fair man (so the Englishman Dr. Moore describes him) of a genteel address and cheerful countenance, with an habitual smile,' and with an amiable weakness for children and animals. He had been put where he was by his reputation as a democrat in the National Assembly, and by the reaction against the authors of the massacre of the Champ de Mars. Living in a grand house, and drawing a salary of five thousand a year, the Mayor of Paris could snap his fingers at the Paris department in the modest person of the Mayor of Saint-Denis, or of Bourg-la-Reine.

Yet Pétion was hardly master of his own Mairie. He had quarrelled with his old town-fellow Brissot about the war, and he was quarrelling with his old partner of the Constituent Assembly, Robespierre, about the Jacobin club. A man of no real convictions, he was exploited by determined republicans—Manuel, *procureur* of the Commune, Danton, one of Manuel's deputies, Panis and Sergent, *administrateurs* of the police and of the National Guard. He was made to follow public opinion, not to lead it; and he would pay the penalty of popularity-hunting.

Dumouriez's *grand tumulte* on June 15th was no false alarm. The dismissal of Roland, Clavière, and Servan roused the democratic sections. Three of the most adventurous—Saint-Marcel, Quinze-Vingts, and Gobelins—asked the Commune for leave to parade on the 20th, the anniversary of the Tennis Court oath, wearing their old uniforms of '89, and carrying arms, in order to present a petition to the king and the assembly. They intended also to plant a 'tree of liberty' on the terrace of the Feuillants. This pleasant custom, borrowed from the May Day ceremonies of the old regime, had recently become so popular that by now some sixty thousand young oaks or poplars (its Latin name *populus* made it appropriate) had been planted in the country, and many in the capital.

An armed petition was illegal, and the Commune refused to consider the application. The sections determined to proceed without its consent. There followed an amusing but disastrous skirmish between the municipality (Pétion) and the department (Roederer), both of which wanted to avoid the responsibility for keeping order, and the odium of calling out the National Guard. They remembered only too well what had happened on July 17th a year ago, and they were ready enough to shelter behind the ambiguities of *Titre IV* of the constitution. It is the mayor's duty, says the *procureur*, to prevent an illegal gathering, and to suppress any disturbance of the public peace. It is due to the fears of the *procureur*, insists the mayor, that he must ask the commandant of the Guard to double his sentries round the palace and the parliament-house, and to increase the number of his patrols. The department pretends to the last moment that the sections will not be armed. The commune vainly urges the sectional commanders to obey the law. They reply that they cannot answer for their men. As a result, the palace is left to face a popular demonstration almost without defence.

At eight o'clock on the morning of June 20th the *procureur* of the department and the Minister of the Interior were assuring one another that the day would pass off quietly, when news came that a large crowd was marching with arms and guns into the West End. By nine o'clock the authorities were calling in vain for troops to defend the Tuileries.

From the Salpêtrière in the south-east marched men of the Observatoire and Montreuil sections. From the Place de la Bastille in the east came the Quinze-Vingts of the *faubourg* Saint Antoine, and the Gobelins of the *faubourg* Saint-Marcel. Meeting at the Hôtel de Ville, some eight thousand in number, under the popular brewer Santerre, and soon swelling to twenty thousand, they surge westwards along the rue Saint-Honoré—'an immense quantity of people,' report the municipal officers, 'of both sexes, and of every age, armed and unarmed, a large number of them in the uniforms of grenadiers, fusiliers, or chasseurs, with their banners in their midst.' When challenged, they declare that they have no intention of breaking the law; they have only come 'to present their respects to the National Assembly, to celebrate the anniversary of the Tennis Court oath, and to plant a may-tree in memory of that occasion.'

They arrive at the Parliament-house. A few of the petitioners are admitted to the bar. It is soon clear that the peaceful intentions of the *section-naires* who organized the procession have been over-ridden by more violent elements. Their orator makes a threatening speech. 'In the name of the nation,' says Huguenin, 'whose eyes are fixed on this city, we have come here to tell you that the people is alert (*debout*), fit for any emergency, and ready to make a supreme effort to avenge the majesty of the outraged nation'; and he appeals to the right of 'resistance to oppression' guaranteed by Article II of the Declaration. 'The sovereign People,' he cries, 'is here to judge the friends of arbitrary power. The Executive Power itself (the king) is at issue with the assembly, as is proved by the dismissal of patriot ministers. Is the happiness of a free people to depend on the caprice of a king? Ought this king to have any will but that of the law? The people says, No! The people's life is worth more than that of any crowned tyrant. Liberty cannot be even temporarily deposed (*suspendue*): but the Executive Power, if it fails to act, must be. It is not right that any one man should overrule the will of twenty-five millions.'

Huguenin's harangue was cheered by the Left, and by the public in the galleries. The demonstrators were by now bursting open the doors of the *manège*. They were allowed to troop through the hall, shouting *Vivent les patriotes!* and *A bas le Véto!* Some of them displayed the repulsive banners of the Fourth Estate—an old pair of gentlemen's breeches (*culottes*), or the bleeding heart of a calf (*cœur d'aristocrate*). There followed an hour's singing and dancing, and the planting of the tree of liberty, not at the Feuillants, but in the garden of the Capucin convent close by. Then the mob broke through the iron gates into the Tuileries gardens, and flowed round by the river-side to the courts at the back of the palace. Santerre trained his guns on the *porte royale*. By this door, by another facing the terrace of the Feuillants, and by three wickets (*guichets*) in the Louvre, all carelessly or

F.R.—18

treacherously left open by the municipal officers, the crowd was able to enter the Tuileries.

The royal family had been expecting an attack at any time during the past twenty-four hours. They had strengthened the palace guards with armed nobles and men from the royalist section of Filles de Saint-Thomas. At about four o'clock in the afternoon they heard the sounds that had haunted them ever since the night of October 5th—a wild shouting, a smashing down of doors, and a rush of feet up the stairs. This time there was no escape. Louis was forced back, protected by a few faithful guardsmen, into the embrasure of a window, whilst the mob poured into his room, crying, 'Down with the veto!' and 'Recall the ministers!' He listened patiently to a harangue by the butcher Legendre. He calmly said that he stood by his rights under the constitution. He allowed a *bonnet rouge* to be placed on his head. He drank to the health of the nation.

After two hours—he dared not risk his popularity earlier—Pétion arrived, and made a speech, and moved the crowd away; but not before they had poured into another room, in which the queen, with Madame Elisabeth, the Dauphin, and his sister, had taken refuge behind a table and a group of guards, and were exhibited to the public, by showman Santerre, like freaks at a country fair. It was not till ten o'clock at night that the palace was at last cleared and quiet, and that the king and queen could feel themselves safe from the violence of the sovereign people. An hour later the Minister of the Interior wrote to the departmental directory, asking that steps should be taken to prevent the repetition of such disorders. Roederer once more passed on the request to Pétion; and Pétion, now that the danger to his reputation was over, arranged to increase the garrison of the Tuileries.

'This June 20th,' wrote the lawyer Lavaux, many years afterwards, 'I was walking aimlessly in the Tuileries gardens amidst the din of the armed mob invading the palace, when I was accosted by M. Perronet, the engineer of roads and bridges. We were both deploring such an outrage to the royal dignity, when we were interrupted by a young man, whom I should have distrusted, but for M. Perronet's reception of him. He looked like a soldier: his eyes were piercing, his complexion pale; he had an uneducated accent, and a foreign name. He spoke his mind freely about the disorderly scene before us, and said that if he were king such things would not be tolerated. I paid little attention to this remark at the time: but later events recalled it to my mind: for the speaker was Bonaparte.'

There were many who agreed with the young Corsican. The blow of June 20th had missed the king: but it had fallen on the crown. 'The constitution,' Morris noted that evening in his diary, 'has this day I think given its last groan.' The monarchy was doomed. Yet the first result of the affair seemed to be a reaction of moderate opinion in favour of the king—a reaction which included a grudging respect for the coolness with which Louis, incapable of taking an initiative, had met a dangerous situation thrust

upon him. Whilst the 'patriot' municipalities generally applauded what had
been done, the reactionary departments sent in wordy protests, and the Paris
directory, which had already (June 12th) denounced the 'criminal preach-
ments' (*prédications*) of the Jacobin club, now suspended Pétion and Manuel
from their posts. Roederer had been against this measure, and ironically
congratulated Pétion on a martyrdom which brought him undeserved
sympathy.

Another protest had more important consequences. From his camp at
Maubeuge, four days before the affair of June 20th, Lafayette had addressed a letter to the assembly attacking the *faction jacobite* as the cause of
political disorder, and demanding the suppression of club regime in the
capital. Now, feeling that his worst fears had been realised, he hurried to
Paris (June 28th), to demand the punishment of the authors of the outrage at
the Tuileries, to offer his services to the king and queen, and to appeal to the
patriotism of his old comrades of the National Guard. It was a brave but a be-
lated gesture. It could do nothing against the universal distrust in which the
hero of '89 was now held. The deputies indicted the general for deserting his
command. The king rejected all suggestions of escape from the man who had
so long presided over his imprisonment. Louis was blindly pinning his hopes
of safety on the constitution, which, as Salamon bitterly remarked, he knew
by heart, though he was the only person who still observed it. The queen,
inexorable in her hatred, encouraged the mayor to prevent Lafayette from
addressing the National Guard. Royalists suggested that, despised by the
aristocrats, and hated by the Jacobins, he was only seeking an excuse
to go over to the enemy. The crowd burnt him in effigy in the Palais-
Royal.

Lafayette returned to the front in despair, and sent the assembly a
final letter—his political testament. He had never, he said, changed his
principles, his opinions, or his language. He still believed (as he told Morris
on June 29th) in 'the American constitution, with a hereditary Executive
Power.' But his army did not share a creed which might have been well
enough three years ago; and without his army he was powerless. In Kellermann's camp at Wissembourg a fortnight later an army order decreed that
the cap of liberty should be the regimental mascot. It would be the privilege
of the oldest non-commissioned officer, or of the bravest man in the army, to
carry it at the head of the column. There was no place for such as Lafayette
beside that republican emblem, nor any career for him in the country which
had adopted it. Within six weeks he was arrested whilst in flight to England,
and immured in an Austrian prison.

Lafayette's family never lacked moral courage. Thirty-eight years later
he presided over the establishment of a monarchy as nearly as possible like
that of Louis XVI. A hundred and fifty years later (July 9th, 1940) his
great-grandson was the only member of the French Senate to vote against
the destruction of the Third Republic, the last defender of the Rights of Man.

It was soon apparent that the main effect of the successful demonstration of June 20th had been to encourage direct action by the Paris sections. The ban imposed by the department could be defied, because there were no troops to enforce it. So long as Pétion was mayor, the municipality could be trusted to put the telescope to its blind eye. The debate on the affair of June 20th had shown that the deputies, having condoned previous breaches of the law against armed petitions, dared not now make a stand against them. Indeed they went further. The suspension of Pétion and Manuel by the department had been confirmed by the king. The assembly revoked it. One Girondin after another expounded the theme that the real criminal of June 20th had been Louis himself. They saw no remedy for the dangers facing the country but the removal of the king and the king's ministers.

Vergniaud led the attack. After an elaborate appeal to the people, he declared that it was not enough to punish the ministers for failing to deal with the counter-revolutionary priests and nobles. There was, he reminded the House, a clause in the constitution which stated that 'if the king puts himself at the head of an army, and directs its forces against the nation, or if he does not formally oppose such an enterprise undertaken in his name, he shall be deemed to have abdicated the throne.' This clause had been added after Louis' flight a year ago, and it should now be the ground of their proceedings against him. They should put out an address, warning him that his present policy was viewed with 'profound horror' by the nation, and asking for a 'plain declaration of his intention either to triumph or to perish with the people and the constitution.' They should at the same time declare a state of national emergency (*la patrie est en danger*): the effect of this would be to put all administrative bodies on a permanent footing, to mobilise the National Guard, and to enforce a kind of national registration—the compulsory wearing of the tricolor cockade.

Vergniaud's speech was an oratorical triumph: but it was a week before the assembly accepted his proposals. Dumas disputed his view that the ministers were to blame for what had happened at the front, and denied that the king's acts amounted to constitutional abdication. The Robespierrist bishop, Torné, declared that there was no hope in the constitution, and proposed that the assembly should assume dictatorial powers. The philosophic Condorcet defended the rule of law, and maintained that the constitution provided all the powers necessary to deal with the situation. He drafted an address to the king, begging him to 'choose between the nation which made him king and the factions which were quarrelling over the partition of his power.'

The debate was interrupted on July 7th by the curious incident known as 'Lamourette's kiss' (*le baiser de Lamourette*). Lamourette, a man of fifty, was constitutional bishop of Lyon, and a representative of the Rhône and Loire department. He proposed that the deputies should drop their unreal differences, and affirm their common faith in the constitution. Such was the unction of the bishop's appeal, if not the force of his argument, that the members of the Right and Left rushed forthwith into each others' arms, and shared their sentiments and their seats.

Soon, however, it became known that Pétion and Manuel had been suspended, and that their arrest had been approved by the king and his Feuillant ministers, who were at that moment blessing the assembly's unexpected act of faith in the constitution. The deputies reflected that advantage was being taken of their feelings to represent them as enemies of republicanism, which more of them every day were beginning to think the only remedy for the situation. The enthusiasm of a moment gave way, as it had done on a famous summer night three years before, to a temper of cold suspicion. At the Jacobin club Billaud-Varenne said it was as though 'Nero had embraced Britannicus, or Charles IX held out his hand to Coligny'; and he called Lamourette's kiss no better than a kiss of Judas.

On July 10th the ministers appeared in a body in the assembly, presented a report on the critical state of the country, and announced that they had just resigned. The excuse for an action which could hardly mend the situation was that three of them had been attacked by Brissot the day before. The real reason seems to have been an attempt on the part of Lafayette's party to make the king accept an anti-Jacobin ministry before the declaration of a national emergency gave Paris an opportunity to attack the Tuileries. Whatever the motive of this move, its results were not what its authors expected. Robespierre was at last convinced that the time had arrived for the Jacobins to come out into the open, and to call for the deposition of the king, and the summoning of a national convention.

As the temperature of the Jacobins went up, that of the Brissotins went down. Their republicanism cooled. They made an eleventh-hour attempt to save the throne, at the expense of the king. A letter drafted by Gensonné, and signed also by Vergniaud and Guadet, was sent to Boze, the court painter, for the eye of the king. In this document the deputies for the Gironde urged Louis to appoint a democratic ministry, to disarm his body-guard, and to present its weapons, as a patriotic gesture, to the army. They urged him to prove, by publishing his private accounts, that he was not spending public money on counter-revolution. They urged him to propose the appointment of a patriot tutor for the Dauphin, to sanction a decree dismissing the senior officers of the National Guard (they were suspected of aristocracy), and to displace Lafayette from the command of his army. Ten days later Vergniaud wrote again. Both overtures were snubbed by the king. He would make no further concessions. He would meet popular pressure by an appeal to force. He could not find ministers among men he had thought to be his friends. He would sooner have no ministers at all than seek them among men he knew to be his enemies.

It remains something of a puzzle whether this move on the part of the Brissotin leaders was due to jealousy of their Jacobin opponents, and represented an attempt to anticipate and outbid any offer they might make to the crown; or whether it was due to the fear that in the coming struggle victory might after all lie with the king. In either case their two-faced policy contrasted poorly with the single aim of their rivals; as the failure of June 20th contrasted with the success of August 10th.

The Fête of Federation fell this year three days after the declaration of the national emergency. It was marked by two significant features. The usual ceremony on the Champ de Mars (or, as it was now called, de la Fédération) was preceded by another, which the king did not attend—the laying of the foundation-stone of a Column of Liberty on the half-dismantled site of the Bastille. Though Louis had vetoed the Paris camp decree, and Terrier, the Minister of the Interior, had instructed the departments to prevent the march of armed bodies to the capital, yet the usual number of *fédérés* was vastly increased by volunteers on their way to the front. Monneron took the opportunity to reissue a number of medals commemorating the *pacte fédératif* of July 14th, 1790. Nevertheless what had then been a civil festival was now a military review; and what had then been an expression of loyalty to the monarchical constitution was now almost a demonstration against the king.

Excluded from the Place de la Liberté, Louis took pains to ensure his presence on the Champ de la Fédération. He told the assembly that it was his wish to see the two powers of government united at the altar of the country, and to join in receiving the loyal vows of the nation. But when the day came, he ventured no further than the lowest step of the altar, wearing under his coat a breast-plate of two thicknesses of taffeta. As he walked from his place to the altar, his powdered head and embroidered coat almost disappeared from sight amongst the throng of dark-haired black-coated citizens around him; and the queen's eyes filled with tears of apprehension. No one could fail to be aware that the real hero of the day was not the king of France, but the mayor of Paris. In the evening federals in *bonnets rouges* crowded the Palais-Royal, shouting *Vive Pétion!* and *Pendez Lafayette!* Fresh from the dangers of the Champ de Mars, Louis may well have reflected that he would be running no greater risk upon a real battlefield. He clung to his determination to appeal to arms. Paris did not see him again until it saw him on the scaffold.

Of the three thousand federals who reached Paris by July 18th, only one in three had come for the usual pleasure-trip to the capital. Two-thirds intended to pass on to the camp at Soissons, and thence to the frontier, to meet the invader. Some two thousand had already done so by the 24th: another six thousand followed by the end of the month. Many of these men had no shoes or stockings, and some no shirts. Yet they were the pick of the active citizens from the provinces, the nucleus of the Grand Army. Those who went on played no part in the events of August 10th. Those who stayed behind soon joined in the plans that they found afoot to rid the country of the arch-enemy on the home front.

What these plans might involve some knew better than others. The correspondence of the Brest federals suggests that they were persuaded against their better judgement to remain in the capital, and to take part in the attack on the Tuileries. But the Marseillais came with a clear intention of dethroning the king. They had received their marching orders a month ago from their clever young delegate Charles-Jean-Marie Barbaroux. Barbaroux had been sent to Paris in February to put the case of the patriots of Marseille against the royalists of Arles and Jalès. He had out-stayed his mission there, finding the experience of a revolution in eruption more fascinating than his old study of the extinct volcanoes of Ollioulles, and the conversation of Madame Roland's drawing-room more alluring than Marat's lectures on Optics.

'It is no use hoping,' he had written to the municipality of his native town on June 21st, 'that the court will change its policy, unless we give it more to be afraid of than any insurrection of the *faubourgs* Saint-Antoine and Saint-Marcel. We must either give the Executive Power a fright it will not forget, or let ourselves be destroyed by it, in the name of the constitution. The simplest way of frightening it is to put into effect of our own will the decree for the formation of a National Guard camp at Paris, at the same time very much increasing the number of citizen soldiers contemplated in the decree. Marseille could provide six hundred men.'

And so they had mobilized, and marched; and on July 30th they entered Paris. The five hundred and sixteen National Guardsmen of Marseille and Toulon had been picked for their moral and physical fitness as carefully as Rhodes Scholars. They were men who, as Barbaroux said, 'knew how to die'. As they marched they sang the *Chant de guerre de l'armée du Rhin*, which Rouget de Lisle had written for Diétrich of Strasbourg, and Diétrich had sung there, on April 26th, to a tune harmonized by Madame Diétrich from Dalayrac's opera *Sangine*. A month later it had been sung again by Mireur of Montpellier at Marseille. Now it sounded for the first time in the streets of Paris, where they called it the *Hymne des Marseillois*.

Feasted in the Champs Elysées, and billeted in the Chaussée d'Antin close by, some of the Marseillais engaged in a brawl with Guardsmen of royalist sympathies. Others found themselves approached by Gouverneur Morris, now American ambassador, with proposals to sell their services to the court. But their help was urgently needed by the patriots for the attack upon the Trojan horse of the Tuileries. They were accordingly induced to follow the Brest federals to more democratic quarters at the Cordeliers convent in the revolutionary Théâtre français section, where they would be under the eye of Danton and his associates. The assembly invited them to its debates, and made each man an allowance of one and threepence a day.

The Jacobins fraternized with them, and worked them into their plans for the coming assault on the Tuileries.

It was now certain that the demonstration of June 20th would have a more violent sequel. Already at the Jacobins on July 15th Danton's bitter young secretary, the ex-Oratorian teacher, dramatist, and pamphleteer, Billaud-Varenne, had outlined a programme for the next insurrection. Exile the king, he had said: dismiss the generals: elect a National Convention: transfer the royal veto to the people: appoint a new Civil Service: arrest Luckner and Lafayette: deport all public enemies: exempt the poor from taxation. This programme was repeated almost intact in a strongly worded manifesto drawn up by Robespierre, and declaimed by a federal orator at the bar of the House. It would do as well as any other: indeed, the last clause would have made any policy popular. The real question was, how it would be carried out. Where could a revolutionary army be found strong enough to conquer the resistance that the court, now thoroughly alarmed, might be expected to offer? There were only two sources of armed support— the National Guard and the provincial federals.

Already (July 15th) a co-ordinating committee had been formed of one federal from each department. Within this body soon appeared a secret committee of five members. Vaugeois of Blois, Debesse of the Drôme, Guillaume of Caen, and Simon of Strasbourg were names as little known in Paris as they are to history: but they were the authors of a movement that shook France. They met at Duplay's house in the rue Saint-Honoré, where Robespierre had his lodgings, in a room occupied by their fifth member, Antoine, the mayor of Metz, during his visits to Paris. They conferred with a group of section-leaders hardly better known than themselves—the journalists Carra and Gorsas, Alexandre and Lazowski of the Saint-Marcel quarter, Fournier 'the American,' Westermann (the only soldier among them), the baker Garin, Anaxagoras Chaumette, and a few more.

Santerre was there too: he was, in fact, the indispensable link between those who made the plot and those who carried it out—the insurrectionary sections of the East End. It was Santerre whom Chambonas, the newest Minister of War, had made the most determined efforts to win over to the king's side on the eve of June 20th. It was Santerre who, persuaded by the cautious Pétion not to march on August 5th, fixed the evening of August 9th, the day set down for the debate on the king's deposition, as the hour for the attack.

The federal troops could not march without the help of the National Guard: the National Guard could not march without the leave of the sections. How had this situation come about? Why did the use of the armed forces of the capital rest upon the decision, not of one authority, but of forty-eight?

Considered as an area, the city of Paris was one of three districts included in the Paris department. Considered as a community, its six hundred thousand citizens were a commune, like any town in the country with six thousand inhabitants, or any village with six hundred. Considered as a self-governing body, it was a municipality; but the word *commune* was popularly applied to it in this sense too. In view of its great size, the city had been sub-divided, for the elections of 1789, into sixty districts. These districts had been destroyed, and the city sub-divided afresh, by the Municipal Law of 1790, into forty-eight sections. The intention had been that each section should contain about the same number of active citizens. The total number of active citizens was between eighty-two and eighty-three thousand; there were on an average from seventeen to eighteen hundred in each section.

Each section conducted the affairs of its part of Paris through a mass meeting (*assemblée générale*) of all its active citizens. Its most important function, that of police, was entrusted to a *commissaire de police*, assisted by sixteen *commissaires de section*. For the other purposes of local administration the sections formed almost as many committees as a modern Borough Council. There were *comités civils* and *comités révolutionnaires* (Vigilance Committees): there were *comités de bienfaisance* (Relief Committees), *comités militaires*, *comités d'agriculture*, and *commissions des salpêtres*, for providing gunpowder. Each section had its own J.P. (*juge de paix*) and Magistrates' bench. It might set up special committees to organize work for the unemployed (*ateliers de charité*), or Tenth-day festivities (*fêtes décadaires*), or open-air suppers for the poor (*banquets populaires*).

But the primary function of the sections, sitting not as *assemblées générales*, but as *assemblées primaires*, was to elect, by a tiresomely compli-cated process, the hundred and forty-eight members of the Paris municipality. This body included three concentric circles of authority. All its members were elected by the sections, but in different ways. The inmost circle (*bureau*) consisted of the mayor, the *procureur*, two deputy *procureurs* (*substituts adjoints*), and sixteen *administrateurs*. The mayor, the *procureur*, and his deputies were elected individually by voting in all the sections. Each section then elected three of its own members to form the rest of the municipal body. From amongst these hundred and forty-four they elected the sixteen *administrateurs* to complete the *bureau*. The *bureau* was enlarged into the *corps municipal* by the addition of another thirty-two members, elected by the sections, like the *administrateurs*, from amongst the hundred and forty-four. The *corps municipal* became the *conseil général de la commune* when it sat along with the remaining ninety-six members (*notables*) who had not been elected either amongst the sixteen or amongst the thirty-two.

The result, if not the intention, of this arrangement was that every section could be sure of having three of its own men on the *conseil général*, but could not be sure of having any on the *corps municipal* or the *bureau*. It meant that any group of twenty-five out of the forty-eight sections might have a majority on the *conseil-général*, but that they could never count upon having a majority on the *corps municipal* or the *bureau*. Everyone knew that the occasional meetings of the hundred and forty-four had less influence on the policy and action of the municipality than the more frequent meetings of the forty-eight, or the daily confabulations of the twenty. The more active and enthusiastic sections felt that they were being excluded from power. Their resentment had made itself felt at the recent elections (November, '91—February, '92). Not only had the progressive sections secured a majority on the General Council: they had also elected Pétion (mayor), Manuel (*procureur*), Danton (*substitut-adjoint*), Panis, and Sergent (*administrateurs*) on to the *bureau*.

The sections, like the districts, had never been content to remain occasional electorates. They inherited the personnel and the premises of the districts. They carried on the political rôle which had made the districts disliked by the assembly, and had led to the restrictions of the Municipal Law two years ago. Their active citizens could meet, not only for elections, not only when convoked by the *corps municipal* on the demand of any eight sections, but also whenever fifty active citizens moved the President of their section to summon a meeting. Their committees met in rooms permanently lent or hired for the purpose. For an assembly of the whole section they generally repaired to the parish church. The municipality made grants towards these and other expenses, proportionate to the size of the section. The sections were, therefore, political debating societies as well as local administrative authorities. They combined, as the assembly did, the functions of a legislature and of an executive. As the departments decentralized the government of France, so the sections decentralized the administration of Paris. At a moment of crisis the city had forty-eight wills instead of one.

On July 25th the assembly recognized the *permanence* of the sections: they could now meet as often as they liked. On the 27th they set up a *bureau de correspondance* to co-ordinate their views and actions. On the 30th they decided to admit the disfranchised passive citizens to their debates. The way was now cleared for the organization of a mass movement against the government.

But how would the sections stand, if it came to a trial of arms? The original establishment of the National Guard amounted to some sixty thousand men—a thousand drawn from each of the sixty districts. It was still so organized in 1792. At best only two-thirds of the active citizens of each section were armed. But the municipal law of 1790, by rearranging the sixty districts into forty-eight sections, had destroyed the local loyalty and significance of the Guard. As one of the sections complained in May, '92, a single battalion might now include men from several sections, and a single section might contribute men to several battalions. The old comradeship was gone: the old keenness was half destroyed. The ancient banner of Henri II no longer waved over the patriots of the Popincourt section. The volunteers of he Pères de Nazareth no longer carried the royal arms of Louis XIV. The *Almanach militaire de la garde nationale parisienne* was out of date. The popular *manuels* and *catéchismes* of drill and musketry no longer contained he text of the constitution, or a commentary on the Rights of Man.

A further reorganization was carried through at the end of October, '91, without enough consideration for the many interests it involved. The *bureau militaire* was soon flooded with complaints from old corps such as the *maréchaussée de l'île de France*, which found itself suppressed, and from the *garde soldée*, whose numbers had been reduced from five thousand to seven hundred, and whose pay was nearly fifty thousand pounds in arrears. Meanwhile the assembly, no doubt for political reasons, stubbornly upheld the very unmilitary arrangement by which, since the decree of February 10th, 92, the command of the Guard had been shared by each of its six battalion commanders (*chefs de légion*) in succession for two months at a time. It was suspected, too, that the *aristos* were making great efforts to monopolize the higher commands. The Commander-in-chief of the moment, the royalist Mandat, showed reactionary sympathies which almost made the public regret Lafayette.

In any case, who could order the Guard to march? Probably the municipality, perhaps the department, possibly the ministers; for there was a conflict of claims. Certainly none of these authorities could enforce their orders without leave of the sections. For, as Pétion reminded the assembly on the eve of the insurrection, the same active citizens who marched in the Guard debated in the sections; and from their decision there was no appeal.

Of the forty-eight sections only fourteen could certainly be relied upon to take part in the coming attack. In the eastern part of the city was the densely populated Gobelins section, with its tanneries and its royal tapestry works, and the Quinze-Vingts—the scene of the still remembered Réveillon riot, and the centre of influence of that popular and prudent dispenser of beer and sedition, Santerre. In the south was the Théâtre français section, the home of Danton, Desmoulins, Marat, Manuel, and other leaders of the Left. With it went the Luxembourg, Croix-rouge, and Fontaine de Grenelle sections— the artists' and journalists' quarter. In the centre was a group of superior working-class sections—the Lombards, Mauconseil, Ponceau, and the parish in which the *enragé* priest, Jacques Roux, preached Christian republicanism to the poor inhabitants of the Gravilliers district. In the west was the bourgeois Jacobin district of le Roule, and Robespierre's section of the Place Vendôme, or les Piques. This reckoning still left the constitutional or royalist sections as three to one. But they were so little organized or enthusiastic that they were soon either absorbed into the insurrectional movement by the influence of such agitators as Chabot, Merlin, and Basire, or swept aside by it. On August 3rd forty-seven out of the forty-eight sections had petitioned for the deposition of the king. On the morning of the 10th as many as twenty-eight were ready to risk their lives for it.

One incident contributed decisively to this change of mind. On August 1st there were published in Paris the documents generally known as Brunswick's Manifesto. Both the Declaration of July 25th and the Additional Declaration of the 27th were signed by the Prussian general, and bore the hall-marks of the Prussian mind—a dense belief in the efficacy of threats and an inability to recognize anyone else's point of view. But they had been drafted in Paris, and probably at the Tuileries. Gouverneur Morris noted in his diary the main points of the manifesto a fortnight before it was issued at Metz. It was in fact fathered upon Brunswick by the *émigré* de Limon and by Mirabeau's old secretary, Pellenc. It represented what the court and the aristocrats, in their more than German blindness, thought likely to intimidate the French people, and the politicians of Paris.

The Duke declared that his aim was 'to put an end to anarchy in the country, to stop the attacks directed against the throne and the altar, to re-establish the rule of law, to restore to the king the safety and liberty of which he has been deprived, and to enable him to exercise his legitimate authority. He threatened with military execution, and the burning of their homes, any civilians who opposed his march. He said that if any attack were made on the Tuileries, or any violence offered to the king and queen—if, indeed, they were not immediately released—he would exercise 'an exemplary and unforgettable vengeance, by delivering up Paris to military execution and complete destruction'. He added, as an after-thought, that if the royal family were removed from Paris, any town that connived at such a proceeding would share the fate of the capital.

Brunswick's manifesto, and the official declarations issued at the same time from Vienna and Berlin, acted as a counter-irritant to the party quarrels and suspicions which were paralysing the national defence. Popular anger was concentrated upon the court, the emigrants, and the foreign powers. On the very day that the manifesto was published Lazare Carnot propounded to the assembly that theory of 'a nation in arms' which was to be the secret of the revolutionary victory. 'From the moment when danger exists,' he said, 'every citizen is a soldier'; and he carried a decree for the manufacture of a weapon which could be issued to every Frenchman who was not vagrant, a beggar, or a traitor. These pikes were rude weapons from eight to ten feet long: they had been out of date since the days of Marshal Saxe: but Napoleon agreed with Carnot that they were serviceable, and thought it worth while to employ them for the defence of Paris in 1814.

Louis, realizing too late what the consequences of the Manifesto might be, tried in vain to dissociate himself from it. In a message to the assembly on August 3rd he pretended that the document was not authentic. He took the opportunity to express his disquietude at the internal quarrels which (he asserted) were the chief cause of military defeat. It was his intention, he said, to remain faithful to the constitution, and to increase his efforts in the national cause. The message was received with scepticism, and a royalist

roposal to print it was thrown out. It was, said a speaker at the Jacobins
he same evening, only a manœuvre: Louis wished to anticipate the next
1ove against him. In fact his only hope of safety lay in seizing the initiative,
nd asserting his authority by force. 'In the present state of things,' wrote
Aorris to Jefferson on August 1st, 'it seems evident that if the king be not
estroyed, he must soon become absolute.'

Both sides knew that this was now the issue. On August 3rd Pétion
rought to the assembly a petition from forty-seven out of the forty-eight
ections of Paris calling for the forfeiture of the throne (*déchéance*), and for
he summoning of a National Convention. The Brissotin majority, as fearful
y now of republicanism as their predecessors had been a year ago, stood only
or the king's suspension. The petition was referred to the reactionary Com-
nittee of Twelve, and was put down for debate on the 9th. The deputies
rgued, as procrastinators have always argued, that 'anything might happen
1 a week.'

They were right. The insurrection, which had been two months preparing, could no longer be delayed. One premature rising was stopped on
uly 26th, and another on August 5th. Pétion, whilst encouraging the court
o think that he could prevent an insurrection, was nursing the sections till
he moment when their action would be as unanimous and effective as
ossible. The more violent sections had sent in petitions of their own backing
hat of August 3rd. But on the 5th there was still a majority against direct
ction; and a group of counter-revolutionary sections—Bibliothèque (or
'illes de Saint-Thomas), Arsénal, and Henri IV—had publicly expressed
heir disapproval. Even the federal petition presented by Varlet on the 6th,
hough it testified to the unity of the country, and contained a more com-
rehensive programme than that of Billaud-Varenne, was felt to be, like its
redecessor, a move in the Jacobin party game.

It was the assembly itself which finally gave the majority to the insur-
ectional sections, and precipitated the outbreak. On August 8th, after two
ays' debate, the deputies threw out a motion for the impeachment (*décret
d'accusation*) of Lafayette in respect of his conduct on June 28th. This
efiance of popular feeling made it clear on which side the assembly stood.
f it would not vote for the punishment of a disloyal general, it was not likely
o vote for the deposition of a treacherous king. If it condoned an attempt to
issolve the Jacobin club, it was not likely to accept a democratic revision of
he constitution. The Parliament-house would make common cause with the
alace. Nothing was now left but to reassert the constitutional right of
1surrection, and to re-enthrone the Sovereign People. The People, by the
ecessities of the case, was the people of Paris: but the presence and support
f the federals, the representatives of the People in the provinces, gave them
he right to speak and act for the whole nation.

All the fateful night of August 9th the sections sat in consultation. At eleven o'clock the Quinze-Vingts, always the leaders, proposed that each section should appoint three of its members on to a body with instruction 'to recommend immediate steps to save the state' (*sauver la chose publique*) During the night twenty-eight sections answered this invitation. It was their representatives who constituted the Insurrectional Commune. It was too large a body to do more than sanction the detailed preparations already made by the organizing committees: but it was the body finally and publicly responsible for the rising of August 10th.

The municipality was already in session. From midnight till three o'clock next morning the old and the new, the legal and the insurrectional communes sat in adjoining rooms at the Town Hall. The illegal body organized the attack on the Tuileries. The legal body, by recalling the officer in charge of the troops at the Tuileries, disorganized its defence. Between six and seven in the morning this farcical situation was brought to an end. The Insurrectional Commune informed the municipal body, in a formally worded resolution, that they had decided upon its suspension; but they would retain the mayor (Pétion), the procureur (Manuel), the deputy-procureur (Danton) and the administrators in their executive functions. They were at this time a body of eighty-two, the skeleton of an assembly that ultimately numbered two hundred and eighty-eight. Within an hour of their seizure of the Town Hall the attack on the palace began.

It might be thought that Paris was running no great risk in attacking the Tuileries, and that democratic historians have given to the affair of August 10th a factitious air of heroism. Such was not the general opinion at the time. The king had failed to buy off the popular leaders. According to Malouet thirty-seven thousand pounds had been paid to Pétion and Santerre for worthless promises to stop the insurrection. He had rejected the last-minute advice, not only of Vergniaud and Guadet, who were now alarmed by turn of affairs they had themselves brought about, but also of his loyal old minister Malesherbes, to abdicate the throne. He was determined to defend the Tuileries. His supporters had anticipated and prepared for the attack long beforehand, and were confident of success. A plan of defence, drawn up by a professional soldier, had been adopted by the Paris department on June 25th: for it was their official duty to safeguard the Executive Power. The palace was easy to defend. It was garrisoned by the only regular troops on either side—nine hundred veteran Swiss mercenaries (rumour made them four times as many); and these were backed by nine hundred and thirty *gendarmes*, two thousand National Guards, and from two to three thousand Chevaliers de Saint Louis, and other royalist volunteers. Five thousand men should have been an ample defence; though it appears that by some oversight, they were seriously short of ammunition. Police spies reported to the commune that underground passages had been constructed by which additional troops could be secretly introduced from their barracks.

This, then, was no Bastille affair. The popular leaders might well hesitate to throw an uncertain number of half-trained and untried volunteers, followed by an undisciplined mob armed with pikes, against so formidable a fortress. The supporters of the throne might well expect victory.

Whilst resolution wavered, treachery and weakness found a way. Three men were in the palace, late that night, whose presence should have guaranteed the safety of the royal family—Pétion, the mayor of Paris, Roederer, the procureur of the Paris department, and Mandat, the commandant of the National Guard and the officer in charge of the troops detailed for the defence of the Tuileries. All three failed the king. Pétion professed that he had come to defend the royal family; but about two o'clock in the morning, hearing himself threatened by a group of royalist gunners, he obeyed a (possibly prearranged) summons to the Parliament-house, reported that all precautions had been taken to keep the peace, and retired ingloriously to the *Mairie*, where (he said) he was confined by orders of the Insurrectional Commune. Roederer's first act was to assure the royal family, who (as Morris heartlessly puts it) had been 'sitting up all night, expecting to be murdered,' that there would be no attack. His second act, when a series of bulletins from Blondel, the secretary of the department, made it certain that an attack was coming, was to persuade Louis to abandon the defence of the palace, and to put himself under the protection of the assembly. Mandat, after seeing to the defence of the palace, was persuaded by Roederer (it was his third and most fatal mistake) to obey a treacherous summons from the Town Hall. There he was put under arrest, and shortly murdered; and his command was transferred to Santerre.

Thus when, at about seven o'clock in the morning, the head of the federal column was seen debouching on the back of the palace, there was no one to order the defence. Louis, sleepily reviewing his garrison, 'in full dress, with his sword at his side, but with the powder falling out of his hair,' was greeted by some of the National Guards with cries of *Vive la nation!* and *A bas le véto!* Hating violence, and dreading bloodshed, he listened willingly to Roederer's suggestion that he should abandon the defence of the palace. In vain the queen urged that they should stay and fight. Before a shot had been fired the royal family were in sad retreat across the gardens to the door of the Parliament-house. There the king was given a seat by the President, and listened, with his customary air of bland indifference, whilst the deputies discussed his fate. The queen sat at the bar of the House, with the Dauphin on her knees. She at least knew the tragedy of their situation.

The king had deserted his garrison; but he had not countermanded the defence. The Swiss and the *gendarmes* withdrew from their outlying posts into the palace, and the National Guard went over to the people. In the first phase of the fighting the defenders succeeded in clearing the insurgents out of the court (*carrousel*) behind the Tuileries. In the second phase the attackers, reinforced, pushed them back into the palace. Louis, hearing from the *manège* the sound of firing, wrote on a scrap of paper, which can still be read in the Carnavalet museum, 'The king orders the Swiss to lay down their arms at once, and to retire to their barracks.' To obey this order at such a moment meant almost certain death. Some of the Swiss fell at their posts: some sought sanctuary in the Parliament-house: some, trying to retreat by the gardens, were surrounded, carried off to the Town Hall, and put to death beneath the statue of a king who would at least have shown more appreciation of their loyalty—Louis XIV. Out of the nine hundred only three hundred survived.

The total losses on the king's side were perhaps eight hundred. On the side of the insurgents three hundred and seventy-six were either killed or wounded. Eighty-three of these were federals, and two hundred and eighty-five members of the National Guard—common citizens from every branch of the trading and working classes of Paris, whom a day's adventure had turned into heroes. Hair-dressers and harness-makers; carpenters, joiners, and house-painters; tailors, hatters, and boot-makers; locksmiths, laundry-men, and domestic servants—over sixty callings were represented there. Two women combatants were among the wounded; and passive citizens, who had been thought too insignificant to have a vote, lay dead upon the ground they had won for the republic, still clasping their clumsy pikes. For this was a people's victory.

CHAPTER XVI

COMMUNE

La nation veut se rendre libre: son ambition est noble, car l'homme n'est pas fait pour être esclave de la volonté d'un autre hômme; mais chez une nation populeuse, grande, spirituelle, et légère, que deviendra cette révolution?—(CASANOVA: Paris, c. 1760).

THE medal struck by the Paris commune to celebrate the rising of August 10th was inscribed, 'In memory of the glorious combat of the French people against tyranny at the Tuileries.' It was a people's victory. It was also a people's vengeance. The capital had been preparing the event for two months. The country had been expecting it for two years. An Englishman on his way to Paris heard from fugitives some days beforehand that an insurrection would break out on August 9th. The people spoke with indifference about the deposition of a king whom a few years before they had regarded as almost divine. Their mood was one of cheerfulness and gaiety.

On every market-place between Calais and the capital travellers passed 'trees of liberty,' planted sometimes, like the constitution, so carelessly that their leaves were already withering, but crowned with a cap of freedom, and

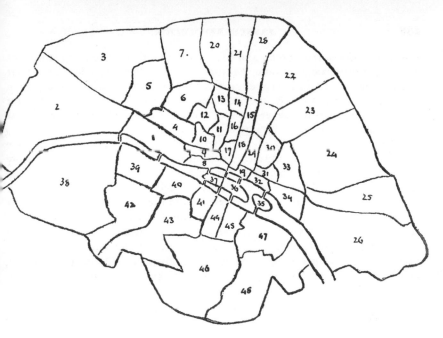

THE PARIS SECTIONS IN 1792
With the number of their ' active ' citizens.

1. Tuileries, 1700.
2. Champs-Elysées, 900.
3. Roule, 1,300.
4. Palais-royal, 2,400.
5. Place-Vendôme, 1,200.
6. Bibliothèque, 1,500.
7. Grange-Batelière, 1,500.
8. Louvre, 2,000.
9. Oratoire, 1,900.
10. Halle-au-Blé, 1,900.
11. Postes, 1,800.
12. Place-Louis XIV, 1,400.
13. Fontaine-Montmorency, 1,100.
14. Bonne-Nouvelle, 1,600.
15. Ponceau, 2,300.
16. Mauconseil, 1,700.
17. Marché-des-Innocents, 1,100.
18. Lombards, 2,500.
19. Arcis, 1,800.
20. Montmartre, 700.
21. Poissonière, 800.
22. Bondy, 1,400.
23. Temple, 1,700.
24. Popincourt, 1,300.

25. Montreuil, 1,500.
26. Quinze-vingts, 2,000.
27. Gravilliers, 3,300.
28. Saint-Denis, 1,300.
29. Beaubourg, 2,300.
30. Enfants-Rouges, 1,800.
31. Roi-de-Sicile, 1,800.
32. Hôtel-de-Ville, 1,700.
33. Place-royale, 1,900.
34. Arsenal, 1,400.
35. Ile-Saint-Louis, 1,100.
36. Notre-Dame, 1,700.
37. Henri IV, 900.
38. Invalides, 1,100.
39. Fontaine-Grenelle, 2,000.
40. Quatre-Nations, 3,900.
41. Théâtre-français, 2,600.
42. Croix-rouge, 1,600.
43. Luxembourg, 2,100.
44. Thermes-de-Julien, 2,000.
45. Sainte-Geneviève, 2,800.
46. Observatoire, 1,700.
47. Jardin-des-plantes, 2,200.
48. Gobelins, 1,200.

gay with ribbons, red, white, and blue. In the churches the painted images sported patriotic cockades, and the iron grilles had been torn down to make patriotic pikes. In one chapel a few old women would be on their knees, hearing mass: in another commissioners would be taking down the names of volunteers for the army. In the beer-houses of Paris fish-wives and *sansculottes* danced to the strains of the *Ça ira*.

On the terrace of the Tuileries a frail ribbon had kept back the people till the moment of the assault. Then they came in their thousands, and 'their march was at the rate of perhaps five miles an hour, without running or looking aside, rushing along the streets like a torrent, and attending wholly and solely to the object they had in view.' On the morning after the assault the terrace, the gardens, and the courts of the Tuileries were crowded with sightseers, who gazed with curiosity at the scarred walls, the broken windows, the burnt-out barracks, and the stripped bodies of the slaughtered Swiss. Everywhere emblems of royalty were torn down, and the images of kings overthrown. These spectators, it was remarked, were not the ragged *canaille* of the old regime, but women in white linen and muslin gowns, with large caps and low-heeled shoes, wearing gold necklaces and gold earrings: the men, of whatever rank, wore the plain clean coats of *citoyens*: they were better dressed and better mannered since the revolution had come to give them equality and self-respect. For days the public walks were 'crowded with men, women, and children of all conditions, with the most gay unconcerned countenances imaginable.' A stranger 'could not possibly imagine that the ground he is walking over was so lately covered with the bodies of slaughtered men.'

For forty-eight hours, broken only by uncomfortable nights at the neighbouring Feuillants, the king and queen, the king's sister, and his two children sat in one of the press boxes (*loge du logographe*) of the *manège*, whilst the deputies discussed what should be done with them. Louis had been received by the assembly as an outraged king. When the fighting went against him, the deputies still showed their sympathy by decreeing his suspension, not his dethronement. Guadet afterwards said that this was in order to avert a regency. Vergniaud said that it was done to enable the Convention to declare a republic. The real intentions of the Girondins were perhaps shown by the proposal to appoint a tutor for the Dauphin, under a clause of the constitution which only came into effect during a regency. This would isolate him from the king, and enable him to be treated as a hostage for Louis' good behaviour. When the Tuileries had fallen, and it became necessary to provide for Louis' captivity, the deputies tried to secure his instalment in the comfortable apartments in the Luxembourg palace, which had been sealed up since his brother, the Comte de Provence, fled from them a year ago. Failing that, he might be accommodated at the Ministry of Justice in the Place Vendôme. But the commune claimed Louis as its prisoner: and the commune was inexorable. The Luxembourg was said to have secret exits, probably underground; and the garden wall was too low for safety. The Ministry was too closely surrounded by other buildings. First the Bishop's Palace was suggested. Then only the Temple would suffice—and not its residential wing, but its grim baronial tower (*Petite Tour*), with the narrow windows, the deep ditch, and the unclimbable walls of a medieval keep. Its only occupant at this time was M. Barthélemy, Keeper of the Archives of the Order of Malta. He was ruthlessly evicted; and there, on the third day, the royal family were interned.

Cléry's journal, which went through many editions from 1798 onwards, gave the world a *valet-de-chambre's* view of Louis' five months' imprisonment. Ten years later, under the Bourbon restoration, the reminiscences of the Duchesse d'Angoulême, of Hue, Lepitre, Turgy, Moelle, and Goret enabled a compassionate public to reconstruct every detail of the royal martyrdom. The physical sufferings of the royal prisoners were, indeed, somewhat mitigated by the services of over twenty attendants, including a kitchen staff of ten, whose wages came to three thousand pounds a year, and by a food bill of two hundred and fifty pounds a week—for republican tradesmen were still royalist in their charges. Nor was Louis deprived of the reading which now became his only recreation. His library at the Temple included some fifty books of devotion, and twenty books of travel, together with many classical authors, Hume's *History of England*, and Robertson's *History of Scotland*. In effect most of the hardships of the Capets, as they were now called, were those inseparable from close confinement. They were needlessly increased only by the bad manners which *sansculotte* sentries assumed in order to show their equality with *ci-devant* royalties, or by fresh restrictions imposed, as time went on, by the cruelty which springs from fear.

The Jacobin press amused its readers by publishing the *Complainte* of Louis' Bourbon ancestors, the *Désespoir* of Antoinette, the *Grandes reproches* of the royal children, or the *Mea culpa du ci-devant Véto*. The commune received almost daily reports on every detail of the imprisonment: the construction of the continuous wall and the twelve-foot ditch and draw-bridge which were to make the tower even more secure; the organization of the garrison of fifty men, twenty-five chosen in turn from each legion of the National Guard, who were on duty day and night; or the lessons Louis gave to his children, the books they read, and the games and puzzles with which they tried to relieve the endless *ennui* of captivity.

One day it is proposed to deprive the king of the star, the *cordon rouge*, and the other 'symbols of feudalism' that he wears on his coat. Another day it is proposed to reduce the number of dishes served at the royal dinner-table. The *Journal des débats* is supplied for Louis' reading, and thirty Latin books for the instruction of the Dauphin; but all possible weapons are taken away, from razors and pocket-knives to scissors and tooth-picks. When the cold weather comes, the queen has to ask the commune for winter clothes. The prisoners are now separated from one another, and only meet for meals—a senseless act of cruelty towards any mother with two young children.

But the warders seem to have doubted whether princes had human feelings, rather than have wished to outrage them. 'These crowned heads have an entirely different nature from ours,' wrote the naïve patriot Madame Jullien on August 18th; 'they have no souls; they eat and sleep just as usual; they play backgammon, and do not seem to think of a calamity (*the bloodshed of August 10th*) which has filled us with horror.' The ingenuous Cubières, whose report was laid before the commune on December 21st, was astonished to find Louis reading a breviary, and observing the fasts of the church. When Malesherbes, who, though he called Louis *le Roi*, seemed 'an honest man,' told him that the king's Catholic convictions would never allow him to commit suicide, 'I realized,' said Cubières, 'that though I have no love for religion, yet there are conditions under which it might be worth something.' Indeed, the quiet dignity and simple piety which Louis learnt in captivity compelled a measure of respect from his warders. It was after his execution that the regime began which turned the Dauphin, before his premature death, into a depraved slanderer of his mother, and his sister, the only one of them who survived, into an implacable enemy of the revolution.

The leaders of the assembly had made a last-minute attempt to prevent the Jacobin *coup d'état* by inducing the king to recall the Brissotin ministry. When this failed they tried to save the constitution by proposing to summon a National Convention, and by decreeing the king's suspension, instead of his deposition from the throne. In the matter of his imprisonment they were forced to give way to the commune, when any further attempt to help the king would have compromised them beyond repair. But they were not disposed to surrender the relics of government left to the legislature by the fall of the Executive Power. They therefore tried to represent August 10th as an extension of June 20th. They would never admit that it had been an attack upon the Parliament-house as well as upon the palace. The constitutional status of the assembly could be preserved by the fiction that the session of August 9th had never been adjourned. They appointed a standing committee of twenty-one (*commission extraordinaire*) with Vergniaud as *rapporteur*, to carry on the administration. The small number of deputies who still had the courage to present themselves (many of them stayed at home, writing letters of protest against assaults made on them for voting against the impeachment of Lafayette) took a fresh oath 'to maintain liberty and equality, or to die at their posts.' They drew up an elaborate scheme by which the departmental authorities, under the supervision of their own Vigilance Committee (*comité de surveillance*) should deal with crimes against the state. They listened anxiously to reports from the provinces, where, upon the whole, the municipalities supported the action of Paris, whilst the departmental directories rejected it. They even suspended a few directories which declared the *coup* of August 10th to have been illegal.

At the front, many important officers hesitated whether or not to transfer their allegiance from the king to the assembly. Only Lafayette, after attempting to organize resistance in the Ardennes, threw up his command, and crossed the frontier. Dumouriez, Luckner, Kellermann, and Montesquiou remained to lead the republican armies to victory. The interim government was saved, as its predecessor had been saved a year ago, by the necessity of meeting a national emergency.

In the provinces the emissaries of the assembly, carrying the official account of August 10th, clashed and sometimes quarrelled with the emissaries of the commune, whose version of what had happened was not quite the same. In the capital the authority of the Brissotin 'rump' was hotly disputed by the organizers and victors of August 10th, who considered that, until a National Convention could be summoned, France should be ruled by Paris, and Paris by the Insurrectional Commune.

A great part of this difficulty might have disappeared, if there had been effective and influential ministers to take the place of the *pouvoir exécutif*, and to stand between the country and the capital. There was indeed a ministry, but it contained only one man who could do what was needed. One of the first acts of the assembly after the fall of the throne had been to declare that the late ministers had lost the confidence of the nation, and to ask its *commission extraordinaire* to draw up a plan for the organization of a new ministry. Until the Convention met, the Brissotins hoped to keep their control over the legislature, and to extend it to the executive. Guadet accordingly proposed that the assembly should nominate five 'provisional' ministers for the Interior, War, Taxation, Marine, and Foreign Affairs. They were to be elected in that order, and the first appointed was to act for the rest until all the places were filled. On Isnard's motion three of the vacancies were at once supplied by the reappointment of Roland (Interior), Clavière (Taxation), and Servan (War). Later, Monge was elected Minister of Marine, and Lebrun Minister of Foreign Affairs.

There remained a sixth ministry, which Guadet had omitted from his list. The department of Justice, as originally defined by the decree of April 27th–May 25th, '91, might seem a pale shadow, beside that of the Lord Privy Seal. It had since acquired importance from the increase, if not of justice, at any rate of judicial proceedings and imprisonments during the war period. The Minister of Justice would incur the responsibility and the odium of dealing with the popular demand for vengeance on the 'criminals' of August 10th. The assembly saw an opportunity of appointing to this post one who had already been offered it at the time of the formation of the Brissotin ministry—one who would carry weight with the commune, of which he was an official member, without committing his patrons to approval of the recent insurrection, in which he had played an undistinguished part. Thus it was that they nominated Georges Danton; and he was elected by over two hundred votes in an assembly which had been reduced by abstention to less than three hundred members.

Danton was for half a century the scapegoat of the August revolution and of the September massacre, as Robespierre was of the Jacobin dictatorship and of the Terror. Rehabilitated by the neo-Jacobin historians of 1848, he became the chief hero of republicanism and of national defence, until a determined attempt was made, half a century later, to put Robespierre on his pedestal. Danton would have laughed at the irrelevant little men discussing his venality and his vices. It is more certain that he took bribes than that he did anything to earn them. It is more certain that he had vices than that he was enslaved by them. He was one of the best classical scholars of the revolution, a book-collector, and widely read in English and Italian literature. His library included copies of Shakespeare, Pope, and Dryden. He could talk English with Tom Paine and Italian with his mother-in-law, Madame Charpentier. He knew his Rabelais as well as his Corneille. Yet he was able to express the ideas of the moment in language that any *sansculotte* could understand. He lived in open-minded, open-handed comradeship with men who could be liked, but scarcely respected. He indulged in occasional bouts of politics as a change from the pleasures of domesticity; and lived his public life, as he lived his private life, in a spirit of generous ruffianism. A *grand seigneur de sansculottisme* (the phrase is Garat's), he was the very reverse of Robespierre. Danton improvised, where Robespierre planned ahead: Danton scoffed, where Robespierre sermonized: Danton trusted and understood, where Robespierre idealized and intrigued: Danton piloted the country to victory, whilst Robespierre pointed it to virtue. How could Robespierre's sleek Puritanism fail to be offended at every turn by Danton's Rabelaisian honesty? Mirabeau, had the two met, would have recognized a rival—a man with the same virility, the same arresting ugliness, the same power of leadership. But Danton had something Mirabeau could never match—a natural sympathy with the humanity and heroism of the man in the street.

Those who appointed Danton must have hoped that his reputation as a democrat and a demagogue would reconcile Paris to the decidedly dull virtues and dimmed prestige of his colleagues in the ministry. There is little evidence that his part in the insurrection of August had made him a popular hero. He left Paris a few days before the day fixed for the rising, to attend to family affairs at his country home, Arcis-sur-Aube. He came back to the capital on the evening of the 9th, and was called from his bed late that night to attend to his duties as deputy-procureur of the commune. He played an uncertain part in the proceedings of the insurrectional commune which took its place early the next morning. It was not his section (*Théâtre français*) but Santerre's (*Quinze-Vingts*) which led Paris to the attack on the Tuileries.

There can, however, be no question that the new Minister of Justice overshadowed his colleagues as completely as the commune overshadowed the assembly. They met at his house. He set their political step. His energy organized the national defence. His view of the international situation gave them a foreign policy. But even Danton could not restore popularity or prestige to men doubly compromised by their association with a deposed king and with a discredited assembly. His best work was done as a free-lance. His real function was that of liaison-officer between the assembly and the commune, the government and the people.

Danton's colleagues on the *conseil exécutif provisoire,* as the new ministry was named, were in no position to control either the country or the capital. They were no longer ministers of the crown, but employees of the assembly. Their executive work was hampered by a civil service inherited from the monarchical regime. Their patriotism was rendered suspect by the too obvious attempts of Roland and his wife to fill the subordinate offices of state with personal friends—Champagneux, Lecamus, Lanthenas, Buzot—and to exploit their powers in the Girondin interest. It was suspected that the elegant dinners given twice a week at the Ministry of the Interior were used by Roland's political clique to ventilate their hostility against Paris and the commune. It was hinted that departmental funds were being spent on party propaganda. It was rumoured that plans were afoot for the transfer-ence of the government to Lyon or Marseille, the alternative capitals of a new republic in the Midi. It was noticed that whilst some of the old police spies (*agents de police, observateurs, mouchards*) such as Collenot d'Angre-mont or Soltho-Douglas (as the French spelt his name) had been indicted as royalists, others such as Bachelu, Jourdain, and Cabanis merely transferred their allegiance to the new Ministry of the Interior. It was well known that the minister's official letters were not infrequently dictated by the minister's wife, and signed *Roland, née Phlipon.* There was even a day when Madame Roland made a speech at the bar of the assembly, and walked through the hall amidst the applause of the deputies. But the public galleries were silent. 'They know better,' Marat sourly remarked, 'than we do.' Within six months the minister had fallen, and the minister's wife was in prison. Ro-land's virtues alone were merely tiresome: seconded by his wife's, they became a menace to republican government.

The residual legatee of the monarchy, the insurrectional commune, had no credentials for government except its willingness to govern, and any success its rule might achieve. It was pestered from all sides by advice, good and bad. It was forced to balance the claims of deputies and ministers, sec-tions and clubs. It became a clearing-house for ideas and expedients in municipal management and national defence. It had no assured control over either department of government. But it profited by its recent victory to exploit the weakness of the assembly. It extorted a grant of five thousand pounds towards the 'extraordinary expenses' of the August revolution; and it succeeded, during the next few weeks, in securing the passage of a considerable programme of radical reforms. Some of these were, no doubt, justified by the critical state of the national defences: others expressed only the demands of a class which believed that it deserved some return for its sufferings on behalf of the revolution.

Amongst these measures was a decree giving municipalities extensive police powers, under the supervision of the departmental and district directories; a decree abolishing passive citizenship, and introducing manhood suffrage; a decree suppressing the remaining feudal charges without compensation; and a decree increasing the *biens nationaux* by putting confiscated *émigré* property up for sale in small lots, with payments spread over fifteen years. There were also decrees dissolving the remaining religious orders, deporting non-juror priests, secularizing the registration of births, deaths, and marriages, reducing the age of marriage, widening the grounds of divorce, outlining a scheme of national education, and abolishing all social qualifications for commissions in the army. The needs of poor purchasers were met by calling for an immediate report on the scheme for issuing a new bell-metal currency in small denominations. These coins were to range in value from five *sols* (twopence half-penny), to three *deniers* (half a farthing). They were to bear the head of Liberty in place of that of Louis XVI.

The opportunity was also taken to initiate two reforms in the government of Paris which were to have important effects in the months that followed. The commune determined to administer a *coup de grâce* to its old enemy, the Paris department, and to obtain effective control over the National Guard.

The old directory had resigned on the eve of August 10th: but the assembly had ordered it to be replaced by a fresh election. The commune was soon faced by a new department, 'provisional' in name, but in fact a dangerous weapon in the hands of a hostile assembly determined to exercise its right of supervision under the new police decree. Urged by Robespierre, at this time a hot champion of the independence of the sections, the commune attempted to get the powers of the new body limited to matters of taxation. For the moment it failed. The assembly's refusal was the first shot fired in the Girondin reaction against the 'dictatorship' of the Paris commune.

Within ten days the deputies conceded, under another head, more than they had gained. One handicap under which the people had lain during the recent rising was the lack of *liaison* between the forty-eight sections of the capital and the sixty battalions of the National Guard. This hindrance to ochlocracy was now removed. The Guard was reorganized on a sectional basis. Each of the little republics into whose hands the government of Paris had fallen could in future count upon its own men, its own muskets, and (if it were fortunate enough to possess any) its own guns to reinforce its political opinions. In July, '91, the National Guard had been used by the legally constituted commune against the people. In August, '92, it had been used by an insurrectional commune against the crown and the constitution. In June, '93, and July, '94, it would be used in a civil war between political parties. The history of the country would be determined by the armed sections of the capital.

The militarizing of the sections, and the opening of their assemblies to those who had so lately been passive citizens, gave point to a formula which now appeared for the first time at the head of the official acts of the commune —'The fourth year of Liberty, the first year of Equality.' The control of the revolution had at first been transmitted downwards from the middle to the lower class of society. It was now beginning to reverse its direction. Initiative was passing from the constituted authorities, whether the assembly elected by the whole country, or the commune appointed by the people of the capital, to unconstituted gatherings and unofficial leaders. It was also passing, though slowly, from the middle to the lower *bourgeoisie*.

This social change can be verified from the published lists of national and communal representatives. There was, in fact, surprisingly little difference in age, origin, or social status between the deputies of the Commons in '89, '91, and '92. The ultimate direction of the revolution remained in the hands of the class which began it. Its national orbit was little affected by the aberrations of the capital. When the quarrels of Jacobin and Girondin had ended on the same scaffold, the beneficiaries of the new order belonged to the same class of society as the men of 1789.

As it was in the country, so it was, for the first part of the period, in the capital. A comparison of the personnel of the Paris commune of '90 with that of '91 shows almost exactly the same professional make-up. Of a hundred and thirty-one members of the commune of '90, forty-four were lawyers, forty-two merchants or tradesmen, eighteen officials, twelve men of letters, artists, or journalists, six doctors, six priests, and three officers in the army. Of a hundred and thirty-five members of the commune of '91, forty-six were lawyers, forty-three merchants or tradesmen, sixteen officials, sixteen men of letters, five doctors, five priests, and three officers.

But in the constitutional commune of '92, which included many new members appointed during the winter and spring, there is already evidence of a change of balance. Of fifty-two whose professions can be ascertained twenty are merchants or tradesmen, and only sixteen lawyers; and within this class the shop-keepers (*marchands*) have increased their numbers at the expense of the merchants (*négotiants*). An analysis of the professions of the insurrectional commune of August 10th is conclusive. Out of two hundred and one members no less than a hundred and four are *marchands* or *négotiants*: lawyers have sunk to thirty-one: art and literature, with thirty-four members, are better represented than before: there are nineteen officials, four doctors, five priests, and four officers.

In this revolutionary executive, the nominees of the democratic sections, there are only two workmen (*ouvriers*)—one cobbler and one jeweller. The working class may listen to speeches, and carry pikes. The direction of their movement is still in the hands of the men who can read a paper and write a petition, who can sit on a committee and stand on a platform—the lawyers, journalists, petty officials, and, in ever-increasing proportion, the small employers of labour, whether in shops, factories, or transport. Yet, though they are in a minority, the most active leaders of the insurrectional commune are still lawyers and journalists. It is this class which supplies the majority of the twenty-one who act as President or Secretary during the week of August 10th-17th.

As the revolution went on, it was becoming more and more difficult to say what meaning should be attached to a word which was increasingly used by speakers of all parties—'the people' (*le peuple*). Mirabeau in the 'National Assembly' debates of June, '89, had used it in the sense which it bore in the preamble to the American constitution—'We, the people of the United States'; and he had defended an ambiguity which alarmed some of his hearers. By common consent the term no longer included the privileged orders, the *ci-devant* bishops and nobles, the First and Second Estates of 1789. But did it mean the whole residue—both the active and the passive citizens? Did it include, along with the Third Estate, what some were beginning to call the Fourth Estate, the disfranchised proletariat? Did it mean the *populus*, the whole population, or did it mean specifically the lower orders, the *plebs*—a class hitherto so despised that no word had been provided for it in the French language? The orators used the ambiguous word in whatever way best suited their argument. The sections cut the knot by admitting the Fourth Estate to their counsels, and by calling themselves indiscriminately *sansculottes*.

One result of the employment of civilian guards and volunteers in the fighting of August 10th was the 'dictatorship' of the commune. Another result was a cry for vengeance on the 'murderers' raised by the relatives of those who had fallen. The families of professional soldiers would have taken their losses more philosophically. Even volunteers might have reflected that the casualties inflicted on the enemy were more than double their own. Such was not the temper of the *fédérés* and *sectionnaires*. The assembly, being in no position to offend the people, was quick to promise a court-martial (August 11th). It then delayed the execution of the decree, hoping that the agitation might die down. But the commune did not forget. It was not content with a court which could only try soldiers. It demanded one which could try civilians also. It must be a tribunal set up for this sole purpose (*cour d'exception*), and judging without appeal.

On August 17th the deputies gave way, and set up a special court, sitting in two panels, under eight judges, with jurymen nominated by the sections. Four days later the trials began. Within a week three 'criminals' of August

10th had been condemned to death. But still the public was not satisfied. Several sections demanded more and quicker decapitations. The provocative ceremony of the 26th, commemorating on the scene of their victory the 'French citizens who had died for liberty,' and suggesting vengeance on 'traitors and tyrants,' showed that there was a growing danger of the people taking the administration of justice into their own hands, and lynching those whom the courts were too slow to execute.

At the end of August, '92, the nine principal prisons of Paris contained some two thousand six hundred prisoners. Under the dilatory and divided care of the department, which was responsible for the prison buildings, and of the commune, whose *administrateurs de police* supervised the prisoners, these establishments had become increasingly over-crowded and insecure. There had once been hope of improvement. John Howard's first-hand description of French prisons in Paris and in the provinces was published in 1777, and revised, after further visits, in '80, '84, and '89. It gives the impression that, thanks to a liberal enactment of 1717, French prison management was in many ways more enlightened than that of other countries. Even before Howard's book was translated into French by Mlle de Kéralio in '88, it had inspired Louis XVI to pull down two of the worst prisons, and to transfer their inmates to the better quarters and more civilized regime of La Force. There was an interesting moment when Jeremy Bentham himself suggested an experiment with his 'Panopticon' system of prison management, and even offered his own services as Governor.

But bad customs drove out good. La Force soon fell back into the old ways; and when part of it was burnt down in January, '91, many of its prisoners were sent back to older establishments. Fresh quarters were designed at the Madelonettes; but they were not ready eight months later, though the work (it was reported) could have been done in a fortnight. Another plan, to fit up Saint-Lazare as a prison, had also hung fire for a year past. A report in favour of separating different classes of prisoners had never been acted upon. Roland's inquiry in May, '92, whilst finding no evidence for the personal ill-treatment of prisoners, showed that the prisons were dangerously over-crowded, insanitary, and unsafe. But his complaints to the department and the commune came too late.

At the Châtelet, which was dreaded by the most hardened criminals, five hundred persons on trial, or under arrest, were crowded into rooms barely large enough for half that number. A few who could afford to pay for the privilege slept *en pistole*, with a mattress under them: the majority lay on straw (*en paille*). A dangerous prisoner might languish and die in solitary confinement (*en cachot*). It was the same at the Conciergerie and La Force. Only at the aristocratic Abbaye all the inmates lay on mattresses, not more than six in a room, and were allowed, with their *soupe, bouilli, et entrée*, a bottle of wine a day.

Shut up in the dark for twelve hours out of the twenty-four, the prisoners had nothing to do. Some spent the time gambling. Some, working by the light of linen wicks soaked in salad oil, engraved counterfeit *assignats* with nails or shoe-buckles on paper smuggled in from a shop across the road, and sold them at half their face value to the visitors who were their accomplices For in day-time little attempt was made to segregate the prisoners either from one another or from their friends outside. Watrin, the Governor (*concierge-greffier*) of the Châtelet, was a mild and overworked man. His warders were untrustworthy; and two depleted companies of gendarmes were unable to cope with their various duties—visiting the prisoners' quarters to see that the doors and windows were intact, patrolling the courtyards, and conducting prisoners to and from the prisons of which they were in charge. Their number should by now have been increased by the addition of another hundred and fifty men; but the decree of June 17th, like so many others, had not been carried out.

One consequence of this casual and incompetent regime was the constant risk of prison-breaking. There had been a series of successful attempts during the autumn of '90, and again in October, '91. The *concierges* were never free from the fear of its happening again. The general public, outside the small number who were in league with the prisoners, dreaded nothing so much as the liberation of persons whom, under a safer system, they could have pitied for their sufferings. It might well be feared that in the event of an enemy attack upon Paris, either the prisoners would break out, or the public would break in, to anticipate and prevent such a rising.

On August 14th, '92, the care of the police and prisons of Paris, hitherto delegated to four *administrateurs*, had been entrusted to a Vigilance Committee (*comité de surveillance*) that included fifteen other members of the municipality. This body was replaced, a fortnight later (September 2nd) by a committee of eleven, on which Panis and Sergent, the two most active *administrateurs*, still played the leading parts, and to which was added the ominous name of Jean-Paul Marat.

A tablet on the little Hôtel du Lion d'Or at Boudry, near Neuchâtel, reminds the traveller that *le Tribun de la Révolution Française* had a Swiss mother. His father was a Spanish doctor forced, by becoming a Calvinist, to leave his country. Jean-Paul, born in 1743, spent a vagabond youth in foreign parts, studying and practising what passed at that time for medical science. For ten years before 1776 he was a well-known figure amongst the foreigners who frequented the coffee-houses of Soho, including amongst his acquaintances the artists Antonio Zucchi and Amelia Kauffmann, and the diarist Joseph Farington. 'He was,' says Farington, 'a little man, slender, but well made. Of a yellow aspect, he had a quick eye. He had a great deal of motion, seldom keeping his body or limbs still. He was thin, discontented, and abused the establishments which existed.' His scientific pamphlets, his medical cures, and the Wilkite political views which he embodied in his most considerable work, *The Chains of Slavery*, made him known in Newcastle and Edinburgh. He joined a well-known Masonic Lodge, and purchased a medical degree at St. Andrews. But his frenzy for publication put him constantly in debt, and drove him to undistinguished, if not dishonest ways of earning a living. There are almost sufficient grounds for identifying Jean-Paul Marat, during some otherwise unaccountable gaps in his English career, with 'John Peter Le Maître, alias Mara,' who taught French first at Warrington Academy, and then at Oxford, where he lived with a wife in a house at the corner of the Broad and the Turl, and had a child christened at St Michael's in the Corn; who robbed the Ashmolean collection of a number of valuable medals; fled, pursued by Sir John Fielding's runners, to London, Norwich, and Lichfield; was arrested at Dublin, imprisoned in Oxford Castle, and condemned by the Vice-Chancellor's court to the hulks at Woolwich.

However this may be, Marat reappeared in Paris in 1777 as a doctor attached to the household troops (*médecin des gardes du corps*) of the Comte d'Artois. During the ten years before the revolution he built up a fresh reputation as a fashionable practitioner, working remarkable cures by means of a secret concoction (*l'eau factice anti-pulmonique*) which proved on analysis to contain little else but chalk and water. He was known in more learned circles as an ambitious and cantankerous candidate for a place in the Academy of Science, on the strength of a number of optical experiments of doubtful value. When in 1783 Robespierre made his mark as a barrister by defending a householder of Saint-Omer against the charge of endangering his neighbours' lives by erecting a lightning-conductor, Marat was called by the other side as an opponent of Franklin's invention. Charlatanism could go no further.

The outbreak of the revolution found the unsuccessful candidate for the Academy at a dangerous age, and in a dangerous temper. The news of the fall of the Bastille (such is his own account) raised him from a sick-bed. He abandoned medicine and scientific research, and became a democratic journalist. A candid friend of the people—*L'Ami du peuple* was the title of his first paper—he never flattered them, and won their respect by telling them that they were unfit to rule. He believed and was not afraid to maintain that a dictatorship was the only remedy for the disorders of popular government. Giving up (he declared) but two hours of the twenty-four to sleep and one to meals and domesticity, he spent six hours of such leisure as his parliamentary duties allowed in listening to the grievances of the poor, writing petitions for the oppressed, receiving denunciations, and editing his paper. He had not (he said) allowed himself a quarter of an hour's recreation for three years.

Marat's habitual disrespect for accepted opinions gave him a reputation for far-sightedness which he did not deserve. He suspected everyone, and generally proved to be right in doing so. But he had no eye for proportion, and no sense of humour; his denunciations added to the evils they were meant to cure. With surgical callousness he was prepared to clear the way for a new order of society by amputating the old. Decapitation seemed to his half-Spanish mind the obvious prelude to a democratic dictatorship.

The main business of the first Vigilance Committee of the commune had been to fill the Paris prisons. The main business of the second Vigilance Committee, during the short Indian summer of its existence, was to empty them. Within three days of its appointment (September 2nd–5th) nearly half the prisoners had been murdered. This is not to say that the committee was wholly, or even mainly, responsible for the prison massacres. The causes were more remote: the agents were more various.

At Mainz, on July 19th, the Emperor and the King of Prussia had agreed upon a plan for the invasion of France. The spear-head of the attack was to be a Prussian army under the Duke of Brunswick advancing by the historic route from Coblentz through Trier to Verdun. It was to be supported by Austrian armies spread out on either flank, from the Netherlands to the Swiss frontier. The two sovereigns estimated their total effectives at about a hundred and thirty thousand men. To these might be added four thousand eight hundred armed *émigrés*. To meet this force the French could count on no more than ninety-three thousand men, disorganized by defeat, deserted by their royalist officers, and distracted by the uncertainties of the political situation.

The enemy, anxious not to enter the country till harvest-time, when his army could count on subsistence, advanced with extreme deliberation, and took over a fortnight to move from Trier to Verdun at the rate of some three and a half miles a day. Yet there could be no disguising the direction of his march. On August 12th the frontier was crossed at Sierck. On the 20th Longwy was invested. The German guns opened, and started a few fires. It capitulated on the 23rd. On the 30th Verdun was attacked in the same way. After fifteen hours' bombardment part of the garrison mutinied; the commandant blew out his brains; and the town surrendered. The invader was within a hundred and forty miles of Paris.

At this critical moment the republic was saved by the slowness of Brunswick, and by the energy of Danton. If the Prussians had advanced more quickly, the throne might never have fallen, or the government might have been forced to take the advice of the Brissotin leaders, and to evacuate Paris. Without Danton's leadership, the movement might never have been started which sent city volunteers to the front, from September 2nd onwards, at the rate of eighteen hundred a day. Professional caution was worsted, as so often before and since, by the audacity of the amateur. Within three weeks the invader would be turned back towards the frontier.

But already Paris was in a ferment. Sectional meetings were being held for the choice of electors to the forthcoming Convention. Domiciliary visits were being made, both officially and unofficially, in search of arms. Volunteers were enlisting and equipping themselves for the front. Fresh placards appeared every day at the street-corners. The red flag of national emergency flew on the Town Hall. Workmen tramped out every morning to fortify Montmartre. Every day volunteers marched away to swell the chaotic mobilizations at Chalons, Soissons, or Reims. They were 'accompanied as far as the Barriers'—so an English traveller describes the scene—'by their women, who were carrying their muskets for them; some with large sausages, pieces of cold meat, and loaves of bread stuck on their bayonets, and all laughing, or singing Ça ira.' How seldom in French history had such a spectacle been seen before! How often since it has recurred! Here was an atmosphere in which heroism and violence might flourish side by side.

On Sunday, September 2nd, Paris heard of the investment of Verdun. The barriers were at once closed, signal-guns were fired, the church bells were set ringing, and proclamations were issued exhorting good citizens to march to the front. 'The tocsin you will hear to-day,' cried Danton, 'is not an alarm, but an alert. It sounds the charge against the enemies of our country. For victory we must dare, and dare, and—dare again. So France will be saved.'

The enemies of the country were not all outside the walls of the capital. With every mile that the Prussians approached nearer to Paris the counter-revolutionaries on the home front grew more confident. With every rumour of treachery at Longwy or at Verdun Parisians grew more conscious of the number of *ci-devant* nobles, refractory priests, and suspicious-looking foreigners whom they passed in the streets of the threatened capital. Stories began to spread, as they had spread at the time of the king's flight, of a royalist rising in the prisons.

On this same Sunday morning (September 2nd) the new Vigilance Committee met for the first time at the mayor's official residence. Marat had been escorted there by an armed crowd from his section, the *Quatre nations*. From the *Mairie*, early in the afternoon, four carriages set out to carry twenty priests to the prison at the Abbaye of Saint-Germain-des-Près, about half a mile away. As soon as the carriages arrived outside the prison, the priests were dragged out by members of the section, and murdered. Perhaps the murderers were the men who had accompanied Marat to the *Mairie* a few hours before. Certainly Marat, who had already been inciting the volunteers to lynch the prisoners before they left for the front, did not disapprove. Certainly the committee, when they sent a convoy of priests, unguarded, to a prison in Marat's section, must have known that they might be attacked. Such was the beginning of the massacre: without it, the rest might never have happened.

From the murder of priests outside the Abbaye it was an easy step to the murder of prisoners inside. From priest-killing at the Abbaye it was an easy step to priest-killing at the Carmelite convent (*Carmes*) in the neighbouring Luxembourg section. Then there was a pause, from six to eight o'clock in the evening. A determined effort at this moment should have prevented further trouble. The commune, indeed, sent commissioners to the prisons; but their only instructions were to protect debtors, and prisoners lying under civil charges. The assembly was asked to send some of its own members, and did so; but no attention was paid to them by the murderers. The same evening the killing began again. It continued for two more days, at the Châtelet, the Bernardins, the Conciergerie, Saint-Firmin, the Bicêtre, and the Salpétrière. At La Force it did not end until September 7th.

The original motive of the murders was soon forgotten. At the Châtelet the victims were from two hundred and fifteen to two hundred and twenty thieves and debtors: at the Bicêtre, a kind of reformatory, a hundred and sixty to a hundred and seventy boys and girls: at the Salpétrière, a women's prison and penitentiary, thirty-five prostitutes. Out of the total of eleven to thirteen hundred killed, the non-political victims were as three to one. Yet the massacre was not indiscriminate. Improvised tribunals gave a semblance of justice to popular vengeance, or popular fear. At the Abbaye, Maillard, the hero of July 14th and October 5th, produced a warrant from the *administrateurs* of the commune, and marked off the names on the prison list (*écrou*). The silver-rimmed spectacles through which he deciphered the names and the gold watch by which he timed the proceedings are still treasured by his last living descendant. At the Salpétrière the women were brought one by one before a 'court nominated by the people.' The killing was in most cases carried out by small bands, not of hardened criminals or professional cut-throats, but of middle-aged tradesmen and *patrons* (working employers), with a few ex-soldiers, federals, and gendarmes, armed with clubs, swords, and pikes. The murderers at the Abbaye included carters, carpenters, and cabinet-makers; hat-makers and cobblers; jewellers and watchmakers. They were provided with drink by the section, and were promised twenty-four shillings each by the commune if they did not plunder the bodies of their victims.

It is natural to inquire whether the authorities did anything to stop the massacre. The commune was responsible for maintaining order in Paris. Acting through the mayor (Pétion) and the Commandant (Santerre) it could order out the National Guard, the only armed force in the capital. Its responsibility was therefore the greatest. It had, in fact, consistently supported the sections in their demand for popular vengeance on the 'criminals' of August 10th. It was not likely to bring much pressure on the sections to parade their contingents of the Guard. Its General Council was not sitting at the time when the massacre began. When it met in the evening, it ordered the combing-out of petty delinquents from the prisons, and it sponsored the attack on the Conciergerie. On the second evening, and during the subsequent three days of the massacre, it did no more than despatch commissioners to the prisons. There is a strong suspicion that, when all was over, it paid the murderers for their work. The inference is that the commune contained a majority of members in favour of a 'prison purge', and a minority too weak to resist them.

The assembly, over which the unprincipled ex-courtier Hérault de Séchelles presided for the first time on September 2nd, adjourned at four o'clock without hearing of the killing at the Abbaye. At the evening session it sent out commissioners, at the request of the commune. It shares the responsibility of the commune for allowing the massacre to begin again at eight o'clock that evening, and for failing to stop it afterwards. On September 3rd it had no difficulty in rescuing from the Abbaye the deputy Jonneau. It made no attempt to save others. It was content to charge the city authorities to see that persons and property were respected, and to call on the mayor for a daily report on the situation. Worse, it circularized the sections and departments with Roland's apologia for the first day's massacre.

The ministers cannot escape their share of responsibility. The respectable Roland claimed afterwards not to have heard of what was happening till September 3rd. He then wrote a long letter to the assembly, excusing the *effervescence* of the people, and describing the massacre as *une sorte de justice*. The next day, finding that the killing was not over, he ordered Santerre in the name of the nation and the government to employ all legal means to prevent attacks upon person and property: and he wrote a second letter to the mayor and the President of the assembly lamenting the continuance of disorder, and calling attention to the dangerous position of the survivors at the Abbaye. Danton, as Minister of Justice, and the man of the moment, was more likely than anyone else to be listened to. He did nothing, unless he prevented Robespierre from directing the attention of the murderers to Roland, Brissot, and other prominent Girondins. There is a well-known story that on the day after the battle of Valmy he boasted of his part in the massacre to the young Jacobin who was afterwards King Louis-Philippe. He may well have done so. It might be written of him, as it was written of Hugh Speke, who claimed the credit for the Irish Night of 1688, that 'he was a man quite capable of committing such a villainy, and quite capable also of falsely boasting that he had committed it.'

Pétion, who had lost much of his popularity and influence since August 10th, seems to have done nothing on his own account, whatever may have been his part in the proceedings of the commune. Appealed to by Roland on the 4th on behalf of the Swiss at the Abbaye, as well as by those in charge of the Salpétrière and La Force, he contented himself with passing on the messages to Santerre; he asked him at the same time to make sure of the safety of the royal prisoners in the Temple.

As for Santerre, it could hardly be expected that one who had so often exploited the popular will would now oppose it. The murderers may well have counted on the non-intervention of the National Guard. The only order Santerre gave on the first two days of the massacre was one for the removal of the dead bodies from the Conciergerie. He seems to have taken

no action on the appeals that he received from Roland and Pétion, though h
took a solemn oath at the bar of the House that he would die, if need be, i
enforcing the law. He was accused afterwards of having boasted that h
could have stopped the massacre, but that he would have preferred the credi
of perpetrating it; and he did not deny that he had said so.

Manuel, the *procureur* of the commune, and his deputy, Billaud-Varenne
made futile appeals to the murderers at the Abbaye and at La Force. On th
7th, when the massacre was over, Manuel proposed the erection of a specia
court to punish those responsible for it. The fact was that all the municipa
authorities were in a very weak position, when it came to enforcing order
The control of the National Guard was in the hands of the forty-eigh
sections: the control of the police had been entrusted to the Vigilanc
Committee, which was doing more to encourage than to repress the
massacre.

The action of the Vigilance Committee provoked the first murders: it
tacit approval encouraged the rest. Marat would not shrink from carryin
out his own advice. He, if any one man, was responsible for the massacre
Nor was this all. On September 3rd, when the assembly published Roland'
letter, the Committee issued to the departmental authorities all over th
country a missive announcing that 'some of the ferocious conspirators de
tained in the prisons had been put to death by the people,' and urging that
similar course should be followed in the provinces. This letter was printed a
Marat's press, and circulated under seal of the Ministry of Justice, probabl
by arrangement with Danton's secretary, Fabre d'Eglantine. It is unlikel
that Danton himself was ignorant of it.

The sections did not ordinarily meet until five in the evening. Th
resolutions that some of them sent in, calling for the purging of th
prisons, were probably drawn up in view of what had already happene
at the Abbaye and at the Carmes. But it was their encouragement tha
caused the renewal of the massacre that evening, and on the following days
There was, in fact, hardly a public body or a political leader in Paris wh
could honestly say, ' I am innocent of the blood of this just person.' Most o
them, perhaps, would have agreed with what young Basire wrote to hi
mistress. 'A sensitive man,' he said, 'can only wrap his head in his cloak
and hurry past the dead bodies, to take sanctuary in the temple of the Lav
—thinking not of individuals, but of the people as a whole.'

Public opinion, perhaps, must be held ultimately responsible for wha
happened. Yet it has to be remembered that in a city as large as Paris a priso
massacre, like the fall of the Bastille, might not be generally known for som
time outside the quarter in which it took place. September 2nd was a Sunday
The shops were closed, the people were holiday-making, and news travelle
more slowly than on a week-day. During the days that followed, the bette
citizens were preoccupied with the preparation of camps and fortification
outside the city. Deputies set out at five o'clock in the morning to supervis

the work. 'Actors, dancers, musicians, stage-hands, and scene-shifters' from the Théâtre Montansier had volunteered to form a labour company. The *pensionnaires* of two other theatres declared that they would be proud to defend to the death the love of liberty and equality which they had so often professed on the stage. Few were in a mood to cavil at the more brutal way in which others expressed their patriotism. When the massacre became generally known, public opinion was at first apathetic, if not approving. As the killing went on, there were fears of a general attack upon persons and property, and middle-class disapproval asserted itself. The *Moniteur* waited until September 6th to see which way the elections were going, and then published an apologia for the massacres. Other papers followed suit.

The attitude of the lower orders was a point into which the Englishman, Dr. John Moore, who was then in Paris, particularly inquired. The opinion of a Parisian acquaintance quoted by him deserves attention. 'Their rage,' he said, 'is seldom excited, but by the high price of bread, when the only remedy they think of, is the dragging of a baker or engrosser *à la lanterne*: there would terminate their thirst of blood; they never would have a wish for the death of other prisoners, if they were not wrought upon by wicked and ambitious men.' Nevertheless there were many who viewed with indifference or even favour proceedings in which they were too fastidious to take a part. Audot at eighty remembered visiting the Abbaye as a boy of ten when the killing was just over. There were two piles of dead bodies—one of priests, which had been dismembered, and one of lay victims. They had been dragged together by the feet, leaving a trail of blood. The *pavé* was being washed down, and the kennel was running red. The circle of spectators opened out, saying, 'Let the child have a look.'

'Necessity made this execution inevitable,' wrote a Parisian in his diary on the night of September 2nd: 'part of Paris is starting tomorrow for the army: the city will have no men left in it: this crowd of unfortunates might have cut our throats while the men were away. It is sad to have to go to such lengths. But it is better (as they say) to kill the devil than to let the devil kill you.' Such was the popular view among Parisians.

Outside Paris, in the more royalist, clerical, and what could by now be called counter-revolutionary parts of France, the massacre was repudiated as yet another crime of city mob-rule, and a beginning was soon made in the compilation of a new martyrology. In the provinces more closely connected by position or sympathy with the great republican centres—Paris, Lyon, Marseille, or Bordeaux—the occasional lynching of priests or other suspects had been common enough that summer to make Marat's invitation of September 3rd superfluous.

But at Orléans lay a number of prisoners under charges of *lèse-nation*, waiting for trial by the dilatory *haute-cour*. As early as August 11th the Mauconseil section of Paris had demanded the transference of these prisoners to the capital, so that they might be judged by the special court set up on the

17th. This demand was backed by the commune on the 23rd. In vain the assembly ordered the removal of the prisoners to safer custody at Saumur. A force of two thousand National Guardsmen marched from Paris, with the connivance of Santerre, and carried off fifty-three prisoners under the eyes of the protesting magistrates (*grands procurateurs de la nation*). Fournier 'the American,' who was in charge of the convoy, was urged by Roland to stop at Etampes. He professed himself unable to do more than divert its march to Versailles: here the authorities of the Seine-et-Oise department might be able to protect the prisoners from the popular vengeance which had just emptied the prisons of Paris. But they had scarcely arrived at Versailles when they were set upon, at the door of the town gaol, and massacred (September 9th). The murderers were local people, including two vine-dressers, and a cobbler and his wife. Alquier, the President of the departmental tribunal, who took care to be in Paris when the prisoners arrived at Versailles, believed that Danton was privy to this crime. Roland, convinced of Fournier's good faith, defended his part in the affair, and helped him to recover his expenses from the assembly.

No document illustrates the August revolution and the September massacre more realistically than the list of accounts settled by the treasurer in connexion with work done for the General Council of the Commune. Here are a few of the items.

To sieur Menu, for a rope to pull down the statue of Louis XV in the Place Louis XV, £5.

To J. B. Baillard, for conveying to the Town Hall on a hand-cart the silver plate found in the church of Saint-Gervais, 6s.

To Delore, for two torches, 5s., and to the widow Binet, for the hire of 16 horses, both for the proclamation of the decree giving passive citizens the rights of active citizenship, £3 4s.

To Mme Michel, of the ribbon shop, Rue aux Fers, for 351 *aunes* of tricolor ribbon at 45 *sous*, £39 9s. ; and for 280 woollen cockades at 3d., £4 4s.

To Blondeaux, for 4 horses that drew the guns to the Tuileries on August 10th, 24s.

To the porter Mazoyer, whose duty it was to recover property found on the dead bodies, and to return it to the General Council of the commune, 24s. ; and to three persons who supplied carts, £3.

Expenses of a commissioner of the commune who superintended the burial of bodies brought from the prisons on Sept. 3rd and 4th, at three cemeteries, 9s.

The same, for other commissioners, who provided quick-lime for the destruction of the bodies, 4s.

To Gil . . . and Pet . . . for the time they and their comrades put in, during two days, *à l'expédition des prêtres de Saint-Firmin*, £2 8s.

To Jol . . . , for carts that made five journeys carrying bodies from the abbaye of Saint-Germain on Sept. 2–3, 30s.

To a painter who defaced the coats of arms on the collars of horses belonging to the *ci-devant* Prince de Condé, 5s. 2½.

For the provision of a carriage to convey two commissioners to the Bicêtre and Salpétrière, in order to appease (*calmer*) the citizens, 25s. 6d.

To Elevé, upholsterer, for the provision of a desk and chairs every day from Aug. 22nd to Sept. 1st in the amphitheatre of the Place Saint-Martin, for receiving the names for voluntary enlistment, 10s.

The narratives given by English eye-witnesses—the traveller John Moore, the *chargé d'affaires* William Lindsay, or the secret agent George Monro—are sufficient evidence of the repugnance which the prison massacre aroused in foreign minds. Even to modern feelings, hardened by a long course of pogroms, purges, and executions, something of spectacular horror still attaches to the dark and dreadful scenes of September, 1792. Was this, then, the justice of the people?

CHAPTER XVII

CONVENTION

Je l'ai dit, dès l'origine de cette Convention; c'est la troisième révolution que nous avons à finir, la révolution de l'anarchie. Nous ne pourrons la terminer qu'en établissant une bonne constitution à la place de ce système de désorganisation et de despotisme qu'on voudrait perpétuer.—(BRISSOT, March 24th, 1793.)

IT had been argued by the abbé Maury in April, 1790, that the so-called National Assembly had no right to the powers it claimed to possess. 'To produce a national assembly,' he insisted, 'the whole nation would have to rise against its government, ignore its king, and give its assembly plenary powers.' The abbé thought he was putting an impossible case. It was now an accomplished fact. August 10th had seen Paris and the provinces united in an attack upon the Parliament and the throne. All the hopes of the country were now placed in a National Convention, the re-embodiment of the absolute power of the sovereign people. Yet in this twilight of constitutional government Frenchmen moved uncertainly, seeing forms of authority, but not knowing whether they were real. The king of the French had been suspended; but France was not a republic. The accomplices and agents of the royal counter-revolution were either dead or in exile; but nothing had been done to bring Louis himself to trial. A constitution had been enacted; but was it still in force? Ministers had been appointed; but were they a constitutional executive? Only a Convention could tell.

The elections of '92 began, according to pious precedent, with a mass, and ended with a *Te Deum*. They coincided with the Prussian advance on Paris, and with the massacre in the prisons. The electoral assembly of Paris held its first meeting on September 2nd, and chose its first deputy on September 5th. The voters may have been preoccupied; but they refused to be hurried. Both in the primary and in the electoral assemblies separate scrutinies were held for each place to be filled: it was not surprising that it took the section *des Piques* four days to choose sixteen electors, and the electoral assembly of Paris eighteen days more to agree upon the names of twenty-four deputies. Owing to the length of these operations, the abstention of aristocrats and anti-republicans, and the fear of victimization, if one voted inadvertently for what might turn out afterwards to be the wrong side, the electoral meetings were very poorly attended. Sometimes unfair pressure was exercised upon the voters by *bourgeois* proprietors on one side or by Jacobin enthusiasts on the other. The electoral assembly of Paris refused to count the votes of delegates who had belonged to an anti-Jacobin club, or who had signed the 'Petition of the twenty thousand' against the proceedings of June 20th. Nor was it without design that the decree of May 27th for the deportation of refractory clergy was revised on the first day of the elections, so as to require a class which might well influence the country vote to leave France within a fortnight.

Such precautions may have been unnecessary. Everywhere the first thought of the electors was for the national defence, and their second thought for a new constitution. In this respect the country showed a remarkable unanimity. In the whole of France only eleven primary assemblies wished for the retention of the monarchy. Of the electoral assemblies there was not one but tacitly voted for a republic—though only Paris used the word, and instructed its representatives to press for it. When the deputies had been chosen it was found that not one of the seven hundred and fifty had stood for election as a royalist. Since August 10th there had been a fresh exodus of the king's friends. Even the loyal Malouet, barely escaping with his life, was now in England, wondering why a system that worked in Guiana did not work in France. As for the prison massacre, most of the electors may never have heard of it: if they did, they were more influenced by the Paris volunteers than by the Paris murderers.

Though only a million voters went to the polls, there is no good reason to doubt that they represented the will of the five million Frenchmen who in '92, as in '89, enjoyed the franchise. Majorities begin revolutions; minorities carry them on. The peasantry, who constituted the mass of the electorate, were by this time generally satisfied with what the revolution had done for them. They had never been deeply concerned with the political programme of Paris. They were quite uninterested in the controversies between Jacobin and Girondin which occupied the early months of the Convention. All they asked was that the government should leave them alone to exploit their new

MODERN

Beheading Machine,

AT PARIS.

VIEW OF

La Guillotine;

OR THE

By which the unfortunate LOUIS XVI. (late King of France) suffered on the Scaffold, January 21st, 1793:

THE EXECUTION OF LOUIS XVI

From a contemporary English broadside.

freedom from feudal charges, and their new access to the land. They regretted the monarchy, but they would not fight for its restoration. They welcomed the war, but they would resist recruitment. Like most country populations, they were the joy of the first generation of reformers, and the despair of the second.

In '92, as in '89 and '91, the electors chose for their representatives men of mature age and social standing. Though the statutory age for election was twenty-five, only ten per cent of the deputies were under thirty-one: nearly seventy-five per cent were between thirty-one and fifty: fifteen per cent were over this age. The junior member, Saint-Just, was only a few days over twenty-five. The 'father of the House,' old Longqueue of Chartres, was seventy-four, and had been born within three years of the death of Louis XIV—so short a space of time separated the new France from the old. As to professions—every other man was some kind of lawyer. About forty-seven per cent called themselves *conseiller, avocat, procureur, notaire, juge,* or *homme de loi*; and of the ten per cent who held official posts many had some legal qualifications. Business men, merchants, manufacturers, and tradesmen made up another ten per cent. The representatives of art, literature, and science (about six per cent) included a remarkable number of professors and teachers. Medicine was well represented by another six per cent; so were the church (six per cent) and the fighting services (eight and half per cent). The landed interests, doubtless owing to indirect election, were under-represented with only six per cent, mostly *propriétaires* and *cultivateurs.* There were also a few travellers or men of leisure (one was in Norway at the time, and never took his seat), as well as actors, colonial deputies, and others more difficult to classify. It is surprising to find, among these enemies of the old order, seven Marquises, and a Prince of the blood royal.

It is commonly asserted that there were only two working men among the nine hundred deputies who sat in the Convention at one time or another between '92 and '95. Noel Pointe was a munition-worker (*ouvrier armurier*) from Saint-Etienne. Jean-Baptiste Armonville was a weaver (*ouvrier cardeur de laine*) from Reims, whose motherless children lived on charity until his deputy's pay enabled him to set up house in Paris. But others who did not call themselves *ouvriers* might well be classed as working men: Bernard des Sablons, a mason's son, who married a vine-dresser's daughter, and worked on the land; Boiron, a cooper, who died in the village where he was born; the Abbeville baker, Duquen; Gaudin, who had been a gunner in the coastguards (*cannonier garde-côtes*) during the war with England; Montégut, a ditcher or grave-digger (*fossoyeur*); perhaps Panis, an unspecified *employé* of the *caisse du trésor royal.* But in fact class representation was neither expected nor desired. The National Convention was to consist of representatives of the nation.

Nothing is more remarkable, in this first democratically elected assembly, than the number of deputies who lived and died in the same district, if not in the same village; who were lawyers or tradesmen there, as their fathers had been before the revolution; who became judges or mayors there in '90–'91; and who sat as local deputies in '92. The drift of clever young men from the provinces to the capital ended too often in those days on the scaffold; but many of the men of '92 returned to end their lives in their native place, full of years and reminiscences. The Convention grew out of the soil of France. It was because the deputies loved their *pays* that they left it to serve their *patrie*.

Amongst these representatives of young France there sat, as a gesture of Girondin free-mindedness, an Englishman, Thomas Paine. It had been provided in the final draft of the constitution of '91 that under special conditions the assembly might grant naturalization to any foreigner wishing to reside in France, and willing to take the civic oath. The Legislative Assembly, not content with inviting the collaboration of that pattern of Girondism, Jeremy Bentham, and accepting copies of his works, along with those of William Godwin, chose William Priestley, in consideration of his father's eminent services to science and politics, to be the first Englishman naturalized under this clause. Two months later, on the eve of the elections to the Convention, it was proposed by M. J. Chénier that French citizenship should be granted unconditionally to distinguished foreigners whose writings 'sapped the foundations of tyranny, and prepared the road to liberty.' On August 26th Guadet, after leaving out some of Chénier's nominees, and putting in some of his own, read out to the House a list which included six Englishmen. They were Joseph Priestley, Thomas Paine, William Wilberforce, Thomas Clarkson, James Mackintosh, the adversary of Burke, and David Williams, the Deist. All of these accepted the honorary citizenship bestowed upon them, and thus became eligible to the Convention. Only two —Priestley and Paine—were sufficiently well known to the electors to be nominated. Only Paine, whose recent publication of the second part of the *Rights of Man* made his absence from England desirable, accepted election, and took his seat in the assembly.

For a month after the capture of the Tuileries the palace remained empty and untouched. When Roland was directed by the locksmith Gamain to the discovery of the iron safe in the king's room, he may well have reflected what admirable quarters might be found here for the new assembly. It was Roland who, on September 15th, laid before the deputies Vignon's plans for converting the *salle des machines* into a parliament-house. This was a huge apartment on the ground-floor of the central block of the building, a hundred and thirty feet long, forty-five feet broad, and sixty feet high. It had been used as a theatre ever since Molière's *Psyche* was performed there in 1671. Thomas Gray, who saw *Pandore* there in 1739, pronounced it 'one of the finest in the world.' Roland hoped to have this room ready for occupation by November 1st. But the work took much longer than was expected, being held up partly by lack of funds, and partly (it was complained) by a tendency of the labourers to down tools in order to watch the executions in the neighbouring Carrousel, where the guillotine stood until its removal to the Place de la Révolution. By the end of March it was possible for the *comité de défense générale* to occupy two rooms prepared for it: but it was a long time before space could be found, and furniture provided, for the other twenty-seven committees transferred from their old quarters in the Capucins, Feuillants, and elsewhere.

Some, notably the *comité de salut public*, were placed in the southern block of the building, the Pavillon de Flore, which now bore in large letters the name ÉGALITÉ: others found accommodation in the Pavillon de Marsan, on the north, now called LIBERTÉ. The central block, the Pavillon de l'Horloge, was now marked UNITÉ, and surmounted by a cap of liberty in red serge. Here, by the great door and grand staircase, where the Swiss had made their last stand for monarchy, now passed the rulers of the first French republic.

Here too was the *salle des séances*. The deputies viewed their new parliament-house with admiration, but with some uneasiness. Their old seats in the *manège* had been crowded, but companionable. It had been easy to accost a friend across its narrow floor, or to insult an enemy. Now the deputies' seats were ramped in a great semicircle against one of the long sides of the hall, six deep in the middle, and nine deep at the ends. In the middle of this semicircle, on floor level, approached from behind, was the bar: opposite it, in the centre of the other long wall, were the President's chair, from a design by David, the secretaries' tables, and the speaker's desk. Public seats were provided behind the deputies' block, and at each end of the hall. The walls were decorated with classical correctness, and embellished with busts of classical heroes—Demosthenes, Lycurgus, Solon, and Plato for Greece; Camillus, Publicola, Brutus, and Cincinnatus for Rome.

There inspiration ended. The place was very difficult to speak in. If the orator kept his voice down, it could not be heard: if he raised it, the sound echoed unintelligibly in the huge spaces between the pillars and the ceiling. When the numbers of the assembly began to dwindle, the hall was found far too large, and the isolated deputies felt themselves to be dominated by the governing clique and its permanent officials. The terrace of the Tuileries was too far from the sound of the President's bell, and too large for small gatherings of counsel or opposition. It would be interesting to speculate how far the decline of democratic government has been due to the reversion, in the arrangement of its meeting-places, from a rectangular to a circular parliament-house, from the model of the college chapel to that of the theatre and the arena.

By one of the great coincidences of history, the day on which the National Convention met to elect its officers was also the day on which the national army won its first victory. On September 20th, at Valmy in the Argonne,

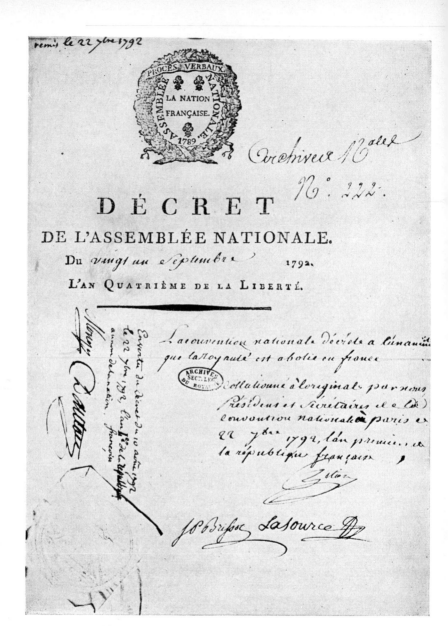

THE DECREE ABOLISHING THE THRONE

It is signed by Pétion as President of the Convention on September 21st, 1792, and countersigned by the Secretaries, Brissot and Lasource. The Ministers of Marine (Monge) and of Justice (Danton) signed it next day in the margin. They first dated it '4th year of Liberty,' and then corrected this to '1st year of the Republic.'

the Prussian invader was brought to a standstill, and forced to retreat. On September 21st, amidst profound silence, the proposition was put to the assembly, 'That royalty be abolished in France,' and was carried with cheers. On the 22nd came the news of Valmy. On the same day it was decreed that 'in future the acts of the assembly shall be dated, *First Year of the French Republic.*' Three days later the corollary was added, to guard against federalism, that 'the French Republic is one and indivisible' There was no formal or ceremonial declaration of a new regime, as in 1848, 1871, or 1875. The monarchy had been abolished, but not the monarchical constitution. A republic had been proclaimed, but it remained to enact a republican government. The country was little more republican in feeling or practice than it had been at any time since Varennes. But it must now be a republic, because it no longer has a king.

In a note added to his *Travels* on April 26th, 1792, Arthur Young records that when news came of the French declaration of war against Austria, all the company declared that France must be beaten. The French army, they said, had no discipline; the French people would never take orders. Young himself, without venturing on prophecy, disputes this view. The French army may be undisciplined; but the frontier fortresses—Lille, Metz, Strasbourg—are very strong. The French finances are in disorder; but what does public credit matter, if the nation can be saved? The internal troubles of the country will not produce a civil war. The French are fighting to a man for liberty; their enemies, the Austrians and Prussians, mix as badly as oil and vinegar, fire and water. When this passage was written, it must have seemed madness to prophesy a French victory. How did the miracle of Valmy come about? How were the disasters of Longwy and Verdun so signally avenged?

The troops which stood their ground at Valmy included the men who had fled at Mons and Tournai five months before. They had that disgrace to avenge, they had seen twenty weeks' service under new commanders, and their resistance was stiffened by thirty-five guns of the best artillery in Europe. They were, though they did not know it, the advance guard of the *grande armée.* Napoleon's weapons were already being shaped for him by generals trained in a new school—Menou, Custine, Montesquiou, Dumouriez, Kellermann, Dugommier, Kléber, Serrurier. Amateurism was reinforcing professionalism. The traditions of the old army were being diluted with the intelligence of the new. Side by side with Marceau, Joubert, Hoche, Championnet, and Desaix served Ney, Soult, Lannes, Murat, Davout, Macdonald, Grouchy, Drouot, Marmont, Victor, Oudinot, Jourdan, Masséna, Augereau, Pichegru, Bernadotte, Junot, Moreau, Brune—soldiers in whose exploits the revolution would live a new life long after it was dead in the hearts of the politicians.

The situation at the end of the first week of September was critical. The Prussians had occupied the two crucial passages of the Meuse—Stenay and

Verdun—on the direct roads from Trier to Paris. They had separated the army of Dumouriez in the north-west (Sedan) from that of Kellermann in the south-east (Metz). Only one obstacle now lay between them and the capital—the thickly wooded line of hills separating the Meuse and the Aisne, called the Argonne. On September 4th Dumouriez, marching south, occupied Grand-Pré, the central of the three passes through this obstacle, about equidistant from Stenay and Verdun. Attacked here, he fell back southwards, ten days later, behind the Aisne to the little town of Sainte-Ménehould, on the road for Chalons and Paris: it was the place where the king had been recognized on his flight to the frontier a year before. Meanwhile Kellermann was marching round from Metz to meet him. The two armies joined hands on the 19th.

They were only just in time. On the 20th the Duke of Brunswick, who had followed Dumouriez southwards, determined to attack. Though he was now between the French armies and Paris, he dared not leave them undefeated behind him. They had some fifty thousand men, of whom thirty-six thousand were effectives, against his thirty-four thousand. They were strongly posted on the hills each side of the windmill of Valmy, a few miles west of Sainte-Ménehould. In spite of discouraging reports from Massenbach, his chief of staff, he did not believe that their half-trained volunteers would stand against his regular troops. So he ordered the assault. To his surprise the Frenchmen on the hill-top did not budge; with Kellermann sitting his horse undaunted at their head they met the advance of his infantry, and the fire of his guns, with answering volleys, and cries of *Vive la France!* and *Vive la nation!* His infantry could make little headway against their musketry, and the devastating fire of the old royal artillery. They could get no further than half-way up the hill-side. He had no choice but to sound the retreat.

The losses were small—three hundred dead on the French side, a hundred and eighty on the Prussian. The next day Kellermann retired to a fresh position, where he expected to be attacked again. But the enemy, weakened by sickness, disheartened by unexpected resistance, and with his communications endangered by his march across country, had no heart for further fighting, and only asked for a safe return to the frontier. Valmy was indeed the French Thermopylae that Dumouriez had promised Servan, in his boastful way, a fortnight before, and he a luckier Leonidas.

Ten days before the battle the historian Gibbon, writing from Lausanne, had confessed to Lord Sheffield that though 'on every rational principle of calculation' the Duke of Brunswick must succeed in reaching Paris, yet sometimes 'when his spirits were low, he dreaded the blind efforts of mad and desperate multitudes fighting on their own ground.' Ten days after the battle Morris could not believe that the Prussians were really in retreat. The poet Goethe, who had committed himself with Brunswick's army to what seemed an easy adventure, now warned his friends of the significance of their defeat. 'Here and to-day,' he said, 'begins a new age in the history of the world. Some day you will be able to say—I was there.'

The strategy of the generals was seconded by the intrigues of the politicians. Ever since he came into office, Danton, aided by Lebrun, had been trying to buy off the Prussians. On September 3rd instructions had been sent to Desportes, the French agent accredited to the little court of Zweibrücken, to try to detach Prussia from Austria. Three days after Valmy, in reply to suggestions from Dumouriez, the king of Prussia sent the French general a note in which he outlined the conditions of an armistice. They were that he should treat with Louis XVI personally; that all propaganda should cease; that Louis should be restored to liberty; and that France should keep 'a government suitable to its best interests.'

At this time no one in the army knew that France was a republic. But it was possible to accommodate the terms of the note to the situation which Westermann found when he brought it to Paris on September 25th. Next day Lebrun informed the Convention that the government would refuse to negotiate till the Prussians were once more beyond the frontier. Yet the despatches which Westermann took back to the army included an offer to Frederick William not merely of a separate peace, but of a French alliance; and meanwhile Dumouriez was doing his best to conciliate the King of Prussia. But when news came of the fall of the throne, and of the imprisonment of the king, Brunswick issued another manifesto (September 28th) in terms no less threatening than that of July, whilst Frederick William broke off negotiations, and ordered his troops home.

The retreat began ten days after the battle, and continued unopposed, indeed assisted, by French generalship and diplomacy, over the same muddy and malaria-stricken ground as the advance two months before. Dysentery ended what defeat had begun. The French troops followed rather than pursued the enemy along a road littered with dead men and dead horses. They had orders neither to fire on the Prussians, nor to plunder them. Within a month of Valmy (October 23rd) the invader was once more beyond the frontier. So ended a campaign to which Bismarck pointed, after Sadowa, as a precedent for his plan of not forcing further hostilities upon a defeated foe.

The effects of the Prussian retreat were felt all along the front. Lille, after a brave week of resistance to bombardment, was relieved on October 5th. The next day Dumouriez was given supreme command of the army of the north; and his newly won prestige soon overcame all arguments against an invasion of the Netherlands. He answered the call of the people of Liège, and crossed the Belgian frontier. Exactly a month later (November 6th) the victory at Jemappes added a Marathon to his Thermopylae. Within two months the fall of Namur (December 2nd) turned invasion into conquest. Further south, Montesquiou had occupied Chambéry on September 24th, and Anselme had entered Nice on the 29th.

The Girondins were jubilant. 'We must never rest,' wrote Brissot to Servan on November 26th, 'until the whole of Europe is ablaze. There must be no slackening of our endeavour. We must take the offensive. We must issue manifestos in French and Spanish. We must electrify every mind, either to make revolution, or to accept it. If once we push our frontier to the Rhine, if once there are free peoples on both sides of the Pyrenees, then our liberty will be firmly established.' This crusading spirit was not unmixed with worldly considerations. 'The national will and the interests of the republic,' wrote Dumouriez to Kellermann on the 25th, 'demand that we should winter beyond the frontier:' so the cost of supporting the French armies could be borne by those whom they had liberated. The timid and censorious Roland had another motive in mind. 'The thousands of men we have under arms,' he said, 'must march as far away as their legs will carry them: otherwise they might cut our throats.'

So the advance went on. By October 21st the army of the Rhine, under Custine, had occupied Speyer, Mainz, and Worms. At the end of November the frontier districts of Porrentruy and Delemont declared their independence from the Empire, and became the French department of Mont-Terrible. Everywhere the regular troops of old Europe seemed to be falling before the volunteers of new France. Everywhere the Rights of Man were eclipsing the Divine Right of Kings. At Vienna the Imperial cabinet was reading a gloomy despatch from Mercy (October 3rd) in which he declared that the attempt to restore the French monarchy by force of arms was *une chimère, une désastreuse folie*. In Paris, beneath the dome of the still unfinished Panthéon, a third national hero now lay beside Mirabeau and Voltaire—Beaurepaire, the commandant of Verdun, who, as his epitaph proudly recorded, had 'preferred to kill himself rather than to make terms with tyrants.'

It was a national misfortune that at the very moment when the generals were widening the frontiers of the new republic, the politicians were splitting it up from within. Every representative assembly tends, like Caesar's *Gallia*, to be divided into three parts—a Right, a Centre, and a Left. In the Convention of 1792 these normal differences were aggravated by the fact that one out of every three deputies had already sat either in the Constituent Assembly of '89 or in the Legislative Assembly of '91. The party badges of the old parliaments were worn by the members of the new. Nearly a hundred of these men remembered with what fear of popular violence they had removed from Versailles to Paris in October, '89, and with what dread of popular republicanism they had fired on the demonstrators of July, '91. Nearly two hundred of them had fresh in mind the insurrection of August, and the September tyranny of the commune. It was only three weeks since the prison massacre. There was too much that they could not or did not want to forget.

The leaders of the majority were men who had learnt their republicanism
in the academic atmosphere of a Bordeaux debating society, or a Sunday
supper at Marseille. Their friends were persons of property and leisure.
Their commercial constituencies lived under allegiance to the laws of
supply and demand. They believed that every question of state could be
settled by an appeal to reason and conscience. These Girondins, as they came
to be called, provided no party organization or programme for the *Brissotins*,
Buzotins, or *Rolandistes* who generally accepted their leadership; but they
enjoyed dining together, and airing their common dislikes; they indulged a
nice taste in political nepotism; and they nourished an ambition, based on a
sincere belief in their superior talents, to monopolize the government of the
country. Never comfortably at home in Paris, and making little attempt to
understand the Parisian point of view, they left the lower circle of that
political inferno, the sections, and even the middle circle, the clubs, to their
astuter rivals, the Jacobins.

Hitherto *Girondin* had been a geographical expression, and *Jacobin* the
name of a club. Now a group of deputies from the Gironde gave their name
to a party, and a non-party club began to identify itself with the political
opinions of a group of Paris representatives. The Jacobin leaders were men
little different from their opponents in origin or up-bringing. They believed,
as the Girondins did, in the war, the republic, and the Convention. They
were no less idealistic, and no more humanitarian. But they had a greater
regard for the interests of the common people, they had less respect for
political shibboleths, and they had an extra capacity for realistic, and if necessary ruthless experimentation.

In a parliamentary assembly of a modern type the complementary
qualities of Jacobin and Girondin might have stimulated one another, and
so provided a healthy rivalry of alternative governments. It was not so
in the Convention of '92. This was a body whose business was not to
administer a constitution, but to make one. This was a body in which it was
thought suspicious that a group of statesmen should dine and talk together.
This was a body whose destructive critics might never be required to become
constructive legislators, and whose members had no responsibilities towards their constituents other than those which they had towards the
nation as a whole. Under such conditions differences that might have spread
healthily outwards grew unhealthily inwards. Opposition became unforgivable. Divergences of opinion started fatal feuds. If the blame for this lay
more with the Girondins than with the Jacobins, it was because they were
the stronger party in the assembly—they monopolized the Presidency up to
the middle of November—and they could have afforded to be generous.

Yet it may be doubted whether generosity would have been interpreted
as anything but weakness. The commune had, no doubt, tried to forestall
attacks by dismissing its notorious Vigilance Committee, and by calling for
its accounts. Danton had made overtures to Brissot, and had tried to establish

his respectability by proposing (September 21st) the perpetual maintenance
of the rights of property owners. Marat was, as usual, prepared to think
any new assembly better than its predecessor. But was Robespierre any more
ready than Roland to forgive or to forget? Was Desmoulins likely to resist
the temptation to urge on the combatants with his diabolically clever pen?
Was he likely to refrain from attributing the worst motives to the men whom
he called the *Flegmatiques*—those who, like Pétion, Barère, Condorcet, or
Rabaut Saint-Etienne, 'tried to mediate between Brissot and Robespierre,
Danton and Roland, as the abbé d'Espagnac stands to profit either by a rise
or by a fall in the funds'?

During the early meetings of the Convention the deputies had sat indiscriminately, where they pleased. But it was noticed that, as the quarrel
between Jacobins and Girondins developed, they grouped themselves to the
right and left of the President's chair, whilst the extreme Jacobins found a
place of vantage in the higher seats at one end of the hall, which came to be
called the Mountain (*montagne*). Right and Left could, indeed, have no
fixed meaning. The President's place was soon moved from the north to
the south side of the *manège*. Within eight months the sessions were moved
from the rectangular riding-school to the semicircular arena of the *salle
des machines*. But the subtle influence of proximity remained.

The controversies that shook the Convention during the autumn of '92
may almost all be viewed as episodes in Roland's crusade against the capital.
'Loving liberty, because it is indispensable to the happiness and perfectibility
of the human race; sacrificing private interest to public good, because that
is the first duty of man in society; speaking the truth without reserve, and
practising justice without fear; indifferent to life or death, since the one
gives conscientious employment, and the other offers the hope of repose'—
such is Madame Roland's account of the chivalric mood in which her
elderly Paladin girt on his pen-sword Durandal before the gates of Paris.
In fact, Roland's feelings were not always at this high level. He had a
personal feud with the commune. He could never forget the massacre of
the prisoners, in which his enemies had nearly compassed his death, and his
associates had betrayed him into condoning their crime. His resentment
against the commune was ready to exploit the old feeling of the provinces
against the capital. It had long been held that Paris consumed more than its
share of the resources of the country. It was now suggested that Paris
grasped more than its share of political power, and aimed at a dictatorship
over the eighty-three departments.

From the moment that the Paris police, as well as the National Guard,
falls under the control of the commune, Roland initiates at the Ministry
of the Interior a *bureau de l'esprit public*, to propagate sound opinion, and to
penalize unsound. Already in mid-September, whilst Pétion is assuring the
assembly, in daily reports, that all is well, Roland insists upon the need of an

armed force to keep order in the capital, and summons the mayor and the commandant of the Guard to the bar of the House to be reminded of their duties.

In his first ministerial report (September 23rd) Paris is Roland's main objective. He complains of its disorderliness, of the difficulty of maintaining its food supply, and of the impoverishment of its charitable funds owing to the abolition of tithe and octroi. In October he finds fault with the irregularities practised in the municipal elections: one of the sections had even enfranchised domestic servants. From beginning to end of his ministry he misses no opportunity of showing his dislike of the citizens and of the city authorities. Their conduct was certainly exasperating: but his method of dealing with them—that of a conscientious schoolmaster who does not know how to keep order—made matters worse than they need have been. Madame Roland wrote too often: Roland acted too seldom. Their more important circulars alone, the work of five months at the ministry, fill a volume of two hundred and sixty closely printed pages. Their achievements could be put in very small compass.

Roland's suggestion of an armed guard under the control of the Convention was taken up by his friend Buzot on September 24th, and became the subject of a special report on October 8th. The plan was too provocative to be accepted by an assembly already suspicious of Girondin intrigue. Its object was achieved indirectly by the deputies of Bouches-du-Rhône, whose leaders, Barbaroux and Rebecqui, were *Rolandistes*, working against Robespierre, Marat, and the commune. A fresh detachment of *fédérés* was summoned from the Girondin departments. They arrived in Paris on October 20th, and were welcomed by a battalion of their predecessors of July which had refused to leave the city. Within a month as many as sixteen thousand provincial volunteers were demonstrating against the Jacobins, and resisting all attempts to send them to the front. This was a strange contribution to public order, and reminded Parisians unpleasantly of the foreign troops which another unpopular government had called to its aid three years before.

As the autumn goes on, Roland's suspicions assume fantastic shapes. He is ready to believe that six thousand daggers of a particularly murderous pattern are being manufactured at Birmingham for use in the next Paris mob-rising; or that three hundred armed men are coming from Bordeaux to assassinate the inhabitants of the East End; or that Barras has discovered at Nice proofs of a plot to invade France. His second report (October 24th) is an elaborate *réquisitoire* of six thousand words, summarizing the unhappy state of the capital. The administration, he says, is powerless, the commune is despotic, the people are misled, the police is badly directed, and the Convention fails to take a firm line. In the debate on this report Robespierre defended his constituents, and Danton remarked, not without reason, that Roland's indictment should have been brought, not against the capital, but against the revolution. That was the true source of 'this national fever, which has worked miracles enough to astonish posterity.'

If Roland's acrimony causes offence, so does his officiousness. In the mysterious robbery of the crown jewels from the *garde-meuble* on the night of September 16th he personally conducts the police investigations, from Paris to Bordeaux, and from London to Amsterdam, with the assurance of a Scotland Yard detective over-riding the incompetent efforts of a County constabulary. Thirty suspects are interrogated, and half a dozen sentenced to death. It is not Roland's fault if his agent in London has to be recalled without recovering the missing gems, or if his own resignation leaves the mystery half unsolved.

By this time the assembly was not only bored by Roland's constant complaints: it was also annoyed at his clinging to office. After Gensonné's 'Self-denying ordinance' of October 27th, when Danton remained a deputy, but ceased to be a minister, Roland was persuaded by his friends to retain the ministry. At the end of November he was denounced to the Convention by the commune. In December he lost the support of the reorganized department of Paris. By the end of the year he was thinking of resignation, and his wife sat at a writing-table piled with threatening letters, 'turning with delight to nature, which, in this sad world, seems to offer no refuge but the grave.' Roland's ultimate resignation, in January, '93, was in terms expressing his willingness to remain in office till his successor was appointed. As always, his motives were unimpeachable. But his enemies were tired of being reminded of them. His virtues did as much harm as other men's vices.

Roland's attack on Paris was not the only part of the Girondin campaign which miscarried. The party had hoped to strengthen its hold on the executive by the appointment of Pache (October 20th) to succeed Servan, and of Garat (October 19th) to succeed Danton. Jean-Nicolas Pache was a Swiss of forty-six with country tastes, formerly a protégé and employé of Necker, who had come to Paris to educate his children, and who had made himself indispensable to the Rolands as secretary and audience. He no sooner became a minister than he quarrelled with his patrons, deserted their party, and went over to the Jacobins. Joseph-Dominique Garat, a Basque literary man of forty-three without force of character or political principles, the younger and more liberal of two brothers who had sat in the Constituent Assembly, still attended Girondin dinner-parties, but inclined towards Jacobinism as soon as he entered his office. It became his hopeless mission to mediate between the two parties.

Meanwhile the personal animosity with which some of the Girondins attacked the Jacobin leaders discredited their cause, and drove waverers into the opposite camp. Robespierre, who had recently turned a deaf ear to all the blandishments of Madame Roland, was accused of royalism by her protégé the novelist Jean-Baptiste Louvet, who published his charges under the strange and provocative English motto: 'In politiks there exist onless two parties in France. The first is composed of philosophers, the second of Thieves, Robbers, and Murderers.' Robespierre used an easy opportunity to demolish his opponent, and to strengthen his reputation as the most dangerous man in the assembly. Danton's overtures to Brissot were rejected, and a Girondin attack on his financial honesty destroyed all hope of his support. Marat, whom no party would acknowledge, was needlessly antagonized, and met his accusers with a republican frankness which increased his hold on the people. Even the scheme for a Convention guard gave the Girondins little advantage. The Jacobins fraternized with the federals, and soon made them as good Parisians as themselves.

The blunders of the Girondins, and the obvious unfitness of their leaders for the business of government, gradually weakened their hold on the Convention, and on the country. One proof of this which attracted attention at the time, and was to have important consequences a year later, was the political conversion of Georges Couthon. Couthon had come to the Legislative Assembly from Clermont-Ferrand with a provincial reputation as a poor man's lawyer, and with marked anti-monarchical sentiments. His proposals for the king's reception by the deputies, his championship of the Châteauvieux heroes, and his hatred of Lafayette doubtless commended him to Robespierre, who addressed him as *mon ami*, and confided to him his hopes and fears on the eve of August 10th. Like Robespierre, Couthon stood for the rights of the common people. It was he who had demanded the total abolition of feudal exactions six months before the victory of August made it practicable. It was he who insisted at the first session of the Convention that any new constitution should be subject to a popular referendum. But he was a member for France; he wore no party badge; and it was by no means certain that his sympathies would be with Paris and the Jacobin party.

On October 11th a Constitutional Committee had been appointed, seven of whose nine members were Rolandists. The next day Couthon, who was crippled with rheumatism, wheeled himself painfully to the Jacobin club in his invalid chair, was carried by his friends into the tribune, and made one of his infrequent speeches. It announced his conversion to Jacobinism. 'It is no good making pretences,' he said: 'you can take it from an old man, though a young republican (Couthon was in fact thirty-seven), that there are two parties in the Convention. One consists of persons of extremist principles, limited resources, and anarchical tendencies; the other consists of shrewd, cunning, and extremely ambitious intriguers. The Girondins are for the republic, because that is the national mandate: but they are also for aristocracy, because they want to keep their influence, and to have at their disposal the appointments, the emoluments, and the financial resources of the republic.' Where, he asked, could this faction be resisted and overthrown? Where, indeed, but in the Jacobin club? 'Here the revolution was planned, here it was carried through. Jacobins and deputies stand together. He who deserts the club is a traitor, worthy only of the execration of his country.'

A desperate attempt was now made to rally the forces of Girondism in view of the struggle which was seen to be approaching. Jean-Antoine-Joseph, *ci-devant* baron De Bry, had earned the nickname 'Tyrannicide' by proposing, in August, '92, the formation of a body of twelve hundred volunteers to assassinate kings and the commanders of enemy armies. On December 23rd Thibault introduced a report to the effect that the provinces were indignant at quarrels in the assembly, and wished to liquidate the Opposition (*les factieux*). De Bry took the opportunity to call on his colleagues to close their ranks, to rise to the height of their responsibilities, and to destroy the elements of disorder and dissension in the Convention and in the capital. 'Is Paris,' he asked, 'to be the prey of a handful of ambitious egoists, who see in these changing times only a fresh opportunity to increase their fortune, or to improve their position?' He challenged the deputies, in vague but eloquent words, to be ready to shed their blood for their country.

De Bry's view of the situation was the same as Couthon's, but with the party labels neatly reversed. He was supported by the trimmer Barère, who hoped to be in a position to profit by the defeat of either party. The sitting ended with a series of resolutions calling for a report on the state of Paris and of the country, and appointing six commissioners to co-operate with the Executive Council in 'all measures necessary for the maintenance of the laws, the preservation of liberty, and the defence of the republic.' Such was the first hint of the Committee of Public Safety. Some more drastic proposals which De Bry seems also to have favoured, such as the setting up of a special court to deal with crimes of *lèse-nation*, and the outlawry of persons guilty of conspiracy, show how little difference there was between Girondin intention in '92 and Jacobin performance in '93.

The moment had now come which, for the past three months, both parties in the assembly and all classes in the country had been anticipating. The king's trial could be no longer postponed. The royal prisoners in the Temple were perhaps thinking that the quarrels of the deputies had put them out of mind. They were perhaps hoping that a Girondin Convention would be able to save them from a Jacobin commune. But there could be no repetition of the reprieve of 1791. The retreat of the invading armies removed the fear of war which had hitherto prevented the punishment of the royal traitor. The evidence which the retreat brought to light of atrocities committed by the *émigré* battalions embittered public feeling against the real authors of the Brunswick manifesto. As the Girondin hold on the assembly weakened, and as the clubs came under the influence of a sterner and better-organized Jacobinism, it became evident that retribution was at hand.

As early as October 10th Robespierre's section *des Piques* had hinted that

only the king's trial could prevent more violent designs on the Temple.
A few days later the Robespierrist Bourbotte declared in the assembly that
demands for the trial were coming in from all parts of the country. It was
replied that a Commission of Twenty-four was already considering the
'crimes of the ex-king.' Ten days later Mailhe, one of the ablest lawyers of
the Gironde, promised on behalf of the *comité de législation* an immediate
report 'on questions relating to Louis' trial.' The matter, he explained, was
not difficult, but must be very carefully dealt with. The Long Parliament
had been blamed, not for executing Charles I, but for trying him too hastily.
By the end of the month translations of the proceedings in Westminster Hall
began to appear on the bookstalls round the *manège*, and to be hawked in the
alleys of the Palais-Royal. Rühl of Strasbourg, one of the oldest members of
the House, advised deputies to read Milton's *Defence of the English People*.
Scripture was also invoked. A cartoon was on sale in the print-shops showing
the hand that wrote Belshazzar's sentence on the palace wall: but its
doom was now pronounced on the traitor 'Louis the Last'—'you have been
weighed in the balance, and found wanting.' If these precedents aroused
any scruples, they were brushed aside by the Jacobins. The deputies, they
declared, were either afraid of awkward revelations at the trial, or they
feared that, if they condemned Louis, their rest might be disturbed by
les revenans, supernatural hauntings.

On November 6th Dufriche-Valazé introduced the report of the Commission of Twenty-four. It was based on a mass of papers handed over by
the Vigilance Committee of the commune a month before, and it was
believed to contain, along with exposures of political corruption, indisput-
able proofs of the crimes of the ex-king. From this compromising source
Valazé produced his evidence that Louis' apparent simplicity had long
covered a double game. There were particulars of payments to the widow
of the Marquis de Favras, to non-juror priests, and to counter-revolutionary
papers. There was evidence of Louis' investments in the *pacte de famine*,
and of his subsidies to the *émigré* army. There were Bouillé's accounts for
the expenses of the flight to Varennes.

Whilst the deputies were still discussing the value of Valazé's revelations,
Mailhe's report (November 7th) took up the 'previous question'—could the
Convention try the king? There were here two problems: could the king
be tried ; and could he be tried by the Convention?

Tit. III, Cap. II, Sect. I of the constitution laid it down (Art. II) that
'The person of the king is inviolable and sacred.' It provided for a regency
(Sect. II) only in case of the king's minority, or of his madness (Art.
XVIII). It envisaged one means, and only one, by which the throne might
become vacant. If within a month of being invited to do so by the Legislature
sitting or summoned at his accession, the king fails to take the oath of allegiance to the nation and the law, 'he shall be deemed to have abdicated' (*il sera
censé avoir abdiqué la royauté*). But after the return from Varennes two fur-

ther clauses had been added, extending the grounds of abdication. Art. VI provided that 'if the king puts himself at the head of an army, and directs its forces against the nation, or if he fails formally to oppose such an enterprise executed in his name, he shall be deemed to have abdicated.' Art. VII provided that if the king left the country, and failed to return within a time fixed by the legislature, 'he shall be deemed to have abdicated.' Art. VIII further provided that 'After abdication, whether express or legal, the king shall rank as an ordinary citizen (*sera dans la classe des citoyens*), and can be accused and judged as a citizen for acts committed subsequent to his abdication.'

The republican petitions of July 16th and 17th, '91, had gone upon the assumption that Louis' flight to Varennes constituted an abdication. The clauses drafted by the anti-republicans who suspended Louis instead of deposing him excluded this interpretation (Art. VII), and guarded his inviolability (Art. VIII) against all eventualities. Either he had abdicated, or he had not abdicated. If he had not abdicated, he was still king, and inviolable: if he had abdicated, he was a mere citizen, but he could not be accused of the crimes that had brought about his abdication. There were, however, two possible escapes from this dilemma, and Mailhe indicated them both. First: the king's inviolability under Sect. I of Tit. III, Cap. II of the constitution must be interpreted in the light of Sect. IV, dealing with the responsibility of ministers. It only applies (he maintained) to those acts of the crown for which a minister is held responsible. For these acts the king's minister is accountable, and the king himself is inviolable. For other acts the king himself is accountable: his inviolability no longer applies. Secondly: the Legislative Assembly, being subordinate to the constitution, could not judge the king, though it ventured to suspend him. The Convention, being the sovereign people in council, is above the constitution, and cannot be bound by constitutional limits. The nation, acting through the insurgents of August 10th, has deposed the king: the nation, represented by the Convention, has the right to judge him. The sovereign people recognizes no royal prerogatives, and is bound by no forms of law. It might have murdered Louis in August. It can still execute him in November.

The assembly showed its approval of Mailhe's argument by ordering that his report should be translated into every language, and circulated throughout the departments and the armies. In the debates and divisions that followed, and that occupied the whole time of the assembly—seven hours a day—for two months, it was remarked that a serious and almost solemn air prevailed, and that the President's frequent appeals to the deputies and to the public not to applaud or demonstrate enabled the House to discuss reasonably and (until the last few days) with unaccustomed calm the most difficult decision they were ever likely to face. The number of publishers who found it worth their while to print detailed accounts of the debates (Buisson in seven volumes, Perlet in eight, Dufort in two, all dated 1793) shows how seriously and how widely the issue was discussed outside the House. Posselt's *Unparteyische Geschichte* is evidence that the trial was closely followed across the Rhine. The opinions of the general public were expressed in such a spate of pamphlets as had not been seen in Paris since the early weeks of the revolution.

In the preliminary discussion (November 13th) opinion was deeply divided as to whether the king should or should not be tried. The President had before him two urns, into which were put the names of those who wished to speak. One was marked POUR, the other CONTRE, and he drew the names at hazard from each in turn. Not only the speakers, but also those who failed to get a hearing, were allowed to print and circulate their opinions at the public expense. Bundles of these pamphlets—some three hundred and fifty of them, ranging from legal arguments to passionate appeals—can still be found in the top shelves of historical libraries. There was a surprising variety of points of view. Some speakers (Morisson, Lefort) thought that, now Louis was deposed, nothing more could or should be done. Others (Fauchet, Rouzet) maintained that capital punishment was against the laws of nature, or unworthy of a free people. Louis should be kept alive, as a warning to other kings, and as a security against pretenders to the throne. Others scouted all constitutional scruples, arguing either (as Grégoire, or Paine's letter of November 21st) that a royal trial would be a stimulus to world-wide revolution, or (Robert, Saint-Just) that there was no need for a trial, and that Louis should be executed out of hand. He was never a commoner, said Saint-Just, always a king: and kingship itself is a crime (*on ne peut point regner innocemment*).

On November 20th an unexpected turn was given to the situation. Roland received information from a locksmith named Gamain of the existence of a secret safe in the Tuileries. It was a curious story. Gamain's father had worked at Versailles under Louis XV. The son, at the age of eighteen, had been given a room in the palace where Louis XVI, as Dauphin, had indulged his favourite hobby. This man had been summoned to the Tuileries in May, '92, to construct an *armoire de fer* in the king's private room. On his return he was taken violently ill. Six months later, persuading himself that he had been poisoned, he went to Roland, and revenged himself by revealing the secret. His story, as presented in Peyssard's report of May 17th, satisfied the Convention, and he was voted an annuity. The evidence has since disappeared from the archives.

When Roland heard Gamain's story he went to the palace, and opened the 'iron chest.' It was found to contain a mass of private papers: when printed they filled two octavo volumes, and over six hundred and fifty pages. Amongst them were projects for the king's flight, instructions to refractory priests, a correspondence between Calonne and Pitt, particulars of Mirabeau's scheme for royalist propaganda, and suggestions for the bribery of Pétion, Santerre, and other popular leaders on the eve of the August revolution. Whatever fuel this discovery might provide for political *autos-da-fé*, (Roland, of course, was accused of suppressing documents damaging to his friends), it doubled the demand for the king's punishment, and vastly reinforced the case against him. Even before the papers were published, the commune was protesting against any further delay in bringing Louis *le Parjure* to trial. He might die in prison, and they would be suspected of poisoning him.

On December 3rd and 4th Robespierre seized the opportunity to deliver two of his most effective speeches—speeches which were decisive in hurrying on the trial, and in making it a party issue. Away, he cried, with the moralistic prejudices of the old regime! Forms of law are for those who have no principles, and want to keep up appearances. It is absurd to invoke a constitution that our every act denies. Whatever was right on August 10th is right now. A trial would merely be an opportunity for royalist propaganda. Louis declared war on the revolution, and he has been defeated. His life is forfeit. The only duty of the Convention is to judge him here and now. By judging Robespierre meant condemning to death—*il faut le condamner sur-le-champ à mort, en vertu d'une insurrection.*

A few days later (December 10th) Robert Lindet introduced the report of the commission 'on the crimes imputed to Louis Capet.' He traced, step by step, from documentary evidence, the course of the king's unhappy resistance to the revolution. In '89, instead of taking the popular side, he had tried to treat the assembly as his predecessor had treated the *parlements*, until the fall of the Bastille drove him to dissemble. He had vetoed the charters of the revolution, and summoned fresh troops, until October 5th forced him to a second surrender. In '90 he still carried on counter-revolutionary intrigue through Mirabeau and Mirabeau's agents. In '91, whilst professing fidelity to the constitution, he planned the flight to Varennes: its true aim, civil war, was proved by the manifesto that he left behind him. He was privy to the massacre of the Champ de Mars, and to the Declaration of Pillnitz. He encouraged counter-revolution at Avignon and at Arles. He used the Civil List to buy votes, and to finance the emigrants. In '92 he allowed his ministers to neglect the army and navy, and helped on the foreign invasion by vetoing the Paris camp, and by forcing Servan and Dumouriez to resign. Finally he organized the *coup* of August 10th, and rounded off his course of deceit by plotting to overthrow the very constitution which he had previously used as a cover for his counter-revolutionary intrigues. For proof of many of these charges Lindet relied upon the documents newly drawn from the 'iron chest.' There was, indeed, as little need for proof as for exaggeration. The acknowledged facts were sufficiently damning to anyone who believed in the revolution. There was hardly a deputy who doubted that Louis was guilty.

The next day the king was brought in a closed carriage from the Temple to the Tuileries, and questioned for nearly three hours at the bar of the

House. The deputies were solemnly reminded by the President that the eyes of Europe and of posterity were upon them. They listened in profound silence whilst he put to the prisoner a series of questions based on Lindet's report. Louis was quite unprepared. He had not been shown the questions beforehand. He had no counsel to assist him. Some of his friends hoped that, like Charles I, he would dispute the competence of the Convention to try him. Others hoped that he would appeal to the people. That was not Louis' way. He sat patiently in his wooden chair, 'plainly dressed in an olive silk coat, and looking remarkably well.' He neither protested against questions which were too long and complex for a plain Yes or No; nor did he ask for time to consider his answers. He always did his best to extemporize a reply. His simplicity was disarming. But it could also be cunning. When asked about the Mirabeau episode, he said that 'he had forgotten all about it.' Questioned as to the 'iron chest,' he denied any knowledge of it. Confronted by documents in his own hand-writing, he disowned them. But 'when he was accused of shedding the blood of Frenchmen, he raised his voice with all the consciousness of innocence, and in a very strong tone of indignation replied, "No, sir! I have never shed the blood of Frenchmen." His spirit (says the Englishman who recorded the scene) was evidently wounded at this charge, and I perceived a tear trickle down his cheek.'

As soon as Louis had left the House, it was proposed, and ultimately agreed, that he should be allowed to choose counsel to prepare his defence. He nominated two of the oldest and most distinguished members of the Paris bar. Guy-Jean-Baptiste Target, the only lawyer in the French Academy, declined, on the ground of age and infirmity, and salved his conscience by publishing, in the form of *Observations* on the trial, a defence of the king, and a denial of the competence of the Convention. François-Denis Tronchet, a man seven years his senior, accepted the invitation as a matter of duty. Malesherbes, a still older man, whose seventy-one years might have excused him from so onerous and dangerous an office, wrote to give his services. 'I was twice called in,' he said, 'to advise him who was then my master'—Malesherbes had been a member of the *conseil du roi* in 1774 and 1787. 'Then everyone envied my good fortune. Now that many people find it dangerous, I still hold it my duty to serve him.' If Tronchet had refused to act, there would have been no lack of substitutes. The Convention received over twenty letters from persons offering to take his place: they included Malouet and Lally-Tollendal, who were in exile, and Olympe de Gouges, the authoress of *Zamor et Myrza*, who described herself as a 'free and loyal republican' convinced of Louis' guilt as a king, but of his harmlessness as a citizen. The Comte de Roffignat gave an even greater proof of devotion. He wrote from Madrid offering to die in the king's stead.

The two counsel soon found the work too heavy for them. It took five hours to sort out the papers sent them on December 16th, and many more were added later. They accordingly invited the help of a younger man,

Raymond-Romain, Comte de Sèze, a Bordeaux barrister who had of recent years made his home in Paris, and who had secured the acquittal of the royalist Bezenval in '89. It was de Sèze who, on December 26th, made the king's formal defence, when he appeared for the second time at the bar of the Convention. He had only ten days in which to study a mass of documents whose authenticity and completeness he could not control. He sat up the last four nights before the trial writing out his speech. If it reads dully, it must be remembered that Louis refused to allow the customary appeals to the emotions. It has at least been admired by lawyers for its technical skill.

The defence fell under two heads. One was a legal argument to prove that Louis' trial was unconstitutional: the other was a historical argument to refute the charges brought against him. For the first, de Sèze relied upon the king's 'inviolability'. Louis had never 'abdicated' under the terms defined in the constitution: he was therefore still unindictable. To say that he had already been judged by the nation on August 10th was rhetoric, not argument. If he is now to be judged as a citizen, where are the forms of justice? Is the Convention a Court? Can his accusers also be his judges?

As for the charges, de Sèze did his best to meet them, one by one: but this part of the defence carried little conviction. He was on his strongest ground in dealing with what seemed to the deputies Louis' greatest offence. He argued that the king had done no more, on August 10th, than officially defend himself, with the concurrence of the municipal and departmental authorities, and with the help of the National Guard, against an armed insurrection. He added that he had capitulated, in order to avoid bloodshed, before a shot had been fired. Louis himself, speaking to the deputies, 'perhaps for the last time,' protested once more against the charge of having wittingly shed French blood. 'I think,' he said, 'that I should have been saved from such a reproach by the repeated proofs of my affection for my people.'

When the king and his defenders had left the House, some deputies were for proceeding at once to consider the verdict. The majority, having come so far at such a deliberate pace, saw no reason for sudden hurry, and voted for further consideration. Thus on the 28th Buzot was enabled to start a Girondin attempt to postpone the decision, and to disown responsibility for it. He argued as the republicans had argued after the return from Varennes (July 17th, '91). In any settlement of the monarchy, the whole country ought to be associated with the assembly. There should be a plebiscite of the departments, an appeal to the sovereign people.

The debate which followed, and which postponed for another week the hour of decision, anticipated many of the stock arguments for and against a referendum. But the issue was really one of political tactics. The Girondins hoped, and the Jacobins feared, that an appeal to the departments would evoke the latent royalism of the country-side, and make it impossible for the deputies to carry the trial to its logical end. Barère, as so often, expressed the feeling of the non-party majority. He emphasized the prudent deliberation (*sage lenteur*) with which the House had discussed the fate of the king, and said that it would be both cowardly and superfluous for a national convention to go back to the country which it represented, and which had entrusted it with the decision of this very question. 'It is for you to vote,' he ended, 'before the statue of Brutus, before your country, before the whole world. It is by judging the last king of the French that the National Convention will enter into the fields of fame.'

On January 14th it was at last decided that three questions should be put to the deputies: first, Is Louis guilty? second, Do you wish your decision to be referred to the people? and third, What punishment does Louis deserve? It was added, next day, that votes would be given aloud, from the tribune, and that the speaker might give reasons for his decision. Absent members could send their votes in writing. If any failed to vote without good cause, their names would be posted, with the censure of the House.

The voting began the same day, and went on till ten o'clock at night. On the question, Is Louis guilty? six hundred and eighty-three out of seven hundred and forty-eight deputies voted, Yes. Twenty-eight were absent. Of thirty-seven who qualified their answers, the majority only doubted their right to judge the king. It was a practically unanimous verdict. On the question, Do you wish your decision to be referred to the people? two hundred and eighty-six votes were cast for a plebiscite, and four hundred and twenty-five against. It was a Jacobin victory.

There remained the crucial question, What punishment does Louis deserve? Here a close division was expected, and it was important to settle beforehand the majority required to carry a decision. Characteristically, the Girondins would rather have no decision than a Jacobin one: the Jacobins would risk a defeat, if there was any chance of a victory. Lanjuinais proposed that a two-thirds majority should be required. Danton retorted that the war and the republic had gone by a bare majority: why should not the fate of the king be decided in the same way? Such was the usual procedure of the House: and it was adopted. The Jacobins were by now growing confident of victory, the Girondins apprehensive of defeat. An almost hysterical letter from Roland addressed to the Convention at eight o'clock on the morning of the 16th protested against the closing of the city barriers by the commune, which he interpreted as the prelude to another September massacre.

The voting on the final issue began at eight o'clock on the evening of January 16th, and lasted till the same time on the 17th. For twenty-four hours one deputy after another mounted the tribune, and gave his vote either for the exile, or for the imprisonment, or for the death of the king. Sometimes a few words of explanation were added, sometimes a speech of considerable length.

The satirical Mercier has elaborated a strange and unforgettable scene. The end of the hall (he says) was transformed into a sort of lounge, where ladies in charming *negligées* were eating ices and oranges, drinking liqueurs, and receiving the compliments and greetings of their friends. The public galleries were full of foreigners, and people of every class, who drank wine and brandy as if it had been a tavern. Bets were offered and taken in all the neighbouring coffee-houses. The faces of those who went to the tribune were rendered more funereal by the pale gleam of the lights, as in a slow and sepulchral voice they uttered the one word, Death! Here were deputies calculating whether they would have time for dinner before they gave their vote. Here were women pricking cards with pins, to count the votes. Tired deputies fell asleep, and had to be woken up to vote. The scrutineers could be seen slipping away a vote, now and again, in order to save the unhappy king. The scene (ends Mercier) can never be described as it really presented itself. History will never be able to record it. History, indeed, tells of no more momentous decision made by so narrow a margin, unless it be that taken in the House of Commons on the Reform Bill in March, 1831.

When at last the votes were counted, it was found that out of seven hundred and twenty-one deputies present and voting three hundred and sixty-one had voted for death without qualification, and seventy-two for death with reprieve (*sursis*). Two hundred and eighty-eight had voted either for imprisonment or exile, sometimes substituting death in case of foreign invasion. The number three hundred and sixty-one was a majority of one, and no more. If twenty-six of the seventy-two qualified votes were added, as they fairly might be, there could be no doubt of the feeling of the majority of the deputies. Louis must die. But the idea of a reprieve was so attractive to timid or merciful minds that an additional vote was taken on this issue. On the 19th Louis' last hope of life was removed by three hundred and eighty votes to three hundred and ten.

More was at stake in these divisions than the life of a deposed king. They determined the immediate fortunes of two political parties and the ultimate fate of many of the seven hundred voters more than twenty years afterwards. It had been agreed before the final division that lists showing the vote cast by each deputy, and recording a censure against anyone absent without cause, should be circulated throughout the departments. Desmoulins was certainly not the only deputy whose family had written from the country begging him not to vote for the king's death; he could easily excuse himself (his father suggested) on the ground that he had condemned Louis in his paper, and could not vote impartially.

As the *appel nominal* went on, special note was taken of the votes cast by the Girondin leaders and their sympathisers. Would they stand together with the unanimity of the Jacobin deputies for Paris, of whom twenty-one out of twenty-four, including the king's own cousin, Orléans, voted for the death penalty? Whether they would not, or dared not, only their consciences could tell. Nearly all the leaders—Vergniaud, Guadet, Gensonné, Louvet, Brissot, Buzot, Barbaroux, Pétion—voted for death. Of those generally reputed their followers, fifty-seven out of a hundred and sixty-nine, or about one in three, cast their votes the same way. In the division on the plebiscite it was the same story: several of the leaders voted against it, and about a third of their followers. The long list of *appelans*, as those who voted for the plebiscite were called, was used for the proscription of a party; and some of those who had tried too late to save the monarchy were numbered among the regicides who, if they escaped a republican guillotine, ended their lives as outlaws and exiles under a Bourbon restoration.

Louis heard on the afternoon of January 20th that his execution was fixed for the next day. He asked for three days' respite in which to take leave of his family, and to prepare for his end. He was allowed everything except delay: for the *comité militaire* feared attempts either to lynch him, or to rescue him on the way to execution. So the king sent for his sister's confessor, the abbé Edgeworth, a non-juror priest of Irish birth, and prepared for immediate death.

That evening he said good-bye to his wife and children. At six o'clock the next morning—it was Tuesday, January 21st—he received communion. About half-past eight he left the Temple in a closed carriage, surrounded by troops. Santerre, on horse-back, was at the head of the convoy. Armed citizens drawn up two deep along the two and a half miles of the route prevented any attempt at rescue. At the corner of the rue Saint-Denis the Baron de Batz, with a small group of royalists, called for volunteers to save the king: *A nous, ceux qui veulent sauver le roi!* But it was in vain. The constant beating of drums drowned any cries of sympathy that might have been heard. The Marquis de la Tour du Pin and his wife were listening at an open window of their house in the suburbs for the sound of musketry which would mean that a rescue had at least been attempted: but it never came.

A cold mist still hung over the Place de la Revolution. Troops surrounded the guillotine. Behind them a great crowd waited, some on piles of building materials, some on the terrace of the Tuileries gardens, to see the end. Whole families were there—mothers with their nurses and their children. Louis, after five minutes spent in prayer, left the carriage, and took Edgeworth's arm to mount the scaffold. When he reached it, he signed to the drummers to be silent, and said in a loud voice, 'My people, I die an innocent man' (*Peuple, je meurs innocent*). . . At an instant order from Berruyer, passed on by Santerre, the drums beat again, and no more could be heard: but to the men who pinioned him Louis added, 'I hope that my blood may secure the happiness of the French people.' A moment later the blade fell, and the executioner held up the severed head to the crowd, amid universal shouts of *Vive la nation!* It was, the official witnesses noted, 10.22 a.m.

Louis' three-cornered hat with the tricolor badge was auctioned from the scaffold. His hair and hair-ribbon were sold by the headsman's assistant. His brown coat with the blue enamel buttons was divided, and distributed to the crowd. Some of them dipped handkerchiefs, swords, or scraps of paper in his blood. Many danced round the guillotine, singing the *Marseillaise*. But old M. Favart's most vivid recollection of the day was that he was called as a child into his mother's darkened room, and told to kneel down and pray for the king's soul, at the moment of his execution.

The body and the severed head were buried the same day in the cemetery of the Madeleine. They were placed between the victims of Louis' marriage fête, twenty-three years before, and the Swiss soldiers killed on August 10th. It was ordered that the grave should be dug ten feet deep, as though to bury the Bourbon monarchy beyond hope of resurrection.

In the afternoon the theatres opened as usual, and the *cafés* and *cabarets* were filled with care-free Parisians, discussing the crime of the hour, the theme of indignant addresses from all over the country—the murder of a Jacobin deputy, Le Peletier, by a royalist assassin, who had intended Orléans to be his victim. The capital, as the mayor reported to the commune, remained perfectly calm, though the fear of disturbance justified the extravagance of keeping the street lamps burning during a few moonlit nights. Parisian royalists might pass from hand to hand relics or mementos of the martyr. The only medals that record public sorrow for the death of the French king betray by their wording that they were struck in Germany.

A week later, in his quarters at Villingen, the Prince de Condé attended a mass for the repose of the soul of the 'royal martyr,' and recognized the Dauphin as king of France, under the title of Louis XVII. From his place of exile the Comte de Provence wrote to the Comte d'Artois telling him of their elder brother's death, and adding that the Dauphin was not likely to survive him long. 'Whilst you shed tears,' he said, 'for those near to us, you must not forget how useful their deaths will be for the country. Comfort yourself with this idea, and reflect that your son is, after myself, the heir and hope of the monarchy.' How these Bourbons loved one another!

CHAPTER XVIII

GIRONDINS

The Girondists, who were the first republicans in power, were men of enlarged views and great literary attainments: but they seem to have been deficient in that vigour and daring activity, which circumstances made necessary. Men of genius are rarely either prompt in action or consistent in general conduct: their early habits have been those of contemplative indolence; and the day-dreams with which they have been accustomed to amuse their solitude, adapt them for splendid speculation, not temperate and practicable counsels.— (S. T. COLERIDGE: Addresses to the People.)

A WEEK after the king's execution the *Annales patriotiques* regaled its readers with an article headed 'Remarkable epochs in the life of Louis Capet.' The writer suggested that 21 was Louis' unlucky number. April 21st, 1770, was the date of his unpopular marriage, and June 21st the same year the date of the wedding fête at which hundreds of sightseers had lost their lives. January 21st, '82, was the celebration of the birth of the Dauphin, whose premature death cast a gloom over the court during the early months of the revolution. June 21st, '91, was the day of Louis' arrest at Varennes. September 21st, '92, was the day of the abolition of the monarchy. January 21st, '93, was the day of the king's execution. What the *Annales* could not tell its readers was that this series of coincidences was to have a retributive sequel. It could not foresee that the foundation of the republic and the execution of the king would lead the revolution into an expansionist policy involving conflict with almost every power of Europe. It could not foretell that at Trafalgar (October 21st, 1805), Vimiera (August 21st, 1808) and Vittoria (June 21st, 1813) France would lose command of land and sea. It could not foretell that, after their final defeat at Leipzig, the revolutionary armies would be driven back behind the frontiers they had crossed just 21 years before.

For two months after the victory of Valmy the republican armies marched out from Paris and across the frontiers, full of zeal and patriotism, but without any clear notion either of their aims, or of the means of attaining them. It was assumed that Belgium and Nice, Savoy and the Rhine-land would welcome republican freedom. If they failed to do so, was it to be forced upon them at the point of republican bayonets? It was hoped that they would offer hospitality to the troops that liberated them. If they did not, were they to be compelled to contribute towards their entertainment? Each separate general— Anselme, Montesquiou, Custine, Dumouriez—acted as he thought best. After a month or two of French occupation the inhabitants of Belgium and of the Rhine-land showed clearly enough their dislike of military requisition-ing, and their distrust of the depreciated paper money in which their bills were paid. On the approach of a Prussian force (December 2nd) the population of Frankfort rose, and massacred part of the French garrison.

These experiences brought about a reaction from Girondin optimism towards the disillusioned realism that was to inspire the Jacobin regime. Evidently it was not enough to offer the benefits of the revolution to peoples unable to appreciate them. They must be actively assisted to rid themselves of the obstacles to appreciation—the agents and institutions of the old order. Revolution would not come in Germany, any more than it had come in France, by the light of nature. It must be worked for, fought for: it must not only be coaxed, but coerced. Furthermore, political converts must learn that it is their duty to support their missionaries. Republican propaganda is expensive. Republican *assignats* are excellent for expenditure, but useless as receipts. Republican assistance must be paid for in hard cash, or in its equivalent in kind.

It is one of the weaknesses of a national assembly that it responds too quickly to changes of popular temper. On November 19th, without waiting for the advice of its Diplomatic Committee, the Convention voted a decree that caused alarm in every court in Europe. It promised brotherly assistance (*fraternité et secours*) to any people wishing to regain its freedom. 'We cannot rest,' was Brissot's gloss on this text, 'until all Europe is ablaze. What puny projects were those of Richelieu and Alberoni, compared with the world-wide risings, the gigantic revolutions, that we are called upon to achieve!' A month later (December 15th), whilst artistes paid by the government were singing the *Marseillaise* to puzzled audiences at Ghent, Brussels, and Liège, the assembly adopted by acclamation, and almost without amendment, a consequential decree proposed by Cambon to regulate 'the measures to be taken by French generals in countries occupied by the armies of the republic.'

Although Cambon spoke in the name of the committees of War and Diplomacy as well as of Finance, his proposals were obviously inspired by the need of cash. The Convention, he argued, had declared war only on the rich: it wished to remain at peace with the poor. *Guerre aux châteaux, paix aux chaumières* was its watchword. It must now enforce this policy in the liberated areas. It must make war upon wealth; and by making war upon wealth it will make war self-supporting. The French generals will therefore proclaim, in every place they occupy, the abolition of all existing tithes, taxes, and feudal charges. They will suppress all the existing authorities, and proclaim the sovereignty of the people. They will then 'take under the protection of the republic' all property belonging to the government, to corporations, and to public undertakings in the country; and they will set up a 'provisional administration nominated by the people' to collaborate with commissioners appointed by the Convention in the disposal of these resources.

Beneath this apparently harmless arrangement lay a system of exploitation

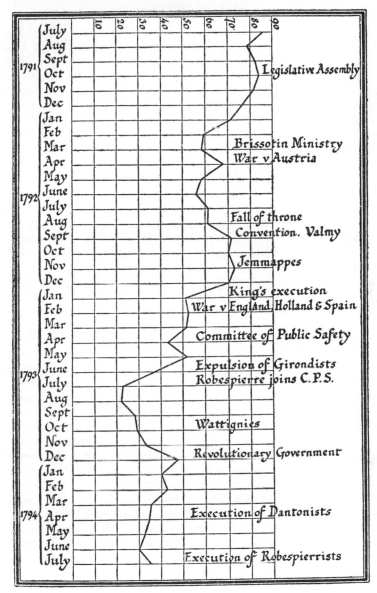

The chart shows data with values along the top axis (10, 20, 30, 40, 50, 60, 70, 80, 90) and months along the left side, grouped by year:

1791: July, Aug, Sept, Oct, Nov, Dec
1792: Jan, Feb, Mar, Apr, May, June, July, Aug, Sept, Oct, Nov, Dec
1793: Jan, Feb, Mar, Apr, May, June, July, Aug, Sept, Oct, Nov, Dec
1794: Jan, Feb, Mar, Apr, May, June, July

Event labels on the chart:
- Legislative Assembly
- Brissotin Ministry
- War v Austria
- Fall of throne
- Convention. Valmy
- Jemmappes
- King's execution
- War v England, Holland & Spain
- Committee of Public Safety
- Expulsion of Girondists
- Robespierre joins C.P.S.
- Wattignies
- Revolutionary Government
- Execution of Dantonists
- Execution of Robespierrists

THE DEPRECIATION OF THE ASSIGNAT

Showing the exchange value in *livres* (metal) of 100 *livres* (paper), and the connection of the variations with contemporary events.

which Napoleon himself could hardly have improved. The abolition of taxes, as Cambon explained in his introductory speech, would create a trustful mood in which *assignats* could be unloaded upon the country. The French army of occupation would buy all it needed at the price of worthless paper. The French government would confiscate all the specie in the country. Later it might need to have recourse to additional taxation (*contributions extraordinaires*). The raising of such money would not be left to the military, whose methods might cause a foreign tax-payer 'to regard our principles with undeserved disfavour.' It would be entrusted to the 'more tactful methods' of civilian administrators, who, by extorting money only from the rich, 'would make the people love liberty': for they would contribute nothing themselves, and yet they would have a hand in the spending of all that was collected.

The decree of December 15th caused an even worse impression abroad than that of November 19th. 'More even than all the previous transactions,' as Pitt said in the House of Commons seven years later, 'it amounted to a universal declaration of war against all thrones, and against all civilized governments.'

Dumouriez saw clearly that Cambon's plan would endanger his position in Belgium, and make his further advance impossible. In spite of his protests, it was at once put into practice. Thirty commissioners set to work. Within a month Cambon could congratulate himself on having extracted, in the name of friendship, over six million pounds. It came chiefly from the coffers of the Catholic Church; and it was done at the cost of alienating a Catholic people. It was not to be expected that the economic advantages of reunion with France which were to make Ghent the rival of Reims and Lyon would outweigh the anti-clericalism, the exactions, and the petty tyranny of the French occupation. It soon became impossible to hold the country, except by force. Annexation was the only alternative to insurrection. The 'reunion' of Belgium to France was voted under military pressure. It could be maintained only by an army of occupation. It could be extended only by a policy of conquest, which would turn the most indifferent of France's friends into the most tenacious of her foes.

French affairs had always held an important place in Pitt's policy of 'peace, retrenchment, and reform.' He had worked steadily to keep peace between the two countries. His first attitude towards the revolution was to regard it as a political plague that might incapacitate our hereditary enemy, without endangering our own security. Both the interests of Britain and the prejudices of George III would be best served by the continuance of the constitutional monarchy of Louis XVI. Pitt had accordingly kept out of the Conference of Pillnitz, and the anti-French coalition. He had been forward to recognize the constitution of 1791. At that period, as Burke reported, Pitt and Grenville seemed to be 'quite out of all apprehension of any effect from the French Revolution on this kingdom, either at present or at any time to come.' 'We shall go on as we are,' Pitt had declared, 'till the day of judgment.' He had therefore taken steps, in January, '92, to reduce our armed forces. As late as February 17th, the day on which Paine published the second part of the *Rights of Man*, he had told Parliament that he expected fifteen years of peace. When, two months later, France declared war on the Emperor, he was careful to assert British neutrality. When he was informed on August 4th of the imminent danger of the royal family, he expressed his sympathy, but refused to intervene. It was not till the throne had fallen, and the republican armies passed to the offensive, that he became seriously concerned.

On the news of August 10th, Lord Gower, the British ambassador, was recalled from Paris. The new ministry set up by the Legislative Assembly was not recognized in Whitehall. The French ambassador, the Marquis de Chauvelin, was not given his passports, but he was put into diplomatic quarantine, and remained on in London, uninvited and unaccredited, to do what he could for his new government, and for the pacific policy of Danton and Lebrun. He was overshadowed by his unofficial adviser, the ex-bishop of Autun. Disowned by his family, denounced by his diocesan clergy, and excommunicated by the Pope, Talleyrand had found consolation in foreign travel, and in a secular occupation exactly suited to his great talents. Others came and went—Lebrun's old school-fellow the abbé Noël, the Dantonist lawyer, Pierre Benoist, and Bernard-Hugues Maret, afterwards Napoleon's Duc de Bassano.

Up to the middle of October some of these hopeful diplomatists believed that, if supplied with sufficient *assignats*, they could build 'a bridge of gold' across the Channel. But after the September massacre Noël felt bound to report that British opinion had hardened against the revolution, and against its noisy but not numerous sympathisers in England. George III was already believed to favour war. Yet Pitt still clung to neutrality. It was hoped that he might do more. Less than a week after Valmy Noël wrote to Lebrun outlining the terms on which he believed it would be possible to induce the British government to mediate between France and Prussia, and to bring about a general peace.

These negotiations, which never seem to have got beyond the back door of the Foreign Office, were wrecked by the French proceedings in the Netherlands. Speaking with 'republican frankness' in the Convention on September 26th, Lebrun counted on economic interests to keep England and Holland neutral during Dumouriez's invasion of Belgium, and made play with the idea that the store of diplomatic bribes he had found at the Foreign Office—'snuff-boxes, watches, and the like'—would now be replaced by 'iron, the metal of liberty.' It was a vain hope. The victory of Jemappes on November 6th, the capture of Brussels a week later, the 'liberation' decree of the 19th, the opening of the Scheldt (November 27th), the plans for exploiting the country put into force by the decree of December 15th, and its subsequent annexation, forced Pitt to intervene. Chauvelin had already been warned of this change of front on November 29th, and Maret on December 2nd. When Parliament met on December 13th Pitt had no difficulty in passing an Aliens Bill, augmenting the navy, and initiating a blockade of the French coast. On the last day of the year Grenville penned a despatch to Chauvelin which was almost an ultimatum.

On January 1st, '93, a newly appointed Vice-admiral of the republican navy addressed the Convention on the international situation. Armand-Guy-Simon de Coetnempren, Comte de Kersaint, had served in the navy since he was a boy, and had taken a lead in all naval discussions in the assemblies of '91 and '92. War with England, he asserted, was now inevitable. Corn-ships bound for Brest and Bayonne had already been seized in the Thames. England, with all its political parties united by war, would be the heart of a hostile maritime coalition. Only from the Irish, the Scotch, and the English Jacobins could any sympathy be expected. He went on to anticipate Napoleon's two favourite plans. First, France must attack England through her commerce, and destroy her financial resources, the heart of her power. *La fortune publique d'Angleterre* (he said) *se trouve presque entièrement dans sa banque*. Secondly, she must transport an army of a hundred thousand men across the Channel, and dictate terms 'upon the ruins of the Tower of London.'

There was still time, perhaps, for the Girondin leaders to withdraw from this bellicose position, which some of them felt to be alien to the true principles of their party. At a meeting at Clavière's house on January 11th Brissot read a report that he intended to make to the Convention the next day. David Williams, who had been brought over from England to help in drafting the new constitution, protested against its more provocative passages. Brissot promised to tone them down. But he failed to do so. His excuse shows the real motive for the war. 'It was the Committee's doing', he told Williams: 'if we had hesitated (*to declare war*), the Jacobins would have seized power.'

Brissot's speech the next day said nothing of this fear. It only showed his anxiety to put the blame of the war upon England. England had refused to recognize the French republic. England had resented the opening of the Scheldt. England had confiscated French goods, and legislated against aliens. England had rearmed, contrary to the terms of the treaty of Paris. He stressed British weakness, saying that we had neither the population nor the financial resources to engage in another war. He ended by proposing to send an ultimatum, whose form must have reminded his hearers of the unfortunate message to the Emperor two years ago. They could hardly look forward with confidence to this fresh adventure. Was the republican navy of '93 likely to be as successful against the chief naval power of Europe as the army of '92 had proved itself to be against the chief military power? Would the victory of the Ardennes repeat itself in the English Channel? For the second time within twelve months France was following Brissot into an adventure that offered little hope of success. Nevertheless the French people entered upon the new war as light-heartedly as upon the old. The *Patriote français* records that on January 27th, after the ceremonial planting of a Tree of Liberty in the Place du Carrousel, the band played the *Carmagnole* and the *Ça ira*, 'which so electrified every soul, that the municipal officers, headed by the mayor, danced round it; and at seven o'clock at night they were still dancing.'

On January 10th it had been determined to invade Holland, and to secure, while there was still time, the wealth of an even richer bank than that of London. But Dumouriez did not receive his orders until the 31st, ten days after the execution of Louis XVI, and too late to anticipate the outbreak of war with England. As soon as the news of the king's death (January 21st) was known in London, Chauvelin was required by an Order in Council, dated the 24th, to leave the country. At Blackheath, on his way to Dover, he met a French courier carrying instructions, dated the 22nd, for his return to Paris. On February 1st the French republic declared war on England.

Seeing the position in which France found herself in February, '93, it was a pity that the war could not be waged on paper. Her politicians were ready with admirable plans for conducting and financing military operations; but her armies and her *assignats* were rapidly depreciating in value.

Edmond-Louis-Alexis Dubois-Crancé had spent thirteen years of his youth in the King's Guard at Versailles: he had been one of the most active and useful members of the Military and Finance Committees in the National Assembly of '89: he had since served in the republican army. No deputy in the Convention knew so much as he did about military organization. On January 25th he brought forward a plan for the recruitment of three hundred thousand volunteers, and for the creation of eight armies, totalling more than half a million men. Some of these armies were to stand on the defensive on the southern frontiers. One was to be detailed for the invasion of England —an enterprise often planned, and at last thought feasible 'under the regime of liberty.' The rest were for the main offensive against Austria and Prussia. Dubois-Crancé followed up this proposal, on February 7th, with a consequential scheme for the fusion of the old army with the new. The regulars were to be diluted with volunteers. Two volunteers were to serve by the side of each professional soldier. The pay and the conditions of service were to be the same for all, except that volunteers need not sign on for more than one campaign. The men were to choose their own officers, a proportion of places being reserved for members of the old army. This *amalgame*, as it was called, cleverly combined the virtues of two systems, and laid the foundations of the *grande armée*.

About the same time Sieyès, applying his mathematical mind to military affairs, and deserting precedent for 'the natural fitness of things,' evolved what Saint-André called a 'metaphysical' division of the War Office into three parts—a *ministère*, a *directoire*, and an *administration*; whilst Cambon, announcing that this was to be a Money War, and reviewing the financial situation (which was none of the best, seeing that the last four years had barely yielded the tax of one), proposed to pay for the war by a fresh issue of *assignats* to the value of forty millions sterling.

Whilst Cambon's *assignats* were still in the press, and Sieyès' metaphysical War Office before the assembly, and long before Dubois-Crancé's recruits could be enrolled, Dumouriez was facing a fresh crisis on the northern frontier. He had left Paris on January 26th 'with despair in his heart.' His plan for the invasion of Holland was to advance in the centre on Dordrecht and Rotterdam, whilst his right was guarded by Miranda in the Aix-Maestricht region, and his left by Dutch insurgents in Zeeland. But already the decree of December 15th had filled all Belgium—his base of operations, and his line of retreat—with seething discontent. Soon the king's execution made it certain that England would come into the war on the side of her Dutch allies. The Austrian army behind the Meuse grew stronger every day. His own troops were weakened by inaction, desertion, and lack of supplies. His army stood at little more than half its former strength.

Yet the real danger of the coming campaign did not rest in these discouraging circumstances. In a military emergency Dumouriez's elastic courage might well carry him on a rebound from despair to victory. The crisis was not on the battle-field, but in the mind of the general. It was no secret among Dumouriez's friends in Paris that he detested the Girondin government. His feud with Pache, the Rolandist Minister of War, was notorious. But the replacement of Pache by his friend Beurnonville, which Danton secured on March 4th, did not reconcile him to the policy and administration of the Executive Council. As a soldier he would defend the Belgian frontiers. As a soldier he would even have a gambler's throw at the invasion of Holland. But as a politician—and the revolution had inextricably mixed the rôles—his ambition was to settle the war by negotiation, and to use his army against the French government.

On February 3rd he wrote hopefully from Antwerp about the interview he hoped to have with Lord Auckland, the British ambassador, with a view to a peaceful settlement. He did not know that France and England had already been two days at war. The negotiations never took place. Dumouriez, with a fresh grievance against the Girondin government, fell back on an alternative scheme. He would use his position in the Netherlands to set up that country as an independent state. With the Netherlands as a bribe he might still purchase British neutrality, or at least British inaction. With the Netherlands as a threat he could coerce Paris into getting rid of the Girondin government, if not of republicanism. The ultimate issue might be a monarchical restoration: it might be an Orléans regency for the Dauphin: it might be a military dictatorship. His mercurial mind was ready for any eventuality. Meanwhile he would conceal his designs beneath an apparent acquiescence.

There is some reason to think that at this juncture in his career Dumouriez was not only an intriguer, but also a traitor. On April 26th the Swedish ambassador at St. Petersburg informed his government that the Empress had recently received particulars of an arrangement between Dumouriez and Clerfayt, one of Coburg's commanders, under which the attack on Holland, and the dispositions of the French armies on the Meuse and the Rhine, had been concerted with the Austrians before the beginning of the campaign. If the Baron de Stedinck was correctly informed, Dumouriez never intended his invasion of Holland to succeed; Miranda's defeat had been arranged; and Neerwinden was a move in the game which brought Dumouriez's army within striking distance of Paris.

Whatever the truth of this story, which gained credit from Dumouriez's reputation for intrigue, the campaign fell out as might have been foretold. Before the French centre reached Dordrecht, the right, under Miranda, collapsed, and Dumouriez's communications were compromised. At first he persisted in his advance. It was not till March 8th that he obeyed a peremptory order from Paris, and retired. Soon the retreating armies were defending themselves in the heart of Belgium. On March 18th they were disastrously defeated at Neerwinden, east of Louvain.

Now was the opportunity for Dumouriez to carry out his move against the government. Already, a week before the battle (March 11th), he had issued proclamations annulling Cambon's decree of December 15th. Plate taken from the Belgian churches was to be restored: revolutionary clubs were to be closed: emissaries of the government were to be arrested. On the 12th he had written defiantly to the Convention, blaming the War Office for the loss of Holland. Danton and Delacroix, who had recently returned from Belgium with particulars of Miranda's reverse, were at once despatched to recall Dumouriez to a sense of his duties. They met him at Louvain, two days after Neerwinden, amid the debris of his army, quite unrepentant. He refused to withdraw his proclamation of March 11th or his letter of March 12th, saying that his attitude was entirely justified by the conduct of the government. All he would do was to ask the assembly to suspend judgement until they received the report of this interview. According to Danton, their conversation then moved onto more dangerous ground. Dumouriez showed the commissioners a letter he had received from Roland, asking his help for a scheme to destroy the Jacobin party, and especially Danton. Whatever passed between them, Dumouriez remained in command of his army, and the commissioners returned to Paris.

Whilst they were on their way, Dumouriez opened communications with the enemy. On the 25th he had a conversation with an Austrian officer afterwards known to history as Quartermaster-general Mack. It was agreed between them that the Austrian army, which had been following the French retreat as politely as Dumouriez had followed Brunswick the year before, should halt at the frontier, whilst the French commander marched on Paris.

The next day another group of emissaries arrived from the capital. Roland's letter had asked Dumouriez's help for the Girondins against the Jacobins. Proli, Pereira, and Dubuisson came on behalf of the Jacobin club, to offer him their help in the dissolution of the Girondin Convention, on condition that he set up a Jacobin dictatorship. Dumouriez, in reply, made no secret of his wish to dissolve the Convention. But his object in doing so, he said, was to restore the constitutional monarchy of 1791; and the only rôle for which he cast the Jacobins was that of his assistants in saving the queen's life, and in dispersing the seven hundred and forty-five tyrants of the Convention. A few days later (April 2nd) following an official letter from Lille, Beurnonville, the Minister of War, with three commissioners of the Convention, came himself to Tournai. His instructions were to deprive Dumouriez of his command, and to bring him under arrest to Paris. Three more commissioners stayed behind at Lille. They may well have doubted whether a self-willed general at the head of his troops would so easily capitulate to a handful of politicians armed only with the majesty of the law. Dumouriez, having nothing to gain by compliance, promptly arrested Beurnonville and his companions, and handed them over to his Austrian friends, to be held as hostages for the safety of the prisoners in the Temple. They were, in fact, exchanged, two years later, for Madame Royale, the only survivor of that unhappy family.

Dumouriez had now burnt his boats, and made a supreme attempt to carry his army towards Paris. But it was a hopeless venture. The artillery refused to move. He was outlawed by the remaining commissioners at Lille. He escaped the bullets of his own men only by galloping into the enemy's lines. A few days later an English traveller saw him at Stuttgart, bowing to the crowd, as he got into his carriage and took the road for Ratisbon and Vienna—'A little man with a red face, and looked clever.' So for the second time in two years France showed that it would not be dictated to by its generals.

Whilst the generals and politicians were intriguing to destroy the government, the people were rallying to save the country. In Paris the call for troops was answered almost as enthusiastically as the year before. Within five days five hundred volunteers had left for the front, and within ten days nearly four thousand. True, they were ill-armed, ill-disciplined, and ill-fed. The ordinary difficulties of an extemporized army were increased by the crowds of women who insisted on marching with them; nor had any provision as yet been made for families who stayed behind, deprived of their wage-earners. It had not been foreseen that munition-workers and civil servants would desert their comfortable posts to go to the front. All kinds of unexpected problems were raised by the very patriotism of the Parisians.

This spirit was not shared in some of the outlying provinces. On the same day as Dumouriez's defeat at Neerwinden news was received of a serious insurrection in the west. Sunday, March 10th, was the date fixed for the first enrolment in the national levy of three hundred thousand volunteers. In the Vendée, the coastal department lying between La Rochelle and the mouth of the Loire, March 10th was the signal for an armed rising in almost every centre of recruitment. On the 11th a body of fifteen hundred men attacked Machecoult in the neighbouring department of Loire Inférieure, and murdered the commandant of the National Guard, the constitutional *curé*, the *juge de paix*, and many others. Another three thousand insurgents defeated republican troops at Saint-Florent, and sacked the headquarters of the district. At Jalais, two days later, Jacques Cathelineau started his career as a leader of revolt by routing a government post. On the 14th he won the first battle of the civil war by overwhelming the village of Chémillé, with its two hundred defenders. On the 15th he repeated his success over five hundred republicans at Cholet. The whole of the Vendée was now up in arms.

The rising was of a kind and on a scale that might have embarrassed any government. Of the three hundred thousand inhabitants of the Vendée, some seventy-five per cent were scattered in small villages throughout the roadless labyrinth of rough hills and narrow valleys called the Bocage. It was an ideal country for guerrilla fighting, and almost impossible for scientific warfare. Dumouriez himself was reported to have said, 'If I wanted to wage a civil war, I should choose the Vendée.' The people were amongst the most ignorant, cruel, and religious in the country. They lived on familiar terms with a boorish squirearchy. They obeyed every behest of a pious and fanatical clergy. They suspected and disliked the bourgeoisie of their few small towns, who tried to enforce the regulations of a distant and almost foreign government.

The Vendeans had taken part in the *jacquerie* of '89, and had snatched the benefits which the revolution offered them. But they had done so too easily to feel grateful for their improved lot, or to exhibit anything better than a cupboard-love patriotism. They had been easily roused against the Civil Constitution of '90–91 by priests who did not so much resent the nationalization of church property as the secular spirit in which the assembly had carried it out, and who might have accepted the popular election of bishops and clergy if it had not carried with it the obligation of the civil oath. Nowhere in the country was so much passion spent in the vendetta against the *assermenté* clergy. Nowhere was the *curé intrus* more likely to be chased out of the parish, or to have the parsonage burnt over his head. By the side of the priest who had refused the oath stood the squire who longed to avenge the death of the king, the farmer who would not sell his corn for depreciated paper-money, and the peasant who did not see why his sons should be marched off by a government he disliked to fight an enemy he had never seen.

Thus, though the levy of February, '93, called for only four thousand men out of a population of three hundred thousand, it rekindled all the old resentments into a sudden blaze of violence and vengeance. The movement had its charter too. A declaration from twenty-one parishes which was read in the Convention on March 23rd demanded 'No enlistment, no forced labour (*corvée*), no requisitioning, no taxation without local consent, no searching of houses, and complete freedom of worship, speech, and publication.' Grievances, however legitimate, could not be discussed with rebels. For the moment the government must fight for its life against a civil as well as a foreign foe; against women who believed that the 'Blues' (as they called the republican troops) would eat their infants; and against men who went into battle fresh from absolution, and were convinced that if they were killed they would rise again the third day, and go straight to heaven.

The assembly showed its alarm at the situation by decreeing the death penalty (March 19th) for all rebels taken with arms in their hands, and the confiscation of all their goods. For a month attempts were made to stem the revolt with local detachments of National Guards, and with a few regular troops detached from the Belgian front. But all that could be done by such means was to localize the insurrection. The treachery and desertion of Dumouriez had already damaged the Girondin party. Their inactivity and irresolution in face of this fresh crisis seriously shook their position in the Convention and in the country. Their Jacobin opponents spied an opportunity to compass their downfall.

Now was seen the inconvenience of government by a democratic assembly without a party system. The seven hundred and fifty members of the National Convention had been elected without regard to any political grouping or party programme. Their primary duty was, indeed, neither to legislate, nor to rule, but to draw up a constitution. The Executive Council of ministers had been appointed by the assembly, but was not constitutionally accountable to it. The standing committees which advised the Convention and the special committees which supervised the ministry were expedients hardly consistent with a healthy 'separation of powers.' As visitors to Oxford or Cambridge look in vain for the University, so visitors to the Convention looked in vain for the Government. There was none. The government policy was the view of the majority of the members present and voting upon each separate issue. The government personnel was the group of speakers which most commonly commanded the assent of the House. Consistency and continuity of policy could be secured only if such a group succeeded in packing the committees with their supporters, appointing their friends to ministerial or administrative posts, and carrying the divisions in the assembly by their eloquence or by their intrigues. They might also exploit their views in the clubs, the sections, and the press. If they failed, there was no law or custom of the constitution which compelled them to resign. If they fell, there was no Opposition to take their place. Some other group, perhaps, might be able to make a better use of their methods, and achieve in its turn a temporary ascendancy.

But how could a new government be formed? In the last resort, parliament would look to the people to get it out of its difficulties, not by a general election, but by an appeal to force. If the representatives of the sovereign people could not rid themselves of a group of deputies whose policy had lost the confidence of the country, the sovereign people itself must exercise its constitutional right of insurrection, and force a new group and a new policy upon the national assembly. A change of government could only be brought about by something resembling a fresh revolution. Since the assembly resided in Paris, the sovereign people meant the active citizens of the sections. The party that commanded the capital could control the revolution.

The moment for popular intervention has not yet come. The *deus ex machina* must be kept for the last scene of the political drama. During the first five months of 1793 the stage is being set for the climax of June 2nd. The Girondin group had seized power during the scramble for the spoils of royalism six months before. It is now being gradually extruded from the key positions in the government and administration. For the partisans and nominees of Girondism are gradually being substituted the partisans and nominees of Jacobinism. The governing party is being pricked and harried round the arena until the time comes for the *coup-de-grâce* of a popular insurrection.

Only two members of the Provisional Executive Council of August, '92, remained in office till June, '93. They were Clavière, the Minister of Finance, and Lebrun, the Minister for Foreign Affairs. On January 21st, after defying constant attacks in the press, the clubs, and the Convention, Roland was challenged by Robespierre and Danton to publish the accounts of his *bureau d'esprit public*, and this institution was suppressed. None of the Girondins would take up the defence of their most unpopular minister. The next day he resigned. Only Louvet made some attempt to carry on his unlucky campaign against Paris. Roland was succeeded at the Ministry of the Interior by the cautious and colourless Garat. The unchallenged organization of a considerable espionage system soon afterwards showed how artificial had been the agitation against Roland's *bureau*. At the War Office the Girondins had been able for a few weeks (February 4th–March 29th) to replace their great disappointment, Pache, by Dumouriez's friend, the Marquis de Beurnonville. He was now, by that friend's action, in an Austrian prison. His successor, Jean-Baptiste-Noel Bouchotte, was a soldier who had risen from the ranks, and a thorough-going Jacobin. Jean Dalbarade, who replaced Monge as Minister of Marine on April 10th, was another Jacobin, a nominee of Danton. Louis-Jérôme Gohier, who became Minister of Justice on March 20th, had been Garat's understudy, and carried on his negative policy. Thus by the middle of April the Girondins had lost practically all hold on the executive and administrative side of the government.

The Jacobin capture of the ministries might have mattered less, if the Girondins had still controlled the special committees which, in the emergency of the spring of '93, took over so many ministerial functions. But the *comité de sûreté générale* set up in October, '92, had been reduced in January '93, from thirty to twelve members, all of whom were Jacobins; and the more powerful *comité de salut public*, which replaced the *comité de défense générale*, was similarly reduced from twenty-five to nine (afterwards twelve) members, of whom seven belonged to the non-party Centre, and two, Danton and Delacroix, to the Jacobin Left.

As with the special committees, so with the standing committees. When the Convention began its work in September, '92, it followed the precedent of the previous assemblies by appointing twenty-one standing committees representative of all parties in the House. The membership of these committees remained substantially the same until the autumn of '93. It would be uninforming as well as tedious to inquire how far the Girondin influence on them yielded to Jacobin influence, owing to the casual replacements that came about during these twelve months through death or resignation. Where party feeling ran highest, as in the Constitutional Committee, it was in any case easier for the Jacobins to obstruct their Girondin rivals than to remove them; and it was almost as effective.

In a modern legislature it is easy to tell the state of a government majority by an analysis of the division lists, or by the number of lines under a party whip. The Convention had no party organization, and seldom divided by *appel nominal*. Only one division during this period can fairly be appealed to as a test of party allegiance—that on the impeachment of Marat; and on that occasion more than half the deputies were not in the House. There is, however, one safe indication of party strength—the fortnightly election of Presidents and Secretaries of the assembly. Of the nineteen Presidents and sixty-six Secretaries who held office between September 20th, '92, and May 30th, '93, nine Presidents and twenty-eight Secretaries came from the group of sixty-three deputies who can fairly be called the nucleus of the Girondin party. If the whole party, as designated in the proscription lists drawn up by their rivals, numbered a hundred and eighty-three out of the seven hundred and fifty members of the Convention, it appears that they nominated to these key positions more than four times as many candidates as their proportion entitled them to do. This preponderance continued up to the eve of the June revolution. Out of the last five Presidents elected before the end of May, four were Girondins.

Thus whilst the Girondin party was losing its hold on the ministries and the committees, it still retained its majority in the assembly. Indeed, it took some trouble to do so. It is noticeable that not one of the sixty-three leading Girondins appears among the eighty-two representatives sent out on civil mis-

ions under the decree of March 8th, and only one among the fifty-eight sent
out on military missions under the decree of April 30th. But this manœuvre
defeated its own ends. The Jacobins might be lost to the assembly. Scattered
over the provinces, and among the armies, they had every opportunity to
spread their opinions, and could all the more effectively appeal for outside
help to eject the Girondin leaders from their artificial stronghold in the
Convention.

In Paris itself the future lay with the party which could control the press,
the clubs, and the sections. The remnants of the royalist party still attacked
Jacobins and Girondins with impartial spite. But the royalist papers had disappeared with the fall of the throne. Suleau and Bonnefoy had been murdered; du Rozoy had been executed; the royalist presses had been broken
up; the 'royal' type had been handed over to Marat. Since the rout of the
royalist press the field of journalism had been disputed between their victors.
On the Girondin side were Brissot's *Patriote français*, Gorsas' *Courrier*,
Dulaire's *Thermomètre*, Carra's *Annales patriotiques*, Condorcet's *Chronique*,
and Louvet's *Sentinelle*. On the Jacobin side were Marat's new paper, the
Journal de la république, Fréron's *L'Orateur*, and Hébert's *Père Duchesne*.
The Girondins had the better of it, both in the number and quality of their
papers. It was no accident that on March 9th their opponents forced a
decree through the House requiring deputies who were also editors to opt
between professions which gave them a plural voice in politics. It was no
accident that the Jacobin rioters of March 10th began their operations by
breaking up the printing-presses of the *Patriote*, the *Annales*, and the
Courrier. Soon Desmoulins' malicious *Histoire des brissotins* (May 19th)
and the inflammatory pamphlet *Rendez-nous nos dix-huit francs* by the
Cordelier Lebois overwhelmed the enemies of the Mountain, and indeed
the whole central party of the Marsh, with every sort of accusation. The
more incredible the charges were, the more likely they were to be believed.

But the spoken word was, if less pervasive than print, more direct in its
appeal. It was through the clubs, the sectional meetings, and the popular
societies that the Jacobins were best able to organize, almost unopposed, the
armed intervention of the sovereign people.

There were at this time, particularly in the southern and eastern districts
of Paris, too many unhappy members of the class who, in the words of a
government spy, 'begin life in the workhouse (*la Pitié*), and end it in Bedlam
(Bicêtre): who spend fifty shillings a week when they have as much, and
five shillings when they have no more, so that they never have anything in
their pockets, and cannot save.' These are the people, Dutard goes on to say,
who helped in the storming of the Bastille, and in the attack on the Tuileries;
who form the *claques* in the gallery of the assembly, and the audiences at the
Palais-Royal; and who are ready to rise again, if only from envy of those who
have never had to pawn their watches and their jewellery to pay the butcher
and the baker. These men knew little of the revolution except that it had

left them as poor as it found them. They could have given little account of the democratic theory which allowed them to impersonate the sovereign people. They had neither the initiative nor the discipline to organize an insurrection. But so long as they remained ill-housed and ill-fed, and were not compelled to enter the army, they would, for free beer, or a franc a day shoulder a pike, and march into the West End, to do as their temporary employers told them. Hitherto they had confined themselves to such shop breaking expeditions as that of February 25th–26th, instigated by Marat and led by Jacques Roux. But at any moment they might be exploited by more dangerous leaders, and for more political ends.

The difficulties and dangers of the situation in the spring of 1793 were apparent to any independent observer. In an interesting letter to Danton dated May 6th, Tom Paine analysed the position as he saw it. He has stayed on in France, he says, instead of returning to America, in the hope of seeing the principles of the revolution spread throughout Europe. Now he despairs of this event. The internal state of France is such that the revolution itself is in danger. The way in which provincial deputies are insulted by the Parisians will lead to a rupture between the capital and the departments unless the Convention is moved elsewhere. France should profit by American experience in this matter, and hold its Congress outside the limits of any municipality. American experience shows (he thinks) that the *maximum* (price-control) cannot be worked on a national, but only on a municipal basis. Paine also insists on the need of staying the inflation of the paper currency. But the greatest danger he signalizes is 'the spirit of denunciation that now prevails.' 'Calumny is a species of treachery that ought to be punished as well as any other kind of treachery. It is a private vice productive of public evils; because it is possible to irritate men into disaffection by continual calumny.' Paine was right. But his own friends of the Girondin party were principally to blame for what had happened; and now it was too late to avert their punishment.

The first sign of what might follow was given by the 'days of March' (March 8th–10th, '93). The news of Miranda's reverse in Belgium had much the same effects in Paris as the news of the fall of Longwy and Verdun six months before. Now, as then, Danton was the man who rode in the whirlwind, if he did not (as his enemies alleged) direct the storm. On January 31st he had linked the reunion of Belgium with the attainment of the 'natural frontiers' of France—the Atlantic, the Rhine, the Alps, and the Pyrenees. On March 8th he carried a decree for the raising of fresh troops and deputies were sent round the sections, and into the departments, 'to beg them, in the name of the country, to fly to the help of their brethren in Belgium.' On March 9th, in order to engage public sympathy, Danton secured the release of all persons imprisoned for debt. On the same day he supported a more dangerous demand, already made by Desfieux and Carra, for the set ting up of a special court to punish enemy agents. The Assembly raised cries of 'September!' Danton retorted that if such a court as he proposed had existed six months ago, the prison massacres would have been averted. In point of fact the tribunal of August 17th had failed to prevent the September massacre; and the *tribunal extraordinaire* which was now set up was destined to exploit rather than to restrain the 'justice of the people.'

Paris was not slow to respond to these incitements. Manifestos issued by the Cordeliers club, the *société des fédérés*, and the *Quatre nations* section threatened vengeance on Dumouriez and his Girondin supporters. On March 9th an Insurrectional Committee proposed to march on the Convention, and to expel the *appelans*—the deputies who had voted for the plebiscite during the king's trial. Santerre's National Guards, aided by the Brest *fédérés*, prevented in the first week of March a *coup d'état* which they promoted in the last week of May. What might have been an insurrection became a riot. A Jacobin crowd attacked the headquarters of the Girondin press. The offices of Condorcet's *Chronique* were sacked; and Gorsas escaped over his garden wall, whilst a mob broke up the printing-presses of the *Courrier*.

Was there any ulterior design behind these activities? Were the March days a riot that went wrong? Should it have led to a political revolution? Little importance need, perhaps, be attached to the arrest of Fournier *l'Américain* on the charge of threatening to murder Pétion, or to Vergniaud's assertion that March 9th had been intended as 'a St Bartholomew's Eve for patriots.' But was it a pure accident that Dumouriez chose this very moment for his acts of defiance against the Girondin government? Was it a pure accident that Danton, whose call for volunteers started the crisis in Paris at a moment so convenient for Dumouriez's plan of intervention, should choose this moment (March 10th) to attack the Executive Council, and to propose the abolition of the rule which excluded deputies from the ministry? Though he was careful to disclaim any ambition to be himself a minister, the *Patriote* published a list in which he figured amongst a group of his associates as Minister of Foreign Affairs; and there was no lack of enemies who accused him openly of aiming at a dictatorship. Robespierre, in the notes he supplied to Saint-Just for his indictment of the Dantonists, accused Danton on no better evidence than hearsay (*on m'a assuré*) of having offered to finance the insurrection which would give Dumouriez an opportunity to march on the capital. The Robespierrist Arthur repeated this charge at the Jacobins a year later. Two years later Barère repeated it again in a report to his constituents which he embodied in his untrustworthy Memoirs. This testimony is of little value, unless on the principle that 'what I say three times is true.' But it gains a little credit from the ambiguous and perhaps suspicious conduct of Danton in his dealings with Dumouriez; and it is not unbelievable in view of Danton's part in the movement which brought him to the scaffold a year later.

The sequel to the March days was not long delayed. On April 1st the insurrectional committee of March 9th reappeared as a *comité central de salut public, correspondant avec les départements*. Its originators were the same 'ten or twelve persons who habitually met at the café Corazza, to drink beer,' signalized in Garat's report of March 19th, but exculpated by his slackness or cowardice from responsibility for the previous disorders. They included Collot d'Herbois, Chabot, Proli, Desfieux, Guzman, Tallien, Varlet, and Lajowski. They met at the Évêché or Archevêché, the twelfth-century episcopal palace standing on the south side of Notre Dame, in the Jacobin section *de la Cité*. Their aims were to 'save the state' (*salut public*), to correspond with the departments, and to insist on the right of every constituency to control the votes, and, if necessary, to revoke the powers of its representatives. Their summary programme was a simpler one: Down with the Gironde!

A few days later (April 5th) the Jacobin club, under the presidency of Marat, issued an inflammatory address to the departments. 'Friends,' it said, 'we are betrayed. To arms! There is counter-revolution in the government, and in the National Convention. There, in the citadel of our hopes, our criminal representatives pull the strings of the plot they have contrived with a horde of despots coming to cut our throats!' Such a challenge could not be ignored. Answering an attack by Robespierre on April 12th, Guadet read it out to the deputies, and demanded the impeachment of its author. By two hundred and twenty votes to ninety-two, a motion was carried for the indictment of Marat. The *appel nominal* showed the parliamentary strength of Girondism, and has been used as a clue to the membership of the party. But the majority were living in a fool's paradise. Twelve days later Marat was triumphantly acquitted by the new *tribunal extraordinaire*.

Paris had turned down its thumb against the Girondin government. Marat's acquittal was the signal for execution. Two days later representatives of thirty-five sections met at the Mairie, and drew up a list of twenty-two Girondin deputies, 'guilty of the crime of felony against the sovereign people.' Next day the mayor himself presented this list to the Convention, demanding, in the name of Paris, their expulsion from the assembly. The Convention characterized the petition as an insult; but this did not prevent the commune from sending a fresh deputation on April 20th to defend its view. This time the Jacobins were strong enough to carry a vote giving the petitioners 'the honours of the session.' There the matter rested for the moment. The commune was not yet in a position to press its advantage. But the preparations for the attack went on.

A month later came a counter-attack by the Gironde. It was led by their most alarmist orator, Maximin Isnard, who was in the chair of the assembly from May 16th to May 30th. The occasion was the continuance and recrudescence of insurrectional meetings held at the Mairie, and with the connivance of the city police. As the Minister of the Interior seemed unable to enforce order, the Girondins sought to do so by direct action. Guadet had proposed the suspension of the municipality. On Barère's motion a less provocative step was taken. A *commission extraordinaire* of twelve members was set up, to inquire into the recent proceedings of the commune and sections. Three days later (May 24th) this body ordered the arrest of those whom it regarded as the ring-leaders of the insurrectional movement—Michel and Marino of the police department, Varlet of the Post Office, Brichet of the *messageries*, and Hébert, *substitut-procureur* of the commune, and editor of *Père Duchesne*. On the 27th two more men were arrested—Dobsen and Protain of the section *de la Cité*—because they had refused to submit their minutes to the scrutiny of the commission. The resentment of the commune at these arbitrary acts was reflected in a snap vote in the assembly which dissolved the commission (May 27th). Before it could be reinstated, the opportunity was taken to release its prisoners. The reception of Hébert by the commune, and of Varlet by the *Droits de l'homme* section, was a defeat for the Girondins hardly less ominous than the acquittal of Marat.

The opportunity was not missed by the sections, which for six months had been watching every move of the Girondin party, and working on its weaknesses. On the night of May 30th the sovereign people was once more in travail, and gave birth to three committees—one of twelve members of the Paris department and sections, one of nine delegates of the sections, and one of twenty-five, which included the majority of these two committees along with some additional members. This was the final embodiment of the *comité central révolutionnaire* which was to organize the coming insurrection. Most of its members were comparatively young men, and little known. Varlet had, indeed, made his name as an agitator; Hassenfratz held an important post in the War Office; Dobsen had been foreman of the jury in the tribunal of August 17th; Rousselin edited the *Feuille du salut public*. But who had ever heard of the printer Marquet, who presided over the Central Committee, or of its secretary Tombe? Who had ever heard of the painter Simon of the Halle-au-Bled section, of the toy-maker Bonhommet, of Auvray, an usher from Montmartre, of Crépin the decorator, of Caillieaux the ribbon-maker, or of the *déclassé* aristocrat Duroure, who haunted the gambling-saloons of the Palais-Royal? What speculations might not be suggested by the note still legible in the margin of Hanriot's marching orders for June 1st—*Bonsoir, ma bonne amie; vous êtes fort jolie?* Yet these unknown men were the voice of the people; and their banner, with the brave inscription, *Insurrection et Vigueur*, was to lead the march on the national parliament. They were all Parisians; and it might be noticed, at a time when public disorder was too readily put down to foreign intrigue, that they were all Frenchmen: for the Spaniard Guzman was expelled from the committee, almost as soon as he appeared on it, as *un intrigant bien suspect*.

These men were not novices in revolution. Their plan was clear and confident. It was to be an orderly and bloodless insurrection. The technique of August 10th would be used again, with Lenin-like precision—but with a difference. No armed resistance was to be expected from the present occupants of the Tuileries. François Hanriot, the hard-faced ex-clerk of the *octroi*, newly appointed commandant of the National Guard, need not fire a shot. Nor, since the poorer patriots were to be paid a penny an hour for their services, was time any great object. So, from the ringing of the tocsin at three o'clock on Friday morning, May 31st, till after sunset on Sunday, June 2nd, the contest of wills went on, between the rival representatives of France and Paris, the Convention and the commune, the Tuileries and the Town Hall.

Hanriot's first care was to seize the key positions—the Arsenal, the Place royale, and the Pont neuf. Next the barriers were closed, and prominent suspects arrested: they included Madame Roland (her husband escaped) and Clavière. In a tumultuous meeting of the assembly the Jacobins carried a decree finally abolishing the Commission of Twelve. There for the moment the insurrection halted. Both parties went to bed not dissatisfied with the day's work, and relieved that no blood had been shed. June 1st too passed quietly. But by the evening Hanriot had placed four hundred men and thirty-two guns outside the Tuileries. Inside the building a number of deputies, mostly of the Left, reassembled to deal with an ultimatum from the commune, requiring them to decree the arrest of their Girondin colleagues. This request, to gain time, they referred to the *comité de salut public.*

No more grace was allowed. Early on June 2nd another deputation from the commune demanded an immediate answer to their ultimatum. When it was refused, they retired, shaking their fists at the deputies of the Right. All this day the Convention sat behind closed doors. Within, the spectators in the public galleries clamoured for the resignation or arrest of the Girondin leaders. Without, some three to four thousand Vendée volunteers, flanked by Hanriot's guns, and backed by a vast crowd of citizens in their Sunday garb, exercised the silent but relentless pressure of the sovereign people. In answer to Barère's appeal to their generosity, a few of the victims—Isnard, Fauchet, Lanthenas, Dusaulx, Barbaroux—consented to their suspension. Lanjuinais refused, saying that the deputies were no longer free agents, and emboldened them to declare the sitting over. They made an attempt to leave the Tuileries. When they appeared at the doors, headed by their President, Hérault de Séchelles, they found both the court and the terrace barred by an angry crowd. In the Place du Carrousel Hanriot met their challenge by ordering his troops to stand to arms. At the Pont-tournant Marat, though himself a deputy, urged the soldiers to hold firm. The few voices raised in favour of the Girondins were drowned by cries of 'Bleed the Convention!' (*Purgez la convention: tirez le mauvais sang!*). The deputies could do nothing but return to their seats, and accept Couthon's motion for the suspension and internment (*arrestation chex eux*) of twenty-nine Girondin members, together with the ministers Clavière and Lebrun.

'To-day a palace, to-morrow a prison' (*Aujourd'hui sur le trône, et demain dans les fers*): such, writes Madame Roland from her cell in the Abbaye, is the righteous man's reward. The Girondin memoir-writers never ceased to assert, in louder and less philosophical language, not only their righteousness, but also the brutality of their treatment. Yet there was truth in the almost apologetic contention of the Jacobins that June 2nd was a triumph of constitutional reason over unconstitutional reaction. The sovereign people, they maintained, had merely reasserted its rights against a government which had ceased to represent its views; and it had done so by the only means known to the law—what Augustin Robespierre called a 'moral insurrection.' The right of petition had been backed by a threat of force, no more.

Not only so. On May 30th the crowds in the market had dropped on their knees as a procession of the Host passed by. The insurrection had been carried out with an almost ritualistic solemnity. The Jacobin club and the sections had publicly resolved to stake their lives on the security of property (*de mourir plutôt que de laisser porter atteinte aux propriétés*). Not a drop of blood had been shed; not a pane of glass had been broken. If there had been violence, it was no more than that used by the Commission of Twelve, when they arrested their Jacobin victims.

The Girondins owed their defeat as much to their friends as to their foes. The Committee of Public Safety had suggested the appointment of the Commission of Twelve, and had then failed to support it. The Paris department, the traditional enemy of the commune, antagonized by Roland, and influenced by the Cordelier Dufourny, had given a show of legality to the revolt by consenting to the formation of the Insurrectional Committee. The central party in the Convention, which had so long kept the Gironde in power, now voted for the suppression of the Twelve, and the arrest of the Twenty-nine. Such might be the fate of any political party that outstayed its welcome in a national assembly.

It had out-stayed its welcome in the country too. Wherever the commercial middle class controlled the local authorities, wherever they benefited by the sale of the national property, by the cheapening of production costs, and by a share in the contracts for the army, there Girondin republicanism had at first received firm support. But as soon as the incompetence of the government changed the hope of victory into fear of civil war, as soon as foreign markets were closed by the British blockade, this cupboard-love patriotism came round to the Jacobin side. Where its best friends thus betrayed it, Girondism was not likely to find much support among the town and country workers, who suffered from the economic effects of victory as well as of defeat, and to whom small differences of political colour were imperceptible. The country-people would take their cue from the priests, to whom all anti-clericals were obnoxious, or from the Parisians, who had turned down their thumbs against the Girondins. The Popular Society of Besançon had despatched a representative to Paris. He carried an address urging the Jacobins and Girondins of the assembly to compose their quarrels in the name of their common patriotism. Briot arrived in the capital at the end of May; but he found no opportunity to deliver his message until June 11th. Ten days had revolutionized the political outlook. He hurriedly turned his speech into an apologia for his department, and wrote to his friends at Besançon urging them to adhere to the victorious Jacobins.

It was the Jacobin contention that the expulsion of the Girondin deputies was necessary for the free and effective functioning of the national parliament. Only without them could the Convention give the country the lead for which it was asking. Only without them could the revolution return to its proper course, and hold on towards its true destiny. 'The men of July 14th and August 10th,' wrote Pache, the Jacobin mayor of Paris, to the departments, 'have risen once more. They have demanded the arrest of those who aimed at federalizing France, of those who, by libelling Paris in the departments, tried to kindle the flames of civil war. They have asked that attention should at last be paid to the necessities of the people, for whom and by whom the revolution was assuredly brought about.' Pache went on to say what those necessities were, in terms which must have been almost as embarrassing to the incoming Jacobins as bitter to the outgoing Girondins. 'Come,' he cries to the people, 'and tell us what you want—nay, what you demand. A constitution? Yes, it is for that we have risen, and our insurrection will not be in vain. The sovereignty of the people? Yes, we rose because it was outraged. Security of property? Yes, for it was to prevent its violation during a popular rising that we carried arms in our hands. Order and Peace? Yes, because they will never exist until we have got rid of intriguing and ambitious men who would destroy and partition the country. The defeat of an enemy whose presence defiles the soil of the republic? Yes, and we shall never exterminate them so long as we arm brother against brother, and cut one another's throats.'

On the new republican coinage, which was just beginning to appear, the table of the constitution was increasingly crowded out by unfamiliar symbols—the Roman fasces surmounted by the cap of liberty, the cock, the eye of vigilance, a bunch of grapes and a sheaf of corn, denoting a rather problematical abundance, the scales of justice, and the oak-leaves of victory. On Parisian house-fronts could now be seen the inscription, suggested by a resolution of the department on June 29th, *Unité, indivisibilité de la république: Liberté, Egalité, Fraternité, ou la mort*, surmounted by tricolour pendants, and caps of liberty.

Twice within a year Paris had saved France. For the second time it demanded as its reward the government of the people by the people.

CHAPTER XIX

FEDERALISM

En nous faisant naître à l'époque de la liberté naissante, le sort nous a placés comme les enfants perdus de l'armée qui doit combattre pour elle et la faire triompher; c'est à nous de bien faire nôtre tâche et de préparer ainsi le bonheur des générations suivantes.—(MADAME ROLAND: August 18th, 1790.)

WHEN Pache said that behind the rising of June 2nd was a popular demand for a constitution, he was expressing an important but an unpalatable truth. It was the desire for a constitution which had inspired the resistance of the National Assembly to the royal will in June, '89. It was the fear of destroying this constitution which induced its authors to restore the king to the throne in September, '91. It was to remodel the monarchical constitution on republican lines that the Convention had been summoned in September, '92. The wish to have a constitution was no less strong in June, '93, than it had been three years before. It was, perhaps, stronger. The country had grown used to constitutionalism, and was becoming unhappily aware that the dangers of arbitrary government had not disappeared with the execution of 'the tyrant,' Louis the Last. And yet eight months had passed since the inauguration of this new constitution-making assembly, and not a clause of the promised measure was yet on the statute-book. The constitution of 1791 was not, indeed, a *bloc*. It had been gradually brought into action: it did not suddenly disappear. But the whole of Tit. III, Cap. II–IV, dealing with the Monarchy and the Executive Power, would have to be recast in view of the abolition of the crown; and large changes were needed in Cap. I; for public opinion had long ago rejected the franchise imposed under the anti-republican reaction of 1791.

Republicanism was now the only wear. Though Louis' head still appeared on coins struck in Paris and at the provincial mints in the early months of 1793, yet, for the people as a whole, royalism had died on the scaffold of January 21st. Orleanism, long discounted by everybody who knew the Duke, was destroyed when, on September 15th, '92, the Paris commune voted him the surname Egalité, and when, four days later, the Paris electors appointed him, on a doubtful vote, the last of their deputies. Of foreign candidatures for the empty throne, that of the Duke of Brunswick did not survive his letter of July, '91, and his manifesto of July, '92; and the mere suggestion of the Duke of York ruined Carra's career. August 10th was a popular mandate for a democratic regime, a manhood franchise, and the right of the people to recall or overrule its representatives. This programme was soon found to be unattainable except under a republican constitution. The word *république* was, indeed, used on September 22nd only because it seemed absurd to speak of 1792 as 'the fourth year of Liberty,' The republic itself was not proclaimed. It was not even mentioned in the *Moniteur* till four days later. But this did not imply any lack of republican enthusiasm. The decree abolishing monarchy had been greeted in the streets with cries of *Vive la république!*; and the provinces had shown themselves quite as eager as the capital to welcome the new regime. The suspicion of federalism which America and Switzerland had attached to the word were removed by declaring, on September 25th, that 'the French republic is one and indivisible.' Even those deputies who could not forget July 17th were reconciled to the prospect of a republican constitution.

The constitutional Committee set up by the Convention on September 29th consisted—such was already the stress of party rivalry—of two Jacobins, Danton and Barère, four Brissotins, Brissot (later replaced by Barbaroux), Pétion, Vergniaud, and Gensonné, and three non-party men, Sieyès, Paine, and Condorcet, who were known to have ideas about constitution-making. Of these last, Sieyès' reputation made him indispensable; but fear or fastidiousness prevented him from contributing anything to what he must have foreseen would be regarded as a party document. Paine's ignorance of French confined him to submitting an important memoir, and to talking things over with his friend Condorcet. More help was given by another Girondin sympathiser from across the Channel. Early in November Brissot wrote to David Williams, asking him to come to Paris as a guest of the government, and to help in drafting the new constitution. The author of the *Letters on Political Liberty* accepted the invitation. He did not attend the meetings, but he submitted *Observations* on the constitution of 1791, and suggestions for its improvement, which were used by the Committee. The bulk of the work, both in discussion and drafting, fell upon Cordorcet.

A spoilt child of the eighteenth century, and a disciple of Turgot and the Encyclopaedists, Condorcet had been driven by a cold and incommunicable passion for human betterment into the ranks of the republicans, and was now the most distinguished apologist for Girondism. The constitution presented to the Convention on February 15th was essentially his work. Its elaborations were due to the refinements of his philosophic mind. Its failure was the measure of his unpopularity with both political parties. Its fate showed that France had outgrown the ideas of the eighteenth century.

What with Girondin indecision, Jacobin obstruction, and the hundreds of communications supplied, in answer to the invitation of October 19th, by amateur constitution-makers, over four months had already been consumed in drafting the new constitution, and the country was coming to regard the interim government as a permanency. Now another two months elapsed, whilst the committee adjourned, and the critics studied its work. When Condorcet faced the House again on April 17th, it was with the knowledge that his project had had a bad press, that the Jacobin club

Le citoyen Doulcet de pontécoulant est un lache
D'avoir Refusé de me défendre, lorsque la chose
était si facile. Celui qui la fait s'en est aquité
avec toute la Dignité pofable, je lui en conserve
ma reconnaissance jusqu'au dernier moment

Marie de Corday

CHARLOTTE CORDAY'S LAST MESSAGE

Written between her trial and execution. 'Le citoyen Doulcet de Pontécoulant est un lache d'avoir refusé de me défendre, lorsque la chose était si facile. Celui qui l'a fait s'en est acquitté avec toute la dignité possible. Je lui en conserve ma reconnaissance jusqu'au dernier moment. Marie de Corday.' (Her full name was Marie-Anne-Charlotte.)

359

was instructing a rival constitutional committee to draft an alternative measure, and that the Convention had set up a fresh committee of six members, from which his own name was markedly omitted, to report on the many constitutional projects sent in by private members, and other would-be legislators. Worse: everything of Girondin origin was now discredited by the disasters in Belgium, and by the rising in the Vendée. After some desultory discussions of the new Declaration of Rights, and a fortnight's debate on general issues, the assembly proceeded to consider the new measure clause by clause. By May 29th it had dealt with six out of the three hundred and sixty-eight articles of Condorcet's constitution.

By this time Paris was beginning its anti-Girondin insurrection. The *comité de salut public* suddenly reversed its obstructive policy, added to the Constitutional Committee five Jacobins—Hérault de Séchelles, Ramel, Saint-Just, Mathieu, and Couthon—and instructed them to produce a constitutional plan as quickly as possible. The work was done in a week. 'Those who construct oppressive governments, and anti-democratic systems (*i.e. the Girondins*)'—so the introductory report naïvely announced—'compile their schemes laboriously. Frenchmen who are true patriots (*i.e. the Jacobins*) have only to look into their hearts to find the republic written there.' What the new committee certainly found written on their hearts was a desire to win over the Girondin electorate. 'We were unanimous,' they admit in the same report, 'in wishing to produce as democratic a document as possible. We have an inner feeling that our constitution is perhaps one of the most popular ever drafted.'

When, just ten months later, Hérault de Séchelles was on trial for his life, it pleased his ruthless young accuser, Saint-Just, to decry his part in the constitution of '93. But it is certain that the draft submitted to the committee on June 9th, introduced into the Convention on the 10th, and adopted, in spite of Girondin obstruction, on the 24th, was substantially the work of this elegant aristocrat, amorist, and bibliophile, equally at home in a queen's boudoir and an actress's dressing-room, who passed across the revolutionary stage almost as rapidly as did his constitution from fame to oblivion.

It would be idle to study a constitution that never came into force, were it not that a comparison of Hérault's proposals with Condorcet's, and of both with the constitution of 1791, illustrates the difference between the Girondin and Jacobin points of view, and shows how far the revolution had drifted from its original moorings.

Here, for instance, is a third Declaration of the Rights of Man—rights which one might suppose sacred enough to have remained unchanged, at least for two years. In his preamble to it Hérault restores (with how much sincerity, who can tell?) the dedication to the Supreme Being that Girondin austerity, which Robespierre called 'atheism,' had removed.

The Rights themselves, in Condorcet's draft, are a historical charter, guaranteeing the social contract (*la base du pacte social*). In Hérault's constitution they become once more what Mirabeau had made them, and almost in Mirabeau's words—a standard of statesmanship.

In the Declaration, as in the body of the Jacobin document, there is evidence of the new rulers' intention to tighten the curb of government. Liberty, it is now noticed, follows Equality, instead of preceding it. The change might be thought accidental, but for others that go with it. A reference, more in the spirit of an electoral address than of a constitutional document, to 'recent memories of (*Girondin*) despotism' is coupled (Art. 7) with the granting of a fresh right—that of public petition and peaceful assembly. Condorcet had trusted the laws to guarantee society against oppression, and had been content to add that 'methods of resistance must be determined by the constitution'. Hérault, with a practical ruthlessness prophetic of the Jacobin regime, says bluntly (Art. 27), 'Any individual who usurps the sovereignty of the people shall be instantly put to death by free men,' and adds (Art. 35), 'When the government violates the rights of the people, insurrection is, for the people as a whole, or for any portion of it, the most sacred of its rights and the most indispensable of its duties.' Thus the Jacobins are commended for their recent rising, and armed against future oppression.

They are, it is true, deprived of any such public control over private property as might have encouraged their socialistic tendencies (Art. 16). But they are consoled by definite promises (where Condorcet could only offer vague assurances) of 'work or the dole' (Art. 21); and they are informed, in language new to the revolutionary statute-book, that 'the aim of society is the happiness of all (*le bonheur commun*), and that their rights are something not merely to be claimed, but to be enjoyed (*jouissance*, Art. 23).

When the reader passes to the body of the constitution, he finds that Condorcet's draft has been hurriedly but drastically revised in the Jacobin interest. It was cumbered with unnecessary detail; and it was designed to satisfy the national needs by what seemed to a good Girondin the obvious way—keeping his own party in power. Hérault, being pressed for time, summarised or ignored the complications. Being a good Jacobin, he tried to turn the Girondin devices to the discomfiture of their inventors.

He could not offer a wider franchise than Condorcet, who had already removed the disqualification of passive citizens and domestic servants. But he made a generous provision for foreigners, whom the Girondin proposals unaccountably omitted—a provision all the more remarkable at a moment when France was carrying on an unsuccessful war against a coalition of eight European states, helped by the seditious activities of resident aliens. He nearly granted his country-women the vote which they still lack, after a century and a half of political progress. He struck out Condorcet's requirement of a higher age (twenty-five) for candidates for election, and threw all offices open, as the Constituents had done, to men of twenty-one.

Condorcet's machinery for elections was not only exceedingly complicated—a fault which was remedied in the new constitution: it also contained the anti-democratic provision that every vote should be given in writing. The effect of this would be to disqualify a vast number of illiterate voters. The feudal and clerical country-side and the socialistic proletariate of the cities would both be disfranchised: the voting-power of the middle-class minority would be immensely multiplied. Hérault could hardly miss so obvious an opportunity. Jacobinism stands for free and equal franchise. 'Elections,' he announces, 'are conducted either by ballot or vivâ voce (à haute voix), at the choice of the voter. In no case may a primary assembly prescribe a single method of voting. The scrutineers accept the votes of those who, being unable to write, prefer to vote by ballot' (Art. 16–18). Moreover for the first time France is to have a system of direct election. The primary assemblies are grouped into réunions representing about fifty thousand citoyens. Each assembly votes directly for a deputy. The resulting votes are pooled at the centre of the réunion. The candidate who gets most votes, above an absolute majority, is elected. It is not clear how any single candidate could obtain a majority, unless all the assemblies of the réunion voted on the same list of names: this is presumed, but not provided for. Still, nothing could be more democratic.

The Girondins knew that they were losing control of the executive; the Jacobins wished to subordinate it to the Committee of Public Safety. Both therefore aimed at reducing the power of the ministry. Both covered their design by submitting the ministers to a form of popular election. Condorcet still kept seven distinct ministries, filled by direct election. Hérault set up a Ministerial Council (conseil exécutif) of twenty-four members, nominated by the legislature from a list of candidates elected by the departments. This unwieldy body could have no initiative. It would inevitably be subservient to the legislature which appointed it, and to the committee which supervised it. The ministers were to be housed under the same roof as the assembly, and could be summoned before it at any time (Art. 75–6). Only a short step remained to the Administrative Councils of April, '94.

Both constitutions made an important distinction between laws and decrees. Laws were enactments of a general and permanent character: decrees were of particular or local application, and subject to reconsideration. Condorcet, in his anxiety to prevent hasty legislation, had submitted both laws and decrees to an elaborate procedure. Every measure had to obtain two readings in the House. If it survived these, it was printed, and submitted to the scrutiny of a constantly changing committee (bureau). It might also be challenged by a referendum—an American device which Condorcet kept in reserve as the last weapon of conservatism. Hérault, by a master-stroke, kept some of these precautions, but for laws only; he exempted decrees from them all. Le corps législatif propose des lois, et rend des décrets. (Art. 53.) An examination of the topics that could be dealt with by decree shows how free the new legislature would have been to decide the most important questions of state without even the formality of printing. The only important concession made was the inclusion of the declaration of war under the category of laws. Even laws now escaped from the scrutiny of the *bureau*; and the referendum became practically unworkable (Art. 58–60). The Jacobins would use it against the Girondins to confirm their constitution. They would make sure that it could not be used against themselves.

There was one other significant change. In order to weaken the communes, the centres of Jacobin influence, and to subordinate them to the departments, the strongholds of Girondism, Condorcet had hit on the idea of regrouping the country population into *grandes communes*. These larger units were to be so composed that no cottager should be more than two and a half leagues from the grand-communal centre. This was to apply on a large scale the plan by which the sixty Paris districts had been regrouped into forty-eight sections; and it would have the same disorganizing and anti-democratic effects. Local loyalties would be broken up. Voting and debating would be discouraged. Accordingly Hérault returned to the forty thousand communes of 1791. To a Jacobin, who thought of the provinces not so much in terms of administration as in terms of voting power and popular propaganda, there could never be too many centres of national sovereignty.

Towards the end of the constitution of '93 there is abundant evidence that Hérault was unduly hurried. He excused his omissions by claiming that 'a republican charter must be concise,' and by leaving it to the new assembly to fill in the 'merely facultative and administrative details.' But there are so many gaps and loose ends in the document that it is difficult to suppose it was seriously intended for the statute-book. It bears all the signs of an attempt to supplant the Girondins in popular favour. It has much of the loose and rhetorical phrasing of an electoral address. Its submission to the country by the plebiscite of July was in effect a call for a vote of confidence in the authors of the recent insurrection.

On January 1st, '94, the official figures of the plebiscite were published, though the votes of over four hundred cantons were still missing. It appeared that the constitution had been approved by 1,801,918 votes to 11,610. In face of such unanimity on the part of the minority—in some departments not more than one in eight—who troubled to record their votes, it was a matter of little concern that the acceptance of the constitution had already been celebrated by David's elaborately symbolical *Fête de la Nature* five months before (August 10th); and only cynics remarked that for three months the country had already been ruled, without regard for this or any other constitution, under a decree (October 10th) which made 'the provisional government of France revolutionary until the peace.'

The steps by which the Convention prolonged its life are not difficult to trace. On the morning after the *repas frugal* and the *pantomime* that ended the festival of August 10th, the assembly met to consider its dissolution, and

the election of a *corps législatif* under the new constitution. The natural
disinclination of the deputies to give up power and emoluments which they
had enjoyed for less than twelve months was supported by arguments based
on more respectable grounds. They reminded themselves of the critical
position of the foreign war, and of the insurrections in the provinces. They
remembered that they had promised the country a civil code and an education bill, neither of which they had yet found time to enact. They reflected
that not only the Jacobin club, but also the delegates of the provincial
electorates who were still in Paris wished them to remain in power. Was it
surprising that they decided to do so?

But it would be a little indecent to bury the new constitution as soon as it
was born. Accordingly it was decreed that, with a view to the forthcoming
elections, the communes should be instructed to draw up fresh lists of all
qualified electors. It was calculated that, by the time these lists were ready,
the Convention would be so firmly established that the question of its
replacement would be no longer worth raising. And so it was. Within
two months (October 10th) the emergency government was sanctioned
for the duration of the war, and the constitution of '93 was indefinitely
postponed.

This could not have been done simply by the intrigues of a party, or the
threats of a mob. It meant that, with the substitution of Jacobin for Girondin
leadership, the Convention was making good, and winning the confidence
of the country. It meant that Jacobinism was now identified with the
revolution—Jacobinism in the ministry and the committees, Jacobinism in
the clubs and sections, Jacobinism in the armies and the provincial communes. It meant that anti-Jacobinism, whether at home or abroad, whether
amongst the royalists who could not forget January 21st, or amongst the
Girondins who could not forget June 2nd, was identified with counter-revolution. For better or for worse, the French people would have it so. The
dictatorial regime of the Jacobin group was not imposed upon the Convention from outside: it was evolved from within. The licence they used was by
leave of the nation, and would last just so long as it was used in the national
interests.

In the assembly a succession of Jacobin Presidents, and the packing of the
committees with Jacobin nominees, enabled business to be conducted with
an order and speed hitherto unknown. The removal of the Girondin leaders
made an end, for the time being, of personalities in debate. Their opponents,
not yet strong enough to risk more drastic measures, allowed them to live at
home, each under the eye of a National Guardsman. They could visit and
entertain their friends. They could work for their restoration to parliamentary freedom. They could write letters such as those in which Valazé
rejected an amnesty, Vergniaud demanded the punishment of the authors
of June 2nd, or Pétion required the reinstatement of the proscribed deputies

Clavière and Lebrun, though under provisional arrest, were still allowed to do the work of their ministries. Barère's report of June 6th proposed sending deputies as hostages to the departments whose representatives had been arrested. Saint-Just's report of July 8th denounced as traitors only the nine Girondins who had evaded arrest, or who had roused revolt in the provinces. He proposed to try five others as their accomplices, and to restore nineteen 'misguided' deputies to their places in the assembly. Neither of these plans was adopted. But it was not until more than four months after their expulsion that the Girondin leaders paid the final penalty for their failure.

For this punishment, when it came, the Girondins were themselves to blame as much as their opponents. They might have exploited the uncertainties of the Committee of Public Safety. They might have taken advantage of the hesitation shown in the reports of Barère and Saint-Just. They might have played on the popular demand for a constitution. Instead of this, they exasperated their enemies, and alienated their friends, by declaring open war on the Convention. From arguments they appealed to arms. Morris had told Washington that they would do nothing. 'The greater part of them,' he said, 'have only *parole* energy.' But in fact twenty out of the twenty-nine expelled from the House on June 2nd escaped from Paris forthwith; and they were followed by some of the seventy-five deputies who had protested against their expulsion. Before he evaded his careless guards, Barbaroux despatched urgent demands for troops to Marseille. 'It was the Bretons and Marseillais,' he reminded his fellow-townsmen, 'who reversed the tyrant on August 10th. It was a Breton (Lanjuinais) and myself who stood up against the assassins of June 2nd. It is for the Bretons and Marseillais once more to save the republic from these Jacobin anarchists (*désorganisateurs*).'

Federalism since June 2nd had ceased to be a political theory, and had become the programme of an armed insurrection. In November, '89, Brissot had attacked the new departmental system on the ground that it divided France into 'a number of federated republics.' Better Rousseauists remembered that Jean-Jacques had advised the Poles to 'extend and perfect the system of federal government,' as 'the only one which combines the advantages of large states and small.' But the predominance of Paris, symbolised in the annual festival of Federation, gave this federal state the beginnings of unity and indivisibility. War made unity a necessity, and federalism a crime. The victory of the Jacobins was built on this conviction. The Girondins, as usual, found themselves in two minds. Brissot, never a federalist, maintained that he was fighting to free the Convention from Jacobin control, and to ensure its free leadership of the country. Barbaroux and the Rolands contemplated without much regret the abandonment of Paris, and the waging of a civil war against the Convention. They planned, as other Frenchmen planned seventy years and again seventy years later, a Ligue du Midi, or a government of Vichy.

The Girondins did not find it difficult to exploit the grievances of the provinces. Under their influence the desire of the middle class to stabilize the revolution, the half extinguished royalism of the country-side, the food and currency grievances, and the dull resentment of the towns against the capital, broke into open revolt. The west was already ablaze. Now from new centres—Limoges, Toulouse, Bordeaux—the trouble spread northwards, and reinforced the revolt in the Vendée. In the south the annexation of Avignon had prevented an earlier outbreak of federalism. Now insurrections at Marseille, Nîmes, Toulon, Grenoble, and Lyon carried on the encirclement of the capital. The peasants of the Jura and the brigands of Corsica joined in a movement they did not understand. On this side the danger was distant and doubtful. More serious was the threat from the north-west. Here were seventeen of the Girondin leaders, including Buzot, Gorsas, Pétion, Louvet, Guadet, and Barbaroux. Here was general Wimpfen, the hero of the defence of Thionville. Here was the royalist Comte de Puisaye, with two regiments of cavalry from the Cherbourg command. Here, at Evreux and Caen, within striking distance of Paris, backed by departments traditionally separatist, and by districts almost as discontented as the Vendée, rebel troops were already advancing on the capital. The civil war that Mirabeau foresaw and that Louis dreaded had begun.

The unity and indivisibility of the republic, proclaimed as a dogma less than a year ago, was now disputed by the greater part of the country. Sixty departments of the west and south were in revolt against twenty of the north-east. But the contest was not so one-sided as geography might suggest. The federal revolt was, in general, the work of an official and propertied minority. Outside a few centres, it got little active or persistent help from the common people, or from the municipalities. It was compromised by its connexion with royalism and clericalism, and by the suspicion of foreign support. Paris, with its wealth, its concentrated numbers; Paris, the centre of administration and communications; Paris, the base of the armies on the northern and eastern frontiers, was in a position to strike hard, and to strike in any direction.

Nevertheless the revolt was put down less by arms than by decrees. A skirmish in the Seine valley, in which neither side mustered more than four thousand men, a scattered campaign in the Midi, and two interminable sieges, showed the difficulties of a military decision. The real cause of the Jacobin victory was a moral offensive which divided the insurrection by bribing its humbler adherents, and weakened it by giving easy terms to those who deserted its standards. A series of emergency measures removed the last obstacles to the peasant ownership of the land, increased the salaries of minor officials, and lowered the exemption level of taxation. The new constitution went far to win the support of the middle and lower classes. The rebel administrations were given an opportunity to draw back. Only to the 'traitors' themselves, and to the insurgent cities, would no mercy be shown.

In the end the Vendeans alone, refusing to listen to their 'fellow-citizen' Robert Lindet's appeals, remained unreduced and irreconcilable.

Up to the middle of July the outlook for the rebels must have seemed hopeful. On the first day of the month came news of the revolt of Corsica. On the 5th the deputies from Vernon declared that the camp-fires of Wimpfen's army were almost visible from Paris. On the 11th Couthon reported bad news from Lyon, and Cambon denounced a royalist plot to put the young Dauphin on the throne as Louis XVII. The debate on Saint-Just's report which began on the 15th showed how unready the victors of June 2nd were to administer a *coup de grâce* to the vanquished. As late as the 23rd Conédic was writing confidently to Barbaroux, proposing that when the federal troops entered Paris the Jacobin leaders should be promptly tried and executed 'in the Swiss military manner' on the Champ de Mars, beside the altar of the country. But already the turning-point had come. On July 13th, at Pacy, the Breton rebels had fled at the first shot from the republican troops; and the rapid submission of Normandy showed how superficial the revolt had been.

On the very day after the victory at Pacy the decisive weapon which the Jacobins still lacked was put into their hands by the Girondins themselves. Marat was assassinated by Charlotte Corday. She was a young woman of twenty-five, an aristocrat by birth, but brought up in country simplicity. The heroic blood of the poet Corneille was in her veins, and his stoic precepts in her heart. Caen was her Domrémy: Raynal supplied her 'voices'. She came to imagine herself another Joan, called as a royalist to avenge the death of 'her Dauphin,' Louis XVI, and as a patriot to rescue her dear France from its Jacobin oppressors. She had seen and heard the escaped Girondins. She had read Perlet's *Gazette*, the *Courrier français*, and the *Courrier universel*. She took June 2nd to be a national disaster. She made up her mind then and there to kill Marat. Why Marat? The question was put to her at her trial. The answer seemed obvious. Had she not heard him described, along with Robespierre and Danton, as one of the authors of the civil war? Was he not a criminal hoarder (*accapareur*)—had not a man been arrested at Caen and charged with buying up currency for him? Did not everyone outside Paris know that he was a 'monster'? Charlotte (she stubbornly maintained) had no accomplices. She made use of Barbaroux and Duperret only in order to obtain access to the Tuileries, where she intended to murder Marat as publicly as possible. She expected to be lynched by his avengers: so she pinned into her frock her baptismal certificate, and an *Adresse aux Français*, to explain who she was, and why she had done the deed.

When Corday arrived in Paris, she was disconcerted to find that for the last month Marat had not been seen at the Convention. He was ill, suffering from an eruptive skin disease, which he treated by spending long hours in a warm bath. He had just written to the assembly complaining that his letters were not being forwarded to his lodgings. He lived in an old house in the rue des Cordeliers. Like Robespierre, he was surrounded by women—Simonne Evrard, a woman of twenty-nine, whom he had taken to wife in his fiftieth year 'before the Supreme Being, in the vast temple of Nature,' her sister Catherine, his own sister Albertine, Marie Aubin, the *portière* of the tenement, whom he employed to fold up his paper after printing, and a maid named Jeannette. On the day before his death Marat had been visited by a deputation from the Jacobin club. They found him, as Charlotte did, 'in his bath, with a table, an ink-pot, some papers and books by his side, working as hard as ever at public business.'

Early on July 13th Corday bought a butcher's knife at a shop in the Palais-Royal, and drove in a cab to Marat's lodgings. She was refused admittance. She left a note, saying that she would return later, to report on the state of affairs at Caen; and she returned to her hotel. At half-past seven in the evening she drove again to the rue des Cordeliers, and was again refused admission. But Marat heard her speaking to the *portière*, and told them to let her in. He questioned her about the Girondin deputies at Caen, and took down the names of the rebel administrators of Calvados at Evreux, saying that 'they would all soon be guillotined in Paris.' These words hastened his end. Charlotte drew her knife, and stabbed him in the breast. By chance she struck a fatal spot. Marat cried *A moi, ma chère amie, à moi!* but he was dead before he could be moved from the bath.

The murderess made no attempt to escape. She was seized, and taken to the Abbaye, and thence to the Conciergerie. When questioned, she spoke frankly and proudly of what she had done; and whilst in prison she wrote to Barbaroux, telling him the whole story. 'We Parisians,' she added ironically, 'are such fine republicans that no one can understand how a useless female, who could do no good by going on living, could sacrifice her *sang-froid* to save her country' . . . 'I am at peace, and delightfully content,' she ends, in words which might have been written by Corneille himself—*Je jouis délicieusement de la paix.* 'For the last two days my country has been happy, and so have I . . . Tell General Wimpfen that I think I have done more than win a battle for him, by making peace possible.'

Charlotte's deed was the prelude, not to a Girondin peace, but to a Jacobin vendetta. She had struck down the chief critic of the Convention, who gloomily described himself, in the last words he printed, as 'the Cassandra of the revolution.' She had perhaps anticipated by a few months Marat's death on a sick-bed, or on the scaffold. But she had rendered political assassination, for once, almost respectable; and she had made herself immortal. Before her execution she had her portrait drawn for posterity. When she went to her death on July 17th her beauty and grace almost made the crowd forget that she was a murderess.

A young German named Adam Lux, visiting Paris on a deputation from his native town of Mainz, had already been so deranged by the excitements of revolution that he had written to his wife announcing his death in the cause of freedom. Two days after Charlotte's execution he published a pamphlet eulogizing her in almost amorous terms, and an *Avis aux citoyens français* which it was not difficult for his judges to twist into a demand for a Girondin dictatorship. The suspicion of madness did not save him from the guillotine. Nor was Lux the only victim of Marat's avengers. Deschamps, a watch-maker of the faubourg Saint-Denis, was executed almost on the same day for indiscreet remarks about the leaders of the *Montagne*. Lecocq, once a servant of the Rolands, suffered six months' imprisonment before meeting the same fate on the same charge. In November Marie-Anne Bertaux, a handsome woman of forty-two, had been chosen to impersonate Reason at a local fête in honour of 'the Martyrs of Liberty'—Rousseau, Marat, and Le Peletier—and had moved the audience by her patriotic eloquence. Within a month she was indicted, on the word of jealous neighbours, as a friend of Roland, and an anti-Jacobin. She admitted having dined with Roland, whom she described, rather surprisingly, as *un galant homme*. She was thrown into a dungeon of the Conciergerie, and brought out, in March, '94, to be guillotined.

Meanwhile, Marat's youngest brother, Jean-Pierre, who had married a jeweller's daughter at Vandoeuvres, near Geneva, in '91, arrived in Paris with his married sister Marie to acknowledge Simonne Evrard as a member of the family, and to claim Jean-Paul's musket as a relic of the martyr. The elder brother, Henri, heard the news in Russia, where he was teaching French literature at Tsarskoe-Selo under the unrevolutionary name of M. de Boudry.

Charlotte Corday had been asked by her judges, 'Do you imagine that you have killed all the Marats?' She replied regretfully, 'No.' Whilst the artist David set himself to dramatize Marat's end in the most effective of his revolutionary canvasses, *Marat assassiné* (1793), the Jacobin politicians lost no time in exploiting the prestige of the murdered man in the interests of their party. Marat's gruesome lying-in-state at the Cordeliers club, his public burial, more than a year later, at the Panthéon, and the fanatical cult of his memory were, indeed, little to the taste of men who had detested and disowned him whilst alive. But it was noticed that within a few weeks of his murder the Committee of Public Safety started more active measures against the federal insurrection. The *tribunal extraordinaire* was reorganized. The federal leaders were outlawed. The Convention passed (August 1st) a number of disciplinary and almost terrorist decrees. Police control in the provinces was tightened up. Warnings were issued against English intrigue. Orders were given for the trial of the queen, for the deportation of members of the Bourbon family, and for the destruction of royal tombs, wherever they might be found. Steps were taken to purge the higher command of the army, to round up rebels in the Vendée, to arrest foreigners, and to enforce the circulation of the *assignats*. Aimed in every direction at once, some of these blows might strike home. Soon Caen, Marseille, and Bordeaux were in the hands of Jacobin commissioners. Federalism was discredited. The Girondin leaders were in flight all over the country.

On October 15th the Jacobin government, as it could now be called, staged a great political trial, to consummate and advertise the overthrow of Girondism. It was remarkable not only for the number and distinction of the accused men, but also for the judicial methods employed. The trial of the Girondins provided a precedent for the subsequent trials of the Hébertists and Dantonists. It illustrates the rape of justice and mercy by political passion as well as any trial held under the auspices of Ogpu or Gestapo.

No one can doubt from the first moment that this is a French trial, not an English one. No one can doubt that it is being held in a time of war and revolution, not in a time of settled and peaceful government. No one can doubt that its object is not to discover whether the persons tried are guilty, but to justify their execution. This is clearly shown by the procedure. The persons indicted in Amar's charge on October 5th are not the same persons as those who appear before the court on the 15th. Fifty thousand copies of the *acte d'accusation* have been printed and distributed all over the country, and even in foreign parts. Frenchmen and foreigners alike are enlightened as to the intrigues of a criminal party which has long 'distracted (*déchiré*) the republic, and compromised the cause of liberty.' When the trial opens, the papers used by the Prosecution are not ready, and have not been communicated to the Defence. If charges are made in sufficiently general terms, they need not be substantiated. It does not matter, if they are not applicable to some of the prisoners. The chief witnesses are the political opponents of the accused men: they can now say what they like about them, without any fear of the consequences. Such methods may well seem a travesty of justice. But it is to be remarked that the prisoners themselves do not protest against them. It may be inferred that, had the Jacobins been in the dock, and the Girondins on the bench, the case would have been conducted in much the same way.

It is not so much the trial of twenty-one individuals as of the whole party to which they belong. 'We are hearing evidence,' remarks the Public Prosecutor, 'as to the opinions of the accused persons only in order to collect and to bring out the facts which prove that they belonged to an association (*coalition*—it was the word used for workmen's strike unions) for the ruin of the republic.' Again, the President of the court rules that 'If the court were investigating a definite crime, I should not allow evidence as to opinions, but since the issue is a conspiracy against the state, it may be established by proof of the association of the accused: and such proof can be obtained only from the identity of their opinions.' In other words, if it can be shown that seditious opinions are characteristic of the 'set' frequented by the accused, then there is a presumption that they are individually guilty of seditious acts. The witnesses are therefore allowed to make long speeches, giving their impression that such a set existed, and that such opinions were expressed in it. They are allowed to tell stories and to repeat remarks suggesting that one or another of the prisoners has expressed such opinions. They are allowed to allege acts which, though innocent enough in themselves, borrow alarming significance from the opinions that accompany them. Some of the accused persons may object, 'I did not belong to the committee when that was done,' or 'I was not present when that was said.' But if A. was there on the first occasion, and B. on the second, then C., who knew them both, may be presumed guilty of their opinions and of their acts.

No limit of time is set to the opinions for which a prisoner may be indicted. Brissot's Girondism goes back to 1789, when there was no Gironde —indeed, to still earlier days, when there was no revolution. Association at any moment of his career with someone who has since turned out to be a traitor is equally damaging. The distinction between *les patriotes* and *la faction* is as absolute as that between right and wrong. To belong now to the wrong side is to have belonged to it always. The Girondins are in the pitiable embarrassment of *Saint Joan*, when she is convinced by the court that her voices have misled her, and that what she has taken for orthodoxy must have been heresy all the time. The evidence given by one of the witnesses, Boileau, is very instructive on this point. He admits that he was so bewildered by the counter-accusations of the two parties that he was for a moment in error, and became a Girondin. But now that the bandage has fallen from his eyes, he knows where truth resides, and is a Montagnard. 'I have been looking for the truth,' he says: 'I have found it on the Jacobin side; I am now a Jacobin.'—'You ought to have seen,' the President in effect retorts, 'from the acts of the Commission of Twelve, that it was counter-revolutionary: surely you could not have misunderstood the murder of Le Peletier, or of Marat?'—'It was perhaps Marat's murder that opened my eyes,' is all that the turncoat can find to reply.

Since the whole Girondin party was on trial, the charges ranged all over the political field—from such wide but material issues as Brissot's war policy in '91, or Roland's polemic against Paris in '92, to such puerilities as opposing clerical marriage, conniving at the theft of the crown jewels, or deleting from a design for the republican seal the eighty-four stars which symbolized departmental unity. The main heads of the accusation were, as everybody expected, the Rolandist attacks on Paris, the attempt to save the life of the king, the treachery of Dumouriez, the arbitrary acts of the Commission of Twelve, and the federal revolt at Caen and Evreux. Here the facts alleged were so notorious, and the evidence of party opinion so strong, that the prisoners can have had little hope of an acquittal.

Nevertheless their eloquence might prolong the trial indefinitely, and they made good use of the liberty offered them by a procedure less like that of a trial than of a debate. At last Fouquier-Tinville, the Public Prosecutor, in despair of obtaining a conviction, appealed to the assembly. 'It is now five days,' he reported, 'since the trial began, and only nine witnesses have been heard. Each of them wants to give his evidence in the form of a history of the revolution. The accused answer the witnesses, and are answered back. So a debate starts which is as long as the speakers are talkative. Besides, when the discussion of particular points is over, each prisoner will want to make his formal defence. At this rate the trial will never end.' Why, he asks, should there be any witnesses, when everyone, including the prisoners themselves, knows that they are guilty? The court cannot remedy this state of affairs: but the Convention, he suggests, might 'get rid of the formalities which are holding up its progress.' The assembly took the hint, and immediately passed a decree under which, at any time after three days' hearing, the President of the court might closure the trial, if the jury had declared that 'their conscience was sufficiently enlightened.'

At seven o'clock on the evening of the sixth day of the trial (October 30th) the foreman of the jury made the requisite declaration. Three hours later an unanimous verdict of Guilty was brought in against all the prisoners. When they were led back into court to hear the verdict, and to receive the death sentence, some of them cried *Vive la république!*, and some cursed their judges. Valazé stabbed himself in the dock. It is said that as the rest were taken away they scattered *assignats* among the crowd, and cried *A nous, nos amis!* but that the crowd tore up the notes, with counter-cries of *Vive la république!* The Parisians revered the Convention, as they had revered the monarchy, impersonally; they cared little for its members, of whatever party, and would have regarded the death of twenty Jacobins with little more concern than that of twenty Girondins. The next day the condemned men went straight from the prison to the scaffold.

Their lot was perhaps fortunate, compared with that of their comrades at Caen. Outlawed by the decree of July 28th, these men were in the unhappy position of those struck by an Act of Attainder in the seventeenth century. If caught, they could be executed without trial. Anyone who gave them shelter did so at peril of his life. Some of them escaped. Wimpfen, after his defeat at Pacy, hid himself at Bayeux, and avoided arrest. Louvet lay concealed in the Jura, and Meillan in the Pyrenees. A few others—Bergoeing, Delahaye, Duval, Kervélégan, Lanjuinais, Larivière, Mollevaut—somehow survived the Terror. Isnard avoided immediate arrest by resignation, and made a legendary escape. But three—Cussy, Gorsas, and Duchâtel—were recaptured, and executed in Paris—the last two with the leaders condemned in October, the first soon afterwards. On November 6th Courtard and Louis Egalité (as the Duc d'Orléans was now called) followed them to the guillotine; as did Noël on December 8th, Rabaut Saint-Etienne on December 14th, and Masuyer on March 19th.

In June, '94, Guadet and Salle were found hiding in an attic at Saint-

Emilion, near Bordeaux, and were executed within two days (June 19th). Birotteau too was caught and executed at Bordeaux. Pétion, Buzot, and Barbaroux were in hiding close by, writing melancholy memoirs, and composing eloquent prayers for vengeance on their enemies. They tried to escape across the Spanish frontier. But the country-side was on the alert. Barbaroux, to avoid capture, shot himself, but was still alive when dragged to the guillotine at Bordeaux (June 25th). Pétion and Buzot, hiding in a forest, but seeing no hope of escape, blew out their brains. Their dead bodies were found half eaten by dogs, and were buried where they lay.

Of other prominent Girondins, Chambon was discovered and shot down in the village where he had taken refuge: Lidon shot himself to avoid arrest: Condorcet was found dead in prison—it was said that he had taken poison: and Clavière stabbed himself in prison. Roland, when he heard of his wife's death, left his hiding-place at Rouen, and walked out into the country. Hopeless and exhausted—it was a wet, stormy night—he turned off the road, and stabbed himself to death. A note was found on his body: 'Whoever thou art that findest me lying here, respect my remains: they are those of a man who died as he had lived, in virtue and honesty.'

Of the sixty-three leaders of the Girondin party, only twenty-five survived the revolution, and died in their beds. The last of them, if he was really so, le Doulcet de Pontécoulant, was still alive in Paris in 1853, six years after Lamartine's fantastic *Histoire des Girondins* had transformed his old associates into an apostolic band of saints and martyrs. Did he think of Charlotte Corday's last message (*see p. 359*)? Did he ever meet Sieyès, who was still living in Paris; or Thibaudeau, whom the historian Aulard remembered meeting as a boy in his park at Tours—a dry erect old man, his neck swathed in a vast black cravat? Did they fight the old battles over again? Or did they ever read, in that 'wild savage book,' born in the 'blackness, whirl-wind, and sorrow' of Carlyle's soul, eighteen years before, one of the shrewdest pages ever written on the failure of the Gironde?

'The weapons of the Girondins (he had written) are Political Philosophy, Respectability, and Eloquence. The weapons of the Mountain are those of mere Nature; Audacity and Impetuosity which may become Ferocity, as of men complete in their determination, in their conviction. The ground to be fought for is Popularity: further, you may either seek Popularity with the friends of Freedom and Order, or with the friends of Freedom Simple; to seek it with both has unhappily become impossible. With the former sort, and generally with the 'Authorities of the Departments, and such as read Parliamentary Debates, and are of Respectability, and of a peace-loving monied nature, the Girondins carry it. With the extreme Patriots again, with the indigent Millions, especially with the Population of Paris, who do not read so much as hear and see, the Girondins altogether lose it, and the Mountain carries it. It must be owned likewise that this rude blustering

Mountain has a sense in it of what the Revolution means; which these eloquent Girondins are totally void of. Was the Revolution made, and fought for, against the world, these four weary years, that a Formula might be substantiated: that Society might become *methodic*, demonstrable by logic; and the old Noblesse with their pretensions vanish? Or ought it not withal to bring some glimmering of light and alleviation to the Twenty-five Millions, who sat in darkness, heavy laden, till they rose with pikes in their hands? '

The philosophic spy whose letters to Garat during the summer of 1793 enliven a dreary scene of party strife would have applauded this judgement. He quotes with approval a Jacobin friend, an ex-aristocrat, as saying, 'The Jacobins are consistent: the Brissotins are not. The aim of the latter was to set up an aristocracy of wealth, of trade, of landed property. They refused to see that such men are the scourge of humanity, living and thinking only for themselves, and ready to sacrifice everything to their egoism and ambition. Now the Jacobins have come into power. They wish no harm to these Moderates; but they intend to make them co-operate with the *sansculottes*, to force them to empty their money-bags, and to sell their wares more cheaply.'

Yet Dutard has doubts whether even the Jacobins know how to commend their views to the people. 'I never see the name Marat or Robespierre at the foot of a poster,' he writes, 'without saying to myself—What a pity these fellows are so clever, and so out of touch with the point of view of those they are supposed to govern. They are just like the old court and aristocracy. They seem to think the people have quite different souls from themselves, and are incapable of reasoning as they do. I can almost hear them say —The lower orders know nothing of literature, geography, history, or mathematics; they can't dance or play cards or talk to a lady as we do: they are incapable of rational thinking. But no one who lives among the people (he continues) would ever argue so. The people have as much pride and vanity and self-respect as any aristocrat. In their narrow sphere they sometimes reason more soberly than their enlightened brethren: and in time of revolution they have commonly shown themselves more sensible than the educated classes.' What Paris really needs, Dutard concludes, is to be governed by its respectable middle-class married men—those who have made a position for themselves, who are at work all day, with a few employees under them, and who have a wife, and children, and a home. These men are going through an apprenticeship in the art of government. They know how to talk to the people. 'A bottle of wine, a glass of beer, a joke, and a hand-shake— that is what the sansculottes like.'

The reasons both for the eminence of the Girondins and for their failure were, indeed, very like the reasons for the eminence and the failure of the philosophic Radicals in our own Parliament forty years later. When John Stuart Mill first read the history of the French Revolution, he 'learnt with astonishment that the principles of democracy had borne all before them in France thirty years earlier,' and 'the most transcendent glory he was capable of conceiving, was that of figuring as a Girondist in an English Convention.' But as time went on, he was forced to see in the English Radicals the same faults as he saw in the French Girondins. 'The men were honest, and faithful to their opinions, as far as votes were concerned. When measures were proposed flagrantly at variance with their principles, they came forward manfully, and braved any amount of hostility and prejudice rather than desert the right. But on the whole they did very little to promote any opinions; they had little enterprise, little activity'; and in the end 'they sank into a mere *Côté Gauche* of the Whig party.'

It had been a contest for popularity and power, without which no party could save the country. The events of 1793 had shown that the Girondins were incapable of winning the one or of using the other. Would 1794 find the Jacobins more successful? Would the children of this world show themselves wiser than the children of light?

CHAPTER XX

JACOBINISM

Le but du gouvernement constitutionnel est de conserver la République, celui du gouvernement révolutionnaire est de la fonder. La Révolution est la guerre de la liberté contre ses ennemis; la Constitution est le régime de la liberté victorieuse et paisible. Le gouvernement constitutionnel s'occupe principalement de la liberté civile, et le gouvernement révolutionnaire, de la liberté publique.—(ROBESPIERRE, 5 nivôse, An II.)

THE executions of October 31st, 1793, advertised the beginning of the Jacobin regime commonly called the Terror. But there was no exact point at which a man ceased to be a Girondin, and became a Jacobin; and there was no exact point at which the country changed over from a Girondin to a Jacobin government. The process of 'softening' started behind the battle-front. It was due, not to the shock-troops of argument, but to the para-troops of hard fact. There had been going on, ever since the king's flight, and the outbreak of war, a gradual change from decentralized and decontrolled methods of government to methods that were centralized and controlled. Power had been passing from the men who believed in persuasion to the men who believed in compulsion. Hardly a measure was decreed in '93–4, hardly an institution was set up, which had not precedents and origins in '91–92. Party propaganda might represent Girondins as obstructionists, and Jacobins as innovators. National safety and the rules of political warfare might demand the destruction of one set of leaders, and their replacement by another. Popular opinion might suppose a violent cleavage of policy, and speak as though there had been no dictatorship before the rule of the Committee of Public Safety, and no intimidation before the Terror. History must rule otherwise.

Those who feared the tyranny of a many-headed Convention more than the tyranny of a king, and clamoured for a new constitution, could be reminded that the National Assembly itself had come into power by a *coup d'état*, and had kept itself in power, without much thought of its mandate, for over two years. Those who mourned the doctrine of the Separation of Powers could be asked to remember that the Constituent Assembly, whilst refusing to interfere with the king's appointment and dismissal of ministers, had constantly intervened in the executive government of the country. Behind the 'extraordinary' powers of the 'governing committees' of '93–4 lay a long history of *comités des recherches, comités de surveillance,* and other emergency bodies. Behind the 'dictatorship of the commune' lay the arbitrary Electors of '89, and the half-autonomous districts and sections of '89–91. Martial law, control of the press, and political courts were not unasked for or entirely unrealized before the August revolution. The Insurrectional Committee which carried through the rising of August 10th, and the Insurrectional Commune which, during the following weeks, imposed its will on the government, stood in the same 'revolutionary' relationship to the constituted city authorities as the dictatorial Convention did to the relics of the constitution of '91, and to the germs of the constitution of '93. They used the same theory of direct popular sovereignty; they applied the same methods of centralized control; they resorted in the same way to the easiest weapon of a minority government—terrorism. The removal of the Girondins, like the removal of the king, did not reverse the engine of state. It only released the brakes which had hitherto retarded its progress.

Thus to the strict eye of legalism the *comité de l'Evêché* of May, '93, was no more unconstitutional than the *assemblée générale des Electeurs* of July, '89, and the *comité de salut public* no more dictatorial than the *commission des douze*. Nevertheless, to the Parisian citizen who lived under both, there must have been a world of difference between the Girondin and Jacobin regimes.

Both in its origin and in its functions the National Convention was well suited to be the main instrument of a 'revolutionary' government. Its members had been freely elected by all Frenchmen of the age of discretion. It embodied, as not even the Constituent Assembly had done, the General Will. It brought into political being and action the Sovereign People. It exercised at one and the same time legislative, executive, and constitution-making powers. The rising of June 2nd had accelerated and eased its working by purging it of the Opposition. The decree of December 4th organized it more efficiently. The Nation in Council remained for the next

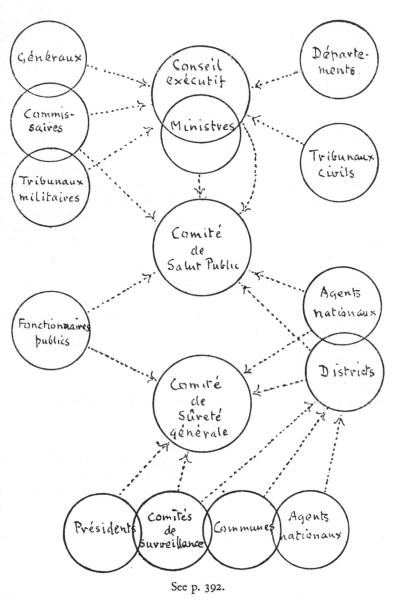

JACOBIN CENTRALISATION
under the decree of Dec. 4, 1793.
(each ·····> represents a written report every ten days)

See p. 392.

three years the ultimate authority for everything that was done. It never abdicated its powers. It never shirked its responsibilities. Ministers, committees, commissioners, generals, were all its agents and its nominees. Their acts were its acts. If laws were passed, if victories were won, if traitors were executed, it was equally the work of the Convention, done in the name of the Sovereign People.

The seven hundred and sixty-five deputies who embodied the General Will remained in the old *manège* till May 9th, '93: then they transferred their sessions to the more dignified but less friendly *salle des machines* of the Tuileries. Now that their quarters were larger, their numbers became less. Absenteeism, for one cause or another, had reduced attendance in the Legislative Assembly, before the August revolution, from seven to six hundred: the number of votes cast in the important division on the impeachment of Lafayette (August 8th) was six hundred and thirty. The Convention was slow to assemble. Only three hundred of its members were present when the republic was proclaimed on September 22nd. Over seven hundred deputies recorded their votes at the trial of Louis, when it was dangerous not to do so. But only three hundred and sixty took part in the critical party division (April 13th) on the impeachment of Marat. Perhaps at that time as many as two hundred were absent on government work, or with other good reason. Twenty-nine more were removed by the purge of June 2nd; and another seventy-three by the imprisonment of their sympathizers. There were still so many absentees that the Convention threatened (June 14th) to fill their places by calling up their *suppléants*. Most of the deputies then returned to their duties: a month later not more than fifty were still missing. Absenteeism was not easily excused: if the attendances dwindled again, till there were seldom more than three hundred and fifty members in the House, and sometimes under two hundred, it was principally due not to indifference, but to causes which are common to most representative assemblies in time of war. Probably half the deputies were absent at one time or another, and often for long periods, on work of national importance in the provinces, or at the front.

The Convention sat every day from ten o'clock in the morning till four or five in the afternoon, and very often again for another two or three hours after eight or nine in the evening. Twelve members remained in the House all night, to deal with urgent despatches from the front. The first two hours of the morning session, when attendance was apt to be thin, were usually given up to the reading of addresses, the receiving of petitions, and other affairs of minor importance. After midday the main business of the day might not be interrupted, except by special leave of the President. But an omnicompetent and still slightly Quakerish assembly could not be bound by absolute rules. Safeguards against hasty legislation which the previous assemblies had retained were now thrown away. Measures not involving legislation or affecting the constitution, and therefore not needing to be sealed by the Executive Council, were not infrequently proposed and carried during a single sitting. The second reading nominally required for legislative or constitutional acts might be dispensed with whenever a measure was thought essential for the government of the country. A decree could then be introduced at any moment, and passed in a few minutes, by a majority of the deputies rising in their places. With the disappearance of party issues, the *appel nominal* was rarely resorted to. No deputy need give a reason for his vote, or have his personal responsibility called in question.

Another change would have been noticed by a visitor familiar with the ways of previous assemblies. Seldom, except when a committee was presenting a report, or a government spokesman expounding a policy, was the House expected to listen to the long written discourses which had been the pride and penance of earlier days. It was not until the last months of the National Assembly that the deputies had acquired the faculty of debating. In the Legislative Assembly a new style of oratory was introduced by men who had learnt to dispute the issues of the day in provincial clubs and committees; and the burning topics of the war and the republic kindled a fresh blaze of eloquence. The speakers of the Convention were the pick of both previous assemblies, and their talents were sharpened by personal feeling. Never had invective been carried to such heights of rhetoric as in the weeks preceding June 2nd. But now, almost suddenly, oratory was put aside, and the debates became cold and businesslike. The war, the necessities of administration, and the cessation of personal and party controversy, introduced a new technique of debate, less like that of an eighteenth-century Academy, and more like that of a nineteenth-century Parliament.

It requires some discrimination to establish the text of the revolutionary speeches. None of the publications which professed to report the debates in the assembly was a Hansard. If all the speeches in the Convention had been extemporized, we should be as uncertain of what Vergniaud or Robespierre said as we are of what Pitt, or Fox, or Sheridan said in some of their earlier speeches. Were it not that so many orators spoke from a manuscript, which they handed to the editor of the *Moniteur* when they left the tribune, history would be dependent upon the summaries made by a dozen distracted reporters, and blue-pencilled according to the fancy of a dozen partisan editors.

The first and best reporter was Maret, the future Marshal, whose *bulletin*, originally composed for his own interest, and afterwards printed privately (September 12th, '89), was embodied in the *Moniteur* after February 2nd of the following year. For the early weeks before the appearance of the *Moniteur* (November 24th, '89) Le Hodey's *Journal des Etats-généraux* gave the liveliest summaries. Early in '91 the same editor started the *Journal logographique*, in which the speeches were reported by the naïve device of employing fourteen scribes, each of whom in turn took down as many of the orator's words as he could follow: these fragments were after-

wards pieced together, if possible with the help of the speaker, and formed
an almost verbatim report, including the stumblings of the speaker, and the
interruptions of the audience. The business was said to cost sixty pounds a
day; it would hardly have been attempted, but that it was financed by the
king, who hoped that so literal a reproduction of the debates would discredit
the assembly amongst those who valued good French and good manners.

The *Logographe* disappeared with the throne on August 10th. The best
reports were now those of the *Moniteur*, the *Journal des débats*, and the
Républicain universel or (from December 24th) *Républicain français*. But
none of these can always be trusted to be impartial. There exists a letter
from the parliamentary reporter of the *Moniteur* to Robespierre, dated a
fortnight after the expulsion of the Girondin deputies, in which he asks for
Jacobin patronage on the ground that he has habitually given more space to
Jacobin than to Girondin speakers. The claim is not borne out by an
examination of the reports: but that it should have been made is sufficient
proof of the untrustworthiness even of the better papers.

The transference of the assembly from the *manège* to the Tuileries
enabled more members of the general public to attend its debates. Within a
month the expulsion of the Girondins, and the dwindling numbers of the
representatives, removed most of the reasons for doing so. It may, indeed, be
doubted whether the debates of the Assembly were ever influenced as
much as tradition asserts by the presence in the public galleries of its master,
the people. Did any great importance attach to that *gros petit vieux, tout
rabougri*, M. Saule or Sole, who for three years (according to Dutard) used
a voice *assez perçante, toujours bien humectée*, to direct the applause of the
tribunes? Seldom, perhaps, had this pressure so little effect as during the sober
debate on the king's trial. Seldom, perhaps, had it so much effect as during
the bitter debate on the expulsion of the Girondins. The sovereign people
would not seriously intervene except when some question was discussed of
special concern to Parisians.

There were, in any case, subtler and more powerful interests at work
under the Jacobin regime—the fear of being 'purged' from one's club, the
fear of being deprived of one's *carte de civisme*, or the fear of losing one's
eighteen shillings a day. Even these considerations cannot have much
affected the non-party members who still formed the majority of the House,
who voted for Jacobin or Girondin measures alike, if they thought them for
the good of the country, and who acquiesced in the proscription of every
faction in turn, as soon as it seemed to put its own interests before the
interests of the republic.

Whatever the influence of the gallery upon the public meetings of the
Convention, it could not extend to the committees, whose work was no less
important a part of parliamentary life than it had been under the previous
assemblies. The first thing the Convention did was to appoint two bodies to
settle the number and composition of its committees. It had always recog-

nized, though it rejected Mathieu's proposal (September 29th, '92) to enact it, a distinction between standing committees (*commissions fixes*) and special committees (*commissions éventuelles*). In addition to the special 'governing' Committees of Public Safety and General Security, twenty-one standing committees were set up, with membership varying from three or six to twenty-four (the commonest number) or even forty-eight.

But three of these committees soon disappeared from the active list. The work of the committee of commerce was taken over by the more formidable *commissaires des approvisionnements*. The Constitutional Committee had done its work. The Diplomatic Committee had none to do, now that the foreign policy of the country was under the supervision of the Committee of Public Safety.

The suspension of the king on August 10th, '92, had left the remaining parts of the constitutional structure of '91 in an anomalous position. The Legislative Assembly carried on for six weeks, under the fiction of an unadjourned session, until it was replaced by the Convention. The old ministers, dismissed on the same day as the king, had been replaced immediately afterwards by new ministers elected by the assembly; and these men remained in office under the Convention. Since three out of the six had served under the king, they were in personnel as well as in status the only constitutional link between the old monarchy and the new republic. Foreign powers still corresponded with them; and it was argued by the Opposition in the House of Commons that their presence might have enabled us to recognize the French republic. But the Ministerial Council inherited a bad tradition. It had come to do little but approve, however grudgingly, the decisions of individual ministers. It never recovered from the unhappy position in which it was placed during August and September, '92, when the government of the country was disputed between the assembly and the commune. Its authority and independence were gradually undermined and finally destroyed by the Committee of Public Safety.

The Home Office (*ministère de l'intérieur*), under Roland, might attempt, with no more than two hundred and fifty officials, to deal with affairs which would nowadays be distributed amongst half a dozen departments. The long and beautifully expressed letters of advice which it despatched into the provinces were quite ineffective in solving the complicated problems of commerce and industry, prisons and food-supply. They were without the backing of compulsory powers. The Ministry of Justice, even under a Danton, could do little more than file reports received from its commissioners upon the administration of judges whom it had not appointed, and whom it could not dismiss. The Treasury (*ministère des contributions et revenus publics*) dealt not only with the collection and spending of public money, but also with the Post Office, the Mint, Woods and Forests, and even Munitions. How far it did so effectively cannot be ascertained, since all its archives disappeared in the fires of the Commune of 1871. The **War Office** and the **Admiralty** (*ministères de la guerre* and *de la marine*) derived new importance from the necessities of national defence. With every fresh levy of troops, with the opening of the offensive on every fresh front, the War Office had to expand its organization. The numbers of its staff were multiplied by four within the year following April, '93. Bouchotte, when Minister of War, complained that he spent his whole time giving monosyllabic answers, and signing his name. It mattered, perhaps, the less now that Carnot, at the head of the war section of the Committee of Public Safety, could do his thinking for him. The most independent of the ministries was the Foreign Office (*ministère des affaires étrangères*). Its traditions and policy remained for a long time those of the old regime. Its personnel, until purged by Dumouriez in '92, included men who had spent thirty or forty years within its walls. But its importance declined, as one state after another broke off relations with the regicide republic.

All the ministries were affected by the growing control of the Convention. This was exercised at first through its standing committees; but after January, '93, the *comité de défense générale*, and after April, '93, the *comité de salut public* took over the supervision of the executive. From June 15th onwards the Committee of Public Safety held its meetings in the assembly room of the Ministerial Council, and required the ministers to attend there every day to report and consult on the affairs of their departments. The decrees of October 10th and December 4th regularized this subordination. Finally, as foreshadowed by the constitution of '93 (Art. 62), the six ministers were replaced, on April 1st, '94, by twelve *commissions*, consisting of two *membres* and one *adjoint* (Foreign Affairs, War, and Marine had one *membre* and one *adjoint*). These *commissions* were attached to the Committee, and functioned as permanent secretariates under the direction of one or more of its members. Only the Treasury was allowed to retain its independence. This change meant that executive power was no longer divided between a minister and a committee of the House, but was concentrated in the hands of a group of deputies: the long taboo against the fusion of the legislative and executive functions had at last been removed.

The principle of the Separation of Powers, the chief constitutional dogma of the eighteenth century, owed its acceptance to the reputation of Montesquieu. It would not have maintained its position, against every argument of common sense, but for a deep prejudice against the old monarchical regime. Obsessed by traditions of Bourbon tyranny, the deputies regarded the king's ministers with nothing less than abhorrence. It was thought shameful even to be seen speaking to a minister. Vaublanc records that he was cut by his friends in the assembly because he was reported to have spent a night at the house of Narbonne, the Minister of War. The deputies would have nothing to do with Mirabeau's practical advice, backed by the legal authority of Thouret and A. Duport, to allow some at least of the ministers to be chosen from the legislature. Even now, after four years of semi-executive activity by legislative bodies, and in face of the plain speaking of another political realist, Danton, they hesitated to acknowledge in theory what they had long allowed in fact. The incoherence of government by a body of seven hundred amateur politicians, who must be at once legislators and administrators, judges and constitution-makers, had forced on the change from Girondin to Jacobin leadership. It was the same consideration which now made Danton urge the need of a closer co-operation between legislature and executive, such as could only be secured if the whole business of government were in the hands of a few chosen individuals. The Convention had inherited one constitutional experiment when it accepted ministers elected by the Legis-lative Assembly. It shrank from another. It preferred a round-about route, and had recourse to government by committee.

The first *comité de salut public*, on which the ex-minister Danton did not hesitate to fill a place, interfered increasingly with the executive; and from this time onwards the Ministerial Council lost much of its power. When, three months later, the first Committee of Public Safety was replaced by the second, Danton's experience of office again led him to urge that the new committee should be called what it really was, the Governing Committee (*comité de gouvernement*). Again the Convention drew back. But the con-stitution and powers of the new body soon showed that there was no hesita-tion in matters of fact. The decree of April 1st, '94, abolishing the ministries, gave all that Mirabeau and Danton had desired.

Whether they were conscious of it or not, the Conventionals thus in-augurated a constitutional expedient of the greatest importance for the future of parliamentary government. It was an expedient due to no disrespect for Montesquieu, and to no desire to imitate England, where a similar experi-ment was being tried. It was an expedient due to sheer political necessity. Robespierre had been right when he said, in his report of December 25th, that the Jacobin theory of government was 'as novel as the revolution that led to it,' and that it was no good looking for it in books by political writers who had never anticipated such an eventuality. It was happy improviza-tion. That is, after all, how constitutional changes are generally made.

The organ of government thought important and competent enough to initiate this great experiment, the *comité de salut public*, was the ultimate shape taken, after a series of transformations, by the *comité de défense générale*. As originally constituted on April 6th, 1793, it was a body of nine deputies elected by the Convention, and deliberating in secret. Its duty was to supervise and speed up the administration. It had power both to suspend ministerial measures, and to dictate orders to the ministers. During the three critical months since April it had undergone two changes. Its personnel had been increased by the addition of five deputies empowered to draft the constitution of '93, and by two representatives of the fighting services, Gasparin and Saint-André. At the same time its political colour had become strongly tinged with Robespierrism. When the committee came under the attack of the Convention for its failure to repress the federal revolt in the Vendée, Normandy, and the Lyonnais, and when the differences between its members made a 'coalition cabinet' unworkable, support was found for Desmoulins' demand that it should once more be reconstituted, without its superfluous or more incompetent members. The Robespierrists seized a heaven-sent opportunity (July 10th). Danton and most of his friends disappeared from the committee. It soon assumed the shape in which it governed France during the next twelve months.

The personnel of the committee, in its successive forms, was as follows:
April 6th (nine members):
      BARÈRE (re-elected, July 10th).
      Delmas (excluded, July 10th).
      Bréard (replaced by Berlier, June 5th).
      Cambon (excluded, July 10th).
      Danton (excluded, July 10th).
      Guyton-Morveau (excluded, July 10th).
      Treilhard (replaced by Gasparin, June 22nd).
      Delacroix (excluded, July 10th).
      LINDET (replaced by Jeanbon Saint-André, June 12th–22nd; re-elected, July 10th).
May 30th (fourteen members):
      HÉRAULT DE SÉCHELLES (formally elected, June 5th; re-elected, July 10th; executed, April 5th, '94).
      Ramel (excluded, July 10th).
      COUTHON (re-elected, July 10th).
      SAINT-JUST (re-elected, July 10th).
      Mathieu (replaced by Lindet, June 22nd).
July 10th (nine members):
      JEANBON SAINT-ANDRÉ (informal member since June 12th).
      Gasparin (resigned, July 27th).
      Thuriot (resigned, September 20th).
      PRIEUR de la Marne.
July 27th:
      ROBESPIERRE.
August 14th:
      CARNOT.
      PRIEUR de la Côte d'Or.
September 6th:
      BILLAUD-VARENNE.
      COLLOT D'HERBOIS.
After September the twelve whose names are in capitals were re-elected as a whole monthly, without further change.

At its first meeting the committee appointed a President, Vice-President, and two Secretaries; but there is no sign of such officers in its subsequent proceedings. After June 13th its work was divided up amongst sections, which dealt with correspondence, foreign affairs, the army, the navy, taxation, justice, and deputations. Each section was under the charge of one or more of the members. Meetings of the whole committee were held in the morning, to allot the work of the day, and in the evening, to report results, to sign decrees, and to discuss matters of policy. This seems to have been done in an informal way. No chairman was appointed; no minutes were kept; and no records of the committee's work remain but the resolutions and correspondence drafted and signed by its members.

The special responsibilities of each member may be judged, in a general way, from the letters or orders (*arrêtés*) which he drafted in his own hand, or was the first to sign (*en premier*). If we are to believe the evidence given by Carnot at the trial of Billaud and Collot eighteen months later, the countersignatures of other members were a formality prescribed by law, but carrying no personal responsibility. He had, he said, frequently counter-signed orders about which he knew nothing, or of which, had he known their contents, he would have disapproved. This reads like the excuse of an individual member seeking to escape the odium of the committee's terrorist policy. Doubtless counter-signatures were sometimes given carelessly by such members as happened to be available. But when specially important decisions had to be made, or specially important documents had to be signed, trouble was evidently taken to secure a full attendance. Resolutions were then drafted and signed on the spot. If a member dissented from the common policy, he could refuse his signature. If he gave it, he shared the responsibility. The haphazard way in which signatures are appended to the resolutions of the committee carries out this convention of collective responsibility.

There was never a Prime Minister, or *Président du conseil*. If the committee is called 'Danton's government' from April to July, and 'Robespierre's government' afterwards, the expression is excusable, but inexact. Danton's hot forcefulness and Robespierre's cold efficiency gave to each an informal leadership, but no more. The one presided over the creative phase of the committee's work, the other over its consolidation and growth. These two were, besides, the best-known politicians, and stood out in the public eye amongst a group of men whose ability was administrative rather than oratorical, and whose personal qualities were relatively unknown. They were easily credited with acts for which they were perhaps only one-twelfth part responsible; and their obscurer colleagues were not infrequently glad to have it so.

The committee met at eight o'clock in the morning every day of the week, and remained at work till ten o'clock at night, or even later. The 'politicians' might spend part of the time in the Convention, or at the club. The 'workers' would have little time to cultivate popularity. Some of them remained almost as unknown to the general public as the secretaries of Napoleon. The small room with its sparse furniture, and the green-covered table round which the committee met to discuss the fate of the revolution, contrasted rather self-consciously with the luxurious setting of the old *conseil du roi*. The secret and autocratic methods of the old regime were less foreign to the pose of the Provisional Government; but they were tempered with a new austerity befitting republican manners. The cold and formal way in which (if Barras is to be believed) the committee received the reports of its agents was in studied contrast with the ill-balanced enthusiasm of a popular assembly, or of a Parisian mob.

The register of attendance, which cannot always be trusted, suggests that during the year from July 26th, '93, to July 26th, '94, there were only twenty-five days when the committee did not meet, and that those members who were in Paris attended with untiring regularity. There is no need to reject the commonly accepted division of the committee into the 'workers' who stayed at their desks and the 'politicians' who attended the meetings of the Convention, or travelled on missions to the armies and the provinces. But everything was as fluid and informal as it is apt to be in a time of national emergency and constitutional improvisation.

Amongst the 'workers' of the Committee France was fortunate to be able to count an engineer officer of forty, Lazare-Nicolas-Marguerite Carnot. Historians, in their admiration for Carnot's administrative achievements, have attempted to explain away his part in a terrorist regime, when they might rather have reflected how necessary he must have thought it to be. Carnot was, not only by temperament, but by the choice of a branch in the service which debarred him from high promotion, a student-soldier of a type peculiarly French. He was already the author of papers anticipating modern discoveries, and of ideas which had been crowned by more than one learned Academy. His patriotism had refused an invitation to enter the service of Frederick the Great. He had led the attack in the Legislative Assembly against the *émigré* princes. He had given up attendance at the Jacobin club because he could not acknowledge loyalty to any lesser cause than that of France. A keen believer in military discipline and army reform, he was realist enough to see a use both for medieval pikes and for modern steam-boats. His reputation for sound, if silent, work on three committees of the Convention, and his success in several missions to the front, marked him out as the man best fitted to organize victory for the republican armies.

Carnot's principal assistant was another engineer of his own age. Claude-Antoine Prieur-Duvernois was deputy for the Côte d'Or. A man of many talents, a member of the Dijon Academy, and of the Natural History Society of Paris, Prieur was best known as the author of *L'Art du militaire*— a book of instruction for all branches of the army—and as the inventor of the decimal system of weights and measures. Whilst Carnot directed the disposition of the armies, and drew up the plans of campaign, Prieur organized the supply of arms and munitions without which Carnot's work would have been of no avail.

The third of this group was Jean-Baptiste-Robert Lindet, a man of forty-six, with an immense reputation for good sense. He had made his name as the pacifier of Normandy, and as the chief draftsman of the first Committee of Public Safety. He now showed himself an extremely efficient Quartermaster-general; and his sphere of action was soon extended over the whole field of commerce, agriculture, and food-control.

The Admiralty, a department of less traditional importance than the War Office, was fortunate to find a competent supervisor in André Jeanbon, generally called Jeanbon Saint-André, an ex-captain of the mercantile marine, who had once been a Protestant minister and preacher. A man of forty-four, he was transferred from the *comité de la marine*, and spent most of his time on missions to the naval ports—an itinerant 'worker,' trying to extemporize a republican navy.

That the Committee was not merely a Jacobin clique, a party of political associates, was shown by the addition to it of two men of a very different type and temper from Carnot, Prieur, or Robert Lindet. Jacques-Nicolas Billaud (he added Varenne to his name when he married) had been an unsuccessful actor and teacher, till he settled in Paris as a lawyer a few years before the revolution, and made a name as an anti-clerical, anti-ministerial, and anti-Lafayettist pamphleteer. Now, at thirty-seven, after several political missions, he was President of the assembly, and entered the committee the day after a speech calling for the execution of Clavière, Lebrun, and the queen.

Jean-Marie Collot d'Herbois, a man of the same age as Jeanbon Saint-André, was an actor-dramatist whose plays had been popular on the Paris stage so lately as '90–91. He had become almost famous as the author of the *Almanach du Père Gérard*, and as the organizer of the fête in honour of the mutineers of the Châteauvieux regiment. A member of the Insurrectional Commune of August, '92, he had defended the prison massacre, and had proposed the decree of September 21st, inaugurating the republic. In several missions he had shown himself both severe and self-effacing. Like Billaud, he had been President of the Convention. Both men had found fault with the work of the committee. Both men represented the discontented elements of the capital. Their continued opposition might give substance to dangers which were already threatening the government from the groups that framed the Hébertist plot six months later. They were accordingly silenced, as Carnot admitted afterwards, by being put on to the committee, and were diverted from Paris politics by being made responsible for the arduous correspondence carried on with the government agents in the provinces.

Pierre-Louis Prieur (de la Marne) was the same age as Billaud-Varenne. One of the most active legislators of the Constituent Assembly, secretary to the *comité de mendicité*, administrator of the Marne department, and organizer of the defence of Champagne in '92, Prieur was a revolutionary of long standing and loud views, whose honesty and hard work had become almost proverbial. He was, however, so often absent on missions that he played no great part in the routine work of the committee.

Georges-Auguste Couthon (thirty-seven) and Louis-Antoine de Saint-Just (twenty-six), the youngest member of a committee whose average age was less than that of the assembly, were Robespierre's closest associates. He had many admirers, but few friends. His link with Couthon was probably a likeness of character and outlook. His link with Saint-Just was probably the attraction of opposites. Couthon, like Robespierre, was a 'poor man's lawyer,' a Puritan, and an invalid; like Robespierre, he cultivated a certain elegance in his dress and surroundings; like Robespierre, he rode revolutionism on the curb, and used the spur. Saint-Just was everything that Robespierre would have liked to be—young, handsome, adventurous, and sure of himself. The older man was flattered by the younger man's open discipleship, and learnt more than he cared to admit from his cleverest pupil. The younger man dedicated an idle past upon the altar of a devotion which at last gave him something to live for.

Couthon and Saint-Just were frequently away from Paris—the one taking cures for his crippling rheumatism, the other leading the republican armies to victory. Robespierre was thus driven into an uneasy and uncongenial partnership with the most ubiquitous member of the committee, Bertrand Barère. Whilst the 'workers' were tied to their desks, or travelling in the provinces, Barère was always at hand, the most regular attendant of them all, and the most indispensable. When, at the end of a long discussion, the other members of the committee were too tired or too confused to formulate a conclusion, Barère would sum up the debate in a few lucid words, and draft a resolution that expressed the sense of the meeting. A man of the same age as Billaud, Couthon, and Prieur de la Marne, he was one of those adaptable, conciliatory, and essentially unprincipled politicians whose value is recognized by every Prime Minister, because they can always be trusted to carry out an administrative task efficiently, to deal tactfully with an unpleasant situation, and to find excellent reasons for supporting whatever may be the policy of the moment.

Barère does not deserve—no statesman could deserve—the tremendous indictment of Macaulay. But he was a Trimmer who never made that designation a title of honour: he was a time-server with no truth in him. His whole career was, like one of his own *carmagnoles*, an advertisement of feats which had not been performed, and of virtues which had never existed. Assisted by the most transitory member of the committee, the ex-aristocrat Marie-Jean Hérault de Séchelles, Barère made himself specially responsible for diplomacy, education, and the fine arts; but he was as ready to turn his hand to a new task as his mind to a new idea. His facility for change should have earned him a longer article in the *Dictionnaire des girouettes*.

Robespierre himself was added to the committee as its most experienced parliamentarian, its most acceptable orator, and (had he been left outside) its most dangerous critic. He interested himself, more perhaps than his colleagues liked, in the affairs of every department. His belief in the spoken word, and his readiness to dogmatize any part of the Jacobin faith, marked him out as the natural *rapporteur* of the committee, just as Saint-Just's air of ruthless detachment made him its most effective *accusateur*. Robespierre was the best known and most admired Jacobin in the country. He was easily credited with a supremacy which he did not possess, and with designs upon a dictatorship which he was the last man to entertain. Yet as a minister without portfolio, with access to every department of government, he had more opportunity than the rest to look ahead, and to think out a common policy.

The note-book (*carnet*) that contains his rough memoranda for the last three months of 1793 (Saint-Just had one like it marked *Notes militaires*) is very suggestive of Robespierre's key position on the committee. It contains more than one hint of ideas which took shape in the ordering of the committee's work, the remodelling of the Revolutionary Tribunal, the cult of the Supreme Being, the Law of the 22nd *prairial*, and the *bureau de police générale*. Nor can there be much doubt that Robespierre's special interest lay in those activities of the committee which caused most public apprehension, and which labelled its regime the Government of the Terror. In Opposition a devotee of absolute liberty, in Government Robespierre became a convinced disciplinarian. In his youth he had been an opponent of capital punishment—a fact remembered by the editors of the journal *Le Robespierre* in 1848, when they used his name to cover their principle, *Abolition de la peine de mort*. Now, at thirty-five, he believed in the guillotine as the sovereign method for purging vice from the body politic; though he was always hoping, as terrorists have always hoped, that he had reached the point of transition from compulsion to persuasion, and that the next execution would be the last.

Such were the men who, though subject to re-election every month, established a year's unchallenged supremacy. Such was the committee to which a constitutional scruple denied the title of *comité de gouvernement*, but which became, by leave of the Convention, and by the enlargement of its powers, the actual government of the country.

The original reference of the committee (by decree of April 6th) was 'to supervise and speed up the administration in charge of the Provisional Executive Council.' It was authorized, 'in urgent circumstances, to take measures of general defence (for it was the heir of the *comité de défense générale*) both external and internal.' The ministers were ordered to carry out its orders (*arrêtés*). It was given a draft of two and a half million pounds on the Treasury for secret expenses: the money was spent chiefly on police work, but partly in grants to local Jacobin clubs, and to propagandist newspapers. On the day that Robespierre joined the committee (July 27th) its power to arrest its own agents was extended to all 'persons suspected or warned.' On August 2nd its Treasury draft was doubled. The decree of October 10th showed what was meant by the 'revolutionary' regime it set up, when it placed the Executive Council, the ministers, the generals, and all the administrative authorities under the supervision of the committee. All *mesures de sûreté*—a wider term than *défense*—are now within its scope, and it nominates generals for appointment by the Convention.

Under the decrees of December 4th the committee becomes the hub of an administrative universe. It receives constant reports from the districts, the essential agents of provincial government, and from the government representatives attached to the armies. Through the Executive Council it is in close touch with the generals, the tribunals, and the departmental authorities. It is particularly entrusted with the conduct of foreign diplomacy. It signs an ambassador's credentials; it sanctions his instructions; and it reserves the right to correspond directly with the government to which he is accredited. On March 13th the climax of dictatorial power was attained when the committee was empowered to suspend from office any public official in the country. Its autocracy was now curtailed only by the caution of its employer and paymaster, the Convention. The still independent *comité des finances* limited its drafts on the public purse. The rival *comité de sûreté générale* had still to be consulted in police matters, and in the direction of the Revolutionary Tribunal.

It is customary to call the *comité de salut public* the Committee of Public Safety, and the *comité de sûreté générale* the Committee of General Security. *Salut* would be better translated 'salvation,' and *sûreté* 'police.' The first was an emergency body, set up at a moment of public danger to save the country. The second was a permanent body, with a long-term policy of police safeguards to secure the country against counter-revolution.

The senior of the two in standing, the Committee of General Security was also in one sense the more important: it dealt with persons rather than policies; and its investigations supplied the data for the administrative decisions and appointments made by its junior but more powerful rival. Perhaps, if its records were as open to inspection as those of the Committee of Public Safety, its importance would be found to be above its reputation. Certainly the younger committee could not afford to quarrel with the elder. When it did, it fell.

Since its formation on October 17th, '92, the Committee of General Security had passed through a bewildering series of changes, both in the number and in the political colour of its personnel. Since March 16th, '93, it had been predominantly Jacobin. Since October 13th, '93, it had consisted of fourteen members; and these, like those of the other committee, were renewed without change until July '94. Its rooms were in the hôtel or maison de Brionne, on the east side of the Tuileries, opening on to the Place du carrousel. Two of its members were there every day from twelve to four: its general meeting was from eight to eleven at night: a frugal supper was provided by the *restaurateur* Peyron at a total cost of five pounds a month.

The average age of the Committee of General Security was as much above the average age of the Convention as that of the Committee of Public Safety was below it. Vadier of Pamiers, Guffroy of Arras, Rühl of Strasbourg, and Louis of the Bas Rhin were all over fifty. Only one member, Lebas, was under thirty. Again, only four of the fourteen were Parisians. Their seniority, their provincial origin, and their varied experience—they included an artist, a country doctor, the director of a mint, and three members of Protestant families—may have fitted them for the supervision of the four regions into which France was divided for police purposes, and for the management of the hundred and twenty *secrétaires, analyseurs, enregistreurs, expéditionnaires, interprètes,* and other officials whose salaries amounted to more than nineteen thousand pounds a year. Of the four most active members, Grégoire-Marie Jagot, deputy for the Ain, was reputed to be a hard, quarrelsome man ; the ex-Oratorian Jean-Henri Voulland, deputy for the Gard, was a pious Jansenist; and Marc-Guillaume-Albert Vadier, deputy for the Arriège, had a Voltairian temper and a bitter tongue. But none was so feared as Jean-Baptiste-André Amar, deputy for the Isère, a courtly, insinuating, and almost effeminate terrorist, who directed Maillard, Héron, and the other spies and bravoes in the pay of the committee.

Such a body was not likely to work harmoniously with the smaller, younger, more Parisian, and more powerful committee with which the national emergency forced it to co-operate. It was inevitable that the right of arrest granted to a political committee by the decree of July 28th, '93, should lead to clashes with the established jurisdiction of a police committee. It was inevitable that when this same body, in pursuance of powers given it under the decree of March 13th, set up a *bureau de police générale,* with an independent approach to the Revolutionary Tribunal, serious differences should arise. But for a time outward harmony was preserved by arranging joint meetings of the two committees to deal with any important matter that concerned them both. The warrant for the arrest of Danton bears the signatures of eighteen members of both bodies, appended in the haphazard order common in these documents, as though to show their democratic equality, and their joint responsibility.

In its reaction against the old centralized regime, and in its desire to stimulate local patriotism, the revolution had created a hierarchy of departmental, district, and communal bodies almost out of touch with either the legislature or the executive. These bodies might be more efficient, but they were no easier to control, when dominated an by energetic *maire* or by an ambitious *procureur-général-syndic.* The latter, indeed, might rule his *département* through its *directoire* almost as independently as Louis XVI's *intendants* had ruled their *généralités*. It was an essential aim of the Jacobins to remedy this state of indiscipline, and to restore a seventeenth-century control.

In the important *Décret constitutif du gouvernement révolutionnaire* (December 4th, '93), the Convention regularized the provisional government inaugurated two months before. The two 'governing' committees and the Council of ministers became the focal points of a centralized bureaucratic system such as France had never before experienced. If the system of ten-day reports from every authority in the country had been carried out (*see p.* 377), the central government would have been buried under a mass of documents 'thick as autumnal leaves in Vallombrosa,' and its work would soon have become impossible. That the Committees were in any case exceedingly busy is sufficiently proved by the twenty-six volumes in which Aulard reprinted a selection from the papers of the Committee of Public Safety, and by the rumoured dimensions of the still unpublished *Répertoire de la correspondance* of the Committee of General Security.

Jacobin austerity soon impressed itself upon the bureaucracy, as upon every branch of the new regime. The circular which Robespierre's fellow-townsman Herman, once judge of the Revolutionary Tribunal, now Commissioner of Civil Administration, issued to the civil service in May, '94, is of more than passing interest. 'The civil servant,' he wrote, 'must above all shed his old dress, and put off that mannered politeness, so inconsistent with the bearing of a free man, which is a relic of the time when some men were ministers, and others were their slaves. We know that the old forms of government have already disappeared: we must forget even what they looked like. Simple and natural manners must take the place of the artificial dignity which was often the only virtue of the head of a department, or of a chief clerk. Decency and an unaffected seriousness are all the manners needed by men occupied in public affairs. The essential quality of Man in the order of Nature is to stand upright. The nonsensical jargon of the old ministries must be replaced by a simple style, clear, and yet concise, free from expressions of servility, from obsequious formulae, stand-offishness, pedantry, or any suggestion that there is an authority superior to that of reason, or of the order established by law—a style which adopts a natural attitude towards subordinate authorities. There must be no conventional phrases, no waste of words.'

Those who incurred the serious displeasure of the committees were fortunate if they did not experience imprisonment, and risk execution. But both punishments were, considering the circumstances, humanely inflicted. Except in the matter of overcrowding, the state of the Paris prisons in '93 was better than it had been the year before. They had been thought over-crowded in September, '92, when they contained two thousand five hundred prisoners. The daily returns issued after August, '93, show that they now contained nearly eight thousand—about twice as many as the London prisons contained at this time in a normal year. Though little attention seems to have been paid to Doublet's report in '91, or to Giraud's report in '93, there is nothing in the reminiscences of Riouffe, Beugnot, Beaulieu, or other prisoners under the Terror to suggest that they were treated with unusual harshness. They had to put up with the over-crowding, discomfort, and lack of air and exercise inseparable from any prison system in the eighteenth century. But money or interest could usually obtain better food or bedding; friends or relations of the prisoners found access to them surprisingly easy; and the frail tenure of life among the inmates, like that of a public air-raid shelter, encouraged a democratic friendliness of which many of them had never known themselves capable. The gaolers, generally picked men, and well paid, had no reason, least of all any political or racial hatred, for ill-treating their prisoners. Many of them knew that their own position was almost as precarious.

As for the method of execution, it was regarded as a privilege, it was believed to be painless, and it certainly saved time. Decapitation, once a monopoly of noble birth, and the only form of execution that bore no stigma of dishonour, was now the right of the humblest *citoyen*. It was the experience of those who attended executions, and an excuse for making them a public entertainment, that the victims died instantaneously, and that the severed heads bore no expression of pain. Decapitation by the old Tower Hill method was out of the question for any nation that had escaped from barbarism, and did not deliberately return to it. It was said in 1792, when the question was first raised, that there was not a Jack Ketch in all France who would undertake to do his work quickly and painlessly: in any case (it was pointed out) a fresh sword or axe would be required for each execution. The obvious alternative was a beheading machine, such as had been employed for the execution of common criminals at Halifax, and of an Earl of Argyll at Edinburgh in 1661—a machine such as might still be seen at work by travellers in eighteenth-century Italy. The *guillotine* was better so known from the ingenious Dr. Guillotin, who suggested the idea of it, than as *louison* or *louisette*, from Louis, the Secretary of the College of Surgeons, who collaborated in carrying it out. After an experiment on dead bodies at the Bicêtre, it was first used for the execution of a highway robber on April 25th, '92. Its first political victim (August 21st) was the 'royalist agent,' Collenot d'Angremont, the first organizer of the National Guard. It was not the use of the guillotine, but the abuse of it, which became horrible. If Sanson had been forced to do his work by hand there would have been scenes like that at the execution of Monmouth, and the Terror would have been stopped within a week by a general outcry against its cruelty. The guillotine had another advantage. Mechanized execution made judicial murder the quickest way to get rid of a political enemy, amidst the indifferent regard, if not the applause, of the general public. It took only half an hour to execute the twenty-one Girondins in October, '93. In June, '94, the execution of the sixty-one *chemises rouges* victims was carried through in forty-five minutes.

Both the Constituent and the Legislative Assemblies had from time to time sent out their own members into the provinces as *représentants en mission*, to deal with matters which required personal investigation, or the authority of a deputy. The Convention, faced by a permanent state of civil and foreign war, and by the sabotaging of local government by incompetent or ill-disposed officials, made extended use of the same method. In March, '93, eighty-two deputies were despatched into the provinces, with wide-reaching powers, to raise recruits, and to regulate local administration. In April it was decreed that three representatives should always be attached to each army in the field; they enjoyed unlimited powers, and the right to employ whatever agents and to spend whatever monies they might think expedient. At the end of the same month (April 30th) the powers and duties of *représentants près les armées* were further defined; and they were required to send in a daily account of their expenses to the national Treasury.

These agents of the central government were not always welcomed or assisted in the provinces. The local authorities had to be warned (May 16th) that they must carry out their orders. Soon (July 17th) their regulations were given the status of *lois provisoires*, unalterable except by the Convention. The influence of travelling representatives was already considerable: it was further increased when their mission kept them stationary in a particular department, or with a particular army. Their functions then became almost those of the Bourbon *Intendants*, or of the Napoleonic *Préfets*.

The representatives on mission relied upon local advice and local help. The decrees against suspects were enforced by the Vigilance Committees (*comités de surveillance*) set up all over the country by the law of March 21st, '93. The purging (*épuration*) of local authorities was carried out by the Popular Societies (*sociétés populaires*). The Popular Societies, like so many other Jacobin weapons, had been forged by the Girondins. As long ago as April, '91, Madame Roland's friend Lanthenas had commended the idea of them to Bancal des Issarts, and had hoped that they might be financed by Lafayette. They passed under various names—*Amis de la constitution, Amis de la liberté et de l'égalité, société républicaine, société patriotique*. They were in effect groups of 'keen men' who 'ran' the revolution in their town or village, and they generally echoed the opinions of the Jacobin club in Paris, to which they were often affiliated. As the revolution moved from right to left, the Popular Societies moved with it. As the Jacobin club became more closely identified with the Jacobin party, so did they. They constituted an active and sometimes tyrannous minority in communities which still favoured the ideas of '89. They insisted on 'keeping up to the height of the revolution' people who often wished to be left in peace to enjoy its benefits, and who had little stomach either for the heroics or for the ferocity of post-Girondin republicanism.

The Societies were thus well-fitted to act as the spies and censors of the Jacobin regime. They advised the visiting representative as to the choice of fit persons for municipal office. At the request of the Committee of Public Safety (November 13th, '93) they drew up a list of citizens in their districts whom they considered worthy of public employment. They were, in fact, an early and imperfect venture in that control of a people by a party which has been brought to a climax by the twentieth-century dictatorships. 'Vigilant sentinels'—so the Committee addresses them—'holding the advanced posts of public opinion, they sound the alarm in every danger, and against every traitor. It is in the sanctuary they provide that patriots sharpen the weapons of victory.'

It is not to be assumed that the Popular Societies flourished equally everywhere. The flowing stream of the revolution had many backwaters. In the district of Ervy in Aube seventy-three communes could only support thirteen societies—two founded in '92, seven in '93, and four in '94. Their membership averaged about eighty, but sometimes fell to fourteen. Their attendances were irregular. Their answers to party questionnaires were evasive. In such districts the Popular Societies lay under a suspicion of *modérantisme*. In others, according to reputable witnesses, 'the whole population trembled before the arrogance of a handful of lawyers calling themselves *société populaire*; and all real power was in their control.'

It had become apparent, during the troubles of May, '93, that the National Guard was no longer sufficient for all the duties of the Home Front. 'How can one expect great activity or energy,' asks a spy's report, 'of men who, continually on guard, and exhausted by their duties, spend most of their time on camp-beds, or go home as soon as their spell of duty is over, leaving their posts short-handed, or unattended?' The Convention had more than once rejected Girondin demands for a special Guard to defend its liberties against the alleged threats of the Paris mob. It had grown tired of hearing popular petitions for the use of force against hoarders and profiteers. Now, with their customary flair for exploiting the ideas of their critics, and diverting the energies of the dangerous elements in the capital, the Jacobins sanctioned the creation of an Emergency Army (*armée révolutionnaire*).

On April 5th Danton had blocked a Girondin decree for a Convention Guard by declaring that what was really needed was an *armée des sansculottes*, to overawe the aristocrats. Robespierre supported this idea in the Jacobin club a few days later. On May 13th there was an important debate in the General Council of the Commune. It was declared that a situation had arisen not unlike that which Paris had experienced eight months before.

Great numbers of volunteers were marching to the front, leaving the working class unprovided for, and the capital at the mercy of rich counter-revolutionaries. It was therefore proposed that two measures should be taken. One was the disarmament and arrest of all suspected persons. The other was the establishment of a paid army of *patriotes peu fortunés, véritables sansculottes*, on the model of that created by the patriot Chalier at Lyon. Its duties were at present obscure. If the Hébertists had their way, it would certainly be set to enforce the food regulations, and to secure the food-supply of the capital. It would not be allowed to take over the functions of the National Guard, if the Jacobins could prevent it. But Danton, who was forward in proposing so many terrorist measures, certainly saw in the Revolutionary Army an instalment of the general payment and arming of the *sectionnaires* which he hoped would distract them from more serious political ambitions.

The formation of this force was sanctioned by the Convention on June 4th, and the Commune authorized enrolment a week later. But for three months the scheme hung fire. The *sansculottes* were not forward to volunteer. It was not till Barère presented a fresh decree (September 5th) that the Revolutionary Army was actually set on foot. The force, for which Carnot drew up a *règlement* four days later, was to consist of six battalions of infantry, each a thousand strong, and six squadrons of cavalry. It would have part use of the guns of the National Guard. Its members, men of twenty-five to forty not belonging to any other force, would choose their own junior officers, and would be paid 1s. 8d. a day. The government was careful to keep control over the personnel of a body which might easily become a hindrance rather than a help to the enforcement of order. The final choice of recruits was entrusted to a committee on which the department was represented alongside the commune; and the commanding officers were appointed by the Committee of Public Safety.

One way or another, it was six weeks before this rather ragged Home Guard paraded before the Convention. The infantry was then seen to be led by the actor Ronsin, Parein, a lawyer's clerk, and the jeweller Boulanger. Grammont, another actor, was Ronsin's Chief of Staff. At the head of the cavalry rode the embroiderer Mazuel. In a week's campaign, they boasted, they would purge the suburbs of Paris of 'a host of traitors, hoarders, and ill-disposed persons.' They showed their spirit by singing patriotic songs before the General Council of the commune.

The government had changed its views, since the spring, about the use it would make of the Revolutionary Army. It now needed all the help it could get against the federal revolt. A decree of October 10th provided for the employment of the new force against counter-revolutionaries, and fore-shadowed the billeting of garrisons on troublesome towns. The Jacobins were not sorry to be able to disperse fifteen hundred undisciplined men in small bodies over some ten departments. Detachments were sent as far afield as Laon, Caen, and even Brest. The risk of armed mob-rule in Paris was further lessened when the main force of nearly two thousand men marched off in mid-October under Ronsin, Parein, and Boulanger to help in the punishment of the rebels at Lyon.

The Revolutionary army did some good work in the provinces. It inspected barns, checked stocks of food, requisitioned supplies for the army, and provided escorts for the grain convoys. But its chief merit, in the eyes of a government bent on centralization, and jealous of local initiative, was that it could be alleged as an excuse for disallowing and disbanding unofficial forces of the same kind. Chalier's Lyon experiment had been repeated elsewhere—by Ysabeau and Tallien at Bordeaux, by Saliceti, Gasparin, and Albitte at Marseille, by Ysoré and Duquesnoy at Lille. It had already been found advisable to remove Doppet's *légion franc des Allobroges* from Paris, and to attach it to the army of the Pyrenees. Legal sanction was given to this policy by the decree of December 4th, which provided (Sect. III, Art. 18) for the disbanding at twenty-four hours' notice of any revolutionary army other than that established by the Convention, and forbade the raising of any such force in future.

But even one such organization was enough to cause friction with the municipal authorities, especially in districts out of sympathy with Parisian Jacobinism. There were frequent clashes between the military and the civilians. The Revolutionary Army, as Augustin Robespierre had warned his brother, was likely to become counter-revolutionary. When the Hébertists were executed, a place was found on the scaffold for Ronsin. Three days later the disbanding of his force was moved (March 27th) by the same man, Barère, who had proposed its embodiment six months earlier. Then the Jacobins had been forced to give way to a popular demand: now they had no more need to do so. Thus a dangerous experiment and a dangerous example came to a timely end.

In a circular addressed to the departments a fortnight after the enactment of the decree of December 4th, and designed to soften a blow which deprived them of half their powers, the members of the Committee of Public Safety were at pains to expound what they called *le génie des lois révolutionnaires*. 'Failings inherent in the mistakes, or rather in the faults of the Girondins have (they claim) been eliminated; everything worth keeping has been remodelled, but retained. In particular, two great vices of federalism have been corrected—its decentralization, and its delays.' How far was this Jacobin claim justified?

The departmental directories had always been an obstacle to quick and easy relations between the Convention and the communes. They were therefore deprived of all responsibility for the enforcement of the law, and were confined to the ordinary functions of a local authority. These *fonctions d'édilité*, however floridly described, consisted of no more than a general

supervision of trade, of roads and canals, of the national property, and of
taxation. The departmental *conseils-généraux*, *présidents*, and *procureurs-
généraux-syndics* were suppressed. The superiority of the department to the
district and commune disappeared. The 'supervision (*surveillance*) of revolutionary law' was handed over to the districts, and its enforcement (*application*) to the Vigilance Committees of the communes.

This removal of an intermediate wheel in the administrative machine
made possible a further measure of centralization. The districts and communes, which now became, for most purposes, the units of administration,
found that their permanent officials (*procureurs-syndics* or *procureurs*) were
to be replaced by government officials (*agents nationaux*) with roaming
commissions and overriding powers, and in constant communication with
the Committee of General Security. True, for the present these functions
were to be exercised by the existing officials: but at any moment a *commissaire* might arrive from Paris, an *épuration* might be ordered, and the control
of local affairs might be taken out of the hands of the local people. Such a
system was too elaborate. The Committee had neither enough agents nor
enough time to deal with the complicated affairs of five hundred and fifty
districts, and forty thousand communes. Napoleon was probably well
advised when he restored, in the form of his *préfets*, a single administrative
authority for each department.

The elimination of the departments was intended to contribute to the
second great object of Jacobin administration, speed. The December
decree was not content with enjoining that all reports, lists of names, and
correspondence must be punctually supplied. It contained a whole section
of twelve articles, headed *Envoi et promulgation des lois*, to provide for the
prompt publication of its orders. A special commission of four members,
with a private printing-press, was charged with the duty of publishing and
circulating a *bulletin des lois* to officials all over the country. It was expressly
provided that even the less important decrees should be sent out within three
days of their enactment. The best commentary on these provisions is a
decree of March 27th, '94, which shows that, nearly four months afterwards, no *bulletin* had yet appeared. The press was not available: paper
had to be manufactured : the official addresses were not known: the postal
authorities were not ready to handle the parcels. In fact, the first number of
the *bulletin* appeared in the middle of June, '94, and contained the *Loi du 22
prairial*, the swan-song of the Jacobin regime. Meanwhile it was left to the
representatives on mission and to the national agents to circulate the laws
that governed their action, when and as they could. It does not require
much imagination to realize the confusion and delays thus involved, or to
picture the state of mind of an ignorant country mayor trying to grapple
with an imperfect series of successive and sometimes overlapping regulations.

In view of such difficulties, it was a little hard that public officials should
have been warned that 'the piercing eye' of the Committee of Public Safety

'scrutinized their most secret acts,' and should have been threatened with the ferocious punishments prescribed in Section V of the December decree— punishments ranging from long terms of imprisonment, the loss of civic rights, and the confiscation of property, to the death penalty for a *contrefacteur du bulletin des lois*. Section V was, no doubt, a salutary warning to the considerable number of royalists and federalists who still clung to office, and to such members of the Jacobin party itself as took easy money in government posts. But it inevitably stifled initiative, and encouraged a dull if not an idle routine. There was point as well as humour in the complaint of a father of thirty-eight children, of whom thirty-two were boys, that most of the administrative posts were occupied by bachelors, and that these men 'spent their time in the café, the gambling-saloon, and the brothel, unless they were at the office, reading plays, and practising shooting.'

'He's too original for my taste.' The remark was made by Augustin Robespierre about Joseph Lebon: it might be taken as a motto for all such regimes. Over-centralization sterilizes variety, and breeds stupidity. The Jacobins, indeed, were not theorists, but practical men dealing with an emergency. They had none of the mass-stupidities nowadays called ideo-logical: no racialism, no anti-Semitism, no militant and exclusive national-ism. Their mild attempts to conscript the labour, to requisition the means, or to mould the minds of Frenchmen would be thought laughable by present-day professors of these arts of government. Their spying was not inquisitorial, their punishments were not refined by torture, their method of liquidating their political enemies was the humanest they could devise. They retained, in their most ferocious moods, a sense of proportion and a sense of humour which saved them from the lowest depths of degradation. But they could not escape the fate of all governments which substitute compulsion for per-suasion, and put servility before service.

It is sometimes objected that the Jacobin regime was government by a minority. If stress is to be laid upon the word 'minority,' it has to be proved that the three thousand Jacobin clubs in the provinces did not represent the mass of revolutionary opinion; and that the body of nearly two million active citizens who recorded their approval of the constitution of '93 had no right to pledge the support of the other two millions who abstained from voting. If stress is to be laid rather on the word 'government,' it may be suggested that all government is, on analysis, minority government, and that no fault need be found with this, so long as the governing minority has the confidence of the majority, and an effective sovereignty resides in the whole people. If the French people delegated too much of its activity, during the years '93–4, to its Jacobin rulers, it may well have done so, not because it lacked the spirit to rebel against a regime that it grew to dislike, but because it lacked the desire to overthrow a regime which it continued to trust.

Much turned, in either case, upon the feeling that this was a period of transition, from which a new order would soon emerge, worth waiting for, and, if need be, worth suffering for. 'It is your task,' Saint-Just had said, 'to build a city whose citizens treat one another as friends, guests, and brothers. It is your task to re-establish public confidence, and to make it understood that revolutionary government means, not war or conquest, but the passage from misery to happiness, from corruption to honesty, from bad principles to good principles.' But would the transitional period ever end? Would the clearsightedness which dictated Jacobin aims triumph over the stupidity involved in Jacobin means? Robespierre had laid it down as the motto of revolutionary government that intimidation (*terreur*) was disastrous without patriotism (*vertu*), and patriotism powerless without intimidation. But if intimidation became the order of the day, might it not sap the foundations of patriotism?

Such was the problem which the Jacobin regime had yet to solve.

CHAPTER XXI

CIVIL WAR

Eadem illos deum ira, eadem hominum rabies, eaedem scelerum causae in discordiam egere.—(TACITUS, Hist. II. 38.)

THE Jacobin control of the Convention lasted fourteen months, gradually strengthening its hold over the country, until it ended in the dictatorship overthrown in July, '94. The period may be divided, without more violence than always accompanies the vivisection of history, into four parts.

From June 2nd, '93, when the Girondin deputies were expelled from the assembly, until July 27th, when Robespierre joined the Committee of Public Safety, the Jacobins were still too weak to exploit their victory at home, or to win another in the field. The surrender of Mainz and Valenciennes in the last week of July marked the bankruptcy of Girondin militarism. An intensification of the British blockade, an extension of the revolt in the provinces, and the beginnings of the *enragé* troubles in Paris combined to make the government's position very difficult.

The reorganization of the Committee of Public Safety (July 10th) re-invigorated the government almost as much as the inauguration of the Convention itself a year before. The replacement of Danton by Robespierre opened a second period (July 27th–December 4th), during which an amazing change was brought about in the face of affairs. The Girondin leaders were outlawed or executed. All the resources of the country were mobilized for war. Military successes were gained on four fronts, at Hondschoote, Wattignies, Cholet, and Lyon. A centralized administration converted

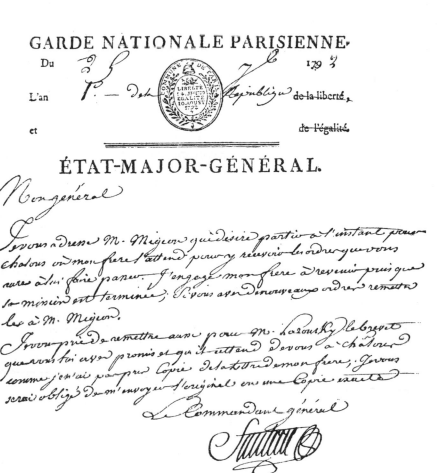

GARDE NATIONALE PARISIENNE.

Du ... 179...

L'an ... République de la liberté,

et ... de l'égalité

ÉTAT-MAJOR-GÉNÉRAL.

[handwritten letter]

Mon général

Je vous adresse M. Mijeon qui désire partir à l'instant pour Châlons où mon frère l'attend pour y recevoir les ordres que vous aurez à lui faire passer. J'engage mon frère à revenir puisque sa mission est terminée; si vous avez de nouveaux ordres remettez les à M. Mijeon.

Je vous prie de remettre aussi pour M. Larousky le brevet que vous lui avez promis et qu'il attend de vous à Châlons comme j'en ai pas pris copie de la lettre de mon frère; je vous serai obligé de m'envoyer l'original ou une copie exacte

Le Commandant général

[signature]

A LETTER BY SANTERRE
As Commandant of the National Guard.

France, for the duration of the emergency period, into a rationed, disciplined fortress.

But there were soon signs of fresh trouble. The *enragés* showed themselves insatiable. The anti-clericals let their passion carry them beyond reason. On the very day after the decree of December 4th had regularized the Jacobin government Desmoulins published the first number of a paper whose unavowed aim was to restore the easier standards of a Dantonist regime. The Committee of Public Safety, having either to abdicate or to assert its monopoly of power, chose the way of force. A period which had begun with a threat of dictatorship ended with the reality of it. At the crisis of Germinal, Year II, first the Hébertist and then the Dantonist opposition went to the scaffold.

The final period (April 5th–July 28th, '94) is that of the supremacy and fall of a Robespierrist regime divided by internal feuds, disliked for its plans to enforce public decency and discipline, discredited by an unsuccessful economic policy, and undermined by the hidden enemies and half-revealed victims of its power.

In June, '93, France had been at war for more than a year. Frenchmen were beginning to see that an adventure lightly and unadvisedly begun could not so easily be abandoned. It must be carried through, whatever the cost, to victory or death. A state of war, which the most solidly established government can never face without the fear of change, is doubly dangerous to a newly founded regime. Already the unhappy king, staking his fortunes on foreign intervention, had lost both his throne and his life. Already Brissot and his friends had been overwhelmed in the disaster provoked by their bid for power. Already the people were regretting the temper in which they had allowed themselves to be exploited by ambitious or treacherous leaders. Their just anger with the *émigrés*, and their natural resentment at foreign interference, which inspired the gallant volunteering of a year ago, seemed remote and unmeaning in the disillusionment of a long war. What began as a glorious adventure had become a dull round of duty and danger. The minority who had opposed the war-fever of '91–2 because they foresaw military defeat, the designs of the court, the ambitions of Brissot, and the political influence of the generals, could now point to the truth of all their predictions. A fresh danger had been added which might also have been foreseen—the exploiting of the nation's necessities by speculators, profiteers, and the agents of foreign powers. Called both by ambition and by a sense of duty to relieve the failure of the Girondins, the Jacobins would need great energy, and indeed ruthlessness, to deal with a very dangerous situation.

It was defeat in the field which had brought the new government into power : only victory in the field could establish it. The aim expressed in the title of the Committee of General Security could be attained only by the means expressed in the title of the Committee of Public Safety. The way to *sûreté générale* was through *salut public*. The Jacobins could win the support of the sound majority in the Convention and in the country only if they saved the land, the homes, and the food of the people against attempts to destroy the integrity of the republic.

It was a single war, but a war upon three fronts. There was a foreign enemy in the east, a Catholic-royalist enemy in the west, and a federalist enemy in the south. The revolt in the north-west, partly owing to the incompetence of its leaders, and partly owing to its isolation from the centres of revolt in the south, had already collapsed.

Bordeaux, though free from serious economic troubles, had not escaped political controversy. Almost every play staged at the Grand-théâtre by its enterprising manageress, Madame Dorfeuille, from Chénier's *Charles IX* to Laya's *Jean Calas* and *L'Ami des Lois,* had led to anti-Jacobin demonstrations by the *société populaire de la jeunesse bordelaise;* till it became one of the aims of the Jacobin regime to purge the local stage. In this reactionary atmosphere the news of June 2nd caused an outbreak of anger against Paris and the Convention. The local representatives on mission were expelled from the town. A committee was set up to organize ' resistance to oppression.' There was talk of raising an army of eighty thousand men to co-operate with Custine, the commander of the northern army, and with Houchard, the commander of the army of the Moselle, in a combined march on the capital. By August Bordeaux was full of priests, emigrants, and aristocrats. Their threats against the Jacobins were encouraged by the presence of refugee Girondins from Caen—Guadet, Pétion, and Barbaroux. The Convention seemed for a time to be faced with a serious revolt. But military measures proved, after all, to be unnecessary. Finance ruled the situation. Although it confiscated a hundred and thirty thousand pounds of government money, the municipality of Bordeaux was unable to feed its swollen population, still less to equip an expeditionary force against Paris. In September it tamely allowed itself to be replaced by an Insurrectional Commune (as it would have been called in Paris) composed of commissioners elected by the sections.

This apparently Jacobin victory should have ended the affair. But it did not. The exiled representatives of the Convention doubted the republican zeal of the Insurrectional Commune, and refused its invitation to return. It was not until the middle of October that Baudot and Ysabeau, Tallien and Chaudron-Rousseau at last considered that enough of their enemies were in prison to prove the repentance of the Bordelais, and to guarantee their own safety. On the 16th they entered Bordeaux by a symbolic breach in the town walls. Their first care was to set up a court-martial (*commission militaire*), which during the next nine months tried over eight hundred ' rebels,' and put nearly three hundred of them to death. But this, thought their secretary-spy, Peyren D'Herval, was not enough.

There must be something in the atmosphere or in the social make-up of Bordeaux that gave even its Jacobin justice a taint of Girondin clemency. When the citizens at last imprisoned him for the excesses of his Vigilance Committee, D'Herval sent word to his masters in Paris. In March, '94, Tallien had to defend himself before the Committee of Public Safety against charges of loose and luxurious living. In April Jullien, the youngest and most intelligent of the government's travelling commissioners, arrived at Bordeaux. He dismissed Ysabeau, restored Peyren, and hunted down the outlawed Girondins. When news came, on July 31st, of the fall of Robespierre, he proceeded, with admirable presence of mind, to arrest Lacombe, the President of Tallien's court-martial, and sent him, a week later, to the guillotine. Thus everyone's idea of justice was satisfied, except that of the victims.

At Marseille, as at Bordeaux, the municipal government set up by the revolution had hitherto lived on friendly terms with the mercantile class which paid the rates and maintained the commercial prosperity of the town. It had even profited by the food-shortage of '91–2 to build up an import trade in grain from overseas. It was not long since Marseille had been proud of its republican spirit. It had sent federal troops to Paris, to Aix, and to Arles. There had been Marseillais among the men who guarded Louis' scaffold on January 21st. But the dictatorship of the Paris commune had offended the pride of the capital of the Midi; and the British blockade had swept its ships from the seas. At Marseille, as at Bordeaux, the news of June 2nd caused an immediate outbreak against the headquarters of Jacobinism. Boisset and Bayle, the representatives of the Convention, were expelled from the town. The Jacobin club of the rue Thubaneau was closed. The *comité général* of the sections declared an insurrection against the government. On June 6th a joint meeting of local authorities— municipal, district, and departmental—proposed to summon a commission representing all the southern departments. It was to meet at Bourges—so far north was the movement expected to spread—and was to mobilize an army which Barbaroux, from his confinement in Paris, urged should march on the capital, and 'extinguish anarchy.'

Like Bordeaux, Marseille was soon filled with malcontents of the usual kinds ; but they included, as befitted so cosmopolitan a centre, foreign spies, and foreign speculators. Even citizen Egalité, the *ci-devant* Duc d'Orléans, was to be found there. But little was accomplished. As at Bordeaux, Girondin enthusiasm was soon discouraged by lack of supplies. When, in mid-August, the advance of government troops threatened actual starvation, the municipality wrote to Lord Hood, the admiral in command of the British fleet blockading the port, offering, in return for his help, to proclaim Louis XVII king of France. This was too much for the patriot elements in the city. Encouraged by Carteaux, the Convention general, they fraternized with the municipal troops, and with a battalion that Toulon had sent to help in the rebellion. When the republicans attacked, the Marseillais refused to fight. On August 25th Carteaux and his men, with a group of Paris representatives, entered the town. The revolt was over.

As at Bordeaux, so at Marseille the downfall of federalism was followed at first by a regime of local Jacobinism. When that failed to show the requisite ruthlessness, its place was taken by a repressive system directed from Paris. Between August and October the pre-federal authorities resumed control of the town ; the Jacobin club reopened its doors ; the revolutionary tribunal resumed its operations. But if the Bordeaux air bred indifferentism, the air of Marseille bred plutocracy. The rich merchants shirked their share of taxation, and invested their wealth abroad. The speculators found that fresh profits could be made by evading the food regulations, or by smuggling goods through the blockade. Even the guillotine, which by the end of August had despatched a promising number of federalists, found its work impeded by interest and bribery. During five months of municipal management the execution-rate was not more than half that of the *commission militaire* which followed.

In October the mild Albitte was replaced by the ruthless Barras and Fréron. Paul-François-Jean-Nicolas Barras was a man of aristocratic birth, who had at one time served in the Colonial army, till the experiences of the fall of Pondicherry turned him from war to politics. He was less of a Jacobin than he pretended to be, and less of a philanderer than he liked to be thought. His present mission qualified him to become the patron of Bonaparte, and the effective ruler of France. Louis-Marie-Stanislas Fréron, a Jacobin journalist, had been Robespierre's contemporary at College, and was now a supporter of his regime. A year later he would do his best to compass his death, and to blacken his fame. These respectable emissaries of the central government proclaimed a policy of repression. *La terreur*, they said, *est à l'ordre du jour.*

They began by doubling the rate of executions : they ended by attempting to destroy the very identity of the third largest city in France. Not merely were federalist buildings to be pulled down. Marseille itself was to disappear from the map. The place was henceforth to be known as *Sansnom*, 'the Town without a name.' This indignity was, however, disapproved of by the government, which had already inflicted it upon the guiltier Lyon. Six weeks later Maignet, a new emissary, arrived from Paris, and the order of January 6th was revoked. In March the court-martial was again replaced by the tribunal, which, borrowing new zeal from its predecessor, carried out within a little more than a month a hundred and twenty-eight executions.

Even that was not the end. The decree of April 16th should have transferred all political trials to Paris. But there were still so many prisoners at Marseille that a special *tribunal d'Orange* was set up to deal with them. The new court, adopting methods devised by Couthon, and soon adapted to Paris by the law of the 22nd Prairial, carried out its work so efficiently that in less than two months another three hundred and thirty-two heads had fallen on the scaffold. When the storm had passed, the prosperity of Marseille was in ruins. Its merchants had fled, its wealth was dispersed, the privileges of its port had been abolished. French repression had completed what the British blockade had begun. In maps of '95 Marseille appears in the smallest type and is no more than a *chef-lieu de district*.

The importance of Toulon lay less in its inconsiderable trade in oil and cloth than in its naval port—the finest on the southern coast of France, and the base of the French Mediterranean fleet. Here Malouet had been *Intendant de la marine*. Here Robespierre had supported the municipality in a contest with the naval commandant, the Comte de Rions, and had been rewarded with the honorary citizenship of the town. When this six months' controversy was closed by a vote of the assembly (January 16th, '90), the local patriots fell out amongst themselves. The Jacobin club and municipality were on one side, the Girondin sections and naval establishment were on the other. As elsewhere, the Jacobin coup d'état of June, '93, brought matters to a head. Within a month Toulon had set up a Girondin committee ; it had thrown the local representatives, Bayle and Beauvais, into prison ; it had sent help to the Marseillais. The rebels had counted on a Girondin revenge. When news came of the collapse of the federal revolt in Normandy, and of the fall of Marseille, Rear-admiral Trogoff committed the unforgivable offence of treating with Admiral Hood for the surrender of his ships and forts, in return for help in the defence of the town against the Jacobins, and in the restoration of the Bourbon monarchy. This he did in defiance of the feeling of his men. Five thousand of them under Rear-admiral Saint-Julien, the second in command, were allowed by Lord Hood to sail in four of the least serviceable of their ships, under a flag of truce, to Rochefort, Lorient, and Brest. When the republican armies arrived near the town, they found its inner harbour crowded with a disarmed French navy, its outer basin occupied by foreign men-of-war, and its forts manned by nearly seventeen thousand British, Spanish, Piedmontese, Neapolitan, and French royalist troops.

The siege of Toulon outlasted by two months that of Lyon. It has been too often treated as an episode in the early career of the Corsican 'artillery general of outstanding merit, citizen Buonaparte,' whom Augustin Robespierre mentioned in a letter to his brother on April 4th. It has too seldom been treated as the climax of the civil war. It was a serious and difficult operation, during which two generals were recalled in disgrace. The besieging army had to contend not only with a troublesome terrain, but also with lack of food, money, and ammunition. Couthon, his temper as well as his health troubled by the climate of Lyon, had offered to go to Toulon, and to 'burn it down.' The Committee of Public Safety, with more sense of realities, preferred to send Robespierre's brother, with the Corsican Saliceti, to supervise the siege. Here was an instance in which the political and military authorities seem to have worked harmoniously together. The final despatch of Augustin Robespierre, describing in true war-correspondent style the assault of December 27th, shows that it was a gallant as well as a successful operation.

It was a misfortune that Barras and Fréron, who were already executing 'republican vengeance' on the Marseillais, should have had their commission extended to Toulon. As soon as the town fell they took over the repulsive business of punishing the rebels. 'Toulon,' wrote Fréron, 'shall be rased to the ground ; its inhabitants shall be put to the sword; the English, Spaniards, and Neapolitans shall be drowned.' The threat was almost carried out. The British fleet, indeed, made its escape, burning or carrying off a great part of the French navy, and taking on board nearly fifteen thousand refugees. But nothing could save the rest. Fréron was soon able to report that twelve thousand workmen had been requisitioned to pull down the town. 'Every day since our entry,' he added, 'two hundred Toulonais have been shot. Already eight hundred have been executed.'

Not even the dagger of Charlotte Corday struck a blow more fatal to Girondism than the news announced in the Convention during the debate of June 2nd, that Lyon had risen against the government. Bordeaux, Marseille, and Toulon were important centres of maritime trade or sea-power. But they lay as far from Paris as could be. Their defection was a frontier, almost a foreign affair. Even the Vendée revolt, so much nearer home, could be localized, and did not threaten the heart of the country. But Lyon was the second city of France, almost a rival capital. It had been the seat of Roman rule and the centre of the Roman road-system north of the Alps, at a time when Paris hardly existed. It had known eighteen centuries of civic life, and nearly five hundred years of communal self-government. It boasted a population of some hundred and fifty thousand souls. Its happy position at the junction of the Rhône and the Saône made it the gate-way of the Midi. Its industries provided a quarter of all the exports of the country. Its magazines contained the military stores of the southern armies. The rebellion of Lyon was a menace to the whole Jacobin regime. The presence within its crowded walls of a large and discontented class of workers, whose last rising had been cruelly repressed only seven years before, increased the risk of a general conflagration.

The manner as well as the moment of the rising emphasised the challenge. Lyon, like Paris, had its sections, its active citizens, and its new municipality organized under the law of 1790. Lyon, like Paris, had a Jacobin club a city militia, and a patriotic press. There was the same feud between an aristocratic department and a democratic commune. There were the same food troubles, the same provocative extremes of poverty and wealth. Lyon too had its Bastille ; and the fall of the Château de Pierre-seize (September 9th, '92) had been accompanied by acts of savagery which showed that the cut-throats of Lyon had nothing to learn from the *septembriseurs* of Paris.

But beneath this apparent likeness the republicanism of Lyon had developed on lines of its own. It was from Lyon that Madame Roland, whose house may still be seen there, wrote, in the early months of the revolution, of 'a social inequality more marked, more stubbornly resented, and more fanatically defended' than in Paris, and described the crowd of 'petty officials and financiers, the sons of bakers or inn-keepers, who hate to see their relations rising in the social scale, and anathematize the revolution.' It was of the Lyon district that a German traveller wrote in February, '92, 'No one thinks of sacrificing an atom of his own interests for the good cause,' and 'Here the one thing that everyone covets at all costs is peace, and the security indispensable to business.' This foreigner foresaw that owing to the rise of prices, and the depreciation of the *assignats*, the Lyon working class would soon be in a deplorable situation. In fact, during the winter of '92–3 the number of persons in need of relief was estimated at over twenty thousand.

Yet all this did not explain why a city which had professed its loyalty to the revolution of August 10th, and to the republic of September 21st, should take up arms against the government of June 2nd. The reason lay in the social and occupational solidarity of a great industrial centre ; a solidarity strange to the cosmopolitan make-up of the capital; a solidarity which enabled the well-to-do merchants and tradesmen who monopolized municipal office to command the support of the active citizens of the clubs and sections, even whilst they intrigued with royalists and counter-revolutionaries; a solidarity which drove the Jacobin minority into violent reprisals hardly paralleled elsewhere. Here was a Girondism *in excelsis*, and the *de profundis* of Jacobinism.

The execution of Louis XVI was seized upon by the Lyon Jacobins as an opportunity to assert themselves. Marie-Joseph Chalier, a businessman of forty-six, of Piedmontese origin, organized an armed following, and announced his intention of purging the city of 'all aristocrats, moderates, egoists, speculators, hoarders, usurers, and priestly fanatics.' His 'revolutionary army' carried out this programme by arresting, and sometimes murdering, the richer and more reactionary citizens. After a long struggle, Bertrand, one of his followers, was forced into the mayoralty. The arrival of Dubois-Crancé and a Jacobin deputation in the middle of May gave to a provincial outpost of Jacobinism the sanction and support of the capital.

But by now the Girondins were alive to the danger of an attack upon their persons and property. They formed anti-Jacobin clubs in the sections. When these were closed, they organized an armed attack upon the Town Hall. On May 29th, a day never forgotten by good Lyonnais, bitter street-fighting broke out. Four hundred citizens fell: but victory remained with the anti-Jacobins. Their local revenge was mild. Only Chalier, and Riard, one of his followers, were executed. A subscription was opened to relieve the victims of both parties. But it was not to be expected that the new Jacobin government would overlook so striking a defiance of its authority. Six months before, Lyon had shown Paris the way to a Jacobin dictatorship: now it had relapsed into Girondism. Chalier, the hero of March, was the martyr of May. At the very time when Jacobinism was triumphing in Paris, it was being overthrown at Lyon. On the very day (June 1st) that the Paris sections were preparing to surround the Convention and to force the expulsion of the Girondin deputies, the *conseil général de la commune de Lyon* issued a manifesto denouncing the local Jacobins as 'anarchists,' and encouraging their betrayal to a newly constituted Police Committee. Within a few weeks Lyon was joining with Marseille, Toulon, and other rebel districts of the Midi in plans for a concerted march on Paris.

When it was realized how firmly the new government in Paris was holding its position, the victors of Lyon would willingly have drawn back. They even tried to conciliate the Jacobins by passing a resolution approving the constitution of '93. But an intercepted letter from Dubois-Crancé showed that their repentance came too late. Within two days of the reconstitution of the Committee of Public Safety (July 12th) the Convention had declared Lyon to be 'in a state of rebellion against the republic,' and had prepared an armed force to repress the revolt. The city was already marked down for revenge. Kellermann and a republican army might at any moment appear outside its walls. The Lyonnais chose as their leader Perrin de Précy, who had fought with the Swiss in the defence of the Tuileries, and prepared to stand a siege. It was a tense moment. The whole issue between Jacobinism and Girondism, between federal and centralized republicanism, was to be decided by a duel to the death between Paris and Lyon.

A last effort to avoid civil war was made by Robert Lindet, the ablest conciliator whom the government could have employed; but it failed. On August 8th Kellermann appeared before the city, and called on it to surrender. When it refused, the bombardment began. Red-hot cannon-balls bounced along the streets, and set the buildings on fire. The defenders were reduced by cowardice or desertion from twenty-five thousand to not much more than six thousand men. The reinforcements that they expected from Marseille never arrived. The republican army grew in numbers every day. When the garrison were summoned to give up their general and his staff, and to surrender at discretion, they refused. But at last, after two months' siege, in which two republican armies were engaged, and a vast amount of ammunition was expended, the city was forced to capitulate.

Couthon, the senior representative of the central government, believed that no punishment would suffice short of the extermination of the citizens taken under arms, the ruin of the richer civilians, and the removal of the poorer population to some more patriotic part of the country, where they might 'change their nature, and become useful citizens.' It was in this spirit that the Convention, almost before it was certain of the fall of Lyon, published the famous decree for its destruction. A *commission extraordinaire* was set up to punish the rebels *militairement et sans délai*. The inhabitants were to be disarmed. The rich quarters of the town were to be pulled down. The name Lyon was to be struck off the map; and such parts of the place as might still be standing were to be called Ville-affranchie (Freed-town). 'Upon the ruins of Lyon,' it was decreed, 'a column shall be set up, to bear witness to posterity of the crimes and punishment of the royalists of this town, with this inscription :—"Lyon made war on liberty: Lyon no longer exists." ' With this savage enactment went a covering letter from the Committee of Public Safety, written by Robespierre, instructing the representatives at Lyon to carry it out *avec une sévérité inexorable*.

Couthon approved of this policy; but he was hardly the man to enforce it. Three weeks later (November 4th) he was superseded by Collot d'Herbois, Fouché, and Châteauneuf-Randon. To them were added, on November 25th, the officers in command of the *armée révolutionnaire* sent to help in the work of repression—Ronsin, Boulanger, and Parein. These were the men responsible for a punitive regime which lasted till the recall of Fouché to Paris on March 27th, '94. Their executive was a *commission temporaire*, or *de surveillance républicaine*, of twenty members, set up on November 10th, which divided its attention between the city itself and the surrounding department. Their working orders, the Instruction of November 16th, provided for the abolition of aristocracy, the arrest of all suspected persons, the taxation of the rich, the increase of agricultural production, and the extirpation of religious fanaticism. But what was most significant was the spirit in which these measures were to be carried out. 'A revolutionary agent,' says the Instruction, 'may do anything. He has nothing to fear, except failure to reach the level of republican legality. He who anticipates this, or goes beyond it, or even seems to have passed its goal, may not yet have reached it.'

The history of the punishment of Lyon may be studied in the records of the three courts—the *commission militaire* (October 12th–November 28th), the *commission populaire* or *Dorfeuille* (so notorious became the name of its President, the husband of the theatrical manageress of Bordeaux), and the *commission révolutionnaire* or (for similar reasons) *Parein*—which, in less than six months, tried over four thousand prisoners, and condemned nearly half of them to death. The first of these courts dealt with combatants, the second with non-combatants, and the third, which superseded them, with both. It was the *commission Parein* which, sometimes trying twenty prisoners an hour, and using the firing squad as well as the guillotine, carried out the bulk of the executions at the rate of twenty-eight a day for two months on end. It was this court, too, which, encouraged by Collot d'Herbois, was guilty of a piece of brutality remarkable even in this dreary and distasteful record of violence—the mass-shootings (*mitraillades*) of December 4th–5th.

Other parts of the Instruction were carried out with the same almost religious ferocity. The fortifications of the city, and the houses of its richer inhabitants, were systematically destroyed; a representative struck the first ceremonial blow. The 'martyr' Chalier's remains were disinterred, and given public burial. His head—a sacred, and (thanks to the guillotine) a portable relic—was carried by Collot to Paris, and presented to the Convention. The ex-Oratorian Fouché, fresh from his anti-clerical experiments at Moulins and Nevers, found the extirpation of fanaticism specially congenial, and on November 30th staged in the church of Saint-Jean a festival of Reason. At Saint-Roch Monvel lectured on the poetry of the pagan Lucretius. Their labours were protected by the *sansculottes* of the Revolutionary Army, and blessed by Hébert's *Père Duchesne*, which now printed a special edition at Lyon. Only depopulation proved to be impracticable.

Perhaps it would have been better if some such plan could have been carried out. It was hardly to be expected that a factious and intractable people would forgive their injuries, unlearn their violence, and rebuild a prosperous Lyon on the rubble-heaps of Ville-affranchie. The recall of Fouché gave the place a short respite. With the fall of Fouché's enemy Robespierre the Girondins had their revenge on the Jacobins, and a White Terror raged at Lyon only less ferociously than the Red Terror which had preceded it. Under the Directory the place gradually returned to political convalescence. It remained for Bonaparte to restore, under careful supervision, a municipality which had proved so unfit for self-government, and a mayoralty which had been the cause of such bitter strife. With the re-erection of the buildings which had been pulled down came a revival of the industries upon which alone the peace and prosperity of the town relied.

The insurrection in the west was not due to the *coup d'état* of June, '93; it was an inheritance from the Girondin regime. It was a very different affair from the rebellions in the south. The rebels in the Vendée and the surrounding districts were peasants and farmers, led by nobles and priests. It was not a productive area. The only great sea-port likely to be affected was Nantes: fortunately it was situated on the remoter south bank of the Loire. The Vendée revolt did not, like that of Bordeaux or Marseille, appeal to the commercial bourgeoisie, or, like that of Lyon, to the industrialists. It had few friends in Paris, and no champions in the assembly. Its supporters—Catholic gentry, non-juror priests, and emigrant aristocrats—were of a kind to discredit it with patriots of all colours. The loss of the west as a recruiting-ground might be serious; but it did not contain an arsenal like Lyon, or a naval base like Toulon. The revolt in the Vendée was not so much a malignant growth bound to spread as an infection that could be isolated and destroyed.

On May 31st, '93, the Committee of Public Safety received a report on the situation in the west from the Duc de Gontaut de Biron, the aristocratic commander-in-chief of the *armée des côtes maritimes*—the three coastal commands whose headquarters were at La Rochelle, Nantes and Brest, and Cherbourg. The Vendée revolt (they learnt) had now acquired a policy, had chosen leaders, and had adopted tactics justified by success in the field. It disowned both the Breton particularism of La Rouerie's earlier movement, and the compromising patronage of Coblentz. It entrusted its leadership in ideas to the priests, and its leadership in arms to such Catholic and royalist gentry as would enlist for the crusade. The eloquent and fanatical abbé Bernier had summed up the aims of the rebels (May 27th) as 'the restoration of the Catholic faith, and of a king who could be a father of his people.' Civil and ecclesiastical councils had been set up to recover the church lands, and to restore the tithes. A military council had taken Jacques Cathelineau from a weaving-machine in his native village as one fitted by his courage and piety to be the Jeanne d'Arc of a new deliverance, and to save France from the alien tyranny of an anarchical Convention. The 'Whites'—officers and men alike—wore a hundred emblems, but no uniform. They fought with whatever weapons they could command. They marched in crowds, but attacked like scouts, by ambush and alert. They used a countryman's knowledge of the ground, and were as quick to mobilize as they were to scatter and escape.

The government troops, the 'Blues,' were of too many origins. They included dragoons of the old army; *corps francs* such as Rossignol's *Vainqueurs de la Bastille*, Westermann's *Chasseurs du nord*, or the *Légion germanique*; battalions specially recruited to deal with the 'brigands'; and freshly brigaded drafts from the foreign front. They were commanded by too many rival generals, and the generals were supervised by too many civil commissioners. The military jealousies of the field were increased by the political animosities of the capital.

Fortunately for this nondescript army, the rebels were divided too. There was a moment in the middle of June when they might have marched on Paris: they preferred to attack Nantes. The assault failed, Cathelineau was fatally wounded, and their army broke up. After three months' stalemate, the surrender of Mainz, so fatal to the eastern campaign, freed fifteen thousand good troops for the western front. At first the new army, rashly dividing its forces, was doubly defeated at Torfou and Caron (September 18th–19th). But early in October four republican columns converged on Cholet, where the rebels were decisively beaten, and driven across the Loire (October 17th). Two months later the relics of the White army were cut to pieces at Mans (December 10th) and Savenay (December 23rd).

These victories were the beginning of a punitive regime which lasted throughout the winter. Civil or military commissions, criminal tribunals, and courts-martial, using *fusillades* or *guillotines ambulantes*, put to death no one will ever know how many armed or unarmed, conscious or unconscious enemies of the republic. The *noyades* at Nantes, like the *mitraillades* at Lyon, were the climax of a ferocious vengeance wreaked by Frenchmen on Frenchmen, in the name of the revolution that they had all helped to make, and had all sworn to defend. Their author, Jean-Baptiste Carrier, has become a legend for wholesale and sadistic murder; and rightly. Even the piety of a descendant has rescued only a handful of domestic virtues from the wreck of his reputation. Carrier's assistants of the *Compagnie Marat* and the Revolutionary Committee of Nantes were commonplace citizens of the lower middle class. They included coopers, carpenters, hair-dressers, watch-makers, and small shop-keepers, along with a sprinkling of river-side merchants and contractors. They were the same people as those who staffed the local municipality, and frequented the local Jacobin club. The whole episode provides a striking example of the power of civil war to degrade the nature of a man below that of a beast.

In the Vendée, as at Lyon, it was found impossible to stamp out insurrection by the judicial murder of one in every five hundred of the population. A movement older than the Jacobin regime outlasted it. Rebellion reappeared south of the Loire, and spread north of it, in the new form of *Chouannerie*. In the autumn of '94, after the fall of Robespierre, the Convention reversed the policy of the previous twelve months, and tried conciliation. But the negotiations were bungled on one side, and abused on the other. In the summer of '95 fighting broke out again. Though its royalist allies were almost exterminated at Quiberon (July 22nd), the insurrection dragged wretchedly on. The Directory was forced to leave to Bonaparte the credit of its final pacification.

Historians whose countrymen have seldom fought one another, and who have no personal experience of civil war, find it hard to explain the savagery of the campaigns in the Vendée. They may, if they will, attribute something of what happened to the cruelty of the old feudal and penal system. They may attribute something to the ignorant brutality of a country population whom it had been the church's endeavour less to civilize than to save, and whom the priests were inciting to a holy rebellion. They may reflect, too, that the reprisals of the republican troops, whose behaviour was little better than that of the rebels, were provoked by the unprofessional conduct and tactics of civilian forces generally far outnumbering their own. Summarily, this was not a routine campaign against an enemy with whom there is a political but not a moral issue: nor against one who, because he is a foreigner, is expected to behave badly. It was a punitive expedition, an almost Albigensian crusade, against political heretics, and traitors to a common faith. It was, in effect, that most bitter and cruel of all wars, a war of religion.

Because the war was fought in this temper, conciliation, though thrice talked of, and twice tried, could not succeed until the fires of passion had burned out, and both sides felt that force had failed. For the same reason, other remedies that common sense might suggest were inapplicable. Economic reforms might have deprived the Lyon silk-workers of their grievances: they would have been useless to the peasants of the Vendée. Exemption from recruitment would not have satisfied the Catholics, nor a concordat those who objected to military service. It was either too early or too late for the republican propaganda and education to which Jullien looked for the regeneration of Brittany. Political concessions were neither to be asked nor to be received from a government which the priests taught their people to anathematize as atheistic and anarchical. There could be no more compromise between Whites and Blues than between Fascists and Communists. So the shooting and the guillotining went on.

Thus ended half a year of hard-won victory at home and abroad. The time had come, the Jacobins felt, for a national triumph. On December 30th Paris staged one of David's most spectacular pageants, 'in honour of the capture of Toulon, and the other victories of the republican armies.' The day began at seven o'clock with a salvo of artillery from the west end of the Île de Paris. Armed deputations of a hundred men from each of the forty-eight sections marched to the garden of the Palais national (the Tuileries), taking with them wounded soldiers, whom they 'respectfully' placed in triumphal cars dedicated to the fourteen armies of the republic. Now the procession was formed. First in the order of march came a detachment of cavalry, preceded by trumpeters and followed by sappers; then forty-eight cannon, drawn by artillery-men of the sections; groups of citizens representing Popular Societies, Revolutionary Committees, the law-courts, the commune, the department, and the ministers, all carrying appropriate banners. They were followed by the Conquerors of the Bastille. Then came the fourteen triumphal cars. In front of them marched girls dressed in white, with tricolor sashes, carrying laurel-branches. Between them marched armed detachments from the sections, led by flag-bearers, and chanting songs of victory. After them marched the members of the Convention, surrounded by a tricolor ribbon—a symbol of their unity—held by the oldest and the youngest soldiers in the country. Last of all, preceded by the band of the National Guard, came David's masterpiece, the car of Victory. Victory herself stood on a pedestal composed of Roman rods and axes, the *faisceau national*: at her feet were fourteen crowns, from which issued fourteen laurel-wreaths interlaced with tricolor ribbons, and carried by fourteen chosen soldiers.

The procession marched first to the Temple de l'Humanité (the old

Hôtel Dieu), where the bands played, and the President of the Convention made a speech to the Invalides; then on to the Champ de Fédération (Champ de Mars), where a hymn was sung in the Temple de l'Immortalité, and the white-robed girls laid their laurels on the triumphal cars. Finally, cheered by the 'warlike music' of the band, and the 'triumphant chanting' of the people, the General Council of the Commune led the wounded warriors back to the 'civil and fraternal banquet' that ended an edifying day.

Chapter XXII

CONQUEST

All reasonable chances are in favour of a confederacy such as was never opposed to the ambition of Louis the Fourteenth ; but, after the experience of last year, I distrust reason, and confess myself fearful for the event. The French are strong in numbers, activity, and enthusiasm ; they are rich in rapine ; and, although their strength may be only that of a frenzy fever, they may do infinite mischief to their neighbours before they can be reduced to a strait-waistcoat.—(EDWARD GIBBON : Feb. 18th, 1793.)

THE French revolution developed by adaptation to circumstances, not by the working out of a formula. Nowhere was this better shown than in its foreign diplomacy. In the Foreign Office (*ministère des affaires étrangères*), if anywhere, prescription and tradition might be expected to reign. The Foreign Office dealt with matters which fell outside party differences, and which the ordinary deputy could not claim to understand. It might be expected to keep its professional aloofness, its almost family solidarity. It might be expected to profit, more than any other department of government, from the taboo against the interference of the legislature with the executive. Yet, almost from the first, the foreign policy of the revolution was determined by declarations of the National Assembly, and the work of the ministry was interfered with by committees of the House.

Such may well have been the thoughts of the ex-abbé who, in April, '93, sat in the ministerial chair of the Foreign Office. A clever boy of uncertain parentage, Pierre-Marie-Henri Tondu had been educated, like Robespierre, at episcopal expense at the College of Louis-le-Grand. He had begun an ecclesiastical career as a member of the Oratoire, under his father's name of Tondu. Before long he threw up Orders for the army, and the army for journalism, and reappeared, with his mother's name added to his father's, as Lebrun-Tondu. Expelled from France for too freely expressing his views about the American war, he settled at Liège, and became editor of the *Journal général de l'Europe*, which became so popular that it was said that clerical Liégeois preferred it to their breviaries. But here, too, Lebrun's liberal opinions led to exile, and the loss of his business, so that he was glad to borrow money from the English political agent, W. A. Miles. Returning to Paris in '91, he associated at first with Carra, Robert, and the early republicans; then with Dumouriez, who took him to the Ministry of Foreign Affairs in March, '92. Diplomacy had since become his profession.

From March to June, '92, Lebrun had worked under Dumouriez; from August 12th till October 11th, he had worked with Danton; after Danton's retirement from the Ministry of Justice he was wholly responsible for the foreign policy of the revolution. He had now been in office eight months—a longer period than any of his predecessors except Montmorin. Working under difficulties created both by the prejudices of foreign governments and by the provocations of his own, Lebrun had done something to transplant the diplomatic traditions of the eighteenth century into revolutionary soil. His level-headed ability had met with an exceptional degree of confidence on the part of the Girondin Convention, and of the Diplomatic Committee which, following the precedent of the two previous assemblies, it had set up to co-operate with his department.

But three months ago, during the crisis caused by the king's trial, and by the extension of the war, the assembly had appointed a special committee of twenty-five, called *comité de défense générale*, to co-ordinate the work of the ministries. Since then Lebrun had never known when he might not be summoned before a body whose meetings were held two or three times a week, and which could be attended by any amateur diplomatist or newswriter, to debate high questions of public policy. The inconvenience of this was, indeed, so obvious that a new committee of twenty-five, called *comité de salut public*, had been substituted for the old (March 25th); but this, though more secret, still contained too many members, and too many political partisans. It had therefore just been replaced (April 6th) by a homogeneous, secret, and powerful body of nine, the 'great' Committee of Public Safety. The Diplomatic Committee had meanwhile (May 23rd) disappeared. Lebrun found himself once more under the direction of his old chief, the most forceful member of the new committee, Georges Danton.

Danton and his friend Delacroix were in a minority on the committee. They represented the rising influence of the Jacobin Left, or, as it was coming to be called, the Mountain. The other seven members were Jacobin 'Independents,' of whom the most distinguished was the indispensable Pierre-Joseph Cambon. Cambon had led the attack on Dumouriez, and cannot but have had his suspicions of Danton's collusion with Dumouriez's anti-republican intrigues. It was inevitable that Danton should be put in charge of the diplomatic business of the committee ; but with him was associated the cautious and ambiguous Barère.

Lebrun knew what Danton's policy had always been, and had generally agreed with it. He had never concealed his dislike of Brissot's war. He had seconded the attempt to restore diplomatic relations with the powers after

August 10th. He had supported the negotiations with the Prussians after Valmy. He may even have sympathized with the obscure advances made by Dantonist agents in England with a view to saving the king's life; though officially he kept his hands clean. On the day that the Convention declared war on England he entrusted David Williams with a letter to Lord Grenville expressing the regret of the Foreign Office. Though France had now no accredited representatives at any European court, its unofficial envoys could go everywhere. Though it was at war with a coalition of eight states, not all of these were equally committed to hostilities. It would be many months yet before British subsidies welded their various aims into a formidable war machine. It was not, perhaps, too late to prevent so great a threat to the republican armies, and so great a set-back to the peaceful development of the republican state.

Hitherto the fundamental weakness of Danton's peace policy—that it was belied by the provocative attitude of the Convention, and by the belligerent tone of his own speeches—had been unaccountably ignored. To this extent, at any rate, Lebrun had been successful in keeping up the traditions of the old Foreign Office. His detachment from the other departments of government was worthy of a d'Argenson or a Vergennes. But perhaps it was not too late to remedy the disharmony between profession and practice. One lesson of the Dumouriez affair had not been entirely lost upon the Convention. It could not be concealed that the disasters in Belgium, and the entry of England into the war, had been largely due to the decrees of November 19th and December 15th. Danton was not alone in thinking that these declarations had antagonized peoples as well as governments, and that they had created unnecessary difficulties for the republican arms. Many would welcome their public repudiation.

On April 13th the Convention received a letter from the representatives with the northern army enclosing some proclamations issued by the Austrian general, Cobourg. Robespierre moved that they be not read, on the ground that such communications encouraged a defeatist attitude. He ended by demanding outlawry and the death penalty against anyone proposing negotiations with the enemy. Danton cleverly turned this attack upon the policy of appeasement to his own advantage. Robespierre had gone too far. His extremism made it possible for Danton to criticize the decree of November 19th, and to propose in its place a new declaration to the effect that France would not interfere with the affairs of its neighbours, but would punish with death any attempt to negotiate that compromised the principles of the republic. This formula won the votes both of the war party and of the defeatists. All that Robespierre could do was to secure the addition of an amendment securing the rights of those peoples to whom support had already been given or promised.

The declaration of April 13th ran as follows:—'The National Convention declares, in the name of the French people, that it will not interfere (*s'immiscera*) in any way with the government of other powers. But at the same time it declares that it will sooner be buried (*s'ensevelira*) under its own ruins than allow any power to interfere in the internal affairs (*régime*) of the republic, or to influence any new form (*création*) of constitution that it chooses to adopt. The Convention decrees the death penalty against any person who proposes to negotiate or treat with enemy powers which have not first solemnly recognized the independence and sovereignty of the French nation, and the indivisibility and unity of the republic, founded on liberty and equality.'

This rhetorical gesture was broadcast to all the world by Barthélemy, the French ambassador in Switzerland. All possible stress was laid upon the conciliatory language of its first clause. Emissaries of the Foreign Office informed suspicious diplomats that republican missionaries would respect the right of every people to keep its own form of government. France would engage its enemies in what Danton later described as a new kind of hostilities (*une dernière sorte de guerre*)—war by negotiation. Negotiations were then begun, with all the apparatus of secret agents and unofficial conversations that Lebrun inherited from the old regime. The main objects were clear:— to divide the coalition, and to localize the war. The main fields of diplomatic intrigue were prescribed:—England, Austria, and the lesser powers.

Danton and Lebrun inherited from the old regime something more serious than a diplomatic technique. They inherited a historical prejudice derived from the wars of Louis XIV and XV. They imagined that Austria was the real enemy, not England. If they had been present at the council of war held by the allies at Antwerp on April 8th, they would have discovered that Austria felt less resentment for the defeat of Valmy and the conquest of Belgium than England did for the surrender of Yorktown, and the loss of the American colonies. They would have realized that whilst the Emperor demanded no territorial rewards, so long as he could see a Bourbon upon the French throne, the King of England intended at all costs to keep Dunkirk, and his colonial conquests. They would have known that the fight with Britain was a fight to the death.

The Dantonist Committee of Public Safety came into power on April 6th. It may not have been till a day or two later that Danton and Barère assumed effective control of the work of the Foreign Office. It is therefore unsafe to attribute to Danton the beginnings of the overtures to England, or even to Austria. Already on April 2nd a certain J. T. Matthews, a friend of David Williams, had been sent to London with a letter from Lebrun asking Lord Grenville to receive a French plenipotentiary: the intention was to employ Maret, who had previous experience of such negotiations. Grenville's reply (May 18th) was not encouraging. He appeared to ignore the decree of April 13th. He refused to see any emissary of the republic until the Convention altered its attitude towards other nations, and gave the allies satisfaction, security, and indemnification. Lebrun wrote again, this time with the approval of Danton, waiving any demand for the recognition of the republican government. Grenville replied that negotiations on this basis would be better addressed to the generals in the field. Accordingly two fresh agents, Forster and Pétry, were instructed to get into touch with General Murray, under cover of negotiating an exchange of prisoners. But before anything came of this plan, it was brought to an end by Danton's fall from power (July 10th).

It never had any prospect of success. Lebrun overestimated the effects of the decree of April 13th. Danton underestimated the hostility of a country which had in the past provided himself, and other political exiles, with an impartial asylum. How unlikely it was that Parliament would agree to any terms tolerable to the republic may be judged by the small amount of support given to Fox's periodical proposals for the ending of the war during '93–4.

The negotiations with the Emperor were pursued with the same disregard for probabilities. As long ago as March 25th Austria had formulated terms that France could not possibly accept: they included the return of Avignon, the cession of Alsace-Lorraine, and the drawing of a new Franco-Belgian frontier on the Somme. Cobourg's negotiations with Dumouriez were disowned by the Antwerp conference on April 8th, and he was forced to publish next day a proclamation withdrawing the armistice he had offered and the undertakings he had given four days previously.

Nevertheless, on April 5th the Jacobin Proli, who had already been employed on a mission to Dumouriez, wrote a letter to his mother at Brussels which he afterwards asserted had been dictated by certain members of the Committee of Public Safety, suggesting that the Austrian government should ratify the armistice with Dumouriez, and send a negotiator to the French frontier. In the same strain, when General Dampierre, who had superseded Dumouriez, was informed by the Austrian General Clerfayt of the cancellation of the armistice, his answer (April 8th) was to suggest that it should be extended, whilst arrangements were made to exchange 'certain persons under arrest in Paris'—by this he must have meant the royal family in the Temple—for the deputies arrested by Dumouriez. This exchange, he thought, might make it possible to resume peace negotiations. A few days later (April 11th) Custine, the general in command of the Rhine army, is found making similar overtures to his opponent, Wurmser; and on April 13th another French general officer, Chérin, discusses the Austrian terms with Cobourg and Colonel Mack. The coincidence of these various negotiations with Danton's decree of April 13th certainly suggests that they were not discouraged by the Foreign Office. As late as April 20th, in a letter to Descorches, Lebrun still speaks of the likelihood that Austria will make peace.

The Emperor's real intentions were expressed only four days later in the instructions that he sent to Cobourg and Wurmser. 'All your diligence,' he wrote, 'ought to be directed to one end. We must profit by the confusion and disunion which prevail in France to seize their fortresses, to obtain a firm foot-hold on their territory, and to carry My arms as far as possible.' They were warned to listen to no propositions that did not bring them military advantages. 'It is only by prosecuting the war as vigorously as possible that we shall secure a quick and honourable peace.'

The object of the negotiations with Prussia was the same as it had been after Valmy—to detach Frederick William from the Emperor. This part of Lebrun's policy was not put in hand until the failure of the English and Austrian negotiations was becoming obvious. Early in May Félix Desportes, formerly attaché at the little court of the Duke of Zweibrücken, and Dubuisson, a friend of Proli, were instructed to open conversations. Their go-between was to be the Duke's minister Esebeck, who was in prison at Metz. But nothing more was achieved than a fruitless conference with the Baron de Luxbourg, one of the King of Prussia's chamberlains.

Later again, Sémonville (May 23rd), once an agent of Mirabeau, was accredited to the court of Tuscany, and Maret (June 18th) to the court of Naples. Both were commissioned to say that the queen's life would be spared, in return for assistance in securing peace. Both emissaries were arrested by the Austrian government on their way to Italy, and imprisoned at Milan.

The death of Marie-Antoinette's champion, Gustavus III, suggested a Swedish alliance, and Lebrun had great hopes of his negotiations with de Stael, under which France offered a considerable subsidy in return for the promise of troops. But this scheme too broke down. At Constantinople the Marquis Descorches de Saint-Croix—not the only one of Lebrun's agents whose aristocratic title looked strangely out of place on republican credentials—urged the partition of Poland as an inducement to Turkey to renew its traditional French alliance. At Warsaw Parandier, in the best tradition of the *secret du roi*, held out hopes of a Polish *revanche*. In Switzerland special trouble was taken to undo the bad impression caused in a sister republic by the massacre and disbanding of the Swiss Guard. As the result of several concessions, the Diet of July declared for neutrality, and for the defence of the Swiss frontier against Austrian aggression. This minor success was all that Lebrun could boast.

By this time the Convention was alive to the failure of the 'war by negotiation.' On the very day (April 24th) that the Emperor was sending his bellicose instructions to the Austrian generals, Robespierre returned to the attack which had failed ten days before. He now proposed to insert in the Constitution four Articles asserting the brotherhood of man in the struggle against 'kings, aristocrats, and tyrants'; and Barère read out a proclamation by the Committee to the armies denouncing the pacifists. 'Their cry,' he said, 'is Peace and Royalism: yours must be the Republic and War!'

Barère, always the first rat to desert a sinking ship, followed up this declaration against the policy he had been supporting at the Foreign Office by a speech (May 3rd) saying that the French government left it to the enemy to initiate peace negotiations. The attack was taken up a few days later by Louis Pio, a naturalized Italian who had once been an embassy secretary at Naples, and was now employed in Lebrun's office. Not content with denouncing his chief to the Committee of Public Safety, he sent Lebrun a 'free and frank' letter, saying why he had done so, and published it in Marat's paper (May 13th).

Before the month was up, the Jacobin coup d'état of May 31st–June 2nd put Lebrun in the anomalous position of carrying on under nominal arrest a policy in which no one now believed. He was accompanied every day to the ministry by a gendarme. A few days later Danton was excluded from the Committee; before the end of the month the Foreign Office was handed over to Deforgues, under the supervision of Barère and of Hérault de Séchelles, who had been a member of the Diplomatic Committee in the previous Assembly.

Hérault had given pledges to the revolution as a Hero of the Bastille, and as President of the Legislative Assembly during the September massacres. He had proved his Jacobinism in the chair of the Convention on May 27th–28th and June 2nd. He had drafted the Jacobin constitution of '93. Nevertheless his royalist past, his connexion with Danton's shadier associates, his disdain for political shibboleths, and his loose and luxurious way of life rendered him obnoxious to strict Robespierrists. The airs and advantages of a man of the old regime, which made him so serviceable at the Foreign Office, became a fresh cause of offence when the policy he favoured fell under the suspicion of defeatism, and when the negotiations he carried on in Austria, Switzerland, and the United States were compromised by the indiscretion of such agents as Proli, Dubuisson, and Genêt.

The accession of Robespierre to the Committee of Public Safety at the end of July was fatal to Hérault's career. Robespierre suspected that his foreign policy was little different from that of Danton and Lebrun. He was jealous of a popularity which carried Hérault to the Presidency of the Convention for a second time (August 4th) a fortnight before his own first election. He disliked seeing his rival pontificating on August 10th at the fête in honour of the new constitution. He would be quick to seize any opportunity of discrediting the 'Alcibiades of the Convention.' Hérault himself provided an occasion by his indiscreet conduct during a mission to Alsace at the end of October. Hearing of attacks upon him, he demanded his recall, and two months later defended himself with temporary success against the charges of his enemies. But there was no place for him now in a committee packed with Jacobin stalwarts, and no hope remained for a foreign policy of appeasement.

Barère now made another *volte-face*, and took his orders from Robespierre.

The first clause of the declaration of April 13th was silently dropped: the second became the rule of foreign policy. Instead of conciliation, defiance: instead of promises to keep off, warnings not to intrude: instead of diplomatic ambiguities, the weapons of war. Hitherto the foreign policy of the revolution had been supervised by men who had travelled, and knew something of the world—Mirabeau, Talleyrand, Brissot, Dumouriez, Danton. It was now in the hands of an Arras lawyer and a councillor of the *sénéchaussée* of Bigorre. Both were men of very confined experience, who had never been outside France. There is little evidence that they made any serious attempt to understand the European situation.

Robespierre's reputation as an international statesman rested on his speeches of November 17th and January 28th. They are full of boasting and abuse; but they contain no policy, unless it be the declaration that England, not Austria, is the real enemy, and that France must keep on good terms with countries such as Switzerland and the United States, from which it draws supplies of meat and corn. Since England is the arch-enemy, France becomes the champion of the small nationalities. England, politically rotten, may be expected to perish at any moment by internal revolution:— had not Paine been telling his French friends this ever since the spring of '91? The Jacobins have only to display their republican virtues, and they will win the support of the neutral states. France, Robespierre proudly asserts, is necessary to the universe. Without France, liberty would cease from off the earth.

The rhetorical *carmagnoles* in which Barère celebrated the victories of the French arms were appropriate footnotes to Robespierre's defiance of Europe. Jacobinism would henceforth cease to negotiate, and pin its whole faith on the final argument of realistic diplomacy—war. Its new motto would read *La victoire ou la mort*. At sea this meant that the Girondins' free-trade ideas would be replaced by the protectionism which their economic adviser Ducher, fresh from seven years' experience in the United States, had vainly urged as the only means of defeating British competition. The Navigation Act of September, '93, launched France on a voyage which ended in the Continental System. On land Robespierre's new policy meant twenty years of war, and the absorption of the Jacobin republic into the Napoleonic empire.

England had planned the First Coalition on the traditional lines of her foreign war policy—subsidies on the continent, and mastery at sea. Between February and September, '93, she took Holland, Russia, Sardinia, Spain, Naples, Prussia, Austria, and Portugal into her pay. France seemed not to have a friend left in Europe. But there was little agreement between the motives and aims of the allies. Three of them—Sardinia, Naples, and Portugal—merely furnished mercenaries. Two—Spain and Russia—co-operated only in the coastal blockade. The two most important—Prussia and Austria—had hopes of territorial or financial indemnities. If these failed, their support might at any moment be withdrawn.

Such aims met with little encouragement in England. Replying on May 30th, '94, to Fox's Fourteen Resolutions, Pitt declared: 'The present is not a contest for acquisition of territory; it is not a contest for power and glory; as little is it carried on merely for any commercial advantage, or any particular form of government; but it is a contest for the security, the tranquillity, and the very existence of Great Britain, connected with that of every established government, and every country in Europe.' He went on to say, 'We have no desire to conquer France; we wish only to free it from a system of tyranny equally oppressive to itself and dangerous to its neighbours; which can, in the first instance, only exist by the misery of its subjects, and menaces in its progress the destruction of regular government.' He concluded that 'while that system, with which we now contend, continues in France, we can have no peace upon any terms short of absolute ruin and dishonour.' Pitt was in fact preaching what would nowadays be called an 'ideological' crusade, calculated to enlist anti-Jacobin zeal all the world over. But his war-aims did not exclude more mundane considerations; and some of these offended his allies. It was not unnatural that, if England annexed the West Indian islands, and was suspected of designs on Dunkirk and Toulon, Prussia should resent Pitt's grudging attitude towards the partition of Poland, or Austria his refusal of a foot-hold in the Netherlands. It was understandable that Spain should take alarm at our colonial pretensions, and withdraw from the alliance.

Even in a military sense the coalition was not so strong as numbers should have made it. The allies encircled France from the English Channel to the Pyrenees with three hundred thousand men. But considerable detachments of the international army never came into action, or were prematurely withdrawn. Pitt himself failed to take military advantage of opportunities offered in the Netherlands, at Toulon, and in the Vendée. Upon the crucial front, where it was as essential for Cobourg in '93 as it had been for Brunswick in '92 to make a rapid advance on Paris, delay succeeded delay—at Condé, at Valenciennes, at Mainz, at Landau, at Dunkirk, at Maubeuge. When at last in mid-October Wurmser crossed the Rhine opposite Wissembourg, there was no corresponding invasion in the north. In the first week of September Houchard had defeated Freytag at Hondschoote, and had relieved Dunkirk. On October 15th Jourdan's decisive victory over Clerfayt at Wattignies had freed Maubeuge. The north-east frontier was saved. The invaders retired. The campaign was over.

How had the republican government achieved a victory which no one would have dared prophesy, and which took all Europe by surprise? The answer was, through the national spirit, the new army, and the Committee of Public Safety.

The composite or extemporized forces with which the republic tried to make headway against foreign invasion and civil rebellion during the early summer could never have won the victories of the autumn. They were the best that could be expected from a system of voluntary recruitment, supplemented by local requisitioning. But it had been obvious for a long time that something more was required. The appeal for volunteers in '91 had brought in good men, but only half the number needed. Requisitioning in '92 had filled the ranks with inferior and often unwilling fighters. Both classes had rejected appeals to stay with the colours. During the winter of '92–3 the army of Valmy and Jemappes was reduced to little more than a skeleton force.

Nevertheless the old method of recruiting was tried once more. A decree of February 24th, '93, ordered the levying of three hundred thousand men—roughly the estimated number of the allied army. That so large a force would be forthcoming as volunteers was unlikely, in view of the king's execution, the political dissensions, and the economic discontents of the winter. It was therefore provided that the numbers should be made up, if necessary, by local designation, or by the drawing of lots. A crowd of commissioners was sent into the provinces to help on the recruiting campaign. In spite of every effort less than half the necessary number was procured.

It became clear that the Convention must fall back on a suggestion made two years before, and tried out on a small scale by representatives in some of the departments—a *levée en masse*, or wholesale compulsory enlistment. This plan was proposed by a deputation of the *fédérés* of August 10th. It was debated in the Convention on August 12th, '93. It was again urged on a hesitating government by Danton on the 19th. It finally took shape in Carnot's decree, as it is generally called, of August 23rd. It was enforced throughout the country by the *fédérés* themselves: eight thousand of them worked as *commissaires des assemblées primaires* under the direction of representatives on mission in the departments.

The Committee of Public Safety had seen that, if compulsion were to be made palatable, it had better be made as nearly universal as possible. What all suffer, none so much resent. Accordingly the introductory report proclaimed that 'all Frenchmen, whatever their sex or age, are called by their country to defend liberty.' 'Henceforth (it said) the republic is a great city in a state of siege: France must become one vast camp, and Paris its arsenal.' The first Article of the decree laid it down, in language as new as it was ominous, that 'From this moment until that when the enemy is driven from the territory of the republic, every Frenchman is commandeered (*en réquisition permanente*) for the needs of the armies. Young men will go to the front: married men will forge arms, and carry food: women will make tents and clothing, and work in hospitals: children will turn old linen into bandages: old men will be carried into the squares to rouse the courage of the combatants, and to teach hatred of kings, and republican unity.'

It was the first example in modern history of the deliberate mobilization of a nation for the purposes of war; and it was, as yet, a national war without the vices of nationalism. 'War,' Carnot himself had declared, 'must not be nationalized. The name of France must be feared, but not hated.' Again, he had instructed the republican army:—'Respect all objects of worship: respect the cottages, the women, the children, the old people: whatever place you enter, do so as the people's benefactors.'

The appeal for equality of self-sacrifice met with an answer that showed there had been no need to add to the Declaration of Rights a Declaration of Duties. It was not found necessary to go beyond the first class of *réquisitionnaires*—those aged from eighteen to twenty-five. This class alone provided four hundred and twenty-five thousand men; and successive drafts from the same age-group, together with the flow of volunteers, kept the republican armies up to strength for the next five years.

But it was another matter to arm, equip, feed, and train such vast numbers of recruits: and there still remained the problem, how to combine the new troops with the old, so as to form a homogeneous army. For equipment and commissariat it was necessary to organize what would nowadays be called a Ministry of Supply and a Ministry of Munitions. The first was the work of Robert Lindet. The second was the work of Prieur de la Côte d'Or.

On October 31st Lindet was recalled from a mission in the Calvados, where he had been notably successful in dealing with questions of food-control, and was asked to take charge of a Ministry of Supply on behalf of the Committee of Public Safety. Nearly a year before (November 4th, '92) Roland, Pache, and Monge had set up a *directoire des achats* to centralize the purchasing funds and powers of their three departments—the Interior (including Paris), the Army, and the Navy—in the hands of a committee of three business men. The three directors were Bidermann, a Swiss, Cousin, and Marx-Beer, a Strasbourg Jew. Their names, the method of their appointment, and the size of their salaries, gave rise to not unnatural suspicions. But so long as the Girondins monopolized the ministries, the system continued.

Something of the kind was in fact indispensable. When Roland resigned, and Beurnonville succeeded Pache at the War Office, the *directoire* was swept away, and the ministers were once more free to place their contracts where and as they pleased. The scandals which ensued soon made it clear that a government which is dependent on private capital for financing and on private enterprise for organizing commissariat must protect itself by setting up a Ministry of Supply.

Accordingly on October 22nd the Convention returned to the Girondin plan, and set up a *commission des subsistances* under three commissioners with reassuringly French names—Raison, Goujon, and Brunet—and with Tissot as General Secretary. The work of the new Commission was divided into three departments. One dealt with the supply of food, another with its distribution, and a third with accounts. Though they met twice a day, and seldom sat for less than four hours on end, the Commissioners confessed a fortnight later that they were barely able to deal with the varied and difficult questions with which they were faced—the requisitioning of supplies for Paris, controversies with manufacturers about the price of clothing materials, the establishment of food-stores (*greniers d'abondance*) for the army, the purchase of meat from abroad, the organization of river transport, the drawing up of price-schedules for the Food Control, and the hundred other affairs which fill the voluminous minutes of their proceedings. But Lindet, working all day and every day, created competence out of chaos, and succeeded in winning from the generals, not wont to be over generous in such matters, a reputation second only to that of Carnot as an organizer of victory. Within five months (March 22nd, '94) Cambon was able to announce that the cost of the upkeep of the army was only half what it had been a year ago, when it was a third of its present size.

No less formidable was the work undertaken at the Ministry of Munitions by Prieur de la Côte d'Or. The archives of the Committee of Public Safety contain, amongst more than a thousand papers in Lindet's hand, two hundred and sixty important resolutions dealing with arms, and eighty-two dealing with gunpowder, all of which were passed during the year beginning July, '93. Metal was commandeered from every discoverable source, including church bells and railings. Forges were set up everywhere: over two hundred and fifty could be counted in the squares, boulevards, and gardens of the capital. Convents were transformed into factories; cellars were scraped and dug for saltpetre; and thirty thousand pounds of gunpowder were produced every twenty-four hours from the great works at Grenelle. At Meudon experiments were carried on in the new science of aeronautics. The first war-balloon, floating above the French lines at Fleurus, was as wonderful as the first air-machine that flew over the same front in 1914. Nor was that the only invention used by an amateur army. When the news of the fall of Quesnoy was signalled to Montmartre, a hundred and twenty miles away, in the space of an hour, by Chappe's new semaphore, it seemed nothing less than a republican miracle.

A solution long advocated was at last supplied to the problem of army-building. This was the *amalgame* of '93–4. It included two operations, neither of them easy—the co-ordination of the different kinds of voluntary and requisitioned troops into a single body, and the fusion of this force with what was left of the old army. Only so could there be an end of the confusion, indiscipline, and expense involved in the coexistence of so many rival forces. Only so could the experience of the old soldiers be wedded to the enthusiasm of the new.

The *amalgame* was long opposed by officers who feared to lose their commissions, and by soldiers who disliked changing their uniforms. It was denounced by arm-chair critics who feared that republican liberty would be sacrificed to the idol of military esprit de corps. But by the end of '93 the first part of the operation had been forced through, and the government had at its disposal two hundred and thirteen battalions of regulars and seven hundred and twenty-five battalions of volunteers and *réquisitionnaires*, all wearing the national blue uniform, and all detached from their old regimental or territorial traditions.

It remained to combine four hundred and twenty-six of the new battalions with the two hundred and thirteen old battalions, so as to form two hundred and thirteen half-brigades, in which there was one old soldier to every two new. Of the rest, some were drafted into battalions still below strength, and some were formed into supernumerary half-brigades of reserve. Finally the half-brigades were grouped into divisions of six to eight thousand men, and these into thirteen armies, nominally of a hundred thousand men, but actually varying in effective strength from forty thousand to a hundred and thirteen thousand. The whole totalled some three-quarters of a million men. The so-called fourteenth army, the *armée révolutionnaire*, was disbanded under a decree of October 6th, '93.

How were the new armies officered? Under the *amalgame* of February, '93, one out of every three captains and lieutenants was chosen by the men themselves, and two were promoted by seniority of service. In the higher commands the claims of seniority could be overruled, on the advice of its commissioners, by the Committee of Public Safety. A new principle now began to decide important appointments in the army. During the whole year from April, '93, to April, '94, the War Office was under the control of Jean-Baptiste-Noël Bouchotte, a soldier who had risen from the ranks of the republican army, and shared the popular distrust of the old royalist officer class. Bouchotte's *sécrétaire-général* was F.-N. Vincent, a leading member of the Cordeliers club, an associate of Ronsin and Hébert, and the chief exponent of the policy of direct action by the *sansculottes* in the conduct of the war. A people's army, he held, must have popular generals.

As early as May, '93, when it was becoming difficult to find competent officers for the army, Bouchotte asked for the removal of all nobles and suspects, of whom a considerable number still hoped to pursue their career under the republic. When, in July, the Committee of Public Safety submitted to the Convention the names of staff officers for eleven armies, there was a public outcry, because some titles of nobility still appeared upon the list. When, on July 28th, news came of the betrayal of Mainz by the aristocrat Custine, the War Minister was given a free hand to deal with appointments as he pleased. Soon he discovered for himself the absurdity of replacing competent generals, for the accident of a *de* before their names, by officers whose only qualification was their patriotism. The new generals had to be chosen carefully, and the choice took time. It was not until the summer of '94 that the operation was completed, and the Birons, Dillons, Custines, Beauharnais, and Montesquious of the old army were replaced by the Hochs, Klébers, Marceaus, Desaixs, Jourdans, Pichegrus, and Bonapartes of the new.

France had now a national and democratic army, manned and officered by plain *citoyens*, who *tu-toied* one another when off duty, and settled their differences before a civil jury. It was inevitable that a new discipline based on *fraternité* should issue in a new technique, relying not on mechanical movements and ordered fire-control, but on numbers, unanimity, and *élan*. Military bands were sent to the front, to encourage the troops by playing the *carmagnole*. Carnot, a trained engineer, and once a convinced believer in the pre-Guibert strategy, had been converted by the success of Barthélemy's aggressive plan for the '93 campaign from reliance on fortresses and defensive manœuvring to the doctrine of attacking and destroying the enemy. He now embodied the new tactics which this strategy demanded in a famous Order (Feb. 2nd, '94).

' The general rules,' he wrote, ' are always to manœuvre *en masse*, and on the offensive ; to maintain strict but not too detailed discipline ; to keep the troops in constant readiness, without over-working them; to employ the utmost watchfulness on sentry-go ; to use the bayonet on every possible occasion ; and to follow up the enemy without pause until he is completely destroyed.' Thus was Danton's *L'audace, toujours l'audace!* translated into terms of war.

Such tactics might win surprising results. But they were still unemancipated from the old strategical ideas, the old drill-book (the *règlement* of '91), and the old weapons—the *fusil* of '77, which was not accurate much beyond a hundred yards, and Gribauval's cannon, which fired a four-pound shot perhaps five times as far. Napoleon owed his victories, more than he ever admitted, to the makers of the republican army. He owed his ultimate defeat to his failure to abandon its mass-tactics long after they had ceased to justify the loss of life they involved.

In February, '93, when the war began, the French fleet, or ' sea army ' (*armée de mer*), as it is still called by writers of the mid-19th century, was almost a match for the British, if not in the number of its ships, yet in their construction, and in the weight of their broadsides. It had three ships (counting only those ready for sea, or fitting, and in good condition) carrying a hundred and twenty guns, and five carrying a hundred and ten : against these we could only bring five hundred-gun ships. But we had four ninety-eights, one ninety, and twelve eighties against their ten eighties, whilst of seventy-four-gun ships we had sixty-one to their sixty-two, and could add two sixties and twenty-eight forty-fours. That is, we had a hundred and thirteen ships of the line, which were regarded in the eighteenth century as the capital ships of a navy, to their eighty ; but in the number of guns carried, and the weight of metal fired, the advantage on our side was no more than a sixth.

The real handicap under which the French lay was that the personnel of their old navy, and the traditions of its service, had been broken up by the revolution. On land, enthusiasm might compensate for inexperience. At sea, nothing could take the place of expert seamanship and gunnery. An army can, up to a point, be extemporized; a navy cannot. It was easy and amusing to rename the *Commerce de Bordeaux* (for fear that 'such mercantile names might encourage egoism and *modérantisme*') the *Bonnet Rouge*, or to give republican baptism to the *Royal Louis* (now *Républicain*), the *Sceptre* (*Convention*), the *Dauphin-Royal* (*Sansculotte*), and the *Couronne* (*Ça Ira*). It was impossible to find republican officers fit to take the place of the aristocrats who had served under Suffren or d'Estaing, or suddenly to accustom *sansculotte* fishermen to the training and discipline which had so nearly defeated England in the American war.

For two years, under a series of aristocratic Ministers of Marine, the old order survived almost unchanged. The white flag, with a tricolor in one corner, which now flew at the mast-head, was the utmost concession the old navy would make to a new allegiance: and the assembly had ordered (October 21st, '90) that the men should in future cheer the Nation and the Law along with the King. At Toulon in '89 and at Brest in '90 there were demonstrations against the Comte de Rions, reputed the ablest flag-officer in the navy, whom Suffren himself had designated as his successor. Discipline could no longer be preserved by royalist officers among revolutionary crews. The drastic remedy was therefore tried of democratizing the whole navy.

By the decrees of April 22nd and 28th, '91, commissions were given to men from the lower deck, or from the merchant service. In the following year the trained corps of seamen-gunners was replaced by marines under artillery officers. When the war broke out in '93 this experiment was still in the making. Saint-André, whose experience as a sea-captain was thought to qualify him to supervise the navy, introduced a fresh rule by which naval officers could be chosen by election, like those of the army. As in the army, it was found impossible to replace all the aristocratic officers in the higher commands. About one naval officer in three still belonged to the old royalist establishment.

Two disastrous incidents showed the dangers of a transitional period. At Toulon, in August, the Comte de Trogoff, the Rear-admiral in command of the Mediterranean fleet, surrendered his ships and port to the British, against the wish of his men. At Brest the Atlantic fleet refused an order to sail under its admiral, Morard de Galle ; and Saint-André could only restore discipline by sending six mutineers to Paris for execution, dismissing a number of officers, and introducing a severe code of punishments. By the Toulon affair France lost some thirty ships, either burnt or captured by the enemy. By the Brest affair it at least acquired a new class of republican officers, one of whom, Villaret-Joyeuse, commanded the French fleet with great credit at the battle of the First of June.

Under such conditions France could not hope to beat superior numbers and better-trained crews in fleet actions. But serious damage might still be done to the enemy in single-ship actions, or by privateering. Being the first to declare war, the republic had, in February, '93, captured over seventy British ships lying in French ports. Privateering carried on this success. It was a branch of the service particularly popular amongst sailors who disliked discipline, and hoped for private gain. It was encouraged by the ex-privateer Dalbarade, whose regime as Minister of Marine ran concurrently with that of Bouchotte at the War Office, from April, '93, to April, '94. Privateering inflicted heavy losses on our unprotected coastal shipping. Some of the privateers had made as many as sixty prizes before they were themselves captured by the British navy. Ten years later we were losing four hundred ships a year.

Both on land and at sea it was now frankly acknowledged that the republican forces must live on the enemy. The republican motto, *Vivre libre ou mourir*, was translated, 'Loot or starve.' A resolution of the Committee of Public Safety dated September 18th, '93, instructs generals in command of forces entering enemy countries to destroy all fortresses, bridges, canals, and sluices, and to take up all paved roads. They are to disarm the inhabitants, to take hostages from amongst the most notable citizens, and to exact contributions in cash or kind, especially from wealthy and privileged individuals, and religious bodies. They are to requisition everything of possible use for the equipment of the army, and to send to the rear whatever they can spare in the way of food, forage, horses, cattle, fuel, cloth, and other such commodities. They are to seize and send home church plate, treasury funds, and 'all portable public property'; and they are to forward inventories of all these articles to the Committee, and to the Ministry of War.

Such was the model for Napoleon's campaign in Italy three years later. A special instruction made it applicable also to naval commanders making a descent upon an enemy coast-line. With what senseless brutality such orders were sometimes carried out will be remembered by those who have read Zachary Macaulay's account of the attack on Sierra Leone by a French naval squadron in September, '94.

The means by which the Committee of Public Safety kept itself informed about the state of the armies, and the behaviour of the generals, and the channel through which it conveyed its orders, was the *représentants en mission aux armées*.

This was not a new method, though it was used in a new way. More than two hundred years before, when Henri II was re-establishing the royal authority, he sent *intendants* with his armies, as well as into the provinces, and newly conquered territories ; one of them, Pierre Panisse, helped to pacify Corsica in 1555. In the next century Richelieu attached *intendants* to most of the French armies, with almost viceregal powers. After the Fronde, Le Tellier, who had himself been *intendant de la justice, police et finance et vivres* with the army of Italy, regularized the institution of *intendants d'armées*, giving them power to punish looting, to regulate the soldiers' pay, to superintend the commissariat, hospitals, billeting, clothing, and equipment of the troops, to assist the general in the negotiation of treaties, and even to interfere (by correspondence with the king's ministers) with his conduct of a campaign.

This civil control over the army, this royal precaution against over-powerful generals, was maintained throughout the 18th century. Dubois-Crancé, the pioneer of army reform during the Revolution, must often have heard his father talk of his experiences as *intendant de police et des finances* attached to the Duc de Richelieu's army during the Seven Years' war. A similar practice obtained in Holland ; and its use by the Scotch emigrants against the enterprise of Argyll inspired one of Macaulay's angriest denunciations.

During the early years of the revolution, whilst the royal army was gradually breaking up, and the civil authorities could use the National Guard to keep order, there was little reason for the legislature to transgress the sacred principle of the Separation of Powers by interfering with the control of the army by the executive. During the period of Girondin predominance the Legislative Assembly refused several requests from generals in the field for the attachment of representatives to their armies, on the ground that military duties were incompatible with those of a deputy. But this did not prevent occasional interference with military affairs. Two deputies, Cahier and Duveyrier, were despatched to investigate the Nancy affair in September, '90. When Barnave, Pétion, and Latour-Maubourg were sent to bring Louis back from Varennes in June, '91, they were empowered to give orders to the military as well as to the civil authorities. A national crisis would overrule a constitutional principle.

During the foreign invasion of '92, Carnot and two other representatives were sent (July 31st) to organize defence at Soissons ; and a few days later they were despatched again with other deputies to the armies of the North, the Centre, and the Rhine. The Separation of Powers fell with the fall of the throne; and on August 11th the *commissaires de l'Assemblée nationale aux armées*, as they were now called, were given authority to suspend, and if necessary arrest, disloyal generals, and to take any steps that might be required for the national safety. It was by their means that Lafayette was driven into exile, and his army saved for the republic.

The precedent once established, the practice was found too useful not to be extended. If the old army had needed civilian control, still more did the new army need it, during the difficult times of the treachery of

Dumouriez, the second invasion, and the civil war. How could the daily affairs of thirteen armies be conducted, except with the advice of trusted agents upon the spot? Cambon's law of April 30th finally reorganized and regulated the service. From four to twelve representatives were permanently attached to each army, according to the importance of the command. Their functions were to exercise an active supervision over ministerial agents, government contractors, and military officers. They had power of provisional appointment and dismissal. They could organize recruitment, commissariat, and propaganda. There was in effect no limit to their powers, except the fear that their actions might be disowned by the Committee of Public Safety.

Dressed in the military-looking coat, sash, and plumed hat designed by David, the *représentant* sat by the general's side at courts-martial or councils of war, and rode by his side into battle. He was the general's equal, indeed his superior. For had he not the ear of the government? Was he not the living symbol of the memorable fact that this was no longer a professional but an amateur army, self-disciplined by liberty and equality, and inspired not by *esprit de corps*, but by *esprit de nation*?

The old army had been a miniature of the old order, with its fixed class-distinction between officers and men, its caste-like separation from civilian society, and the completeness of its allegiance to the king. The new army was no less a specimen of the new order. Created, no longer to fight by the side of a professional army, but to take its place, it was something new in the world of war. It was the first nation under arms. The new popular levies took up military life not as a profession, but as an occupation. They kept their social equality, their civil rights, and their political opinions. They hated nothing so much as war, unless it were to be backward in the fight for freedom.

A REPUBLICAN COMMISSAIRE
From a painting by David.

Chapter XXIII

OPPOSITION

Mais, quand le peuple est maître, on n'agit qu'en tumulte ;
La voix de la raison jamais ne se consulte ;
Les honneurs sont vendus aux plus ambitieux,
L'autorité livrée aux plus séditieux.
Ces petits souverains qu'il fait pour une année,
Voyant d'un temps si court leur puissance bornée,
Des plus heureux desseins font avorter le fruit,
De peur de le laisser à celui qui les suit. . . .
Le pire des états, c'est l'état populaire.

(CORNEILLE : *Cinna,* Act II, Scene I.)

ONE result of the Jacobin *coup d'état* of June, '93, was to concentrate the patriotic energy of the country in the hands of the political party best able to use it. Another, not so beneficent, was to turn all other parties into ' factions,' and all counter-revolutionary activities into attacks upon the government. In peace-time, and under a parliamentary regime organized on party lines, such attacks might have been a healthy stimulant. Carried on during a time of foreign and civil war, and in a country that knew no tradition of political compromise, they became, in effect, a third campaign, fought not with rifles and swords, but with manifestos and speeches, in which the reward of victory might be only a postponement of the penalty of defeat—death at the hand of the public executioner.

Opposition took as many forms as there were interests that ran counter to those of the government, or grievances against its rule; but it was embodied in four main kinds of counter-revolution.

There were first the relics (the popular metaphor was *queues*) of parties already discredited or destroyed—royalists, emigrants, aristocrats, refractory priests, federalists ; politicians who had turned back in '89 or '92, or who had been turned out in '93 ; landowners lamenting their rights or their rents ; and the nameless crowd of officials and investors whose fortunes had sunk with the wreck of the old regime. Next came those whose opposition consisted in isolating or exaggerating parts of the government programme, in such a way as to compromise the whole :—the *enragés,* as they were called, who exploited the demands of the city poor for the punishment of hoarders and profiteers, and for the control of food-prices ; or the anti-clericals and ' atheists,' with their attacks on the Catholic church. The third class was that which, without overtly attacking the government, brought discredit upon it by disreputable conduct—the so-called ' Rotters ' (*pourris*), who made corrupt money out of the revolution by cornering, speculation, or profiteering, and spent it in luxurious and immoral living ; whose friends were foreigners or suspects, and whose influence tainted the Convention and committees themselves. Lastly, there were coming into view two parties whose opposite aims might have seemed innocent echoes of what was in the mind of leading Jacobins, but became the most dangerous of all when they began to suggest an alternative government—the so-called Hébertists and Indulgents.

When the day of reckoning came, it was convenient for the Jacobins to confound all these forms of opposition under a general charge of conspiracy (*conspiration*), or of attempting to discredit the Convention (*avilir la représentation nationale*). In the great political trials of Germinal agitators and atheists, terrorists and moderates, middle-class parliamentarians and believers in the direct action of the *sansculottes*, sat side by side in the dock. But the historical eye, seeking, like that of Providence, to read the heart, discovers almost as many differences in degrees of guilt as there were names on the long list in the hands of the Public Prosecutor.

Six months after the execution of Louis XVI the monarchy was still being persecuted with a vindictiveness which can only be explained by fear. The queen, more hated than the king had ever been, was closely imprisoned in the Temple, with her son the Dauphin, her daughter Madame Royale, and Louis' younger sister Madame Elisabeth. But the Comte de Provence, who had escaped when his brother was recaptured, now called himself Regent for the young Dauphin, whom he hoped to restore as Louis XVII, along with the Catholic religion and the Bourbon constitution. He would admit only such reforms as Louis XVI had freely promised. ' Tolerant towards persons (was his motto), intolerant towards principles.' Royalism was still formidable in parts of the provinces : even in Paris, boxes were on sale containing locks of Louis' hair, or scraps of the coat that he had worn on the scaffold. Royalists held key positions in the civil service, and in the fighting forces. Emigrants and secret agents were constantly urging foreign courts to intervene on behalf of the royal family. The Temple buzzed (as the Tuileries had buzzed) with rumours of cypher correspondence, and legends of escape.

Can it be wondered that, where so much hatred was kept alive by the tradition of Bourbon tyranny, and so many interests threatened by any return of the old regime, there should have been a demand for the completion of the work of January 21st ? At the beginning of August ' Capet's widow ' was placed in solitary confinement in the Conciergerie. Even here she was visited by an Englishwoman, once an actress at Drury Lane, now living in Paris under the name of Mrs. Atkyns, who suggested a plan of escape. Soon another such intrigue (the so-called *conspiration de l'oeillet*) gave an excuse for the next step towards the scaffold; and on Oct. 3rd the Convention ordered the immediate trial of the queen.

Dilatoriness now gave place to indecent haste. When the queen saw her counsel, on the afternoon before the trial (Oct. 13th), she had not

MARIE-ANTOINETTE ON HER WAY TO EXECUTION
From a pencil sketch by David. See p. 436.

received the *acte d'accusation*, and did not know what the charges might be. It was not till the morning of the 14th that Fouquier-Tinville, who was to accuse her, received the nine hundred documents on which the prosecution was based. Taken through a dreary and useless round of historical questions, Marie-Antoinette replied that at each turn of Louis' policy she had only consented as a wife; but everyone in court was convinced that she had advised as a queen. Not content with the general belief that she was a Messalina, Hébert produced in evidence statements made by the young Dauphin, which went to prove her an Agrippina too. The indecency of the charge, and the dignified way in which it was answered, nearly turned public opinion in her favour. But, as she came away, she heard a woman remark, ' Look, how haughty she is ! '

She had, indeed, no chance of life, and nothing to live for. Sentence and verdict were pronounced in the early morning of Oct. 16th. At half-past four, whilst she wrote a farewell letter to Madame Elisabeth, charging her with the care of her children, Fouquier-Tinville was ordering the troops for 10 o'clock next day. David's cruel sketch of her in the cart on the way to execution (made, they say, from the window where he sat with the lovely Madame Tallien), shows her defying death, and a hostile mob, with Habsburg disdain. The crowd which had been waiting for two hours in the Place de la Révolution clapped when she appeared, and acclaimed her execution with cries of *Vive la République !*, throwing their hats into the air. They nearly lynched a soldier who stooped beneath the scaffold to dip his handkerchief in Austrian blood. From the provinces there soon followed a flood of addresses, congratulating the Convention on the brave blow it had struck for justice and freedom.

Philippe Egalité, whose portrait had disappeared from the walls of Carlton House since he voted for his cousin's death, followed the queen on Nov. 6th, and Madame Elisabeth six months later. There remained only the Dauphin and Madame Royale. Even Hébert did not propose to execute a girl of fifteen and a boy of eight. It was easier to let the Dauphin die in prison (1795), and to exchange his sister two years later, when the danger of a royalist restoration was over, for the Jacobins arrested by Dumouriez on April 1st. But there are still some royalists who believe that the Dauphin survived in the person of one of many Pretenders; and there are others who support a Bourbon claimant to the throne of Louis XVI.

Most of the '*aristos*,' as they were now called, were in prison or in exile ; but there remained a few whose local popularity, or honest acceptance of republican principles, enabled them to live on undisturbed in their country estates, save perhaps for the closing of their family pew, or the pulling down of their feudal gate-posts. Some of them consoled themselves, like Ferrières, with the hope that the prestige and tradition of nobility would survive the destruction of its outward privileges.

There is a common belief that the aristocracy supplied most of the victims of the guillotine ; but this was not so. The most superficial analysis of the names given in the register of the Paris municipality shows that the number of ex-nobles executed by the Revolutionary Tribunal, from November, '93, to March, '94, was always less than the number of priests and members of religious orders, or of persons holding appointments in the forces or civil services. During the last three months of the Terror, indeed, the aristocratic victims exceeded the ecclesiastical, but without equalling those of the official class, whilst they were far outstripped by members of the middle and lower orders.

The number of priests, monks, and nuns who came before the Tribunal shows that there were still men and women who put religion before life, and attempted to carry on the work of the ' refractory ' church, whilst intriguing against the government that persecuted it. Their influence was behind every counter-revolutionary movement, especially in the west and north. The same politicians who hoped to suppress superstition by introducing the Revolutionary Calendar soon found it advisable to discourage the anti-clerical excesses of some of their most efficient agents, and set about devising a state worship which might conciliate rather than antagonize the religious instincts of the common people.

Militant Girondism, or the federal insurrection, was crushed during the autumn of '93. But the Parisians had long memories, and short mercies. Mme Roland was dragged from a happy imprisonment in Sainte-Pélagie and the Conciergerie to a radiant martyrdom before the statue of Liberty. Marie Gonze (or Mme Aubry), a widow, who had offered to defend Louis at his trial, and who had acquired notoriety as a political writer under the name of Olympe de Gouges, was condemned to death (Nov. 3rd) for a pamphlet proposing an appeal from the government to the people. The cruel circumstances of Bailly's execution showed that the people of Paris had never forgiven his part in the Martial Law of July, '91, and in the massacre of the Champ de Mars. Not only the prisons, but the cafés and clubs of the capital still contained men who dreaded the charge of complicity with Mirabeau, Lafayette, or Dumouriez—the discredited heroes of '89–'92, and who professed an exaggerated patriotism when they thought themselves overheard by the *mouchards* or *moutons* whom the government set to spy upon them.

Roland's purge of the Home Office, and Dumouriez's purge of the Ministry of Foreign Affairs, had at best substituted a Girondin for a royalist personnel. It was commonly complained in December, '93, that the administration was full of men who, under a mask of loyalty, were secretly working against the republic. But many of these, like the *aristo* officers of the army and navy, could not easily be replaced. The government showed little sympathy for the methods by which Vincent and his friends sought to ' sansculottize ' the staff of the War Office, or to enforce inquisitorial *cartes de civisme* upon candidates for public employment.

Discontent in the country-side was due less to political controversy, which did not interest the peasantry, than to economic troubles, exploited by royalist and clerical counter-revolutionaries. True, land-purchase became easier every day. The *émigré* land sold after '92 went in smaller lots and at lower prices than the *biens nationaux* hitherto on the market. The land, too, freed from tithe and feudal charges, was worth twice what it had been before the revolution. Yet there were complaints of the profits made by bourgeois speculators in real estate, not without the connivance of the official vendors, and of the disproportionate share of the land that fell to prosperous town-dwellers. Again, the Jacobins made little attempt to enforce agricultural reforms, which they knew to be expedient, upon a peasantry stubbornly attached to old-fashioned individualistic methods ; so that the country-side benefited less than it might have done from the freeing of the soil. Yet, politically speaking, the solid advantages that the revolution had won for the farmer gradually prevailed over the loyalties of the old regime, and created that wide basis of proprietorship upon which French prosperity has rested ever since.

A more serious discontent was remedied by the ingenuity of a retired grocer, now the most competent financier in the revolutionary government. Necker, as long ago as '81, and Lebrun again in '90, had called attention to the chaotic state of the National Debt. The *rentiers* (national bond-holders), a large and important class, particularly in Paris, held government stock of half a dozen different issues. Not only was the payment of interest unduly complicated and expensive, but political dissension was caused by the fear that a royalist restoration might repudiate republican investments. It was to deal with both these troubles that Cambon carried through the operations summed up in the *Grand Livre* of August, '93. This measure consolidated the various forms of public debt, paid a uniform five per cent interest, imposed a tax on investments analogous to that on land, and enabled *assignats* to be used for the purchase of national bonds as well as of national property. The main result of this transaction was to secure for the republican government the financial support of some forty-five thousand *rentiers*, many of whom had previously put their faith in the overthrow of the new regime. If only such methods had been tried more often, instead of the guillotine!

Serious as some of these opponents were, the government of '93 had less to fear from its old enemies than from its new friends. In order to defeat the Girondins, the Jacobins had courted the working-class sections of Paris. They were now asked to pay for this support by economic concessions and controls which puzzled and alarmed their supporters amongst the property-owning classes.

Nobody could deny that the inhabitants of the *faubourgs* Saint-Marcel and Saint-Antoine had a strong case for consideration. Economic causes and conditions were not indeed studied then as they are now by card-indexers and statisticians. Many of the evils from which the poor suffered were put down, for lack of scientific analysis, to some 'foreign plot.' But three economic factors at least could be easily recognized—monetary inflation, commercial stagnation, and rising food-prices.

As to inflation, and its accompanying depreciation, sufficient evidence is now available to set out diagrammatically the monthly variations in the value of the *assignats* throughout the revolution, and even to note the local aberrations which, as in the price-diagrams of the eighteenth century, illustrate the lack of a financial control-centre in the body politic. The main points that emerge from this evidence (*see p.* 337) are clear enough. During the two years preceding May, '93, *assignats* had depreciated slowly, with occasional recoveries, from about ninety to about fifty per cent of their face-value. In May they stood at about the same level as in January. Between May and July they sank suddenly to not much more than twenty per cent. of their face-value, and made no recovery until September. Certain results inevitably followed this disastrous fall:—hoarding and exportation of metal currency; speculation in paper money; refusal of vendors to accept *assignats*; and a steep rise in prices.

These evils might have been countered in a time of flourishing trade and commerce. But the luxury-trades had been hit by the ruin or exile of the spending classes. The necessity-trades were monopolized by the needs of the army. Foreign commerce, fairly prosperous till February, '93, had since been ruined by civil war, the British blockade, and the attempt to stop inflation by the prohibition of exports. Of many of these things the man in the street understood nothing ; but he knew at once when his daily food and fuel cost more, and when his wages failed to meet his wife's demands for the week's house-keeping.

In the autumn months of '93, before the price-fixing law of September 27th, coffee, which had now become a popular drink, cost from 4s. 5d. to 5s. a pound, milk 6d. a pint, fresh butter from 1s. 5d. to 2s. a pound, sugar 1s. 1d. a pound, and eggs 2d. each. The price of a small cabbage was from 6d. to 8d. ; 10d. would purchase only half a gallon of peas or beans ; candles were 2s. 2d. a pound, soap (so bad that it ' ruined the washing') 3s. 5d., whilst lard at 1s. 8d. a pound 'looked like cart-grease,' and at 1s. was ' little better than poison.' Coal cost from 4½d. to 10d. a bushel, and tobacco 3s. to 4s. a pound. There were bitter complaints, too, of middlemen's profits, and of charges for transport. Goods bought at midday for five shillings were sold (it was said) at one o'clock for ten. Fuel merchants charged eight shillings for delivering a load of wood, and then it was under weight.

Such, no doubt, are the grievances of small buyers in every age, and all the world over : but when it is remembered that the French working man's average wage in '89 was only ninepence half-penny a day (if he were a mason or carpenter he might make one and threepence), the seriousness of the situation is evident. No wonder the poor man, puzzled by increases of price that he could not understand, supposed that someone was bribing the tradesmen to make life difficult for him, and raised the cry of conspiracy.

In his trouble, to which neither Girondin nor Jacobin politicians seemed to pay much heed, the Paris workman found champions in a small group of people on the extreme left of the Jacobin party whom, because they loudly upheld the claims of the Have-nots, the Haves called *enragés* : a century later they would have been 'labour agitators.' Some of these men forced themselves upon the attention of the Assembly and of the Commune. Jean Varlet, a well-educated and well-to-do young enthusiast, was always ready with provocative speech, or an inflammatory placard, demanding the prevention of hoarding, speculation, and profiteering. Jacques Roux, the middle-aged *vicaire* of Saint Nicholas-des-Champs, a friend of Marat, a leader of the Cordeliers club and of the Gravilliers section, was a popular open-air preacher of political sermons, in which he never shrank from supporting extremes either of legislation to prevent food-shortage, or of terrorism to put down counter-revolution, and to enforce the rights of the people. These were regarded as the leaders of the party. Amongst their followers were Théophile Leclerc, who had made his reputation as a champion of revolution at Martinique, and as Chalier's colleague at Lyon; and Claire Lacombe, an actress, who presided over the women's *société des républicaines révolutionnaires.*

The *enragé* movement was not confined to the capital. Many a country town or wayside village contained unconscious precursors of Babeuf and Marx. At Orléans Taboureau de Montigny, a lawyer and pamphleteer, had already worked out an economic programme designed to protect the poor consumer against exploitation by producers and profiteers— a programme which anticipated the *maximum*, the *greniers d'abondance*, and other expedients of '93-4. At Meymac in Corrèze an ex-priest named Charles Jumel edited a Jacobin paper, and championed the cause of an exceptionally indigent peasantry : but when he made the mistake of trying to introduce his followers to the cult of Reason they raised a riot which began in breaking his head, and ended in a visit by a republican troop and a travelling guillotine.

In general the *enragés* knew as little of economic theory as their opponents. The issue was as old and as simple as it could be. The Haves clung to their property, the Have-nots demanded a livelihood. To the Haves the state was a policeman : to the Have-nots it was a relieving officer. To the Haves liberty meant the right to live comfortably : to the Have-nots equality meant the right not to be too poor, or too hungry. Here for the first time since '89 the revolution produced a clear-cut class-issue. For the first time the revolutionaries of the street-corner seriously challenged the revolutionaries of the assembly.

Lack of food was nothing new in Paris : but the revolution had given Parisians a new spirit to resent it, and to insist upon a remedy for it. A shortage of sugar in January, '92, due to political troubles in San Domingo, and shortages of corn in March and September, owing to the invasion and the inflation of the *assignats*, failed to move the Girondins from their policy of *laissez-faire* tempered with requisitioning. In the spring of '93 (February 25th–26th) a shortage of soap and other necessities led to the looting of some grocers' shops. Varlet preached a crusade against free trade, and Roux against hoarding. But a demand for the fixing of the price of grain was refused by Jacobin as well as Girondin deputies. It was not until May 4th that the first *maximum*, or Price-control Act, was forced upon an unwilling assembly by the aid of Jacobin politicians who needed the support of the crowd to overthrow their Girondin enemies.

The success of the alliance of June 2nd encouraged the *enragés* to enlarge their demands. The *maximum*, sabotaged by the ill-will of producers and officials, must be enforced by a Revolutionary Army. The Convention must be purged again by the expulsion of the *appelans*. The Committee of Public Safety must be reconstituted. This encroachment of an economic party upon the field of politics brought the *enragé* leaders into alliance with Vincent and Ronsin, the advocates of direct action by the people ; it was an alliance ominous for the future of both parties. During the summer the Jacobin government was too much embarrassed by the federal revolt to deal with opposition on the home front. The Hébertist-*enragé* coalition was able to exploit its advantage in more than one direction. A law against hoarding (*accaparement*, July 26th), the provision of *greniers d'abondance* for the storing of requisitioned food-supplies (August 9th), and the reaffirmation and extension of price-control (September 11th, 29th) were conceded rather than favoured by the government.

But as the war went better in the provinces, the Jacobins stiffened their attitude towards the demands of their former allies. The Convention had no love for agitators who exploited its troubles, and compromised legitimate grievances by associating them with a dangerous political programme. Early in September Roux was arrested. Varlet and Lacombe soon followed him to prison. The Women's Revolutionary Society was closed. Five months later Roux killed himself, to avoid coming to trial.

The grievances that the *enragés* had expressed remained. The remedies that they had formulated were taken up by more powerful partisans either of parliamentary or of direct action. It is, however, significant that this is the only group of French revolutionaries of this period to attract the sympathetic attention of Russian Bolshevist historians. The professors of Communism consider that, whilst they were neither socialists nor communists, the *enragés* went further in that direction than other Jacobins, and may be regarded as a link between the economic ideas of Mably and Marx.

On November 29th, '91, the Legislative Assembly had passed the first penal decree against the refractory clergy, threatening with deprivation those who failed to take the requisite oath of allegiance. The war which broke out four months later encouraged both resistance and repression. On May 27th a fresh decree authorized the departmental authorities, under certain conditions, to expel non-juror clergy from the country. After the fall of the throne came a stiffer measure (August 26th) ; all refractory clergy were to be exiled within a fortnight. Nevertheless many remained in the country, and some in their cures. The outbreak of insurrection in the west in March, '93, was largely the work of priests irreconcilably opposed to the revolutionary church. Not unnaturally the Convention hit back with a decree (April 23rd) which put all non-jurors, including ex-clergy and ex-members of religious orders, into the class of suspects, punishable by exile, or, under some conditions, by death.

During the next few months anti-clericalism, stimulated by war-fever, led to a definite attempt to destroy the influence of a cult which was becoming identified with counter-revolution. The de-Christianizing movement, as it is generally called, was never officially acknowledged by the Conventionals, unless their sanction of clerical marriage, their substitution of republican *décadis* and festivals for the Sundays and Saints-days of the Catholic calendar, or their attendance at a famous service at Notre Dame in honour of Reason be so interpreted. But the campaign was enthusiastically and, indeed, earnestly prosecuted by certain popular societies, and by certain deputies on mission, as well as by the Paris Commune.

In October, Fouché, in the course of a mission to the departments of the centre and west, came to Nevers, where the Popular Society was ready for any measures against the clergy. Encouraged by Chaumette, himself a Nevers man, and the chief exponent of Parisian anti-clericalism, he posted up an *arrêté* in which he declared that the French people recognized no privileges but those of law, justice, and liberty, no cult but that of morality, and no dogma but that of its own sovereignty. He prohibited services, religious emblems, and clerical dress in public; and he enforced the burial of the dead of every sect in a common grave-yard, whose only emblem was to be an effigy of Slumber (*Sommeil*), and whose only inscription was to be, 'Death is an eternal sleep.'

Fouché's campaign was not directed only against the refractory clergy, or the friends of fanaticism. One of his victims was the abbé Glaize, the constitutional curé of Glux, who had welcomed the revolution, and was living comfortably in his parsonage with a man-servant, a daily maid, and two cows, on a hundred pounds a year. Glaize was popular with his parishioners, and on good terms with the municipal officers. He was prepared to conform to Fouché's reasonable demands. But when he failed to publish from his pulpit the decree of Oct. 10th, he was arrested, and spent a month in prison. He was liberated by the intercession of his parishioners, but soon afterwards he had to flee from Glux, never to return. By such persecution the church setttlement of 1790 was undermined, the new Gallicanism aligned itself with the old Papalism, and the way was prepared for the Catholic reaction of 1801.

Pierre-Gaspard, or (as he preferred to call himself, after the irreligious Greek philosopher) Anaxagoras Chaumette, had tried his hand as a seaman, a surgeon, and a school-master, before he took to political journalism, and attached himself to the Cordeliers club in Paris. A sentimental moralist, credulous and exploiting credulity, idealistic and envious, Chaumette lived on his wits, and showed how dangerous Rousseauism might be to little minds. With a head full of undigested ideas, he would support indifferently pacifism and republicanism, anti-clericalism and a General Strike. A ring-leader on July 17th, '91, and President of the Insurrectional Commune of August, '92, he remained one of the most influential leaders of the lower middle class in Paris.

As the organizer of a systematic ' purge,' and as the founder of a federation of Popular Societies, Chaumette had affinities with the Hébertists ; but it was as an anti-clerical that he most offended the official leaders of Jacobinism. Amongst the papers he kept whilst *procureur* of the Commune is a list of measures taken during October and November, '93, to de-Christianize the capital. Ministers, of whatever sect, were forbidden to function outside their churches. The vessels used in the chapel of the Town Hall were sent to the Mint, and the altar-linen made into shirts for soldiers. Church books were sold to grocers, for packing-paper ; leaden coffins were melted down in the munitions factories ; religious images were mutilated, and relics burnt. Audot in his old age recalled how at the age of eleven, just after his first communion, he had helped to carry church vessels in procession to the Convention.

It was seriously proposed in the name of equality that bishops should give up their mitres, crosses, and episcopal rings, and that when church towers overtopped secular buildings they should be pulled down:—it was thus, according to local tradition, that the parish church of Saint-Jean de Maurrienne in Savoy lost its spire, during Albitte's regime in the department of Mont-Blanc in *Pluviôse*, '93. The statues on the west front of Notre Dame were spared from destruction (it was said) only because the astronomer Dupuis found among the carvings over the side doors evidence for his planetary theories.

On the invitation of the Commune many sections renounced Catholicism, and closed their churches, or dedicated them to new saints, and new forms of worship. At Vitry-sur-Seine, on December 10th, a service was held in the Temple de la Raison (formerly the parish church), at which

' a big girl in a white dress decked with ribbons, and carrying a *bonnet rouge* on the end of a pike,' stood on the altar, supported by busts of Voltaire, Rousseau, Marat, and Le Peletier, whilst patriotic hymns were sung, and the Rights of Man proclaimed ; all being done with ' decency, gaiety, and even magnificence.'

At Havre the publication of Romme's Revolutionary Calendar (October 5th) was made the occasion for an elaborate *fête décadaire* in honour of Reason under the patronage of the representative Delacroix ; this was a month before the similar ceremony in Paris. At Reims (October 7th), on the ruined steps of the pedestal from which Louis XV's statue had already been thrown down, the representative Rühl solemnly broke in pieces the *sainte ampoule*, the most famous relic of Catholic royalism in the country, the flask of ointment given by St. Remi to Clovis, and used at every coronation of a French king. The popular society of Blois closed all the churches in the town, recommended the cult of Reason, and advised good citizens to stay at home, practise virtue, and obey the law ; ' for that is the long and short of Gospel morality, and of the teaching of its author, the *sansculotte* Jesus.' At Nancy, Faure induced all the clergy to renounce their Orders, and made a ceremonial bonfire of their licences in the nave of the cathedral.

Chaumette, like his friend Fouché, was seriously concerned about the insanitary gloom of Christian funerals and church-yards; he thought that burial in towns should be forbidden, and that graves should be marked, not with emblems of death and decay, but with bright flowers, and signs of hopefulness. But he did not confine himself to reasonable reform. He took part in the destruction of the reliquary of Sainte-Geneviève, and of the holy oil-flask at Tours. He approved of the fête in honour of Chalier at Ville-Affranchie (Lyon), when church vessels were carried on a donkey's back, and church vestments thrown into a bonfire. He organized the Feast of Reason in Notre Dame (Nov. 10th). He encouraged Gobel, bishop of Paris, Thomas Lindet, bishop of l'Eure, and a number of constitutional priests to make a public renunciation of their Orders (Nov. 9th).

Such proceedings could not but offend a government which needed the support of the Catholic working class both in town and country, and which feared the bad effect of anti-Christian propaganda upon Catholic opinion abroad. A decree of Dec. 6th therefore reaffirmed liberty of worship ; and Chaumette himself, denounced by Robespierre as an atheist and an aristocrat (for theism, he held, was democratic), was arrested at the same time as the Hébertists, and executed on April 13th.

To the Hébertists de-Christianization meant an attack upon ' superstition and fanaticism ' ; it is likely enough that the common people saw in it little more than a new method of stopping clerical propaganda against the revolution, and of procuring fresh currency for the Treasury. Already, by decrees of Nov. 6th, '90, and March 3rd, '91, the plate of all suppressed churches and monasteries had been sent to the Mint ; and some unofficial pillaging had followed the revolution of August 10th, '92. A return made by Cambon of the amount of such plate, including some voluntarily contributed by a Jewish synagogue and by the Protestant church of Saint-Louis-du-Louvre, with some more from less voluntary *émigré* sources, shows that by Jan. 18th, '94, when the de-Christianizing movement had by no means reached its climax, the value of this plunder was already nearly a quarter of a million sterling. It constituted an appreciable addition to the national resources.

Did any more direct result follow from the de-Christianizing campaign ? Nothing is more difficult than to estimate how far (whether as cause, result, or accompaniment of the closing of so many churches) religion was actually losing ground at this time. An English traveller noticed that the sale of books of devotion had fallen off, and that beggars, instead of asking for charity *pour l'amour de Dieu,* now cried *Vive la nation!* These were changes of fashion, rather than of faith. Probably the lack of opportunities for worship, and some degree of persecution, weakened the weak Christians, and strengthened the strong. There is little reason to think that in the long run the church was deeply affected, either for good or bad, by a movement essentially superficial and transitory.

Nevertheless there is evidence, coming from too many sources to be ignored, of a disregard for moral appearances, if not of morality, which showed itself in the public life of Paris at this time, and which coincided, at least, with the 'attack on religion.' Louis Marie Debost, a provincial lawyer, and a good Jacobin, came to Paris in August, '93, to express to the government the admiration of his native town, Bourg-en-Bresse, for the new constitution. His account of this visit was, indeed, written after he was released from a Jacobin prison, a year later, and is coloured by a natural resentment. But it is probably no great misrepresentation of the appearance of the capital.

' In the neighbourhood of the Convention,' he writes, ' amongst the crowds walking up and down, the only papers on sale were *Père Duchesne,* and other gutter-press publications. Here one heard people of repulsive appearance saying that the existence of God was a hoary superstition, that Hell was a myth, and man a being without a soul, who ought to indulge all the pleasures to which his nature prompted him, without concern either for religion or for moral principles. In accordance with this view, indecent prints and obscene books were on sale ; and nothing was left undone to destroy morality, or corrupt the public mind. Here, again, were men shouting at the top of their voices about conspiracy, talking for ever about the guillotine, gloating over the next execution, and reporting beforehand whose head would be the next to fall. . . . Further on you would find two men standing on chairs, with ready-made lists of questions and answers, one of whom spoke for the Revolution, and one against it, but with a foregone conclusion in favour of the Mountain. This amused the idlers, and put simple folk off their guard, so that they were an easy prey for pick-pockets. In the cafés, where people dined at a common table, one found police spies who tried to get into conversation with foreigners, and to turn the conversation on to the affairs of the day, so as to induce them to give opinions for which they could be denounced to the police. If you so much as went out of doors for a stroll, you could hear the market-women say to one another, 'Do you see that fellow ? He looks like a counter-revolutionary. He's got *guillotine* written all over him.'

The ' Rotters ' (*pourris*) were not a political party. They were the men who, whatever their political views, dishonoured the revolution, in the eyes of good Jacobins, by taking bribes, embezzling public money, putting their friends into overpaid posts, cheating the government over army con- tracts, speculating in *assignats*, or practising other forms of what is nowadays summarized in the word ' graft.' There can have been few situations in modern history which offered so many temptations to practitioners of this disreputable art. Ample funds, in ministerial hands before August, '92, and in those of royalist agents afterwards, were available to corrupt patriot editors and politicians. The rapid fluctuations of the paper currency were a constant encouragement to speculation. The frequent purging of public departments made Jacobin jobbery almost a public duty. The conduct of two wars, the equipment and provisioning of thirteen armies, gave every opportunity for dishonest contracting, and illicit profiteering. The lack of government control made corruption as easy as it was attractive to men for the most part badly paid, irresponsible, and affected by the loosening of moral principles that accompanies a revolution.

It was Robespierre's pride that he was inaccessible to bribery and in- different to gain. There were others of the Jacobin leaders who, when they died, left little or nothing behind them. But incorruptibility was not a common virtue. Mirabeau, constantly living beyond his means, had been for months in the pay of the court. His successor in popularity, Danton, cannot be absolved without inquiry from the charge of corruption that contributed to his downfall. Thanks to a series of investigations, Danton's financial circumstances are uncommonly well known. The facts may be put in the form of a Balance Sheet for the years '87–'94.

Receipts	£	*Expenditure*	£
Capital in '87	600	Purchase of practice	3,900
Borrowed.	3,000	Loans repaid	3,000
Second wife's dowry	2,000	Professional expenses	2,000
Salary as *procureur*	450	*Biens nationaux* bought	2,835
Salary as minister	833	House bought.	1,265
Salary as deputy	750	Property purchased	2,248
Balance	7,615		
	15,248		15,248

How was this deficit of over seven thousand pounds made good ? How was Danton able to repay the money he borrowed, and to live more than comfortably, keeping up four establishments, and a private carriage ? There is no reason to suppose that his legal practice was ever remunerative enough to meet such charges. The suggestion cannot be avoided that he owed his wealth to the acceptance of bribes.

Brissot, Bertrand de Moleville, and Lafayette all assert that he was bribed by Montmorin, the Foreign Minister, in October, '89, though their estimates of the amount vary from five to fifteen thousand pounds. Mirabeau says that Danton received fifteen hundred pounds out of the secret fund that he (Mirabeau) administered in the king's interests a year later. His statement was confirmed by Talon, the agent through whom the payment was made, when questioned by Napoleon's police in 1804. At the time of the king's trial, Ocariz, the Spanish ambassador, distributed over a hundred thousand pounds in bribes to those who might save Louis' life. He approached the British government through the abbé Noël, a friend of Danton, who was in touch with him at Liège at the moment of the transaction. Would Danton risk the charge of royalism for nothing? Did not his attitude during the vote on the king's death suggest that he had made, but failed to carry out, some such promise ? It is likely enough in this instance, and not unlikely in the other two instances, that he had received bribes.

Other charges that have some evidence behind them cannot be ignored. It was said that Danton received money from the Duc d'Orléans to insert the suggestion of a Regency in the manifesto of July 16th, '91 ; that he was given two thousand five hundred pounds by the court on the eve of August 10th, '92 ; that he spent on his private purposes part of the secret funds, totalling over twenty-seven thousand pounds, entrusted to him as Minister of Justice ; that he carried off loot from Belgium in '93 ; and that he passed in '89, and was paid in '93, as a secret agent of the British government.

Danton's great services to his country may perhaps outweigh an amoral indifference to bribery : he probably made money, as he made friends, easily and unfastidiously. The same defence cannot apply to a group of deputies, Danton's associates, who were the principals in one of those complicated *affaires* which periodically plunge French political life into the atmosphere of an American crook film.

The Compagnie des Indes, a big over-seas trading corporation, founded by the Bourbon minister Calonne, and protected by the Girondin minister Clavière, attracted the envious attention of a group of unscrupulous Jacobins, who, in July, '93, saw in it an opportunity for a financial operation that would bring them both credit and profits. In public they attacked the Company for evading the decrees of August, '92, which required the registration of its stock, and the payment of a five per cent tax, as well as for cornering, profiteering, and subscribing to the royalist cause.

In private they contrived to control the liquidation of the Company's affairs in such a way as to secure considerable profits for themselves, and for the friends on government committees who connived at their proceedings. They did not even shrink from the falsification of an important document, to further their designs.

The first of this group in alphabetical order (the order of delinquency is not so easy to determine) was Basire, a man of 29, who had left a wife and child at Dijon, under a separation allowance, to live with a mistress in Paris, where he became a member of the *Comité de Sûreté générale*, and frequented the salon of the feminist courtesan and Dutch spy, Etta Palm, *alias* the Baronne d'Aelders. The second, François Chabot, had been a Capucin monk for nearly twenty years before he became a republican, married a German wife, and shared the financial intrigues of her foreign relations. Like Basire a member of the *Comité de Sûreté générale* until its purge in September, '93, the ex-monk was a moral *malade imaginaire*, never so happy as when denouncing his friends' misdeeds, or confessing his own weaknesses : his letters from prison touch the lowest depths of terrified self-abasement.

The third of the group, Delaunay of Angers, was a clever lawyer, and a member of his local Academy, who sat on the Left both of the Legislative Assembly and of the Convention. His weak character was at the mercy of any woman, and his membership of the *comité des finances* offered temptations which he could never resist. The fourth, Fabre of Carcassonne, who fancifully called himself d'Eglantine from a prize he claimed to have won at the *jeux floraux* of Toulouse, had spent his youth as a strolling player, artist, and poet. He came to Paris in '87, as the author of that delicate little pastoral, *Il pleut, il pleut, bergère*, and produced a series of comedies that recalled the manner of Molière. His wit and easy morals commended him to Danton, and to Danton's less reputable friends. Julien, the last of the five, was a Protestant pastor from Toulouse, oddly associated with the ex-monk Chabot in left-wing Jacobinism and financial speculation. His position as a member of the *Comité de Sûreté générale* and a commissioner for the printing of *assignats*, backed by the hospitality of his mistress, Mme de Beaufort (for he, like Basire, had left his wife and child at home), gave him special prominence in the India Company affair.

In October the conspirators fell out. Fabre, strong in the confidence of Danton and Robespierre, denounced Chabot for his foreign connexions. Chabot and Basire, to distract attention from themselves, informed against their associates, and tried to implicate them in the Hébertist and foreign plots. The charges against Fabre and Hébert were for the moment ignored. All the rest, accusers and accused alike, were thrown into prison.

In the investigations which followed, more and more people became involved, till hardly any well-known name was free from some smear of suspicion. The representatives of the India Company itself escaped notice in the pursuit of persons who were perhaps less to blame :—members of the *Comité de Sûreté générale*, the *comité des finances*, the *comité d'agiotage*, or the Paris department, who might have connived at the plot, foreigners who were said to be spies, *fournisseurs* who had made undue profits out of government contracts, or financiers who were supposed to be using foreign money to foment disorder, and to aggravate the food-shortage; together with a crowd of their agents, mistresses, and business acquaintances. Not all of these came to trial ; but many disquieting discoveries were made, and many suspicious persons were brought to light from the dark under-world of the revolution.

Jean-Pierre-Louis, Baron de Batz, *grand sénéchal* of the Duchy of Albret, had served in the Spanish army, and sat in the Constituent Assembly as deputy for the nobility of Nérac. He now lived with an actress in Paris, and was believed to have attempted to rescue the king, on his way to execution, and the queen from her cell in the Conciergerie. His country house at Charonne, searched after the Baron himself escaped, was said to have been the centre from which the India Company conspiracy was planned and financed. The abbé d'Espagnac, a disreputable priest of aristocratic birth, had been denounced years ago by Mirabeau for profitable speculations in the shares of the old India Company. Now, a prominent Jacobin, trading under his valet's name as the Compagnie Masson, he obtained army contracts from Dumouriez and Servan. From one of these he was shown to have received more than a quarter of a million pounds a month, whilst expending only twenty-five thousand.

The brothers Gotlob and Emmanuel Dobruska were Austrian Jews whom the Emperor had rewarded with a title for their services as army contractors during the Turkish war. Now, changing their name to Frey, they appeared first at Strasbourg, and later in Paris, giving money to patriotic funds, and dinners to Jacobin politicians, whilst losing no opportunity for a profitable investment in the corn trade, or in privateering. Chabot's marriage to Léopoldine Frey involved them in the India Company affair. Another Austrian, Proli, said to be an illegitimate son of the statesman Kaunitz, and well known in Paris banking and literary circles, had been employed by Danton and Lebrun at the Foreign Office in confidential peace negotiations with Cobourg and the Austrian government. He was also involved with Hébert and his associates in activities which brought him under the suspicion of the government. One of his acquaintances in this circle was the Spanish adventurer, Guzman, whom he had met during the Vonckist rising in Belgium, and whose speculations, financed perhaps by shares in a gambling-saloon, were covered, like those of the Freys, by generous contributions to patriotic funds.

Some bankers, a class naturally suspect, but generally well able to protect themselves, were involved in the India Company affair. Amongst them were the brothers Simon, army contractors in '92, living handsomely on their profits in '93, cultivating political connexions, and even claiming arrears of eighty-five thousand pounds from the government. Like their fellow-bankers Boyd, Kerr, and Walckiers, the Simons disappeared, whilst their name-sake the socialist Saint-Simon was arrested, and their agent Rose carried on his duties as an usher in the Convention under the guard of two gendarmes. Walckiers, the head of the London and Brussels bank, Veuve Nettine et Cie, which negotiated Austrian loans, and financed the Vonckist movement, easily fell under suspicion of being an Austrian agent in Paris, where he had taken refuge after the failure of the Belgian revolution.

The inclusion of so many foreigners in the purge of October, '93, suggests that they had taken advantage of the generosity of the revolution towards a class which, under modern conditions, is one of the first to suffer. It was not until France had been at war with England for six months that steps were taken to intern foreigners, or to sequestrate their property. This was due to the discovery of alleged proofs of a fantasy which had long haunted the public mind, and was, indeed, more useful to alarmist orators in its imaginary than in its real form :—' Pitt's plot.' Chabot of course knew all about it, and spun it into the complicated texture of his denunciations ; but Barère, too, in his speech of Aug. 1st, Robespierre on Nov. 17th, and Desmoulins, in the first number of the *Vieux Cordelier* (Dec. 5th), made it a main thesis of political argument. What, if any, were the facts ?

Both the Spanish ambassador and the Polish agent, writing from Paris in the autumn of '89, assume that it is in England's interest to subsidize disorder in France ; but they give no evidence that this was being done. Mme de Stael quotes her father's statement (and no one was better placed than Necker to make it) that in his time the British government was quite innocent of any such policy. All the available evidence suggests that Pitt's attitude, up to within a short time of the declaration of war, was one of almost pedantic neutrality. This was W. J. Croker's conclusion, after questioning every surviving member of Pitt's administration. Again, no grounds were ever found for the suggestion that Pitt's bankers, Boyd and Kerr, had made improper use of the funds they held for their many English clients. Only three pieces of evidence have been produced to suggest that public money was passing from England to France for purposes of political corruption, or to justify the belief of most Parisians in '94 that anyone who introduced English words into his talk, or had English guineas in his purse, was an agent of Pitt.

In the course of a speech on August 1st Barère read out two documents which he said had been found on an Englishman arrested at Lille. One was a letter in English, dated June 29th, but without signature or address, in which an agent of ' Milord ' (also called ' H.R.H.', and evidently the Duke of York) gave instructions to ' the President of the Committee, at Saint-Omer ' for the payment of secret-service money. ' C.', a friend of Lamarlière (dismissed from the command of the northern army a week before), was to be given five hundred pounds for information supplied, and to be asked to report on the state of the French ammunition supply, and on the camp at Cassel. Phosphorus matches were to be provided to start fires in forage-stores. Stapleton (perhaps Gregory Stapleton, Superior of the English College at Saint-Omer) was promised a reward for his zeal. Steps were to be taken to discredit *assignats*, raise prices, and corner essential commodities. Assassinations (it was urged) had best be attempted by disguised priests and women.

There was only one sentence in this letter that referred to the British government : ' Pitt,' the writer said, ' approves of Milnes' plans.' This is apparently a reference to W. A. Miles, who on July 10th had forwarded to Pitt an offer from M. de la Colombe, formerly aide-de-camp of Lafayette, to raise an army in the Auvergne, and to join in the fight for the restoration of the French monarchy. It is certainly not evidence that Pitt approved of the designs referred to in the body of the letter. But that such plans were afoot, and that a body of secret agents had been organized, with the knowledge of the Duke of York, to carry them out, can hardly be denied except on the supposition that the document, which exists only in the form in which Barère printed it as an appendix to his speech of August 1st, was edited, if not invented, for the purposes of propaganda. The second paper that he produced, described as 'notes extracted from an English portfolio,' contained memoranda of payments, correspondence, and meetings with agents between January 21st and July 2nd. Among the correspondents appear Dillon (presumably General Arthur Dillon, who was implicated in a royalist plot) and Dumouriez; among the agents Stapleton (again), Hunter, Morell, Duplain, and others only represented by initials. The activities of the note-writer extend from Lille and Dunkirk in the north of France to Caen and Nantes in the west, and Tours, Blois, and Orléans in the centre—all of them places in which disorders are known to have broken out. Here too are several references to relations with London, but without mention of names.

The third piece of evidence is the following letter, addressed to the banker Perregaux, and found among Danton's papers.

Whitehall. Friday 13
(presumably September, 1793)

The information which you have lately sent us has been very satisfactory to 12. We desire you to continue your exertions, and to advance 3000 livres to C.D., 12000 to W.T., and 1000 to De M., for the essential services they have rendered us *en soufflant le feu*, and carrying the Jac. (*Jacobins*) to a paroxysm of fury. We hope that by their endeavours, and those of others whom we shall soon send over, the old 7 (*monarchy ?*) will be again re-established, or at least the present o (*anarchy ?*) be prolonged for several years. Staley (*probably Stanley, denounced in a spy's report as an agent of Pitt*) brought your last. We are determined to grant C.D.'s request. You'll be pleased to advance him the 18,000 livres, and be kind enough to assist him in discovering the channels in which the money may be most successfully distributed. We have a great deal of business to transact today in the office, which circumstance obliges me to subscribe myself, pro S. . .e,

Your most humble obedient servant,

N.

This document, described as ' written on foolscap, with every appearance of official origin,' is evidence that ' S. . .e ' and ' N,' acting for ' 12,' are paying secret agents, apparently ' sent over ' from England, to provide information, and to foment counter-revolution. So far as is known, it was not used against Danton at his trial, nor against Perregaux, who, in spite of his acknowledged English connexions, continued to be protected and employed by the Committee of Public Safety. There, for the present, the matter rests.

In all these factions, whether royalists, *enragés*, ' atheists,' *pourris*, or foreigners, there was much to disquiet a moralist, but little to alarm a government. By the end of the year '93 most of their leaders were either in prison or in exile. But just as, during the summer, Jacobin vengeance on the Girondins had been delayed until the federal revolt and the murder of Marat provided an opportunity, so during the winter the factionists remained in prison, and investigations went slowly on, until the atmosphere of suspense and suspicion caused the real enemies of the government to show their hand, and enabled the Jacobins to stage two great political trials, in which they hoped to destroy the Opposition once and for all.

The first of these trials is generally called the Hébertist trial. It was not merely because his cowardice was likely to dishearten the defence that Hébert was given the seat of honour in the dock. His long revolutionary career, his position as *substitut-procureur* of the Commune, and his editorship of the most widely-read paper in the country, made it natural that a movement he had patronized (if only to increase his circulation) should bear his name. The Hébertists were in reality a party with wide ramifications, and had supporters everywhere. Their political headquarters was the Cordeliers club, a centre of opposition to each successive legislature. Their administrative centre was the War Office, where Bouchotte's secretary for appointments, F.-N. Vincent, was exploiting theories of popular control over the Executive. Their social rendezvous seems to have been the café Corazza in the summer, and in the autumn the café Chrétien. Vincent, with his provocative championship of sansculottism in politics, was, perhaps, the most representative man in the movement. His following among the personnel of the army and ministry for whom he had found employment made him one of the most powerful. With him stood his friend Ronsin, commandant of the Revolutionary Army; Momoro, one of the founders of the Cordeliers, a republican hero of July, '91, and August, '92, and a member of the Paris department ; Javogues, deputy for Rhône-et-Loire, and an anticlerical terrorist at Mâcon ; Carrier, the notorious *noyadiste* of Nantes ; and the Dutch banker de Kock. Vincent could some-times look for support to Chaumette, the *procureur* of the Paris Commune, to Hanriot, the commandant of the National Guard, and even to Hérault de Séchelles and Collot d'Herbois, both members of the Committee of Public Safety.

The Hébertist programme was not on paper ; it could only be inferred from the speeches and acts of its supporters; but it may be summed up in one phrase : government of the people by the people. Its origin could be found in the armed intervention of the sections on August 10th and June 2nd. Its opportunity lay in the fact that so many key-positions in the govern-ment, both central and local, were held by men who owed their rise to the working-class movement. Its chief activity consisted in the endeavour to purge the personnel of the War Office, the local administration, and the civil services of all non-patriots.

This was well enough in theory ; but the standard of patriotism was set by the popular societies, and its instrument was an ' identity card ' (*certificat de civisme*), the requirements of which were stiffened up by a series of resolutions of the Paris commune. Eventually (December 2nd) no citizen could hope to be free from suspicion who could not satisfy his section that he had served in the National Guard since '90, that he had paid his taxes and ' patriotic contributions ' for '91 and '92 ; and that he had not held more than one paid post at the same time, or written anything ' against liberty,' or belonged to any club ' proscribed by public opinion,' or been ' purged ' from any popular society, or signed any such petition as those against the marriage of clergy, or the burial of Voltaire in the Panthéon.

The attempt to enforce such inquisitorial tests not only endangered many genuine patriots ; it also embarrassed the ministries, departments, and other public authorities, who wished to engage officials for their competence, not for their patriotism. The persecution of General Custine (though more was at issue than his aristocracy), and the championship of the incompetent General Rossignol, showed where such a policy might lead when applied to the army. This was not all. The patriotic purge was to be enforced, the food-supply of Paris to be secured, and the wholesale execution of ' public enemies ' to be carried out (here the Hébertists stole two popular planks from the *Enragé* platform) by a Revolutionary Army, recruited among the working men of the capital—a rival to the still mainly middle-class National Guard.

Here already was plenty to alarm the government. But there was worse to come. The idea behind the purging of the civil service was that under patriot control the ministries should recover the rights they had recently surrendered to the Committee of Public Safety. The War Office, in particular, was to make its own military appointments, and to conduct the war on its own responsibility. This was a proposition that Carnot and his colleagues could not possibly accept. It amounted to a demand for the suppression of the Provisional Government. It would probably be followed by an agitation for the introduction of the constitution of '93.

Looked at from another angle, the campaign for popular control of the administration, if it were only that of the food-supply, involved the substitution of a mandatory for a representative theory of government. It involved the direct control of the Convention and Commune by the sections. What that might mean was clear enough from the association of the Hébertist movement with the Cordeliers club, and its satellite *sociétés populaires*, whose provocative motto had always been, ' the restoration of order means the restoration of the old order.' Faced by such ideas, was it surprising that the government took alarm at what looked like an attack upon the Jacobin regime, and a reaction towards constitutional Girondism, if not the anarchy of mob-rule ?

This, then, was the situation at the end of '93. In order to throw back the foreign invasion, and to stamp out civil war, the Jacobins had set up an emergency government. They had concentrated the executive power in the hands of a dictatorial committee. They had restored discipline and efficiency to the administration by means of commissioners and courts-martial. These methods had been largely successful, and the country was not ungrateful. But owing to their preoccupation with war, and their need to conciliate the politicians who had helped them to overthrow the Girondins, and the people who manned their armies and made their munitions, the government had allowed too free a hand to certain factious elements behind the ' home front '—royalists, *enragés*, de-Christianizers, *pourris*, and Hébertists. They had even gone part of the way with these subversive movements. They had put off the punishment of the Girondins ; they had accepted the *maximum* ; they had patronized the cult of Reason ; they had exploited foreign financiers; and they had employed the Revolutionary Army. When the time came for vengeance on the Gironde, they used the resentment of the victims of Bailly and Lafayette. When the *enragés* became an embarrassment, they enlisted the trading interests to destroy them. When the ' atheists ' and profiteers fell out, they let them denounce one another, and dig their own graves. But when they found the *affaire*, as is the way with *affaires*, widening, so as to implicate their own friends, when they discovered designs not merely to exploit the weaknesses of the government, but to challenge its authority, then they had either to abdicate, or to use force and intimidation. Such was the dilemma which the Jacobins solved by the *coup d'état* of Germinal, Year II.

Chapter XXIV

GERMINAL

Jim said: 'Y'ought to think only of the end, Doc. Out of all this struggle a good thing is going to grow. That makes it worth while.'

'Jim, I wish I knew it. But in my little experience the end is never very different in its nature from the means. Damn it, Jim, you can only build a violent thing with violence.'

'I don't believe that,' Jim said. 'All great things have violent beginnings.'

'There aren't any beginnings,' Burton said. 'Nor any ends. It seems to me that man has engaged in a blind and fearful struggle out of a past he can't remember, into a future he can't foresee nor understand. And man has met and defeated every obstacle, every enemy except one. He cannot win over himself. How mankind hates itself!'

(JOHN STEINBECK: *The Dubious Battle*.)

On February 27th, '94, the Cordeliers club, after listening to an anti-Dantonist resolution from the *société populaire des droits de l'homme et du citoyen*, decided to print it and post it up, declaring that ' public opinion is the final court of appeal against disloyal deputies.' On March 4th it approved the prospectus of a new *Ami du peuple*, which was to denounce *les mandataires infidèles du peuple*, and it resolved to drape with mourning the copy of the Declaration of Rights which hung on the wall of its place of meeting, 'until the people has recovered its sacred rights by the destruction of the faction.'

The ' faction ' was that of Danton, Desmoulins, Fabre, and their friends, who were constantly attacking the Hébertists ; but the demand for vengeance seemed to envisage the Jacobin party as a whole. Vincent spoke of ' a conspiracy more formidable than Brissot's, and one that will be fatal to liberty, unless the threat of the guillotine is used unsparingly against the enemies of the people.' Carrier, fresh from his drownings at Nantes, deplored a tendency to be sorry for the victims of terrorism, and declared, amid loud applause, ' The weapon you must employ against these villains is insurrection—yes, a holy insurrection (*une sainte insurrection*).' Even Hébert, his courage gradually kindled by the cries of his audience, denounced prominent Jacobins, called Desmoulins an agent of Pitt and Cobourg, hinted that Robespierre was misled (*égaré*), if no more, and ended by backing Carrier's appeal. ' Insurrection ? Yes, insurrection ! and the Cordeliers will not be the last to give the signal for the death of the oppressors ! ' Two days later the section Marat, led by Momoro and Ducroquet, declared itself on the alert (*debout*) ' till the assassins of the people are exterminated.'

There had been too many long faces at the Cordeliers on the 4th, and a reaction soon followed. At the Jacobins, two days later, Collot d'Herbois asked the club to support the government against popular agitation. Carrier tried to explain away what had happened. Next day a Jacobin deputation to the Cordeliers proposed that the two clubs should be reconciled. The moderates had no wish to see themselves compromised, as they had been in July, '91, by the extremists. It was the Hébertists' last chance to draw back. The veil covering the Declaration of Rights was torn off, and presented to the Jacobins ' as a symbol of union and fraternity.' But the gesture came too late, and was disowned by the extremists. Ronsin on the 7th, in a speech printed by the club, persisted in the original demand for action against ' a faction even more disastrous than those of Brissot or Orléans.' Vincent supported him on the 9th. On the 12th Dufourny counter-attacked the popular societies that Vincent and his friends had organized in the sections. Evidently the Hébertists, not content with alienating the Jacobins, were falling out among themselves, and losing popular support.

Now was the time for the government to strike. It so happened that, just at this moment, the deputy Sergent reported that his friend Haindel of the hôtel de Philadelphie had overheard a conversation in which one of those in the confidence of the conspirators had given away their plans. These plans were reported to include the massacre of all the members of the Convention and Jacobin club, the liberation of the prisoners at the Luxembourg and Abbaye, the seizure of the Pont-Neuf and Mint, whence money would be distributed to the people, and the proclamation of a king. Rumours better attested said that the aim of the movement was to set up Hébert, Vincent, and Ronsin as a Triumvirate, or Ronsin alone as *Grand Juge*, a kind of dictator.

However unlikely any of this might sound, it was heaven-sent material for propaganda. The assembly at once passed a decree declaring that ' any person who usurps the power or attacks the safety and dignity of the Convention is an enemy of the people, and will be put to death.' It reinforced all the penalties of the decree of 14 *frimaire*, and instructed the Revolutionary Tribunal to proceed against the conspirators. Fouquier-Tinville was summoned before the Committee of Public Safety to receive instructions. The same night the Hébertists were in prison. A week later they stood in the dock.

The Hébertist trial was, like all French trials, a public debate (*débats*) ; but, to a greater extent even than the trial of Louis, or of the Girondins, it was a debate designed as government propaganda. Not only was the dock packed with representatives of every cause which might bring odium on the Hébertist prisoners ; but an official report of the trial was issued (*Procès instruit et jugé au tribunal révolutionnaire*), carefully edited by the judges who tried the case. In this report the attempts of the Defence to inculpate or discredit members of the government, or their friends, were omitted, and a discreet turn was given to embarrassing evidence. True, the Defence too issued a report designed to compromise the Prosecution ; but this appeared under a name (*Bulletin du tribunal révolutionnaire*)

Copper sol of 1793.

Copper 5 centimes of 1794.

Siege-piece of Valenciennes, 1793.

REPUBLICAN COINAGE

which carried the unpleasant associations of a *Newgate Calendar*, and enjoyed but little vogue.

St-Just's *rapport* had already shown how vague, and therefore how dangerous, the charges against the Hébertists could be. It was a long-winded sermonizing argument, in the Robespierre manner, based on the assumption that republican government implies a ' guarantee ' that the people will be ' just and virtuous,' or, in other words, submissive and co-operative, and that anything threatening this public temper must be ruthlessly attacked. There are two factions (says Saint-Just)—one too moderate, the other too extreme ; and both are incited by a foreign conspiracy of refugee spies, posing as patriots, who carry out the English plan of disquieting the people by food-shortage, or corrupting it by luxurious excess. Their vantage-ground is the popular societies, where civil servants forget their duty in plots against the government. It is a choice between a right and a wrong idea of public happiness (*bonheur public*), between a life of idleness and intrigue, or an active and austere co-operation in the Republic of Virtue. Indiscipline and immorality are twin forms of ' federalism,' attempts to break the disciplined unity of the country.

But this *étatiste* philosophy, with its close anticipation of views familiar enough to a later age, would be far above the heads of a patriot jury. It was necessary to find charges which the man in the street could understand. The essential crime of the Hébertists was accordingly said to be a design to overthrow the government, or, as the verdict more picturesquely put it, ' a conspiracy against the freedom and safety of the French people, encouraging civil war by arming citizens against one another, and against the authority of the law ; in pursuit of which aim the conspirators intended to dissolve the national Convention, assassinate the deputies, seize the national sovereignty, destroy the republican government, and put a tyrannical power in its place.'

In this comprehensive charge Ronsin and Mazuel of the Revolutionary Army, Vincent, Leclerc, and Bourgeois of the War Office, Momoro of the Paris department, and some minor officials were most clearly envisaged. Towards the end of February Vincent had posted a *placard* in the Halles, inciting the market-women to demand the dissolution of the Convention. Since then, anonymous letters had been found, and another poster put up, calling for an insurrection. Someone had scrawled *anthropophage* ('cannibal') under Robespierre's name on a notice signed by members of the *Comité de salut public*. Insulting remarks had been scribbled on the walls of public buildings.

This was good enough evidence in a state trial. But neither Committee nor Convention was over-popular, and it would be advisable to give the conspiracy a more alarming turn. So the organizers of the Revolutionary Army, designed to secure the food-supplies of Paris, found themselves charged with artificial famine (*disette factice*), or a plot to starve the capital.

To give colour to this sinister indictment, Ducroquet and Descombes, who had made themselves unpopular by requisitioning supplies, were also put in the dock, and Fouquier-Tinville set on foot elaborate inquiries, extending far beyond the city boundary, in the hope of finding some scraps of evidence for the fantastic theory of the Prosecution. He looked in vain ; for it was soon clear that no conspiracy was needed to account for the unpopularity of the *maximum*, or the breakdown of the food-supplies of Paris.

An even surer way was then found to discredit the movement : the suggestion was made that it had been financed from abroad ; and the *amalgame* was strengthened by the appearance in the dock of the Prussian Cloots, the Belgian Proli, the Dutch banker de Kock, and three dubious Foreign Office agents, Desfieux, Dubuisson, and Pereira.

Finally, in the hope of obtaining fresh evidence against the conspirators, one Laboureau, a minor official of the War Office, was sent to spy on them in prison, on the understanding that he would be acquitted at the trial. Thus, when Vincent's weakness for ' purging ' (*épurations*) led him to make lists of fellow-prisoners favourable and unfavourable to his cause, colour could be given to the suggestion that the Hébertists were planning another September massacre; or when it was reported that Pereira had offered 300 lb. of tobacco to anyone who could discover a single counter-revolutionary act in his career, it was evident that he was attempting to pervert the course of justice.

When the time came for questioning the prisoners, no charge, it seemed, was too trivial, if it could discredit them with the jury and with the public. Momoro (it was said) had insisted on housing the War Office in the Luxembourg, where it would be under the influence of Vincent's Popular Societies. Vincent himself had made fun of the deputies' official costume. Pereira had been on friendly terms with Beaumarchais. Kock's luxurious dinners to Hébert, Vincent, and Ronsin became a capital indictment. Hébert three years ago had robbed a friend of some clothes and bedding. Ducroquet had confiscated a rabbit, a turkey, and three dozen eggs which might have gone into the public supply. Laboureau's evidence did not add much weight to these heavy charges. He only knew five of his fellow-prisoners by sight. Of these Vincent was suspicious. His letters to his Nanette suggest that he was confident of acquittal. Momoro's grievance (said the spy) was that members of the Dumouriez gang—Proli, Pereira, Dubuisson— had been put in with the Hébertists to compromise them ; not to mention the *aristo* Laumur, and his equally rascally accuser, Westermann. Hébert was in a state of collapse and despair. Only Ronsin frankly admitted that there was no chance of an acquittal. ' This,' he said, ' is a political trial,' and the speeches at the Cordeliers on March 4th are enough to convict us. But the party will be avenged some day. ' Liberty cannot perish ; and those who are now sending us to death will follow in their turn.' He was right.

The execution, if one can believe the official version in the *Moniteur*, was popular, and the crowd amused itself by taunting Hébert, who showed too clearly his terror of death, in the language of the blustering *Père Duchesne*. On the same day the Cordeliers club started a drastic purge of its membership, and the Convention disbanded the Revolutionary Army. Hébertism was dead.

But the most dangerous part of the Opposition remained alive. Behind the *enragés* and ' atheists,' who were not politically formidable, and need only be given enough rope to hang themselves, had grown up the Hébertist threat to the government. Behind the Hébertists there now emerged another party that aimed at the overthrow of the Jacobin monopoly of power. This was the party of the ' indulgents,' or Dantonists. Writing to his brother from Nice on April 4th, Augustin Robespierre said that he did not think Hébert and his followers were the real leaders of the new conspiracy. 'I have always suspected (he said) that the chief plotters are the two big D's of the Convention.' He wrote, without knowing it, only two days before Danton and Delacroix went to the scaffold.

The Dantonists were more dangerous to the government than the Hébertists. They were not more sincere in their aims, or more violent in their methods. But their leaders were men of greater political prestige, and directed their attack with more subtlety. Fabre, Chabot, and Basire had this great advantage over their fellow-conspirators in the India Company affair, that they were the first to turn king's evidence. The *Vieux Cordelier* never enjoyed the circulation of *Père Duchesne* ; but Desmoulins stood nearer the centre of government than Hébert. The real leaders of Hébertism—Vincent, Ronsin, and Momoro—were club and section men, not deputies. Of the fourteen Dantonists to be executed together on April 5th nine were members of the Convention, and six had sat on the ' governing ' committees. Above all, the nominal leader of the conspiracy was the only man in France who might have become the popular head of a rival government—Georges Danton.

' Indulgence ' was only one characteristic of the Dantonist party ; but it was perhaps the most dangerous to the government. It gave to the Opposition the support of a crowd of unpolitical sufferers from the Jacobin regime —the families and friends of those whom it had imprisoned or punished ; the officials whom it had dismissed ; the speculators, agents, and profiteers with whose gains it was interfering ; or the persons of easy means and easy morals who resented the drill and strain of parade-ground patriotism. It was to these people that Desmoulins spoke, with his specious claims for clemency, and Danton, with his frank appeal to the natural man.

One of Desmoulins' many indiscretions had been to issue a public protest in February, '92, against police attempts to interfere with gambling. ' Let us beware,' he said, ' of connecting politics with moral regeneration— a thing at present impracticable. Moralism is fatal to freedom.' (*C'en*

serait fait de notre liberté, si elle reposait sur les moeurs.) The historian
Louis Blanc had it from Godefroy Cavaignac, the deputy's son, that Danton
in his cups would declare that the revolution was a battle, and that the
time had come for the victors to divide the spoils—luxurious houses,
exquisite food, silk and gold, and the women of their dreams. This moral
laxity was odious to the Jacobin Puritans of '94.

A more charitable account of Danton's sober intentions is that given
by Garat, his successor in the Ministry of Justice, who had several conversations with him after his return to Paris in November, '93. The aims
of what Garat nevertheless does not hesitate to call a conspiracy were, he
says, to restore a regime of law and justice for everyone, and of clemency
for the enemies of the state ; to grant an amnesty to the Girondin deputies
expelled from the Convention ; to revise the Constitution of '93, and fit
it for national use ; to work for peace with other European powers ; to
revive commerce and industry by free trade, and subsidize art and science ;
and to end the inquisitorial system of identity cards (*certificats de civisme*).
Safety on the home front would be sufficiently secured by good government,
and a victorious army.

Every one of these proposals, except perhaps the encouragement of culture, involved serious criticism of the Jacobin regime. But Danton's means
must have seemed to the government even more ominous than his ends.
They were, according to Garat, to bring about a change in public opinion
through such papers as the *Vieux Cordelier*; to work for a coalition between
the Left and what remained of the Right in the Convention, so that they
might combine to resist ' the despotism of the two committees ' ; to detach
Robespierre and Barère from Collot, Billaud, and Saint-Just, the only members of the *Comité de salut public* regarded as irretrievably committed to 'the
policy of extermination ' ; and at the same time to increase the power of the
committee, so that it might either justify itself by a really republican policy,
or come to the bad end its tyranny deserved. An alternative plan was to
purge both government committees, and to put into power a party of
' wide, generous, and truly national outlook.'

This policy was already backed in the press. Camille Desmoulins
had become an editor because a stammer, overcome for a few minutes during
the excitement of July 12th, '89, prevented ' Monsieur Hon-Hon ' from
airing his views in any other way. An undeniable talent for journalism,
and a head easily turned by flattery, led him on from the patronage of Mirabeau to the friendship of Danton, and to the company of a prosperous
self-indulgent set of men who hated Jacobin Puritanism. A moral coward,
he was frightened by the very publicity he courted, and would tell his father
how he longed for the quiet of his home at Guise—*O ubi campi Guisiaque !*
But he always fluttered back into the flame of Paris, trusting his safety,
and that of his dear Lucile and Horace, to the freedom of the press, and the
favour of his friends in both Jacobin camps.

By the summer of '93 Desmoulins had lost faith in the revolution, which seemed only to have substituted new political vices for old ; but he clung to what the old regime had not provided—the possibility of reform. His *Vieux Cordelier*, published during the winter of '93–4, was a running commentary on the Indulgent campaign, and one of its chief causes of offence to the government. Encouraged by the success of his cruel and mendacious *Histoire des Brissotins* (May 19th) in ruining the Girondins, he calculated on the continued support of his old school-fellow, Robespierre, for a similar attack upon the Hébertists, whom his friend Fréron, writing from the army of Toulon, was denouncing as agents of Pitt and counter-revolution. But he forgot the difference between a pamphlet, to whose one fatal thrust there can be no *riposte*, and a paper, whose repeated stabs may wound an enemy without disabling him.

Léd on by love of his own talent, and by the fallacy that he was deluding Danton's enemies, he gradually shifted his aim from a rival faction to the government, and from Hébert to Robespierre. His first number, published, significantly, on December 5th, the day after the decree of the 14th *frimaire* had set up the Provisional Government, backed Danton's effort to save Fabre, Chabot, and Basire (November 26th) by attacking their Hébertist accusers as atheists. This, he calculated, would please Robespierre ; Robespierre, indeed, saw and passed this number of the paper in proof. In his second issue (December 12th) Desmoulins again supported Robespierre by attacking Cloots and Chaumette. But he did it in such a way as to suggest an attempt to undermine the government, and he did it on the very day that a motion was being moved in the Assembly to purge the Committee of Public Safety. His indiscretion brought him a public rebuke from Robespierre at the Jacobin club. His third number, perhaps already in print (December 15th), unmasked a definite attack on the government of the Terror.

But now, alarmed at his own boldness, he tried to draw back. On December 24th (No. 4) he published a proposal, not for an amnesty, but for a 'condoning committee' (*comité de clémence*)—a tactless attempt to exploit Robespierre's own clemency against Terrorism. On January 5th (No. 5)—the very day on which Fréron, in a letter to Lucile, begged her to urge caution— he printed a plain apology, though unfortunately tempered by personal attacks on Hébert, and on Nicolas, the government printer, a *protégé* of Robespierre. This day there was another scene at the Jacobins, where Robespierre openly denounced Desmoulins. On the 6th he publicly described the *Vieux Cordelier* as expressing ' a thoroughly pernicious *modérantisme,*' which aimed at discrediting and dissolving the Convention : and he ended by assuring ' all faithful Montagnards ' that, once ' a few more serpents were crushed,' victory lay within their grasp. Both Fabre and Desmoulins were thereupon expelled from the club.

But the latter still persisted in his dangerous course. *Vieux Cordelier*

No. 6 (January 25th) coincided with a series of Indulgent attacks in the Convention, and was a criticism of the economic policy of the government. The extant fragments of No. 7, which was never published, show that it would have contained personal attacks on members of both governing committees, on Robespierre's ' Jansenist ' republic of virtue, and on the war policy of the government, ending with a demand for the introduction of the constitution of '93.

In view of such evidence, surprise might be felt, not that the Montagnards proscribed the Dantonists, but that they put off their proscription so long. For two months the conspiracy was allowed to go on, side by side with that of the Hébertists, until, in the last fortnight of March, both factions were struck down at one blow. The delay was partly deliberate. It was hoped that accusers and counter-accusers, when imprisoned together, might provide fresh evidence for the government spies who listened to their conversations, and might thus more thoroughly compromise themselves. Another cause of delay was the attempt, shown in the *maximum* decree of February 21st and the so-called 'Laws of Ventôse' (February 26th, March 3rd), to conciliate the working-class support which made Hébertism, for the moment, the more serious enemy. A third cause of delay was the illness which kept Robespierre and Couthon away from the Committee of Public Safety during the second part of February, whilst Billaud-Varenne and Saint-André were absent on missions. The unexpected outburst at the Cordeliers club on March 4th showed that conciliation had failed. The return of the Jacobin leaders precipitated a crisis long foreseen and at last unavoidable.

On March 12th a joint meeting of the Committees of Public Safety and General Security decided to proceed first against the Hébertists. It was not until the 30th, a week after the execution of Hébert, that they arrested the Dantonists. This fact has given rise to the idea that the Jacobins deceitfully used the latter party against the former, and then ungratefully sent it to the same fate. This was not so. The official Jacobin view, expressed alike by Robespierre, Couthon, and Saint-Just, was that both factions were a danger to revolutionary orthodoxy, and a threat to the government that embodied it—the one by an excess and the other by a defect of republicanism. Besides, even if the Hébertists had not been so forward to challenge the Committees by their action of March 4th, it would have been good tactics to deal first with the party that had most vulnerable points, and least political credit. The condemnation of the lesser men, especially upon a variety of charges, made it easier afterwards to indict the more important persons with whom, either as *enragés*, atheists, *pourris*, or foreign agents, they could be implicated.

The Dantonists seem to have thought, until the last minute, that their political position made them immune from attack. Even after the imprisonment of the Hébertists they were for arresting Héron, an agent of the Committee of General Security (March 18–20). Danton himself, perhaps counting on his old friendship with Robespierre, felt confident that the Jacobins ' would not dare ' to attack him. There is evidence, indeed, that it was a long time before Robespierre would give way to the demands of Billaud for the proscription of Danton ; though it may be doubted whether he was weighing the claims of comradeship, or the chances of success.

One thing is certain. So soon as his neat little signature was added to the warrant of March 30th, Robespierre set himself to provide, in the form of foot-notes to Saint-Just's draft indictment of the Dantonists, charges against the prisoners in general, and Danton in particular, so cruel and spite-ful as to suggest that he had been long nourishing envy, hatred, and malice against a man to whom he was naturally antipathetic, and whom accident alone had made his friend.

On March 31st the Assembly listened in profound silence whilst a proud and impassive youth demanded the death of nine of his older colleagues, and seven of their associates. Barras, in after life, never forgot Saint-Just's dramatic progress to the tribune, or the monotonous gesture of his hand, with which, like the falling blade of the guillotine, he punctuated his speech.

As in his indictment of the Hébertists, Saint-Just preferred general to specific charges. Patriotism, he began by saying, must show itself pitiless to enemies of the Revolution, whatever their past reputation. There had always been, since the first days, a party royalist at heart, and in league with foreign powers. This party had taken the form, now of Orléanism, now of Brissotism, now of Hébertism, and finally of Dantonism. The special seat (*foyer*) of this faction was the administration, where civil servants were attempting to sabotage and to overthrow the government. Its special vices were self-aggrandisement, an easy-going clemency, and a failure to hate the Girondins, Brissotins, and other enemies of the Republic. Its specific crime, here and now (Saint-Just ended), is that it aims at the dis-solution of the Convention and of the Committees by bringing in the con-stitution of '93.

In the verdict, five days later, these charges were condensed into two. Six of the prisoners were found guilty of ' a conspiracy aiming at the re-establishment of the monarchy, and the destruction of the national repre-sentation and the republican government '; and the other nine (for one was acquitted) of ' a conspiracy aiming at discrediting and debasing the national representation, and destroying by corruption the republican government.' The special characteristics, then, that distinguished the Dantonists from the Hébertists in their common attempt to overthrow the government were royalism and corruption.

Royalism was easily proved. At every turning-point in the five years' course of the revolution it had been possible to make a right or a wrong choice, and to associate with the right or the wrong people. The Robespierrists who now ruled the country had in each case (it was understood) made the right choice, and associated with the right people. Those who, at any of these turnings, had gone the other way, or had associated with the wrong people, shared a common crime, and were guilty, not merely of their own error, but of the errors of all. The Jacobin who is a Dantonist in '94 was probably a Girondin in '93, a Brissotin in '92, and a royalist in '91.

The court was not concerned with proving each, or indeed any of these charges : it was enough to show the prisoner's connexion with any one political heresy to establish a presumption that he was guilty of them all. Such particular charges as might be added were no more than speculative attempts to confuse the issue, and to prejudice the jury. Thus Danton's actions at every crisis of the revolution are twisted against him. If he supported the republican petition of July 17th, he was responsible for the massacre that followed ; if he made peace proposals to England, he was to blame for the war.

Oddly enough, the truer charges that might have been brought against him—his taking of bribes, or his Belgian loot—were ignored. Indeed, the second main accusation, that of corruption, was little used. Amar's report on the India Company affair touched only a few of the prisoners, and some who were not on trial at all : in any case it was not a political indictment, and so did not bear on the real issue. But as prejudice had been created against Vincent and Ronsin by putting them by the side of Cloots, Proli, and de Kock, so Danton's unproved corruption was given colour by the inclusion among the prisoners of the Jewish brothers Frey, the profiteer d'Espagnac, and Guzman, the Spanish adventurer.

The trial opened with every appearance of justice. The prisoners were separately questioned by a judge ; they were encouraged to choose counsel ; they were allowed to designate witnesses, and to challenge the jury. From the first they played to the gallery. Danton, asked his address, replied, ' It will soon be Nirvana (*le Néant*), and my name will be inscribed in the Panthéon.' Desmoulins gave his age as ' Thirty-three, the same as that of the *sansculotte* Jesus.'

The *débats* lasted four days, and most of the prisoners took advantage to the full of the opportunities given them of working on the feelings of the court and of the public. Danton, in particular, whose examination took up most of the second day, defended himself against Saint-Just's charges by pointing to his reputation for audacity and patriotism. ' Audacity,' retorts the President, 'is an attribute of crime ; innocence is characterized by calm.' What the court wants is not general protestations, but specific answers to specific charges. Let Danton follow Marat's example, and earn a similar acquittal. For a time this advice is followed; but it is a casual, discursive defence, with interludes of violence which at last exhaust even Danton's energy. He agrees to let the other prisoners have their turn.

Delacroix asks to be allowed to call some fellow-deputies as witnesses. The Public Prosecutor objects, on the ground that the Convention as a whole is for the prosecution, and its individual members, therefore, cannot be witnesses. But there was, in fact, nothing illegal in the demand ; and when it was loudly reiterated by other prisoners the next day, public sympathy veered towards their side. Ultimately, after an agitated exchange of notes with the Public Prosecutor, Herman, the presiding judge, ordered an adjournment, and Fouquier-Tinville wrote to the Convention, asking what should be done. He must somehow, he knew, secure a conviction. His own position, as official assassin of one party in the pay of another, was none too secure.

When the committees received his letter, they were already considering a report from a prisoner in the Luxembourg to the effect that a plot was on foot there to rescue the Dantonists, and to murder the members of the governing committees. The coincidence was convenient. Saint-Just hurried to the Convention, and declared that the ' revolt ' of the criminals in the dock exposed the country to 'the greatest danger with which liberty had ever been threatened,' and that it was a proof of their guilt. Accordingly the committees, congratulating themselves on their *surveillance héroïque*, proposed a decree by which the President of the court was to ' use all the means provided by the law to make his authority respected, and to repress any attempt on the part of the prisoners to disturb the public peace, or to interfere with the course of justice.' ' Any person (it was decreed) under a charge of conspiracy who resists or insults National Justice shall forthwith be deprived of the right of defence (*sera mis hors des débats*).'

Nor was this all. It was alleged afterwards that the jury were shown evidence against Danton that was never produced in court—perhaps a suspicious letter from abroad, perhaps the far more compromising document bearing his signature (with evidence that it was used at the trial, and passed into the possession of Robespierre) in which he suggested means of escape to the queen a few days after August 10th. By some such means the jury were ' convinced,' and the trial closured on the fourth day, amid the protests (*sorties indécentes*) of the prisoners. They were hustled out of court. In their absence the jury found all but one of them (Lullier) guilty, and the judges condemned them to death.

Their behaviour in prison, and on the scaffold, was in character with their reputations :—Desmoulins scribbling off a reply to Saint-Just's charges, or crying for the loss of his Lucile ; Fabre lamenting a play that he could now never produce ; and Danton mixing broad jests with threats of vengeance. An eye-witness in the rue Saint-Honoré saw the prisoners go to their execution. ' Three carts painted red, each drawn by two horses, and escorted by five or six gendarmes, passed at foot's pace through a huge silent crowd, which could show no joy and dared show no sorrow. Each cart carried five or six of the condemned men. I can remember clearly (he says) only the first, because it contained two faces that struck me with surprise and horror. One was that of Danton, the principal victim. His huge round head, as he stared proudly at the dull mob, bore an expression of impudence, and on his lips was a sneer of anger and indignation. The other was Hérault de Séchelles—the once smart and fashionable lawyer—all broken down, with shame and despair on his face, his head bowed, his black hair cut short and ragged, his neck bare, his body half covered by a shabby brown dressing-gown.'

It is said that, at the place of execution, Hérault, the first to mount the scaffold, tried to embrace Danton, but was prevented by the executioner: 'The fools!' said Danton; 'they can't prevent our heads kissing in the basket'; and, when his own turn came, 'Don't forget to show my head to the people; it's worth the trouble!'

There were no public protests against the execution of a national hero. At the Convention, when the arrests were first reported, it had required the intervention of Robespierre and Barère to defeat Legendre's outspoken demand that Danton—'as pure a patriot as himself'—should be given an opportunity to answer his accusers at the bar of the House. But at the Jacobins the same evening, in spite of another protest by Legendre, Saint-Just's report was read again, amidst general applause. On April 1st the Convention, as though already assuming that the constitutionalist plot was scotched, abolished the Executive Council, and turned the six Ministries into twelve administrative commissions directed by the Committee of Public Safety. On the 5th it listened, apparently without shame, whilst Vadier and Couthon congratulated it on a heroic victory. The admiring addresses from provincial communes were only less numerous than on the occasion of the Hébertist executions. Probably some of them found it too much trouble to write again so soon.

The most significant thing, perhaps, to one who studies the conduct of the trial, is the trust shown in the impartiality of the Revolutionary Tribunal. Legendre was faithfully expressing the attitude of the man in the street when he ended his assertion of Danton's innocence by saying that ' he left it to the court ' (*il s'en rapportait au jugement du tribunal révolutionnaire*). That this confidence was the strongest card in the government's hand can hardly be doubted, for they had every means of assuring that those they accused would be convicted. That they exploited this advantage to the point of abuse is equally certain. The popular belief in ' republican justice ' became the chief excuse and the chief encouragement of the Terror.

The guillotine of Germinal, Year II, destroyed the leaders both of the parliamentary and of the non-parliamentary opposition, and left the government free to do as it would, until its members should fall out among themselves, and provide fresh victims for the guillotine of Thermidor, Year II.

Only four months of life now remained to the Jacobin regime. They were four months of unmitigated dictatorship. But since no two dictatorships are alike, except in their restrictions on private liberty, it is important to establish the special character of that set up by the Montagnards from April 1st to August 1st, 1794.

The ultimate authority for everything that was done was still the Convention, a body of men drawn from the professional and business classes, the elected representatives of two-thirds of the nation. True, this assembly was now decimated, by the absence of many of its members on 'government work.' It had been deprived by the recent proscriptions of any effective Opposition. Its meetings were thinly attended, its proceedings were orderly, and its subservience to the Governing Committees was all that could be desired. But the Convention never surrendered the power of the purse; and it always contained enough enemies and critics of the government to remind the majority that the Assembly was a master who might at any moment revoke his orders and dismiss his servants.

The powers of the Committee of Public Safety, the main organ of dictatorship, were now completed (April 1st) by the transformation of the six ministries, which Carnot's engineer mind had discovered to be ' the main-springs of monarchy, wheels within wheels of aristocracy, and fulcrums of fanaticism,' into twice as many commissions, each dealing with a specialized field of administration, and reporting daily to the Committee. The Committee shared out amongst its members the supervision of the clerks (*commis*) who directed these commissions, and ' reserved to itself the right of thinking for the government ' (*la pensée du gouvernement*). But it was no accident that the *commission des finances* was, like the rest, purely administrative, and that the Treasury remained under the direct control of the Convention.

The Committee of Public Safety soon took advantage of the powers given it by the decrees of March 13th and 17th to nominate new officers (*parquet*) to the Commune. Three days after Hébert's arrest, and the day before Chaumette's, it appointed substitutes for both, and on March 28th made the younger Payan (not the editor of the *Anti-fédéraliste*) *agent national*, or executive head of the administration of Paris. No one could have been better qualified to secure the Committee's control over the commune ; Payan's hostility both to extremists and to reactionaries, combined with a genuine care for the interests of the common people, made him, more than any other of the Jacobin leaders, an understudy of Robespierre.

At the same time as the Committee secured control over the officials of the commune, it proceeded to a thorough purge of its personnel. It dismissed thirteen *administrateurs de police*, and filled their places with other members of the commune. The whole body, already reduced in numbers, was in effect dominated by government nominees. On May 10th Pache himself, the mayor, was arrested, in a back-wash of the Hébertist affair (he had been one of rumour's candidates for the post of *Grand Juge*), and was replaced by the more subservient Lescot-Fleuriot. The purge was complete.

The same process went on in every sphere. Many of the representatives on mission, whose independence had so often embarrassed the government, were recalled, and were replaced by national agents. The departmental directory of Paris, reconstituted by the decree of December 4th, came under the direct control of the governing committees. Revolutionary Committees and Popular Societies, especially those intended for women or children, found themselves either purged or abolished.

This was the beginning of a campaign to make the revolution respectable. Robespierre's expensively powdered hair, and Saint-Just's high stock and earrings, were no less a rebuke to the slovenliness of republican manners, than the staid proceedings of the government committees were a rebuke to the dirty, drunken, and smoke-laden atmosphere of the sectional meetings described by Pétion, Malouet, and other anti-Jacobin memoirists. The privileged Jacobin club was filled with functionaries, and wearied with a constant round of official business. Of the three-score papers which had enjoyed popularity since '89, only half a dozen remained, with as many more of later origin ; and these confined themselves to discreet news, and government propaganda.

The stage, one of the last free institutions in the capital, was by now forced to obey the orders of the Convention, or of the commune. The producer of *La chaste Suzanne* had to cut out a scene referring to the king's trial. *Le Cid* offended by representing a king in too amiable a light, and *Mérope* a widowed queen. A decree of August ordered performances of *Brutus, Guillaume Tell,* and *Caius Gracchus*, and threatened to close any theatre that ' tended to deprave public opinion, or to revive the shameful superstition of royalism.' This ban was enforced a month later against *Paméla*, which was denounced for a too tolerant attitude towards politics and religion : the theatre was closed, and the company put under arrest.

Pache's contemporary in the Home Office was Paré, a carpenter's son, who had risen from a clerk's stool in Danton's office to be secretary of the *conseil exécutif provisoire* in '92. It was in keeping with the new technique of government that he should have spent the winter in perfecting the spy-system inaugurated by his colourless predecessor, Garat. Garat had done little more than take over from Roland the discredited *bureau d'esprit public*, under its director, their common friend, Champagneux, and turn it from propaganda to espionage. Its *observateurs* were appointed by himself, and not infrequently from among his own acquaintances ; they could report to him personally at any time, either by word of mouth or in writing ; and the seven whose reports survive were evidently men of intelligence and education.

Paré increased their number to twenty-four, but included only two of

Garat's friends. They now reported officially to the Committee of Public Safety, in writing, every day, so that their communications should have increased the already mountainous correspondence of Robespierre and his colleagues by seven hundred and twenty letters a month. Actually, according to a list which has survived, not many more than sixteen hundred reports were sent in during the seven months from mid-September, '93, to mid-April, '94. At that date Paré's organization disappeared along with his ministry. In future the spies addressed themselves to the new *commission des administrations civiles, police, et tribunaux*. Did the Jacobin government ever reflect that, in organizing this system, they were returning to the methods adopted by the royalist ministers, Delessart and de Moleville, under the regime of ' the tyrant ' whom they had so lately destroyed ?

' The Revolution,' wrote Saint-Just, himself a strong advocate of this Puritanical policy, ' is frozen.' To an age of fire had succeeded an age of ice. Even in the campaigns of '94 a cold efficiency was beginning to replace the casual heroism of '93. There were now seven hundred thousand men under arms, and they were better trained than ever before. Schools of Artillery and Engineering had been set up. At the Cadet College (*Ecole de Mars*) at Sablons four thousand picked youths lived under canvas, and were taught, under hard conditions, 'brotherhood, discipline, simplicity, good behaviour, and patriotism; how to hate kings, and how to use their arms.' With such reserves, and with a Carnot to draw up plans of campaign, the republican army had nothing to fear from any adversary.

It was a good moment to follow up the victories of the previous autumn. Kosciusko's revolt in Poland was likely to draw the Prussian army eastwards, and to leave no more than 150,000 English and Austrians in the Netherlands. Early in May Clerfayt's retreat from Courtrai and Tournai cleared a way into the country west of the Scheldt. A month later (June 26th) Cobourg was decisively beaten by Jourdan at Fleurus: Barère boasted that no quarter was given to the 'slaves and brigands' of the Imperial army. On July 10th a French army once more entered Brussels, throwing the English back into Holland, and the Austrians back on to the Rhine. In the Pyrenees, too, the Spaniards were retreating, and September saw a French invasion of Catalonia. But the temper of the war had changed. On none of these frontiers—north, east, or south—did the armies of '94 fight as enemies of kings, or as missionaries of republicanism. They fought for loot, and for peace; not even, as Barère put it, to conquer, but merely to win (*non pour conquérir, mais pour vaincre*).

In the war at sea, not even this cold satisfaction was allowed. The loss of Corsica was an inevitable result of the destruction of the Mediterranean fleet at Toulon. The loss of the West Indies followed immediately from the revolt of San Domingo, and British command of the western Atlantic. Though Villaret-Joyeuse made a good fight of it on the First of June,

Barère thought it necessary to create the legend of the *Vengeur* to put 'French courage' into the hearts of a disappointed public.

Soon signs were not wanting that the Jacobins were falling into the most dangerous snare of dictatorship. They were beginning to despise the people ; to lecture them instead of consulting them, to force them instead of persuading them, to keep them excited by trifles instead of exercised by responsibility, to feed them on fables instead of telling them the truth. The anniversary of the king's execution was celebrated in the assembly by a procession of Jacobins through the House, whilst a military band played patriotic tunes. Robespierre found an eponymous hero for Jacobin patriots in the young Barra, who at the age of thirteen, surrounded by rebels in the Vendée, and told to say *Vive le Roi*, cried *Vive la République*, and died. His body, said Robespierre, would be buried in the Panthéon with the honours given to Rousseau or Voltaire : a picture of his martyrdom, promised Barère, would be set up in every schoolroom in the country.

A public competition was advertised for designs for roofed arenas, in which, during the winter, the triumphs of the republic could be celebrated by patriotic community-singing (*chants civiques et guerriers*). In *Floréal* the Committee took in hand a programme for the *embellissement* of the Tuileries quarter, of which Napoleon himself might have been proud; and it was a real disappointment to them that guards had to be provided to prevent the public from damaging the statuary in the 'national' garden. Other *arrêtés* of the Committee invited artists to send in designs for a bronze statue of Rousseau to be erected in the Champs Elysées, for a column in the Panthéon in honour of soldiers who had died for their country, and for monuments in bronze or marble representing ' Nature regenerated ' (on the ruins of the Bastille), ' Liberty ' (on the Place de la Révolution, one of the sites of the guillotine), or ' the French People overthrowing feudalism.'

It had long been a counsel of prudence for ex-aristocrats to drop the titular *de*, or to adopt less conspicuous surnames : thus the Comte de Saint-Simon, perhaps warned by his mistaken arrest in place of the banker Simon, had become Claude-Henri Bonhomme. But now, lest there should be any doubt whether Paris, and indeed France, was wholly republican, streets and communes too changed their names, and recorded, until the next revolution, the heroes and achievements of Jacobinism. Mont-Martre became, by an obvious and easy transition, Mont Marat, the Tuileries the Palais National, the Palais-Royal the Maison Egalité, the Champ de Mars, the Champ de la Réunion, the Place des Vosges, the Place des Fédérés, and Notre Dame itself the Temple de la Raison.

In the provinces between three and four thousand communes are known to have been rebaptized into republican names. This easy profession of patriotism became so common that the Convention at last set up a commission to regulate and restrain a practice which it had at first encouraged.

It would be a pity if what had been a punishment at Lyon (now Commune-Affranchie), at Toulon (Port-de-la-Montagne), in the Vendée, now known as *le département Vengé,* or in the Gironde (Bec d'Ambès) should elsewhere be vulgarized as a matter of parochial pride. It was a fine republican gesture to abolish (October, '93) the ' royalist ' terms *ville, bourg,* and *village.* Rebaptism was by now a good old custom of the Revolution. But whereas the new names of '89 had honoured Liberty or Law, those of '90 National Unity, and those of '91 Equality, now Jacobin jargon was all the fashion. Several villages named after Saint-Bonnet transferred their faith to his homonyms Bonnet-Libre, or Bonnet-Rouge ; Saint-Pierre de Moutier became Jacques-Bonhomme ; and other proscribed saints were replaced by Sans-Culotte, Sans-Préjugé, Décadi, or Le Peletier. The prefix Mont-, in honour of the Jacobin ' Mountain,' was adopted by more than three hundred communes, with little regard for their geographical situation.

No living statesman was commemorated, unless the village of Ami-de-la-vertu adopted this name as a compliment to Robespierre. He, indeed, received several requests that republican children might bear his name, and at least one offer of marriage from a female admirer who was anxious to perpetuate it. At republican baptisms it was not uncommon for children to be given such names as Tullie and Mucius Scaevola (these were twins), Pimprinelle Décadi, or Nonidi Violette. Thus republican language invaded common life, till even on the playing-cards of patriots the King of Hearts was replaced by the Genius of War, and his Queen and Knave by Liberty of Worship and Equality of Duties ; whilst other packs displayed a King of Sages, a Queen of Virtues, or a Jack of Heroes.

It was a time of reasoned change rather than of wanton destruction. Frenchmen had little reason to love the Middle Ages. Eighteenth-century taste condemned everything Gothic. It would not have been surprising if the revolution had led to a wholesale abolition of the monuments of feudalism. But it was not so. The attack on the royal tombs at Saint-Denis, ordered by a decree of August 1st, '93, was carried out with such care that a modern visitor sees them much as they were before their ' desecration.' Paris churches were closed or secularized. But for fourteen destroyed during '91–4 forty-three were destroyed between '95 and '99, and twenty-six between 1800 and 1814. It was neither revolutionary Philistinism nor hatred of religion; it was the zeal for improvement, and the fear of barricades, which proved disastrous to the streets, the houses, and the churches of Old Paris.

Meanwhile a *commission des monuments* set up by the Convention (October 18th, '92, August 27th, '93), and replaced by a *commission des arts* the following year, organized the collection and preservation of works of art, which were in less danger of destruction than of loss by dispersion and looting. Such loss was, of course, particularly to be feared in connexion with libraries and museums; and on October 23rd, '93, the Convention prohibited 'removal, destruction, mutilation, or any kind of alteration (under pretext of removing symbols of feudalism and royalty) in libraries, collections, or museums.' Two years later Lenoir formed the nucleus of the *musée des monuments français* which inspired young Michelet to write his history of the French people.

It was the same with the national archives. The Constituent and Legislative Assemblies had preserved no documents previous to 1789 ; decrees of June 19th and Aug. 19th, '92, had even ordered the burning of all title-deeds of nobility, and charters of seigneurial rights ; and a good deal of authorized destruction had in fact been perpetrated. The Girondin Convention, no less destructive, but more economically minded, preferred to sell such documents, or to hand them over to the fighting services for use as cartridge-paper. As late as 1853, accounts of the 15th century were found in French artillery magazines. But in November, '93, the Jacobin government, wishing to safeguard its rights to the ' national property,' collected all the title-deeds that could still be found into the Louvre, and so laid the foundations of the great collection now known as the *Archives nationales*.

It showed, perhaps, some loss of original enthusiasm, but it was also a sign of political stability, that the revolution was beginning to live upon its past. Robespierre and Saint-Just, austerely meditating a Republic of Virtue, might be planning an even brighter future for their fortunate fellow-citizens : the man in the street preferred to wear his medals, to hoard his savings, and to hope for a return to the amenities of 1788. He had grown accustomed to using *citoyen* for *monsieur*, and *tu* for *vous*— for since November, '93, this sign of *fraternité* had become habitual in the civil service and in the army; but he used it much as a Communist may use the term 'comrade' half officially, and without feeling that it commits him to an inconvenient intimacy.

To the normal Frenchman, closely attached to the soil, and interested in new ideas only so far as they contributed to the old artistry of common life, the superficial changes of the revolution were, like *tutoiement*, a passing fashion, from which he expected to return to a familiar, if now more amenable old-fashionedness. Did not his favourite speakers still clothe their *sansculotte* ideas in the elegant literary style of the old Academies ? Even the crusade which Barère inaugurated on January 27th, '94, to banish Bas-breton, Basque, and provincial patois, and to make the six hundred thousand Frenchmen who knew no French use the language of the Declaration of Rights, seemed to most people artificial and impracticable.

Meanwhile the national language had been enriched by a whole vocabulary of revolutionary terms—not only a rich if short-lived growth of derivatives from personal names, such as *brissotin, rolandiste*, or *maratiser*, but also words of such general and permanent use as *civisme* (not found before

'89), *centraliser* (dating from the Jacobin regime), *alarmiste, antisocial, modéré, réactionnaire,* and many more. Modern French was in fact being created, not by deliberate propaganda, but by unconscious infection, not by educational theory, but by practical convenience.

In art it was the same story. David, the pageant-master of the republic, gave all his talent to expressing the ideal virtues of the revolution in symbolical and artificial compositions in the classical style he had learnt from old Vien, and had recast in the sculpture-galleries of Rome. Yet no contemporary artist learnt more from the revolution, and no pictures reproduce with more appreciation the crude and colourful vitality of revolutionary Paris than the portraits he painted of Jeanbon Saint-André or Le Peletier, of M. Sériziat or La Maraichère.

In 1794 the spirit of the eighteenth century was wrestling with the spirit of the nineteenth century for the soul of the revolution. Which would prevail ?

CHAPTER XXV

DICTATORSHIP

Perhaps these governors, inspectors, policemen are needed ; but it is terrible to see men deprived of the chief human attribute : love and sympathy for one another. . . . That is why I feel so depressed when I am with these people. I am simply afraid of them. And really they are terrible, more terrible than robbers. A robber might, after all, feel pity, but they can feel no pity ; they are inured against pity as these stones are against vegetation. That is what makes them so terrible.—(TOLSTOY : *Resurrection.*)

THE legend-makers say that when Danton, on his way to the guillotine, passed Robespierre's house in the rue Saint-Honoré, he prophesied, *Tu me suis !*—' You will be following me soon ! ' Nothing seemed less likely. Robespierre's Jacobin government had cleverly used the indiscretions of its enemies to achieve a position of undisputed power. It had waited until each faction in turn challenged its political leadership, and had then crushed them one by one. The only danger, it might be thought, now came from within. Would the ill-assorted members of the governing committees, when rid of their common enemies, fall out among themselves ?

This was in fact what happened. Yet it might never have led to the fall of the Jacobin regime, but for three aspects of Jacobin policy which lost it the support of Paris and France. These were its economic measures, its police system, and its treatment of the church. When the Robespierrists appealed for popular support against their enemies in the Convention, it was dislike of the laws fixing prices and wages, and regulating the sale of food, which alienated their former friends. When Robespierre's opponents

EXTRAIT

DU REGISTRE DES ARRÊTÉS

DU COMITÉ DE SALUT PUBLIC

DE LA CONVENTION NATIONALE,

Du *Cinq Messidor*, deuxième année de la République française, une et indivisible.

Le Comité de Salut-Public, considerant que l'Instruction est un des besoins les plus pressant des Citoyens, et que ceux qui la répandent remplissent des fonctions Publiques dont ils ne peuvent être détournés sans danger.

Arrête

Que le Citoyen, Geoffroy, Professeur du Muséum, d'histoire Naturelle, est autorisé à se faire remplacer dans sa Garde les jours où il a des Leçons à faire au Muséum.

Signé au Registre, Collot-D'herbois, Billaud-Varenne, Barère, Robespierre, Couthon, Carnot, Lindet, C. A. Prieur.

Pour Extrait.

Carnot   C. A. Prieur

A. Lindet

au cit: Geoffroy

A DOCUMENT OF THE COMMITTEE OF PUBLIC SAFETY

Authorizing Citizen Geoffroy to obtain a substitute to do his duty in the National Guard, in order that he may lecture at the Museum of Natural History.   Signed by Carnot, C. A. Prieur, and R. Lindet.   Dated June 23rd, 1794.

tried to organize his downfall, it was hatred of the tribunal and the guillotine which provided them with their strongest argument. When the Jacobin regime finally collapsed, the force that had done most to undermine its position was popular Catholicism.

France, one of the richest agricultural countries in Europe, could not grow enough corn to keep itself alive. England, with a smaller proportion of its people on the land, with a less fertile soil, and with a less favourable climate, was more nearly self-supporting. In France occasional famine (*disette*) might afflict any part of the country after a bad harvest ; there was chronic fear of bread shortage in the large towns ; and the feeding of Paris was a constant anxiety to the government. The revolution inherited from the incapacity of the old regime three problems—the redistribution of grain in the provinces, the supply of food for the towns from the country-side, and the provisioning of Paris. The Convention, whether it wished it or not, was committed to a system of state-control (*réglementation*) which, though resented in detail, was demanded in principle by a population accustomed to look to the government for the protection of its property and for the provision of its needs. It inherited from the Bourbon monarchy the uneasy task of providing cheap bread for the labourer without endangering the profits of the farmer, the miller, or the baker. The republican commune of Paris was faced with the same fear of bread-queues and food-riots as its predecessor, the royalist municipality.

It is only necessary to glance through the proceedings of the commune and sections during '93–4—the *rapports, projets, ordres, arrêts, avis,* and *interdictions* of authority on the one side, and the *appels, adresses,* and *pétitions* of the public on the other—to realize what a large part the problem of food played in the varied interests of Paris administration. Of what use was it to appeal for recruits, to requisition arms, and to organize the manufacture of gunpowder, if all the time there were queues at the bakeries, and a shortage of sugar, meat, and fuel ? Of what use was it to restrict ' fifth column ' activities by the issue of *cartes civiques*, of what use was it to imprison suspects, or to regulate public morals, if all the time it was necessary to control the sale of chickens and lamb, and to distribute amongst the hungry sections of the capital ' four hundred and fifty barrels of salt pork,' or ' seventy-eight thousand pounds of lard, ham, and goose-legs ' from the Pyrenees ?

Certain old remedies for food-shortage in the provinces had been tried, and had failed. The concentration on wheat-growing led to neglect of the principle of rotation of crops, and prevented the introduction of greens and potatoes. There was seldom a sufficient surplus of grain in good harvest areas to make up the deficit in bad harvest areas. If there was, transport was made difficult by bad communications, and by the obstinate objection of the peasantry to the moving of grain-stocks. If the export of corn from

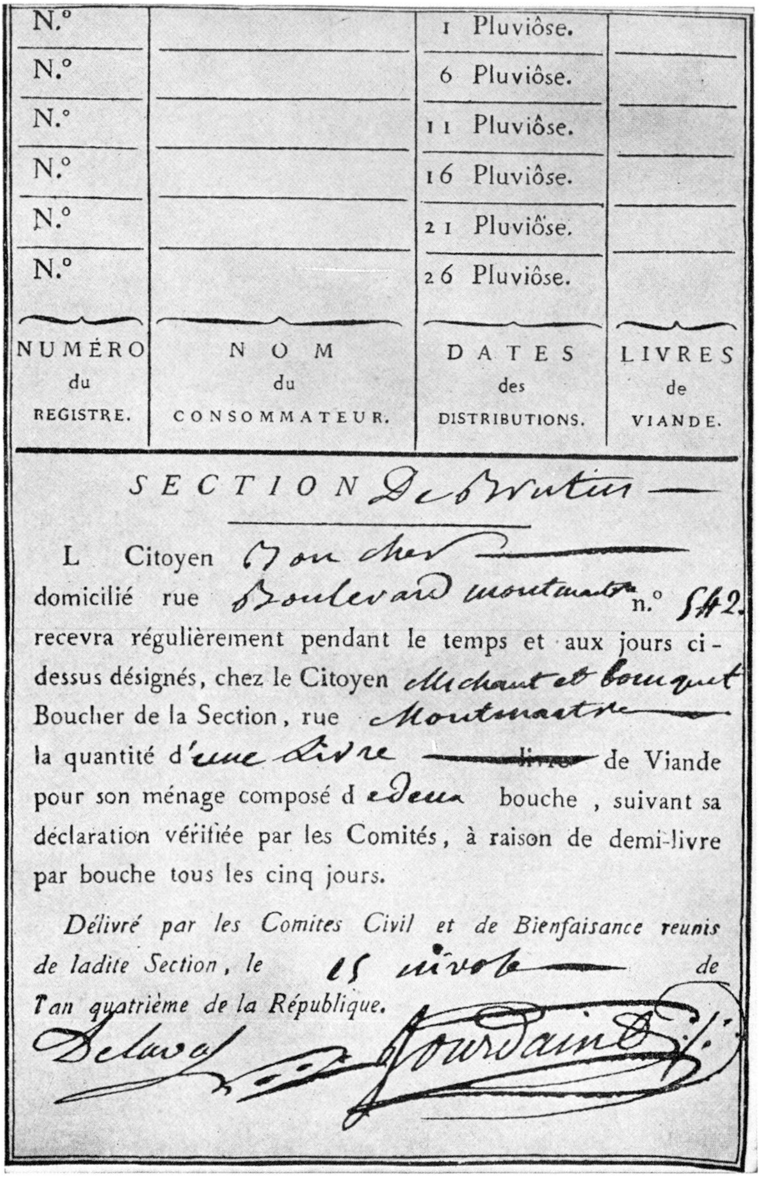

N.º		1 Pluviôse.	
N.º		6 Pluviôse.	
N.º		11 Pluviôse.	
N.º		16 Pluviôse.	
N.º		21 Pluviôse.	
N.º		26 Pluviôse.	
NUMÉRO du REGISTRE.	NOM du CONSOMMATEUR.	DATES des DISTRIBUTIONS.	LIVRES de VIANDE.

SECTION *Debrutus*

L Citoyen *Bon cher*

domicilié rue *Boulevard montmartre* n.º *542*

recevra régulièrement pendant le temps et aux jours ci-dessus désignés, chez le Citoyen *Michant et bouquet*

Boucher de la Section, rue *Montmartre*

la quantité d'*une livre* ————— livre ————— de Viande

pour son ménage composé d *e deux* bouche , suivant sa déclaration vérifiée par les Comités, à raison de demi-livre par bouche tous les cinq jours.

Délivré par les Comites Civil et de Bienfaisance reunis de ladite Section, le 15 *nivote* ————— *de l'an quatrième de la République.*

Delavos *Jourdain*

A REPUBLICAN FOOD-CARD

Entitling Citizen Boucher, of the Boulevard Montmartre, to receive a pound of fresh meat from his butcher for a household of two persons every five days. Dated January 4th, 1796.

he country was encouraged in order to increase production, its immediate effect was a panic amongst the ignorant country-folk, who imagined that hey were being starved in the interests of profiteers.

The means by which Paris was kept alive was the organization of three zones of supply. The inner zone consisted of the river-side lands within fifteen or twenty miles of the capital. The growers in this area were under compulsion to send their surplus supplies to the Paris markets. The middle zone covered the nearer parts of Normandy, Picardy, and Champagne, within a radius of fifty to a hundred miles of Paris. Here there was less good land ; the cost of transport was higher ; and Paris buyers had to face the competition of other big towns. But generally these areas supplied enough food to make up the deficiencies of the inner zone. In any emergency such as a bad harvest, or a change in the river-level that stopped the working of the Seine water-mills, it became necessary to purchase food from all over the country, or to import it from abroad. Italy, Sicily, North Africa, England, Holland, and Poland were all drawn upon. Havre was the main port of supply, Rouen the *entrepôt*, and the lower Seine the channel by which Paris was fed.

During the twenty years before the revolution the average annual consumption of meat in Paris was seventy thousand oxen, a hundred thousand calves, three hundred thousand sheep, and thirty-six thousand pigs. The breeding of live-stock was, for a variety of reasons, very backward in France, and home-grown meat had to be supplemented from a number of distant sources. A flourishing monopoly of the supply of Irish salt meat was carried on between Cork and Nantes.

The orthodox modern method of regulating food-supplies by means of ration-cards or food-coupons was not tried until the autumn of '93, and then only for bread, the staple food of the Paris poor. On October 29th the commune ruled that heads of households should make a declaration of the amount of bread they required. They would then be given bread-cards, valid for one month, entitling them to receive that amount from their baker. The municipal Food Office (*administration des subsistances*) would supply the bakeries with the necessary amount of flour. But the returns were not completed till December 11th, and the cards were not ready till the 22nd. The system came into force on Christmas Day.

In April, '94, this system was extended from bread to meat. The government bought the live-stock. The municipality slaughtered it—not very hygienically, perhaps, since the slaughter-house was at the City Hospital. One butcher from each section purchased as much meat as he required, and distributed it at the rate of half a pound per household every five days. The meat-supply was made particularly difficult, during '93-4, by the needs of the army, and by the outbreak of civil war in some of the best stock-raising areas. One market which ordinarily supplied six or seven hundred head of oxen could now only provide a tenth of that amount.

In April, '93, the Vendée rebels captured a convoy of four or five hundred head of cattle, and massacred their escort, including twenty butchers.

It was one of the claims made by the *Almanach des gourmands,* whose 'eight fat little volumes' delighted the indulgent diners of the Bourbon restoration, that the amenities of the table d'hôte had disappeared during the Terror, when 'people dined in solitary gloom, each sitting apart at a small table, consuming his portion in silence, and paying no attention to what his neighbour might be saying or doing.' Perhaps it was so. But the fare was by no means unplentiful. Had such a diner entered Véry's, in the Palais-Royal, he would have found on the menu a choice of six soups, eight hors d'œuvre, eight beef entrées (including three varieties of 'bifteck'), seventeen chicken and game entrées, nine more of fish, three of mutton, and six unclassified, seven roasts (amongst which figured 'plum-bouding'), and four sweets. The wine-list showed nine white wines, eight *vins de liqueurs,* nine liqueurs, and *punch au rhum* at threepence a bowl.

Such fare was, no doubt, beyond both the means and the desires of the Jacobin patriot. When Madame Jullien invited the Robespierres and Robert Lindet to a republican dinner, her outlay was :—milk and cream, 7d.; two loaves, 1/- ; vegetables, 3d.; salad, 5d.; oil, 1s.; vinegar, 6d.; pepper, 2½d. ; cheese, ½d. ; cider, 9d. ; and a fowl—the *pièce de résistance*— 8/5d. : total, for five persons, 13/2d.

The working man, who could not afford a fowl, had to pay 1/- for a pound of rice, or for a *litron* of groats, dried pease-flour, plums, or grape jam. Honey, cheese, raisins, figs, nuts, and almonds cost him from 1/4d. to 1/8d. a pound. The price of potatoes varied from 1/8d. to 6/- a bushel, according to the competing demand for them by manufacturers of ladies' face-powder.

One of the great difficulties that beset the regulation of the food-supply was a natural practice which abnormal conditions might at any moment turn into a crime—hoarding (*accaparement*). Arthur Young, indeed, defends what he calls 'monopolizing' as Nature's method of equalizing supplies. The speculator who buys grain when it is plentiful in the autumn, and sells it when it is scarce in the spring is really (he thinks) a public benefactor. He prevents the consumer from being wasteful in the autumn, and he prevents him from starving in the spring. If he makes a profit out of the transaction, he deserves to. If it is asked—Why should not the state do the same thing, without raising the price of grain ? Young's answer is—It cannot, without a system of storing, which experience has proved to be expensive : the money would be better spent on improving agriculture.

However this might be, the Jacobins soon found it necessary to penalize hoarding, which compromised every attempt to keep the markets supplied with food, and put up the price of supplies for the army. It was their hope that, if hoarding could be dealt with, it might not be necessary to proceed any further with the even more difficult experiment of fixing prices (the *maximum*). Their first law against *accaparement* (July 26th, '93) simply made it a capital crime. Hoarding was defined under three heads :— failing to expose purchased stock for sale ; allowing it to perish ; and failing to make, or falsifying, returns of stock in hand. The imperfections of the Act were obvious. It did not deal with domestic hoarding. It treated a big wholesale concern like the Compagnie des Indes in the same way as a village shop. It was enforced by an army of local *commissaires*, who were suspected, not always unjustly, of connivance with the hoarders. Informers were rewarded by receiving a third part of confiscated stock. There was no appeal from the judgement of the criminal court, or the Revolutionary Tribunal.

No one in Paris had been more forward in the cause of republicanism than François Robert. Was he not the author of a republican pamphlet published as long ago as December, 1790 ? Had he not drafted the famous manifesto of July 17th, '91 ? But his greatest sacrifice to the cause had been his marriage to Mlle Kéralio. For though his wife was, to Madame Roland's jealous eye, ' a witty little woman, clever and acute,' she was also the editress of the *Mercure national ;* and her husband was soon involved in the bankruptcy of the only republican paper that circulated in monarchical Paris.

In his embarrassment Robert accepted the friendly help of Danton, who made him his secretary, and secured his election to the Convention. Finding his eighteen shillings a day inadequate to pay his debts, he hit on the unlucky expedient of buying eight barrels of rum, with the intention of reselling them at a profit. Soon afterwards the law of July 26th included *eau-de-vie* amongst the articles which it was a capital crime to hoard. But was rum *eau-de-vie* ? Robert thought not, and tried to sell. His section, which disliked his political views, and had a grudge against his wife, took the opposite view, and accused him of *accaparement*. For four months he went in fear of the guillotine, and never outlived the ignominious nickname, Robert-le-rhum.

When a business man named Gaudon, who had unwittingly made a false declaration, had to be saved from the guillotine by a special decree of the assembly (December 22nd), it was agreed that the Act must be amended. Osselin's proposal (September 19th) to confine capital punishment to the hoarding of necessities had offered too many points for criticism. After a series of debates, punctuated by impatient demands from the populace, the assembly enacted the law of the 12th Germinal (April 1st, '94). This set up a regime of returns and regulations, suppressed the *commissaires*, and retained the death penalty only for the crime of knowingly allowing food-stuffs to perish. Thus, after more than eight months' delay, the working-class population of Paris had no real safeguard against the operations of hoarders, speculators, and profiteers other than the good faith of the middle-class trading community. It was not merely, they argued, a confession of economic failure; it was also a proof of Jacobin indifference to the needs of the people.

It is impossible to distinguish in practice between anti-hoarding legislation and requisitioning, or forced sale. The first is the negative and the second the positive method of dealing with the same abuse. Duquet, the *commissaire* of the Champs Elysées section, was only one of many such officials who found himself in a difficult position. He was constantly being pressed by a number of rival or complementary authorities—the Committee of Public Safety, the commune, the War Office, the Ministry of Munitions— to requisition supplies. He was constantly met, on the side of the producers and owners of what was wanted, by hoarding, falsification of returns, and obstruction of all kinds. Out of seven hundred returns of stock he was only able to verify six. He prosecuted twenty-three persons, and obtained only eight convictions. He ended by concentrating on the line of least resistance, and spent his time requisitioning church railings for the munitions factories.

Requisitioning might be a serious burden in country districts near the front. In Haute-Garonne, which was on the lines of communication of the armies of the Pyrenees, the representatives attached to the generals commandeered rations for passing troops, fresh meat, flour, and fodder, arms, powder, metal, and rope, clothing, boots, and *sabots*, bandages and dressings. Horses, mules, and oxen had to be provided, and carts for camp use, or for the transport of commissariat. It was the difficulties experienced in securing military supplies at reasonable prices which had more than anything else to do with the next step in the economic organization of the republic—the *maximum*.

The attempt to fix prices was nothing new. Gibbon records that when there was a bad harvest in Syria in A.D. 362, and the cost of bread went up at Antioch, ' the fair and reasonable proportion was soon violated by the rapacious arts of monopoly,' and the Emperor Julian was forced to fix the price of corn. Diocletian's edict, earlier in the same century, (A.D. 301) was a more ambitious measure. In a preamble whose language shows where the Popes learned their Latin style the Emperor asserts that in spite of the *pax Romana* the growth of avarice and luxury has become ' almost a religion amongst unprincipled and shameless men.' He therefore intends to remedy this evil, in the interests of the whole community, and with special intention for the needs of the army, which is being charged from four to eight times as much as it should be. He appends a schedule of maximum prices, and prescribes, for any infringement of it, the penalty of death. The schedule includes all kinds of food, many clothing materials, metal, timber, jewellery, and even pens, ink, and paper. The scheme embraces a detailed regulation of wages, and of charges for the hire of vehicles.

Under the old regime attempts had been made from time to time to determine a fair price for the staple food of Frenchmen, by establishing a fixed relation between the price of wheat in bulk and the cost of a loaf of bread. Since the revolution began, some occasional and unofficial experiments of the same kind had been made to deal with local bread-riots. The government had always shrunk from a more comprehensive treatment of what it knew to be a very difficult problem.

The first *maximum*, described as ' a decree dealing with *subsistances*,' was demanded by the Paris department on April 18th, '93, and forced upon the Girondins by popular agitation just a month before their fall. The Act of May 4th confined its operations to the raw material of the people's staple food—flour. It obliged producers to make a return of their stocks. It forced them to sell in the open market. It empowered the government to requisition grain from one district in order to supply it to another. It fixed the price of grain in each department at the average market price ruling between January 1st and May 1st, '93, and it arranged that this price should be reduced by a tenth on the 1st of each subsequent month. It prescribed the usual penalties of fines and confiscation, and enacted that for ' deliberately and with evil intent spoiling, wasting, or hiding grain ' the punishment should be death.

Various defects in this Act became apparent during the summer. Millers had to be forbidden to trade in flour, and their stocks were requisitioned for the public needs. Absolute prices had to be fixed for some kinds of grain. After an anxious conference between the local authorities and a debate in the assembly (June 24th, 27th), the operation of the law was extended to salt, fuel, and some other necessities of life. The second *maximum* (September 29th) embodied and enlarged these changes. No less than forty commodities, including food and drink, fuel, metals, clothing, shoes and *sabots*, were now dealt with. The prices of certain necessities were fixed absolutely—fuel at the price of 1790, plus a tenth; tobacco at 5d. (smoking) and 10d. (plug) a pound ; salt at a penny a pound ; soap at 1/1d. a pound. The price for all the rest was to be that ruling in 1790, plus a third. Wages were to be fixed too, but at the rate of 1790 plus a half :—this would increase their purchasing power by the difference between a half and a third. The penalties attached to the Act now included one for refusing to work at the scheduled wage-rate.

The second *maximum* worked little better than the first. The variations of price, as between one district and another, were an irresistible temptation to speculators and profiteers. When prices were fixed too low, producers refused to sell, and the markets were empty. Bordeaux was overflowing with red and white wines which the merchants declined to supply at the controlled price, in the hope of breaking down the *maximum*. When prices were fixed too high, consumers could not afford to buy, and the larders were empty. Both buyers and sellers were haunted by suspicion of the fast depreciating paper money in which every transaction had to be carried out.

Within less than two months a final attempt was made to deal with an almost insoluble problem. It was entrusted to the newly constituted *commission des subsistances et approvisionnements* (October 22nd). The commissioners were instructed to draw up a new schedule of prices, on the basis of returns from all the seven hundred and fifty districts in the country. This was no longer to be fixed on the constantly changing market prices, but on what was believed to be the more stable level of prices at the place of production, manufacture, or import. The year 1790 was still to be the standard. To the price ruling in 1790 was to be added five per cent profit for the wholesaler, ten per cent profit for the retailer, and the cost of transport from the place of production to the capital (*chef-lieu*) of the district. The resulting sum would be the price paid by the purchaser. The suspicion could not but arise that this arrangement was designed chiefly in the interest of producers' and middlemen's profits. It was strengthened by a provision which allowed compensation to manufacturers or tradesmen who found their capital reduced, in consequence of the maximum, below five hundred pounds.

It took the commissioners more than three months to collect and tabulate the returns. It took the national agents another month to adapt the *tableaux* to the local conditions of their districts. The calculation of the cost of transport alone was extremely complicated: different rates had to be allowed for transport by main roads and secondary roads, by river and canal, and even up-stream and down-stream. It was not until March, '94, that the first schedules were issued. The results were as disappointing as ever. The speculations of the 'black market' continued almost unchecked. The refusal to accept *assignats* was unabated. Working-class consumers bitterly resented having to find out of their fixed wages safe profits for middle-class shopkeepers. Producers who were not satisfied with limited profits withheld their goods from the market. The only appreciable advantage of the new plan was that the requisitioning of large stocks by the government for army purposes at the *maximum* rates did something to stabilize prices, and to stop the depreciation of the paper currency.

The control of wages (*maximum des salaires*) seemed to the Jacobin government a corollary of the control of prices (*maximum des denrées*). So long as they were indebted to the workers for support against the Girondins, they might resist this conclusion. When they were first in a position to free themselves from this obligation, they had inserted the principle of wage-control into the *maximum* law of September 29th, but had softened the blow by stabilizing wages at a slightly higher level than prices. So long as it remained under Hébertist control, the Paris commune administered this system with a lenient eye to the interests of the poor. Such complaints as there were came chiefly from the employers, whose men took advantage of the concession to strike for yet higher wages. In March '94, the masons and carpenters threatened to stop work unless they were paid at what were then the exorbitant rates of six shillings a day for skilled work, and three and fivepence a day for unskilled work.

But when (April 21st) two hundred workers in a tobacco factory petitioned for a rise in wages, the Robespierrist Payan reminded them that the Loi Chapelier was still in force. He declared them guilty of illegal assembly, and put their leaders in prison. The same attitude was adopted a week later by the *administration des subsistances* towards the transport workers. The bakers' apprentices were informed that under the decree of March 11th their services had been requisitioned by the Convention, and that any demand for higher wages would bring them under the formidable penalties of the Law of Suspects.

As a result of these incidents the *corps municipal* issued on May 5th a proclamation to the working class. It said that certain ill-disposed persons, in order to foment counter-revolution, had spread amongst the government munition-workers a spirit of revolt, for which the penalty under revolutionary law was death. It invited good citizens to denounce these agitators. It declared that workmen guilty of leaving their employment would at once be brought before the courts.

The requisitioning of labour as a means of breaking strikes was not confined to munitions factories. When there was a shortage of labour at harvesttime, prisoners were set to work in the fields ; under a decree of July 8th soldiers and able-bodied civilians could be commandeered to help in the work. When a body of civil service officials at Grenoble went on strike, because their salaries did not enable them to meet living expenses estimated at a hundred and eighty pounds a year, their services were requisitioned, and they were forced to carry on.

Ultimately, when threats proved ineffective, and economic distress was being exploited by the political Opposition, the *maximum des salaires* was revised. But it still failed to win the approval of the Paris workers. They demonstrated against it on the very day of Robespierre's last appeal to the sections (July 27th). They greeted the execution of the members of the commune on July 29th with cries of *A bas le maximum* !

Nor was this the only point at which Payan's Robespierrist policy touched the rights of the workers. He attempted to deprive them of an easily used and easily abused privilege of earning one and eightpence a day by attending the sectional assemblies. He kept a close watch on the Revolutionary and Popular Societies formerly associated with Hébertism, and assisted in purging or closing them down. He attacked the street suppers (*repas fraternels*) recently organized in the poorer parts of Paris, because, he said, they encouraged a false security and familiarity under the guise of celebrating national victories. If Payan thought, as he claimed, that his regime was one of 'kindness and generosity,' he underestimated the offence it might give to a class that remembered its services to Jacobinism, and felt that it had been cheated of its reward.

Like most governments which are afraid of the common people, the Jacobin dictatorship combined relief with control, and allowed its subjects considerable privileges, provided they made no political use of them. Whilst strikes, bread-queues, and street-banquets were suppressed, and whilst the law was enforced against dishonest tradesmen and discontented workmen, attempts were made to ease the life of the aged and infirm. Their gratitude, it was reckoned, would go far to disarm popular opposition.

It had been recognized from the beginning of the Revolution that the old haphazard overlapping of voluntary charities must give place to some national system of poor relief ; but neither the Constituent nor the Legislative Assembly had found time to put in hand the radical changes recommended by the third report of the *comité de mendicité*, and codified in its *projet de décret* (September 27th, '91). It remained for the Convention to carry out the promise embodied in the constitution of '91 that all public utility services should be put on a national footing. Meanwhile the hospitals (under the *bureau de l'Hôtel Dieu*), the out-door relief system (under the *grand bureau des pauvres*), and the administration of the various funds that supported these charities, remained under the supervision of the municipality. By a series of laws during '93-'94 (March 19, June 28, October 15, May 11) the Convention at last set up a Poor Law on national and logical lines, to provide assistance for all who needed it, at the expense of the state. Unfortunately, it was never put into working order ; and the Directory fell back, in despair of perfection, on a modified version of the pre-revolutionary regime.

Hospital endowments had been excepted from the destruction of feudal revenues, and from the nationalization of church property. But many of the old charities had suffered from the economic backwash of the revolution ; whilst the mass of poverty in the towns, if not in the country-side, had been increased by the rising cost of living. Some new form of assistance became necessary to deal with an unemployed class which might at any moment become a political danger.

The first remedy to be tried was the Parisian *ateliers de charité*, or Relief Centres, where paupers domiciled in the capital were given paid work, whilst outsiders were sent back to their homes, and the sick and infirm placed in hospitals. But this system, already employed in '89, and regularized by decree of May 30th, '90, was changed three months later (August 31st) into a less centralized and uniform grouping of *ateliers*, both in Paris and the provinces, some for active workers, and some for weaklings. The dole was now fixed at a lower level than local wages. So matters remained till March, '93, when the Convention, recognizing it as a public duty to provide work or subsistence, decreed that an annual grant should be distributed by the departments, on a poverty basis, either in the form of wages, or of outdoor relief, or of care in an institution. The administration of this charity was left to paid *officiers de santé* and voluntary *agences de secours*.

The last clause of this measure promised that ' mendicancy would be suppressed ' ; and six months later (October 15th) a serious attempt was made to do so. Relief Works were, as before, provided for able-bodied paupers ; but begging, and even the giving of charity to beggars, was made an indictable offence, and mendicants were either confined in *maisons de répression*, or, if stubborn vagabonds, transported.

The results of this punitive policy were disappointing. The highways were reported to be fuller than ever of sturdy young tramps, who fled from the recruiting officers, and extorted food from the villagers by threats or violence. Travellers stopping at country inns were surrounded by women and girls who would rather beg than go into domestic service. The government was forced to requisition workers who would not offer their services. The capital itself was beset by beggars of all kinds ; some produced faked certificates, others claimed to have lost sons in the Vendée, or to have been robbed by brigands, others again pretended to have lost an arm or a leg fighting for the Republic.

Meanwhile the really deserving poor were provided for by a decree of June 28th–July 8th, which helped mothers in child-birth, made allowances for children, apprenticed poor boys, and gave relief to the aged. Some of the provisions of this bill are of more than passing interest to an age which rightly prides itself on its social services. It encouraged large families, though without eugenic design, by making allowances in respect of every child after the second. It made no discrimination against foundlings (tactfully called *orphelins*), or against illegitimate children, giving unmarried mothers the same attention as married women. It compelled all children supported by the state to be inoculated against small-pox.

A year later (May 11th, '94) Barère drafted an even more comprehensive measure, to deal with the problem of rural poverty. Every department was to draw up a *Livre de la bienfaisance nationale*, in which the authorities of each district inscribed every tenth day (*décadi*) the names of needy labourers, artisans, and mothers and widows with children. All these classes received state pensions and sickness benefit. True, the generosity of the scheme had limits. Only six hundred names (four hundred labourers and two hundred artisans) could ordinarily be entered for each department ; if more wanted relief, they must wait their turn of seniority. The candidates must produce a medical certificate saying they have worked for twenty to twenty-five out of their sixty years : they then qualify for a pension of eight pounds a year for labourers, or six pounds for artisans. In addition, three hundred and fifty mothers and a hundred and fifty widows in each department receive allowances of three pounds a year for themselves or their children, and sickness benefits at the rate of three to five pence a day. Once a year, at the capital of every district, there was to be held a festival of Misfortune (*malheur*), at which the Book of Beneficence would be read aloud, the beneficiaries receive their pensions, and 'the dignity of the agricultural profession and the usefulness of the mechanical arts be celebrated by a speech, and the singing of patriotic hymns.'

There were in the Paris prisons in the early summer of 1794 between seven and eight thousand suspects awaiting trial. How many there may have been in the whole of France can only be inferred from the interested statements of the critics of Jacobinism ; Lecombe in '94 said a hundred thousand ; Boudin in '95 said eighty thousand : the latter figure may be accepted provisionally. If these eighty thousand suspects had been priests or *émigrés*, their property would have been forfeit to the state, and might have been ear-marked for special use; for instance, Madame du Barry's effects, valued at ten thousand pounds, were given to the *commission des subsistances*. Why not, then, by means of a preliminary examination, anticipate the conviction that would no doubt follow if these prisoners were brought to trial, and treat their property in the same way? It would not be worth very much, perhaps, at any one moment ; for it has been estimated that only twenty-two per cent of the suspects executed, and presumably of those in gaol, came from the aristocratic and upper middle classes. But it was anticipated that, as quickly as old prisoners were put in the dock, new suspects could be found to fill their cells ; so that a steady income might be expected from the sale of confiscated property.

It was this improvement of revolutionary justice that Saint-Just had in mind when he declared in the Convention on February 26th that ' the property of a patriot is sacred, but the goods of a conspirator are at the disposal of the unfortunate ; they (*les malheureux*) are the powers that be : they can dictate to governments which neglect their interests.' The same day a decree was passed saying that ' the property of recognized enemies (*personnes reconnues ennemis*) of the revolution will be sequestrated for the benefit of the republic : these persons will be kept in custody till the end of the war, and then be banished for life.' For this purpose the *comités de surveillance* were to send in lists of all prisoners under arrest since May 1st, 1789, and of all arrested in future. Another decree, five days later (March 3rd), ordered every commune in the country to draw up a list of ' indigent patriots,' who were to be compensated with the goods so acquired. Such were the ' Laws of Ventôse.'

In making these proposals Saint-Just seems to have aimed at detaching popular support from the Hébertists, whose rising followed so soon after (March 4th), and at winning it for the Jacobin dictatorship based upon their destruction and that of the Dantonists. But he may have meant more. His *Institutions républicaines*, written at this time, though not published till six years after his death, suggests that he regarded the Laws of Ventôse as a first step towards a systematic expropriation of the propertied classes in favour of the poor, and the creation of an economic democracy to balance and reinforce the political democracy of the Robespierrist republic. If this was really the intention of the scheme, it is easy to understand the different ways in which it was received :—enthusiastically by the *sansculottes*, though it could never have provided more than a drop in the ocean of their demands ; suspiciously by property-owners who were not as yet in prison, but foresaw the temptation to put them there; and inimically by middle-class and sometimes anti-Robespierrist officialism.

The Laws of Ventôse were in any case badly drafted, and unworkable. They were badly drafted: it was never clearly understood whether 'recognized enemies' included all imprisoned suspects, or only those designated by the 'popular commissions' set up to examine their *dossiers* and to classify them either for banishment or for trial. They were unworkable: the difficulty of collecting and collating returns of prices from seven hundred and fifty districts was as nothing compared with the difficulty of examining the *dossiers* of eighty thousand prisoners, and equating their property with the needs of indigent patriots nominated by forty thousand municipalities. A special department had soon to be set up to deal with the mass of correspondence between the governing committees and the *comités de surveillance* of the communes. The help of the representatives on mission had to be invoked to prevent over-zealous authorities from seizing the goods of all suspects indiscriminately, and to persuade suspicious paupers that they were not being enrolled for transportation over-seas.

After two months (May 13th) it was possible to set up two *commissions populaires* to make a first classification of the prisoners. But already a fresh obstacle had appeared. The Committee of Public Safety began to act without consulting its partner, the Committee of General Security, which it felt to be hostile to the new policy. The members of the latter committee withdrew their facilities for corresponding with the local authorities. They soon took fresh offence. The Law of the 22nd Prairial, designed to empty the prisons, and to make room for more suspects, was sprung upon them by Robespierre and Couthon. Their police jurisdiction was infringed upon by the *bureau de police générale*. They took the opportunity of Robespierre's temporary withdrawal from the Committee's work to suspend the operation of his friend Saint-Just's favourite scheme. It was not until the middle of June that the *commissions populaires* published their first decisions on the cases submitted to them, and not till a month later that these decisions were examined and approved by the governing committees.

The publication, on June 19th and 21st, of the first lists of suspects condemned to deportation can hardly have been reassuring to either the friends or the enemies of the Laws of Ventôse. An attempt had apparently been made to comb out well-to-do prisoners. About seventy-five per cent of those dealt with were members of the aristocracy or middle class. But the confiscated property of fifty such persons, however wealthy they might be, would not satisfy many indigent paupers.

On the other hand, who would be safe in future, if sentences of deportation were to be passed upon all those who at one time or another had been ' partisans of Lafayette,' had ' disapproved of June 20th,' or had ' opposed the Châteauvieux fête ' ? What person of any social position or culture could deny that he had ' consorted with people of his own class,' or with *gens comme il faut ?* How many reasonably patriotic Frenchmen could escape the charge of aristocracy when defined as ' having done nothing for the revolution ' ; or the charge of fanaticism, if it meant ' having been in close relations with the clergy'? How many had not been guiltless of such dangerous indiscretions as 'hoping some day to put their servants back into livery,' saving a set of coffee cups 'with portraits of the last tyrant, and his agent Necker,' or having on some piece of family plate or jewellery 'symbols of feudalism'?

When, three days later (July 22nd), steps were at last taken to organize similar *commissions* in the provinces, such alarms must have been widespread. But they were unnecessary. The concession to the Robespierrists came too late. Within a week Saint-Just was dead, and his great plan died with him. An empty ledger marked *Exécution des lois des 8 et 13 ventôse* is all that remains of a scheme that might have begun an economic revolution.

The upshot of all these attempts to keep the people contented and docile was rather different from what their authors had intended. The working classes felt that they were getting less than they deserved ; the propertied classes feared that they would be asked to give more than they desired. The economic policy of the Jacobins satisfied nobody, and contributed powerfully to their fall.

A second principal cause of the fall of the Jacobin dictatorship was its abuse of the judicial power which circumstances had placed in its hands. There had grown up, alongside the emergency government of the Committee of Public Safety, an emergency system of justice, as natural in its origin, as necessary in a time of national danger, and as dangerous, if stretched beyond its proper use. Two conditions at least would have to be observed if the regime of military courts and revolutionary tribunals was not to turn against the government. It must be used only against proved enemies of the people ; and it must not clash too obviously with the regime of the ordinary courts of justice. Both these danger-signals were fatally overrun in 1794.

Paris had resented recourse to Martial Law in '89, because its judicial background was the hated Châtelet and the haughty Parlement. It had disliked it in '91, because the new judicial system was not yet in working order, or embodied in the constitution. In '92 Paris called for a special court to punish the ' criminals ' of August 10th. But this was at a moment of anger, and in the heat of war. Though this court ' working night and day ' (said Danton) conducted more than sixty trials in two months, and was deep in the mysterious affair of the crown jewels, it could not escape the charge of being a *tribunal de sang*, and it was abolished by the Convention.

Conversely, there was no intention to surrender the rights of the reformed judicial system so lately set up. The only complaint was that its administration had fallen into the hands of the propertied middle class, and still showed too much of the old discrimination against the rights of the poor. Accordingly, one of the first acts of the Convention (Sept. 22nd, '92) had been to order the reconstitution of all the courts on more democratic lines : any citizen might now be elected to a judgeship, as he might to any other public function, if he was twenty-five years old, and neither a pauper nor a domestic servant. A year later, as part of the emergency settlement of December 4th, these appointments were no longer made by popular election, but through nomination by the Committee of Public Safety or the *comité de législation*. Doubtless these bodies sometimes used their powers to appoint friends of the government. But the ordinary courts never lost their reputation for independent justice, or ceased to point a contrast with the increasingly arbitrary procedure of the Revolutionary Tribunal.

The minutes of the weekly conferences between the judges of the six Civil Courts of Paris, from December, '91 to March, '93, show a sensible and on the whole successful struggle of regular justice against political adversity. Thus, during the crisis of August, '92, the work of the civil courts was held up by the sectional duties of the judges, by the disappearance of the *commissaires du roi* attached to the tribunals, by the business of taking the new oath of allegiance, and by the absence of so many lawyers on war duty, or other emergency occupations.

Criminal justice was similarly obstructed. The establishment of the *tribunal criminel provisoire* of August 17th was followed by two months' complete inactivity in the ordinary criminal courts. It was not till November 15th that the Convention ordered the reopening of the *tribunal de police correctionnelle*, whose functions had been temporarily usurped. Many questions had then to be faced :—the status of prisoners released during the disorders of August ; the age-qualification of barristers, and the necessity of their holding *certificats de civisme* ; or the nature of the cases heard before the *tribunal de famille*. Nevertheless both civil and criminal courts were soon functioning as before. And as in Paris, so in the provinces. Where (as in La Manche) the records of a local *tribunal criminel* have been studied, they show that justice was administered fairly and efficiently.

The crisis of March, '93, brought the first of a series of decrees setting up and strengthening the Revolutionary Tribunal. That of March 10th created a *tribunal criminel extraordinaire* consisting of twelve jurymen, five judges, and a public prosecutor, to deal—as the comprehensive formula put it—with ' every counter-revolutionary enterprise, or attack upon the liberty, equality, unity, or indivisibility of the republic, or the internal or external safety of the state, as well as all plots tending to the restoration of royalty, or the establishment of any other authority hostile to the liberty, equality, or sovereignty of the people.' The jurisdiction of the court was to be the same, whether the accused were ' civil or military officials, or plain citizens.' Three weeks later, when the court held its first sittings, a fresh decree (March 15th) settled its procedure, and another of April 5th transferred from a committee of the House to the Public Prosecutor the essential duty of receiving accusations, and of turning them into arrests and prosecutions.

It is to be noticed that the Convention never relaxed its control over the Tribunal. Throughout the period of the Terror, and whatever rights were delegated to the ' committees of government,' prosecutions continued to be initiated by decree of the Convention ; and the assembly always retained its veto on the indictment of deputies, ministers, and generals.

Improvised in a military and political crisis, and always a subject of party controversy, the tribunal was forced to start work before either its personnel, its procedure, or its stipends were finally settled. So many of the persons designated for the office of judge or juryman excused themselves from a troublesome and perhaps dangerous responsibility, that the court carried on with a provisional jury until the end of June. A month later the public prosecutor complained that it was impossible for three judges to do the work of eight. The second section of the tribunal contemplated by the decree of March 10th had not even come into being. But the Jacobins were now in a position to enforce their policy, and by the end of August the whole court was in working order. On Sept. 5th it was further subdivided into four sections, sharing a president and three vice-presidents, sixteen judges, and sixty jurymen, whilst the public prosecutor was allowed five assistants. Two sections were now to prepare business in chambers, and two to sit in court, conducting the trials. But even this procedure was too slow for a government that was beginning to feel its power ; and both the Girondist and Dantonist trials were closured by special decrees.

So things remained until the *coup d'état* of Germinal, '94, when it was enacted (April 16th) that all charges of conspiracy (*conspiration*) should be transferred from the provincial courts to Paris. It now became necessary to lay down legal frontiers between ordinary and extraordinary justice ; and this was done by the law of 19 Floréal (May 8th). The upshot of this Act was that the criminal courts continued to hear charges of tampering with labour or loyalty (*embauchage*), and *assignat*-forging, and to deal with *émigrés* and outlaws, and with the offences of minor officials, whilst charges against major officials, and, generally speaking, all cases of counter-revolution, were reserved for the Revolutionary Tribunal.

The latter was now not so much a court as a corporation. Its professional and whole-time judges and jurymen were appointed by the Convention, and received the same salaries as the deputies themselves—about three hundred and twenty-five pounds a year. The President and the Public Prosecutor were paid nine hundred pounds, and were given rooms in the Palais de Justice, where meals were provided by the *concierge*. The routine work was carried on by a crowd of *clercs* and *huissiers*.

It was by now becoming a serious concern to the deputies how long their legislative immunity would stand up against a Judiciary so formidably arrayed, and backed by the executive power of the governing committees. The charter of their liberty, the resolution of June 23rd, '89, had been upheld, in a series of test cases, against attacks from both sides. Some thought that it should cover private as well as public delinquencies. Others wished deputies to be treated, outside the House, in exactly the same way as other citizens. The resolution had been reaffirmed in the constitution of '91, and in the Penal Code, which attached the death penalty to any attempt against the individual liberty of a member of the *corps législatif*.

This was satisfactory enough, so long as the danger to parliamentary liberties came only from the king. But when the common enemy had been defeated, the deputy's immunity became a bar to the proscription of Jacobin by Girondin, or of Girondin by Jacobin. In the stress of war and counter-revolution it was thought intolerable that any scruple should prevent the immediate arrest and punishment of a traitor, however highly placed. In April, '93, the natal month of terrorism, the Convention formulated the right (which, in fact, was implied in the resolution of June 23rd , '89) to impeach (*décréter d'accusation*) any of its members suspected of complicity with the enemies of the country. Rejecting an attempt to alienate its control over this process, it decreed that the public prosecutor could not act without previous authorization by its body against generals, ministers, or deputies.

A little later, with the growth in the power of the governing committees, it was agreed to allow the Committee of General Security (July 12th) to seal the papers of any deputy denounced as a conspirator. It was not long before deputies were placed under preventive arrest, and denied the right to defend themselves in the House. The outcome of the Osselin affair (November 12th) was that the Convention delegated to the committees the decision whether, in any particular case, parliamentary immunity should or should not be a bar to impeachment. Though it was still strictly illegal for them to arrest anyone in the privileged categories, there was no effective way of preventing this ; so that the practice became a commonplace of the Terror.

By the spring of 1794 the difference between ordinary and extraordinary justice was so marked that a theory was invented to fit it, and then used to justify a further differentiation. Ordinary crimes, said Couthon in a report to the Convention on June 10th, hurt the individual more than society, and can be tried in a leisurely and elaborate way (*un certain luxe des formes*), even with a kind of partiality towards the accused person: but in crimes of conspiracy the life of a single criminal (*scélérat, ennemi de la patrie*) is balanced against that of the whole people; and here any formality or delay is positively dangerous; 'it is not a question of punishment so much as of utter destruction (*moins de les punir que de les anéantir*).' The Committee of Public Safety therefore proposed to invest the Revolutionary Tribunal with almost complete immunity from the ordinary safeguards of justice, by a decree that might well have served as a model for the *Ogpu* and *Gestapo* of far crueller regimes—the so-called Law of the 22nd Prairial.

Article 4 of this decree laid it down that the object of the court was ' to punish the enemies of the people.' Article 6 defined ' enemies of the people ' as all those who have worked for royal, or against republican, government, compromised the country's war effort, reduced its food reserves, assisted its enemies, or obstructed its friends ; who have spread false rumours, or defeatism, or seditious writings ; or who, as dishonest contractors, vexatious officials, or in any other way, have compromised the liberty, unity, and safety of the republic. These were charges which few could wholly escape. Article 7 allowed the court only two sentences—acquittal or death. Article 9 further encouraged spying and denunciation—duties that more than one decree had already laid upon patriots. The procedure described in Articles 12–17 abolished the preliminary questioning which sometimes enabled an accused person to establish his innocence ; abolished the calling of witnesses (unless the court considered that there was not otherwise sufficient evidence for a conviction) ; and abolished counsel for the defence.

Such was the justice which had been found effective in punishing the rebels of Marseille: such was the justice which during the forty-seven days between June 11th and July 30th sent Frenchmen to the guillotine at the rate of more than thirty a day. It does not excuse the Prairial Law to point out that it did little more than sanction a regime already established, and that in fact the most marked increase in the number of convictions dates not from June, but from March, '94—not from the Prairial Law, but from the *coup d'état* of Germinal. It is one thing to tolerate injustice. It is another thing to enthrone it.

There was yet another article in this law that might carry a most serious threat to constitutional privilege. ' No one (said Article 10) shall have power to indict any person before the revolutionary tribunal, except the Convention, the Committee of Public Safety, the representatives of the people on mission, or the public prosecutor.' Not a word was said about the constitutional immunity of generals, ministers, and deputies. Did this mean that the veto of the Assembly on such proceedings, already delegated o the committees, was now finally surrendered ? Robespierre and Couthon, he authors of the Act, vehemently denied such an interpretation, and the protest of the (for once) unruly deputies was rescinded : but the suspicion emained, and rankled, and played its part in the overthrow of the Robespierrist regime.

The key position in the Tribunal, during the seventeen months of its working, was held by the *accusateur public*, Antoine-Quentin Fouquier-Tinville. This sober, hard-working, and unimaginative official, once a *procureur* of the Châtelet, had, after ten years' penury in small legal posts, obtained a place in the tribunal of August 17th through a family relationship with Desmoulins, the friend of Danton, and had thence passed on to its successor, the Revolutionary Tribunal. His chief ambition was to retain a salary that supported his wife and seven children. He spent almost every hour of the week in his office at the Palais de Justice, sifting evidence, compiling *dossiers*, writing eighty or ninety letters a day, and drawing up lists of prisoners to be brought to trial.

At his trial, after Thermidor, before a leisurely parody of his own tribunal, Fouquier maintained (and so did his colleague, the judge Herman) that he never dealt with individual members of the government, but only with the committees. He was only once (he said) at Robespierre's lodgings, and did not even know Couthon's address, or Saint-Just's. Every evening between ten and eleven he crossed the Pont-neuf, accompanied by four *gendarmes*, from the Conciergerie to the Tuileries, to make his reports to the governing committees. He submitted one list of persons tried today, another list of persons to be tried tomorrow, and sometimes a provisional programme of trials for ten days ahead. A few questions might be asked by the tired Committee men. A name might be added, or struck out. The new list was signed. Copies of it were made (there was always danger of mistakes here). Carts were ordered for tomorrow's procession to the scaffold (Fouquier knew within one or two heads how many would be needed). And so to bed.

Fouquier justly complained that he was being made the scapegoat of a system of which he had been merely the agent. It was not his fault if it had been abused. He was not responsible for spiteful denunciation, arbitrary arrest, or unjust imprisonment. He did not find the verdict, or pronounce the sentence. He was not to blame for the mentality of the professional jurymen—' good *sansculottes*, honest men, children of nature (*des hommes purs, des hommes de la nature*),' as one of themselves naïvely remarks ; nor for that of the judges, whose consciences were sometimes at the mercy of their political connexions, or financial needs. His duty was simply to draw up *actes d'accusation*, to compose *réquisitoires* based on the evidence submitted to him, and to ask for the conviction of the accused. The papers he left fill six hundred *cartons* in the *archives nationales*. The marks of his red pencil show how methodically he picked out effective points against the prisoners.

He claimed at his trial that he had taken every precaution to prevent abuses or mistakes of justice. Such things were alleged at the time, often on no better evidence than the gossip of some court usher or juryman, and they have since been exploited by partial or sensational historians :— stories of private revenge, false evidence, mistaken identity, or tampering with the jury ; stories of lost documents, unopened letters, lists altered, or signed in blank, and so forth. Whatever the truth of these tales, it was never suggested that Fouquier's prisoners had been deliberately ill-treated, or that his executioners had done anything to increase the bitterness of death.

The worst features of the system lay not in its occasional errors, or its inevitable cruelties, but in the cold efficiency with which it carried out an abominable policy. Those made it disliked, but this made it feared. The callous *tricoteuses* who counted the falling heads on the Place de la Révolution might grow sentimental over a handsome face, or be sorry for a victim too young to die. The shopkeeper who put up his shutters when the carts went past his premises in the rue Saint-Honoré might deplore the bloodshed as well as the injury to his trade. It was the dull, deep resentment of the common people who had lost relatives or friends, it was the livelier fears of those who might yet be proscribed, that fired the determination to be done with the Tribunal.

Along with the rapid increase in the total number of convictions that followed the *coup d'état* of Germinal, and that was accelerated again by the law of the 22nd Prairial, went two features which must have been specially alarming to Parisian citizens. One was the disproportionate increase in the convictions, as compared with the acquittals. The other, even more ominous, was the fact that most of the victims were no longer priests, aristocrats, or even government officials, but undistinguished members of the middle and lower classes.

First, as to the proportion of acquittals. These are the figures, month by month, during the winter of '93–4, up to the 22nd Prairial.

Nivôse	167 accused	61 condemned	101 acquitted
Pluviôse	198 ,,	68 ,,	106 ,,
Ventôse	206 ,,	116 ,,	79 ,,
Germinal	218 ,,	155 ,,	59 ,,
Floréal	525 ,,	354 ,,	155 ,,
Prairial	408 ,,	281 ,,	? ,,

These figures explain themselves.

Secondly, as to the social incidence of the Terror. It is not always possible, from the defective lists available, to discover the profession of the victims ; but the following tables are approximately correct :—

Period	Number	Clergy	Nobles	Army	Officials	Middle class	Lower class
April . .	203	18	45	25	43	42	30
May . .	302	21	41	34	49	83	74
June . .	599	43	57	25	86	143	245

During July the lists were so carelessly kept that less than half the names (831 in all) have any profession attached to them : the corresponding figures are :—

July . .	386	21	o	40	27	132	166

The full significance of these figures is not, however, seen until they are stated in (approximate) percentages :—

April . .	(200)	9	$22\frac{1}{2}$	$12\frac{1}{2}$	$21\frac{1}{2}$	21	15
May . .	(300)	7	14	13	16	28	25
June . .	(600)	7	$9\frac{1}{2}$	4	14	24	41
July . .	(400)	5	0	10	7	33	$41\frac{1}{2}$

It needed no statistician to show that the victims of the Tribunal, in the summer of '94, were no longer common enemies, whether *aristos*, or treacherous generals, or dishonest officials, but ordinary citizens of the professional and working classes, such as the 9 shopkeepers, 11 clerks, 9 employés, 7 soldiers, 6 innkeepers, 4 weavers, 4 clock-makers, 3 grocers, 3 domestic servants, 7 day-labourers, and 27 *cultivateurs* who perished between July 1st and 27th.

Some of these were doubtless executed as food-hoarders, a class to which no public pity would be shown : indeed there were those who declared that painless execution was too good a fate for such enemies of the people, and would have repeated, for their benefit, the prison massacres of September, '92.

Generally speaking, the audience at the Revolutionary Tribunal were as pleased when a ' patriot ' was acquitted as when a ' criminal ' was condemned. At an execution (when no one doubted that all were criminals rightly convicted) there might be some jeering at the victims, especially if they showed signs of fear. Courage was always admired. But few were not shocked at the execution of three sisters of 22 25, a boy of 16, or an old man of 84. Others, as a government spy reported in February, '94, who had applauded the arrest of political suspects and rich egoists, murmured at the incarceration of their employer, or of the family wage-earner, perhaps denounced by worse patriots than themselves; and they asked when these innocent men would be released from prison.

A month later such talk was more outspoken. ' *Eh ! mon Dieu !*, said one woman to another, Shall we never grow sick of bloodshed ?—Only, replied the other, when there are no more criminals.—It doesn't cost much to kill a man, said a third.—If they guillotined us for our thoughts, said another, they would have their work cut out.—Don't talk so loud, was the final remark ; they might hear us, and pinch us too.' For such fears were increasing, especially since the publication of the names of those who had signed the anti-Jacobin petitions of the eight thousand and the twenty thousand in June, '92 ; and heads were shaken over the grim prophesyings of dying men.—' Citizens (one had cried), beware lest you contaminate the soil of liberty with blood ! '—and another, ' It will be your turn next, perhaps tomorrow ! '

The fear of government spies was not without foundation. The minutes of the *bureau de police* show that on May 15th, '94, the Committee of Public Safety commissioned one Guérin to carry out the *surveillance intérieure* of Paris, at a salary of two hundred pounds a year. He and his four assistants (they were ultimately increased to ten) were to frequent public places in the city, note down the names, occupations, and addresses of people guilty of any crime, and make daily reports to the Committee on intriguers and conspirators whose movements and haunts they had discovered. Such reports as have survived deal with secret correspondence, confirmed gambling, profiteering, and speculation in *assignats*. It was a formidable and well-organized system of espionage.

Life was not very cheerful in Paris in the summer of '94. The streets were almost empty of carriages. Dress was simple, often slovenly. Conversation was less free. The lists of lodgers that hung on the front doors, and the grim inscription, *Egalité ou la mort,* that was daubed on so many walls and house-fronts, were a constant reminder of the seriousness, if not the precariousness of existence. Where life offered so little amusement, it became almost a sport to play with death, and the police had not always to search for victims.

Dupré told Desmoulins of a girl in the rue Saint-Honoré, who said to her friends, ' I want to be guillotined ; I don't see why I shouldn't be talked about as well as another.' For a long time the authorities refused to make a martyr of her. When everything else failed, she opened her window, and shouted at the top of her voice, *Vive le roi, Vive le roi!* This time the police could not refuse to arrest her. At her trial she denied indignantly that she had been drunk. ' I was as sober as I am now,' she said, and started shouting again, *Vive le roi !* ' Good-bye, my dear friends,' she said, on the way to the scaffold ; and just before the blade fell she turned her head towards the crowd, and remarked, ' Good-bye, rabble (*canaille*), good-bye ! '

Perhaps the change of public feeling between '89 and '94 was well enough illustrated by the print that showed a Frenchman still dancing with Liberty, Equality, and Fraternity under a symbolical tree of Freedom : but his eyes are bandaged, he is groping in vain for the cap of liberty, the triangle of equality, and the hand of fraternity. Life has become a game of blind man's buff ; and there is a fifth figure in the group, whose hand is nearly touching his—a skeleton carrying a scythe, whose name is Death.

It is a sobering reflexion, for a historian who believes in human nature, that the terrorist regime of 1794 was directed by moralists, and inspired by the ideal of a regenerated state. In his famous *Report* of February 5th *on the principles of political morality that should guide the national Convention in the internal administration of the Republic*, Robespierre had defined the Jacobin Utopia as ' the peaceful enjoyment of liberty and equality, and the reign of eternal justice,' embodied in a state in which 'every soul grows greater by the constant sharing of republican sentiments.' Instead of an 'easy-going, frivolous, and discontented people' he would create 'one that is happy, powerful, and stout-hearted.' He would replace the vices and follies of the monarchy by the 'virtues and the amazing achievements of the Republic.'

To reach this result, Robespierre can see no means but compulsion. ' If the basis of popular government in time of peace,' he goes on to say, ' is virtue, its basis in a time of revolution is both virtue and intimidation— virtue, without which intimidation is disastrous, and intimidation, without which virtue is powerless (*la vertu, sans laquelle la terreur est funeste ; la terreur, sans laquelle la vertu est impuissante*).' It was no accident that the Law of the 22nd Prairial appeared within two days of a great festival by which Robespierre hoped to dedicate France to a religious profession of virtue and patriotism.

The promoters of this festival were not ignorant of the message expounded by the Major and Minor Prophets of Nationalism— of Voltaire's moral Christianity, of Raynal's state-controlled church, of Mably's *Etre Suprême*. But what they had most in mind was assuredly the famous chapter of the *Contrat Social* (corroborated in the first of the *Lettres écrites de la Montagne*) in which Rousseau, finding religion necessary for society, and thinking Christianity too other-worldly to stand up against political tyranny, defines the Civic Religion that is to take its place.

' It is essential for the state (he had said) that every citizen should have a religion to make him love his duties. It is the function of the sovereign to define the articles of the civic creed, not quite as religious dogmas, but as social aspirations (*sentiments de sociabilité*)' ; no one is to be forced to believe them, but anyone who does not is to be banished ' as incapable of sacrificing, if need be, his life to his duty.' The dogmas which demand this unquestioning obedience are ' the existence of a Divinity that is powerful, intelligent, and benevolent, that foresees and provides ; a future life, in which the good are rewarded and the bad punished ; and the sanctity of the social contract and of the laws.'

A footnote to this passage made it clear just how much the philosopher was concerned with the practical needs of the state, just how little with conviction of truth. Caesar, he recalled with approval, when defending Catiline, had argued for the mortality of the soul; Cato and Cicero, to refute him, ' never troubled to reason the point out, but merely showed that Caesar was talking like a bad citizen, and propounding a doctrine that was dangerous to the state.'

Such, they believed, was the position in which the Jacobin dictators of '94 found themselves. Frenchmen were not unwilling to fight for their country, and for the benefits which the revolution had given them. But they were less ready to agree that the national emergency justified the Jacobin dictatorship, or to obey the laws that enforced its rule. The more confident the government became of its power, and the more sure of its aim, the greater its need of a religious sanction for its claims upon the obedience of its subjects. This sanction must come either from the old religion of the country, or from a new. The Civil Constitution had been a serious attempt to annex the Catholic church to the revolutionary state. It had by now only too obviously failed. Could anything be found to take its place?

Yes ; for there had been growing up, side by side with Catholic worship, a semi-religious cult of the revolution, whose creed was the Declaration of Rights, whose dogmas were Liberty and Equality, whose symbols were the tricolor cockade and the *bonnet rouge*, and whose sacraments were federative oaths taken at the altar of the country, and dancing and singing round the tree of liberty. With its use of French instead of Latin, with its processions, its banners, its hymns, and its sermons ; with its burning of incense before the new tables of the law, with its confessional of club and sectional ' purges,' and its discipline of prison, exile, and guillotine, the religion of Patriotism provided just the means that Jacobinism needed to exploit the stock-in-trade of the Catholic church, and to find work for the unemployed supernaturalism of the common people.

This patriotic cult had originated, not as a rival, but as an auxiliary of popular Catholicism. The priest, after parochial mass, might accompany the municipal officers to the altar of the country, and lead their patriotic devotions. There was, in the early days, enthusiasm enough to inspire both the old rites and the new. But with the clerical schism caused by the Civil Constitution came a hardening of popular superstition on one side, and of popular anti-clericalism on the other. The constitutional church was denied the support of patriotic religion. Revolutionary enthusiasm was left at the mercy of a provocative secularism.

This was the situation of which advantage had been taken by the ' dechristianizing' movement, whether in the hands of philosophical anti-Catholics such as Fouché and Dumont, or of anti-government agitators such as Hébert or Chaumette ; whether indulging popular Rabelaisianism in masquerades of the Mass, or expressing a shallow intellectualism in the cult of Reason or Nature before the altar of Notre Dame. De-christianization had been officially discouraged, but still went on. In March, '94, Le Carpentier, on mission in La Manche, had announced that ' internal peace requires the annihilation of priestcraft.' Siblot at Evreux a month later had introduced fresh measures against the clergy with the formula, ' WHEREAS in every age priests have been the scourge of society . . .' Against such action toleration was not easily enforced.

There was another possible remedy. It might perhaps be thought that Hébertism had discredited any attempt to provide an alternative to the constitutional church. But the government did not think so. The Jacobins had never been averse to borrowing ideas from the enemies they overthrew. Condorcet's constitution, Roux's *maximum*, and Fabre's calendar were now part of the government programme : why not Chaumette's religion of Reason ? But it would have to be rebaptized, like any royalist commune, and provided with a new creed and a new ritual. Such was the task entrusted by the committee to its most sincere Rousseauist, Robespierre.

Eighteen months before, he had defined his attitude towards the Catholic church in a remarkable speech opposing Cambon's proposal to withdraw all financial support from the constitutional clergy. He had begun with a profession of faith. ' To me,' he had declared, ' God is he who created all men for equality and happiness, he who protects the oppressed, and exterminates tyrants : the object of my worship is justice and humanity. I do not care any more than others (he went on) for priestly power : it is one chain the more round the neck of mankind ; but it is an invisible chain, that binds the soul, and cannot be broken except by reason.'

The rule of superstition, Robespierre thought, was almost destroyed ; philosophy had banished priestcraft ; and the only dogmas still present in the human mind were those that supported moral ideas, such as ' the sublime and touching doctrine of virtue and equality that was taught of old by the son of Mary to his fellow-citizens.' Soon the gospel of reason and liberty would overrun the world. But that day would only be retarded by hasty attacks on Catholicism. ' If people are, on the whole, emancipated from superstition, they do not, for that reason, regard religion with indifference, or admit that it can be a matter of political calculation. Belief in God is deeply engrained : it is a dogma that the nation connects with its traditional worship, and, through this worship, with its scheme of moral values. To attack Catholicism is to attack popular morality.'

There is no reason to suppose that in May, '94, Robespierre had abandoned the views he held so clearly in November, '92. But he may well have come to think that the dissolution of the old faith was now so far advanced that a non-Christian might be gently substituted for a Christian theism, and a non-Catholic for a Catholic worship. He could see several advantages to be gained in this way, besides the primary one of giving religious sanction to the Jacobin regime. He shared with the *Vicaire Savoyard*, and with a good many more orthodox Catholics, a healthy dislike of fanaticism and superstition ; and he believed it to be part of the Jacobin mission to destroy what was not only a political but also a moral danger. He looked beyond the republic of '92 to a regime of moral patriotism, in which a regenerated religion and a cult expressed in patriotic images would play their part.

But Robespierre was a realist as well as a visionary. He knew that government agents all over France were asking what attitude they should adopt towards the church and the priests—what was the official policy ? He was aware that Catholic and indeed Christian Europe was looking askance at a regime which allowed seven thousand clergy to abjure celibacy, and persecuted thirty thousand who had refused to swear allegiance to the state. To both of these doubts the *Culte de l'Etre Suprême* was to be a convincing answer. The Republic would proclaim its official belief in the essential dogmas of an enlightened Theism. The French people would learn, in the regular and dignified worship of the Supreme Being, to forget the superstitions of Catholicism, and to ignore the differences between constitutional and refractory priesthoods. Catholics, Protestants, and free-thinkers would worship side by side. Europe would acknowledge that the Revolution had achieved the reformation, not only of the Gregorian calendar and of the accepted system of weights and measures, but also of the Christian church.

The Supreme Being (*Etre Suprême*) to whose worship France dedicated herself in the decree of May 7th and the festival of June 8th was at once the Christian God, the philosophic Absolute, and the patron saint of the constitutions of '91 and '93, into both of whose preambles it had been, though rather grudgingly, introduced. The only dogma coupled with the new cult was that of the immortality of the soul. The only religious conduct it recognized was to do one's duties as a man, 'to detest bad faith and despotism, to punish tyrants and traitors, to assist the unfortunate, to respect the weak, to defend the oppressed, to do all the good one can to one's neighbour, and to behave with justice towards all men.'

These admirable precepts were to be enforced by festivals every tenth day in honour of the great events of the revolution, the virtues of humanity, and the blessings of nature. Other cults were not proscribed; but any meeting of aristocrats, or any that involved fanatical or counter-revolutionary demonstrations, would be rigorously punished. Rousseau's recommendation that recusants against the civic cult should be banished from the country was conveniently forgotten : like other of his Genevan suggestions, it was impracticable in a community of twenty-five million argumentative Frenchmen. Besides, had he not, in *Emile*, protested against the 'horrible doctrine' of intolerance ?

More than a month was allowed to elapse between the enactment of the new religion and its inauguration ; partly to make sure that it was known and welcomed all over the country, partly to point the contrast between the improvised cult of Reason and the carefully thought out and elaborately staged worship of the Supreme Being. The welcome given to the new religion, if not enthusiastic, seems to have been sincere, whether as expressed by the Convention and the commune, or by persons as different as the materialist Lequinio, the atheist Maréchal, or the Catholic Grégoire.

The inaugural ceremony, on which David lavished all his talent for symbolical pageantry, and to which Nature (whom some people imagined themselves to be worshipping) contributed a perfect June day, was transformed by a recent attempt on Robespierre's life, and by his election to the Presidency of the Convention, into a personal homage to the High Priest of Jacobinism. At Orléans, ' about half-way up the very handsome steeple of the church '—such is the account of an Irish prisoner who happened to be taken through the town during the festival—' a large board was placed, on which the words *Le peuple français reconnoit l'Etre Suprême et l'Immortalité de l'Ame* were blazoned in large gold letters, with a screen before it. At a signal the screen fell, amidst the firing of cannon and musketry, and bands of music playing, while the multitude responded, *Vive Robespierre !* '

All over the provinces the new cult was inaugurated by national agents and municipal officers, who made praiseworthy, if puzzled, attempts to carry out the intentions of the government, and not infrequently contributed hymns or catechisms of their own composition. Such was, by this time, the variety of religious life in the country, and the confusion of local authorities, that it was found impossible to standardize the new cult. In some places the Catholics took advantage of the coincidence of June 8th with Whit-Sunday to give a ' fanatical ' turn to the observance of the patriotic festival, and the Feast of the Supreme Being was preceded by Mass, and the *Veni Creator*. In other places the Supreme Being was identified with Reason, and the Hébertist inscriptions on the church-fronts remained unchanged. In others again the new religion became a fresh weapon in the hands of the de-christianizers, who penalized, as ' proofs of fanaticism,' the practice of kneeling, or the sign of the cross. There were no doubt many *sociétés populaires* like that of Pouilly-sur-Loire, which made the observance of *décadi* instead of Sunday a test of patriotism, not only for officials (upon whom it was obligatory by the law of Dec. 8th, '93), but for all its members.

But upon the whole this attempt to meet all tastes in religion satisfied none. Its promoters had forgotten that their knowledge of Greek mythology, and their admiration for the heroes of the Roman republic, could not be shared by uneducated *sansculottes*. They had forgotten that religious worship thrives on narrow differences rather than on wide agreements, and that religious faith cannot be expressed by a Lowest Common Multiple of beliefs. Wherever the love of liberty and equality still flourished, wherever there was still a foreign enemy or a French rebel to be defeated, wherever hymns to the *Etre Suprême* could be sung to the tune of the *Marseillaise*, there Robespierre's cult had a few months' vogue: no more.

Attempts were made to popularize private as well as public devotions on the new model. A book of *Maximes et prières républicaines* exhorted the devout patriot, as soon as he rose in the morning, to ' lift his eyes to the heavens, and read there the idea of Divinity ' ; the real worship that God demanded of him was work ; the best service, obedience to the law. Republican versions of the Lord's Prayer were published, with such petitions as ' Give us this day our daily bread, in spite of the vain attempts of Pitt, the Cobourgs, and all the tyrants of the Coalition to starve us out.' But as the dangers of war receded, and the gains of the revolution seemed more assured, patriotism ceased to be a religion. The *culte de l'Etre Suprême* was never abolished : it simply disappeared. When, two years later, seven national festivals were decreed, none was dedicated to the Supreme Being. When, seven years afterwards, the national church was re-established, it was upon the basis of the Catholic creed, the priesthood, and the Mass.

Geneva, the birth-place of Rousseau, was also the home of Calvin. Servetus had been burned there two hundred years before *Emile*. The latest disciple of Rousseau unconsciously became a Calvinist. The *vertu* that Robespierre drew from 18th-century *sensibilité* flamed into a *terreur* lit by the executioners' fires of the 16th century.

Paris—gay, clever, irresponsible Paris—was to become a *Civitas Dei*, a community ruled by the narrow creed and the stern morality of Jacobin orthodoxy. By instinct rather than reason, and with a natural repugnance to unnecessary discipline, Frenchmen refused to submit to an economic experiment, a system of justice, and a state religion, each of which was meant to do them good. They preferred the first and greatest gift of the revolution, which their new benefactors were taking away. They would live unreformed, but free.

Chapter XXVI

THERMIDOR

La révolution est l'ouvrage du peuple ; il est temps qu'il en jouisse.—(Saint-Just.)

The Jacobin dictatorship set up by the *coup d'état* of April, '94, could only hope to remain in power so long as it was dealing successfully with a national emergency. As soon as its political opponents had been destroyed, and its foreign enemies defeated, it would lose the chief force that kept it together. As soon as it began to put forward a long-term policy, and tried to impose on the country a new economic, disciplinary, and moral regime, it would incur public disapproval. But its fall need not have been so rapid, but for other more specific and more intimate causes.

DANTON

From a pencil sketch, perhaps from memory, by David.

ROBESPIERRE

From a pen and ink drawing by Grandmaison in the Convention on 9 Thermidor
An II, the day of his arrest.

A cynic might say that the principal mistake made by the victors of Germinal was to kill too few Hébertists, and too many Dantonists. The Hébertists were a large party of small men, whose fall left adherents in every club, section, and government office in Paris. The Dantonists were a small party of big men, whose fall left resentment, and fear of a like fate, in the minds of members of the government itself. A coalition of both parties would provide a new Opposition well led and widely supported. The dictatorship of the committees and the rule of the guillotine forced this Opposition to carry on its work by intrigue, and created an atmosphere of suspicion in which the reforms and ideals of Robespierrism could not hope to flourish.

This was not all. The dictators themselves grew increasingly conscious of their dangerous isolation. They took offence at one another's failings. The Robespierrist Pharisees disliked and were disliked by the post-Dantonist Sadducees. They were attacked from within the government as well as from without. They too fell in their turn. Their fall dragged down the whole party.

Many points in the interpretation of the events between Germinal and Thermidor are still uncertain. It is unlikely that the private motives and petty intrigues of those crowded fifteen weeks will ever be elucidated. No solution seems likely to hold good that assumes the working out of a single plan, or the clean-cut opposition of two or three parties. Like most revolutions, that of Thermidor included intrigues within intrigues, and turned out differently from what any of its originators expected.

There is ample evidence, whether in Robespierre's papers, or in the correspondence of the Committee of Public Safety, or in the records of the *bureau de police*, that the government was constantly embarrassed by passive but none the less dangerous opposition in the provinces. Some of this opposition came from distrust of the *assignats*, some from dislike of the food regulations, some from survivals of clerical and aristocratic counter-revolution, and some—not the least embarrassing—from the obstructiveness or the excessive zeal of agents and officials of the government.

' Most of the authorities here,' writes Duquesnoy from Mortfontaine on April 28th, ' are Moderates. The Popular Societies are merely a collection of garrison officers and military officials. The poor are fanatically religious. The rich stink of aristocracy. The leading merchants make common cause with the tradesmen in ignoring the food-laws.' From Bar-sur-Ornain Mallarmé reports about the same time that if all the food in the district were evenly distributed among the communes, none of them would have a two months' supply. Within a few days of their consecration to the cult of Reason and Liberty (he says) the churches are filled with peasants hearing mass. In the heat-wave of Thermidor, which this year did not belie its name, the complaints seemed to grow louder. From the department of Cher the national agent reported general dislike and disregard of the *maximum*. In l'Allier there was a serious shortage of food-stuffs. The Jacobin Society of Montereau sent in proposals under twenty-one heads for dealing with the economic crisis.

It was the business of the travelling agents of the government to assuage these troubles. But from every direction came complaints of their quarrels and indiscretions. Guffroy was denouncing Lebon, Loisel was denouncing Dumont, Augustin Robespierre and Maignet were at logger-heads ; so were Jullien and Ysabeau. Under these circumstances it would be better, the committee thought, whilst keeping, for the moment, provincial tribunals in certain centres—Arras, Avignon, or Marseille—to concentrate all the political trials in the capital. The reconstructed Revolutionary Tribunal would not shrink from additional work. The new *bureau de police* was ready enough to deal with the miscellaneous cases referred to it from the provinces —aristocrats, suspects, rebels from the Vendeé, clericals, offenders against the food-laws, and, more particularly, incompetent or dishonest officials.

Here arose a fresh cause of trouble. The *bureau de surveillance administrative et de police générale* (such was its full name), was an emanation of the Committee of Public Safety. It had begun its work on April 13th. It had been reorganized on June 20th. Its personnel consisted of a director, two assistants, and ten clerks. It seems to have been under the direct supervision of Robespierre from April 28th to June 30th, with occasional help from his friends Saint-Just and Couthon. He was probably in close touch with its work till the time of his fall.

The *bureau de police* was thus a possible cause of offence to the anti-Robespierrists of the rival committee. The only point, indeed, in which it trespassed on their territory was in the supervision and prosecution of government officials; and here, as elsewhere, its recommendations were subject to review. Vadier, Robespierre's bitterest enemy on the Committee of General Security, afterwards asserted that the Triumvirs used the *bureau* to release persons whom the committee had arrested, and to arrest persons whom it had released. Such evidence as is available does not support this charge.

But Vadier and his friends could not forget that, since Robespierre's criticism of Amar's handling of the India Company affair, the conduct of the more important political trials had been dictated by the Committee of Public Safety. They could not forget that the reports indicting the Hébertists and Dantonists had been entrusted to the youngest member of the junior committee, Robespierre's protégé, Saint-Just. They could not think it an accident that it was precisely these two men who had been put in charge of the police bureau. They could hardly be expected to regard its activities with an impartial eye.

This antagonism came to a head in several small incidents, which were given undue importance by the temper in which they were dealt with. In the Théot case Vadier attempted to turn the prosecution of a crazy ' prophetess,' who was said to have designated Robespierre as a kind of Messiah, into an attack upon the *culte de l'Etre Suprême*. Robespierre, with some difficulty, quashed the prosecution. In the case of the section de l'Indivisibilité Robespierre tried to secure a prosecution, and failed. His attempt to replace Fouquier-Tinville as Public Prosecutor by a nominee of his own party was defeated.

A letter from Payan to Robespierre, dated June 9th, suggests that the members of the Committee of Public Safety were fully aware of this antagonism, and resented the rivalry of ' men who had neither the genius to initiate a policy nor the modesty to hold their tongues, and accept guidance.' But they may well have disliked identifying themselves overmuch with the defence of the Triumvirs. They might well shrink from the drastic policy of purging or liquidating so powerful a rival. The solidarity of the two committees of government was almost a foundation-myth of the Jacobin regime.

It was no moment to provoke quarrels within the government. Not only in the provinces, but in the capital itself, the prolongation of war conditions, and the suspicion that the emergency government was using them to extend its rule indefinitely, were causing a fresh wave of insubordination among the *sansculottes*. No sooner had Payan dealt with the tobacco-workers, or the Food-controllers with the transport-workers, than there came complaints from the pork-butchers' apprentices. On May 20th it was found necessary to dissolve twelve Popular Societies, and on June 3rd to purge the section Marat. A few days later there was trouble in the government munitions factories. On July 6th there was a strike in a china-factory. During the political crisis of the ten days of Thermidor public protests were made against the revised schedule of wages published on July 2nd.

These signs of economic discontent were serious enough ; but they could be dealt with by police action. Much more dangerous was the tendency to make party capital out of economic troubles, and to revive the political activity of the sections. It was noticed that both the Hébertist rising in March and the anti-Robespierrist movement of July were accompanied by labour troubles in the munitions works under the direction of the Committee of Public Safety. It was suspected that the zeal shown by certain sections to hold fêtes in honour of the Supreme Being was due less to religious enthusiasm than to anti-Robespierrism. The Finistère section had even proposed to mark such an occasion by a public reading of Vadier's report on the Théot case.

A few days later (June 19th) the Montagne section organized what was in effect a public petition in favour of the introduction of the 1793 constitution. There could be no more direct challenge to the Provisional Government. When news came of the crowning victory of Fleurus (June 26th), and when, three weeks later, the government showed its fear of disorder by cutting down to a minimum the celebrations of July 14th, there were fresh signs of disapproval. The Opposition was more than suspected of exploiting the open-air Community Dinners (*repas fraternels*) for political purposes. The ostensible purpose of these entertainments was that patriots of all classes and ages should share whatever food they could contribute, and exchange loyal toasts and brotherly embraces. In fact, less was said in honour of the achievements of Jacobin generals than in dispraise of Jacobin statesmen, and victory was saluted principally as an opportunity for getting rid of an unpopular government.

Jacobinism was a plant that fed less easily on victory than on defeat. How seriously the government regarded these popular demonstrations was shown by the denunciations of Payan, Barère, and Hanriot, and by the abject apology which Garnier-Launay, one of the organizers of the *repas fraternels*, addressed to Robespierre on July 17th. ' My republican brother,' he wrote, ' without thinking, and contrary to my real intentions, I have committed a grave fault, which lies heavy on my conscience. I feel that I must relieve my mind by expressing to you (he uses the republican *tu*) my lively regret. . . . I am so weighed down by remorse and confusion that I dared not face you last night, when the Jacobin club broke up.' He will, he adds, make a public apology tomorrow at his section.

If such abjectness could be inspired by the mere expression of Robespierre's displeasure, it is not surprising that conspiracy was driven into underground courses. In the atmosphere of suspicion that is always generated by a dictatorship all kinds of fears and rumours flourished, and not all the reports of plots need be believed. But some facts are undeniable. The execution of the Dantonists, the attempted assassination of Collot d'Herbois, the promulgation of the Law of the 22nd Prairial, and the banning of the fête of July 14th were all followed by fresh conspiracies.

Ruamps, a republican of long standing, a deputy since '91, an official of the Jacobin club, and a member of the first *comité de sûreté générale*, declared after Thermidor that, with Bourdon de l'Oise and other deputies, he had been working for Robespierre's destruction ever since Germinal. On May 25th the Dantonist Rousselin was struck off the Jacobin club for proposing that members of the Committee of Public Safety should be given military protection. The excuse for proposing this invidious and dangerous privilege may have been suspicion of the plot being organized at this moment by the turbulent Lecointre and his eight deputy assassins, or knowledge of the incitement to murder addressed by the ex-policeman Marcandier to the forty-eight sections of Paris.

Nine months later, in the debate following Saladin's indictment of the surviving members of the Committee of Public Safety, no less a person than Cambon claimed that he had only been prevented from presenting an *acte d'accusation* against Robespierre by the other members of the Finance Committee. The ground of his accusation would have been Robespierre's management of the *bureau de police*. As it was on June 2nd that Robespierre took over this department, Cambon's protest can safely be placed about the same time as Bourdon's plot to murder Robespierre in the assembly (June 11th), the day after the promulgation of the Prairial Law. *Bureau* and *Loi* were parts of the same offence. Another plot, by one Rouvière, was reported on June 30th.

Finally, a certain Legray, a member of the Revolutionary Committee of the Museum section, was arrested on July 20th on a charge of having expressed, *à propos* of the fête of the 14th, 'extremely unpatriotic sentiments.' He had, it was alleged, attacked the Committee of Public Safety and the Revolutionary Tribunal, and had stated that the sections would soon be asked to demand ' the constitution, the Rights of Man, and the destruction of the infinitely oppressive revolutionary government.'

It can hardly have been a mere coincidence that on the following day a woman named Lambert was arrested, and charged by Saint-Just with an attempt upon his life. Nor was this the only attempt to assassinate a prominent Jacobin. Léonard Bourdon had been wounded on March 16th. Collot d'Herbois was shot at by a man named Admiral on May 23rd. Robespierre himself believed that his life had been endangered by a foolish if not feeble-minded imitator of Charlotte Corday, a girl named Renault, who tried to obtain access to him the following night. He had received a number of threatening letters; and, though terrified of assassination, he was not unwilling to pose as a martyr.

The attack upon Robespierre as the reputed head of the government put his colleagues in a dilemma. They must either dissociate themselves from him, and risk his enmity, or make common cause with him, and risk being involved in his fall. This awkward situation explains some of the most puzzling features in the internal quarrels of the committee. It shows why Collot d'Herbois and Billaud-Varenne were so hostile to the Triumvirate, why Barère tried to conciliate Robespierre, and why Robespierre himself refused to accept an olive-branch that was offered to him on the point of a dagger.

The Committee of Public Safety had never been a homogeneous body. It was a Coalition Cabinet. Its members were kept together less by comradeship or common ideals than by calculation and routine. Some had the soldier's outlook, some the politician's, some that of the man in the street. Circumstances had denied to any of them the experience and stability that make a statesman. The press of business which at first prevented personal quarrels also produced tired nerves. Trifling differences were exaggerated into the issues of life and death. As with most parties of men forced into narrow companionship, whether in an Arctic hut, a Himalayan tent, or a College Common Room, mannerisms assumed the dimensions of moral lapses. Small disputes estranged them from one another. They fell into rival groups, which found it almost impossible to work together. Soon all that united them was a common task, and a common fear.

Billaud-Varenne and Collot d'Herbois had joined the committee as critics, and continued to dislike parts of its policy. Billaud could not forget that the constitutional decree of the 14th Frimaire was largely his work, and he resented Robespierre's patronizing exploitation of it. They had quarrelled over the proscription of Danton, which Robespierre had resisted. Billaud disliked Robespierre's virtuous poses. He had hinted a comparison, in a speech as early as April 20th, with ' that knave Pericles, who used his popularity to conceal the chains he was forging for the Athenians.' References on other occasions to the tyrant Pisistratus were not unnaturally taken in the same sense. It was known that Billaud detested the *culte de l'Etre Suprême.*

Collot d'Herbois knew that the Triumvirate suspected him as a friend of the Hébertists, and as Fouché's fellow-terrorist at Lyon. He regarded Robespierre, said his old friend Ruamps, as ' the most dangerous enemy of liberty.' He could not forget that when he was nearly murdered, perhaps by mistake for Robespierre, the other had stolen the sympathy, and the martyr's crown. In a speech at the unveiling of a bust of William Tell (July 7th) he urged the Jacobins to imitate the Swiss hero, and to rid France of all its Gesslers. The reference was not missed.

Carnot, a soldier among politicians, had hinted as long ago as April 1st his dislike of Robespierre's patronage of the goddess *Vertu.* He had more than once found reason to resent Saint-Just's amateur interference in the affairs of his department. He did not forget his criticism of the disposal of the French forces at Fleurus, or of the plan for the invasion of Holland. He found one day that two of the best members of his staff had been arrested by Robespierre's *bureau de police,* and he was said to have cried, in the heat of his anger, ' You are a dictator ! ' Carnot in turn was suspected by the Triumvirate of sheltering aristocrats in the War Office, and of selecting generals for their professional instead of their patriotic qualifications. The army paper, *La soirée de camp,* which he started at the end of June, '94, and which appeared daily from July 20th onwards, was undeniably anti-Robespierrist in tone, and seemed to be preparing its readers for the overthrow of a dictator.

That both this journal and the *Républicain français,* edited by His, which held similar views, should have circulated among the troops at the expense of the Committee, suggests that the War Office as a whole was anti-Robespierrist. Carnot's principles and prejudices were certainly shared by his collaborator Prieur de la Côte d'Or. Lindet, too, the key-man of the Committee for home defence, as Carnot was for the foreign war, had been the one member of the committee who refused to sign the warrant for the arrest of the Dantonists, and who objected, on July 22nd, to the decree implementing the laws of Ventôse. Thus five of the ten members of the Committee might be called anti-Robespierrists.

Where groups were so nicely balanced, the rôle of trimmer became all-important. This part was played to perfection by Barère. His patriotic harangues made him as popular in the Convention as his courtesy and his readiness to undertake any duty made him indispensable to the Committee. Barère's chameleon-like changes during the summer of '94 misled Macaulay into thinking him merely despicable. He may have been despicable, but he was also dangerous. His behaviour at this time is the best clue to the inner history of a crisis which he did much to direct.

No member of the committee, except Robespierre, had such knowledge of the revolution. But where Robespierre was constitutionally unable to see more than one side of a question, Barère had made it his business to see both. Where Robespierre made enemies by following, with whatever self-deception, a single line of policy, Barère had, without any pretence, backed every popular cause, and made friends in every powerful camp. Two years ago it had been uncertain whether he belonged to the *Marais* or to the *Montagne*. He soon showed, notably as President of the Convention during the early stages of the king's trial, that he belonged only to the nation, and to the majority of the moment. The Convention, he said, ' would never allow its policy in a matter of public safety to be dictated to it by any section of the people.' This he interpreted to mean that the government should satisfy the demands of any party, so soon as it became sufficiently powerful.

With Barère self-interest marched under the same flag as lack of principle. No one knew better how to make a friend of the mammon of unrighteousness. His recommendations of terrorist measures in the assembly were balanced by *carmagnoles* in honour of the army, and by enlightened patronage of republican literature and art. No one saved so many lives from the executioner as ' the Anacreon of the guillotine.' Such was the man who set himself, with a view both to his own safety, and to that of the country, to reconcile the differences within the government.

From July 1st onwards Robespierre ceased to appear at the Committee of Public Safety. Some of his reasons for taking this course could be conjectured ; some were locked up in his secretive mind. Some of his grievances might yield to treatment ; others were probably incurable. For a month now things had been going badly for him. On June 1st his enemy Fouché had been elected President of the Jacobin club. On the 8th his own *fête de l'Etre Suprême* had been spoilt by trouble in the munitions factories, and by the personal threats of Bourdon and Lecointre. Two days later his Prairial Law had antagonized the Committee of General Security, and had roused bitter suspicions in the assembly. Within a week this antagonism had taken shape in Vadier's spiteful and damaging report on the Théot case. On the 25th had come the unpleasant affair of the section de l'Indivisibilité, and a few days later a scene (not the first) at the committee between Carnot and his friend Saint-Just, which had developed into a general quarrel, and loud charges of dictatorship.

As though these political troubles were not enough, his friend Buissart and his enemy Guffroy had been pestering him with complaints about Lebon's terrorist regime at Arras. He had been compelled to remove his sister Charlotte from Paris, where her indiscretions threatened to compromise his reputation. Worst of all, perhaps, for a physically nervous man, almost every week had brought evidence of some fresh plot against his life, culminating in that of Rouvière, reported to the Committee of General Security on June 30th.

During the remaining three weeks of Messidor Robespierre made occasional appearances at the Jacobins, signed a few papers brought to his lodgings from the Committee of Public Safety, and kept in touch, through Saint-Just, with the work of the *bureau de police*. His colleagues took no public notice, as they might well have done, of his absence from the committee. They executed his ' assassins ' with a vindictiveness which may have been intended to damage his reputation, and to strengthen the change of dictatorship. Collot's speech of July 7th, and Robespierre's own attack on Fouché and Dubois-Crancé on the 11th, were almost the only signs that a battle was preparing. The silence and the uncertainty were more ominous than an insurrection. Probably the public demonstrations about July 14th, and the arrest of Legray on the 20th, hurried on the crisis. Rather suddenly it was brought home to the committee how dangerous their position would be if they were attacked by a coalition between the neo-Hébertists, the Jacobin club, and the Commune under the leadership of Robespierre. There was no time to be lost. Barère's skill must be invoked. Conciliation must be attempted.

One opportunity suggested itself. It was known that Robespierre and Saint-Just attached great importance to the scheme for sequestrating the property of suspects, and distributing it to indigent patriots, inaugurated by the decrees of Ventôse (Feb. 26th and March 3rd). It was known that they chafed under the delays to which their plan had been subjected. It was now three months since the *commissions populaires* needed to work the scheme had been voted, and two months since the first of them had been set up. Not a penny had yet been handed over to the expectant poor. Might it not be possible, by setting this plan in full motion, to induce its author and seconder to support the committee against the latest and (it might be hoped) the last conspiracy ?

That this was Barère's advice may be inferred from the fact that on July 19th–21st the committees suddenly produced three lists of suitable suspects, and that on the 22nd they decided to organize at once the four remaining *commissions populaires* needed to extend the scheme from Paris to the provinces. At the same joint meeting it was agreed that a report should be drawn up condemning the new conspirators, whom Barère described as foreigners and Hébertists. It was no doubt thought that one bait or the other would catch Robespierre. If he saw the hook behind the *commissions populaires*, he could hardly refuse the subtler appeal to his love of an Inquisition.

Everything now turned on the joint meeting of the two committees— one of a series held during this critical time—called for Tuesday July 23rd (5 Thermidor). At this meeting Robespierre reappeared for the first time after an absence of over three weeks. The only official record of the proceedings is a revised text of the decree of the 22nd, simplifying the procedure by which the *commissions populaires* would be set up. But from the several accounts of the meeting given by those who were present it is possible to reconstruct what occurred.

The Robespierrist case was first put by Saint-Just. The enforcement of the Ventôse decrees meant that the Emergency government and the regime of the guillotine would go on until the end of the war. Simultaneously a beginning would be made of the social-economic reconstruction of the country forecast in his *Institutions républicaines*. But Saint-Just knew that the real obstacle to reconciliation with Robespierre was not political, but personal. It was his intransigent temper which gave him the air of a dictator, and made it so difficult for him to forgive an affront. Both Saint-Just and David, therefore, did their best to convince the committees that their judgement of him was unjust. It was useless. Robespierre himself disowned his apologists, and proved, by specific attacks upon Billaud, Collot, Amar, Vadier, and Jagot, that their suspicions of him were correct. He made it clear that it was not new measures he looked to for the millennium, but new men. He remained irreconcilable.

What was to be done? It seems most probable that, having failed to conciliate Robespierre, the committees decided to isolate him. The task of reporting to the Convention on the political situation was accepted by Saint-Just, who had been offended by Robespierre's rejection of his support. As there was now no need to spare Robespierre's feelings, Billaud and Collot asked him to say nothing in his report about the cult of the *Etre Suprême*. For his part, Saint-Just signed a decree which he knew to be disliked by Robespierre and the Jacobin club, removing an artillery detachment from Paris to the army of the North. That evening Barère declared in the Convention that the government was united. The next day, at the Jacobins, Couthon (who now evidently stood with Saint-Just against Robespierre) declared that ' though there might have been personal differences, there had never been any on matters of principle.' On the 25th Barère, in his rôle of Trimmer, could still be heard praising Robespierre, and promising that the reunited committees would rid the country of the 'crowd of clever intriguers' that was tormenting it.

Barère might still hope to win Robespierre over by flattery. Those against whom he had declared war had no alternative but to strike back, and to strike quickly. Who were they? On the Committee of Public Safety, Billaud-Varenne and Collot d'Herbois; on the Committee of General Security, Amar, Vadier, and Jagot; among the deputies, Fouché, Tallien, Cambon, Bourdon de l'Oise, Lecointre, Ruamps, Dubois-Crancé; and others less directly threatened, such as C. Delacroix, Delaunay, Delmas, Garnier-Launay, Fernex, Thuriot, and Léonard Bourdon.

What could they do ? They must attack Robespierre at his weakest point :—not at the Jacobin club, whose *petit bourgeois* audience still hung on his words ; nor at the Commune, where Payan and Lescot-Fleuriot headed a majority of his adherents ; nor in the sections, which, indeed, controlled the armed forces of Paris, but whose choice of sides could never be foretold ; no, but in the Convention itself. The Convention alone had the right, and had already exercised it a year ago, to purge the national representation of undesirable members. The ground may have been prepared beforehand ; at any rate there is evidence that between July 23rd and 26th Fouché and Tallien approached the leaders of the Moderate majority, who had never declared a party allegiance, or abdicated the right of government that they delegated to the committee, with the suggestion that they should lend themselves to the overthrow of the Triumvirate.

What arguments could they use in favour of destroying the unity of the chief organ of government ?—the quarrels within and between the committees, notorious in spite of official disclaimers ? Robespierre's rejection of Barère's olive-branch, and his threats against his colleagues ? The impossibility of working any longer with a man of such intransigent temper? Or considerations which might more closely affect private members—the laws of Ventôse and Prairial, that threatened their property and their lives, or the campaign for republican virtue and piety that seemed likely to make a burden of patriotism ?

Whatever the force of these urgings, the crowning argument was once more provided by Robespierre himself. Convinced of the righteousness of his cause, and confident of his power to sway the majority of the deputies, he addressed to the Convention on July 26th (8 Thermidor) his last and most eloquent appeal. Scouting the charge of dictatorship, and proclaiming the gospel of *vertu*, he denounced yet another conspiracy against the revolution. But this was one which sprang from within the government. It could only be met by depriving the Committee of General Security of its initiative, and by purging both government committees of some of their most prominent members. Names were mentioned :—Carnot and Barère, Collot and Billaud, Cambon, Ramel, and Mallarmé—not enough to reassure others who had already been marked down, but more than enough to suggest that the real aim was to stage one more political trial, and to set up a dictatorship of the Robespierrist faction.

Dictatorship, or martyrdom :—who can say which was most in Robespierre's mind ? To his enemies in the Convention who challenged him, he refused to be more explicit. To his friends at the Jacobins, the same evening, he described the speech in the Convention as his ' last will and testament,' and spoke of ' drinking the hemlock ' of self-immolation. He rejected every suggestion of an appeal to force.

During the night the threatened deputies arranged—it was now easy—that at tomorrow's meeting of the Convention Collot, who happened to be President, or, in his absence, Thuriot, should give the right of speech to Robespierre's enemies, and prevent him from replying. In the meeting-room of the Committee of Public Safety Saint-Just drafted the report with which he had been entrusted three days before. He is said to have turned a deaf ear to the accusations of Collot and Billaud, who had just been expelled from the Jacobin club. But there was another influence against which his young idealism could not harden itself—the mute appeal of Robespierre's martyrdom. At the last minute Saint-Just rallied to his old leader's side. He would throw over the safe bargain of July 23rd for the forlorn hope of victory or death. He would denounce not only Billaud and Collot, but also Carnot and Barère.

The next day (July 27th, 9 Thermidor) the plan for the betrayal of Robespierre was carried out with smooth ruthlessness. Saint-Just, entering the assembly with Robespierre, had scarcely begun his report, when he was interrupted by Tallien. Then Billaud spoke ; then Tallien again. When Robespierre tried to reply, he was met with cries of *A bas le tyran !* Warrants of arrest were issued against the partisans who might have backed him with arms—Hanriot, the commandant of the National Guard, Boulanger, Dufresse, Dumas. He tried to protest ; but his voice was drowned by cries for Barère.

The Trimmer was for once unprepared with a suitable change of front. It was too late for a defence of Robespierre, too early for a *carmagnole* in honour of his defeat. He contented himself with the speech he would have made if the House had heard out Saint-Just, and he supported the government's drive against a new conspiracy. Vadier came next, with a rambling series of charges, which threatened to divide Robespierre's critics. Tallien intervened for the third time—he was clearly the producer of the drama—and roused Robespierre to angry retorts. These were shouted down ; when at last a few of his words could be heard, he was appealing not to the ' brigands ' of the Mountain, but to the ' honest men ' of the Marsh. Thuriot, who was now in the chair, refused him a hearing. Trying to rise above the clamour, Robespierre's weak voice gave out.

At last Louchet of Rodez, one of his own party, a republican, a regicide, and a terrorist, moved his arrest : the motion was seconded by another Montagnard, Loiseau of Château-neuf, and, after a disorderly debate, carried unanimously. Together with Saint-Just, Couthon, his friend Lebas, and his brother Augustin, who claimed to share his virtues and his fate, Robespierre was arrested, and committed to the quarters of the Committee of General Security.

The unexpected solidarity of the Convention threatened not only the Triumvirate, but also the Robespierrists of the Jacobin club and of the Commune. It was not a day on which the whole *conseil-général* met : the inner circle—the *corps municipal*—was discussing a report on the city cemeteries. Its chief officials, Lescot-Fleuriot and Payan, had already been charged by the Convention with the duty of preserving order in Paris. But they remembered August 10th, and were in no mood to put themselves in the position either of a Pétion or of a Mandat. They disobeyed a summons to the bar of the House about 3 p.m. Two hours later, when they heard of the arrest of Robespierre, they at once summoned a meeting of the whole Commune, and passed a number of resolutions—for the sounding of the tocsin, the closing of the barriers, the mobilizing of armed sections, and proclamations to the people of Paris—which made them technically guilty of insurrection against the authority of the Convention. A specially nominated executive committee (*comité d'exécution*) sat on into the night, to deal with any emergencies that might arise. At 7 o'clock the Jacobin club declared itself in permanent session, and informed the Commune of its intention to conquer or to die.

But the time for speeches and gestures was past. The silencing of Robespierre's voice in the Convention meant that the appeal was now to force. The last word lay, as on June 2nd a year ago, with the National Guard, mobilized in its sectional battalions. The personal prestige of the Jacobin leaders still counted for something in most of the sections ; but it had been compromised by the failure of their economic measures, and by the continuance of the Terror. The authority of the Commune, never greatly respected, had been weakened by popular dislike of the recently published scale of wages. Many of its members were suspected of exploiting the *maximum* against their customers or their employees. In the course of the evening, twenty-seven out of the forty-eight sections asked for instructions from the Commune, and thirteen sent troops for the defence of the Town Hall. These included several of the working-class sections of the southern and eastern parts of the city. The remaining twenty-one made no such move. The sections under upper middle-class influence, such as the Lombards, Le Peletier, or Palais-Royal, were only waiting for the right moment to declare for the Convention.

The Convention had adjourned, after the excitements of the afternoon, and did not meet again, to exploit its success, until 7 o'clock in the evening. It had not expected the insurrection with which it now found itself threatened. It heard with indignation that an attempt had been made to rescue its prisoners from the rooms of the *comité de sûreté générale*, and that, two hours later, Hanriot, himself arrested, had in turn been released by another band of Robespierrist troops under Coffinhal, the Vice-President of the Revolutionary Tribunal. A few hours' delay had turned confidence of victory into danger of defeat.

But two things could be done, and there was a man for each. Barère, at last convinced that the Robespierrists would lose the day, carried resolutions annulling the orders given by the commune, and outlawing the impeached deputies as prison-breakers. They could now be arrested at sight, and executed without trial. Barras—it was not forgotten that he had distinguished himself at the siege of Toulon—was put in charge of the military forces that had declared for the Convention.

This strong action had an immediate effect. The wavering sections came over to the side of the government. The Robespierrist troops, tired of waiting in front of the Town Hall, dispersed. The rebel *comité d'exécution*, reinforced during the night by the proscribed deputies, whom the prison governors either refused to receive, or easily surrendered, issued unavailing appeals, proclamations, and warrants of arrest.

At two o'clock in the morning a government force under Léonard Bourdon broke into the Hôtel de Ville. Hanriot and the younger Robespierre tried to escape by the windows, and were picked up injured outside. The crippled Couthon fell down the stairs. The rest were found in the committee room. Lebas had shot himself in the head. Robespierre lay across the table with a shattered jaw: he had apparently tried to shoot himself, and had failed. Saint-Just stood erect, waiting to be taken.

In the neighbouring council-chamber some sixty members of the commune were arrested, and carried off to prison. Ten administrators of police were taken at the *mairie* the same night ; and other members of the party were rounded up during the following days.

The guillotine, which had executed forty-five anti-Robespierrists on July 27th, executed eighty-three Robespierrists on the 27th and 28th. The crowd which had seen Hébert and Danton perish, saw Robespierre go to his death, with the same indifference or distaste for a defeated cause.

Thus a private feud had turned into a public vengeance, and a stroke aimed at three men had slain four score. It can never have been part of Billaud's plan, or of Collot's, to destroy their friends of the commune ; Fouché and Tallien can never have intended to deprive the National Guard and the Revolutionary Tribunal of the soundest exponents of Jacobin terrorism.

Nor were these to be the only points in which the events of Thermidor went beyond the intentions of the conspirators. On the day after Robespierre's execution, Barère, in the name of the Committee of Public Safety, proposed that the Revolutionary Tribunal should carry on its work : there were to be new judges and jurymen, but Fouquier-Tinville was to continue his indispensable work as Public Prosecutor. Furthermore, three deputies of colourless or anti-Robespierrist reputation were nominated to take the places of the Triumvirate on the Committee. Evidently the remaining members counted on staying in office, and carrying on the Jacobin dictatorship, as though nothing more had happened than a party purge.

They were speedily undeceived. Robespierrists might go out, and Dantonists come in ; but the Convention had recovered its initiative, and would put an end, once and for all, to the dictatorial committee government which had ousted it from power. There and then it was decreed that no member of either ' governing committee ' should in future hold office for more than four months, and that their direction of affairs should be shared by the *comité de législation.* Three days later the Prairial Law was deleted from the statute-book, and the Revolutionary Tribunal shorn of its abnormal powers. At the end of August the Commune, which no longer issued orders in its own name, was replaced by a *commission des administrateurs civils* appointed from the ranks of the Convention, and on Oct. 17th by a *commission administrative de police.* In November the Jacobin club was closed. Not merely anti-Robespierrist but also anti-Jacobin reaction was in full flood.

At the beginning of September Billaud, Collot, and Barère left the *comité de salut public :* by the end of the year they were in prison. The *maximum* was suppressed. There was even talk of bringing in a new constitution. In May, '95, after the execution of Fouquier-Tinville, a scapegoat of national vengeance, the Revolutionary Tribunal was finally abolished. In June the very word *révolutionnaire,* the code-word of the whole Jacobin regime, was banned.

The historian is at first puzzled—puzzled, perhaps, as Barère himself may have been—to account for this complete *volte-face.* The simplest explanation seems to be that the middle or moderate party in the Convention refused to be a mere tool in the hands of those who had a feud with Robespierre, or who feared proscription for their crimes ; that they used the power given them against their new enemy, the Triumvirate, to destroy their old enemy, the Commune ; and that they crowned their reassumption of authority by restoring, as nearly as could be, the republican regime of the period preceding the fatal quarrel between Jacobins and Girondins.

But the possibility of doing this depended upon something more than a political coalition. It needed an uprush of public opinion, which, long obstructed by party loyalties, silenced by government intimidation, and diverted by war, could at last declare itself for patriotism, peace, and justice; could at last assure a reasonable enjoyment of the benefits won by the revolution.

The real meaning of Thermidor is not to be found in the twenty-six heads of Lecointre's indictment against the Terrorists, but in the reply made to the unimaginative Louchet, when, three weeks after he had led the attack on Robespierre, he announced in the Assembly (August 19th) that the only way to deal with the dangers which still menaced public liberty was to carry on Robespierre's system of intimidation (*maintenir partout à l'ordre du jour la terreur*). He was interrupted by loud protests, and from all parts of the House there were cries of ' Justice ! Justice ! '—' Justice ? ' retorted Charlier ; ' yes, for patriots ; but for aristocrats the Terror ! ' Thereupon (says the report) ' a great number of voices replied,—" Justice for every man (*justice pour tout le monde*)!" ' It was a cry from the heart of France—France which during the last five years had hoped so much and had been so often deceived. It excused Thermidor. It explained the Revolution.

CHRONOLOGY OF THE REVOLUTION

1789   1st *Year of Liberty*

May

Sat.	3	...	...	...	States-general: reception of deputies
Sun.	4	...	...	...	Procession and mass
Mon.	5	...	...	...	Opening session

June

Thu.	4	...	...	...	Death of Dauphin
Wed.	17	...	...	...	'National Assembly'
Fri.	19	...	...	...	Council at Marly
Sat.	20	...	...	...	Tennis Court Oath
Sun.	21	...	...	...	Council at Versailles
Tue.	23	...	...	...	Séance royale
Sat.	27	...	...	...	Reunion of Orders

July

Sat.	11	...	...	...	Dismissal of Necker
Tue.	14	...	...	...	Fall of Bastille
Wed.	15	...	...	...	First emigration
Fri.	17	...	...	...	King visits Paris
Wed.	22	...	...	...	Murder of Foullon and Berthier

August

| Tue. | 4 | ... | ... | ... | 'Abolition of Feudalism' |
| Thu. | 20 | ... | ... | ... | Declaration of Rights begun |

September

| Fri. | 11 | ... | ... | ... | Suspensive veto |

October

Thu.	1	...	...	...	Versailles banquet
Mon.	5	...	...	...	Women's march to Versailles
Tue.	6	...	...	...	King's return to Paris
Mon.	19	...	...	...	First session of Assembly in Archevêché
Wed.	21	...	...	...	Martial Law

November

Mon.	2	...	...	...	Nationalization of church property
Sat.	7	...	...	...	Decree excluding deputies from ministry
Mon.	9	...	...	...	First session of Assembly in Manège

December

| Sat. | 19 | ... | ... | ... | First issue of assignats |

1790   *2nd Year of Liberty*
February
  Thu. 4 ...   .   King's speech to Assembly
  Fri.   19 ...   .   Execution of Favras
March
  Fri.   12 ...   .   Publication of Livre Rouge
May
  Tue. 11 ...   .   Nootka Sound debate
  Fri.   21 ...   .   Paris Municipal Law
  Sat.   22 ...   .   Decree on right of declaring war
June
  Sat.   19 ...   .   Abolition of Nobility
July
  Mon. 12 ...   .   Civil Constitution of Clergy
  Wed. 14 ...   .   First Fête of Federation
August
  Mon. 16 ...   .   Debate on Nancy mutiny
November
  Fri.   12 ...   .   Castries-Lameth duel
  Sat.   27 ...   .   Clerical oath decreed

1791   *3rd Year of Liberty*
February
  Sat.   19 ...   .   Suppression of octrois
  Sun. 20 ...   .   Departure of King's aunts
  Mon. 28 ...   .   Journée des poignards
March
  Thu. 10 ...   .   Pope condemns Civil Constitution
April
  Sat.   2 ...   .   Death of Mirabeau
  Mon. 18 ...   .   St. Cloud affair
May
  Mon. 16 ...   .   ' Self-denying Ordinance '
June
  Mon.–Tue. 20–21   ...   Flight to Varennes
  Sat.   25 ...   .   Return to Paris
July
  Mon. 11 ...   .   Panthéonization of Voltaire
  Thu. 14 ...   .   Second Fête of Federation
  Sun. 17 ...   .   Massacre of Champ de Mars
August
  Sat.   27 ...   .   Declaration of Pillnitz

1791
September
   Wed. 14 ...   .   King accepts Constitution
   Fri. 30 ...   .   End of Constituent Assembly
October
   Sat. 1 ...   .   First session of Legislative Assembly
November
   Sat. 12 ...   .   King vetoes decree *v.* émigrés
   Wed. 16 ...   .   Pétion mayor of Paris
December
   Mon. 19 ...   .   King vetoes decree *v.* clergy
   Thu. 29 ...   .   Decree disavowing conquest

1792   *4th Year of Liberty*
March
   Thu. 1 ...   .   Death of Leopold II
   Sat. 10 ...   .   Brissotin ministry
   Sun. 15 ...   .   Châteauvieux fête
April
   Fri. 20 ...   .   Declaration of war *v.* Austria
   Sat. 28 ...   .   Defeat and murder of Dillon
May
   Wed. 30 ...   .   Dismissal of King's bodyguard
June
   Mon. 4 ...   .   Paris camp
   Sun. 10 ...   .   Petition of 8,000 *v.* Paris camp
   Wed. 13 ...   .   Dismissal of Brissotin ministry
   Tue. 19 ...   .   King vetoes Paris camp
   Wed. 20 ...   .   Crowd invades Tuileries
   Thu. 28 ...   .   Lafayette's visit to Paris
July
   Sun. 1 ...   .   Petition of 20,000 *v.* June 20th
   Fri. 6 ...   .   Suspension of Pétion
   Sat. 7 ...   .   ' Lamourette's Kiss '
   Tue. 10 ...   .   Resignation of ministers
   Wed. 11 ...   .   ' The Country in Danger '
   Sat. 14 ...   .   Third Fête of Federation
   Mon. 30 ...   .   Arrival of Marseillais
August
   Wed. 1 ...   .   Brunswick's Manifesto
   Wed. 8 ...   .   Lafayette exculpated
   Thu. 9 ...   .   Insurrectional Commune
   Fri. 10 ...   .   Attack on Tuileries

1792
August
Sat.	11	...	...	...	Convention summoned
Mon.	13	...	...	...	Royal family imprisoned in Temple
Fri.	17	...	...	...	Tribunal of August 10th
Mon.	20	...	...	...	Desertion of Lafayette
Thu.	23	...	...	...	Fall of Longwy
Sun.	26	...	...	...	Funeral of victims of August 10th

September
Sun.	2	...	...	...	Fall of Verdun. Prison massacre
Sun.	9	...	...	...	Orléans massacre
Mon.	17	...	...	...	Robbery of Garde-meuble
Thu.	20	...	...	...	Battle of Valmy. First meeting of Convention

1st *Year of Republic*

| Fri. | 21 | ... | ... | ... | Abolition of royalty |

October
| Thu. | 11 | ... | ... | ... | Constitutional Committee |
| Mon. | 29 | ... | ... | ... | Louvet denounces Robespierre |

November
Tue.	6	...	...	...	Battle of Jemappes
Mon.	19	...	...	...	' Fraternité et secours ' decree
Tue.	20	...	...	...	Discovery of ' iron chest '

December
Mon.	3	...	...	...	Decision to try King
Tue.	11	...	...	...	King's interrogation
Wed.	26	...	...	...	King's trial

1793
January
| Fri. | 18 | ... | ... | ... | King condemned to death |
| Mon. | 21 | ... | ... | ... | King's execution |

February
| Fri. | 1 | ... | ... | ... | Declaration of war *v.* England and Holland |
| Sun. | 24 | ... | ... | ... | Levy of 3,000 men decreed |

March
Thu.	7	...	...	...	Declaration of war *v.* Spain
Fri.–Sun.	8–10	...	...	...	The ' March days '
Sun.	10	...	...	...	Revolt in Vendée
Mon.	11	...	...	...	Tribunal extraordinaire
Mon.	18	...	...	...	Battle of Neerwinden
Mon.	25	...	...	...	Comité de défense générale

1793
April
Thu. 4 ... ... Desertion of Dumouriez
Sat. 6 ... ... Comité de salut public
Sat. 13 ... ... Impeachment of Marat
May
Sat. 4 ... ... First Maximum
Fri. 10 ... ... Convention moves to Tuileries
Tue. 21 ... ... Commission of Twelve
June
Sun. 2 ... ... Expulsion of Girondin deputies
Tue. 4 ... ... Armée révolutionnaire
Mon. 24 ... ... Constitution of 1793
July
Sat. 13 ... ... Murder of Marat
Sun. 28 ... ... Girondin leaders outlawed
August
Sat. 10 ... ... Fête in honour of Constitution
Fri. 23 ... ... Levée en masse
Sat. 24 ... ... Cambon's Grand Livre
September
Sun. 8 ... ... Battle of Hondschoote

AN II

Sun. 22 (*Vendémiaire* 1) Revolutionary Calendar
Sun. 29 (*Vendémiaire* 8) Second Maximum
October
Thu. 3 (*Vendémiaire* 12) Impeachment of Girondin deputies
Thu. 10 (*Vendémiaire* 19) Decree on Emergency Government
Tue. 15 (*Vendémiaire* 24) Trial of Girondins
Wed. 16 (*Vendémiaire* 25) Wattignies. Queen's execution
Thu. 31 (*Brumaire* 10) ... Execution of Girondins
November
Fri. 8 (*Brumaire* 18) ... Execution of Mme Roland
Sun. 10 (*Brumaire* 20) ... Fête of Reason in Nôtre Dame
Fri. 22 (*Frimaire* 2) ... Closing of Paris churches
December
Wed. 4 (*Frimaire* 14) ... Revolutionary government
1794
March
Thu. 13 (*Ventôse* 23) ... Ventôse decrees implemented
Sat. 15 (*Ventôse* 25) ... Arrest of Hébertists
Sun. 23 (*Germinal* 3) ... Execution of Hébertists
Sun. 30 (*Germinal* 10) ... Arrest of Dantonists

1794
April
Tue.   1 (*Germinal* 12) ...   Ministry replaced by Commissions
Sat.   5 (*Germinal* 16) ...   Execution of Dantonists
Wed.   16 (*Germinal* 27) ...   Bureau de police générale
May
Wed.   7 (*Floréal* 18)   ... Culte de l'Etre Suprême
Sat.   10 (*Floréal* 21)   ... Execution of Mme Elisabeth
Fri.   23 (*Prairial* 4)   ... Admiral affair
Sat.   24 (*Prairial* 5)   ... Renault affair
June
Sun.   1 (*Prairial* 13) ... Battle of First of June
Sun.   8 (*Prairial* 20) ... Fête de l'Etre Suprême
Tue.   10 (*Prairial* 22) ... Law of 22nd Prairial
Tue.   17 (*Prairial* 29) ... ' Chemises rouges ' execution
Thu.   26 (*Messidor* 8)   ... Battle of Fleurus
July
Sat.   26 (*Thermidor* 8) ...   Robespierre's last speech
Sun.   27 (*Thermidor* 9) ...   Proscription of Robespierrists
Mon. 28 (*Thermidor* 10)   Execution of Robespierrists
Tue.   29 (*Thermidor* 11)   Execution of members of Commune

REPUBLICAN CALENDAR FOR THE YEAR II

Vendémiaire, An. II. Sept.–Oct. 1793		Brumaire Oct.–Nov.		Frimaire Nov.–Dec.		Nivôse Dec. 1793–Jan. 1794		Pluviôse Jan.–Feb.		Ventôse Feb.–March		Germinal March–April		Floréal April–May		Prairial May–June		Messidor June–July		Thermidor July–Aug.	
1	22	1	22	1	21	1	21	1	20	1	19	1	21	1	20	1	20	1	19	1	19
2	23	2	23	2	22	2	22	2	21	2	20	2	22	2	21	2	21	2	20	2	20
3	24	3	24	3	23	3	23	3	22	3	21	2	23	2	22	3	22	3	21	3	21
4	25	4	25	4	24	4	24	4	23	4	22	4	24	4	23	4	23	4	22	4	22
5	26	5	26	5	25	5	25	5	24	5	23	5	25	5	24	5	24	5	23	5	23
6	27	6	27	6	26	6	26	6	25	6	24	6	26	6	25	6	25	6	24	6	24
7	28	7	28	7	27	7	27	7	26	7	25	7	27	7	26	7	26	7	25	7	25
8	29	8	29	8	28	8	28	8	27	8	26	8	28	8	27	8	27	8	26	8	26
9	30	9	30	9	29	9	29	9	28	9	27	9	29	9	28	9	28	9	27	9	27
10	1	10	31	10	30	10	30	10	29	10	28	10	30	10	29	10	29	10	28	10	28
11	2	11	1	11	1	11	31	11	30	11	1	11	31	11	30	11	30	11	29	11	29
12	3	12	2	12	2	12	1	12	31	12	2	12	1	12	1	12	31	12	30	12	30
13	4	13	3	13	3	13	2	13	1	13	3	13	2	13	2	13	1	13	1	13	31
14	5	14	4	14	4	14	3	14	2	14	4	14	3	14	3	14	2	14	2	14	1
15	6	15	5	15	5	15	4	15	3	15	5	15	4	15	4	15	3	15	3	15	2
16	7	16	6	16	6	16	5	16	4	16	6	16	5	16	5	16	4	16	4	16	3
17	8	17	7	17	7	17	6	17	5	17	7	17	6	17	6	17	5	17	5	17	4
18	9	18	8	18	8	18	7	18	6	18	8	18	7	18	7	18	6	18	6	18	5
19	10	19	9	19	9	19	8	19	7	19	9	19	8	19	8	19	7	19	7	19	6
20	11	20	10	20	10	20	9	20	8	20	10	20	9	20	8	20	8	20	7
21	12	21	11	21	11	21	10	21	9	21	11	21	10	21	9	21	9	21	8
22	13	22	12	22	12	22	11	22	10	22	12	22	11	22	11	22	10	22	10	22	9
23	14	23	13	23	13	23	12	23	11	23	13	23	12	23	12	23	11	23	11	23	10
24	15	24	14	24	14	24	13	24	12	24	14	24	13	24	13	24	12	24	12	24	11
25	16	25	15	25	15	25	14	25	13	25	15	25	14	25	14	25	13	25	13	25	12
26	17	26	16	26	16	26	15	27	14	26	16	26	15	26	15	26	14	26	14	26	13
27	18	27	17	27	17	27	16	27	15	27	17	27	16	27	16	27	15	27	15	27	14
28	19	28	18	28	18	28	17	28	16	28	18	28	17	28	17	28	16	28	16	28	15
29	20	29	19	29	19	29	18	29	17	29	19	29	18	29	18	29	17	29	17	29	16
30	21	30	20	30	20	30	19	30	18	30	20	30	19	30	19	30	18	30	18	30	17

MINISTERS DURING THE REVOLUTION

Finance	Foreign	Interior	War	Navy and Colonies	Justice
	Feb., '87 Montmorin	'87 Villedeuil		Dec., '87 Luzerne	
Aug. 25, '88 Necker		July 12,' 89 Breteuil	Aug., '88 Puységur		Aug., '88 Barentin
		Aug. 3, '89 St. Priest	Aug. 7, '89 Tour du Pin		Aug. 3, '89 de Cicé
Sept. 4, '90 Lambert				Oct. 24, '90 Fleurieu	
			Nov. 16, '90 Duportail		Nov. 21, '90 Duport-Dutertre
Dec. 4, '90 Delessart		Jan. 25, 91 Delessart			
May 18, '91 Tarbé				May 16, '91 Thévenard	
				Sept. 18, '91 Delessart	
				Oct. 4, '91 de Moleville	
	Nov. 28, '91 Delessart	Nov. 29, '91 Cahier de Gerville	Dec. 6, '91 Narbonne		
Mar. 23, '92 Clavière	Mar. 17, '92 Dumouriez	Mar. 23, '92 Roland	Mar. 9, '92 de Grave	Mar. 15, '92 Lacoste	Mar. 23, '92 Roland April 13, '92 Duranthon
			May 9, '92 Servan		
June 18, '92 Beaulieu	June 14, '92 Naillac	June 13, '92 Mourgues	June 13, '92 Dumouriez		
	June 17, '92 Chambonas	June 18, '92 Terrier de Monciel	June 17, '92 Lajard		
		July 21, '92 Champion de Villeneuve	July 23, '92 d'Abancourt	July 21, '92 Dubouchage	July 3, '92 Dejoly
Aug. 1, '92 Leroux de Laville	Aug. 1, '92 Bigot de St. Croix				
Aug. 10, '92 Clavière	Aug. 12, '92 Lebrun	Aug. 10, '92 Roland	Aug. 10, '92 Servan	Aug. 12, '92 Monge	Aug. 12, '92 Danton Oct. 19, '92 Garat
			Feb. 4, '93 Bournonville		
		Mar. 14, '93 Garat			Mar. 20, '93 Gohier
			April 4, '93 Bouchotte	April 10, '93 Dalbarade	
June 15, '93 Destournelles	June 14, '93 Deforgues				
		Aug. 15, '93 Paré			

PRESIDENTS OF THE NATIONAL ASSEMBLY

1. *Constituent Assembly*

1.	1789.	June	17 ...	...	Bailly
2.		July	3 ...	...	Duc d'Orléans
3.			3 ...	...	Archbishop of Vienne (de Pompignan)
4.			20 ...	...	de la Rochefoucauld
5.		Aug.	3 ...	...	Le Chapelier
6.			17 ...	...	Clermont-Tonnerre
7.			31 ...	...	Bishop of Langres (de la Luzerne)
8.		Sept.	14 ...	...	Clermont-Tonnerre
9.			28 ...	...	Mounier
10.		Oct.	12 ...	...	Fréteau
11.			28 ...	...	Camus
12.		Nov.	12 ...	...	Thouret
13.			23 ...	...	Archbishop of Aix (Cicé)
14.		Dec.	7 ...	...	Fréteau
15.			22 ...	...	Desmeuniers
16.	1790.	Jan.	4 ...	...	Montesquiou
17.			18 ...	...	Target
18.		Feb.	2 ...	...	Bureaux de Pusy
19.			16 ...	...	Bishop of Autun (Talleyrand)
20.			28 ...	...	Montesquiou
21.		Mar.	13 ...	...	Rabaut Saint-Etienne
22.			28 ...	...	Menou
23.		Apr.	12 ...	...	de Bonnay
24.			27 ...	...	Virieu
25.			29 ...	...	Gouttes
26.		May	10 ...	...	Thouret
27.			27 ...	...	Beaumetz
28.		June	8 ...	...	Sieyès
29.			21 ...	...	Le Peletier
30.		July	5 ...	...	de Bonnay
31.			17 ...	...	Treilhard
32.		Aug.	1 ...	...	André
33.			16 ...	...	Dupont de Nemours
34.			30 ...	...	de Jessé
35.		Sept.	12 ...	...	Bureaux de Pusy
36.			26 ...	...	Emmery

37.	Oct.	9 ...	...	Merlin de Douai
38.		25 ...	...	Barnave
39.	Nov.	9 ...	...	Chasset
40.		20 ...	...	A. de Lameth
41.	Dec.	4 ...	...	Pétion
42.		20 ...	...	de Bonnay
43.		22 ...	...	André
44. 1791.	Jan.	4 ...	...	Emmery
45.		18 ...	...	Grégoire
46.		31 ...	...	Mirabeau
47.	Feb.	14 ...	...	A. Duport
48.		26 ...	...	de Noailles
49.	Mar.	14 ...	...	Montesquiou
50.		30 ...	...	Tronchet
51.	Apr.	9 ...	...	Chabroud
52.		25 ...	...	Reubell
53.	May	9 ...	...	André
54.		25 ...	...	Bureaux de Pusy
55.	June	6 ...	...	Dauchy
56.		18 ...	...	Beauharnais
57.	July	3 ...	...	C. de Lameth
58.		19 ...	...	Defermon
59.		31 ...	...	Beauharnais
60.	Aug.	14 ...	...	de Broglie
61.		29 ...	...	Vernier
62.	Sept.	12 ...	...	Thouret

2. *Legislative Assembly*

1.	Oct.	3 ...	...	Pastoret
2.		17 ...	...	Ducastel
3.		30 ...	...	Vergniaud
4.	Nov.	15 ...	...	Vienot-Vaublanc
5.		28 ...	...	Lacépède
6.	Dec.	10 ...	...	Lemontey
7.		26 ...	...	François de Neufchâteau
8. 1792.	Jan.	8 ...	...	Daverhoult
9.		22 ...	...	Guadet
10.	Feb.	6 ...	...	Condorcet
11.		19 ...	...	Dumas
12.	Mar.	4 ...	...	Guyton-Morveau
13.		18 ...	...	Gensonné
14.	Apr.	2 ...	...	Dorizy
15.		15 ...	...	Bigot de Préameneu

16.	Apr. 29 ...	...	Lacuée
17.	May 13 ...	...	Muraire
18.	27 ...	...	Tardiveau
19.	June 11 ...	...	Français
20.	25 ...	...	Girardin
21.	July 8 ...	...	Aubert-Dubayet
22.	23 ...	...	Laffon-Ladebat
23.	Aug. 6 ...	...	Merlet
24.	19 ...	...	J. F. Delacroix
25.	Sept. 2 ...	...	Hérault de Séchelles
26.	16 ...	...	Cambon

3. Convention

1.		Sept. 21 ...	...	Pétion
2.		Oct. 4 ...	...	J. F. Delacroix
3.		18 ...	...	Guadet
4.		Nov. 1 ...	...	Hérault de Séchelles
5.		15 ...	...	Grégoire
6.		29 ...	...	Barère
7.		Dec. 13 ...	...	Defermon
8.		27 ...	...	Treilhard
9.	1793.	Jan. 10 ...	...	Vergniaud
10.		24 ...	...	Rabaut Saint-Etienne
11.		Feb. 7 ...	...	Bréard
12.		21 ...	...	Dubois-Crancé
13.		Mar. 7 ...	...	Gensonné
14.		21 ...	...	De Bry
15.		Apr. 4 ...	...	Delmas
16.		18 ...	...	Lasource
17.		May 2 ...	...	Boyer-Fonfrède
18.		16 ...	...	Isnard
19.		30 ...	...	Mallarmé
20.		June 13 ...	...	Collot d'Herbois
21.		27 ...	...	Thuriot
22.		July 11 ...	...	Jeanbon Saint-André
23.		25 ...	...	Danton
24.		Aug. 8 ...	...	Hérault de Séchelles
25.		22 ...	...	Robespierre
26.		Sept. 5 ...	...	Billaud-Varenne
27.		19 ...	...	Cambon
28.		Oct. 3 ...	...	Charlier
29.		22 ...	...	Bayle
30.		Nov. 6 ...	...	Laloy

31.		Nov.	21 ...	...	Romme
32.		Dec.	6 ...	...	Voulland
33.			21 ...	...	Couthon
34.	1794.	Jan.	5 ...	...	David
35.			20 ...	...	Vadier
36.		Feb.	4 ...	...	Dubarran
37.			19 ...	...	Saint-Just
38.		Mar.	6 ...	...	Rühl
39.			21 ...	...	Tallien
40.		Apr.	5 ...	...	Amar
41.			20 ...	...	R. Lindet
42.		May	5 ...	...	Carnot
43.			20 ...	...	Prieur de la Côte d'Or
44.		June	4 ...	...	Robespierre
45.			19 ...	...	Lacoste
46.		July	5 ...	...	Louis
47.			19 ...	...	Collot d'Herbois

THE FRENCH DEPARTMENTS IN 1794

SHOWING THEIR NAMES (I), CAPITALS (II), MUNICIPALITIES (III),
POPULATION (IV), AND NUMBER OF ACTIVE CITIZENS (V).

I	II	III	IV	V
Ain	Bourg	468	308,000	40,000
Aisne	Laon	860	408,000	64,000
Allier	Moulins	370	267,000	42,000
Alpes (Basses)	Digne	268	169,000	31,000
Alpes (Hautes)	Gap	186	120,000	23,000
Alpes (Maritimes)	Nice	95	97,000	14,000
Ardèche	Privas	347	290,000	45,000
Ardennes	Mezières	554	248,000	42,000
Arriège	Foix	218	198,000	35,000
Aube	Troyes	483	229,000	43,000
Aude	Carcassonne	450	240,000	39,000
Aveyron	Rhodez	649	372,000	58,000
Bouches du Rhône	Aix	102	323,000	55,000
Calvados	Caen	906	391,000	61,000
Cantal	Aurillac	274	340,000	37,000
Charente	Angoulême	466	340,000	57,000
Charente-Inférieure	Saintes	511	438,000	70,000
Cher	Bourges	313	208,000	35,000
Corrèze	Tulle	298	270,000	42,000
Côte d'Or	Dijon	724	343,000	63,000
Côtes du Nord	Saint-Brieuc	382	524,000	57,000
Creuse	Guéret	313	238,000	44,000
Dordogne	Périgueux	634	433,000	67,000
Doubs	Besançon	628	220,000	32,000
Drôme	Valence	361	247,000	38,000
Eure	Evreux	875	385,000	59,000
Eure et Loire	Chartres	452	357,000	39,000
Finisterre	Quimper	293	286,000	44,000
Gard	Nîmes	409	313,000	52,000
Garonne (Haut)	Toulouse	733	457,000	82,000
Gers	Auch	708	326,000	59,000
Gironde	Bordeaux	569	497,000	77,000
Hérault	Montpellier	334	290,000	49,000

I	II	III	IV	V
Ille et Villaine	Rennes	357	519,000	66,000
Indre	Châteauroux	270	230,000	33,000
Indre et Loire	Tours	315	273,000	40,000
Isère	Grenoble	516	365,000	57,000
Jura	Lons le Saunier	734	280,000	51,000
Landes	Mont de Marsan	387	257,000	40,000
Loir et Cher	Blois	308	200,000	34,000
Loire (Haute)	Le Puy	292	210,000	34,000
Loire Inférieure	Nantes	207	331,000	52,000
Loiret	Orléans	365	286,000	43,000
Lot	Cahors	493	444,000	69,000
Lot et Garonne	Agen	289	412,000	59,000
Lozère	Mende	192	142,000	22,000
Manche	Coutances	684	463,000	78,000
Marne	Chalons sur Marne	697	349,000	54,000
Marne (Haute)	Chaumont	557	223,000	41,000
Mayenne	Lavarne	290	324,000	42,000
Mayenne et Loire	Angers	318	455,000	68,000
Meurthe	Nancy	709	332,000	54,000
Meuse	Bar sur Ornin	595	268,000	50,000
Morbihan	Vannes	227	282,000	44,000
Mont-Blanc	Chambéry	653	?	?
Mont-Terrible	Delemont	122	36,000	7,000
Moselle	Metz	890	328,000	51,000
Nièvre	Nevers	351	236,000	39,000
Nord	Douai	678	448,000	70,000
Oise	Compiègne	728	349,000	62,000
Orne	Alençon	628	382,000	59,000
Paris	Paris	78	647,000	101,000
Pas de Calais	Arras	948	532,000	81,000
Puy de Dôme	Clermont	469	517,000	83,000
Pyrénées (Basses)	Pau	682	188,000	29,000
Pyrénées (Hautes)	Tarbe	513	189,000	24,000
Pyrénées Orientales	Perpignan	249	114,000	17,000
Rhin (Bas)	Strasbourg	578	415,000	65,000
Rhin (Haut)	Colmar	488	283,000	42,000
Rhône et Loire	Lyon	597	579,000	96,000
Saône (Haute)	Vesoul	642	264,000	41,000
Saône et Loire	Mâcon	625	443,000	67,000
Sarthe	Le Mans	418	348,000	54,000
Seine et Oise	Versailles	697	472,000	73,000
Seine Inférieure	Rouen	997	536,000	83,000
Seine et Marne	Melun	572	296,000	48,000

I	II	III	IV	V
Sèvres	Niort	364	259,000	40,000
Somme	Amiens	966	407,000	63,000
Tarn	Castres	373	289,000	48,000
Var	Grasse	214	275,000	56,000
Vaucluse	Avignon	155	193,000	32,000
Vendée	Fontenai	328	306,000	48,000
Vienne	Poitiers	348	258,000	43,000
Vienne (Haute)	Limoges	234	267,000	34,000
Vosges	Epinal	518	289,000	45,000
Yonne	Auxerre	481	365,000	57,000

(For accompanying map see Appendix F.)

APPENDIX F

FRANCE in 1794
showing the départements
and their chef-lieux

INDEX

(The more important references are marked with an asterisk *)

Blaikie, 199
Blanc, 461
Blondel, 287
Boileau, 371
Boissy d'Anglas, 404
Bonhommet, 353
Bonnefoy, 349
Bonne-Savardin, 191
bonnet rouge, 259, 264, 278, 498
Bonneville, 315
Bordeaux, 67*, 118, 413*, 481
Bosc, 62, 93, 196
Bouchotte, 347, 382, 427, 430
Boudet, 207
Boudin, 486
Bouillé (Marquis), 44, 138, 193-4, 198-200, 202, 206-8, 213
Bouillé (C.), 207-8
Bouillon, 36
Bourbotte, 264, 325
Bourdon (de l'Oise), 507-8, 510, 513
Bourdon (L.), 508, 513, 516
Bourgeois, 458
bourgeoisie, 226, 228, 297
Boyd, 450
Boze, 277
Breteuil, 54, 60, 199
Breton club, 82, 102, 109
Brichet, 353
Brienne, 1, 72, 176
Brigny, 204
Briot, 356
Brissac, 34
Brissot, 112, 192, 216-17, 219, 231*, 233-4, 251, 255-7, 267, 269, 272, 318-19, 323, 340, 358, 365, 371, 402, 446, 455
brochures, 12, 145, 210
Broglie, 53-4, 58, 60-1, 63
Broussonet, 16, 230
Brune, 220-1
Brunet, 425
Brunswick, 284, 302, 316-17, 357, 423
Buissart, 511
bulletin des lois, 398
Burdett, 46
bureau de police générale, 391, 487, 504, 505*, 508-9, 511
Burke, 27, 34, 216, 224, 246, 338
Buzot, 146, 231*, 295, 321, 330, 373

Cabanis, 215, 251, 295
cabinet noir, 138, 198
cafés, 91, 110*
Cahier, 431
Cahier de Gerville, 237
cahiers, 10*, 86, 145, 160, 174, 220
Cailleaux, 353
ça ira, 215, 290, 341
caisse d'escompte, 51, 57, 177, 179
Calonne, 327, 447
Cambon, 125, 230, 336, 338, 342-3, 367, 416, 426, 432, 438, 445, 499, 508, 513

Camisards, 79
Campan, 41, 195, 252
Camus, 149
canton, 127
capitalistes, 35, 108, 171
Carlyle, 204, 373
Carmelites, 238
Carnot, 230, 284, 382, 385, 386*, 387, 396, 424-6, 428, 431, 454, 470, 509-10, 513-14
Carpentras, 250
Carra, 215, 280, 350, 357, 416
Carrier, 413, 453, 455
Carteaux, 404-5
Casaux, 90
Castellane, 87
Castries, 196
Cathelineau, 345, 412
Catherine the Great, 152, 179, 210, 248, 343
Cavaignac, 461
Cazalès, 107, 251
cercle social, 109
certificat de civisme, 453, 461, 489
Cérutti, 121, 230
Chabot, 232-3, 251, 448*, 449-50, 460, 462
Chalier, 396-7, 408-9, 411, 440, 444
Chambon, 373
Chambonas, 271, 280
Champagneux, 295, 469
Champ de Mars, 55, 120, 194
Champs Elysées, 97, 121, 212, 225
Chappe, 426
Charles IX, 114, 115*, 403
Chateaubriand, 34, 50, 58, 63, 75, 241
Châteauneuf-Randon, 36, 410
Châteaurenard, 36
Châteauvieux, 263, 488
Châtelet, 100, 116, 132, 136, 191, 200
de Châtelet, 53
Chaudron-Rousseau, 403
Chaumette, 220, 270, 280, 442, 443*, 444, 453, 462, 468, 498
Chauvelin, 339-41
Chénier (M. J.), 114, 313, 402
Chérin, 419
Choiseul, 199, 205
Chouans, 244
church, 140*
Cicé, 32*, 88, 149, 191, 259
citizenship, 183
civil list, 194, 203, 269
civil registration, 296
civil service, 392
claqueurs, 104, 380
Clarivière, 238
Clavière, 258, 293, 340, 347, 354, 365, 373, 447
Clement XIV, 152
Clerfayt, 343, 419, 423, 470
Clermont-Tonnerre, 11, 36*, 254
Cléry, 291
Cloots, 119, 249, 256-7, 459, 462, 465

541